Issues in the Ecological Study of Learning

RESOURCES FOR ECOLOGICAL PSYCHOLOGY

A series of volumes edited by:
Robert E. Shaw, William M. Mace, and Michael T. Turvey

Issues in the Ecological Study of Learning

edited by
Timothy D. Johnston
University of North Carolina
at Greensboro
and
Alexandra T. Pietrewicz
Developmental Learning Center
Fort Pierce, Florida

LEA LAWRENCE ERLBAUM ASSOCIATES, PUBLISHERS
1985   Hillsdale, New Jersey   London

Lawrence Erlbaum Associates, Inc., Publishers
365 Broadway
Hillsdale, New Jersey 07642

Library of Congress Cataloging in Publication Data
Main entry under title:

Issues in the ecological study of learning.

Includes indexes.
1. Learning in animals.   2. Animal ecology.
I. Johnston, Timothy D.   II. Pietrewicz, Alexandra T.
QL785.I85   591.5′1   84-25929
ISBN 0-89859-521-5

Printed in the United States of America
10 9 8 7 6 5 4 3 2 1

Contents

Resources in Ecological Psychology

The purpose of this series is to foster the growth of research on problems in the psychology of perceiving and acting identified by James J. Gibson. Gibson, like all psychologists who study perception, was interested in the relation between animals and their environments. Unlike other students of perception, however, he believed that analyzing environments was just as much a part of the psychologists' task as analyzing animals themselves. He found that these two components, animals and their environments, could not be studied in isolation from one another. That is, they implied one another in a system of mutual constraint. This is not codified in the relations among classical scientific disciplines. The study of environments is usually thought to belong to the physical sciences and animals to the biological and psychological sciences. Classical psychophysics accepted the autonomy of these separate sciences and conceived of their interrelation, as best it could, as a juxtaposition. Seen as a system of mutual constraint, however, suggests the need to tailor both "physical" concepts and "psychological" concepts to one another in a larger system where they are commensurate. This is the essence of what Gibson called his ecological approach which he applied to the study of vision.

The work of Nicolai Bernstein could be seen as an example of a similar ecological attitude applied to the study of action, the coordination of movements in animals. Bernstein's work suggested that action could be studied without reference to environments. Here, biological concepts and physical concepts also would have to be tailored to one another. Since Gibson treated perceiving as a bodily activity in its own right, it was natural for him to view perceiving and acting as an indissociable loop. The coupling of his ideas with Bernstein's forms a natural basis for looking at the traditional psychological topics of acting and perceiving as properties of ecosystems, not isolated animals. If the space-time window on acting and perceiving is enlarged, then this ecological approach may be readily extended to include cognitive variables.

Research on these topics has inevitably led in many directions in many existing disciplines. There is not a shelf in the library, or rarely a single library, where one can go to survey relevant material.

The purpose of this series is to form a useful collection, a resource, for people who wish to learn about what has been done in ecological psychology and for people who wish to contribute to it. The series will include reports of original research, collected papers, reports of conferences and symposia, monographs developing unifying themes, handbooks of technical information, and works from related disciplines outside of psychology.

Robert E. Shaw
William M. Mace
Michael T. Turvey

List of Contributors

Alley, Thomas R.
Department of Psychology
University of Connecticut
Box U-20, Storrs, CT 06268

Bolles, Robert C.
Department of Psychology
University of Washington
Seattle, WA 98195

Coss, Richard G.
Department of Psychology
University of California at Davis
Davis, CA 95616

Galef, Bennett G., Jr.
Department of Psychology
McMaster University
Hamilton, Ontario
Canada, L8S 4K1

Gottlieb, Gilbert
Department of Psychology
University of North Carolina
 at Greensboro
Greensboro, NC 27412

Gray, Lincoln
Department of Otolaryngology—
 Head and Neck Surgery
University of Texas Medical School
Houston, TX 77030

Hazen, Nancy
Department of Home Economics
University of Texas at Austin
Austin, TX 78712

Hailman, Jack P.
Department of Zoology
University of Wisconsin
Madison, WI 53706

Johnston, Timothy D.
Department of Psychology
University of North Carolina
 at Greensboro
Greensboro, NC 27412

Kalat, James W.
Department of Psychology
North Carolina State University
Raleigh, NC 27605

King, Andrew P.
Department of Psychology
Duke University
Durham, NC 27706

Miller, David B.
Department of Psychology
University of Connecticut
Box U-20, Storrs, CT 06268

Owings, Donald W.
Department of Psychology
University of California at Davis
Davis, CA 95616

Pick, Herbert L., Jr.
Institute of Child Development
University of Minnesota
Minneapolis, MN 55455

Pietrewicz, Alexandra T.
Developmental Learning Center
3546 Okeechobee Road
Fort Pierce, FL 33450

Reed, Edward S.
Department of Humanities
   and Communication
Drexel University
Philadelphia, PA 19104

Revusky, Sam
Department of Psychology
Memorial University of Newfoundland
St. John's, Newfoundland
Canada, A1B 3X9

Richards, Jerry B.
Department of Psychology
Emory University
Atlanta, GA 30322

Schleidt, Wolfgang M.
Department of Zoology
University of Maryland
College Park, MD 20742

Shaw, Robert E.
Department of Psychology
University of Connecticut
Box U-20, Storrs, CT 06268

West, Meredith, J.
Department of Psychology
University of North Carolina
   at Chapel Hill
Chapel Hill, NC 27514

Preface

This volume is based on a symposium, also titled *Issues in the Ecological Study of Learning,* that was held at the 1981 meeting of the Animal Behavior Society in Knoxville, Tennessee. We thank the Executive Committee of the ABS for including the symposium on the program for the meeting, and Terry Christenson, the ABS program officer, for helping with organizational details. During the long haul from the oral presentations to the finished volume, several people gave generously of their time and expertise to assist us in editing the manuscripts. In particular, we thank the following individuals for providing careful and thoughtful reviews of the chapters: Jeffrey Alberts, Colin Beer, Thomas Blakely, Steven Braddon, Robert Cairns, Reed Hunt, Cheryl Logan, Jack McDowell, Kelly McLean, Darryl Neill, Jerry Richards, Howard Rollins, Sara Shettleworth, Euclid Smith, and Michael Zeiler.

During most of the time when this volume was being prepared, one of us (TDJ) was supported by funds from NICHHD Grant No. HD-00878 (now HD-17752).

T.D.J.
A.T.P.

Introduction:
Conceptual Issues in the
Ecological Study of Learning

Timothy D. Johnston
Department of Psychology
University of North Carolina at Greensboro

In recent years, an increasing number of behavioral scientists have begun to study the problems of animal learning from a much more ecological, or naturalistic, perspective than has typically been the case in the past. Some workers have been impressed by data from laboratory studies of learning that were difficult or impossible to accommodate within the traditional theoretical frameworks of psychology, and that seemed to demand, in particular, an ecological interpretation (e.g., Bolles, 1970; Rozin & Kalat, 1971). Others have been studying problems of learning that were initially encountered in a naturalistic context and so demanded an ecological approach from the outset (e.g., Pyke, 1981; Vander Wall, 1982). The ecological study of animal learning is one area in which the oft-heralded synthesis between ethology and comparative psychology has proven fertile: Ethological techniques provide a description of behavior as it occurs in the ecological setting (answering the question "*What* behavior might be learned?"), allowing psychological analyses to determine the mechanisms by which the behavior arises (answering the question "*How* is it learned?"). Numerous studies, especially in the area of foraging behavior (e.g., Kamil & Sargeant, 1981; see the chapter by Pietrewicz, this volume), testify to the success of this cooperative endeavour.

As the chapters in this book indicate, the ecological approach to animal learning has been pursued in a number of interesting and profitable directions, and a substantial body of research is now accumulating on the ways in which animals adapt to their natural environments by means of learning. My aim, in this introductory chapter, is to discuss some of the broader conceptual issues that might serve to unify this rather diverse area. The issues I have chosen to discuss do not by any means exhaust those that might occupy a theorist interested in the ecological approach to learning. However, they do provide a sampling of important themes that distinguish the ecological approach from other, more traditional approaches, and that ecological theories of learning should try to elaborate. Before discussing these conceptual issues, however, it may help to put them in perspective by considering some of the historical background to the present situation in the study of animal learning (see also the chapters by Hailman, Gottlieb, and Galef, this volume).

THE PSYCHOLOGICAL TRADITION IN LEARNING

The modern study of learning has historical roots that link psychology with ancient philosophical inquiries into the nature of the human mind, in particular with the problem of the origins of knowledge. The study of nonhuman animals as a means of illuminating that problem is a relatively recent endeavour that originated in the writings of Darwin (1871, 1872), Romanes (1884), and Morgan (1896) toward the end of the nineteenth century (see Gottlieb, 1979). The theme that originated in *The Descent of Man* (Darwin, 1871), and was developed at length in *Mental Evolution* (Romanes, 1884), is that many apparently unique accomplishments of the human intellect are manifest to some extent in nonhuman species also. The development of that theme was partly an attempt to erode the then-prevailing belief that, whatever the theory of evolution might have to say about other organisms, the human species stands apart as a separate, divine creation. Both works are thus to some extent polemical ones, concerned with establishing the case for continuity of descent by pointing to similarities among species.

As a result of this emphasis on continuity of descent, the comparative study of learning inherited from its founders an emphasis on uncovering similarities among the learning abilities of different species, and it has retained that emphasis for most of the past 100 years. However, it should be noted that the theory of evolution is equally receptive to a different emphasis, one that is perhaps more apparent in Darwin's other writings (e.g., Darwin, 1859, 1886) than in *The Descent of Man*. This is that different animals possess adaptive specializations that equip them for survival in the particular environments in which they live. These two issues, of continuity of descent and specialization of adaptation, are familiar sides of the evolutionary coin. The psychology of learning has, throughout its history, tended to emphasize the former to the virtual exclusion of the latter (Lockard, 1971; see Gottlieb, this volume). It is not hard to see how an emphasis on similarities among species, although appropriate enough for an emerging comparative discipline, might lead to the establishment of a nonecological tradition in the study of animal learning. Close attention to the particular ecological conditions under which each species lives would, after all, tend to emphasize the differences among them, rather than their similarities. However, that tradition might not have become so firmly established had it not been buttressed by a belief that was widespread in the early 1900s (and, indeed, much later than that); namely, a belief in the separateness of learning and instinct (see Anastasi, 1954; Marquis, 1930; Pastore, 1949).

Although the proper way to conceive of the relationship between experiential influences ("learning") and genetic influences ("instinct") in the development of behavior continues to be debated even today, it is safe to say that there is little sympathy for any view that insists on a strict separation between the two (Gottlieb, 1983; see also Lehrman, 1970; Schneirla, 1956). Instead, modern developmental theory recognizes that the behavioral phenotype results from a set of epigenetic processes in which experiential and genetic influences are inextricably intertwined—those influences cannot be partitioned in the phenotype at any stage of development. However, it appears that much current research in animal learning tacitly accepts a strong version of the learning/instinct dichotomy, despite cogent and often-repeated arguments against it. Traditionally, the ability to learn has been seen as a property of certain natural systems (variously identified as minds, animals, or brains) that may be studied in any convenient manner that lends itself to controlled experimentation (see Skinner, 1950, for the classic statement of this position). Although it has always been recognized that an animal may have genetic predispositions (instincts) to cope with certain naturally occurring situations in appropriate ways, these have always been viewed as different in kind from whatever learning abilities the animal may also possess (see Eibl-Eibesfeldt, 1961; Lorenz, 1956, 1965; Skinner, 1966; and Watson, 1924, for particularly emphatic statements of this view). Given that perspective on learning, it is easy to see why psychologists have done their best to devise experimental paradigms that bear no resemblance to the animal's natural environment—their very arbitrariness will ensure that the experimenter can study "the association process, free from the helping hand of instinct" (Thorndike, 1911, p. 30).

Thorndike is a most appropriate author to quote in this context, for it was he who introduced the serious experimental study of animal learning into America. Although it is unlikely that many contemporary students of learning would acknowledge a direct intellectual debt to Thorndike, his influence on the field has been profound and enduring. His writings reveal his commitment to the view that learning and instinct are distinct and separate abilities of the animal (e.g., Thorndike, 1899), and in his experimental work he sought a means of effecting that separation in the laboratory. Thorndike argued that, if evolution has provided an animal with the instincts necessary to solve various problems posed by its natural environment, the student of learning must devise unnatural environments in which instinct is of no use and pose problems that only learning can solve. From that point of view, it is clear that the animal must be removed from the context normally provided by its natural environment, so that the learning process can be studied in isolation.

Thus, the learning/instinct dichotomy provided the conceptual justification for a nonecological approach to the study of learning, and that approach, in turn, has inevitably lead to nonecological theories of learning. The weight of tradition continues to support such a view, despite virtually unanimous rejection of its original justification (see earlier), as can be seen in the explicit exclusion of "innate tendencies" from most modern definitions of learning. The definition offered by Hilgard and Bower (1966) is representative: "Learning is the process by which an activity originates or is changed through reacting to an encountered situation, provided that the characteristics of the change *cannot be explained on the basis of native response tendencies,* maturation, or temporary states of the organism" (p. 2, emphasis added).

In recent years, a number of psychologists and biologists have expressed concern that this unwillingness to deal with species-specific capabilities in the study of learning may have produced theories of learning that have little applicability outside the psychological laboratory (e.g., Bolles, 1970; Charlesworth, 1976; Hinde, 1973; Johnston, 1981; Rozin & Kalat, 1971; Seligman, 1970; Shettleworth, 1972, 1983). Those arguments parallel similar concerns in other branches of psychology, such as perception (Breitmeyer, 1980; Brunswik, 1952, 1956; Gibson, 1966, 1979), human development (Bronfenbrenner, 1977, 1979; Fishbein, 1976), human memory (Lachman & Lachman, 1979), and social psychology (Barker & Wright, 1955; Gibbs, 1979; McArthur & Baron, 1983). They may be seen, in part, as a resurgence of the functionalist movement (Angell, 1907; Brunswick, 1956; Petrinovich, 1979), whose proponents included Clark Hull, one of psychology's most prominent learning theorists. Hull's early writings reveal a clear interest in the role that learning plays in enabling an animal to cope with the exigencies of its natural environment (e.g., Hull, 1929; 1943, p. 17), and it is unfortunate that this emphasis should have been lost in the subsequent development of his theory.

Although the call for an ecological approach to the study of learning runs counter to the dominant traditions of the field, it is by no means without precedent in psychology. The recent criticisms of the animal learning tradition by psychologists echo earlier criticisms by ethologists such as Tinbergen (1951, p. 142; see Hailman's chapter, this volume), who recommended an approach to learning based more firmly on ecological considerations than that adopted by psychologists. However, those ethologists who have made learning their special concern, such as Thorpe (1963) and Lorenz (1969), have generally drawn quite heavily on psychological thinking to guide their own analyses of learning, rather than providing an alternative ecological framework. As I have argued elsewhere (Johnston, 1981; Johnston & Turvey, 1980), the conceptual framework of the nonecological tradition in the psychology of animal learning cannot provide appropriate guidance for an ecological approach to learning. Because that framework was erected on explicitly nonecological foundations, it cannot simply be modified to accommodate the ecological viewpoint. Rather, a new, intrinsically ecological framework is needed, one that can help to define the important problems and research foci for an ecological approach to learning.

SIX ISSUES FOR THE ECOLOGICAL STUDY OF LEARNING

An ecological approach to learning may differ from that traditionally adopted by psychologists in a number of important ways. Issues will be raised for which there is little precedent in the study of learning, and we will be forced to develop the theoretical and methodological tools necessary to resolve them. More familiar issues may require a different approach so that they can be resolved in a manner consistent with ecological principles. In the remainder of this chapter, I propose to map out some of the major conceptual issues that seem to be involved in this enterprise and to make a preliminary reconnaissance of the problems to which they give rise.

1. The Nature of Learning

Psychologists have provided a multitude of answers to the question: What is learning? This is not the place to review those answers, except to note that they fall into two categories. Theorists of the behaviorist persuasion define learning in terms of change in behavior, whereas those of more cognitivist tendencies define it in terms of change in internal structures, such as cognitive maps or schemata. From an ecological perspective, behavior remains the important focus for studies of learning. Part of any ecological enterprise is to explicate the relationship that exists between the animal and its environment, and it is through behavior (rather than any internal structures) that this relationship is supported. For the ecologist, therefore, the study of learning must focus primarily on behavior and must begin by asking "What are the patterns of behavior by which this animal interacts with its environment?" (the stage of task description; Johnston, 1981).

It is important to realize that in the ecological lexicon "behavior" is an inherently relational term. Behavior is not a property that can be ascribed to an animal alone; rather, behavior can only be defined in relation to some particular environment. Behavior shares its relational nature with other biological concepts, such as social rank and reproductive fitness. These are not properties of the animal alone, but relationships between the animal and (respectively) its social group and breeding population. Behavior is an aspect of the animal's overall adaptive relationship with its environment and supports the animal's adaptation to certain environmental factors; it can only be described in relation to those factors. In order to describe, say, an animal's foraging behavior, it is necessary to specify, often in some detail, the environment in which the animal is foraging. The foraging behavior of a hummingbird, for example, cannot be described without at the same time giving a description of the location and distribution of the bird's food supply. The spatial orientation behavior of a blackcap warbler can only be described in relation to the ecological scale of the particular orientation problem (for example, migratory orientation vs. orientation during foraging) and to the cues that the bird uses to orient.

Therefore, although the ecologist studying learning focuses on the animal's behavior, he takes a very different approach from the behaviorist. It was a fundamental error of the behaviorist tradition to view behavior as a property of the animal that is independent of its environment; something that could be moved with the animal from one place to another. If behavior is viewed as such a property, then obviously it makes little difference whether we study it in the natural setting or in the laboratory. We can adopt the approach of a morphologist studying properties like hair length or tooth shape, which do not change appreciably according to the context in which they are described.[1] However, because behavior is an aspect of a relationship between the animal and its environment, rather than a property of the animal alone, this approach will not serve for the ecologist.

From an ecological perspective, learning may be defined as the modification or maintenance of the behavioral relationship between an animal and its environment as a result of individual experience. Identifying the involvement of learning in any particular instance requires, therefore, that we first describe the relevant aspect of the animal–environment relationship and then determine experimentally how individual experience contributes to its modification or maintenance (see also Johnston, 1981). For example, if we observe that an animal obtains food from different sources at different times in its life (being fed by its parents when young but feeding independently as an adult, or exploiting different kinds of food during different seasons), we can ask about the role that experience plays in bringing about that change in the animal–environment relationship. Alternatively, if we find that an animal continues to recognize members of its social group despite changes in their appearance as they grow older, we can ask how learning may be involved in maintaining this aspect of the animal's relationship with its social environment.

It is important to see that by defining behavior in relationship to the environment, rather than as a property of the animal alone, the focus of an ecological approach to learning must be on how an animal learns to exploit different *specific* food sources (namely, those that are available to it in its environment), or on how an animal continues to recognize the members of the *specific* social group in which it lives. The animal–environment relationship is specific on both sides; it is a relation between a specific animal and a specific environment, and that

---

[1]In passing, it may be noted that many morphological properties also require a relational definition. For example, colors change dramatically depending on the ambient light, which must therefore be specified if the color of a structure is to be described. Some color patterns can only be detected in restricted regions of the electromagnetic spectrum: For example, the color patterns of some flowers, which attract bees to alight on them, are only revealed in the reflected ultraviolet light, and so their definition depends on a perceiver sensitive to those wavelengths.

mutual specificity is central to the ecological approach to learning (Turvey & Shaw, 1979; see chapter by Shaw & Alley, this volume).

2. The Nature of the Animal–Environment Relationship

If we construe learning to be the modification or maintenance of a relationship between the animal and its environment, the next issue to be resolved must be the nature of that relationship. One approach would be to define it in relatively straightforward physical terms: The animal is an object, bounded by an epidermis, and the environment is that part of the physical world that lies outside the animal. Descriptions of the environment, the animal, and the elements that comprise them would be given in the conventional terms of physics and physiology, as would descriptions of the relationship between those two sets of elements. Such an atomistic style of description has only appealed to a few students of behavior, such as Loeb (1918) and Watson (1924). For most, the interesting point is not that behavior consists of certain physically defined *movements*, but that it consists of *acts*, that is, of sequences of movements that effect consequences for the animal. The difference between these two views, and the value of adopting the latter, was emphasized by Tolman (1932). Tolman acknowledged that acts are dependent on movements but claimed that it is at the molar level of act-description rather than the molecular level of movement-description that the study of behavior should focus. Most modern workers would probably agree with some version of Tolman's claim.

Given that our interest is in the animal as an *actor*, capable of executing actions such as walking, flying, singing, catching prey, or building nests, how should we approach the problem of describing the environment? The answer to that question will have important implications for our theories of learning, because it will largely determine our conception of the relationship between the animal and its environment; and as previously discussed, it is the modification or maintenance of that relationship that we seek to explain. The problem of environmental description has not been seriously addressed by traditional psychological theories of learning (see the chapters by Schleidt and by Gray, this volume), but for an ecological approach to learning, it becomes of paramount importance. Existing theories of learning focus on the question of *how* animals learn; the problem of *what* they learn about has been almost totally ignored. That emphasis is part of what makes current theories of learning nonecological: Whereas they view animals as natural systems whose properties are to be described and explained on the basis of empirical study, they do not view environments in the same way. Instead, the description of the environment (for example, as a set of stimuli that may or may not be associated with reinforcers) is *presumed* by the theory—such descriptions are not based on any empirical study of natural environments. It should also be noted that traditional psychological theories see "the environment" as being essentially the same for all animals (in much the same way as they see processes of learning as being the same for all animals); that is, they fail to recognize that an animal's environment may vary depending on its species, sex, age, and prior experience (Johnston & Turvey, 1980). The ecological approach, by contrast, views "the environment" as defined only in relation to some specific animal, and that view greatly colors the descriptions of environments that will feature in ecological theories of learning.

From an ecological perspective, then, the problem of environmental description is central to the analysis of learning, for we can only understand *how* animals learn if we first determine *what* it is that they learn about (cf. Gibson, 1966, for a similar claim in regard to perception). But a description of the environment in the traditional terms of physics is not appropriate for the study of learning, or indeed of any aspect of behavior. Instead, we must seek a style of description of the environment that more adequately reflects the behavioral nature of the problem, that pertains to the animal as an actor, rather than simply as a complex piece of physiology. Consider, for example, a relatively straightforward action capability (or "effectivity"; Turvey & Shaw, 1979) such as locomotion. In order to describe an animal's environment in regard to its locomotor capabilities, what we need is a description of the substrates and surfaces of that environment in terms of the support they provide for that particular animal's locomotion. The terms of physics do not offer such a description; they are animal-neutral terms that take no account of whether the animal is an elephant, a tree frog, or a pond skater. Yet the various substrates and surfaces of any part of the physical world provide very different locomotor support for those three animals, and a description of their environments that is to inform behavioral study must surely capture that fact. What we need is an *animal-relevant* description, one that is given in relation to the capabilities of the particular animal whose locomotion in being studied (Johnston & Turvey, 1980; Turvey & Shaw, 1979). Such a description identifies the *affordances* of the environment (Gibson, 1966, 1977); it specifies the ecological support that is available for locomotion (or for feeding, orientation, or prey catching) for that particular animal. It is the kind of description that earlier writers sought to capture in the phenomenological concepts of "functional tone" (von Uexküll, 1921; see Schleidt's chapter, this volume) and "valence" (Russell, 1935).

The kind of description of the environment that is required for ecological study can be illustrated by considering how one might approach the problem of orientation from an ecological perspective (Jander, 1975). A nonecological approach would be to describe the environment in terms of the Euclidian relations among its various components, giving the bearings and distances between them (e.g.,: "The home burrow is 42 m N.E. of the drinking site"). What we need, however, is a description in terms of the *ecological* relations among the various components of the environment (Lynch, 1961). Examples of such relations include the concepts of *path* and *barrier*—a path exists for an animal between two points if the animal's effectivities permit it to move from one point to the other. What constitutes a path for one animal (such as a fish) may constitute a barrier for another animal (such as a mouse). Similarly, the path structure of the environment may change for an animal as it grows, and if its condition changes (if it becomes pregnant, or is injured, for example). An ecological study of the learning involved in spatial orientation might then focus on how an animal adjusts its behavior to the changes in the path structure of its environment that are implied by the changes in the animal's effectivity structure as it matures.

In passing, it should be pointed out that physical descriptions of the environment are not irrelevant to the study of behavior. Just as we may describe the anatomical or physiological properties of an animal by virtue of which it exercises certain behavioral capabilities, so we may describe the physical properties of the environment by virtue of which the exercise of those capabilities is afforded. However, such descriptions must, if they are to inform behavioral study, be constrained by the ecological descriptions of affordances and capabilities. Physics and physiology supply the simple variables into which these more complex variables may be decomposed (see Fitch & Turvey, 1979).

The preceding arguments imply that, for the study of behavior and behavioral change, the relationship between the animal and its environment must be construed as a very intimate one. Elsewhere (Johnston & Turvey, 1980; Turvey & Shaw, 1979), it has been suggested that the terms *actor* and *econiche* be used to capture the intimacy of this relationship. A description of an econiche is a partitioning of the simple physical variables describing the environment in terms of the action capabilities of a particular actor. Similarly, a description of an actor is a partitioning of the simple physiological and anatomical variables describing an animal in terms of the affordances of a particular econiche. The actor and the econiche stand to one another in a relationship of mutual implication: Having described the affordances of an econiche, we imply something about the actor that inhabits it; and having described the capabilities of an actor, we imply something about the econiche that it inhabits. Consider, for example, what is implied about some animal (as an actor) by asserting that the unfrozen surface of a pond affords locomotion for it; or what is implied about some environment (as an econiche) by asserting that a mole can burrow in it.

The ecological study of learning must be based on descriptions of both the animal and its environment, but such descriptions cannot be given independently of one another. An understanding of the modification or maintenance of behavioral capabilities that underlie the adaptive relationship between an animal and its environment requires that the nonarbitrary nature of that relationship be recognized. The concepts just discussed offer one way to accomplish this.

3. Describing the Ecological Support for Learning

Answering the question "How does animal A learn behavior B?" involves, in part, specifying the support that the environment provides for learning; that is, it involves specifying the conditions that must be satisfied if that particular kind of learning is to be possible by that particular animal. Because of the intimate relationship that exists between animals and their environments, it is likely that the ecological support for learning varies among different kinds of animals and different kinds of behavioral capabilities. It seems unlikely, for example, that the support required for an indigo bunting to learn the navigational skills involved in migratory orientation (Emlen, 1972) will be at all similar to that required for a sparrow to learn to sing the song of its species (Marler, 1970), and, indeed, the evidence strongly bears out that expectation. The primary requirement for any condition to be seriously considered as part of the ecological support for learning is that it actually exist in the animal's environment, and that it be available to the animal at the time when learning is known or suspected to occur. This in turn requires, once again, that problems of environmental description figure prominently in the ecological study of learning.

In the preceding section, I argued that a description of animal and environment in physiological and physical terms is inappropriate for behavioral study. We might say that those terms provide too fine a grain of description for behavioral purposes (Fitch & Turvey, 1979) and that a coarser partitioning into the more complex variables of capabilities and affordances is required. Only at the coarser grain of description do we find the compatibilities and correspondences between the animal and its environment with which ecological study must deal (Gibson, 1979; Turvey & Shaw, 1979). These arguments pertain to the ecological support for behavior rather than for learning, but a remarkably similar argument has been made independently in regard to the support for learning by Humphrey (1933). Humphrey's argument is that learning theorists have focused on too fine a grain of description, both of the animal and of the environment, for the study of learning. As a result, they have been forced to postulate a variety of mediating constructs, such as memory, associations, and reinforcers, to knit together the elements of their descriptions over the long periods of time typically involved in learning. Humphrey suggested that if we were to adopt a coarser grain of description (in his terms, to describe series of events involved in learning, rather than just the individual events that make up those series), we would see learning not as a mediated processing of information, but as a direct adaptive response to the environment by the animal. Such descriptions would not, of course, explain learning, but they would radically change the kind of explanation that is required. They would also imply an explanation in ecological terms, for, as Humphrey points out, animals are adapted to their natural environments, not to "the environment" in some general, supraspecific sense.

Humphrey's suggestion is for an effort akin to Gibson's (1961, 1966) program of "ecological physics." Gibson based his direct theory of perception on the argument that natural environments provide a much richer source of structured, informative energy for veridical perception than is recognized by traditional theories of perception. Such theories describe the environment in the impoverished, animal-neutral terms of physics and then postulate complex operations within the perceiver that operate on that description (as represented, for example, by the retinal image) to deliver a richly structured perceptual experience. Gibson suggested that we seek a richer, more ecological vocabulary to define informational invariants in the environment that an animal might detect directly, rather than indirectly through the operation of mediating operations (Turvey, 1977). Although this does not solve the problem of how perception occurs, it substantially alters the kind of solution that is required.

What, then, is the appropriate strategy to pursue in describing the ecological support for learning? First and foremost, it must be an ecological strategy; that is, it must focus on the natural environment in which the capability under study is normally learned. We must beware of assuming similarity in the support for learning between species, even in the case of closely related behavioral capabilities. For example, the white-crowned sparrow requires early exposure to a song model in order to learn to sing as an adult but will only learn to sing if the model is the species-typical song (Marler, 1970; but see Baptista & Petrinovich, 1984). The zebra finch, on the other hand, which also requires a song model, will learn heterospecific songs, but only if they are sung by its foster father (Immelmann, 1969). In both cases, the ecological support for learning may be described crudely as "exposure to song," but a more precise definition of the requisite support reveals important differences between the two species.

In at least some cases, the ecological support for learning has been shown to be best described in relatively coarse-grained terms, as suggested by Humphrey (1933), particularly in terms of patterns of elements and transformations of patterns. For example, Emlen (1970) showed that the use of star patterns for migratory orientation by indigo buntings is only learned on the basis of exposure to a *rotating* star field. In this case, the support for learning involves a dynamically transforming pattern of elements, because exposure to a *stationary* starfield will not support the development of the orientation skill. Similarly, Hein and his colleagues (Hein, Gower & Diamond, 1970; Hein & Held, 1967) found that for kittens to acquire visual control over the guided movements of their forelimbs, they must have visual experience with their moving limbs during early development. Exposure to a lighted experience without sight of the limbs, or exposure in a stroboscopically lit environment in which perception of movement is not possible, does not support the development of visual guidance of the forelimbs. Apparently, the ecological support for the development of this behavioral capability involves transformations over patterns of optic texture defined by both the visual environment and the kitten's limbs moving in that environment.

4. Learning and Developmental Systems

Learning and development would seem to be closely allied concepts, because both concern changes in behavior that occur during individual ontogeny. It is curious, therefore, that theories of animal learning should have been so largely nondevelopmental in character, concerning themselves with the behavior of mature, "developmentally stable" animals. The exclusion of developmental thinking from research on learning has its roots in the instinct/learning dichotomy discussed earlier. Instincts were presumed to have a developmental history that is independent of specific experiential requirements, arising as a passive result of neural maturation (Gottlieb, 1976a). Learning and maturation were thus opposed as processes to account for the origins of behavior, and many theoretical articles during the period from about 1920 to 1950 attempted to make rigid distinctions between the two concepts (see, for example, Anastasi, 1954; Marquis, 1930; Mowrer, 1936; Rosenow, 1928; Shepard & Breed, 1913). The distinction was usually drawn on the basis of extrinsic versus intrinsic factors in ontogeny; most writers sought to identify learning with the operation of extrinsic factors and maturation with the operation of intrinsic ones.

Clearly, both external (or environmental) and internal (or genetic) influences are important in the ontogeny of behavior and, equally clearly, the analysis of their respective roles is an important aim for behavioral science. However, our current understanding of development suggests that to insist on a mutually exclusive relationship between them is a mistake. Instead, the proper relation seems to be one of complementarity, a point stressed by embryologists since before the turn of the century (e.g., Weismann, 1894; see Oppenheim, 1982) but too often ignored by both psychologists and biologists studying behavior (for an elaboration of modern developmental thinking on this point, see Gottlieb, 1976a, b; Lehrman, 1953, 1970; Schneirla, 1956, 1966).

The early emphasis by learning theorists on external influences alone as the causative agents in behavioral change has had important repercussions for modern thinking about learning. In particular, it has tended to divorce the analysis of learning from the broader developmental context. Although some investigators have focused their attention on learning in young animals (e.g., Campbell & Coulter, 1976; Johanson & Hall, 1979), this work has rarely been undertaken in a truly developmental spirit, with an eye to explicating the mechanisms that underlie the changing behavioral competence of the developing animal. More usually, the aim has been to demonstrate the presence or absence in the young of certain forms of learning previously described in the adult, and cross-sectional comparison rather than longitudinal analysis has been the rule. McCall (1977) has criticized human developmental psychology for the same shortcoming, although the early history of that field shows a close identification with the "maturational" view, and a concomitant emphasis on intrinsic developmental processes (e.g., Gesell, 1933; McGraw, 1946).

I have already discussed the role that the instinct/learning dichotomy played in fostering a nonecological approach to the study of learning, by its insistence on the use of biologically arbitrary tasks to study learning in the laboratory. The distinction between learning and maturation in development would seem to have reinforced that approach. A view of learning that denies maturational processes to be relevant to its concerns is unlikely to include the study of species-typical behavior, for it is precisely that behavior (usually identified as instinct) that owes its origins to maturation. Tolman (1932) endorsed that view when he claimed that there is a "pragmatically useful distinction to be made between such responses, or immanent determinants of a response, as are due mainly to heredity plus mere normal maturation, and such other responses, as are due primarily to the effects of learning resulting from special environments" (p. 304). The design of such "special environments" became the hallmark of research on learning for the next 50 years.

The concept of "mere normal maturation" has found growing disfavor as our understanding of developmental mechanisms has increased over the same period. The view implied by Tolman's phrase is of behavior passively unfolding in development, requiring no more than the conditions necessary to sustain life itself ("predetermined epigenesis"; Gottlieb, 1976b). However, a considerable body of research now exists demonstrating that the normal environment often contributes actively and essentially to the development of species-typical behavior patterns formerly thought to be "purely maturational." Examples include the pecking response of gull chicks to their parent's bill (Hailman, 1967), the following reaction of ducklings to their mother's call (Gottlieb, 1971, 1980), and the visual coordination of motor activity in mammals (Bauer & Held, 1975; Held & Hein, 1963).

It seems likely that an ecological approach to learning will require, and perhaps also stimulate, a synthesis between conceptions of learning and conceptions of development (Johnston, 1982a). The normally developing organism is subject to interacting external and internal influences, and the way in which those influences promote the modification and maintenance of the animal's behavioral relation with its environment will be a primary focus for ecological research on learning.

5. Learning and Natural Selection

To a large extent, the study of animal learning may be said to owe its existence to the theory of evolution, for it was the concern of Darwin (1871), Romanes (1884), and Morgan (1896) with demonstrating the intellectual continuity among animal species that lead to the rapid growth of comparative psychology after the turn of the century. In the early years of animal learning theory, evolutionary considerations figured quite prominently, but as the study of learning matured, such considerations became less prominent, until they all but disappeared. Where evolutionary theory was applied to the study of learning, as in the work of Bitterman (1975), its application was often very narrow in scope and revealed a limited appreciation of the theory itself (Hodos & Campbell, 1969; Yarczower & Hazlett, 1977; see Gottlieb's chapter, this volume). In recent years, the psychology of learning has rediscovered evolutionary theory (e.g., Rozin, 1976;

Rozin & Kalat, 1971), and there is now considerable debate as to the role that evolutionary considerations should play in the study of animal learning (Bolles, 1970; Hinde, 1973; Johnston, 1981, 1982b; Logue, 1979; LoLordo, 1979; Revusky, 1977; Shettleworth, 1972, 1983).

The ecological study of learning will demand much closer ties with evolutionary thinking than has been the case during most of the history of animal learning theory. A concern with how animals learn about their natural environments inevitably raises the question of how the nature of the environment affects the nature of an animal's learning abilities in the course of evolution. Identifying the selection pressures involved in the evolution of learning is perhaps the most insistent problem posed by considering the relation between learning and evolution, a problem that may be posed both in a general sense and in regard to the evolution of specific learning skills possessed by particular species. In general terms, the problem has been addressed by Johnston (1982b), Plotkin and Odling-Smee (1979), Slobodkin (1968), and Slobodkin and Rapoport (1974). The primary selective advantage of learning is that it permits adaptation to be effected to relatively variable (or unpredictable) aspects of an animal's environment, an advantage that it shares with other forms of developmental plasticity (Bateson, 1963; Levins, 1963; Waddington, 1969). Particular kinds of learning may possess other selective benefits. For example, Thorpe and Jones (1937) suggested that host conditioning in parasitic larvae might act as a reproductive isolating mechanism (see also Smith & Cornell, 1979); a similar advantage has been suggested for the evolution of bird song learning by Hinde (1959) and Nottebohm (1972). The relation between learning and evolution can be seen, on the arguments of the preceding section, to be a special aspect of the broader issue of the relation between ontogeny and phylogeny, which has been a persistent source of concern for evolutionary theorists (e.g., de Beer, 1958; Gould, 1977). It is also allied with the problem of the evolution of life-history strategies, a matter of much current interest among evolutionary ecologists (see Stearns, 1976, 1977). Although the life-history work has been primarily concerned with the evolution of reproductive parameters such as age at maturity, litter size, and number of litters per generation, the evolution of learning skills must be heavily influenced by concurrent selection for those life-history parameters (Johnston, 1982b).

Determining the selection pressures involved in the evolution of the learning skills displayed by particular species is, like all such enterprises, a formidable undertaking. The method of adaptive correlation, pioneered by ethologists in the study of behavioral evolution (e.g., Cullen, 1957; Hailman, 1965, 1976), involves determining correlations between characteristics of different species (in this case their learning skills) and relevant aspects of their environments. Thus, to test the hypothesis that variability in food distribution selects for the ability to modify foraging strategies on the basis of learning, for example, one would identify species that do and others that do not possess the learning ability in question and determine the nature of their food distributions (e.g., Gray, 1981; Gray & Tardif, 1979; see Domjan & Galef, 1983). *Ex hypothesi*, those species that exploit variably distributed food sources will show a greater ability to learn new foraging strategies than will those whose food supply shows a more nearly constant distribution.

Applying the method of adaptive correlation to the study of the evolution of learning is certain to be a difficult task, but it offers the promise of valuable insights into both learning and evolution. The development of formal models for the evolution of particular kinds of learning (e.g., Arnold, 1978; Bobisud & Potratz, 1976) will assist in formulating precise and testable hypotheses about the unexpected correlations. It is, of course, important that attempts to uncover the ecological correlates of particular learning skills do not fall prey to what Lewontin (1979; Gould & Lewontin, 1979) has called the "adaptationist fallacy" of assuming that all characteristics of a particular species, and all differences among species, can be given some adaptive interpretation. A character may become established in a population for other than adaptive reasons, as a result of pleiotropy, gene linkage, or correlative growth effects, for example. This is not a new message for evolutionists (certainly Darwin was well aware of its importance), but the recent excesses of some sociobiologists in that direction make the point well worth stressing.

Appreciating the importance of the adaptationist fallacy in evolutionary analyses lends additional weight to the insistence that an understanding of learning in evolutionary terms be ecologically based. The argument is presented in detail elsewhere (Johnston, 1982b) and is only sketched here. It must be acknowledged that, whatever the psychological bases of learning may be, they are probably very complex, especially in animals with an elaborate central nervous system. It is characteristic of complex systems, well known to computer programmers, that they often respond to input other than that for which they were designed, or in respect to which they have evolved. If selection acts in a population to produce some set of learning abilities that support adaption to certain aspects of the environment, the chances are good that it will also produce other abilities, permitting a developmental response to other inputs. However, these will not normally be revealed because the natural environment does not provide the requisite ecological support, or input. Let us call the former "ecologically relevant learning abilities" and the latter "ecologically surplus abilities." It will be clear that any evolutionary interpretation of learning must keep these two kinds of ability distinct and must seek ways of effecting that distinction in the experimental study of learning. That can only be done through ecological study, for it is the adaptive relationship between the animal and its environment that forms that basis for the distinction.

6. The Mechanisms of Learning

Specifying the mechanisms of learning (answering the question: How do animals learn?) is a primary objective of any approach to the study of learning. Both behavioral and physiological mechanisms are of interest here; generally speaking, the strategy is to define the behavioral mechanisms first and then attempt to uncover their physiological bases.

Two kinds of mechanism have traditionally been proposed to account for animal learning: the formation of associations among stimuli and responses and the elaboration of cognitive models of the environment. Although associationism largely dominates research on animal learning (Jenkins, 1979; Rescorla & Holland, 1976), it is unlikely that associative principles will contribute as broadly to an ecological view of learning mechanisms as they do to the nonecological view, because so many of their fundamental assumptions are explicitly opposed to the ecological perspective. The search for associative principles of learning has been so thoroughly wedded to a belief in the existence of supraspecific learning processes, with a concomitant emphasis on ecologically arbitrary experimental paradigms (see earlier), that the great bulk of research within this tradition is largely resistant to any ecological interpretation. Recent demonstrations of "biological boundaries" to associative mechanisms (e.g., Bolles, 1970; Shettleworth, 1975) have provided cogent criticisms of the associationist tradition (see chapters by Bolles and by Kalat, this volume), but doubts have been expressed regarding the ability of the biological boundaries criticism to generate an alternative approach to the study of learning (Johnston, 1981; Revusky, 1977; see also Revusky's chapter, this volume). On the other hand, it is unlikely that associative mechanisms play no role in learning under natural circumstances. Recent work in food selection, using naturalistic paradigms, suggests that associative processes may well be involved (Pietrewicz & Kamil, 1977, 1979; see also Pietrewicz's chapter, this volume). What is unlikely, however, is that associative principles have the broad explanatory power sometimes claimed for them in regard to learning in general.

Cognitive mechanisms of animal learning originated with Tolman (1932, 1948) and have been undergoing a renaissance in recent years, stimulated, no doubt, by similar developments in human psychology (e.g., Neisser, 1967). Cognitive principles have been most widely proposed in studies of orientation (e.g., Menzel, 1978; Olton, 1979), but they have also been applied in the study of other forms of animal learning (see Hulse, Fowler, & Honig, 1978). As noted earlier in this chapter, the ecological approach to learning focuses on the behavior of the animal, because behavior is what underlies the adaptive relationship between the animal and its environment. However, there is nothing in the ecological approach that precludes the use of cognitive concepts for explaining how that behavior comes about. Whereas classical behaviorism proscribes cognitive theorizing on theoretical grounds, the ecological approach argues only that theories of learning should focus on explaining the modification or maintenance of behavior, not that nonbehavioral terminology must be excluded from such explanations.

My previous suggestion that the ecological approach to learning should also adopt a developmental orientation implies that mechanisms traditionally thought of as developmental, and generally ignored by learning theorists, may well have an important role to play in ecological theories of learning. Modern developmental theory is aimed toward the elucidation of epigenetic mechanisms in which both genetic and environmental influences play a dynamic role in the development of behavior. Much developmental theory is therefore implicitly ecological, because the genetic influences that it must incorporate have been shaped by selection pressures that originated in the animal's ecological circumstances (see Johnston, 1982a; Waddington, 1957; Weismann, 1894). Lack of space precludes an extensive review of the relevant developmental literature, but two important contributions bear mention.

The concept of a "sensory template" (Marler, 1976) identifies a developmental mechanism that may be of widespread importance, and that is particularly amenable to an ecological interpretation. The concept originated with studies of song learning and refers to the fact that in some species of songbird, such as the chaffinch and white-crowned sparrow, in which exposure to a song model is required for normal song development, the model must be the species-typical song or a close approximation to it; atypical song will not be learned (see Marler & Mundinger, 1971; Kroodsma, 1982; see West & King, this volume). Other examples of developmental systems in which specific experiential input is required for normal development have been described (e.g., Gottlieb, 1980; Wiens, 1970), and from an evolutionary point of view, such mechanisms are to be expected, because they protect the system from the consequences of responding to inappropriate kinds of environmental stimulation, Thus, although it may be advantageous for a white-crowned sparrow to learn the particular song dialect of the community in which it is born (Baker, 1982; Marler & Tamura, 1964; Nottebohm, 1972), it would be disadvantageous for it to inadvertently learn the song of some other species, because that would reduce its chances of subsequently finding a mate.

Song learning provides an example of an inductive role of experience, in contrast with either a maintaining or a facilitative role. Gottlieb (1976a) distinguishes these three roles as follows. Maintaining experiences are required to support continued development of a preexisting behavioral skill. Facilitative experiences enhance the development of the skill. Inductive experiences are those in the absence of which the skill does not develop at all. This taxonomy of roles, which has recently been revised and elaborated (Aslin, 1981; Gottlieb, 1981), points to a wider range of experiential effects than is recognized by traditional theories of learning and so implies that, in our approach to the study of learning, we should be willing to consider a wider range of learning mechanisms than in the past.

CONCLUSION

There are two related themes that constitute an ecological approach to the study of learning. The first theme concerns the role that learning plays in the animal's adaptation to its natural environment. Learning evolved as a way in which individuals could adapt, over the course of their lifetimes, to the demands of the particular environments in which they found themselves, and our primary concern must be with the nature and mechanisms of such adaptation. This requires that we study not only the animal that is adapting, but also the environment that is being adapted to. Recent work in animal learning has alerted psychologists to the specificity of learning processes in different species of animal; we must also recognize the specificity of the natural environments in which learning normally occurs. The characteristics of both the animal and its environment contribute to the nature of learning. That does not mean that the use of artificial conditions in the laboratory is precluded by the ecological approach (see Johnston, 1981). On the contrary, we can learn very little about learning without experimentally altering the conditions under which it normally occurs to determine how they contribute to the normal course of learning. But the hypotheses that are tested by such experimental manipulations should be designed to elucidate the role of learning in the normal course of an animal's life; it is no part of the ecological approach to demonstrate simply that animals *can* learn under *some* circumstances. The natural environment, and the behavior that is part of the animal's normal adaptive relationship with that environment, is the essential focus of ecological study.

The second theme concerns the role of learning in the overall life history of the animal, and its relation to other developmental processes affecting behavior. Although it has been a frequent concern of learning theorists to draw a sharp line between learning and the rest of development, that is not a position from which the ecological approach can proceed. Successful adaptation requires that the entire life cycle of the organism, from conception to maturity, be able to cope with the demands of its environment, and processes of learning must be integrated with other developmental processes to ensure success. Many, perhaps most, forms of learning that occur under natural conditions involve predispositions to respond only (or best) to certain kinds of experiential input in certain kinds of ways. The nature of those predispositions is as important a problem for ecological theories of learning as is the nature of the adaptive response, and that requires that our theories be developmental as well as ecological. Only when we can explain the way in which learning proceeds in its developmental and ecological context will theories of learning be able to contribute to a truly *natural* science of animal and human behavior.

REFERENCES

Anastasi, A. (1954). The inherited and acquired components of behavior. In D. Hooker & C. C. Hare (Eds.), *Genetics and the inheritance of integrated neurological and psychiatric patterns* (pp. 67–75). Baltimore: Williams & Wilkins.

Angell, J. R. (1907). The province of functional psychology. *Psychological Review, 14*, 61–91.

Arnold, S. J. (1978). The evolution of a special class of modifiable behaviors in relation to environmental pattern. *American Naturalist, 112,* 415–427.

Aslin, R. N. (1981). Experiential influences and sensitive periods in perceptual development: A unified model. In R. N. Aslin, J. R. Alberts, & M. R. Petersen (Eds.), *Development of perception* (Vol. 1, pp. 45–93). New York: Academic Press.

Baker, M. C. (1982). Genetic population structure and vocal dialects in *Zonotrichia* (Emberizidae). In D. E. Kroodsma & E. H. Miller (Eds.), *Acoustic communication in birds* (Vol. 2): *Song learning and its consequences* (pp. 209–235). New York: Academic Press.

Baptista, L.F., & Petrinovich, L. (1984). Social interaction, sensitive phases and the song template hypothesis in the white-crowned sparrow. *Animal Behaviour, 32,* 172–181.

Barker, R. G., & Wright, H. F. (1955). *Midwest and its children: The psychological ecology of an American town.* New York: Harper & Row.

Bateson, G. (1963). The role of somatic change in evolution. *Evolution, 17,* 529–539.

Bauer, J. A., & Held, R. (1975). . Comparison of visually guided reaching in normal and deprived infant monkeys. *Journal of Experimental Psychology: Animal Behavior Processes, 1,* 298–308.

de Beer, G. (1958). *Embryos and ancestors* (3rd ed.). London: Oxford University Press.

Bitterman, M. E. (1975). The comparative analysis of learning. *Science, 188,* 699–709.

Bobisud, L. E., & Potratz, C. J. (1976). One-trial learning versus multi-trial learning for a predator encountering a model-mimic system. *American Naturalist, 110,* 121–128.

Bolles, R. C. (1970). Species-specific defense reactions and avoidance learning. *Psychological Review, 77,* 32–48.

Breitmeyer, B. G. (1980). Unmasking visual masking: A look at the "why" behind the veil of the "how." *Psychological Review, 87,* 52–69.

Bronfenbrenner, U. (1977). Toward an experimental ecology of human development. *American Psychologist, 32,* 513–531.

Bronfenbrenner, U. (1979). *The ecology of human development: Experiments by nature and design.* Cambridge, MA: Harvard University Press.

Brunswik, E. (1952). *The conceptual foundations of psychology.* Chicago: University of Chicago Press.

Brunswik, E. (1956). *Perception and the representative design of experiments in psychology.* Berkeley: University of California Press, 1956.

Campbell, B. A., & Coulter, X. (1976). The ontogenesis of learning and memory. In M. R. Rosenzweig & E. L. Bennett (Eds.), *Neural mechanisms of learning and memory.* Cambridge, MA: MIT Press.

Charlesworth, W. R. (1976). Human intelligence as adaptation: An ethological approach. In L. B. Resnick (Ed.), *The nature of intelligence* (pp. 147–168). Hillsdale, NJ: Lawrence Erlbaum Associates.

Cullen, E. (1957). Adaptations in the kittiwake to cliff-nesting. *Ibis, 99,* 275–302.

Darwin, C. R. (1859). *On the origin of species by means of natural selection.* London: Murray.

Darwin, C. R. (1871). *The descent of man and selection in relation to sex.* London: Murray.

Darwin, C. R. (1872). *The expression of the emotions in man and animals.* London: Murray.

Darwin, C. R. (1886). *The various contrivances by which orchids are fertilized by insects.* London: Murray.

Domjan, M., & Galef, B. G. (1983). Biological constraints on instrumental conditioning: Retrospect and prospect. *Animal Learning and Behavior, 11,* 151–161.

Eibl-Eibesfeldt, I. (1961). The interactions of unlearned behaviour patterns and learning in mammals. In J. F. Delafresnaye (Ed.), *Brain mechanisms and learning* (pp. 53–73). Oxford: Blackwell's.

Emlen, S. T. (1970). Celestial rotation: Its importance in the development of migratory orientation. *Science, 170,* 1198–1201.

Emlen, S. T. (1972). The ontogenetic development of orientation capabilities. In S. R. Galler, K. Schmidt-Koenig, G. J. Jacobs, & R. F. Belleville (Eds.), *Animal orientation and navigation* (pp. 191–210). Washington, DC: NASA (SP–262).

Fishbein, H. D. (1976). *Evolution, development, and children's learning.* Pacific Palisades, CA: Goodyear.

Fitch, H., & Turvey, M. T. (1979). On the control of activity: Some remarks from an ecological point of view. In R. W. Christiana (Ed.), *Psychology of motor behavior and sports* (pp. 3–35). Urbana, IL: Human Kinetics Press.

Gesell, A. (1933). Maturation and the patterning of behavior. In C. Murchison (Ed.), *A handbook of child psychology* (2nd ed., pp. 209–235). Worcester, MA: Clark University Press.

Gibbs, J. C. (1979). The meaning of ecologically oriented inquiry in contemporary psychology. *American Psychologist, 34,* 127–140.

Gibson, J. J. (1961). Ecological optics. *Vision Research, 1,* 253–262.

Gibson, J. J. (1966). *The senses considered as perceptual systems.* Boston: Houghton–Mifflin.

Gibson, J. J. (1977). The theory of affordances. In R. Shaw & J. Bransford (Eds.), *Perceiving, acting, and knowing: Towards an ecological psychology* (pp. 67–82). Hillsdale, NJ: Lawrence Erlbaum Associates.

Gibson, J. J. (1979). *The ecological approach to visual perception.* Boston: Houghton–Mifflin.

Gottlieb, G. (1971). *Development of species identification in birds.* Chicago: University of Chicago Press.

Gottlieb, G. (1976a). The roles of experience in the development of behavior and the nervous system. In G. Gottlieb (Ed.), *Neural and behavioral specificity* (pp. 25–54). New York: Academic Press.

Gottlieb, G. (1976b). Conceptions of prenatal development: Behavioral embryology. *Psychological Review, 83,* 215–234.

Gottlieb, G. (1979). Comparative psychology and ethology. In E. Hearst (Ed.), *The first century of experimental psychology* (pp. 147–173. Hillsdale, NJ: Lawrence Erlbaum Associates.

Gottlieb, G. (1980). Development of species identification in ducklings: VI. Specific experience required to maintain species-typical behavior in Peking ducklings. *Journal of Comparative and Physiological Psychology, 94,* 579–587.

Gottlieb, G. (1981). Roles of early experience in species-specific perceptual development. In R. N. Aslin, J. R. Alberts, & M. R. Petersen (Eds.), *Development of perception* (Vol. 1, pp. 1–44). New York: Academic Press.

Gottlieb, G. (1983). The psychobiological approach to development issues. In P. H. Mussen (Ed.), *Handbook of child psychology* (Vol. II): *Infancy and developmental psychobiology* (pp. 1–26). New York: Wiley.

Gould, S. J. (1977). *Ontogeny and phylogeny.* Cambridge, MA: Harvard University Press.

Gould, S. J., & Lewontin, R. C. (1979). The spandrels of San Marco and the Panglossian paradigm: A critique of the adaptationist program. *Proceedings of the Royal Society of London, B, 205,* 581–598.

Gray, L. (1981). Genetic and experiential differences affecting foraging behavior. In A. C. Kamil & T. D. Sargeant (Eds.), *Foraging behavior: Ecological, ethological, and psychological approaches* (pp. 455–473). New York: Garland STPM Press.

Gray, L., & Tardif, R. R. (1979). Development of feeding diversity in deer mice. *Journal of Comparative and Physiological Psychology, 93,* 1127–1135.

Hailman, J. P. (1965). Cliff-nesting adaptations in the Galapagos swallow-tailed gull. *Wilson Bulletin, 77,* 346–362.

Hailman, J. P. (1967). The ontogeny of an instinct: The pecking response in chicks of the laughing gull (*Larus atricilla,* L) and other species. *Behaviour Supplement, 15,* 1–159.

Hailman, J. P. (1976). Uses of the comparative study of behavior. In R. B. Masterton, W. Hodos, & H. Jerison (Eds.), *Evolution, brain and behavior: Persistent problems* (pp. 13–22). Hillsdale, NJ: Lawrence Erlbaum Associates

Hein, A., Gower, E. C., & Diamond, R. M. (1970). Exposure requirements for developing the triggered component of the visual placing response. *Journal of Comparative and Physiological Psychology, 73,* 188–192.

Hein, A., & Held, R. (1967). Dissociation of the visual placing response into elicited and guided components. *Science, 158,* 390–392.

Held, R., & Hein, A. (1963). Movement-produced stimulation in the development of visually guided behavior. *Journal of Comparative and Physiological Psychology, 56,* 872–876.

Hilgard, E. R., & Bower, G. H. (1966). *Theories of learning.* New York: Appleton.

Hinde, R. A. (1959). Behaviour and speciation in birds and lower vertebrates. *Biological Reviews, 34,* 85–129.

Hinde, R. A. (1973). Constraints on learning—an introduction to the problems. In R. A. Hinde & J. Stevenson-Hinde (Eds.), *Constraints on learning: Limitations and predispositions* (pp. 1–19). New York: Academic Press.

Hodos, W., & Campbell, C. B. G. (1969). *Scala naturae:* Why there is no theory in comparative psychology. *Psychological Review, 76,* 337–350.

Hull, C. L. (1929). A functional interpretation of the conditioned reflex. *Psychological Review, 36,* 498–511.

Hull, C. L. (1943). *Principles of behavior.* New York: Appleton.

Hulse, S. H., Fowler, H., & Honig, W. R. (Eds.). (1978). *Cognitive processes in animal behavior.* Hillsdale, NJ: Lawrence Erlbaum Associates.

Humphrey, G. (1933). *The nature of learning in its relation to the living system.* London: Kegan Paul.

Immelmann, K. (1969). Song development in the zebra finch and other estrildid finches. In R. A. Hinde (Ed.), *Bird vocalizations* (pp. 61–74). London: Cambridge University Press.

Jander, R. (1975). Ecological aspects of spatial orientation. *Annual Review of Ecology and Systematics, 6,* 171–188.

Jenkins, H. M. (1979). Animal learning and behavior theory. In E. Hearst (Ed.), *The first century of experimental psychology* (pp. 177–228). Hillsdale, NJ: Lawrence Erlbaum Associates.

Johanson, I. B., & Hall, W. G. (1979). Appetitive learning in 1-day-old rat pups. *Science, 205,* 419–421.

Johnston, T. D. (1981). Contrasting approaches to a theory of learning. *Behavioral and Brain Sciences, 4,* 125–173.

Johnston, T. D. (1982a). Learning and the evolution of developmental systems. In H. C. Plotkin (Ed.), *Learning, evolution and culture: Essays in evolutionary epistemology* (pp. 411–442). New York: Wiley.

Johnston, T. D. (1982b). Selective costs and benefits in the evolution of learning. *Advances in the Study of Behavior, 12,* 65–106.

Johnston, T. D., & Turvey, M. T. (1980). A sketch of an ecological metatheory for theories of learning. In G. H. Bower (Ed.), *The psychology of learning and motivation* (Vol. 14, pp. 147–205). New York: Academic Press.

Kamil, A. C., & Sargeant, T. D. (Eds.). (1981). *Foraging behavior: Ecological, ethological, and psychological approaches.* New York: Garland STPM Press.

Kroodsma, D. E. (1982). Learning and the ontogeny of sound signals in birds. In D. E. Kroodsma & E. H. Miller (Eds.), *Acoustic communication in birds* (Vol. 2): *Song learning and its consequences* (pp. 1–23). New York: Academic Press.

Lachman, J. L., & Lachman, R. (1979). Theories of memory organization and human evolution. In C. R. Puff (Ed.), *Memory organization and structure* (pp. 133–193). New York: Academic Press.

Lehrman, D. S. (1953). A critique of Konrad Lorenz's theory of instinctive behavior. *Quarterly Review of Biology, 28,* 337–363.

Lehrman, D. S. (1970). Semantic and conceptual issues in the nature–nurture problem. In L. R. Aronson, E. Tobach, D. S. Lehrman, & J. S. Rosenblatt (Eds.), *Development and evolution of behavior* (pp. 17–52). San Francisco: W. H. Freeman.

Levins, R. (1963). Theory of fitness in a heterogeneous environment: II. Developmental flexibility and niche selection. *American Naturalist, 97,* 75–90.

Lewontin, R. C. (1979). Sociobiology as an adaptationist program. *Behavioral Science, 24,* 5–14.

Lockard, R. B. (1971). Reflections on the fall of comparative psychology: Is there a message for us all? *American Psychologist, 26,* 168–179.

Loeb, J. (1918). *Forced movements, tropisms, and animal conduct.* Philadelphia: J. B. Lippincott.

Logue, A. W. (1979). Taste aversion and the generality of the laws of learning. *Psychological Review, 86,* 276–296.

LoLordo, V. M. (1979). Constraints on learning. In M. E. Bitterman, V. M. LoLordo, J. B. Overmier, & M. E. Rashotte (Eds.), *Animal learning: Survey and analysis* (pp. 473–504). New York: Plenum Press.

Lorenz, K. Z. (1956). The objectivistic theory of instinct. In P.-P. Grassé (Ed.), *L'Instinct dans le comportement des animaux et de l'homme* (pp. 51–76). Paris: Masson.

Lorenz, K. Z. (1965). *Evolution and modification of behavior.* Chicago: University of Chicago Press.

Lorenz, K. Z. (1969). Innate bases of learning. In K. H. Pribram (Ed.), *On the biology of learning* (pp. 13–93). New York: Harcourt, Brace, & World.

Lynch, K. (1961). *The image of the city.* Cambridge, MA: MIT Press.

Marler, P. R. (1970). A comparative approach to vocal development: Song learning in the white-crowned sparrow. *Journal of Comparative and Physiological Psychology Monograph, 71 (No. 2, Pt. 2),* 1–25.

Marler, P. R. (1976). Sensory templates in species-specific behavior. In J. Fentress (Ed.), *Simpler networks: An approach to patterned behavior* (pp. 314–329). New York: Sinauer.

Marler, P. R., & Mundinger, P. (1971). Vocal learning in birds. In H. Moltz (Ed.), *The ontogeny of vertebrate behavior* (pp. 389–450). New York: Academic Press.

Marler, P. R., & Tamura, M. (1964). Culturally transmitted patterns of vocal behavior in sparrows. *Science, 146,* 1483–1486.

Marquis, D. G. (1930). The criterion of innate behavior. *Psychological Review, 37,* 334–349.

McArthur, L. Z., & Baron, R. M. (1983). Toward an ecological theory of social perception. *Psychological Review, 90,* 215–238.

McCall, R. B. (1977). Challenges to a science of developmental psychology. *Child Development, 48,* 333–344.

McGraw, M. (1946). Maturation of behavior. In L. Carmichael (Ed.), *Manual of child psychology* (1st ed., pp. 332–369). New York: Wiley.

Menzel, E. W. (1978). Cognitive mapping in chimpanzees. In S. H. Hulse, H. Fowler, & W. K. Honig (Eds.), *Cognitive processes in animal behavior* (pp. 375–422). Hillsdale, NJ: Lawrence Erlbaum Associates.

Morgan, C. L. (1896). *Habit and instinct.* London: Edward Arnold.

Mower, O. H. (1936). "Maturation" vs. "learning" in the development of vestibular and optokinetic nystagmus. *Journal of Genetic Psychology, 48,* 383–404.

Neisser, U. (1967). *Cognitive psychology.* New York: Appleton.

Nottebohm, F. (1972). The origins of vocal learning. *American Naturalist, 106,* 116–140.

Olton, D. S. (1979). Mazes, maps, and memory. *American Psychologist, 34,* 583–596.

Oppenheim, R. W. (1982). Preformation and epigenesis in the origins of the nervous system and behavior: Issues, concepts, and their history. In P. P. G. Bateson & P. H. Klopfer (Eds.), *Perspectives in ethology* (Vol. 5): *Ontogeny* (pp. 1–100). New York: Plenum Press.

Pastore, N. (1949). *The nature–nurture controversy.* New York: Kings Crown.

Petrinovich, L. (1979). Probabilistic functionalism: A conception of research method. *American Psychologist, 34,* 373–390.

Pietrewicz, A. T., & Kamil, A. C. (1977). Visual detection of cryptic prey by blue jays (*Cyanocitta cristata*). *Science, 195,* 580–582.

Pietrewicz, A. T., & Kamil, A. C. (1976). Search image formation in the blue jay (*Cyanocitta cristata*). *Science, 204*, 1332–1333.

Pyke, G. H. (1981). Hummingbird foraging on artificial inflorescences. *Behaviour Analysis Letters, 1*, 11–15.

Plotkin, H. C., & Odling-Smee, F. J. (1979). Learning, change, and evolution: An enquiry into the teleonomy of learning. *Advances in the Study of Behavior, 10*, 1–41.

Rescorla, R. A., & Holland, P. C. (1976). Some behavioral approaches to the study of learning. In M. R. Rosenzweig & E. L. Bennett (Eds.), *Neural mechanisms of learning and memory* (pp. 165–192). Cambridge, MA: MIT Press.

Revusky, S. (1977). Learning as a general process with an emphasis on data from feeding experiments. In N. W. Milgram, L. Krames, & T. M. Alloway (Eds.), *Food aversion learning* (pp. 1–51). New York: Plenum Press.

Rosenow, C. (1928). One more definition of heredity and instinct. *Psychological Review, 35*, 434–439.

Romanes, G. J. (1884). *Mental evolution in animals*. New York: Appleton.

Rozin, P. (1976). The evolution of intelligence and access to the cognitive unconscious. *Progress in Psychobiology and Physiological Psychology, 6*, 245–280.

Rozin, P., & Kalat, J. W. (1971). Specific hungers and poison avoidance as adaptive specializations of learning. *Psychological Review, 78*, 459–486.

Russell, E. S. (1935). Valence and attention in animal behaviour. *Acta Biotheoretica, 1*, 91–99.

Schneirla, T. C. (1956). Interrelationships of the "innate" and the "acquired" in instinctive behavior. In P.-P. Grassé (Ed.), *L'Instinct dans le comportement des animaux et de l'homme* (pp. 387–452). Paris: Masson.

Schneirla, T. C. (1966). Behavioral development and comparative psychology. *Quarterly Review of Biology, 41*, 282–302.

Seligman, M. E. P. (1970). On the generality of the laws of learning. *Psychological Review, 77*, 406–418.

Shepard, J. F., & Breed, F. S. (1913). Maturation and use in the development of instinct. *Journal of Animal Behaviour, 3*, 274–285.

Shettleworth, S. J. (1972). Constraints on learning. *Advances in the Study of Behavior, 4*, 1–68.

Shettleworth, S. J. (1975). Reinforcement and the organization of behavior in the golden hamster: Hunger, environment, and food reinforcement. *Journal of Experimental Psychology: Animal Behavior Processes, 105*, 56–87.

Shettleworth, S. J. (1983). Function and mechanism in learning. In M. D. Zeiler & P. Harzem (Eds.), *Advances in analysis of behavior* (Vol. 3): *Biological factors in learning*, (pp. 1–39). Chichester: Wiley.

Skinner, B. F. (1950). Are theories of learning necessary? *Psychological Review, 57*, 193–216.

Skinner, B. F. (1966). The phylogeny and ontogeny of behavior. *Science, 153*, 1205–1213.

Slobodkin, L. B. (1968). Towards a predictive theory of evolution. In R. C. Lewontin (Ed.), *Population biology and evolution* (pp. 187–205). Syracuse, NY: Syracuse University Press.

Slobodkin, L. B., & Rapoport, A. (1974). An optimum strategy of evolution. *Quarterly Review of Biology, 49*, 181–200.

Smith, M. A., & Cornell, H. V. (1979). Hopkins host selection in *Nasonia vitripennis* and its implications for sympatric speciation. *Animal Behaviour, 27*, 365–370.

Stearns, S. C. (1976). Life history tactics: A review of the ideas. *Quarterly Review of Biology, 51*, 3–47.

Stearns, S. C. (1977). The evolution of life history traits: A critique of the theory and a review of the data. *Annual Review of Ecology and Systematics, 8*, 145–171.

Thorndike, E. L. (1899). Instinct. *Biological Lectures* (Woods Hole Marine Biological Laboratory), 57–67.

Thorndike, E. L. (1911). *Animal intelligence*. New York: Hafner.

Thorpe, W. H. (1963). *Learning and instinct in animals* (2nd ed.). London: Methuen.

Thorpe, W. H., & Jones, F. G. W. (1937). Olfactory conditioning and its relation to the problem of host selection. *Proceedings of the Royal Society of London, B, 124,* 56–81.

Tinbergen, N. (1951). *The study of instinct.* London: Oxford University Press.

Tolman, E. C. (1932). *Purposive behavior in animals and man.* New York: D. Appleton Century.

Tolman, E. C. (1948). Cognitive maps in rats and men. *Psychological Review, 55,* 189–208.

Turvey, M. T. (1977). Contrasting orientations to the theory of visual information processing. *Psychological Review, 84,* 67–88.

Turvey, M. T., & Shaw, R. E. (1979). The primacy of perceiving: An ecological reformulation of perception for understanding memory. In L.-G. Nilsson (Ed.), *Perspectives on memory research* (pp. 167–222). Hillsdale, NJ: Lawrence Erlbaum Associates.

Vander Wall, S. B. (1982). An experimental analysis of cache recovery in Clark's nutcracker. *Animal Behaviour, 30,* 84–94.

von Uexküll, J. J. (1921). *Umwelt und Innenwelt der Tiere.* Berlin: Springer.

Waddington, C. H. (1957). *The strategy of the genes.* London: Macmillan.

Waddington, C. H. (1969). The theory of evolution today. In A. Koestler & J. R. Smythies (Eds.), *Beyond reductionism* (pp. 357–395). London: Hutchinson.

Watson, J. B. (1924). *Behaviorism.* New York: Norton.

Weismann, A. (1894) *The effect of external influences on development. (The Romanes Lecture, 1894).* London: Frowde.

Wiens, J. A. (1970). Effects of early experience on substrate pattern selection in *Rana aurora* tadpoles. *Copeia,* 543–548. (No volume number)

Yarczower, M., & Hazlett, L. (1977). Evolutionary scales and anagenesis. *Psychological Bulletin, 84,* 1088–1097.

HISTORICAL BACKGROUND AND METHODOLOGICAL ISSUES

It helps in understanding any research area to see how the problems that it addresses developed from earlier lines of inquiry in other fields. The ecological study of learning is connected historically with both biology (especially ethology) and psychology (especially comparative psychology), and the first two chapters in Part I discuss some of the relevant history of these two disciplines. Hailman examines the history of the study of learning from the viewpoint of ethology and shows how the ethological concern with the relation of an animal's behavior to its natural environment has been reflected in studies of animal learning by both ethologists and comparative psychologists. Gottlieb looks at comparative psychology and addresses the specific question of why that discipline, historically the most closely associated with the study of animal learning, has so thoroughly neglected ecological issues. He finds that an important part of the answer lies in the prominence that the concept of anagenesis ("progressive evolution") attained in psychological thinking about evolution during the rise of comparative psychology in the early part of the twentieth century.

Among the historical influences acting on an emerging field of inquiry are the methodological traditions that it inherits from its parent disciplines. The ecological study of learning must draw on both biology and psychology for its research methods and may need to devise new methods when the traditional ones fail. Miller discusses some of the general methodological issues that are raised by the ecological study of learning and shows how they can be addressed by an imaginative combination of ethological and psychological research methods. Many of Miller's general points are exemplified by the particular research programs described in the chapters that make up Part II of this volume.

1

Historical Notes on the Biology of Learning

Jack P. Hailman
Department of Zoology
University of Wisconsin

It may be useful to open a volume on ecological studies of learning with some perspective of our intellectual legacy on the subject. How did it happen that psychologists studied learning as an abstract process in the laboratory divorced from the relevant ecological setting of the species studied? Or how did it happen that the ethologists observing animals in their natural environments felt that they could account for behavior with almost no reference to learning processes?

In this chapter, I look at the orientation of influential researchers by scrutinizing their earlier publications for perspectives on the biological relevance of learning. I was helped by several historical surveys (e.g., Beer, 1963–64, 1980; Boring, 1950; Gottlieb, 1979; K. Heinroth, 1977; Jenkins, 1979; Klopfer & Hailman, 1967; Munn, 1950), from which further perspective may be gleaned. However, none of these references addresses the precise issue at hand, so although the principals treated are familiar, what I have to say about their work may be less so.

It is useful to have some working definition of learning. Unfortunately, the easy approach of considering learning to be anything that authors themselves considered it to be does not work for present purposes because some of the phenomena I want to consider were excluded by certain authors (e.g., Konrad Lorenz said that imprinting had nothing whatever to do with learning). If there be a comprehensive definition, it must be something like this: Learning is a process mediated by factors external to the animal by which its preexisting behavior is permanently altered. A problem with this and similar definitions is the inclusion of phenomena that few would want to call learning: e.g., behavioral changes resulting from neural damage caused by physical accident or an infecting organism.

In response to such problems, many investigators have attempted to ring in the "usefulness" of the behavioral change. Thorpe (1956), for example, defined learning as "that process which manifests itself by adaptive change in individual behavior as a result of experience" (p. 66), and Lorenz (1965) refers to the "adaptive modification of behavior" (p. 5). Such conceptions have the merit of forcing consideration of the ecological context because the adaptiveness of any trait (structure or process) can be judged only against the environment to which it is reputedly adapted. However, saddling the definition of learning with a stipulation of adaptiveness is at once a strength and a critical weakness. The strength of forcing an ecological context is more than offset by the weakness of requiring one to establish adaptiveness in order to call a process of behavioral change true learning. Indeed, the entire evolutionary notion of "adaptiveness" is under scrutiny (e.g., Gould & Lewontin, 1979; Hailman, 1982a; Lewontin, 1978) and it seems undesirable to define *any* immediate process in terms of ultimate causes.

Although it would be relevant to pursue further the ideal formulation (see Hailman, 1982b), for present purposes we may take learning to be any externally mediated process by which existing behavior is changed, if that process has been considered under the rubric of learning by *some* author (but not necessarily by the investigator who studied it). The adaptiveness—or, more broadly, the biological context—of that process then becomes a subject for scrutiny. It is not my assignment to make the scrutiny, but rather to see how those who studied learning viewed its biological relevance.

BACKGROUND

The nineteenth century saw the virtual close of one issue and the opening of another in the biology of learning. Both issues are well known so need be summarized here only to provide the setting for twentieth-century history.

Learning and the Evolution of Behavior

The early French biologist Jean Baptiste Pierre Antonine de Monnet, Chevalier de Lamarck (1744–1829) was the greatest of pre-Darwinian proponents of evolution. Although he made immense advances in many areas of biology and was instrumental in establishing the reality of organic evolution, he is today often mentioned in texts only in conjunction with his discredited notion of the inheritance of acquired characteristics (Lamarck, 1815). In order to account for evolutionary change, Lamarck required a mechanism, for which he suggested that improvements acquired by individuals during their lifetimes could be passed to their offspring. The notion was vague and a relatively minor part of his contributions, especially considering that no science of genetics yet existed, but it is this notion of "Lamarckian inheritance" that loomed large in later evolutionary thinking.

A contemporary of Darwin's was Herbert Spencer (1820–1903), a prolific intellect in the Renaissance spirit whose writings in philosophy, biology, psychology, and sociology continue to influence thinkers today. The principal themes underlying his many contributions were those of continuity, in life forms and processes, and the adjustments of life to its external surroundings. He was a proponent of evolution before Darwin's publications (e.g., Spencer, 1855), and, although he is credited with later coining the phrase "survival of the fittest," he never accorded natural selection a major role in evolution (e.g., Spencer, 1896). Spencer was keenly aware of discoveries in embryological differentiation and translated these notions to evolutionary differentiation in which "Instinct" and "Reason" were points on a continuum without clear lines of demarcation.

Charles Robert Darwin (1809–1882) thus inherited an intellectual climate in which the reality of organic evolution was already established among the intelligentia. His dual contribution was to amass overwhelming empirical evidence for evolution and to provide it with a new mechanism: natural selection (Darwin, 1859). As many writers have pointed out, the notion of selection as the mechanism of evolution troubled Darwin increasingly, and in successive editions of the *Origins of Species* he accorded more and more weight to the Lamarckian notion of acquired characteristics. The missing link was genetics, and the experiments of Gregor Mendel, although published and available, never influenced nineteenth-century evolutionary thinking. Darwin himself proposed a "Lamarckian" mechanism called pangenesis in which "gemules" were sent from all loci in the body to the sex cells so that changes acquired by an individual could be transmitted to offspring (pp. 369–370 in the revised edition of his plant book: Darwin, 1868; repeated in *Descent of Man* on pp. 228 and 231 of the revised edition: Darwin, 1881). Despite Darwin's increasing emphasis on the inheritance of acquired characteristics, he understood clearly that such a notion could not be the sole mechanism of evolution, as in this passage (Darwin, 1897) about nonreproductive castes of social insects:

> For peculiar habits confined to the workers of sterile females, however long they might be followed, could not possibly affect the males and fertile females, which alone leave descendants. I am surprised that no one has hitherto advanced this demonstrative case of neuter insects, against the well-known doctrine of inherited habit, as advanced by Lamarck. (p. 363 of Vol. 1 of the corrected 6th ed.)

Still, Darwin needed "Lamarckian" mechanisms to account for the evolution of behavior, so he turned his attention to learning phenomena in his great behavioral book *The Expression of Emotions in Man and Animals*. Here Darwin articulated his "principle of serviceable associated habits" (see p. 28 of the 1965 reprint of Darwin, 1873), which formulation is very close to the twentieth-century notion of conditioning. Darwin's younger colleague, the biologist George John Romanes (1848–1894), carried Darwin's behavioral views further in two books (Romanes, 1884 and 1889) based partly on notes Darwin had given him. Romanes concluded that there are "primary instincts" evolved through natural selection working on chance variation of obscure origins, and "secondary instincts" that evolve from learned behavior that becomes automatic through "lapsing intelligence."

It was probably Conwy Lloyd Morgan (1852–1936), behaviorally oriented biologist and philosopher, who was most instrumental in laying to rest the Lamarckian notions of the evolution of behavior. His formulation is perhaps best presented in his 1896 book *Habit and Instinct* (pp. 319–321), in which he lays out the steps in behavioral evolution through natural selection.

By the turn of the century the issue of the role of learning in behavioral evolution was largely settled. The principal founder of American psychology, William James (1842–1910), reviewed the issue in the second volume of his monumental *Principles of Psychology* (James, 1890a and b), and came down solidly in favor of the evolution of "most" behavioral "instincts" through natural selection (p. 686). In fact, I believe it was James who really turned the original issue around. Earlier in the work, James (1890b) emphasizes that "every instinctive act, in an animal with memory, must cease to be 'blind' after being once repeated," and consequences of one act "must necessarily either re-enforce or inhibit" (p. 390) the impulse to repeat the act on a later occasion. He summarizes a long development by stating that: "most instincts are implanted for the sake of giving rise to habits, and that, this purpose once accomplished, the instincts themselves, as such, have no raison d'etre in the psychical economy and consequently fade away" (p. 402). This statement would serve as a fair summary of my principal conclusion about the development of begging in gull chicks (Hailman, 1967).

In sum, the continuity of life through evolution, recognized by Lamarck and Spencer, raised the issue of whether learning processes were responsible for the evolution of new "instinctive" behavioral patterns as proposed by Darwin and Romanes. Morgan argued that new "instinctive" patterns arose (almost) solely by natural selection on variation, and James proposed that the functional significance of the instincts was to promote learning processes that ultimately were of paramount importance in structuring an individual's behavior. This initial issue about the biology of learning persisted in some ways into the twentieth century, but I believe that its resolution with James set the stage for the schism that developed between biological and psychological approaches to behavior. Biologists concentrated on the evolutionary adaptiveness of behavior, whereas psychologists concentrated on the individual adaptability of behavior. Before considering these two approaches of the twentieth century, however, let us turn to the origins of the empirical study of learning in the nineteenth century.

Imprinting Forgotten

Douglas A. Spalding (c1840–1877) could have become the founder of either laboratory experiments on learning or naturalistic ethology, but he was neither. Like Gregor Mendel, Spalding published in prominent places and was widely read in his own time, only to be forgotten until his results were rediscovered independently in the twentieth century. Today Spalding's accomplishments are still known only in part, due principally to J. B. S. Haldane (1954), who republished Spalding's 1873 article on imprinting.

Spalding's work may have been forgotten for partly the same reason that Mendel's was: Neither was a university teacher who left students to carry on the tradition. Spalding was trained as a lawyer, removed to Italy for his health, there became interested in psychological issues through his study of art, returned to England to tutor the sons of Lord and Lady Amberley, and in this capacity, with their patronage, conducted empirical studies on animal behavior. The courts upset Lord Amberley's will that Spalding should remain tutor upon his death, and the two sons (the younger of whom was Bertrand Russell) were bound over to a relative for rearing in the tenets of the Church. Perhaps it was just as well, for Spalding died of phthisis in his 30s.

In the 1873 paper on "Instinct" Spalding presented experimental evidence for rejecting the belief that sudden appearance of apparently adaptive behavior early in the lives of baby chicks and other animals can be accounted for as learned stimulus–response associations. He also described the phenomenon of imprinting—without, of course, using that later term—and concluded with a long argument in favor of the Lamarckian notion of the inheritance of acquired characteristics.

Spalding was concerned with the widespread assumption that animals had to learn important stimulus–response associations, just as it was assumed human babies had to learn not to grasp at the moon. Spalding perceived that one could experimentally deprive chicks of certain sensory experiences until they were old enough to be capable of complex motor acts such as pecking at grain. He therefore performed experiments such as opening the egg and trying opaque and translucent hoods on chicks, or rearing chicks in dark felt bags. He (Spalding, 1954) noted carefully their behavior upon the first exposure to natural stimuli and stated that "Never in the columns of a Court Journal were the doings of the most royal personage noted with such faithful accuracy." He established that many responses of the chick require no associative learning of stimuli, as they are performed perfectly on the first opportunity. Nevertheless, Spalding (1954) notes: "But equally certain is it that they do learn a great deal, and exactly in the way that we are generally supposed to acquire all our knowledge" (p. 7). For example, chicks learn not to peck at their own excrement, in one or two trials. And they must learn the appearance of water, at which they first peck cautiously instead of drinking. Furthermore, "not only do the animals learn, but they can also forget—and very soon—that which they never practised." Indeed, in order to study learning experimentally, Spalding (1954) recommends that "students of animal psychology should endeavour to observe the unfolding of the powers of their subjects in as nearly as possible the ordinary circumstances of their lives" (p. 7). This was no offhand recommendation, as Spalding's discovery of imprinting amply demonstrates. Spalding (1954) notes that: "Chickens as soon as they are able to walk will follow any moving object. And, when guided by sight alone, they seem to have no more disposition to follow a hen than to follow a duck, or a human being" (p. 6). Onlookers believed him to "have some occult power over the creatures" that he had imprinted to himself. His sensory isolation experiments, however, demonstrated that chicks have an unlearned attraction to the mother hen's call (a fact rediscovered in the 20th century), so, according to Spalding (1954), in normal circumstances "There is the instinct to follow; and, as we have seen, their ear prior to experience attaches them to the right object" (p. 6). However, imprinting is by no means so simple, for "a chicken that has not heard the call of the mother until eight or ten days old then hears it as if it heard it not" (p. 8). Furthermore, the timing of visual experience also has profound effects as Spalding (1954) asserted:

> Something more curious, and of a different kind, came to light in the case of three chickens that I kept hooded until nearly four days old . . . . Each of these on being unhooded evinced the greatest terror of me, dashing off in the opposite direction whenever I sought to approach it. . . . had they been unhooded on the previous day they would have run to me instead of from me. (p. 8).

Spalding had discovered what later were called "sensitive periods" for learning and was patently puzzled about such phenomena.

Had later research on animals followed Spalding's recommendation to study "the ordinary circumstances of their lives," we might have a better understanding of how learning phenomena work in the natural lives of animals than we do today. Instead, the psychological experimentalists increasingly isolated learning from the natural lives of the animals studied, and the naturalistic ethologists nearly forgot that learning plays any role in behavioral development at all.

LABORATORY LEARNING PARADIGMS

Almost overnight at the turn of the century animal learning became the subject of intense laboratory experimentation, largely in psychology departments of American universities. The questions I ask here are: How did the founding experimenters view the biological context of their work and why did each use the specific experimental paradigm that he did?

Domestic Animals in Puzzle Boxes

Although it could be argued that the development of experimental research on animal learning was gradual, it is just as easy to emphasize the suddenness with which this tradition was independently founded as experiments on various domestic animals in so-called puzzle boxes and rats in mazes. Both paradigms were used just before the turn of the century, the former by Thorndike at Columbia and the latter by Small at Clark University.

Edward Lee Thorndike (1874–1949) began his graduate career at Harvard under William James but quickly moved to Columbia for financial reasons, there extending his work with baby chicks to cats and dogs. His doctoral dissertation was published immediately upon its completion (Thorndike, 1898) and later assembled with newer material into his famous book *Animal Intelligence* (Thorndike, 1911). His principal interest was to see how accidental success at some task promoted stimulus–response associations (Thorndike, 1898):

> After considerable preliminary observation of animals' behavior under various conditions, I chose . . . to put animals when hungry in enclosures from which they could escape by some simple act, such as pulling at a loop of cord, pressing a lever, or stepping on a platform. . . . The animal was put in the enclosure, food was left outside in sight, and his actions observed. (p. 2).

What led Thorndike to concoct such an apparatus? Clearly the experimental situation in no obvious way mimics a natural situation for any wild species, and Thorndike (1898) emphasizes that "None of the animals used had any previous acquaintance with any of the mechanical contrivances" (p. 6).

Thorndike was concerned with two issues that I believe influenced his choice of experiment. First, he wanted to distinguish between simple association and higher mental faculties. Influenced by C. Lloyd Morgan, Thorndike (1898) believed that learned reactions "can all be explained by the ordinary associative processes without aid from abstract, conceptual, inferential thinking" (p. 1). (Bitterman (1969, p. 444) implies that Thorndike probably heard Morgan lecture at Harvard in 1896, thereby receiving the impetus for experimental studies of animals.) Second, Thorndike states that his main purpose "is to learn the development of mental life down through the phylum, to trace in particular the origin of human faculty" (p. 2). Therefore, he required a task that would show how an apparent reasoning process in animals was actually due to stimulus–response association; at the same time the task had to be applicable to a wide variety of animal species. Thorndike emphasized that the particular puzzle box used with a given species was suited to its anatomy, size, strength, etc. so that physical characteristics played no part in his experiments, which deal solely with mental characteristics.

I propose that the inspiration for Thorndike's (1898) apparatus came initially from observing, or at least hearing reports about, the behavior of cats:

Thousands of cats on thousands of occasions sit helplessly yowling, and no one takes thought of it or writes to his friend, the professor; but let one cat claw at the knob of a door supposedly as a signal to be let out, and straightway this cat becomes the representative of the cat-mind in all the books. (p. 4)

I believe that Thorndike here implied that yowling was recognized as simple association, whereas a higher mental process was attributed to the cat that paws at the doorknob, as if the cat understood that the knob opens the door. Thorndike felt that if he could show the latter behavior to be simple association like the former, he would encapsulate the theoretical issue of interest through objective experimentation. And this he did, in the process defining "trial and error" learning (although he was not much interested in analyzing the error part).

Thorndike's comparative aims were laudatory, but his puzzle-box paradigm had an important flaw: Namely, it required tractable animals and therefore was primarily useful for experiments on domestic species. In fact the situation is even more restricted than that, for the experiments worked best with young animals. In his work with chickens Thorndike used baby chicks; although he talks about "cats," he in fact ended up using kittens (as his table of ages clearly shows; Thorndike, 1898, p. 12–13), and at least one of his "dogs" was a puppy (p. 32). No wonder, then, that this pillar of animal learning studies had virtually no relation to the adaptiveness of learning processes shown by adult animals of wild species in their natural environments.

White Rats in Mazes

The other pillar of laboratory learning studies was erected independently at Clark University in Worcester, Massachusetts. A recent institution (founded 1883), Clark quickly became a major intellectual center (partly by robbing the Harvard faculty) and assembled a formidable collection of talent. In 1894, a biologist at Clark named Stewart began using the wild Norway rat (*Rattus norvegicus*) for studies on the effects of alcohol, diet, and barometric changes on activity (Munn, 1950, pp. 2–3). Stewart changed to the more tractable domestic form of albino Norway rats the following year. Also at Clark was Linus W. Kline, a Fellow in Psychology, who published an important paper attempting to define the methodology for animal psychology (Kline, 1899), just a few months after Thorndike's study had appeared in a different journal. Kline's study appears to have been the first to use the white rat as a subject for learning studies, or in Kline's words "to ascertain its susceptibility to profit by experience" (p. 277). It was his colleague and protégé, Willard S. Small, also a Fellow in Psychology, who invented the maze-learning paradigm for the white rat.

Small is best remembered for the second of his experimental studies "of the mental processes of the rat," but the first paper makes interesting reading (Small,

1900). He conducted his studies during the academic year 1898–99, contemporaneous with those of Thorndike but in ignorance of them. Small (1900), quoting from Ernest Ingersoll, believed "an animal should be made to do difficult things only in the line of its inherent abilities" (p. 133), and he set up a series of seminatural experiments in which he carefully observed wild and domestic rats digging, sniffing, eating, and so on. Somewhat like the naturalistic ethologists, Small kept a careful diary of rat behavior and quoted freely from it in his paper.

Small's (1901) second paper gave him a place in the history of comparative psychology because he employed for the first time a maze in which learning by rats was studied. Patterned after one in the formal gardens of Hampton Court Palace, the maze was actually modeled after a diagram in the *Encyclopedia Britannica* (edition unknown), which plan Small "corrected to a rectangular form, as being easier of construction." Munn (1950, p. 3) credits the Hampton Court experimental maze to Edmund Clark Sanford, head of the Clark psychology laboratory, but Small's (1901) actual words are: "I wish especially to express indebtedness to Dr. E. C. Sanford for the initial suggestion" (p. 239), which might refer to either maze learning as a paradigm or the Hampton Court labyrinth as the specific plan. Small constructed three such mazes (p. 208). Thorndike (1898, p. 35, Fig. 13, 14, and 15) had made simple mazes for baby chicks, at first by merely placing books on their edges to serve as walls, but it is Small whose study really began maze learning as an experimental paradigm.

Small's (1901) reasoning in choosing the maze for the experimental analysis of learning is clear:

> the experiments must conform to the psycho-biological character of an animal if sane results are to be obtained. This is not the same thing as guarding against too great difficulties. (*Cf.* the statement in his previous paper quoted above—J. P. H.) The difficulty of two tasks . . . may be identical; yet the problem involved in one may be so different from that in the other, so remote from the animal's racial experience and life habits as to be absolutely outside his capabilities. (p. 206)

Where Thorndike had tried (and failed) to create a paradigm that was "species-independent" by wholly artificial apparatus, Small emphasized mimicking the "life habits" of the species being studied. The white rats were there at Clark; Kline and Small had both used them in previous learning studies, so the problem was to find the most natural experimental apparatus possible (Small, 1901):

> Conforming with such considerations, appeal was made to the rat's propensity for winding passages. A recent magazine article upon the Kangaroo Rat, by Mr. Ernest Seton Thompson, illustrates well the racial character of this rodent trait. Mr. Thompson gives a diagram of the Kangaroo Rat's home-burrow, the outline of which bears a striking resemblance to that of the apparatus used in these experiments. It suggests that the experiments were couched in a familiar language. Not

only do they conform to the sensori-motor experience of the animals, but they also fall in with their constructive instinct relative to home building. (p. 208)

Small's reference is indeed to the famous naturalist better known as Ernst Thompson Seton (1860–1946), born Ernest Evan Thompson. Out of dislike of his father, he introduced his mother's maiden name, Seton, into his own, using various intermediate forms before settling on Ernst Thompson Seton.

I should not leave the impression that Small proposed anything like the evolution of learning processes for modification of specific behavioral complexes or learning processes tied to specific environmental problems faced by the animal. Indeed, much the opposite is true. Small viewed learning as one or several abstract processes and he was much impressed by Thorndike's contrived apparatus (e.g., Small, 1901, p. 233*ff*). Small's primary concern was to make the experiments succeed—by sticking close to the animal's natural history in designing the experimental situation.

Homing Terns, Salivating Dogs, and Pecking Pigeons

John Broadus Watson (1878–1958) was perhaps the investigator having the greatest potential for maintaining ties between biology and psychology. His doctoral work at the University of Chicago under a neurologist in 1903 was quickly followed by an outstanding application of Small's approach in the study of "Kinaesthetic and organic sensations: their role in the reactions of the white rat to the maze" (Watson, 1907). Watson corrected many experimental problems of Small's study and adapted the maze technique for studying sensory processes. Watson went to Johns Hopkins University, where he attracted a brilliant student in Karl S. Lashley (born 1890). Watson is remembered for his founding of "behaviorism" as the study of observable behavior that could do without extrapolations to an unobservable mind or consciousness (Watson, 1913), but that is not our focus here.

Watson recognized that homing is likely to involve learning, as each animal presumably finds its way back to its own specific place. Indeed, psychological journals at the turn of the century contain many papers discussing animal homing. So Watson and Lashley packed off to the field station established on Dry Tortugas by the Carnegie Institute to study homing in sooty terns (*Sterna fuscata*) and later published a landmark paper on that problem (Watson & Lashley, 1915). This study was, in a sense, the last major undertaking of psychological experiments on "natural behavior" until the modern era, and had it not been for personal tragedy such studies might have continued over a long career. However, Watson's "indiscretion" precipitated his divorce in 1920, his resignation from Hopkins, and his general disgrace in the profession. He went in the advertising business (Boring, 1950, p. 644), and, although he continued to publish popular books on behaviorism, he never developed his brilliant start on the analysis of animal learning. His equally illuminating student delved more deeply into sensory functions, then into the brain mechanisms of learning (e.g., Lashley, 1929), never again taking a serious interest in animals in their natural environments.

Ivan Petrovich Pavlov (1849–1936) was a Russian physiologist who won the 1904 Nobel Prize for Physiology or Medicine for research on digestive enzymes, but who is remembered principally as the discoverer of classical conditioning. He began working on salivary enzymes, because these could be collected more readily than others deep within the body, and quickly observed that animals anticipated delivery of food by salivating at its sight or smell. It was then merely a small step to introduce some extraneous stimulus, such as the ringing of a bell, with the food and to show that after many such paired associations a dog would salivate to the sound alone. Because the stimulus–response association depended on this training, Pavlov said salivation was a *conditioned reflex* and the term stuck (Pavlov, 1927). Pavlov's paradigm, now called classical conditioning, helped cement the isolation of learning experiments from the natural history of animals, in which Pavlov never evinced interest.

Burrhus Frederick Skinner (b. 1904) also has a physiological background, working with the great Harvard biologist W. J. Crozier. Perhaps this background sensitized him to naive "physiologizing" of experimental psychologists. His influential contribution was the extension of Thorndike's puzzle boxes to what later became known as the operant conditioning apparatus. Skinner's initial work with rats in fact utilized essentially the same apparatus, but instead of freeing the animal from the cage so it could get to the food outside, Skinner's box simply delivered the food inside (Skinner, 1938). The apparatus was easily modified for the domestic pigeon by replacing the bar pressed by the rat with a key to be pecked, and today more operant studies are probably done with pigeons than rats. The immense convenience of this apparatus, which allowed almost complete automation in delivering reinforcement and recording responses, was well suited to the academic psychologist who could run experiments while teaching and attending to other university duties. It seems clear from Skinner's numerous writings that he firmly believes that learning *is* operant conditioning, and his disciples founded a periodical of operant studies with the monolithic title *Journal of the Experimental Analysis of Behavior*.

Conclusions

It would be wrong to assert that psychological experiments on animal learning lost all touch with biological reality, but it would not be far from the truth. Psychologists who were more interested in the physiological basis of behavior than in the properties of learning did continue to use a diversity of animal species for their studies. Even these comparative psychologists, however, ignored the ecological circumstances to which their species were evolutionarily adapted.

The general view held by the "learning psychologists" was perhaps best expressed by the amazingly productive Clark L. Hull (1884–1952) when he wrote (1943):

> For the optimal probability of survival . . . inherited behavior tendencies must be supplemented by learning. That learning does in fact greatly improve the adaptive quality of the behavior of higher organisms is attested by the most casual observation. But the detailed nature of the learning process is not revealed by casual observation; this becomes evident only through the study of many carefully designed and executed experiments. (p. 68)

Hull may never have become aware of what nonsense he had penned, although I cannot find a matching statement in the revision completed just before his death (Hull, 1952). Even today there is no body of acceptable evidence demonstrating that learning unequivocally improves the adaptiveness of behavior under natural conditions, although many persons today assume along with Hull that it simply must be so. Nor is there as yet good reason to believe that all inherited tendencies must be supplemented by learning.

As readers of the foregoing paragraph in manuscript balked at my assertion that learning has never been shown to be adaptive, a few more words are necessary. Hull's statement about the "adaptive quality of behavior" I take in the usual Darwinian sense of natural selection: Animals showing learning should leave more offspring than those not showing learning, and hence the learners should increase in succeeding generations. Recently (Hailman, 1982a), I have tried to show that the most sophisticated biological studies purporting to demonstrate natural selection of any character, behavioral or morphological, are logically deficient: Even the much-touted case of industrial melanism is open to alternative explanation. I thus stand firmly by my preceding statement that "even today there is no body of acceptable evidence demonstrating that learning unequivocally improves the adaptiveness of behavior under natural conditions." The point in quoting Hull, however, is merely that learning experimenters never even recognized that such issues were in need of empirical study: Learning processes themselves must be studied in detail, they believed, but the adaptiveness of learning may be assumed as obvious from "casual observation."

The dominant view was therefore that (1) there were a limited number of learning types (Hull lists eight "major automatic adaptive behavior devices" in his 1952 book, pp. 348–350) (2) such learning was general and so could be studied in the abstract without relation to specific "inherited tendencies" or environmental circumstances of nature, and (3) such learning was so "obviously" adaptive in the survival of animals that this issue need not even be studied. Although such views may still be held among psychologists isolated from biology, this naive outlook began to fall apart almost simultaneously with Hull's death, for in 1951 Tinbergen's *Study of Instinct* was published in England.

OBSERVATIONS OF CAPTIVE AND WILD ANIMALS

It is an oversimplification to divide views on animal learning into those of laboratory psychologists and classical ethologists, for many important workers have no convenient place in the dichotomy. Yet, in terms of the intellectual legacy bearing on the present topic the dichotomy is a useful device.

It is sometimes said that the classical ethologists were intrepid field observers, but on the whole this was not true. Heinroth, Whitman, Lorenz, Craig, and others developed their concepts by rearing animals in captivity; it was Tinbergen who, almost single-handedly, pioneered the naturalistic observation of and experimentation on animals in their natural environments. The thead that unites the many workers of the ethological tradition was their emphasis on observing the animal in its daily life. When they performed experiments on captive or wild animals the procedures and apparatus were always simple, and the data resulting were more often notebook observations than tables of numbers. The task here is to see how early ethologists, who were primarily concerned with "instinct," viewed the role of learning in the lives of their animals.

Imprinting Rediscovered

Oskar Heinroth (1871–1945) was assistant director of the Zoological Garden in Berlin when the fifth International Ornithological Congress met there in 1910. He had worked closely with a variety of animals in the zoo, making a special study of waterfowl (Family Anatidae), and so reported on his behavioral findings at the Congress under the title "Beiträge zur Biologie, namentlich Ethologie und Psychologie der Anatiden" (Contributions to biology, especially the ethology and psychology of the Anatidae). The published version (O. Heinroth, 1911) has apparently never been translated into English—a particularly unfortunate state of affairs in that this 100-plus-page paper may be *the* start of modern ethology. It was the first paper to use "ethology" in its contemporary sense, the paper that proposed the notion of what became known as fixed action patterns (*arteigene Triebhandlungen,* or literally, species-characteristic driven actions), and the paper in which the "discovery" of imprinting was announced.

Heinroth did not know of Spalding's experiments with baby chicks but discovered the same phenomenon in waterfowl. Here I quote Robert D. Martin's translation from Lorenz (1970), which is the best available published account of Heinroth's words in English:

> Young goslings behave quite differently (from ducklings—J. P. H.). Without any display of fear, they stare calmly at human beings and do not resist handling. If one spends just a little time with them, it is not so easy to get rid of them afterwards. They pipe piteously if left behind and soon follow reliably. It has happened to me that such a gosling, a few hours after removal from the incubator, was content as

long as it could settle under the chair on which I sat. . . . The young gosling shows no inclination to regard the two adults (real geese—J. P. H) as conspecifics: the gosling runs off, piping, and attaches itself to the first human being that happens to come past; it regards the human being as its parent. (pp. 135–136).

Heinroth named this phenomenon *Prägung,* which means "stamping" as in stamping a coin out of metal, and he showed convincingly that the stamping has generality (when imprinted to one person the goslings treated all humans as conspecifics).

Heinroth and his first wife Magdalena later made an enormous empirical contribution to ethology and ornithology by hand rearing almost every avian species indigenous to central Europe. Their results were published in the four-volume *Die Vögel Mitteleuropas* (O. Heinroth & M. Heinroth, 1924–33). Heinroth later published an important paper on avian vocalizations but is probably best known among English-speaking persons for his 1938 book *Aus dem Leben der Vögel* (From the Lives of Birds), which was later revised with his second wife Katharina, and still later translated into English by J. Michael Cullen (O. Heinroth & K. Heinroth, 1958). It is a nice first book about birds, particularly behavior, and encapsulates much of what Heinroth discovered from rearing birds; but this lone English work in no way exhausts the discoveries and thoughts of one of the founders of ethology.

Genesis of an Instinct Concept

Konrad Z. Lorenz (b. 1903) was trained in medicine, presumably to follow in the footsteps of his father, a famous surgeon who is said to have narrowly missed receiving a Nobel Prize. In a sense the elder Lorenz's success launched the son's career in zoology, for the surgeon travelled to America to operate on a millionaire's daughter and with the payment received built a castle in Austria where Konrad kept jackdaws (*Corvus monedula*) and other birds in a seminatural state. His experiences led to correspondence with Heinroth, and together these two inputs were chiefly responsible for Lorenz's development of a sophisticated notion of instinctive behavior.

During the 1930s Lorenz published his major paper on jackdaws and other corvids, followed by three theoretical papers putting forth his general ideas. One of these three, "Der Kumpan in der Umwelt des Vogels" (the companion in the bird's world), appeared almost immediately in a shortened English version in the American ornithological journal *Auk* and much later in a full translation elsewhere. Until 1970, when Robert D. Martin's fine translation of Lorenz's collected works was published, the *Kumpan* paper stood as Lorenz's best-known theoretical statement. However, it is really the earlier paper, "Betrachtungen über das Erkennen der arteigenen Triebhandlungen der Vögel" (Considerations on the identification of species-characteristic driven-actions of birds), that first sets forth Lorenz's general views on animal behavior (Lorenz, 1932; translated as Lorenz, 1970).

Lorenz's (1932) first task was remarkably similar to that of Thorndike: namely, to show that seemingly insightful spatial behavior was in fact the result of simpler learning processes. Lorenz recounted how his jackdaws and other birds solved detour problems (a learning paradigm that was also developed experimentally in psychological laboratories). Lorenz concluded that these problems were solved by "self-conditioning," a notion essentially equivalent to trial-and-error learning in the psychological literature.

Lorenz's framework, however, was the nineteenth-century argument of Spencer that instinct and intelligence lay on a continuum. Lorenz (1970) seemed unaware of the writings of James and others who had virtually settled the basic evolutionary issue by the turn of the century and so had to cover the same ground in his own thinking:

> A very important feature of self-conditioning is the fact that it is quite likely to be based upon an original manifestation of insight. Frequent repetition, accompanied by increasing reinforcement of the relevant pathways, may lead to gradual loss of the original insight component . . . I nevertheless believe that it is quite consistent to dismiss any explanation of the origin of instinctive behaviour patterns from activities involving insight. (p. 60)

Lorenz (1970) then devoted attention to the way in which insight and conditioning are manifest in avian behavior. He noted that "quite often, we can observe behavioural chains which are not inherited as a unitary whole but always possess 'gaps' which are appropriately filled up by self-conditioning or insight behaviour, although these gaps will be properly filled under natural conditions of rearing. In particular, "the recognition of the 'appropriate' object for particular behaviour is frequently *not* inherited," but there is an "instinctive tendency" to try out various objects and then restrict the range through experience.

Lorenz's (1932) chief example of this "filling of gaps by experience" was the behaviour of the red-backed shrike (*Lanius collurio*), which stores its food by impaling the prey on thorns of thornbushes. Ironically, Lorenz (1970) comments in a footnote to his collected works that this turned out to be "a typical case of founding a correct theory on an incorrect observation" because healthy shrikes require no experience to impale prey properly. The early observations by himself, and also by Heinroth and Gustav Kramer, were (Lorenz, 1970, later asserts) made on birds whose physical fitness was subtly suboptimal and so "represent the only known case in which a *pathological defect* of innate behaviour mechanisms was demonstrably *compensated* by learning" (p. 372, emphases his). In any case, Lorenz provided further examples of the "filling gaps by experience," especially in the nesting behavior of certain birds, and named this phenomenon *Erbtrieb-Dressurverschrankung* or *Instinkt-Dressurverschrankung* (literally, driven or instinctive intermixing), for which he used the English term *variable component intercalation*. Lorenz (1970) further stated that he:

> should like to employ the terms *conditioned component intercalation* and *insight component intercalation*. I emphasize at once that the latter is rarely encountered among birds. Even in lower animals, the apparent plasticity of their complex reflex chains is probably largely due to the incorporation of "conditioning links." (p. 66)

In the 1932 paper, Lorenz also gave as an example of his variable component intercalation the recognition of conspecifics among birds. He cited evidence from his own experiences and those of Heinroth and others in which hand-reared birds became attached to their human foster parents, but he did not emphasize the notion of imprinting as separate until his 1935 *Kumpan* paper.

The last identified type of learning in the 1932 paper Lorenz termed "secondary insight of the animal into its own instinctive behaviour patterns" (Lorenz, 1970, p. 67). I cannot find a passage clearly defining this kind of learning so must infer from the long narrative what was intended. In cases where the rearing conditions do not match those of the environment for which the species was evolutionarily adapted, the intercalation may go astray and birds hence come to direct their behavior to inappropriate objects. However, species of high intelligence, such as the ravens (*Corvus corax*) that Lorenz reared, can realize the pointlessness of such behavior gone astray and compensate by simply dropping the behavior from their repertoire; that is, they have some capacity to appreciate the cause–effect relationship of their own behavior, and although they cannot insightfully correct the problem they do at least cease performing acts that have no useful consequences.

A further point of relevance made in the 1932 paper is that behavioral improvements are not necessarily due to learning. Lorenz (1970) addresses the belief that animals improve their performance through practice by citing the example of nest building in birds:

> I am not maintaining that ravens, crows or other highly-specialized birds cannot achieve considerable improvement in nest-building skills on the basis of their learning abilities. But I am utterly convinced that all of the cases so far published, demonstrating that a particular bird built better in a later breeding season than in a previous one (the latter most probably being the uncertain first breeding season in all cases), can be ascribed to general improvements in physical condition. If a genuine learning process could be demonstrated in one given case of nest-building, it would be interesting to determine whether the improvement regularly takes place at the same point in the behaviour chain and thus exhibits the character of a viable component intercalation mechanism. (pp. 71–72)

In sum, the 1932 paper established self-conditioning as the major learning type that facilitated the connections between instinctive components in the behavior of birds and lower animals. Insight, if it occurs, is of a primitive type that initiates the self-conditioning (or trial-and-error) process; imprinting is included in this process (more or less in passing reference), and in highly intelligent birds such as ravens a secondary insight may help suppress unadaptive behavior. Practice, however, plays no role in improving behavior. Finally, Lorenz's (1970) caveat is worth nothing:

> Such variable component links appear to occur frequently in the most advanced vertebrates and they often attain a high degree of complexity in the latter. This renders the analysis of the instinctive behaviour patterns of mammals extremely difficult or even impossible, because of their high level of intelligence. (p. 72).

The *Kumpan* paper, published three years later (Lorenz, 1935), goes over much the same ground with regard to the intercalation process but makes two new points about learning. The first has to do with the evolution of learning abilities and is an explication of the passage just quoted (Lorenz, 1970):

> In my opinion, fixed, instinctive components in a behavioral sequence do not become more labile and increasingly modifiable by experience with increasing development of learning ability and intelligence. It is far more likely that these instinctive patterns drop out completely, one by one, to be replaced by acquired or insight-controlled behaviour patterns. (p. 120)

However, in footnote 49 of the 1970 edition, Lorenz (1970) repudiates this opinion: "This is one of the few fundamental errors of early ethology. Even if a learned behaviour pattern replaces the function of a disappearing fixed motor pattern, this learning process itself necessarily has its own phylogenetically programmed basis" (p. 374). (I do not pretend to understand this later addition. Editors Johnston and Pietrewicz suggest that Lorenz might have felt that the 1935 statement implied that learning had no phylogenetic basis, hence sought to correct this "fundamental error" in the 1970 footnote.)

Although Heinroth and Lorenz had both earlier described imprinting (and unknown to them, so had Spalding), these authors had not formally characterized the process. It was Lorenz (1935) who did so, but his first important point may come as a surprise (Lorenz, 1970): "In my opinion, this process cannot be equated with learning—it is the acquisition of the object of *instinctive behaviour patterns oriented towards conspecifics*" (p. 124, emphasis his). Why imprinting is not learning cannot be decided unless one knows Lorenz's definition of learning, which I have been unable to find in any of his early papers. Thirty years later, Lorenz (1965, pp. 9–10) did define learning as a process of acquiring and storing information other than through phylogenetic adaptation, but this is clearly not what he meant in 1935 when contrasting imprinting with learning. However, he did say in 1935 (Lorenz, 1970) that "the process of imprinting . . . possesses a series of features which are basically different from learning" (p. 127), so it must be these enumerated features that make it separate:

1. Imprinting "can only take place during a narrowly-defined period of time in the individual's life (p. 127).

2. The recognition established by imprinting "cannot be 'forgotten'! The possibility of 'forgetting' is . . . a *basic feature of all learning processes*" (p. 127, emphasis his).

3. "Imprinting involves a peculiar and extremely puzzling selection of the characters of the object: *only supra-individual* characters are fixated" (p. 246, emphasis his).

Lorenz (1970: pp. 127–129) draws parallels between embryological processes and imprinting, concluding that "it would be quite fitting to use the term *inductive determination* for instinctive behaviour patterns whose object is not innately determined in the animal, but imprinted by the environment" (pp. 128–29, emphasis his). This was a sage piece of reasoning, unfortunately marred by his insistence that imprinting is "a quite specific process, *which has nothing to do with learning*" (p. 245, emphasis his).

It seems evident that here (in 1935) Lorenz was still struggling with how to classify imprinting. As noted previously, he had recognized the process in passing in his 1932 paper, there discussing it along with forms of learning such as "primitive insight" which initiates self-conditioning and what he termed "secondary insight" which helps suppress unadaptive behavior. These forms of learning, he felt, were not of great importance in adaptive behavior, and hence a fundamental distinction between "instinctive" and "learned" behavior could be drawn. Sometime between 1932 and 1935 he seems to have realized the crucial importance of imprinting in adaptive behavior and so, to maintain the fundamental dichotomy, separated imprinting from learning processes. The irony, in my view, is that Lorenz may have had in his hand one of the keys to the evolution of learning but let it slip between his fingers: By 1935 he saw the relation between embryological induction and imprinting, but not that between imprinting and other forms of learning. He possessed, in the phenomenon of imprinting, the crucial link between embryological processes and their very special manifestations as higher forms of learning, but the need to dichotomize blinded him to this link.

Field Studies of Behavior

Although Julian Huxley's famous study of the great crested grebe (*Podiceps cristatus*) is rightfully marked as the first ethological field study, it was Niko Tinbergen (b. 1907) who later developed field work into a high art. Tinbergen's early papers were as carefully empirical as Lorenz's were boldly theoretical. Although Tinbergen did publish theoretical papers based on empirical generalizations—about territoriality, social organization, innate behavior, and social releasers—his real summing up did not appear until 1951 as the classic *Study of Instinct*. It is therefore difficult to discern clearly what his early orienting attitudes were toward learning.

Perhaps a significant point is that Tinbergen's first study was almost totally on learning: "Ueber die Orientierung des Bienenwolfes *(Philanthus triangulum* Fabr.)," which concerned how a wasp called the bee-wolf orients in digging and provisioning its nest (Tinbergen, 1932 and 1935). These papers were translated by Tinbergen himself for the first volume of a selection from his numerous works (Tinbergen, 1972). By carrying out simple but systematic experiments of altering landmarks near the nest, Tinbergen discovered in the first paper that the wasp learns a complicated pattern of spatial cues rather than some key feature of the environment. In the second paper he described the behavior by which the female bee-wolf studies her nest locality, and the kind of landmarks she specifically chooses to learn for homing to the nest: patterned, large, three-dimensional objects near the nest that contrast with the background. Such objects are likely to have more permanence than others such as, say, leaves (which could blow away), so evolution has created a learning system specifically adapted to the problems faced by the animal in its natural environment.

The other early study bearing on problems of learning concerned experiments on the gaping behavior of passerine nestlings (Tinbergen & Kuenen, 1939). The study presented models to see what stimuli elicit begging, but the authors attempted to use the results to determine the role played by learning processes in gaping development. They found not only that developmental changes were due almost entirely to "maturation" but moreover that the nestlings were resistant to conditioning to new stimuli. However, according to Tinbergen (1973):

> we believe that learning processes do occur which render certain stimulus combinations *in*effective (i.e., 'carving' out' so-to-speak a small area from the previously broad innate schema). For example, moving twigs and leaves—which possess all the visual characteristics of the optimal stimulus situation—do not evoke gaping, and this can only have been brought about by experience. (p. 49, emphasis his)

Perhaps a more important observation, however, is how a simple process of learning (habituation) can bring about the impression of conditioning (Tinbergen, 1973):

> Finally, in many cases a completely different type of learning process can give the impression that there has been an alteration in the releasing scheme of the gaping pattern. Freshly captured young animals often crouch in response to human presence. When the animals then become accustomed to the new situation, the 'block' on gaping is removed. It could easily be inferred that the animals have 'learned to gape towards the forceps' (with which Tinbergen and Kuenen fed them— J. P. H.). However . . . the pair of forceps fits excellently into the innate scheme

of the gaping response. . . . it is habituation. . . . which . . . lowers the inhibiting effect on gaping. (p. 50)

Insofar as I can tell, Tinbergen made no theoretical statements about learning until Chapter VI of his justly famous *Study of Instinct* (Tinbergen, 1951, pp. 128–150). In this chapter he devoted initial attention to maturational processes of development (pp. 128–142) before considering learning. Then he asked just the right question: "Also, it might be useful to approach learning phenomena from a more naturalistic standpoint than is usually done and to ask, not what can an animal learn, but what does it actually learn under natural conditions?" After considering the question of how to detect a learning process in natural behavior, Tinbergen delved into "the innate disposition to learn" (pp. 145–150) under three heads.

The first topic is what he called *localized learning,* by which he referred to localization within the behavioral repertoire of the species (not localization in space). He (Tinbergen, 1951) states:

some parts of the pattern, some reactions, may be changed by learning while others seem to be so rigidly fixed that no learning is possible. In other words, there seem to be more or less strictly localized 'dispositions to learn.' Different species are predisposed to learn different parts of the pattern. So far as we know, these differences between species have adaptive significance. (p. 145)

He then illustrated this principle from his studies on gulls, those of Watson and Lashley (1915) on terns, his own studies on the bee-wolf, and so on.

The second topic is what Tinbergen called *preferential learning,* in which *what* is learned may be very different even in highly similar situations. For example, the herring gull's (*Larus argentatus*) orientation toward eggs is based on spatial learning, and it will choose inappropriate objects to incubate at the nest site in preference to its own eggs moved just a little distance away. On the other hand, its response to chicks are to the objects themselves, rather than the site at which they are expected to be found. Tinbergen (1951) states: "Here we discover another principle: it seems to be a property of the innate disposition that it directs the conditioning to special parts of the receptual field" (p. 150).

Finally, Tinbergen (1951) considered "critical periods in learning," referring to Lorenz's observations on imprinting, but adding evidence from his own experience. Interesting here is the statement that "some authors doubt whether this process of imprinting is fundamentally different from other types of conditioning and believe that there are only differences of degree between them" (p. 150), thus replacing the link between imprinting and other learning that had become lost since Spalding's time.

It is appropriate to close the dualism between (primarily American) learning psychologists and (primarily European) classical ethologists with *The Study of Instinct.* This book, along with the 1950 *Symposium of the Society for Experimental*

Biology, served as a primary stimulus to get the broad disciplines of psychology and zoology interacting again after a divorce of half a century.

TOWARD A SYNTHESIS

The early 1950s marked a revolution in the study of animal behavior. From within zoology there sprang a new interest in learning processes, their physiological bases, their dynamic relations with processes of instinct, and their adaptive functions. Simultaneously there was a solidification of the classical ethological views, ably summarized in Tinbergen's (1951) *Study of Instinct* and in the works of others, which brought the findings to the attention of laboratory psychologists. And, perhaps more than any other factor, there was vigorous criticism of these ethological views from certain American psychologists. The interchanges that resulted reoriented the research of almost everyone interested in animal behavior and set them groping toward a synthesis, which (in my view) still remains elusive.

Learning as an Adaptive Process

William H. Thorpe typifies a small group of zoologists who had always been interested in learning as a critical part of a species' adaptive capacities. His empirical work in the 1930s concerned olfactory conditioning of insects, followed by several published discussions of learning phenomena, especially in arthropods. His thinking probably had little impact before 1950, when his paper "The concepts of learning and their relation to those of instinct" appeared in the proceedings from the July 1949 Symposium of the Society for Experimental Biology. This symposium gathered together in Cambridge one of the most prestigious groups ever assembled to discuss animal behavior: Represented were sensory and central nervous system physiologists, learning experts and, of course, practitioners of ethology such as Lorenz, Tinbergen, O. Koehler, and G. P. Baerends.

Thorpe (1950) began by asserting that "there are few aspects of animal behaviour that have been more neglected by present-day zoologists than learning," which he defined as an adaptive change in behavior resulting from experience. He noted that there was much to be gained from those who studied conditioning and maze-learning, but "there had been a tendency . . . (for such work) . . . to be too exclusively concerned with a few species, studied under highly artificial conditions, ignoring the immense variety and plasticity of behavior as seen under natural conditions" (p. 388).

Thorpe proceeded to classify, perhaps for the first time in modern zoological literature, types of learning. His classification reflected to some extent the complexities of the processes themselves—the chief characteristics by which psychologists had always classified learning—but also incorporated criteria of what kinds of animals showed the processes and how the learning was related to the adaptiveness of the species' behavioral repertoire. Thorpe's types were:

1. Habituation.
2. Conditioning, type I.
3. Trial-and-error learning (conditioning, type II).
4. Insight learning.
5. Imprinting.

Of habituation, Thorpe emphasized that learning *not* to respond to stimuli that have no adaptive consequences appears in all kinds of behavior and moreover "in animals of all grades of organization" including major groups of invertebrates and even protozoans. He saw habituation as most valuable in terms of stimuli that warn of danger. He considered the similarities between habituation and extinction of a conditioned response, though he concluded that they are not identical processes. However, Thorpe did feel that habituation was a manifest part of trial-and-error learning, such as in the pecking of baby chicks which not only learn to respond positively to food but also habituate to nonfood items.

In order to understand Thorpe's views on Pavlovian or classical conditioning (which he refers to as type I), it is necessary to know first the ethological distinction between appetitive and consummatory behavior, a notion due originally to Charles Otis Whitman, or perhaps to his student Wallace Craig, who prepared Whitman's posthumous works for publication. A fundamental unit of ongoing behavior was conceived as beginning with a variable searching or appetitive complex, which terminates in a consummatory act; for example, a predator's hunting for and then capturing prey. Thorpe noted that Pavlovian conditioning is concerned only with the final consummatory act, in which a new stimulus comes to elicit the act through pairing with the unconditional stimulus.

By contrast, what we would today call operant or instrumental conditioning (Thorpe's type II, which he equated with trial-and-error learning) directly concerns adaptive changes in the appetitive phase of behavior. Here, in contrast with Pavlovian conditioning, which Thorpe (1950) believed can only work through positive reinforcement, the pattern of operant conditioning "depends on whether the reinforcement is positive or negative, i.e., a 'reward' or a 'punishment'" (pp. 392–393).

Thorpe (1950) characterized insight as "the sudden adaptive reorganization of experience or the sudden production of a new adaptive response not arrived at by random trial behaviour" (p. 394). He discussed latent learning (Blodgett's discovery that rats learn mazes through exploratory behavior when there is no food reward for their efforts) and concluded that it is insight, although he remained somewhat ambivalent. He cited Donald K. Adams as having pointed out that "if learning is slow, we call it trial and error, if rapid, we call it insight" (p. 396).

Finally, Thorpe recounted the discoveries of Heinroth and Lorenz about imprinting processes and articulated a principle of imprinting that is implicit in their writings: Imprinting "is often completed long before the various specific reactions to which the imprinted pattern will ultimately become linked are established" (p. 402). Perhaps the most important conclusion, and certainly the most prophetic statement, of Thorpe's (1950) entire paper is:

> But the extreme interest of imprinting lies above all in the fact that its study seems to be more promising than that of any other kind of learning for the understanding of the nature of the perceptual side of instinct and its relationship to plastic processes in general. It needs and would repay full and precise experimental investigation more almost than any other aspect of animal behavior. (p. 403)

A few years after this paper, Thorpe (1956) brought out the first edition of his comprehensive *Learning and Instinct in Animals*, which solidified the points he made in 1950 while producing a comprehensive review of studies broken down by animal groups. Thorpe's contribution was to acquaint zoologists with a vast store of experimental literature on learning while relating these results to familiar behavioral situations in which the adaptive significance of learning seemed obvious. After Thorpe it was simply no longer possible for a zoologist to ignore learning phenomena as a major constituent of any theoretical conception of animal behavior.

Learning as an Ontogenetic Process

Daniel S. Lehrman (1919–1972) was a graduate student in psychology when he launched an attack on the instinct conceptions of the classical ethologists (Lehrman, 1953). His background, however, was replete with influences from zoology, Lehrman having worked as a student assistant to G. K. Noble, having frequently gone bird watching with William Vogt and Joseph J. Hickey (and even Tinbergen, when he visited America), and having interacted at the American Museum of Natural History in New York with the great invertebrate zoologist Libby Hyman and the great evolutionary zoologist Ernst Mayr. Therefore, unlike the majority of psychologists, Lehrman had a deep interest in and extensive knowledge of animals and their natural habitats. This interest led him to a few psychologists with similar interest, such as Frank Beach, who studied hormonal bases of sexual behavior, and particularly T. C. Schneirla (at the time perhaps the world's only "ant psychologist"), who became Lehrman's mentor and graduate advisor. And, perhaps more significantly than one cares to think, Lehrman had a fluent knowledge of German and so he read all the early works of Lorenz and other classical ethologists with comprehension.

What Lehrman (1953) actually said is less important than the profound influence it had on both psychologists and zoologists. His major thesis was that the way in which classical ethologists studied behavior almost automatically excluded their being able to appreciate environmentally caused changes during development. Laboratory paradigms of learning represented merely the explication of general learning abilities in adult animals; more subtle interactions between the developing organism and its environment guided the very ontogeny of behavior. Furthermore, these experientially mediated processes were by no means restricted to stimulus–response connections, as both learning psychologists and classical ethologists often assumed: The very motor acts of behavior developed through interactive processes.

The evidence available to Lehrman was scant, for few investigators had focused on the issues he was raising. It is "safer" to work scientifically within an established framework, such as a particular learning paradigm or an explicit instinct concept, so the vast store of available empirical studies built upon a few conceptions of earlier masters. Even Thorpe had tried basically to interdigitate learning paradigms with ethological instinct concepts while leaving both intact and inserting nothing truly new. So in plowing new ground Lehrman sometimes relied upon evidence that today seems downright silly; for example, following Zing Yang Kuo, Lehrman suggested that the chick's head movements within the egg, caused passively by the beating of the heart, potentiated the development of posthatch pecking movements. As outrageous as such suggestions may have been—and they did provoke lively debate in the literature—they gave new direction to ensuing empirical investigations.

The New Empiricism

The renewed contact between zoology and psychology produced a wave of empirical studies on learning that had no real predecessors. These studies of experiential processes in behavior began in the late 1950s, and I exemplify them for only the ensuing decade, as the late 1960s brings us to a point that begins to stretch the term "historical perspective."

Most prominent in the new empiricism was the fulfillment of Thorpe's hopes about the study of imprinting. Almost immediately there was a wholesale rush to dissect the imprinting phenomenon experimentally, both by psychologists such as Eckard H. Hess (e.g., Ramsay & Hess, 1954) and Julian Jaynes (e.g., 1956) and by zoologists such as Robert A. Hinde (e.g., 1955) and Peter H. Klopfer (e.g., 1956). Almost like an infectious disease, the study of imprinting spread to most of the major behavioral centers of the world and produced such an enormous literature that reviews struggled to keep pace with empirical progress (e.g., Fabricius, 1962; Gray, 1961; Hess, 1958, 1959; Hinde, 1961; James, 1960; Moltz, 1960, 1963; Sluckin, 1965; Sluckin & Salzen, 1961; Smith, 1962 and many later papers and books).

As even today vigorous experimentation continues, it is too early to sum up what legacy behavioral studies will ultimately inherit from this imprinting empiricism. One still unsettled issue seems worthy of pointing out here, as it seems like a mere semantic problem until considered more deeply. Is imprinting a general type of learning, or is it only the process by which a young precocial bird becomes attached to its parent? Recall that Lorenz had said that imprinting had nothing whatever to do with learning, and Thorpe later listed it as a principal category of learning processes. Perhaps the difference is basically a semantic one, but even so it reflects underlying differences in how one conceives of behavioral phenomena. If experimental psychology as a science erred in striving too quickly to generalize learning into a few types, hence blinding everyone to phenomena that did not nicely fit the categories, perhaps zoology erred in the other extreme by refusing to generalize beyond a given-species/given-behavior context. Where between the extremes lies the optimal strategy whereby we simultaneously summarize scientific knowledge yet foster further creative analysis? The question as to how the word "imprinting" should be used encapsulates this general conundrum.

The other principal facet of the new empiricism concentrated on the roles of experiential processes in the development of young animals. This subject is part of many imprinting studies as well, but the focus here is not upon characterizing details of a process that was already known in outline; rather it is following the developmental course of particular kinds of behavior to see how they are experientially influenced during ontogeny. In some cases, imprinting studies gradually led into this second kind of empiricism, as when Gilbert Gottlieb moved from treatments of eggs that would help define the critical imprinting period (Gottlieb, 1961) to direct studies of the embryo itself (e.g., Gottlieb & Kuo, 1965). This new area has since expanded greatly, interesting the embryologists and neurobiologists as well as ethological and psychological researchers.

A similar intellectual development can be traced in psychologists such as Harry F. Harlow. His earlier work on primate behavior had led to the notion of learning sets (Harlow, 1949), a higher level extension of conventional learning paradigms. Harlow then switched his interests to the development of affectional responses of infant monkeys (e.g., Harlow, 1958, 1960), showing among other things that food reinforcement in the form of mother's milk was *not* a key factor in the genesis of "mother love."

Zoologists also began looking more closely at the ontogeny of behavior, as characterized by William Dilger's (1960, 1962) studies of lovebirds (*Agapornis*). He hybridized two species that had different methods of carrying nest material and found that the hybrids tried both methods (somewhat ineffectively), learning slowly over successive nesting cycles to restrict efforts to the more productive method.

The conflict that was formalized in Lehrman's criticisms directed to Lorenz carried through to specific issues between the camps. One such issue, between Schneirla and Tinbergen, was specific enough to be settled in a single empirical test. Tinbergen (Tinbergen, 1951, pp. 76–79; Tinbergen & Perdeck, 1950) said that the chick of the herring gull has an innate, configurational picture of the parent: When the red bill-spot at which the chick pecks was moved to the forehead on a parental model, chicks begged less. Schneirla (1956, pp. 410–411) maintained that this result occurred merely because the spot moved less when on the forehead, considering the way in which the models were moved, and that a configurational stimulus was not involved. The results of a critical test may have surprised both parties, as they did the experimenter. If the movement of the spot is kept constant and at the same distance from the gull chick, the newly hatched chick behaves as Schneirla predicted: It begs equally to models having the spot on the bill and forehead (Hailman, 1967). However, chicks that had had a few days experience with their parents in the nest chose the configurational stimulus with the spot on the bill, as originally thought by Tinbergen. In fact, this and related experiments gave rise to a reinterpretation of Pavlovian conditioning: Perhaps it evolved not for cross-modality linking of something like the sound of a bell with the smell of food, but rather as a means of perceptual development where the conditional stimulus–object (gull configuration) is the same as the object bearing the unconditional stimulus (red spot on bill).

To close the decade from the late 1950s to late 1960s we can note the monumental attempt of Robert A. Hinde to provide "A synthesis of ethology and comparative psychology" in his 1966 book *Animal Behaviour* (revised as Hinde, 1970). He tried, in a manner that no person since has successfully emulated, to integrate virtually all the important phenomena of animal behavior, including everything that might be considered important under the rubric of learning. But history will not stand still for synthesis, and by 1970 there were probably more persons simultaneously conducting research on animal behavior than had made such studies in the entire century since Darwin. Hinde's book was a progress report on the new empiricism and today may be viewed as an introduction to many of the problems with which we still grapple.

Conclusion

It exceeds the bounds of "historical perspective" to specify what it is that we may have learned from the new empiricism ushered in after the middle of the century. We can say, however, that the whole of research on learning was forever changed. No ethologist can any longer seriously believe that the only experiential role in the genesis of behavior consists of connecting instinctive motor acts in a chain. No psychologist can any longer seriously believe that the only kinds of learning are reducible to a few paradigms of conditioning that involve identifiable reinforcement. While deftly avoiding any attempt at summarizing what it is that we currently believe we understand, let me conclude by proposing three areas of further study that might prove especially enlightening.

First, it should prove profitable not only to continue vigorous study of the embryology of behavior and the roles played by experience therein (e.g., Gottlieb, 1976) but especially to link experiential processes more closely with concepts of developmental biology. Lorenz's likening of learning to embryological induction is not, I suspect, merely an apt metaphor: It is a key to fundamental understanding of how highly specific learning processes evolved as extensions of environmentally dependent developmental processes.

Second, we need to pay far more attention to how seemingly irrelevant experiences in the life of an animal potentiate developmental improvement in specific behavioral patterns. For example, the experience of standing upright (whether this merely strengthens muscles or has more complicated effects on coordination) appears to be a major factor in the ontogenetic improvement of accuracy in the begging-pecks of gull chicks (Hailman, 1967). Developmental genetics has shown without doubt that a given gene has multiple effects on wholly different aspects of an animal. We should look vigorously for the analogous multiple developmental effects of given experiences: I suspect they are waiting to be discovered and will contain some interesting surprises.

Finally, if we are to understand the biology of learning in its broadest sense, it will be necessary not merely to study experiential processes in relation to a species' natural ecology, but moreover to enlarge the sophistication of hypotheses concerning the adaptiveness of learning. For example, it simply begs the question to assert that imprinting in gallinaceous birds or waterfowl is "adaptive" in potentiating the choice of a mate from one's own species. Nest parasites—such as the European cuckoo (*Cuculus canorus*) and the American brown-headed cowbird (*Molothrus ater*)—find conspecific mates quite nicely, thank you, without any opportunity for imprinting (see West & King's chapter, this volume). Bateson (1981) proposes that it is not really "species-recognition" that underlies imprinting, but a far more sophisticated need: to find a mate that is neither too closely nor too distantly related genetically, in order simultaneously to avoid inbreeding depression yet retain advantageous aspects of a balanced genotype in the offspring produced. The merit of Bateson's specific proposal is irrelevant; it is the sophistication of his evolutionary thinking that deserves emulation.

SUMMARY

The principal biological issue about learning in the nineteenth century was its role in the evolution of behavior. Darwin endorsed the idea that insightful and conscious acts that become habitual could be transmitted to offspring, although he saw that such "Lamarckian" origin was impossible for behavior of sterile worker casts of social insects. By the turn of the century, Lamarckian notions were largely abandoned, psychologists turning their attention to laboratory experiments on learning and zoologists to observations of natural behavior of animals. The initial experiments (e.g., Small's maze and Thorndike's puzzle boxes) were designed around the natural behavior of the subjects, but psychological studies quickly drifted away from that orientation and the "biology" of learning became restricted to neurological and other physiological variables. In parallel, early zoological studies dealt extensively with the role of learning in behavior in both observations of semicaptive animals and experiments in the field, but this orientation took an increasingly small role as instinct concepts evolved. The prominent exception lay in the rediscovery of imprinting, which process initially was treated as "having nothing to do with learning." At mid-century things began to change rapidly: Contact between psychologists and zoologists was established again through the demonstration that laboratory learning paradigms described important adaptive processes in the natural lives of animals, and through the recognition that both laboratory learning types and instinct conceptions inadequately explained the ontogenetic development of behavior. The intellectual revolution ushered in a wave of new empirical studies in which psychologists increasingly studied natural behavior and zoologists increasingly studied learning processes, both groups intensively involved in the analysis of imprinting. No successful synthesis seems yet to have been wrested from the new facts, and, although we may still be in the explosive phase of the new emphasis, there are already visible signs of largely new and more sophisticated approaches to the biology of learning.

ACKNOWLEDGMENTS

I am indebted to Timothy D. Johnston and Alexandra T. Pietrewicz for most careful readings of the manuscript and numerous suggestions for improvement. An anonymous reviewer provided articulate comments of such erudition that they can have come from only one source, and I thank him. I am especially grateful to Robert A. McCabe for unraveling the mystery of the multiple names of Ernst Seton Thompson, a quandry that proved intractable to the usual library assault.

REFERENCES

Bateson, P. P. G. (1981). Ontogeny of behaviour. *British Medical Bulletin, 37*, 159–164.

Beer, C. G. (1963–64). Ethology—the zoologist's approach to behaviour. *Tuatara, 11*, 170–177 and *12*, 16–39.

Beer, C. G. (1980). Perspectives on animal behavior comparisons. In M. Borstein (Ed), *Comparative methods in psychology*. Hillsdale, NJ: Lawrence Erlbaum Associates.

Bitterman, M. E. (1969). Thorndike and the problem of animal intelligence. *American Psychologist, 24*, 444–453.

Boring, E. G. (1950). *A history of experimental psychology* (2nd ed.). New York Appleton–Century–Crofts.

Darwin, C. (1859). *On the origin of species*. London: Murray.

Darwin, C. (1868). *Variation of animals and plants under domestication*. New York: D. Appleton.

Darwin, C. (1871). *The descent of man and selection in relation to sex*. (Page references are from the revised edition of 1881 published by D. Appleton, New York).

Darwin, C. (1873). *The expression of the emotions in man and animals*. New York and London: D. Appleton. (Quotes taken from the 1965 reprint published by the University of Chicago Press, Chicago and London.)

Darwin, C. (1897). *On the origin of species*, 6th ed. New York: D. Appleton.

Dilger, W. C. (1960). The comparative ethology of the African parrot genus *Agapornis*. *Zeitschrift für Tierpsychologie, 17*, 649–685.

Dilger, W. C. (1962). The behavior of lovebirds. *Scientific American, 206*, 88–98.

Fabricius, E. (1962). Some aspects of imprinting in birds. *Symposium of the Zoological Society, London, 8*, 139–148.

Gottlieb, G. (1961). Developmental age as a baseline for determination of the critical period in imprinting. *Journal of Comparative and Physiological Psychology, 54*, 422–427.

Gottlieb, G. (1976). Conceptions of prenatal development: Behavioral embryology. *Psychological Review, 83*, 215–234.

Gottlieb, G. (1979). Comparative psychology and theology. In E. Hearst (Ed.), *The first century of experimental psychology:* Hillsdale, NJ: Lawrence Erlbaum Associates.

Gottlieb, G., & Kuo, Z. Y. (1965). Development of behavior in the duck embryo. *Journal of Comparative and Physiological Psychology, 59*, 183–188.

Gould, S. J., & Lewontin, R. (1979). The spandrels of San Marco and the Panglossian paradigm: A critique of the adaptationist programme. *Proceedings of the Royal Society of London* (Series B), *Biology, 205*, 581–598.

Gray, P. H. (1961). Imprinting. *Science, 133*, 924–928.

Hailman, J. P. (1967). The ontogeny of an instinct: The pecking response in chicks of the laughing gull (*Larus atricilla* L.) and related species. *Behaviour Supplement, 15*, 1–196.

Hailman, J. P. (1982a). Evolution and behavior: An iconoclastic view. In H. C. Plotkin (Ed.), *Reading and essays in evolutionary epistemology*. London: Wiley.

Hailman, J. P. (1982b). Ontogeny: Toward a general theoretical framework for ethology. In P. P. G. Bateson & P. Klopfer (Eds.), *Perspectives in ethology* (Vol. 6). New York: Plenum.

Haldane, J. B. S. (1954). Introducing Douglas Spalding. *British Journal of Animal Behaviour, 2*, 1.

Harlow, H. F. (1949). The formation of learning sets. *Psychological Review, 56*, 51–65.

Harlow, H. F. (1958). The nature of love. *American Psychologist, 13*, 673–685.

Harlow, H. F. (1960). Primary affectional patterns in primates. *American Journal or Ortho-Psychiatry, 30*, 676–684.

Heinroth, K. (1977). The history of ethology. In K. Immelmann (Ed.), *Grzimek's encyclopedia of ethology*. London and elsewhere: Van Nostrand Reinhold.

Heinroth, O. (1911). Beträge zur Biologie, namentlich Ethologie und Psychologie der Anatiden. *Verhandlung Vth Internationale Ornithologische Kongress*, Berlin.

Heinroth, O., & Heinroth, K. (1958). *The birds*. Ann Arbor: University of Michigan Press.

Heinroth, O., & Heinroth, M. (1924–1933). *Die Vögel Mitteleuropas* (4 vols), Berlin.

Hess, E. H. (1958). "Imprinting" in animals. *Scientific American, 198*, 81–90.

Hess, E. H. (1959). Imprinting. *Science, 130*, 133–141.

Hinde, R. A. (1955). The following response of moorhens and coots. *British Journal of Animal Behaviour, 3*, 121–122.

Hinde, R. A. (1961). The establishment of the parent–offspring relation in birds, with some mammalian analogies. In W. H. Thorpe & O. L. Zangwill (Eds.), *Current problems in animal behaviour*. Cambridge: Cambridge University Press.

Hinde, R. A. (1970). *Animal behaviour: A synthesis of ethology and comparative psychology*. New York and elsewhere: McGraw–Hill.

Hull, C. L. (1943). *Principles of behavior: An introduction to behavior theory*. New York & London: D. Appleton–Century.

Hull, C. L. (1952). *A behavior system: An introduction to behavior theory concerning the individual organism*. New Haven: Yale University Press.

James H. (1960). Imprinting. *Ontario Psychological Association Quarterly, 13*, 41–74.

James, W. (1890a). *The principles of psychology* (Vol. 1). New York: Holt.

James, W. (1890b). *The principles of psychology* (Vol. 2). New York: Holt.

Jaynes, J. (1956). Imprinting: The interaction of learned and innate behavior. I. Development and generalization. *Journal of Comparative and Physiological Psychology, 49,* 201–206.

Jenkins, H. M. (1979). Animal learning and behavior theory. In E. Hearst (Ed.), *The first century of experimental psychology.* Hillsdale, NJ: Lawrence Erlbaum Associates.

Kline, L. W. (1899) Methods in animal psychology. *American Journal of Psychology, 10,* 256–279.

Klopfer, P. H. (1956). Comments concerning the age at which imprinting occurs. *Wilson Bulletin, 68,* 320–321.

Klopfer, P. H., & J. P. Hailman. (1967). *An introduction to animal behavior: Ethology's first century.* Englewood Cliffs, NJ: Prentice–Hall.

Lamarck, M. de (1815). *Histoire naturelle des animaux sans vertebres.* Paris: Verdiere.

Lashley, K. S. (1929). *Brain mechanisms and intelligence.* Chicago: Chicago University Press.

Lehrman, D. S. (1953). A critique of Konrad Lorenz's theory of instinctive behavior. *Quarterly Review of Biology, 28,* 337–363.

Lewontin, R. C. (1978). Adaptation. *Scientific American, 239*(3), 213–230.

Lorenz, K. (1932). Betrachtingen über das Erkennen der arteigenen Triebhandlungen der Vogel. *Journal für Ornithologie, 80,* 50–98.

Lorenz, K. (1935). Der Kumpan in der Umwelt des Vogels. *Journal für Ornithologie, 83,* 137–213, 289–413.

Lorenz, K. Z. (1965). *Evolution and modification of behavior.* Chicago & London: University of Chicago Press.

Lorenz, K. (1970). *Studies in animal and human behaviour* (Vol. I, translated by Robert Martin). Cambridge, MA: Harvard University Press.

Moltz, H. (1960). Imprinting; Empirical basis and theoretical significance. *Psychological Bulletin, 57,* 291–314.

Moltz, H. (1963). Imprinting: An epigenetic approach. *Psychological Review, 70,* 123–138.

Morgan, C. L. (1896). *Habit and instinct.* London: Edward Arnold.

Munn, N. L. (1950). *Handbook of psychological research on the rat.* Boston: Houghton Mifflin.

Pavlov, I. P. (1927). *Conditioned reflexes; An investigation of the physiological activity of the cerebral cortex* (translated and edited by G. V. Anrep). London: Oxford University Press.

Ramsay, A. O., & Hess, E. H. (1954). A laboratory approach to the study of imprinting. *Wilson Bulletin, 66,* 196–206.

Romanes, G. J. (1884). *Mental evolution in animals.* London: Keegan, Paul, Trench.

Romanes, G. J. (1889). *Mental evolution in man.* New York: D. Appleton.

Schneirla, T. C. (1956). Interrelationships of the "innate" and the "acquired" in instinctive behavior. In *L'instinct dans le comportement des animaux et de l'homme.* Paris: Masson & Cie.

Skinner, B. F. (1938). *The behavior of organisms: An experimental analysis.* New York: Appleton–Century–Crofts.

Sluckin, W. (1965). *Imprinting and early learning.* Chicago: Aldine.

Sluckin, W., & Salzen, E. A. (1961). Imprinting and perceptual learning. *Quarterly Journal of Experimental Psychology, 13,* 65–77.

Small, W. S. (1900). An experimental study of the mental processes of the rat. *American Journal of Psychology, 11,* 133–165.

Small, W. S. (1901). Experimental study of the mental processes of the rat. II. *American Journal of Psychology, 12,* 206–239.

Smith, F. V. (1962). Perceptual aspects of imprinting. *Symposia of the Zoological Society, London, 8,* 171–191.

Spalding, D. A. (1873). Instinct with original observations on young animals. *Macmillan's Magazine, 27,* 282–293. (Reprinted in *British Journal of Animal Behavior,* 1954, *2,* 2–11.)

Spencer, H. (1855). *Principles of psychology.* New York: D. Appleton.

Spencer, H. (1896). *Principles of psychology* (2nd ed.). New York: D. Appleton.

Thorndike, E. L. (1898). Animal intelligence: An experimental study of the associative processes in animals. *Psychological Reviews, 2*(4), (*Monographic Supplement, 8*), 1–109.

Thorndike, E. L. (1911). *Animal intelligence*. New York: Hafner.

Thorpe, W. H. (1950). The concepts of learning and their relation to those of instinct. *Symposium of the Society of Experimental Biology, 4*, 387–408.

Thorpe, W. H. (1956). *Learning and instinct in animals*. Cambridge, MA: Harvard University Press.

Tinbergen, N. (1932). Ueber die Orientierung des Bienenwolfes (*Philanthus triangulum* Fabr.). *Zeitschrift für vergleichende Physiologie, 18*, 305–335.

Tinbergen, N. (1935). Ueber die Orientierung des Bienenwolfes II. Die Bienenjagd. *Zeitschrift für vergleichende Physiologie, 21*, 699–716.

Tinbergen, N. (1951). *The study of instinct*. London: Oxford University Press.

Tinbergen, N. (1972). *The animal in its world: Explorations of an ethologist 1932–1972* (Vol. 1). *Field studies*. Cambridge, MA: Harvard University Press.

Tinbergen, N. (1973). *The animal in its world: Explorations of an ethologist 1932–1972* (Vol. 2). *Laboratory experiments and general papers*. Cambridge, MA: Harvard University Press.

Tinbergen, N., & Kuenen, D. J. (1939). Ueber die auslosenden und die richtunggebenden Reizsituationen der Sperrbewegung von jungen Drosseln (*Turdus m. merlua* L. und *T. e. ericetorum* Turton). *Zeitschrift für Tierpsychologie, 3*, 37–60.

Tinbergen, N., & Perdeck, A. C. (1950). On the stimulus situation releasing the begging response in the newly hatched herring gull chick (*Larus argentatus argentatus* Pont.). *Behaviour, 3*, 1–39.

Watson, J. B. (1907). Kinaesthetic and organic sensations: Their role in the reactions of the white rat to the maze. *Psychological Review, 8*(2), (*Monographic Supplement, 33*), 1–100.

Watson, J. B. (1913). Psychology as the behaviorist views it. *Psychological Review, 20*, 158–177.

Watson, J. B., & Lashley, K. S. (1915). An historical and experimental study of homing. *Carnegie Institute of Washington Publications, 211*, 7–60.

2 Anagenesis: Theoretical Basis for the Ecological Void in Comparative Psychology

Gilbert Gottlieb
Department of Psychology
University of North Carolina at Greensboro

Given the overwhelming importance of Charles Darwin's evolutionary ideas in the history of comparative psychology, it seems the height of paradox that ecological considerations have played virtually no role in comparative theory until very recently. It turns out that there are historically discernible reasons for this state of affairs, and these are described and discussed in the present chapter.

ADAPTATION: KEY NINETEENTH–CENTURY CONCEPT

The brilliant psychological scholarship of R. M. Young in his book, *Mind, Brain and Adaptation in the Nineteenth Century* (1970), has made it abundantly clear that the concept of adaptation played a major role in transforming psychology from a primarily philosophical discipline to a scientific one:

> By the end of the nineteenth century, psychologists had provided themselves with the elements of an adequate methodology and an apparently adequate set of explanatory terms on the physiological aspect of their subject. They had also grasped that their field of enquiry was not merely (or, perhaps even primarily) the life of the mind but rather the life of organisms, including men, and their adaptations to their respective environments. What needed explanation was not the representation of reality by the substance mind, but the adjustments to reality by organisms which think, feel, and behave. (p. ix)

Although Young talks about organisms adapting "to their respective environments", nowhere do we find the term or the genuine concept of *ecology* in the writings of psychologists until the most recent era, beginning in the most explicit way in the writings of Egon Brunswik (1952, 1956). So the species-typical or species-specific distinctiveness of behavioral adaptations—the hallmark of ecological thinking—has never been a prominent component of evolutionary theorizing in comparative psychology. In fairness to the great thinkers whose contributions seem damned (or at least diminished) by such an observation, we must remind ourselves that ecology was not practiced much till well after 1900 (Odum, 1959). This lack of appreciation of ecologically distinctive behavioral adaptations is especially fascinating when one considers that for the so-called functional school of psychology an understanding of adaptation to real-life circumstances was a central *conceptual* if not practical theme. Dewey (1900) asserted: "Unless our laboratories are to give us artificialities, mere scientific curiosities, they must be subjected to interpretation by gradual reapproximation to conditions of life" (p. 119).

It was the psychologists' great strength, on the other hand, that evolution and adaptation had been their chief theoretical concerns even before Darwin's publication of the *Origin of Species* in 1859. For example, the psychologist Herbert Spencer was writing in this mode when his *Principles of Psychology* was published for the first time in 1855. (Quotations from Spencer supporting this point appear in the Appendix at the end of this chapter.) Spencer's contribution to casting psychology as an evolutionarily based science is sometimes obscured by the fact that he saw Lamarck's erroneous notion of the inheritance of acquired characteristics as the mechanism of evolution (a view, of course, that Darwin shared as well). As Young (1970) writes:

> The concept of psychology as a biological science based on the evolutionary theory was completely reorienting the science in the half-century following the first statements of Spencer and Darwin. When the mechanism of evolution became more clearly understood, it could find its rightful place within the general approach. Use-inheritance gave way to random mutation and natural selection . . . Although Spencer was wrong about the mechanism of evolution, modern views support his main theme: the adaptations of living things to their surroundings are evoked by problems posed by their environments. (pp. 189–190)

We must certainly ask ourselves with some wonder, how, given this heavy emphasis on evolutionary considerations and the centrality of the concept of adaptation, could these seminal thinkers have overlooked the obvious importance of species-distinctive, ecologically motivated behavioral modifications? I think the answer to this question is, on the one side, methodological and, on the other, theoretical. The remainder of this chapter is devoted to buttressing my conclusion that the failure to realize the highly species-specific nature of behavioral adaptations stems from three problematical sources:

1. The all-too-quick bringing of behavioral study into the laboratory, thus foregoing the extensive field observation that is a necessary precursor to

the design of ecologically valid laboratory experiments (see Miller's chapter, this volume).
2. The widely held, and largely unexamined, notion that the formation and character of associative learning are the appropriate bases for an evolutionary psychology. And, quite apart from those unfortunate predilections,
3. The wide prevalence, nay, ubiquitous popularity, of the concept of anagenesis in the thinking of biologists and comparative psychologists alike.

I discuss these three items in turn. Rather much has been, and is being, written about 1. and 2.; I claim only some originality in adding 3. to the list of conceptual villains. Thus, the main emphasis of the present contribution is on the concept of anagenesis as an influential force in the pervasively nonecological focus of the twentieth-century comparative psychology of learning. It should be noted that the topic of anagenesis is not merely an outdated historical curiosity but is still an active, even if contentious, concept in today's comparative psychology (e.g., Capitanio & Leger, 1979; Demarest, 1983; Masterton, Hodos, & Jerison, 1976; Yarczower & Hazlett, 1977; Yarczower & Yarczower, 1979) as well as in evolutionary biology (Gould, 1976).

LABORATORY STUDY: MAZES AND ASSOCIATIONISTIC LEARNING

Although it is conventional to credit Small (1900) and Thorndike (1898) with initiating laboratory studies of animal behavior (more specifically, animal learning), it should be noted that they merely formalized a trend that had its roots in earlier attempts to bring observational ease, rigor, and control into comparative psychology by observing animals under deliberately confined conditions devised by the observer. Almost all the great figures of comparative psychology (e.g., Lubbock, Morgan, Romanes, Spalding, Mills, Hobhouse) had designed artificial means of some sort to gain a better analytic description and understanding of animal behavior. What Small and Thorndike contributed were (1) highly stereotyped physical situations and (2) a conceptual focus limited to the study of "animal intelligence" from the confines of the associationistic psychology inherited from the nineteenth century (and earlier, of course).

The aims of these earliest pioneers in the experimental study of animal behavior were unquestionably well motivated: If one were to gain control over extraneous variables, enhance observation, and obtain precise description and measurement under replicable conditions, it was clearly necessary to design standard tasks in the confines of the laboratory. These workers were not abiological or nonevolutionary in their abstract conception of the analytic task that lay before them. Here, for example, is a quote from the introduction of Small's (1900) first paper on *An Experimental Study of the Mental Processes of the Rat*:

> The chief difficulty of such experimentation lies in controlling the conditions of the problem without interfering with the natural instincts and proclivities of the animal . . . . an animal should be made to do difficult things only in the line of its inherent abilities. (p. 133)

Although there was no necessary connection between Small's mazes or Thorndike's puzzle boxes and the concept of associative learning as a central feature of animal problem solving, we find the two factors inextricably linked in the experimental comparative psychology of the early twentieth century. Small (1900) goes on to say in the introduction to his experimental studies:

> Their primary purpose was to study the character of the associative processes of the rat: *pari passu* with which, however, would necessarily go a study of the general character of its intelligence as conditioned by its dominant instincts, structural and functional traits, affective life, etc., as well as by the form of the associative processes—indeed as basal to them. (p. 134)

The associationistic theme was of course the indubitable intellectual legacy inherited from the nineteenth century: It was conventional to assume that learning anywhere and everywhere was by association, the laws of which had come down to us in modified form from the Greek philosophers some 2000 years earlier. As is well known, the laws of the association of ideas became the laws of connection of stimulus and response in the service of satisfying organic needs and avoiding pain or punishment (Thorndike's famous Law of Effect).

Because this part of the history of comparative psychology has been rehearsed so many times, it seems unnecessary to go over the same ground in detail once more. The essential deficiencies were an absence of field observations upon which to design ecologically relevant tasks, as well as the historically induced tunnel vision leading to an exclusive concern with the dynamics of associative learning, the relevance of which to all animal ecologies, though untested, went largely undisputed. The disputes, such as they were, were of an entirely theoretical character: the Gestaltists did not raise doubts about the centrality of S–R concepts because of concerns for ecological validity but, rather, because of their belief in the general importance of configural perception or "insight" in animal problem solving (e.g., Köhler's study of learning in nonhuman primates, 1926).

Before turning to a discussion of the concept of anagenesis and its relation to the nonecological flavor of twentieth-century comparative psychology, I would call attention to the fact that there have been some notable exceptions within psychology to the neglect of natural history considerations in the study of animal adaptations, as has been made manifest in D. B. Miller's (1977) comprehensive review.

ANAGENESIS: CORNERSTONE OF THE
COMPARATIVE PSYCHOLOGY OF LEARNING

Because evolutionary thinking is at the heart of the comparative psychology of learning, it is all but inscrutable that ecological considerations have been almost totally ignored until the present time. I think that in addition to the lack of a natural history context for laboratory experimentation, plus the aforementioned preoccupation with association learning, the third "villain" in the piece is the historically exclusive reliance on anagenesis as providing the sole conceptual framework within which to view the evolution of mechanisms of behavioral modifiability. Evolution in this sense has been synonymous with progressive, improved, advanced, or "higher" functioning. Whereas it is true that progressive improvement is one of several evolutionary outcomes of interest and significance, especially as regards behavior and psychological functioning, anagenesis is an evolutionary process that is most likely to be perceived at the supraspecific level; that is, at the level of genera, families, orders, classes, and phyla, not at the level of species or subspecies. Although Darwin's concept of natural selection predicts (or at least favors and supports) improvements in behavioral functions at the species or subspecific level, it will take only a moment's reflection to realize that such improvements would not ordinarily be available or amenable to behavioral or physiological inquiry, leaving, as they do, no fossil remains. This being the case, it is left for us to inquire why it is also not possible to mesh the classical anagenetic viewpoint in comparative psychology with an ecological perspective at the supraspecific level of analysis. For this purpose, it is helpful to review what we know (or, believe we know) about anagenetic trends in learning. To accomplish this task, it is necessary to become somewhat more technical than in the previous sections of this review, an inevitable outcome of having to come to grips with some key concepts in the less familiar area of evolutionary biology.

Ever since the time of Darwin, it has been recognized that evolution includes three nonexclusive processes leading to (1) splitting, diversification and variety of organisms, (2) adaptation and further structural and functional improvement, and (3) stability and persistence of organismic structure and function across geologic time.[1] The names given to these processes by Bernhard Rensch (1959) and Julian Huxley (1957) are *cladogenesis, anagenesis*, and *stasigenesis*, respectively. Although agreement is not unanimous, most workers seem to agree that evolution often proceeds by relatively explosive periods of adaptive radiation wherein a number of new forms are produced. These periods are followed by

---

[1]Simpson (1961) adds a fourth item to the list: extinction. Huxley (1958) regarded extinction as negative persistence rather than a separate process.

both increasing degrees of adaptation, and the greater or lesser persistence or stability of the successful forms. Thus cladogenesis is followed by anagenesis and stasigenesis.

The not uncontroversial classifications that have emerged from this terminology and particular way of characterizing evolution are those of *clade* and *grade*. A clade, according to Huxley (1957), is a delimitable, monophyletic (i.e., genetically closely related) unit produced by cladogenesis (e.g., birds or mammals, or within these larger clades, songbirds or primates). A grade is a particular level in an ascending series of improvements on any given structural or functional unit of analysis in which the animal groups may or may not be closely related from a genetic standpoint (e.g., brain/body ratio; level of problem solving or learning ability or, more specifically, ability to exhibit various forms of associative learning). To exemplify the contrast between clade and grade, whereas birds and mammals are not within the same clade because of the difference in their respective reptilian ancestors, they are in the same anagenetic grade with respect to their similar (although separately evolved) increase in brain/body ratio (described in more detail later).

A concrete example of the anagenetic concept of grade is exhibited in the various levels of social cooperation evident in the very unusual behavior of communal nest weaving in several species of formicine ants. As reconstructed by Hölldobler and Wilson (1983), there are three progressive grades of communal nest weaving in these particular ant species. First of all, each of these species weaves an arboreal nest out of the silk produced by larvae—the silk is essential to bind the nest together. However, it is only the *Oecophylla* species (Grade 3) that exhibits all of the seven forms of activity that represent the most advanced degree of communal nest weaving. In the least advanced form (Grade 1), larvae of the *Dendromyrmex* species contribute silk to the nest but the workers do not manipulate the larvae or otherwise cooperate in adjusting the substrate. In the intermediate species (Grade 2), the larvae contribute silk and the workers perform some but not all of the activities seen in the Grade 3 *Oecophylla* species. The significance of the advanced characteristic of the larvae producing silk before the final instar is its benefit to the colony. By so doing, the larvae have surrendered the ability to construct individual cocoons and thus allow workers to carry and maneuver them effectively because of their smaller size.

Hölldobler and Wilson see the case of *Dendromyrmex* (Grade 1) as especially helpful in envisioning the first step of the evolution in behavior culminating in the communal nest weaving of *Oecophylla* (Grade 3). The only apparent change in larval behavior is the slight addition of releasing some "excess" silk onto the floor of the nest while weaving their individual cocoon. Although the rationale for the progressive grades is clear, the evolutionary reconstruction is speculative. As Hölldobler and Wilson point out, these grades are not cladistically related, each of the species having actually arisen independently from a different ancestor. As will be seen later in the chapter, it is rather more common than one would expect to employ the concept of grade to abstract an "evolutionary" trend from nonevolutionary lines of descent, and the practice occurs in evolutionary biology as well as in psychology.

To return to the main theme, an anagenetic grade for Darwin would have been any evolutionary change in adaptation that permitted a greater or fuller exploitation of the environment. Darwin's concept of anagenesis (though he didn't use the term) stemmed from his belief that natural selection inevitably causes structural and functional improvement but always "in relation to the conditions of life" (cited by Huxley, 1957, p. 455). My own interpretation is that Darwin's conception of anagenesis was much more local and ecologically constrained than our current usage of the concept, and I think that difference lies at the root of the present problem, as I now try to demonstrate.

As I said earlier, whereas we can agree with Darwin that natural selection will almost always bring about some improvement in any given species' adaptation, that must remain a logical inference or speculation as far as behavior and psychological functioning are concerned—there are no fossil traces in which we may discern such improvements. In fact, when one reads the biological literature in search of examples of biological anagenesis, the instances that are recited are usually the readily discerned ones that come from comparing larger (supraspecific) taxonomic units, as, for example, in the evolution of homoiotherms (birds and mammals) from poikilotherms (reptiles), the evolution of the three-cone retina from the single-cone retina, and the like. Such examples, although clearly anagenetic, are quite remote from any direct ecological considerations. It is likely they arose in an explosive period and permitted the animals so endowed to exploit new habitats and niches, where the adaptation could then possibly be refined in a species-specific manner that directly reflected ecological factors. As Dobzhansky, Ayala, Stebbins, and Valentine (1977) point out: "Anagenetic episodes commonly create organisms with novel characters and abilities beyond those of their ancestors" (p. 236).

Although there are many possible defining attributes of anagenetic trends, the least subjective (least arguable) ones are just those that make the improvements ecologically neutral or nonspecific! In his classic book *Evolution Above the Species Level*, Rensch (1959, p. 289) lists the following as typical defining features of anagenesis: (1) increased complexity (differentiation), (2) centralization of structures and functions, (3) special complexity and centralization of the nervous system, (4) increased plasticity of structures and functions, (5) improvements allowing further improvement (partly identical to point 4), and (6) increased independence of the environment and increasing command of environmental factors (progression of autonomy). Rensch's (1959) analysis of anagenesis is the most penetrating I have read and he is in agreement with most other authorities before and after him (e.g., Huxley, 1942, 1957; Simpson, 1949; Spencer, 1855) in recognizing that the interrelated factors of plasticity in ontogenetic development, progress in adaptability, and increased independence of the environment are the hallmarks of evolutionary progress (anagenesis): "In many cases, such increased autonomy is the result of improved sensory and nervous systems" (p. 298).

The preceding review, then, represents the thinking of major evolutionary biologists on the question of biological anagenesis. The trends in improvement that the biologists themselves discern are broad, not species-specific, and ecologically neutral. Little wonder, then, that the same sort of theorizing would be going on in the comparative psychology of learning, even (especially?) among those who knew their evolutionary biology. The premier scholarly work on comparative psychology in this century, Maier and Schneirla's (1935) *Principles of Animal Psychology*, says this:

> The ability which an animal demonstrates in modifying its behavior is largely dependent upon the plasticity of its nervous system. For this reason individual differences in learning ability among animals of the same species become apparent. Among animals of different species this variation in the rate of learning will be much more definite because of the wider difference in neural structure. Comparisons of learning ability between animals, and correlations of differences in learning ability with differences in neural structure will therefore add to an understanding of learning. (p. 346)

Given this orientation, it is not surprising that one looks in vain for the operation of selection pressures or ecological differences between ever more widely separated species. When, for example, birds fail to show evidence of reasoning (in comparison to certain mammals), Maier & Schneirla (1935) conclude: "The bird, though very highly developed in many ways, has a rudimentary cortex, and it is probable that it is largely incapable of reorganizing its experiences [reasoning] in order to adapt to a new situation" (p. 479). This nonecological preoccupation with the connection between anagenetic evolution of cortex and the anagenetic evolution of higher mental processes has been carried through to the present day, reaching its epitome in Harry Jerison's (1973) monumental *Evolution of the Brain and Intelligence* and Gregory Razran's (1971) *Mind in Evolution*.

Since the time of Herbert Spencer it has been traditional to conceive of the progressive evolution of intelligent behavior (learning) as intimately related to the progressive evolution of the brain. Thus, it is of the highest significance that the most recent (and, one assumes, the best) evidence indicates that there was a dramatic increase in the relative size of the brain when the earliest birds and mammals first evolved from their respective reptilian ancestors (Jerison, 1973). The size of the brain relative to the body has continued to increase such that, for example, primates have the largest relative brain sizes among mammals, and *Homo sapiens* has the largest brain among the primates (ibid.). The parallel in the evolution of intelligent behavior is almost perfect, in the sense that experimental evidence from various theoretical outlooks tends to place birds and mammals in a class by themselves as far as learning ability goes (Razran, 1971). Further, the cognitive achievements of primates, and those of humans among primates, tend to stand apart from most other mammals. As at least one viewpoint would have it, the anagenesis of learning ability proceeds in a more or less strict fashion beginning with the invertebrates. Razran (1971) states:

> A vast body of empirical data from both the East and the West attest [sic] to an evolving multiformity of the basics of learning—specifically to an ascending hierarchy of no less than eleven delineated levels: two nonassociative or preconditioned (habituation and sensitization), three conditioning (inhibitory [punishing], classical, and reinforcing), three of perceiving (sensory–sensory learning [sensory preconditioning], configuring, and eductive learning), and three thinking (symbosemic, sememic, and logicemic).

> All levels share some characteristics, but each ascending level is novel in essence and in parameters is not reducible to or deducible from those preceding it, and there are clear phyletic and reactional divides between the levels. Coelenterates are readily habituated but cannot be conditioned. Prevertebrate chordates, such as amphioxi and ascidians, and spinal mammals habituate, become sensitized, but likewise are not conditionable . . . Gill extension in fighting fish is modified by inhibitory (punishing) and classical conditioning but not by reinforcement (reward) conditioning. Otherwise, however, lower vertebrates, including fish, manifest fully both classical and reinforcement conditioning, while most invertebrates (earthworms on) master classical conditioning and higher invertebrates the reinforcement type. On the other hand, sensory preconditioning and learned stimulus configuring is [sic] possible only in birds and mammals; eductive learning . . . in crows, magpies, dogs, and cats but not in pigeons, chickens, ducks, and rabbits. And oddity learning and learning sets in general are largely primate exploits, and symboling an exclusive human achievement. (pp. 310–311)

Other comparative psychologists, even those more in touch with the tenets of evolutionary biology, also emphasize noncladistic, evolutionary grades in intelligent behavior. For example, the touchstone of T. C. Schneirla's (1972) theory of comparative psychology is the anagenetic concept of *levels* in the psychological capacities of animals.[2]

> Of all the factors conditioning the potentialities of individual development and socialization on different levels, the most crucial is the extent to which the central

---

[2]Though I can't be certain, I think Schneirla may have adopted the term level instead of grade to avoid the possibly more typological connotation of the latter. Both terms emphasize organismic capacity without explicit reference to the environment. In this sense, Simpson's (1961, pp. 202–203) term and concept of *adaptive zone* (stable niche) seems the most appropriate of all in that it encompasses the group of organisms and its effective environment. (Huxley, 1958, raised much the same point, only to dismiss it.)

nervous system has evolved. Although it appears that some capacity for learning plays an essential part in socialization on all levels, differences in the learning potential undoubtedly are of first importance in setting limits upon socialization, as upon the relative plasticity of adaptive function in general.

Learning capacity . . . has been demonstrated experimentally even in lower invertebrates such as flatworms . . . Though learning can occur in the absence of cerebral cortex . . . experiments with lower animals show convincingly that it is qualitatively much reduced . . . The maximal accomplishments possible in inframammalian animals such as insects, although impressively complex in some respects, nevertheless show qualitative limitations such as proneness for stereotypy and a sluggish development of habit organization. For example, the learning capacities of ants, evidently at their best in the *Formica* species, are relatively situation-bound and rotelike, resembling the showing of lower mammals (e.g., rats) deprived of much of their cortex . . . The behavior changes which have been reported for invertebrates such as protozoa and echinoderms appear to belong to a distinctive sublearning level, especially since they represent transient effects which do not alter the characteristic behavior pattern in any effective way. (pp. 218–219)

Thus anagenesis permeates comparative psychological thinking as it has evolutionary thought for generations. Psychological and biological improvement is such a pervasive aspect of evolution that Huxley (1958) once suggested that there might be utility in having two separate classifications and nomenclatures, one having to do with grade taxa and the other with clade taxa. Although Simpson (1961) acknowledges that the concepts and terms grade and clade are extremely useful in understanding and discussing evolutionary phenomena, he sees no value in having two systems of classification on that basis. It should be clear from the preceding review that comparative psychologists have in fact been operating on such a premise (two classifications) even though the grade classification has not actually been formalized in the taxonomic sense.

The otherwise well-considered critique of comparative psychology by Hodos and Campbell (1969) did not recognize that there was indeed a theory in comparative psychology; namely a hierarchical classification of adaptive behavior by grade independent of cladistic (i.e., genetic) relationship. Like Simpson, and perhaps most other zoological writers, Hodos and Campbell would see no value in an evolutionary classification scheme that disregarded strict lineal (cladistic) relationships. In this context, it is of more than passing interest that an evolutionary biologist of J. Huxley's stature did see the organizing value of such a scheme, and, in fact, such a classification has been more or less used in comparative psychology since the time of Herbert Spencer!

For the present purpose, it remains only to reiterate that the evolutionary thinking of comparative psychologists has always centered on the ecologically transcendant concept of psychological grade, thus providing the intellectual impetus for the ecological void in comparative psychology since its inception in the nineteenth century. In the event that we have not yet exhausted all the ways of looking at the problem, a novel conceptual integration remains possible. In the meantime, for those who are inclined to paint with a broad brush on the canvas of anagenesis, it may be beneficial to be more keenly aware of the nonecological and noncladistic implications of such toil. On the other side, for those of us who find species-distinctive, ecologically relevant adaptations more to our taste, we should strive toward developing general schemes of behavioral-ecological classification, both within and without cladistic lineages. Within the order Chiroptera (bats), for example, Eisenberg and Wilson (1978) have demonstrated that a relatively large brain is associated with adaptations for feeding on widely dispersed, energy-rich foods that are unpredictable in their spatial distribution. In a similar vein, Jerison (1973) has hypothesized that carnivores that prey upon herbivores or grazing animals have a higher brain/body ratio than their characteristic prey, implying a higher degree of intelligence or learning ability in the former. Unfortunately, a reanalysis of the data for this attractive hypothesis failed to support it (Radinsky, 1978). For certain kinds of ecological variables, e.g., complex interdependent social organization, one may find large brains necessarily covarying with other factors such as long gestation, prolonged postnatal nervous system maturation, degree of homoiothermy, and high basal metabolic rate, as seems to be the case in the class of mammals (Eisenberg, 1981, p. 442).

Thus by examining the traditional literature on the comparative psychology of learning (including the enormous literature on relative brain size), and by attempting to forge systematic links with ecologically relevant behavioral variables pertaining to survival (food strategies, shelter, predator avoidance, parent–young interaction modes, social organization), we may obtain valuable evolutionary insights that could provide a broadly ecological framework for the pursuits of a new comparative psychology. Within this framework, the unique contribution of comparative psychology could continue to be the behavioral spelling-out of the psychological mediation processes (different modes of perception and learning) that may correlate with relative brain size, on the one side, and various ecological trends, on the other. At the least, it would seem fruitful to determine if different mediational modes of perception and learning can be made to correlate with various, even if broad, ecological categories, both within and without cladistic lineages.

ACKNOWLEDGMENTS

This chapter was written in connection with research activities supported by Grant HD–17752 from the National Institute of Child Health and Human Development.

REFERENCES

Brunswik, E. (1952). The conceptual framework of psychology. *International Encyclopedia of Unified Science, 1*, 1–102.

Brunswik, E. (1956). *Perception and the representative design of psychological experiments*. Berkeley: University of California Press.

Capitanio, J. P., & Leger, D. W. (1979). Evolutionary scales lack utility: A reply to Yarczower and Hazlett. *Psychological Bulletin, 86*, 876–879.

Darwin, C. R. (1859). *On the origin of species by means of natural selection*. London: Murray.

Demarest, J. (1983). The ideas of change, progress, and continuity in the comparative psychology of learning. In D. W. Rajecki (Ed.), *Comparing behavior: Studying man studying animals*. Hillsdale, NJ: Lawrence Erlbaum Associates.

Dewey, J. (1900). Psychology and social practice. *Psychological Review, 7*, 105–125.

Dobzhansky, T., Ayala, F. J., Stebbins, G. L., & Valentine, J. W. (1977). *Evolution*. San Francisco: Freeman.

Eisenberg, J. F. (1981). *The mammalian radiations*. Chicago: University of Chicago Press.

Eisenberg, J. F., & Wilson, D. (1978). Relative brain size and feeding strategies in the Chiroptera. *Evolution, 32*, 740–751.

Gould, S. J. (1976). Grades and clades revisited. In R. B. Masterton, W. Hodos, & H. Jerison (Eds.), *Evolution, brain, and behavior: Persistent problems*. Hillsdale, NJ: Lawrence Erlbaum Associates.

Hodos, W., & Campbell, C. B. G. (1969). *Scala naturae*: Why there is no theory in comparative psychology. *Psychological Review, 76*, 337–350.

Hölldobler, B., & Wilson, E. O. (1983). The evolution of communal nest-weaving in ants. *American Scientist, 71*, 490–499.

Huxley, J. S. (1942). *Evolution, the modern synthesis*. New York, Harper.

Huxley, J. S. (1957). The three types of evolutionary progress. *Nature, 180*, 454–455.

Huxley, J. S. (1958). Evolutionary processes and taxonomy with special reference to grades. *Uppsala University Arsskrift*, 21–38.

Jerison, H. J. (1973). *Evolution of the brain and intelligence*. New York: Academic Press.

Köhler, W. (1926). *The mentality of apes*. New York: Harcourt Brace.

Maier, N. R. F., & Schneirla, T. C. (1935). *Principles of animal psychology*. New York: McGraw–Hill.

Masterton, R. B., Hodos, W., & Jerison, H. (1976). *Evolution, brain, and behavior: Persistent problems*. Hillsdale, NJ: Lawrence Erlbaum Associates.

Miller, D. B. (1977). Roles of naturalistic observation in comparative psychology. *American Psychologist, 32*, 211–219.

Odum, E. P. (1959). *Fundamentals of ecology*. Philadelphia: Saunders.

Radinsky, L. (1978). Evolution of brain size in carnivores and ungulates. *American Naturalist, 112*, 815–831.

Razran, G. (1971). *Mind in evolution*. New York: Houghton Mifflin.

Rensch, B. (1959). *Evolution above the species level*. New York: Columbia University Press.

Schneirla, T. C. (1972). *Selected writings of T. C. Schneirla* (L. R. Aronson, E. Tobach, J. S. Rosenblatt, & D. S. Lehrman, Eds.). San Francisco: Freeman.

Simpson, G. G. (1949). *The meaning of evolution*. New Haven: Yale University Press.

Simpson, G. G. (1961). *Principles of animal taxonomy*. New York: Columbia University Press.

Small, W. S. (1900). Experimental study of the mental processes of the rat. *American Journal of Psychology, 11*, 206–239.

Spencer, H. (1855). *The principles of psychology*. London: Longman, Brown, Green, & Longmans.

Thorndike, E. L. (1898). Animal intelligence; an experimental study of the associative processes in animals. *Psychological Review Monographs, 2*, 1–109.

Yarczower, M., & Hazlett, L. (1977). Evolutionary scales and anagenesis. *Psychological Bulletin*, *84*, 1088–1097.

Yarczower, M., & Yarczower, B. S. (1979). In defense of anagenesis, grades, and evolutionary scales. *Psychological Bulletin*, *86*, 880–883.

Young, R. M. (1970). *Mind, brain and adaptation in the nineteenth century*. Oxford: Clarendon Press.

APPENDIX
Herbert Spencer on Evolution and Adaptation

Herbert Spencer's consistently nonempirical, highly abstract focus in his *Principles* maddened both supporters and critics alike—there is no doubt that he seems even "windier" by our standards and expectations. Nonetheless, because of the importance of his influence in starting the science of psychology on its present path, I reproduce here several quotations from Spencer (1855) that give at least the flavor of his evolutionary, even vaguely ecological orientation, including the pivotal role that the concept of adjustment (adaptation) held in his thinking:

> there is invariably, and necessarily, a certain conformity between the vital functions of any organism and the conditions in which it is placed—between the processes going on inside of it, and the processes going on outside of it . . . We find that each animal is limited to a certain range of climate; each plant to certain zones of latitude and elevation. Of the marine flora and fauna, each species is found only between such and such depths. (p. 367)

> Life is defined as—The definite combination of heterogeneous changes, both simultaneous and successive, in correspondence with external coexistences and sequences.

> the broadest and most complete definition of life will be—*The continuous adjustment of internal relations to external relations*. (ibid., p. 368, his italics)

> At the same time that it is simpler and briefer, this modified formula has the further advantage of being somewhat more comprehensive. To say that it includes not only those simultaneous and successive changes in an organism which correspond to coexistences and sequences in the environment, but also those structural arrangements which *enable* the organism to adapt its actions to those in the environment, may perhaps be going too far; for though these structural arrangements present internal relations adjusted to external relations, yet the *continuous adjustment* of relations can scarcely be held to include a *fixed adjustment* already made. But while this antithesis serves to keep in view the distinction between the organism and its actions, it at the same time draws attention to the fact, that if the structural arrangements of the adult organism are not properly included, yet the developmental processes by which those arrangements were established, are included. For it needs but to contemplate that evolution of the embryo during which the organs are fitted to their prospective functions, to at once see, that from beginning to end it is the gradual, that is, continuous, adjustment of internal relations to external relations.

Add to which fact the allied fact, that those structural modifications by which the adult organism better adapted to its conditions—those structural modifications by which, under change of climate, change of occupation, change of food, slowly bring about some rearrangement in the organic balance—must similarly be regarded as continuous adjustments of internal relations to external relations. So that not only does the definition, as thus expressed, comprehend all those activities, bodily and mental, which constitute our ordinary idea of life; but it also comprehends both those processes of growth by which the organism is brought into general fitness for those activities, and those after-processes of adaptation by which it is specially fitted to its special activities. (ibid., pp. 374–375, his italics)

3 Methodological Issues in the Ecological Study of Learning

David B. Miller
Department of Psychology
University of Connecticut

Essays on methodological strategies in the study of species-typical behavior tend to be chided by biologists on the basis that such information has already been acquired by every serious student of zoology and/or ecology as part and parcel of classroom education and research experience, particulary field research. The view that is often expressed is that, although such information is accurate and correct, it does not merit explication because of its presumed pervasiveness in the minds of researchers.

Traditionally, most experimental psychologists have not been greatly concerned with adopting ecoethological techniques in behavioral study. This may be due, at least in part, to psychologists' emphasis on rigorous laboratory control and, perhaps, to the erroneous assumption that field studies cannot be rigorous.

Interestingly, I have heard both biologists and experimental psychologists proclaim that the study of species-typical behavior should be pursued only by properly trained zoologists, that is, by individuals who have received formal training in biology or zoology programs. That some prominent investigators from each of these camps find agreement here (albeit presumably for different reasons) represents an ill-founded ideological marriage of converging views that ought to be torn asunder.

In an attempt to explicate causative and ontogenetic factors influencing behavior, zoologists have increasingly taken to the laboratory. In so doing, they have used some of the good and many of the bad methodological and conceptual principles advocated by their psychological forebears and colleagues. Conversely, psychologists have been reluctant to fully incorporate into their discipline the methodological principles that have successfully guided many ecological and ethological lines of inquiry.

In recent years, it has been exceedingly clear that much can be gained by an interdisciplinary approach to behavioral problems. A revolving door has been established between the field and the laboratory through which some psychologists and zoologists have been passing in an attempt to use techniques unique to each discipline to better understand behavioral processes and mechanisms. Whereas many investigators from both (and related) disciplines have been revolving through that door rather successfully, it remains true that the "external validity" (i.e., generalizability; representativeness; ecological validity) of many lines of experimentation could be greatly enhanced by a better appreciation of certain methodological principles relevant to the ecological study of behavior.

Ecological studies of behavior are primarily concerned with questions about how organisms adapted to deal with those "real-life" situations that are typical for individuals of a particular species. Casting behavioral questions in an ecological framework necessitates a means (i.e., a set of methodological principles or guidelines) by which such questions can be answered. In this chapter, I discuss what I consider to be some of the more important methodological principles that can subserve an ecological approach to the study of learning. It is not possible (nay, it would be absurd!) to present a methodological "cookbook" that would claim to have general applicability. Rather, I try to outline some of the more important conceptual strategies and considerations that investigators interested in an ecoethological approach to behavior in general, and learning in particular, should take into account. (The reader is also referred in Miller, 1977a, 1981, for further elaboration of these ideas.)

CONTRASTING ORIENTATIONS

Ethologists have long argued that the *necessary* first step toward understanding behavior involves observing and describing behavioral events in species-typical settings. Historically, a few psychologists have also embraced this position. However, the prevalent view among most psychologists has been that such normative description is of secondary importance when compared to the manipulative approach characteristic of laboratory investigation (cf. Sackett, Sameroff, Cairns, & Suomi, 1981). Lehrman (1971) discussed these differing philosophies by comparing two types of orientations that investigators have toward their animal subjects. Investigators who have a "natural-history orientation" give primary attention to the behavior of the animal in relation to its natural environment, which includes members of its own and other species. Experimental questions are derived from the natural life of the species. In contrast, the "behaviorist orientation" pays little, if any, attention to species-typical behaviors in natural settings. Such investigators tend to assume that there are "general laws" of learning and that rats are not fundamentally different from humans, nor pigeons from rats. Observation, description, and explanation are replaced by the experimenter gaining control over behavior and predicting how an animal will act as a function of a particular manipulation (e.g., schedules of reinforcement).

Obviously, the natural-history and behaviorist orientations outlined by Lehrman represent endpoints on a continuum of research philosophies in contemporary behavioral science. However, an unfortunate attitude adopted by many scientists is one that assumes mutual exclusivity between these orientations. A frequent response made by such individuals to queries about why they do not concern themselves with experimentally elucidating species-typical behavior is, "I'll study what I choose to study, and you can do likewise." The defensive manner in which variations of this retort are often uttered indicates that such investigators may cling to their orientation by default rather than by explicit choice. For example, traditional psychology departments and many "prestigious" psychology journals have, in the recent past, hardly embraced the natural-history orientation. In fact, some have actively opposed it. One of this century's leading natural-history-oriented comparative psychologists, T. C. Schneirla, had been an Assistant Professor for about 10 years without a raise in rank except from Instructor. "It was shameful, but to most psychologists Ted [Schneirla] was not working on psychologically significant problems except for his interest in ant learning, and even that was considered borderline for psychology" (F. A. Beach, personal communication, August 30, 1976).

Investigators often find themselves working on particular problems or adhering to certain philosophies because of the prevailing Zeitgeist. The natural-history orientation has heretofore been tangential to the Zeitgeist in psychology. It is, therefore, hardly astonishing that the behaviorist orientation has prevailed. It is not unusual that calls for a change are most compelling when they are issued by authoritative figures within a discipline rather than by outsiders. Such calls by comparative psychologists (like Schneirla and Lehrman—i.e., investigators interested in studying underlying mechanisms of species-typical behavior) have not had much impact, probably because comparative psychology has occupied a position outside the mainstream of psychology. Some headway has been made in recent years by developmental and social psychologists who have adopted and advocated ethological and ecological orientations. These orientations emphasize the importance of naturalistic observation in behavioral analysis. It is by appreciating the roles of naturalistic observation that we cross the first bridge toward an ecological study of learning.

In what follows, I outline a tripartite methodological research strategy that provides basic guidelines for an ecological approach to the study of learning. First, one must engage in naturalistic observation of the behavior of the species in species-typical contexts. This enables the investigator to become intimately familiar with the species-typical behavioral repertoire and stimuli, and how these might change across contexts. Second, one must ask questions concerning what kinds of things members of the species learn about in the course of adaptation throughout the life-span. This is the "task description" stage. Finally, in order to examine how animals learn what they do, one must perturb the system by means of experimental manipulation. How one goes about doing this can greatly affect the ecological validity of the behavioral outcomes; thus, I provide one possible scheme that attempts to operationalize what we mean by ecological and nonecological studies.

STEP ONE: NATURALISTIC OBSERVATION ACROSS CONTEXTS

Studying behavior in the settings in which it has evolved and continues to evolve is paramount to an ecological orientation. The term *naturalistic* does not have an absolute meaning but rather is descriptive of relative environmental conditions as viewed by the particular species. Naturalistic conditions can differ radically from one species to the next in the sense that a particular physical environment may be natural for one species but unnatural for another. This point is the essence of von Uexküll's (1934) concept of *Umwelt*, which refers to the fact that different species perceive the same physical environmental features differently and behave differently in accord with their species-typical perceptions. Thus, the natural environment must be defined with regard to the particular species under study. Elsewhere (Miller, 1981), I have defined the natural environment as a habitat in which the species is usually found, one that is self-selected by the species, and, therefore, relatively unrestrained and conducive for reproduction and rearing young (which, of course, is the ultimate measure of "fitness" in the evolutionary sense).

Some species (e.g., rats, pigeons, rhesus monkeys, man) occupy a wide range of qualitatively different types of habitats, such that any attempt to define "natural" for these species is very difficult. It is especially important, when studying such species, to observe their behavior across a wide range of environmental contexts in order to ascertain the extent to which certain forms of behavior are environmentally dependent or independent (the latter referring to behaviors that are universal across contexts). This is particularly crucial when studying the behavior of domestic animals. Certain species-typical behaviors, originally presumed to have degenerated consequent to the intense artificial selection attendant to domestication, have since been found to be exhibited by domestic animals if they are placed in environmental contexts typical of the wild progenitor rather than the domestic breed (e.g., Boice, 1977; Miller, 1977b).

Failure to observe behavior across a range of settings in which members of a particular species are normally found can lead to erroneous conclusions about certain behavior patterns. For example, based only on observations of captive hamadryas baboons at a zoo, Zuckerman (1932) proposed a theory suggesting that sexuality is the primary binding force of primate social organization. Zuckerman's theory, which dominated primate sociobiology for over a quarter of a century, was based on his observation that these captive baboons had bred throughout the year rather than in distinct seasons. Subsequent field studies on a variety of primate species proved Zuckerman's theory incorrect by revealing that under natural conditions some primate species have distinct breeding seasons and that many aspects of primate social organization are quite independent of sexual activity (e.g., Kummer, 1968; Lancaster & Lee, 1965).

More recently, Wallen (1982) has demonstrated the importance of environmental context on the sexual behavior of rhesus monkeys housed either in a 1.4 × 1.2-m cage or in a 15.2 × 15.2-m compound. Wallen found that the females' hormonal condition has more influence on sexual behavior of a male and female pair when the pair is observed in the large compound than when the same pair is observed in the smaller cage. Similarly, McClintock (1981) has observed significant differences in the copulatory behavior of female rats when placed in a small standard aquarium-like enclosure as compared to a large indoor semi-natural environment.

These examples illustrate the impact that context can have on the manifestation of species-typical behavior patterns. Another important factor affecting species-typical behavior that is usually overlooked, or, at least, erroneously assumed to be trivial, is the *range* of normally occurring stimuli to which a developing organism is exposed, both prenatally and postnatally. One reason why this factor is often overlooked is that, from a human perspective, some forms of normally occurring stimuli may be nonobvious, despite the necessary role that they play in the development of species-typical behavior. A recent study by Gottlieb (1982) illustrates this point very well. Briefly, Gottlieb demonstrated that domestic mallard ducklings will respond appropriately postnatally to the species-typical maternal assembly call only if they have been exposed prenatally to the normally occurring *range* of a particular acoustic feature of their own embryonic vocalizations. Surprisingly, exposure only to the *modal* value of the acoustic feature is inadequate and results in a significant developmental lag in normal auditory perception. Gottlieb's finding is both conceptually and methodologically interesting because it demonstrates the importance of assessing not only the modal aspects of species-typical stimuli that affect species-typical behavior but also the range of these elements. Such an assessment is not an easy task and is one that requires extensive observation and description of behaviors and stimuli that might affect such behaviors across species-typical contexts.

An ecological approach to learning can be fostered by an appreciation of the various roles that naturalistic observation play in behavioral study. Elsewhere (Miller, 1977a), I have defined five roles that naturalistic observation can play in comparative psychology. These roles, which are also applicable to areas of psychology other than comparative, are recapitulated in the following sections.

Role One

The first role involves studying nature for its own sake in an initial attempt to observe and describe the sorts of things that individuals of a particular species typically do. This is the essence of Lehrman's (1971) "natural-history orientation." Unfortunately, psychologists tend to relegate this role to the exclusive domain of zoology. Nevertheless, this role is essential for an ecological approach to learning, for it is here that we begin to describe the specific tasks in which organisms engage while interacting with their environment.

Role Two

The second role is a direct extension of the first, particularly with regard to the study of learning. According to this role, naturalistic observations initially serve as a starting point for investigating certain behavioral phenomena and subsequently serve as a point of departure from which to develop a program of laboratory research. A major problem with traditional (i.e., nonecological) approaches to the study of learning is the disregard for linking laboratory-based data with the organism's adaptation to its natural habitat. An ecological approach mandates that such a link be made, and the most profitable way to proceed is by initially observing the organism in its species-typical habitat (or habitats) and subsequently deriving questions for experimental scrutiny.

Role Three

It is not the intent of ecologically oriented investigators to necessarily discard the baby with the bath water; that is, links may exist between existing laboratory learning data and naturalistic adaptations. The third role of naturalistic observation involves validating or adding substance to data previously collected in the laboratory. (This role is similar to the second role, but in reverse order.) This role attempts to provide ecological validity to data previously collected outside of an ecological framework. I hasten to add that this role is not the preferred way to proceed when working within an ecological framework. From an ecological point of view, the preferred role is the second, because that role stresses the importance of deriving one's research questions from initial observation and description of species-typical behavior patterns. However, this third role does provide a means of salvaging existing data and retrospectively casting such data in an ecological framework, if possible.

Role Four

A role of naturalistic observation that is essential to an ecological approach to learning is the identification of so-called species variables (sometimes referred to as biological constraints) for more efficient utilization of animals in experimental situations. When assessing the learning capabilities of members of a particular species, the experimenter must appreciate the sensitivity, specificity, and limitations of various sensory modalities as well as the boundaries of motor output. Taking such information into account is an important step toward assessing learning within an ecological framework. More importantly, failure to do so could lead to erroneous conclusions regarding learning capability. For example, Impekoven (1973) operantly conditioned foot movements in Peking duck (domestic mallard) embryos on the day before hatching. One of two reinforcers was used—either a burst of a mallard maternal assembly call (i.e., a call that the mother duck utters and that ducklings find highly attractive) or a burst of a chicken maternal assembly call (i.e., a call that domestic chicks find highly attractive but that ducklings do not find especially attractive). She found that the response rate (i.e., foot movements) was significantly increased when subjects were rewarded with the mallard call but not increased when rewarded with the chicken call. Had Impekoven used only a species-atypical reinforcing stimulus (such as the chicken call) in this study, she might erroneously have concluded that Peking duck embryos are incapable of modifying their behavior by means of operant contingencies.

Role Five

The fifth role represents a rather special use of naturalistic situations. Some experimental questions can either only be answered effectively, or best be answered, by performing the experimental manipulations in the animal's natural habitat. Thus, one can use the field as a natural "laboratory" to test a hypothesis or theoretical concept via observational techniques and/or experimental manipulation. Individual recognition in the context of territoriality is a case in point. The confines of the laboratory, or even the small size of most outdoor enclosures, precludes the possibility of certain species establishing territories (or at least the kinds of territories that they would defend in the wild). An important component of territorial defense is learning to recognize individuals occupying adjacent territories and to cease responding aggressively toward such individuals once they have established their own territories. Such a field study of habituation was implemented by Falls and Brooks (1975), who found that territorial white-throated sparrows come to habituate to the broadcast of a neighbor's song when the loudspeaker is located in the neighbor's usual adjacent territory. But, when the same bird's song is broadcast from a loudspeaker moved to a different location (i.e., to the territory of a different neighbor), the territorial male behaves as if it is hearing a stranger's song. In a similar vein, the field studies of habituation in white-crowned sparrows by Petrinovich and his colleagues (e.g., Petrinovich & Patterson, 1982) exemplify the kind of experiments that must be carried out in the field if ecologically relevant answers are to be provided for biologically meaningful questions.

STEP TWO: TASK DESCRIPTION

The hallmark of an ecological approach to the study of learning is ascertaining *what* has to be learned by members of a particular species at a particular stage of ontogeny in the course of adapting to their species-typical habitat. Borrowing a term from the literature on artificial intelligence, Johnston (1981) refers to this procedure as "task description." It is not surprising that most psychological studies of learning lack an ecological orientation, for task description of the animal is not easy task for the investigator. Task description entails extensive observation of animals in their species-typical habitat(s) and exhaustive quantitative analysis of these observations in an effort to ascertain precisely *what* behavioral changes might be occurring which suggest that learning is taking place. This rigorous approach is typically adopted by ethologists (e.g., see Colgan, 1978, and Lehner, 1979, for handbooks of ethological techniques), though rarely applied to the study of learning, which, historically, has been relegated to the domain of experimental psychology. Fortunately, as the methodologies of these disciplines have converged, so have many of the behavioral problems that previously had only rarely crossed disciplinary lines. The outcome of this convergence is that some ethologists are now studying species-typical aspects of learning, and some psychologists have, despite Skinner's (1961) warning, taken their "flight from the laboratory" to better understand the tasks that animals face in the course of adaptation. Those who, like Rachlin (1981), dismiss the contributions of ethology to the study of learning by characterizing ethology as a "mass of casual observation, half-hearted experimentation, and theoretical guesswork" (p. 155) are clearly ignorant of the development of that field in the past 20 years.

Criticisms of the ethological approach are usually issued by individuals who ask very different kinds of research questions from those trying to understand ecologically meaningful aspects of learning. This is precisely the distinction that Lehrman (1971) drew in his "behaviorist" versus "natural-history" orientations. Along a similar vein, one can distinguish between two types of questions that reflect different conceptual strategies in behavioral study—*can* questions and *does* questions (McCall, 1977; see also Miller, 1981). "Can" questions attempt to ascertain the capabilities of organisms—"Under certain circumstances, *can* factor X produce behavior Y?" For example, many investigators of human and nonhuman organisms have posited the experimental question, "*Can* infants learn by operant conditioning?" The answer has been resoundingly affirmative. But here is where we encounter the important conceptual argument that differentiates ecological from nonecological approaches to learning. Demonstrations of an animal's capabilities, or behavioral potentials (Kuo, 1976), do not by themselves elucidate the nature of the organism's usual adaptations to its species-typical environment and thereby evade the ecologically significant procedure of task description.

Rather than focusing on "can" questions, ecologically oriented investigators ask "does" questions—"Under typical natural circumstances, *does* factor X produce behavior Y?" The "does" question counterpart for the preceding example is, "*Do* infants learn by operant conditioning in actual family environments?" "Does" questions epitomize task description by asking about normal, species-typical adaptations—questions concerning what kinds of things animals might learn as they interact with the environments in which they have evolved.

The "can vs. does" distinction can be cast in somewhat different terms by considering the concept of developmental plasticity. Plasticity is a highly dynamic concept and has been defined in many ways (Miller, 1981). For the present purpose, I use "plasticity" synonymously with "modifiability" to refer to the extent to which a behavior can be changed with regard to a normative reference point. Additionally, I refer to two subtypes of plasticity that form a continuum with respect to the extent to which a particular behavior pattern or perceptual capability lies within or beyond the range of species-typical variability. These subtypes are depicted in Fig. 3.1.

At one end of the continuum, plasticity denotes the extent of *adaptability* occuring within the range of normal variability for the species. This is the kind of modifiability that an organism exhibits in adapting to its environment throughout its life-span. In essence, this type of plasticity encompasses the kinds of

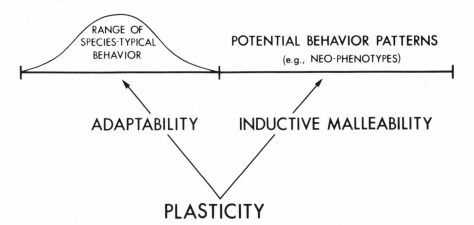

FIG. 3.1   Types of plasticity. One type, adaptability, reflects the range of behavior patterns characteristic of members of a particular species. The second type, inductive malleability, refers to potential behavior patterns that can occur under species-atypical circumstances (such as in the context of experimental manipulation) and that could, at some point, be incorporated into the species-typical repertoire if the unusual circumstances persist and if such behaviors are adaptive under such conditions. These potential behavior patterns are what Kuo (1976) refers to as "behavioral neo-phenotypes."

learning problems that are revealed by engaging in task description and by asking "does" questions.

The other end of the continuum represents the kind of plasticity that encompasses the extent to which behavior can be modified beyond or outside the range of normal variability for the species. This form of plasticity, which I refer to as *inductive malleability* (Miller, 1981), taps into the range of behavioral potentials that an organism has but that typically do not occur outside the situation of experimentally manipulating species-atypical variables. As discussed later in this chapter, these potential behavior patterns are congruous with Kuo's (1976) concept of "behavioral neo-phenotypes." This is the kind of plasticity that has pervaded the search for "general laws of learning" and that represents the sort of "can" questions that elude an ecological approach to the study of learning. (I am not necessarily arguing that general laws might not exist. Rather, we will not be able to specify such laws adequately by focusing our attention on non-ecological forms of learning.) Most studies in which the stimuli and/or response measures have been more or less arbitrarily selected illustrate this form of plasticity. Although the manipulations may be effective in producing a change in behavior, they shed little or no light directly on mechanisms underlying species-typical behavior.

In summary, an ecological approach to the study of learning necessitates task description—the asking of "does" questions by means of intensive observation and description of organisms in species-typical contexts. Such normative description is essential in elucidating the kinds of things that animals learn in the usual course of adaptation.

Learning is *not* synonymous with "experience," but is rather a subset of experience, specifically, a particular form of inductive experience (Gottlieb, 1976). In other words, the intervening variable that we call "learning" is a process that either (1) channels behavior in a particular direction or (2) sharpens or increases the specificity of a behavior pattern. Viewing learning in this manner, one can conceive of innumerable ways that animals might come to adapt to their physical and social environments by means of such a process. It is not unrealistic to expect learning to play a role in the development of many species-typical behaviors, as has already been well documented in feeding (e.g., Cole, Hainsworth, Kamil, Mercier, & Wolf, 1982), individual recognition (e.g., Miller, 1979a, b), migration and navigation (e.g., Emlen, 1969, 1970), habitat selection (e.g., Wiens, 1972), vocal learning (e.g., Mundinger, 1979), and territoriality (e.g., Falls & Brooks, 1975).

STEP THREE: EXPERIMENTAL MANIPULATION

Having identified the kinds of things that animals learn, the final methodological step in the ecological analysis of learning (and, unfortunately, often the *only* step in the nonecological analysis of learning) is experimental manipulation.

Whereas task description tells us *what* animals learn, experimental manipulation assesses *how* they learn (Johnston, 1981).

Experimental manipulation, whether it takes place in the laboratory or in the field, involves imposing upon animals varying degrees of species-atypical conditions (i.e., stimulus, response, and/or context, as discussed later) in an attempt to identify species-typical behavioral processes. Studying "normal" behavioral processes by creating "abnormal" conditions is not necessarily paradoxical to an ecological approach as long as the manipulation has some demonstrable relationship to the learning situation as specified during the task description phase. (A conceptual framework for studying the development of species-typical behavior under species-atypical conditions is discussed in greater detail in Miller, 1981.)

It is the nature of the manipulations that renders any particular learning experiment ecological or nonecological. However, it would be misleading to view the categories of "ecological" and "nonecological" as discrete classes. Rather, the extent of ecological or nonecological content attendant on these categories can be defined in terms of the species-typicality or species-atypicality of each of three dimensions: (1) stimulus objects presented to the animal, (2) responses measured, and (3) the experimental context (i.e., species-typical versus species-atypical setting). This conceptualization renders eight possible methodological dimensions of learning (with varying degrees of ecological content), as represented on the three-dimensional cube in Figure 3.2. These eight categories represent an initial effort toward operationally defining the kinds of experimental manipulations that distinguish ecological from nonecological approaches to learning.

Type 1

Type 1 represents a situation where an animal learns to make a species-typical response in the presence of a species-typical stimulus in a species-typical context. This type of learning situation represents the hallmark of an ecological approach. An example is the playback experiment by Beer (1970) showing that incubating laughing gulls on natural nests (species-typical context) learn to recognize the vocalizations of their own mate (species-typical stimulus) and respond preferentially to his calls over those of a neighbor or a stranger by rising and resettling, calling in return, or flying from the nest and returning with nest material (species-typical responses).

Given this set of ecologically meaningful circumstances, one can proceed to ask the sort of questions posed by investigators interested in underlying mechanisms of learning (e.g., How do gulls learn to recognize their mate's call? Do the calls alone have any reinforcing properties, or must they be associated with a visible mate? Are there mechanisms to guard against habituation to the mate's calls? and so on). Thus, by starting with a set of circumstances that is high in ecological validity, one can begin to assess how learning enables organisms to

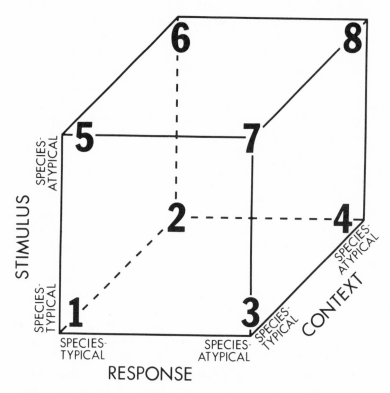

FIG. 3.2 Dimensions of learning. This model provides one way of operation-
alizing the distinction between ecological and nonecological approaches to learning, and various points in between. The numbers refer to types of learning situations
(discussed in the text) that vary in accord with the species-typicality or species-
atypicality of the stimulus, response, and context. Type 1 represents the most
extreme ecological learning situation, and Type 8 represents the most extreme
nonecological learning situation.

adapt to their usual environments. In this manner, learning can be approached
from an evolutionary perspective to the extent that the adaptive phenotypic traits
(i.e., behaviors) resulting from learning processes will generally be favored by
natural selection. This approach places the study of the evolution of intelligence
in its proper perspective as contrasted with certain pseudoevolutionary approaches
that have been adopted previously in nonecological approaches to learning (e.g.,
Bitterman, 1965; but, see also Hodos & Campbell, 1969).

Type 2

Type 2 situations differ from Type 1 only in that the context is now species-
atypical. The ecological character of this situation stems from the notion that
what one does to an animal in the course of experimental manipulation is probably

more important than *where* one does it (Miller, 1981). Two examples merit mention here—one because of its ethological character, and the other because of its relationship to more traditional (though not contemporary) laboratory approaches to animal learning.

The first example involves the effects of prenatal learning on postnatal auditory preferences. Tschanz (1968), working with guillomots, and Impekoven and Gold (1973), working with laughing gulls, found that hatchlings of these species preferentially approach (species-typical response) a loudspeaker broadcasting the particular parental call (species-typical stimulus) to which it had been exposed as an embryo rather than an unfamiliar conspecific parental call. The embryonic exposure and postnatal tests were conducted under laboratory conditions (species-atypical context).

The second example is conceptually important in terms of the history in this century of animal learning paradigms and how, due, in part, to technological advances, the extent of ecological validity attendant to these paradigms has progressively decreased. The thrust of the argument that I wish to present is that "simpler" problem-solving tasks (e.g., detour problems, delayed-reaction problems, and, to some extent, maze-type problems) are methodologically more attuned to an ecological approach to learning than are technologically elegant but ecologically crude Skinner boxes and related learning situations. (An often-overlooked point is that Small, 1901, designed the first rat maze with the explicit intent of mimicking the natural burrow situation and thereby attempting to capitalize on species-typical behavior patterns.) The rationale behind this line of reasoning is that the "simpler" learning situations usually involve species-typical responses (i.e., approach) to species-typical stimuli (i.e., food or water), whereas the Skinner box involves species-atypical responses (i.e., bar-pressing or key-pecking) in the presence of species-atypical stimuli (i.e., discriminative stimuli, such as colored lights, abstract visual patterns, etc.). I should mention here that I classify bar-pressing and key-pecking as species-atypical responses because rats and pigeons do not engage in these behaviors *to locate or capture food* in the wild. It is true that behavior patterns similar to bar-pressing and key-pecking are involved in the *handling of food* to the extent that the food might be manipulated by the rat's forepaws or pecked at by the bird. But in the Skinner box, the animals must emit these responses primarily for the purpose of *obtaining* (i.e., locating or capturing) food rather than in connection with ingesting it, thereby temporally disassociating the behavior pattern from the object at which it is normally directed. Approach-type responses, on the other hand, more closely approximate the actions that occur during the location and capture phase of feeding behavior as it occurs in the wild. Thus, an approach response is deemed species-typical with regard to certain laboratory tasks involving feeding or drinking behaviors.

The example that I think most elegantly illustrates just such an ecological approach to animal learning comes from the Russian literature and is known as the "extrapolation reflex" (Krushinskii, 1962). According to Krushinskii (1962):

"We use the term extrapolation reflex to describe the reaction of animals not merely to some direct stimulus, but also to the direction along which this stimulus proceeds as a result of its regular movement" (p. 181). In essence, this learning situation mimics what often occurs in the field as an animal "stalks" potential prey. The prey is not always visible; yet, it is often highly adaptive for the predator to continue along the same path as the prey at the point(s) where it disappears from sight. This is the sort of feeding-related problem-solving capability assessed in some of the simpler extrapolation reflex problems. For example, a piece of food may slowly be pulled along a straight track as the animal follows it. Then, the food reaches a point along the track where it disappears into either a 3-m-long tunnel or two 1.5-m-long tunnels separated by a 3-5-cm gap where the food is briefly visible. (The situation involving the 3-m-long tunnel is more difficult in terms of sustaining the subject's stalking behavior.) The food continues to move along the track at a mean velocity of 8–10 cm/sec and eventually emerges from the tunnel. Some species (i.e., fowl, ducks, pigeons, rabbits) do not persist stalking when the food disappears into the tunnel; others (i.e., crows, magpies) persist only when the tunnel is separated midway with a small gap, whereupon seeing the food at the gap, the animal runs to the end of the second half of the tunnel and waits for the food's arrival. However, not even crows and magpies completely stalk the nonvisible food in the no-gap situation, though they persist significantly longer (in time) and farther down the length of the tunnel than do other avian species tested.

Other types of extrapolation reflex problems are described by Krushinskii (1962), some involving intricate detour components.

Problems of this type, illustrative of what I have designated as a Type 2 situation involving species-typical stimuli and responses in species-atypical contexts (i.e., laboratories), are far more likely to provide answers to questions of how animals learn to perform adaptation-related tasks than will a multitude of Skinner boxes. Thus, an ecological approach would be fostered if investigators build upon this foundation established by comparative psychologists earlier in this century and by subsequent Russian investigators by designing laboratory situations that tap into the kinds of problems that animals encounter in the wild and discovering how they go about solving these problems—discovering how they learn to adapt and to survive.

Type 3

In the third type of learning situation, an animal makes a species-atypical response in the presence of a species-typical stimulus presented in a species-typical context. This is a most unusual situation and one for which there are few clear-cut examples. But it is not difficult to see why this is the case, for animals usually do not engage in unusual behaviors in the presence of species-typical stimuli in the natural environment.

However, one occasionally finds instances where certain behavior patterns are not typical of most members of a species but are characteristic of certain populations. An example of such a situation is described by Galef (1980, and this volume). Members of certain colonies of wild rats living along the Po River (species-typical context) have acquired a behavior of diving to the river bottom (species-atypical response) to feed on molluscs (species-typical stimuli). Diving for molluscs is apparently not a species-typical response because no members of nearby colonies (having equal access to molluscs) along the Po River have been observed to engage in this behavior. Galef (1980) notes further that feeding behavior patterns in rats tend to be highly idiosyncratic and colony-specific (rather than species-specific).

Along a similar vein, the Type 3 situation may be a paradigmatic example of the way animals that have come to use tools as part of the species-typical repertoire *initially* acquired such skills. We must assume, of course, that at one time such species were not tool users (which is why, upon initial use of a tool, such behavior would be deemed species-atypical) and that such acquired behavior was eventually transmitted by means of social or observational learning, "natural shaping" (Galef, 1980), and/or specific selection.

It would seem that most examples of initial tool use in animals could be explained in terms of this paradigm, so, to illustrate the point, I mention only one example involving the Egyptian vulture, as described by van Lawick–Goodall and van Lawick (1966). This species has incorporated into its repertoire an effective form of tool use associated with feeding. But, again, to relate this example to the Type 3 learning framework, one must envisage what the situation might have been prior to the incorporation of this behavior into the species-typical repertoire. Vultures are scavengers and will often eat (among many other things) unattended eggs found in nests of other species. This poses no particular problem for the vulture until an ostrich egg is encountered, for the thick shell is impenetrable by the vulture's beak. What these birds have learned to do upon finding unattended ostrich eggs (species-typical stimuli) on nests in the field (species-typical context) is to pick up large rocks in their bills and to throw the rocks down on the eggs (species-atypical response) until the eggs split open. (I have assumed in this example that the ostrich egg is a species-typical stimulus due to its egg-like character and the context in which it is found [i.e., natural nests], and because we must further assume that upon initial encounters with these objects, the vultures attempted [unsuccessfully] to extract the contents by species-typical means.)

An interesting concept that is related to the Type 3 learning situation is that of "behavioral neo-phenotypes" (Kuo, 1976). According to Kuo, neonates possess a wide range of possibilities or potentialities of behavior patterns within the limits of species-typical morphological constraints, and the neonate is born with far more behavioral patterns during its lifetime. It is on the basis of these behavioral potentials that "behavioral neo-phenotypes" can be created. The concept refers to new behavior patterns that, having been within the range of behavior potentials, become actualized via experimental manipulation. Kuo argues that the study of these behavior patterns that are either rare or nonexistent in nature can yield valuable information regarding potential evolutionary pathways. In other words, as long as one can demonstrate a potential for behavioral modifiability in development by creating behavioral neo-phenotypes, it is possible that at some later point in evolution selection pressures may, so to speak, call upon this plasticity (i.e., inductive malleability, as shown in Fig. 3.1) and incorporate new behavior patterns into the species-typical repertoire. Thus, in addition to having a strong ecological character, Type 3 learning situations offer an intriguing way to go about assessing the evolution of species-typical behavior from species-atypical behavior.

Type 4

In a sense, Type 4 situations are artificial counterparts of Type 3 situations—all that has changed is the context, which is now species-atypical. Thus, studies of tool using in unnatural settings would exemplify this paradigm. A classic example comes from the work of Köhler (1925), whose chimpanzees, housed in a large enclosure (species-atypical context), learned to join pieces of short sticks (species-atypical response) to make one long enough to rake in a banana (species-typical stimulus) that was otherwise out of reach.

Another example, involving a more "typical" laboratory situation, comes from a paper by Allison, Larson, and Jensen (1967). Rats placed in a shuttlebox in which one side is painted white and the other black seem to have an unlearned preference for the black side. This preference for black was strengthened when the rats were shocked on the white side, but a preference for white was not induced by shocking the rats on the black side. (The preference for black was only weakened.) This preference for black seems explicable on the basis that rats are primarily nocturnal animals that live in dark burrows during daylight. Allison et al. further documented this natural preference for black in a shuttlebox situation (species-atypical context) by training rats to escape from the start compartment to the goal compartment by touching with either forepaw a paddlewheel (species-atypical response) above the guillotine door separating the compartments. The species-typical stimulus in this otherwise highly artificial situation was the black compartment.

Type 5

Like Type 3 situations, Type 5 learning situations are hard to come by because species-atypical stimuli do not usually occur in species-typical contexts. Something has to cause the environment to change in some unusual way, yet not disrupt species-typical responsiveness, for the conditions of this paradigm to be met. In other words, this situation can occur only when species-typical stimuli are suddenly altered, such as by geographical forces, biotic invasions, or by man.

There is one example that illustrates this paradigm, although its relation to learning per se is tenuous or, at best, highly speculative. This example is the responsiveness shown by animals to "supernormal" stimuli. A supernormal stimulus is an artificial (species-atypical) stimulus to which animals respond appropriately (species-typically) and prefer even in the presence of a similar species-typical stimulus. Supernormal stimuli are similar to their species-typical counterparts on at least one dimension (e.g., color, size, shape, etc.); thus, they are not species-atypical in an absolute sense—only in a relative sense, because, in the supernormal stimulus, the common dimension is highly exaggerated beyond the range of species-typicality. A classic example of responsiveness to supernormal stimuli comes from field experiments by Tinbergen (1951) on the incubation behavior of the ringed plover. When presented with an unusually large clutch of eggs consisting of five eggs (species-atypical stimulus) in the field (species-typical context), the bird prefers to incubate (species-typical response) this supernormal stimulus instead of its normal clutch of three eggs. Similarly, if presented with an artificially constructed large egg and its smaller natural egg, the ringed plover prefers to incubate the supernormal stimulus.

In these experiments, it is not quite clear what (if anything) has been "learned"; however, Hogan, Kruijt, and Frijlink (1975) and Staddon (1975) have offered a learning analogy to the responsiveness shown by animals to supernormal stimuli. The analogy involves a phenomenon associated with certain discrimination learning paradigms known as "peak shift" (Hanson, 1959; see also review by Purtle, 1973). In this learning situation, an animal is trained to discriminate two stimuli (for example, different wavelengths) by rewarding responses that occur in the presence of one wavelength (550 nm) and not rewarding respones that occur in the presence of the other (530 nm). Following training, animals respond best (if not almost exclusively) to the rewarded stimulus (550 nm). However, if the animal is tested later with a range of different stimuli, it is often found that the maximum responsiveness has shifted in a direction away from both the previously rewarded and previously unrewarded stimuli (i.e., to 570 nm). This phenomenon is known as "peak shift." The common element shared by peak shift and supernormal stimulus responsivity is the redirection of a response to a novel stimulus. Baerends and Kruijt (1973) properly caution that the relationship may end there and that the two phenomena might be regulated by different processes. This question remains open to experimental scrutiny.

It should be stressed that manipulations involving the occurrence of species-atypical stimuli in species-typical contexts can provide a valuable means of assessing species-typical behavior. For example, if an animal is presented with an altered stimulus and continues to respond in a species-typical fashion, one can conclude that the animal is attending to features of the stimulus other than those that have been altered. Systematically downgrading species-typical stimuli (or, in the case of supernormal stimuli, "upgrading" particular aspects of the stimuli) allows us to assess the critical stimulus features affecting *normal* behavior (Lehrman, 1970; Miller, 1981). It is exceedingly important to bear in mind, however, that the ecological validity of these manipulations is absolutely dependent on the extent to which a species-typical stimulus has been used as a frame of reference. An ecological approach would entail changing a particular feature of a species-typical stimulus (rendering it species-atypical) to assess the extent to which that change affects species-typical responsiveness; a nonecological approach, on the other hand, would involve the use of more or less arbitrarily selected stimuli, as has often been the case in the study of imprinting (discussed later).

Type 6

Type 6 learning situations involve species-typical responses to species-atypical stimuli presented in species-atypical contexts. The laboratory study of filial imprinting in precocial avian neonates serves as a prime example of this situation. Most laboratory studies of imprinting assess the redirection of species-typical preferences toward species-atypical objects in highly artificial contexts. The usual sort of laboratory (species-atypical context) imprinting task might involve a duckling approaching and following (species-typical response) an arbitrarily selected object, such as a moving light or painted three-dimensional ball or cube, or even objects as bizarre as electric trains and inflating balloons (species-atypical stimuli).

Investigators of imprinting, like investigators of general laws of learning, have gone awry in assuming that the processes underlying this nonecological approach to imprinting and the establishment of normal species identification are congruous (see also Miller, 1980, 1981). Recent studies adopting ecological approaches (Johnston & Gottlieb, 1981a,b) have, in fact, raised serious doubts about the role of imprinting in the development of normal species identification. This serves as an excellent example of the lack of process generality that can occur when adopting a nonecological rather than an ecological approach. There is no ecological significance in persistently and intensively studying behaviors that are nothing more than laboratory artifacts.

As discussed earlier in relation to Type 5 situations, Type 6 studies can have ecological validity if the atypical properties of the stimuli have been derived by changing certain features of stimuli that are species-typical, and if the context is not too species-atypical. For example, Emlen (1969, 1970) reared indigo buntings in a planetarium (species-atypical context) in which the star constellations rotated about a non-natural axis (species-atypical stimulus). Upon assessing their premigratory orientation (species-typical response), Emlen found that the axis of rotation is a more important cue than the configuration of the constellations per se. Thus, by carefully manipulating certain aspects of the stimulus configuration within a Type 6 situation, Emlen was able to identify key elements affecting species-typical behavior.

Type 7

The seventh type of learning situation is one that probably occurs rarely because it involves responding in a species-atypical fashion to a species-atypical stimulus in a species-typical context. This situation is similar to that of Type 5 in that something very unusual has to occur in the natural environment in order to provide species-atypical stimuli. In fact, because of the unusual and unlikely circumstances attendant to this situation, clear-cut examples are difficult to come by.

One plausible example that seems to fit the criteria of the Type 7 situation is the opening of milk bottles by great tits, blue tits, and coal tits—an acquired habit that spread throughout the British Isles in near epidemic proportions in the 1930s and 1940s (Fisher & Hinde, 1949). Shortly after milk bottles (species-atypical stimuli) were delivered at the doorsteps of houses (species-typical context, due to its unrestrained character and articulation with the usual foraging habitat that includes lawns, shrubbery, etc.), tits would land atop the bottles and tear open the thin cardboard tops or foil caps (species-atypical response) and proceed to drink the milk off the top. (This learned behavior, which was deemed highly undesirable by those for whom the milk had been intended, was subsequently extinguished, or at least greatly attenuated, by using heavier cardboard caps on the milk bottles.)

Type 8

Type 8 learning situations represent the epitome of the nonecological approach and, coincidentally, the usual manner in which learning has been studied; namely, by assessing species-atypical responses (e.g., bar-pressing, key-pecking, manipulating plastic "junk" objects, as in learning set or oddity tasks, etc.) to species-atypical stimuli (e.g., lights, geometric patterns, artificial tones or buzzers, artificial odors, etc.) in species-atypical contexts (e.g., laboratories and the apparatuses contained therein).

These kinds of studies pervade the contemporary learning literature. It is indeed refreshing to peruse books and journals published before 1940 where elements of an ecological approach abound amid the seemingly crude apparatuses of those times. Since then, investigators of learning became victims of a Zeitgeist that did not concern itself with biologically relevant behavior or ecological validity. Moreover, technology has had a significant impact, enabling experimenters to cease observing the behavior of their animals as experiments are increasingly controlled by complex programming equipment and computers.

Given the lack of contact between these experimenters and their animal subjects, it is hardly surprising that an ecological approach to learning has been shunned.

CONCLUDING REMARKS

It is not difficult to see why nonecological paradigms have been the most popular. In addition to the (often misguided) theoretical and conceptual ideologies that have fostered the nonecological laboratory tradition, laboratories are relatively comfortable places, and they are usually devoid of many of the problems that investigators encounter when attempting to study behavior in species-typical contexts—problems associated with a lack of control. In nature, the investigator has relatively little or sometimes no control over factors that directly influence his or her research, such as weather, loss of subjects to predators, and other practical problems associated with field work. Laboratories, of course, offer their own unique problems associated with housing animals, cleaning their cages, maintaining proper temperature, humidity, diet, and so on. But these problems are usually easier to deal with than the unexpected, unpredictable events that occur in nature.

The reluctance to engage in field work has also obviated the step that is so critical to an ecological approach to learning—task description. Without adequate normative field data, one cannot assess the kinds of things about which animals learn, let alone ask experimental questions about how they solve such problems. Moreover, ascertaining what kinds of stimuli and responses are species-typical cannot be done without extensive naturalistic observation across species-typical contexts. Adherence to theoretical dogma, coupled with the convenience of remaining in the confines of the laboratory, has generated a wealth of learning data that is, for the most part, biologically meaningless from an ecoethological perspective. Such a research strategy has been justified by the unproven assumption that learning is a general process across species and across contexts—a process regulated by universal laws (see Revusky's chapter in this volume for a defense of this "general process" view of learning). Yet, as mentioned previously, by engaging in task description and assessing species-typical responsiveness to species-typical stimuli, it has already been found that the imprinting "process" as typically (i.e., nonecologically) studied in the laboratory is not responsible for the very phenomenon that it had been assumed to explain— species identification. It would be naive to view this as an isolated exception to the "general laws" principle. I suggest that the foundations upon which such presumed laws are based are going to crumble when it becomes fashionable to adopt an ecological approach to the study of learning. Perhaps it is the realization of the demise of these foundations by those who have continued to build upon them that has kept the study of learning alive in its present nonecological form.

ACKNOWLEDGMENTS

This chapter was prepared in connection with activities supported by Research Grant BNS–8013502 from the National Science Foundation. I am grateful to Martha H. Wilson and Benjamin D. Sachs for informative discussions of issues addressed in this chapter, and to Charles F. Blaich and Thomas R. Alley for commenting on the manuscript, though I remain fully responsible for the shortcomings and viewpoints expressed herein.

I owe no small debt to two individuals who have helped me appreciate the importance of the "natural-history orientation"—Robert B. Tallarico, who, as my predoctoral adviser, encouraged me to remove the cataracts obscuring the insights to be gained by field research, and Gilbert Gottlieb, who, as my postdoctoral adviser, performed the "surgery."

REFERENCES

Allison, J., Larson, D., & Jensen, D. D. (1967). Acquired fear, brightness preference, and one-way shuttlebox performance. *Psychonomic Science, 8,* 269–270.

Baerends, G. P., & Kruijt, J. P. (1973). Stimulus selection. In R. A. Hinde & J. Stevenson–Hinde (Eds.), *Constraints on learning.* New York: Academic Press.

Beer, C. G. (1970). Individual recognition of voice in the social behavior of birds. In D. S. Lehrman, R. A. Hinde, & E. S. Shaw (Eds.), *Advances in the study of behavior* (Vol. 3). New York: Academic Press.

Bitterman, M. E. (1965). Phyletic differences in learning. *American Psychologist, 20,* 396–410.

Boice, R. (1977). Burrows of wild and albino rats: Effects of domestication, outdoor raising, age, experience, and maternal state. *Journal of Comparative and Physiological Psychology, 91,* 649–661.

Cole, S., Hainsworth, F. R., Kamil, A. C., Mercier, T., & Wolf, L. L. (1982). Spatial learning as an adaptation in hummingbirds. *Science, 217,* 655–657.

Colgan, P. W. (Ed.). (1978). *Quantitative ethology.* New York: Wiley.

Emlen, S. T. (1969). The development of migratory orientation in young indigo buntings. *Living Bird, 8,* 113–126.

Emlen, S. T. (1970). Celestial rotation: Its importance in the development of migratory orientation. *Science, 170,* 1198–1201.

Falls, J. B., & Brooks, R. J. (1975). Individual recognition by song in white-throated sparrows. II. Effects of location. *Canadian Journal of Zoology, 53,* 1412–1420.

Fisher, J., & Hinde, R. A. (1949). The opening of milk bottles by birds. *British Birds, 42,* 347–357.

Galef, B. G., Jr. (1980). Diving for food: Analysis of a possible case of social learning in wild rats *(Rattus norvegicus). Journal of Comparative and Physiological Psychology, 94,* 416–425.

Gottlieb, G. (1976). The roles of experience in the development of behavior and the nervous system. In G. Gottlieb (Ed.), *Studies on the development of behavior and the nervous system* (Vol. 3). *Neural and behavioral specificity.* New York: Academic Press.

Gottlieb, G. (1982). Development of species identification in ducklings: IX. The necessity of experiencing normal variations in embryonic auditory stimulation. *Developmental Psychobiology, 15,* 507–517.

Hanson, H. M. (1959). Effects of discrimination training on stimulus generalization. *Journal of Experimental Psychology, 58,* 321–334.

Hodos, W., & Campbell, C. B. G. (1969). *Scala naturae:* Why there is no theory in comparative psychology. *Psychological Review, 76,* 337–350.

Hogan, J. A., Kruijt, J. P., & Frijlink, J. H. (1975). "Supernormality" in a learning situation. *Zeitschrift für Tierpsychologie, 38*, 212–218.

Impekoven, M. (1973). Response-contingent prenatal experience of maternal calls in the Peking duck (*Anas platyrhynchos*). *Animal Behaviour, 21*, 164–168.

Impekoven, M., & Gold, P. S. (1973). Prenatal origins of parent–young interaction in birds: A naturalistic approach. In G. Gottlieb (Ed.), *Studies on the development of behavior and the nervous system* (Vol. 1). *Behavioral embryology*. New York: Academic Press.

Johnston, T. D. (1981). Contrasting approaches to a theory of learning. *The Behavioral and Brain Sciences, 4*, 125–173.

Johnston, T. D., & Gottlieb, G. (1981a). Visual preferences of imprinted ducklings are altered by the maternal call. *Journal of Comparative and Physiological Psychology, 95*, 663–675.

Johnston, T. D., & Gottlieb, G. (1981b). Development of visual species identification in ducklings: What is the role of imprinting? *Animal Behaviour, 29*, 1082–1099.

Köhler, W. (1925). *The mentality of apes*. London: Routledge & Kegan Paul.

Krushinskii, L. V. (1962). *Animal behavior. Its normal and abnormal development*. New York: Consultants Bureau.

Kummer, H. (1968). *Social organization of Hamadryas baboons: A field study*. Chicago: University of Chicago Press.

Kuo, Z.-Y. (1976). *The dynamics of behavior development* (enlarged ed.). New York: Plenum.

Lancaster, J. B., & Lee, R. B. (1965). The annual reproduction cycle in monkeys and apes. In I. DeVore (Ed.), *Primate behavior*. New York: Holt, Rinehart, & Winston.

Lehner, P. N. (1979). *Handbook of ethological methods*. New York: Garland STPM.

Lehrman, D. S. (1970). Semantic and conceptual issues in the nature–nurture problem. In L. R. Aronson, E. Tobach, D. S. Lehrman, & J. S. Rosenblatt (Eds.), *Development and evolution of behavior: Essays in memory of T. C. Schneirla*. San Francisco: W. H. Freeman.

Lehrman, D. S. (1971). Behavioral science, engineering, and poetry. In E. Tobach, L. R. Aronson, & E. Shaw (Eds.), *The biopsychology of development*. New York: Academic Press.

McCall, R. B. (1977). Challenges to a science of developmental psychology. *Child Development, 48*, 333–344.

McClintock, M. K. (1981). Simplicity from complexity: A naturalistic approach to behavior and neuroendocrine function. In I. Silverman (Ed.), *New directions for methodology of social and behavioral science* (No. 8): *Generalizing from laboratory to life*. San Francisco: Jossey–Bass.

Miller, D. B. (1977a). Roles of naturalistic observation in comparative psychology. *American Psychologist, 32*, 211–219.

Miller, D. B. (1977b). Social displays of mallard ducks (*Anas platyrhynchos*): Effects of domestication. *Journal of Comparative and Physiological Psychology, 91*, 221–232.

Miller, D. B. (1979a). The acoustic basis of mate recognition by female zebra finches (*Taeniopygia guttata*). *Animal Behaviour, 27*, 376–380.

Miller, D. B. (1979b). Long-term recognition of father's song by female zebra finches. *Nature, 280*, 389–391.

Miller, D. B. (1980). Beyond sexual imprinting. *Acta XVII congressus internationalis ornithologici* (Vol. 2). Berlin: Verlag der Deutschen Ornithologen–Gesellschaft.

Miller, D. B. (1981). Conceptual strategies in behavioral development: Normal development and plasticity. In K. Immelmann, G. W. Barlow, L. Petrinovich, & M. Main (Eds.), *Behavioral development. The Bielefeld interdisciplinary project*. Cambridge: Cambridge University Press.

Mundinger, P. C. (1979). Call learning in the Carduelinae: Ethological and systematic considerations. *Systematic Zoology, 28*, 270–283.

Petrinovich, L., & Patterson, T. L. (1982). Field studies of habituation: V. Evidence for a two-factor, dual-process system. *Journal of Comparative and Physiological Psychology, 96*, 284–296.

Purtle, R. B. (1973). Peak shift: A review. *Psychological Bulletin, 80*, 408–421.

Rachlin, H. (1981). Learning theory in its niche. *The Behavioral and Brain Sciences, 4*, 155–156.

Sackett, G. P., Sameroff, A. J., Cairns, R. B., & Suomi, S. J. (1981). Continuity in behavioral development: Theoretical and empirical issues. In K. Immelmann, G. W. Barlow, L. Petrinovich, & M. Main (Eds.), *Behavioral development. The Bielefeld interdisciplinary project.* Cambridge: Cambridge University Press.

Skinner, B. F. (1961). The flight from the laboratory. In B. F. Skinner, *Cumulative record* (enlarged ed.). New York: Appleton–Century–Crofts.

Small, W. S. (1901). Experimental study of the mental processes of the rat. II. *American Journal of Psychology, 12*, 206–239.

Staddon, J. E. R. (1975). A note on the evolutionary significance of "supernormal" stimuli. *American Naturalist, 109*, 541–545.

Tinbergen, N. (1951). *The study of instinct.* New York: Oxford University Press.

Tschanz, B. (1968). Trotellummen, Die Entstehung der persönlichen Beziehungen zwischen Jungvogel und Eltern. *Zeitschrift für Tierpsychologie* (Suppl. 4), 1–103.

van Lawick–Goodall, J., & van Lawick, H. (1966.) Use of tools by the Egyptian vulture, *Neophron percnopterus. Nature, 212*, 1468–1469.

von Uexküll, J. (1934). *Streifzüge durch die Umwelten von Tieren und Menschen.* Berlin: Springer.

Wallen, K. (1982). Influence of female hormonal state of rhesus sexual behavior varies with space for social interaction. *Science, 217*, 375–377.

Wiens, J. A. (1972). Anuran habitat selection: Early experience and substrate selection in *Rana cascadae* tadpoles. *Animal Behaviour, 20*, 218–220.

Zuckerman, S. (1932). *The social life of monkeys and apes.* London: Routledge & Kegan Paul.

II

THE ECOLOGY
OF LEARNING:
EMPIRICAL RESEARCH

The chapters in Part II present a sampling of current research in which learning has been studied from an ecological perspective. Although it is only recently that the ecological approach has generated widespread theoretical interest, these chapters demonstrate that empirical research of clear relevance has been going on for some time. One of our hopes, in compiling this volume, is that we can both stimulate further work of this kind and provide a broader theoretical perspective to aid in its interpretation.

Obtaining food is an important ecological problem for all animals, and a wealth of research has demonstrated the widespread role that learning plays in the acquisition and modification of feeding behavior. It is appropriate, therefore, that the first three chapters in Part II concern the role of learning in various aspects of feeding behavior. Pietrewicz and Richards review some of the general problems of foraging from an ecological perspective and present data from laboratory experiments that illustrate how ecological questions about learning can be addressed in the psychological laboratory. Kalat assesses results from the study of taste-aversion learning, a research area that was instrumental in stimulating interest in the ecological context of learning. Galef reviews his work on the social transmission of food preferences in rodents, drawing attention to an important mode of learning that is often overlooked by theorists who do not adopt an ecological perspective.

The remaining three chapters in Part II discuss learning in relation to three kinds of behavior where an ecological approach may be especially valuable. Coss and Owings describe the antipredator behavior of ground squirrels and show how the modification of behavior by learning and by evolution are integrated into the production of adaptive patterns of behavior. Hazen and Pick review a wide range of literature on spatial orientation, focusing on the development of spatial abilities in humans. Their chapter illustrates how the ecological approach may be applied to studies of human learning, and how ecological principles may enrich the developmental study of learning abilities. Finally, West and King consider the acquisition of bird song, a research area that is often considered a paradigm case of the ecological approach to animal learning. Nonetheless, West and King show how many important questions that have been overlooked in the past gain new prominence when the problems of song learning are viewed from an ecological perspective, and they present results from their own research program on the cowbird to illustrate the potential fruitfulness of that approach.

As already mentioned, the research presented in Part II is only a sampling of the ecological approach to learning, and it by no means exhausts the range of problems that might be addressed from an ecological perspective. We hope that other investigators will become convinced of the utility of the ecological approach and will find ways to apply it in their own areas of research interest.

4 Learning to Forage: An Ecological Perspective

Alexandra T. Pietrewicz
Jerry B. Richards
Department of Psychology, Emory University

The study of foraging behavior raises numerous and interesting questions concerning the relationship between an animal's environment and its learning abilities. In recent years, the study of this relationship has been directly addressed by both learning psychologists and behavioral ecologists; these investigators have emphasized the complex nature of the animal–environment interaction in foraging behavior (see Kamil & Sargent, 1981). Foraging, whether hunting for prey or finding plant food, is a pattern of behaviors that may be conceptualized as involving a series of problems facing the forager: where to look for food, how to identify it, and so on. The solution to each of these problems is a direct function of environmental factors such as the variability of food supply with changing season, the density of food in various areas, and the distribution (clumped, scattered) of those items. Previous research has focused especially on an analysis of a forager's response to discrete changes in the availability of food. For example, certain predators are sensitive to the profitability of a search in specific niches and change their search path or locus of search with fluctuations in prey density (see review by Krebs, 1973).

Although there has been a substantial amount of research directed at the question of how a forager responds to changes in the availability of food, there has been much less work that focuses on the issue of the specific role of learning, and the ecological factors that affect that process. Some recent work, however, has very elegantly handled such an issue.

Kamil (1978) addressed the problem of the role of learning in the foraging behavior of a Hawaiian nectar-feeding bird (the amakihi). This situation is particularly interesting from an ecological perspective because, once a bird depletes a flower of nectar, that particular flower does not contain enough nectar to make a revisit profitable for some period of time. Thus, it would be highly adaptive for these birds to learn a foraging strategy that would minimize revisits to empty flowers. The first question to be addressed, then, is whether the birds' search pattern is spatially or temporally systematic. Kamil observed the patterns of feeding in these birds and found that they avoided repeated visits to the same flowers, and that they showed a temporal patterning of revisits to specific flowers; that is, the birds tended to avoid revisits to the same flower for about an hour. Kamil ruled out the possibility that this avoidance of a recently depleted flower was due to a spatial pattern of movement through the trees or to visual or other characteristics of depleted flowers. Although these results do not directly provide evidence for a specific learning process, it is highly likely that learning and memory are involved.

Cole, Hainsworth, Kamil, Mercier, and Wolf (1982) more directly assessed learning abilities of nectar-feeders (hummingbirds) in the laboratory. Artificial flowers that could provide a small amount of sucrose solution were presented with two flowers on each trial, one containing food and the other empty. Two types of learning problem were conducted. In the "stay learning" problem, the flower containing food was positioned in the location where the bird had received food in a preliminary phase of the trial. In the "shift learning" problem, the flower containing food was positioned in the location opposite where the bird had received food in a preliminary phase of the trial. In both types of problem, the only cue available predicting food was the prior location of food. Thus, the birds were required to revisit a previous food location, or to shift to a new location for food. Results showed that these birds learned the shift problem significantly faster than the stay problem. The authors point out that shift learning was facilitated by the birds' pretest bias toward a shift response, and, therefore, during shift learning the birds received food reinforcement more often than during stay learning. However, this bias alone did not account for the dramatic differences in the birds' abilities to learn these types of problem. This study presents an example of the relationship between learning and ecological variables, in that these nectar-feeding birds possess a predisposition to learn that is consistent with the demands of their environment. It cannot be determined, of course, whether this predisposition to learn a spatial shift problem is innate or based on previous experiences of the birds in the field. Nevertheless, this research demonstrates that valid predictions about learning abilities can be made based on the study of the ecological variables that are important in feeding.

The role of memory in foraging was specifically addressed by Shettleworth and Krebs (1982) in a study of hoarding birds. Marsh tits store individual items of food in various places and retrieve these items after extended periods of time, up to days. Such a behavior obviously requires some learning or memory mechanism to allow identification of storage sites. Shettleworth and Krebs drilled holes, small enough for a single hemp seed, in tree branches and covered each hole with a swatch of cloth. In order to store a seed in a branch, the bird had to lift the cloth, and the cloth thus covered the stored seed. The branches were set up in an aviary, and the tits were individually allowed to take seeds from a bowl in the center of the testing "forest" and store them in the tree holes. The recovery of stored seeds was then observed. The authors found very strong evidence for the use of memory in the retrieval of seeds. The birds tended to make few errors in seed recovery; they were not only able to recover most of the stored seeds but also searched few empty holes before recovering a seed. Additional evidence for memory was provided by the finding that recovery of seeds was poor if the experimenters moved the seeds during the time between the birds' storage and recovery of the seeds. This result eliminates the possibility that the seed itself provides a cue (such as ordor) that allows the bird to find it. In addition, Shettleworth and Krebs tested for a recency effect of memory. A recency effect is assumed to exist if the most recently stored seeds are retrieved first. The authors found a slight recency effect, which is consistent with the idea that the memory for a stored item may decay over time, or that continued storing may interfere with the memory of a previously stored item. In any case, the authors showed that the behavior of the birds during recovery of seeds was not due to a tendency to follow a fixed route of movement; the only logical explanation of these results is that the birds are able to remember individual storage sites.

In studying the relationship between learning and ecology in foraging behavior, one of the most critical problems is specifying the relevant ecological dimensions and predicting their effect upon behavior. The examples cited previously have rather effectively dealt with these problems; however, often these problems are not as readily solved. Our own work demonstrates the importance of identifying relevant ecological variables. This chapter presents a summary of two types of research conducted in our laboratory. Both research problems focus on the relationship between learning abilities in the laboratory and the problems facing a forager in the wild. In the first section, we report investigations of factors that might affect the way in which a foraging animal (a rodent) first chooses a location for search. The second section presents research on species-typical tendencies to associate certain cues with consequences of feeding in birds. Following a report of this work, we discuss the feasibility of an ecological approach in the analysis of foraging behavior.

SPATIAL CHOICE IN RODENT FORAGING BEHAVIOR

One of the least well-understood dimensions of foraging behavior is the way in which an animal first chooses a location for search, particularly when prior reinforcement or profitability does not predict the present location of food. Although an initial choice of search area could in fact be random, it might be more efficient for the forager to be "guided" to possible profitable areas by the adaptations of its species. The suggestion that the evolutionary adaptations of a species can be seen in individual choice behavior during feeding is prevalent in the experimental research on rodents. Original interest in the relationship between spatial choice and feeding may have been incited by a study by Petrinovich and Bolles (1954). They trained rats in a T-maze to go to one arm, or to alternate arms, for either food or water reinforcement. The most interesting finding was that thirsty rats performed quite poorly on the alternation task, whereas hungry rats showed acquisition of an alternation pattern. The authors suggested at the time that alternation might be a dominant pattern of behavior for hungry rats. Although they later suggested that these behavior patterns might be determined by the weights of the animals rather than by the deprivation condition, much interest was nevertheless stimulated in the relationship between spatial choice and feeding.

More recently, investigation of the possibility that animals have species-typical patterns of spatial choice, and that these patterns affect foraging, or learning to forage, has been conducted by Olton (Olton, Handelmann, & Walker, 1981; Olton & Samuelson, 1976) and Kamil (1978), among others. Olton suggests that consistent patterns of spatial choice in foraging may be categorized as "win–stay" (the animal returns to a location in which it has previously found food) and "win–shift" (the animal moves to an area different from that in which it has previously found food). The "win–stay" strategy is appropriate if food is clumped and the "win–shift" strategy is appropriate if food is dispersed or exhausted in the original location.

That rats have a tendency to alternate is strongly suggested by experimental research. Rats show spontaneous alternation in a T-maze (Douglas, 1966) and rapidly learn a "win–shift" strategy with food reinforcement in a 4- or 8-arm radial maze (Olton, Handelmann, & Walker, 1981; Olton & Samuelson, 1976). In fact Olton has reported that for rats the presence of food is less effective in altering spatial choice than the absence of food. Using a 3-arm radial maze, rats were rewarded with food for either a stay or a shift pattern. They showed an overall tendency to shift rather than to stay, and the tendency to shift was greater when food in the initial choice arm was depleted. Olton also found that rats can learn either strategy when one pattern is consistently rewarded, although the shift strategy is learned more quickly.

Richards (1981) tested rats on various schedules of water reinforcement in a 4-arm radial maze. When water was available at the end of each arm on a CRF schedule, rats exhibited a clear pattern of alternation of arm choice. In fact, the alternation pattern was more pronounced than that previously reported for rats alternating for food (95% of all trials). Richards also altered the probability of water reinforcement on each of the arms. Under this condition, the rats continued to alternate at high frequencies, even though this pattern resulted in shifting to an arm with a low probability of reinforcement. The behavior of these thirsty rats clearly demonstrated a win–shift strategy, even when this behavior reduced the overall rate of reinforcement. These results suggest that the alternation of spatial choice may not be specific to the search for food.

Thus, the evidence for a predisposition in rats to alternate spatial choice is convincing. It cannot yet be determined, of course, to what extent individual experience in food searching plays a role in the development of this behavior pattern. A more critical question from an ecological perspective, however, is whether this strategy is an adaptive response to the distribution of food in the animal's natural environment. Kamil (1978) has provided strong evidence that pattern of spatial choice is such a response to the distribution of food in nectar-feeding birds. Unfortunately, the data for rats are not quite so clear. We suggest, however, that an ecological analysis of spatial choice in rodents be extended to comparative research with species other than rats, in order to further investigate the relationship between spatial choice and environmental variables.

We chose to investigate spatial choice in Mongolian gerbils (*Meriones unguiculatus*) because they were available from other studies being conducted in our laboratory, and also because they are now a relatively common research animal, having retained many of their natural behavior patterns in spite of extensive inbreeding in this country (Thiessen & Yahr, 1977). In addition, there is an increasing data base on gerbils in the current literature on animal learning and behavior. There has been some controversy over whether gerbils display spontaneous alternation in a T-maze (Dember & Kleiman, 1973; Greenberg, 1973), and it has been suggested by Greenberg (1973) that the conflicting results of these studies were due to procedural variations. Our first exploratory study on this issue tested spontaneous alternation rates of gerbils in a T-maze. In the spontaneous alternation procedure, a nondeprived animal is allowed to run from the start box of the T-maze, and to choose an arm of the maze. The arms of the maze do not contain any food or water. In both 2-trial and 6-trial sessions, gerbils alternated at chance levels of performance (48% of trials in the 2-trial procedure, 52% in the 6-trial procedure). The group means, however, are misleading, for there was variability among individual performances, with a range of alternation rates from 0–100% in both conditions. Both male and female animals were tested, but there were no significant differences in performance between the sexes. Thus, it appears that in a test for spontaneous alternation some gerbils are alternators and some are not.

In order to determine whether any individual traits of gerbils are related to patterns of spatial choice, we investigated the following factors as correlates of alternation scores: age, sex, housing condition (individual or group), general activity level, emotionality in an open field, and frequency of scent marking in an open field. Again, alternation was measured with the spontaneous procedure in a T-maze. The only factor that was related to alternation was scent marking. There was a significant negative correlation between alternation scores and frequency of scent marking ($p < .05$, Pearson product–moment correlation). At first glance, it did not seem surprising that scent marking was related to pattern of spatial choice. Previous research with rats (Egger, 1973) has shown that these animals can utilize odor cues in alternation, by avioding an odor trail left on previous trials. Gerbils, however, have been shown to be unresponsive to odor cues in a T-maze (Greenberg, 1973), and our own tests have produced the same result. It is important to note that the correlation between scent marking and alternation in our work was in a negative direction. Animals who marked frequently displayed low alternation tendencies, and animals who marked infrequently displayed high alternation tendencies. Thiessen and Yahr (1977) suggested that frequency of scent marking in gerbils is highly related to dominance; dominant animals mark more frequently than submissive animals. If this is the case, it may be suggested that a tendency to alternate spatial choice spontaneously is related to the social status of the animal. This research also indicates that in the analysis of spatial choice, it is critical to investigate the variables contributing to behavior at the individual level.

If spontaneous spatial choice is in some way related to social status, it could be predicted that animals with different social behaviors would behave differently in tests of spatial choice. This prediction was tested in our laboratory by Kimberly Banks, using Syrian golden hamsters (*Mesocricetus auratus*). Hamsters are relatively solitary animals, and male–female pairs share a territory only during the reproductive season; the females live with the young only until shortly after weaning (Eibl–Eibesfeldt, 1970). On the other hand, Mongolian gerbils are highly social and live in family groups (Thiessen & Yahr, 1977). Thus, it was predicted that these differences in sociality would be reflected in differences in spatial choice in the spontaneous tests. Hamsters were measured for scent gland size to assess dominance, because all pair-encounter tests result in severe aggression and fighting. However, it has been determined that scent gland size is a reliable predictor of dominance in both male and female hamsters. Our results showed that the most dominant animals (male and female) displayed consistent tendencies to alternate spontaneously in a T-maze (l00% of the trials), whereas subordinate animals showed much variability in tendencies to alternate. Thus, it appears that for both hamsters and gerbils, sociality is related to spatial choice. Of course, the social status of the animal may be the result of various developmental and physiological factors, which may in turn affect behavioral biases at the choice point in a T-maze. However, the point we make here is that the presence of a response bias in a laboratory maze may not be a good measure of species-typical foraging strategies in the field, at least in the spontaneous method. Such a response bias may be an individual characteristic and may be only remotely related to foraging behavior in rodents.

To determine whether searching for food, or a motivational state of hunger, affects alternation patterns in gerbils, we tested hungry gerbils in the same T-maze apparatus with food available at both arms. Under this condition, alternation patterns were more frequent than in the spontaneous condition (63.5% of trials in the food condition, 50.0% of trials in the spontaneous condition). However, the animals still exhibited extensive individual variability in alternation for food (0–100%), and nearly 25% of the animals showed a perseverative pattern of arm choice. In fact, the tendency to alternate or perseverate arm choice did not depend on whether the testing condition involved spontaneous alternation or alternation for food ($X^2 = 3.02$, $df = 1$, $p > .05$). Thus, patterns of spatial choice were independent of the presence of food, or the motivational state of the animal, and searching for food does not affect alternation patterns in gerbils.

It is possible that, in this study, the animals did not show any consistent patterns of spatial choice because food was available and independent of the choice behavior on any one trial. Because the animals were, in essence, reinforced almost equally often for a win–stay (perseveration) and a win–shift (alternation) strategy, these data might be explained by general principles of reinforcement. Olton, Handelmann, and Walker (1981) found that although rats are basically win–shift strategists, finding food is less effective in altering spatial choice than not finding food; that is, the tendency to alternate is enhanced if the rat does not find food in the location of initial choice. In order to investigate parallels between rats and gerbils, it was necessary to expose gerbils searching for food to areas in which food is absent. In this study, food was available in both arms of the T-maze for the first trial only; after the first trial and for nine additional trials per session, food was available only in the maze arm to which the animal did *not* respond on the previous trial. Thus, the animal maximizes the probability of reinforcement by adopting a consistent pattern of alternation. If the animal incorrectly perseverates (win–stay) on any one trial, food is absent in the choice arm. After a total of 120 trials per animal, there was no overall or individual increase in frequency of alternation above chance levels of performance (57.5% of trials). Performance was also evaluated to determine the frequency of alternation following a correct response (finding food) and an incorrect response (not finding food). There was a greater tendency to alternate following an incorrect response (68.9% of trials), than following a correct response (48.2% of trials). The difference in performance between these two types of trials was significant ($p < .05$, two-tailed T_D test). These findings are consistent with those of Olton et al. (1981) and suggest that in hungry gerbils spatial choice can be altered by the absence of food. The absence of overall improvement in performance on this alternation learning task, however, is interesting. It may be the case, of course, that many more trials are necessary for improvement, or that any individual response biases in spatial choice may affect performance on this task, or that the level of motivation for food was not sufficient to overcome any response bias.

In another study, we addressed the possibility that gerbils might show consistent patterns of spatial choice in searching for water. Because Richards (1981) had found high rates of alternation in thirsty rats running a radial maze, it is necessary to compare performance of gerbils under a similar motivational state. Gerbils were water deprived for 36 hours and were run for 6 trials, each with water available at both arms of the T-maze. In this test, overall frequency of alternation was high (93.3% of trials), and there was little individual variability in performance (80–100% of trials). It should be noted that in our study with water reinforcement, selection of an arm and the subsequent drinking of water at that arm did not deplete the water supply. In a comparison of data from this study and that of tests of alternation for food, it was found that spatial choice was dependent on the testing condition ($X^2 = 5.61$, $df = 1$, $p < .05$); that is, thirsty gerbils show a tendency to alternate spatial choice, whereas hungry gerbils do not show a consistent response pattern. An ecological explanation of this result may be premature and speculative. There is no way we can assume that the level of motivation for food was equal to the level of motivation for water in these studies. It may be the case that a small amount of water deprivation is more effective in altering behavior than a moderate amount of food deprivation. Perhaps alternation tendencies increase with increased deprivation conditions, and, because water may be more critical to the immediate survival of an animal than is food, the absence of water creates more behavioral arousal than does a temporary absence of food. However, if level of behavioral arousal is directly related to a tendency to alternate, we would expect that individual differences in alternation would be related to activity level. As previously reported, we were unable to establish this relationship in our laboratory.

There is a serious absence of data on the naturalistic foraging patterns of Mongolian gerbils in the field. It has been reported that wild gerbils consume primarily a seed diet, supplemented by herbage (Bannikov, 1954), but the relative abundance and distribution of their food supply in the field has not been studied. In spite of these limitations for a complete ecological analysis of spatial choice in foraging, our laboratory data do provide some suggestions about this behavior. Gerbils show individual variability in the tendency to spontaneously alternate. The absence of food and the presence of water, under appropriate motivational states, increases the tendency to alternate. It may very well be the case that these animals do not possess a species-typical pattern of spatial choice in foraging for food, but that experience with certain distributions of food may shape a particular strategy. This suggestion is supported by the fact that the young remain with the parents from birth (in spring or summer) through the first winter (Bannikov, 1954); in late summer, these animals spend a considerable amount of time collecting and hoarding food. Given this extensive early experience with the parents in food-getting tasks, it is likely that spatial choice in foraging is dependent on experience with the distribution of available food. It is now critical to analyze the role of social experience with adults in the development of feeding behavior, as Galef (this volume) has so elegantly done with rats. Futhermore, the fact that spontaneous spatial choice is related to sociality suggests that a response bias in a laboratory maze may be the display of a complex, multifuntional behavior. It is unlikely that such a behavior is a direct result of foraging patterns, at least in the gerbil. Further comparative research with other cricetid rodents is necessary to determine general principles of the role of this behavior in foraging.

SPECIES-TYPICAL PREDISPOSITIONS IN LEARNING
THE CONSEQUENCES OF FEEDING

Of the problems facing a forager, it is not sufficient only to find the location of a profitable food source. It is also necessary to discriminate between suitable and noxious foods. That animals can readily learn to avoid foods that are followed by illness is a well-documented phenomemon. Kalat (this volume) has summarized some of the major issues surrounding this type of learning, so we will not review them here. However, since Garcia's early work on aversion learning (see review by Garcia & Ervin, 1968), more comparative research has suggested that the type of stimulus associated with gastrointestinal illness varies from species to species, and the association is a direct function of how an animal finds food in its natural environment. Shettleworth (1972a,b) has shown that chickens learn a selective association between visual stimuli and distasteful water, and that the more novel the visual cue the faster the association is learned. Research by Wilcoxon, Dragoin, and Kral (1971) on bobwhite quail demonstrated a selective association between visual characteristics of water and illness, with little learning about taste. These results are intuitively appealing in view of avian foraging behavior in the field. Many avian species are visually guided predators or foragers and respond to the visual aspects of food or prey (Croze, 1970; Dawkins, 1971a,b; Krebs, 1973; Mason and Reidinger, 1982; Murton, 1971; Pietrewicz and Kamil, 1979).

The relationship between the relative salience of visual and gustatory cues in aversion learning and the naturalistic behavior patterns of birds has been questioned recently by Lett (1980). Lett studied illness-induced aversions in quail and pigeons and found that her birds demonstrated weak aversions to visual (color) cues alone. In fact, the birds formed strong aversions to visual cues only when the color cue had been paired with a taste cue during conditioning. Lett suggested that the basis for illness-induced aversions in birds is actually taste, and that the taste cue serves to mediate visual learning by increasing the bird's attention to the color cue. This suggestion is inconsistent with ecological data on foraging in birds because it requires birds to learn about taste in order to learn about the visual characteristics of food; but it should be noted that Lett utilized rather strong solutions of salt or vinegar. However, Lett's results are supported by similar findings by Westbrook, Clarke, and Provost (1980).

One important problem in drawing conclusions about the relationship between the ecological foraging data and the illness-induced aversion data collected in the laboratory is that much of the comparative research on aversions has been conducted with conditioned aversions to water, rather than to food. It seems unlikely that the patterns of food-getting behavior would exactly parallel the patterns involved in the selection of water sources. In fact, some recent research has found that chickens form aversions to food on the basis of visual cues, but not on the basis of taste cues; also, chickens form aversions to water on the basis of taste, but not visual cues (Gillette, Irwin, Thomas, & Bellingham, 1980; Gillette, Martin, & Bellingham, 1980).

It is logical to assume that visual cues associated with food are critical aspects of avian learning in the field. Predatory birds avoid prey with warning (aposematic) coloration (Drickamer & Vessey, 1982), and it has been suggested that in some species the visual cue alone is sufficient for avoidance (Smith, 1975). Seed-eating birds also must utilize visual cues of food without the mediation of a taste cue. Many plants have evolved poisonous seeds as a defense against predation (Skutch, 1975), and there are granivorous birds who avoid certain seeds in feeding, even though those types of seeds are abundant (Handley, 1931; Landers & Johnson, 1976). Because many seeds are encased by a hard shell and are rapidly swallowed by the bird, it is not likely that taste is the most salient cue available to seed-eating birds.

On the basis of this reasoning, we conducted an investigation of the use of visual cues in illness-induced food aversions in Japanese quail (*Coturnix coturnix*). We have used some nonstandard procedures that first should be noted. Typically, research on illness-induced aversions has employed rather gross measures of aversion (for example, the aversiveness of water may be measured by the total intake in a 10–15 minute interval; the lower the intake, the stronger the aversion). In our research, we not only measured total intake of food in testing sessions but also included a measure of the birds' behavioral responsivity to the visual cues associated with food. This responsivity was measured by an autoshaped key-peck response. This procedure, first described by Brown and Jenkins (1968), involves a theoretically interesting response system. A hungry bird placed in a key-pecking chamber is presented with a lighted key and food; the lighted key is always paired with food presentation, but the pairings occur on a variable and unpredictable time schedule. Within about 50 trials or so, the bird begins to peck the key whenever it is illuminated, although pecking is not required for food delivery. It has been hypothesized that because the lighted key reliably predicts food, the key comes to possess incentive properties and elicits feeding-related behaviors. The feeding behaviors directed at the key are topographically similar to species-typical feeding behavior for pigeons (Jenkins & Moore, 1973), and for bluejays, robins, and starlings (Mauldin, 1981).

The basic design of this research was to produce the autoshaped key-peck in quail by pairing food with a certain key-light color (say, blue) until key-peck rate was stabilized. Then, on a conditioning day, the key-light color was changed to a novel color (such as red) for an entire autoshaping session. Following this session, the bird was removed from the test chamber, injected with lithium chloride, and placed back in the home cage. On the next day (following illness), the autoshaping session was conducted with the familiar key-light color, and for daily sessions until key-peck rate was stabilized. Another conditioning session was conducted with the novel key color, followed by poisoning, then stabilization with the familiar key color, and then a third conditioning session. In all sessions, both key-peck rate and food intake were measured. It should be noted that in this procedure, only the visual cue, key color, reliably predicted poisoning. The food in the test chamber was the same food fed to the birds in the home cage. Thus, no taste cue was available to predict poisoning. Because this procedure allows a separation of behavioral responses to the visual cue (pecking) and to the food itself (eating), we were able to assess the relative aversions to both stimuli. A number of different results were possible: The birds could peck the key (associated with illness) and not eat the food that followed this key light, they could eat but not peck the key, they could refrain from both eating and pecking, or they could continue to peck and eat. We predicted, based on the assumption that birds quickly and readily associate visual cues with illness without the mediating variable of taste, that they would develop an aversion to the familiar food paired with the novel key color and would refrain from eating food in the test chamber on novel color days. Also, we predicted that the birds would show an aversion to the visual cue itself, as reflected in decreased pecking at the novel color key. This result would indicate an aversion based solely on visual cues, with no alteration in the taste of food, and the development of an aversion to the visual cue would indicate it to be a salient predictor of illness.

Method

Subjects. The subjects were 10 Japanese quail (*Coturnix coturnix japonica*). Both male and female subjects were used, and they were housed in individual cages. The birds were maintained between 70 and 85% of their free feeding weights by controlled daily feedings of Purina poultry feed.

Apparatus. Testing was conducted in a Lehigh Valley Electronics operant pigeon chamber, the interior of which was adapted for the quail. A hopper-type feeder was located in the center of the front wall. A Gerbrands pecking key, 2 cm in diameter, was placed 10 cm above the wire mesh floor and 8.5 cm to the left of the food hopper. The translucent pecking key could be illuminated from behind by 28v pilot lamps. Colored lenses covering the pilot lamps allowed control of the key-light color. A 7.5 watt houselight provided general illumination inside the chamber, and the sound of a ventilating fan and white noise served to mask extraneous noise. All stimulus presentations, food delivery, and recording of key-peck rate were controlled by electromechanical equipment located adjacent to the test chamber.

Procedure. The birds were first trained to eat from the hopper in the test chamber. Each bird was placed in the chamber for 30 minutes a day, during which time the food hopper was operated 30 times. With each operation of the hopper the bird had a 2-second access to food (Purina poultry feed). After the birds had eaten from the hopper for three consecutive daily sessions, they were exposed to the standard autoshaping procedure (Brown & Jenkins, 1968). This procedure consisted of illuminating the pecking disk with a red or blue light for a duration of 10 seconds; immediately upon the offset of the key light, the hopper was operated, allowing a 2-second access to food. Key light–food pairings were presented on a random time schedule, with an average interval of 1 minute between presentations. Key-pecking had no programmed effect upon the stimulus or food presentations. For five of the birds, the key light in this phase of training was red, for the other five birds the key light was blue. The number of pecks at the illuminated key and the change in body weight of the birds were recorded at the end of each daily session. The amount of food consumed by each bird during a testing session was determined by the change in body weight between the beginning and the end of the session. Any error due to weight loss through defecation was assumed to be random and evenly distributed across the birds. The autoshaping procedure was continued in daily sessions of 30 key light–food pairings until key-peck rate and food intake stabilized.

In the next daily session following stabilization, the key color was changed (to blue or red) so that each bird experienced a novel key color for that session. At the end of the novel key-color session, seven of the birds were injected intraperitoneally with lithium chloride (LiCl) and three of the birds were injected with physiological saline (NaCl), within 10 minutes of the end of the session. Of the birds receiving LiCl, 5 were injected with 0.3 M LiCl at a dose of 2ml/100 g body weight (following Lett, 1980). However, when this dose was found to be lethal for some birds not included in this report, the injections were changed to 0.15 M LiCl at a dose of 2ml/100 g body weight. Of the seven birds receiving LiCl in this study, three birds received the weaker solution. All birds exhibited visible signs of illness (lethargy, watery feces) following LiCl injections.

Following the conditioning session just described, the birds were then continued on daily autoshaping sessions until behavior again stabilized (2 to 6 days). The birds then received another conditioning session with novel key color, then injections. The procedure was repeated until all birds received a total of three conditioning sessions (novel key color–injections).

Results

All birds successfully acquired the autoshaped key-peck response, although there was individual variability in the overall rate of pecking. Figure 4.1 presents a summary of the changes in body weight (food intake) as a function of conditioning trials. The uppermost graph presents the data for the birds receiving LiCl injections. Analysis of change over conditioning trials was evaluated using analysis of variance (ANOVA) procedures. There was no significant or systematic change in body weights across sessions, just prior to conditioning sessions, in which the training (familiar) key color was present. The birds continued to eat food in the sessions with the key color that was not paired with illness. However, there

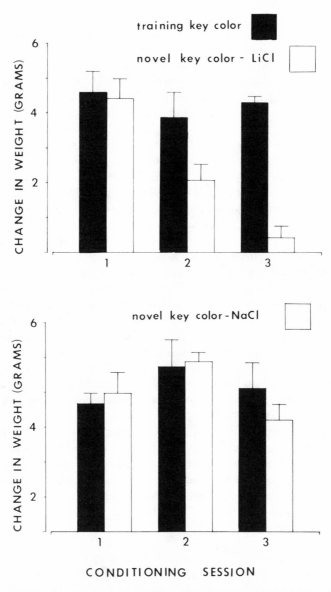

FIG.4.1 Mean change in body weight of birds receiving LiCl and of birds receiving NaCl injections, within experimental sessions. These data are used to assess amount of food intake during these sessions. The dark bars represent change in body weight on the day before conditioning, during the session of exposure to the training (familiar) key color. The white bars represent change in body weight during exposure to the novel key color. It should be noted that for all conditioning sessions injection of LiCl or NaCl did not occur until after the session was over. Thus, during conditioning session 1, the birds had no prior experience with lithium-induced illness, or with saline injections.

was a decrement in food intake in sessions with the novel key color after the first conditioning session. After one session of pairing the novel key color with illness, there was a dramatic decrease in food intake during the next presentation of the novel key color. Another decrement in food intake was displayed for the third conditioning session with the novel color also. This decrease in body weight across conditioning sessions with the novel color was significant ($p < .05$). In fact, some birds exhibited weight losses during these sessions, indicating that no food was eaten, or at least very little, during the entire session. These data for the LiCl birds indicate that with each conditioning session the aversion to the food became stronger. As shown in the bottom portion of this figure, there was no similar effect in the control birds who received NaCl injections. On conditioning sessions 1 and 2, food intake was actually higher (although not significantly) in novel color sessions than in sessions with the familiar (training) color. This result indicates that key-color change and NaCl injections do not systematically alter food intake in test sessions. Thus, the effect exhibited by the LiCl birds is specific to the experience of illness.

Fig. 4.2 presents the effects of these procedures on the key-peck rate, as a function of conditioning sessions. As shown in the upper portion of this figure, the pairing of novel key color with illness resulted in a decrement in key-peck rate in the presence of the novel color. The change in key-peck rate (in the presence of the novel color) across conditioning sessions was significant ($p < .05$). It should be noted, however, that presentation of novel color resulted in a decreased peck rate before poisoning occurred. However, this result suggests that the birds were attending to the change in the visual stimulus and were possibly somewhat neophobic. This effect on peck rate of key-color change was temporary, as reflected in the behavior of the control (NaCl) birds, who recovered high rates of pecking following the first novel color session. There were no other systematic changes in peck rate of LiCl birds, or of control NaCl birds, in the presence of the familiar (training) color. These results indicate that the novel key color–illness pairings produced an aversion to the visual stimulus itself, as evidenced by decreased responsivity to that stimulus.

Discussion

These results support our prediction that birds readily associate visual characteristics, related to food, with illness. The birds here formed strong aversions not only to the food signaled by a visual cue, but also to the visual cue itself. This aversion developed with one instance of illness and no mediating taste cue, and with no change in the type or quality of food. Also, the aversion strengthened with additional conditioning sessions. It might be argued, based on the work by Lett (1980) and by Westbrook, Clarke, and Provost (1980), that had a taste cue been added in this procedure, taste would have potentiated the effect of the visual cue. We do not deny that this result might have occurred, for as Lett (1980)

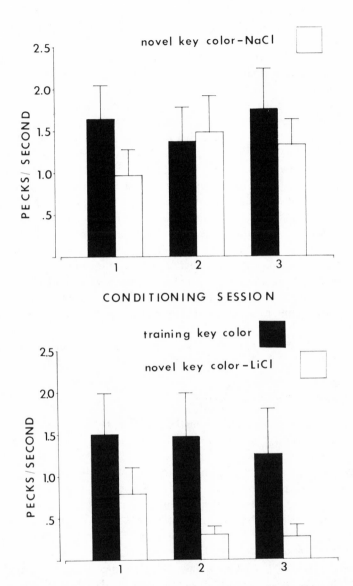

FIG.4.2 Mean key-pecking rates of birds receiving LiCl or NaCl within experimental sessions. The dark bars represent pecking rate on the day before conditioning, and the white bars represent key-pecking rate during exposure to the novel
key color on conditioning days.

suggested, taste may increase attention to the visual cue. We do, however, maintain that for granivorous birds, taste is not a necessary mediating cue for the formation of illness-induced aversions. Ecological data predict that the ability to learn about food on the basis of visual cues has adaptive significance, especially for granivorous birds, and our results support this prediction.

Another interesting aspect of these results concerns the role of novelty in the formation of illness-induced aversions. The use of a novel key color paired with illness produced a strong aversion to both the food signaled by that color and the novel color. In these procedures, the visual stimulus was novel, rather than the food. It has been demonstrated that rats form strong aversions to a novel taste that has been paired with illness, and that such an aversion may be stronger than those formed to a familiar taste (see Kalat chapter, this volume). Our findings do not preclude the possibility that the aversion that developed to both the visual cue and the food it signaled was the result of the development of neophobia, rather than the result of associative learning; that is, the experience of illness may have sensitized the birds to novel, or infrequently presented, visual cues that predict food. At the conclusion of this study, we exposed some birds from the LiCl group to another novel key light (white) and found that pecking, more so than eating, was suppressed compared to the response rate in the presence of the familiar (training) color. Future research should be directed at examining the relative contributions of associative learning and of general neophobic effects, which may result from illness, in the development of illness-induced aversions based on visual cues. Perhaps both the development of neophobia and associative learning are involved in the formation of illness-induced aversion.

General Summary and Conclusions

This chapter presents an ecological analysis of some behaviors involved in foraging, using traditional laboratory tasks in a rather artificial environment. In spite of the testing procedures used, however, we have presented suggestions concerning the way in which learning abilities, displayed in the laboratory, may function in solving problems facing the forager in the field. In the first section, on spatial choice in gerbils, we conducted an admittedly post hoc analysis of the role of this behavior in the animals' natural environment. This analysis allowed us to make some sense of the laboratory results, provided us with a direction for future research, and allowed comparison of this work with the large body of data that has been collected on other rodent species. As Johnston (1981) has suggested, the development of local principles of adaptation will come about following the experimental analysis and ecological description of behavior at the level of individual species. We have begun an attempt to investigate local principles of adaptation by focusing on the determinants and correlates of choice behavior in a rodent species that has not yet been extensively studied from this perspective. This research has led us to the conclusion that a more thorough understanding of the role of spatial choice in foraging can only come about by additional comparative research. Additional species comparisons should focus on the role of individual learning and experience in the development of spatial choice behavior in foraging. We tentatively conclude that alternation bias in spatial choice is not a general characteristic of cricetid rodents but may develop under certain environmental conditions, some of which may be related to social environment or to distribution of food sources.

The second section of this chapter presented a priori predictions, based on ecological data, about the kind of association granivorous birds should be able to learn in the laboratory. Our predictions were supported, and the results strengthen our assumption that learning about visual cues that predict consequences of food choice is an important problem facing these avian foragers in the field. These results also allow us to predict that predatory or nectar-feeding birds, who may be more likely to taste their food than granivorous birds, may utilize taste cues as readily as visual cues in this type of learning. We have additionally concluded that aversions are formed both to food and to the external cues that predict food associated with illness. In this analysis we have been able to generate some hypothetical local principles of adaptation, and these principles will provide the direction of future research.

This chapter additionally serves to exemplify the point that, although a priori prediction of learning abilities based on ecological foraging data is preferable, a post hoc analysis of learning in the laboratory as a function of ecological variables can be valuable in the development of hypotheses about local principles of adaptation. As suggested by Johnston (1981), global principles of adaptation would allow explanation and prediction of the variability in local principles, at the species level. The development of such global principles of adaptation in foraging behavior will be generated through this type of ecological analysis across diverse species.

An ecological analysis of the role of learning in foraging behavior is a powerful approach to the study of learning as adaptation. As mentioned earlier, one of the major problems in this approach is the identification of relevant ecological variables. Our work on spatial choice in rodents, in particular, demonstrates the difficulty in identifying these variables, especially when preliminary field work on the species in question is incomplete. Perhaps one way in which the power of this ecological approach could be increased is to study the development of these behaviors in individual animals. If the relative contributions of selected environmental conditions (such as distribution of food supply) and specific types of experience with those conditions (such as associative learning) were assessed, more valid relationships between ecology and learning could be established. Unfortunately, developmental research is often neglected in the study of the role of learning in foraging. Such an approach would also facilitate the identification of the specific learning processes involved in food-getting behaviors, an area of study that certainly deserves more attention.

ACKNOWLEDGMENTS

This research was supported by grants (4057 and 8164) from the Emory University Research Committee, to the first author, who is now at the Developmental Learning Center, Fort Pierce, Florida 33450.

REFERENCES

Bannikov, A. G. (1954). The places inhabited and natural history of *Meriones unguiculatus*. In *Mammals of the Mongolian Peoples Republic* (pp. 410–415). Moscow: USSR Academy of Sciences.

Brown, P. L., & Jenkins, H. M. (1968). Auto-shaping of the pigeon's key peck. *Journal of the Experimental Analysis of Behavior, 11*, 1–8.

Cole, S., Hainsworth, F. R., Kamil, A. C., Mercier, T., & Wolf, L. L. (1982). Spatial learning as an adaptation in hummingbirds. *Science, 217*, 655–657.

Croze, H. (1970). Searching image in Carrion crows. *Zeitschrift für Tierpsychologie Beiheift, 5*, 1–85.

Dawkins, M. (1971a). Shifts of "attention" in chicks during feeding. *Animal Behavior, 19*, 575–582.

Dawkins, M. (1971b). Perceptual changes in chicks: Another look at the "search image" concept. *Animal Behavior, 19*, 566–574.

Dember, W. N., & Kleiman, R. (1973). Cues for spontaneous alternation by gerbils. *Animal Learning and Behavior, 1*(4), 287–290.

Douglas, R. J. (1966).. Cues for spontaneous alteration. *Journal of Comparative and Physiological Psychology, 62*, 171–183.

Drickamer, L. C., & Vessey, S. H. (1982). *Animal behavior: concepts, processes and methods.* Boston: Willard Grant Press.

Egger, G. J. (1973). The relevance of memory, arousal, and cue factors to developmental changes in spontaneous alternation by rats. *Developmental Psychobiology, 6*(5), 459–468.

Eibl–Eibesfeldt, I. (1970). *Ethology: The biology of behavior.* New York: Holt, Rinehart, & Winston.

Garcia, J., & Ervin, F. R. (1968). Gustatory-visceral and telereceptorcutaneous conditioning: Adaptation in internal and external milieus. *Communications in Behavioral Biology* (Part A), *1*, 389–415.

Gillette, K., Irwin, D., Thomas, D., & Bellingham, W. (1980). Transfer of coloured food and water aversions in domestic chicks. *Bird Behavior, 2*, 37–47.

Gillette, K., Martin, M., & Bellingham, W. (1980). Differential use of food and water cues in the formation of conditioned aversions by domestic chicks (*Gallus gallus*). *Journal of Experimental Psychology: Animal Behavior Processes, 6*(2), 99–111.

Greenberg, G. (1973). Replication report: No spontaneous alternation in gerbils. *Bulletin of the Psychonomic Society, 1*(2), 141–143.

Handley, C. O. (1931). The food and feeding habits of bobwhites. In H. L. Stoddard (Ed.), *The Bobwhite quail: Its habits, preservation and increase.* New York: Scribner.

Jenkins, H. M., & Moore, B. R. (1973). The form of the autoshaped response with food or water reinforcers. *Journal of the Experimental Analysis of Behavior, 20*, 163–181.

Johnston, T. D. (1981). Contrasting approaches to a theory of learning. *Behavioral and Brain Sciences, 4*(1), 125–173.

Kamil, A. C. (1978). Systematic foraging by a nectar-feeding bird, the Amakihi (*Loxops virens*). *Journal of Comparative and Physiological Psychology, 92*, 388–396.

Kamil, A. C., & Sargent, T. D. (Eds.). (1981). *Foraging behavior: Ecological, ethological and psychological approaches.* New York: Garland STPM Press.

Krebs, J. R. (1973). Behavioral aspects of predation. In P. P. G. Bateson & P. H. Klopfer (Eds.), *Perspectives in ethology.* New York: Plenum Press.

Landers, J. L., & Johnson, A. S. (1976). *Bobwhite quail food habits in the southeastern United States.* Tall Timbers Research Station, Tallahassee, Florida (Miscellaneous Publication Number 4).

Lett, B. T. (1980). Taste potentiates color-sickness associations in pigeons and quail. *Animal Learning and Behavior, 8*(2), 193–198.

Mason, J. R., & Reidinger, R. F. (1982). Observational learning of food aversions in Red-winged blackbirds (*Angelaius phoeniceus*), *Auk, 99,* 548–554.

Mauldin, J. E. (1981). *Autoshaping and negative automaintenance in the blue jay (Cyanocitta cristata), robin (Turdus migratorius) and the starling (Sturnus vulgaris).* Unpublished doctoral dissertation, University of Massachusetts, Amherst.

Murton, R. K. (1971). The significance of a specific search image in the feeding behavior of the wood-pigeon. *Behaviour, 40,* 10–42.

Olton, D. S., Handelmann, G. E., & Walker, J. A. (1981). Spatial memory and food searching strategies. In A. C. Kamil & T. D. Sargent (Eds.), *Foraging behavior: Ecological, ethological and psychological approaches.* New York: Garland STPM Press.

Olton, D. S., & Samuelson, R. J. (1976). Remembrance of places passed: Spatial memory in rats. *Journal of Experimental Psychology: Animal Behavior Processes, 2*(2), 97–116.

Petrinovich, L., & Bolles, R. C. (1954). Deprivation states and behavioral attributes. *Journal of Comparative and Physiological Psychology, 47,* 450–453.

Pietrewicz, A. T., & Kamil, A. C. (1979). Search image formation in the blue jay (*Cyanocitta cristata*). *Science, 204,* 1332–1333.

Richards, J. B. (1981). *Effects of reinforcement on choice behavior of rats in a 4-arm radial maze.* Unpublished manuscript.

Shettleworth, S. J. (1972a). The role of novelty in learned avoidance of unpalatable "prey" by domestic chicks, *Gallus gallus. Animal Behavior, 80,* 29–35.

Shettleworth, S. J. (1972b). Stimulus relevance in the control of drinking and conditoned fear responses in domestic chicks, *Gallus gallus. Journal of Comparative and Physiological Psychology, 80,* 175–198.

Shettleworth, S. J., & Krebs, J. R. (1982). How marsh tits find their hoards: The roles of site preference and spatial memory. *Journal of Experimental Psychology: Animal Behavior Processes, 8*(4), 354–375.

Skutch, A. F. (1975). *Parent birds and their young: A study of their behavior.* Austin: University of Texas Press.

Smith, S. M. (1975). Innate recognition of Coral snake pattern by a possible avian predator. *Science, 187,* 759–760.

Thiessen, D., & Yahr, P. (1977). *The gerbil in behavioral investigations.* Austin: University of Texas Press.

Westbrook, R. F., Clarke, J. C., & Provost, S. (1980). Long-delay learning in the pigeon: Flavor, color, and flavor-mediated color aversions. *Behavioral and Neural Biology, 28,* 398–407.

Wilcoxon, H. C., Dragoin, W. B., and Kral, P. A. (1971). Illness-induced aversions in rat and quail: Relative salience of visual and gustatory cues. *Science, 171,* 826–828.

5 Taste-Aversion Learning in Ecological Perspective

James W. Kalat
North Carolina State University

"Above all, do no harm."

—Hippocrates

Hippocrates' advice to physicians is also a key principle of animals' feeding behavior: It is not always possible, or even necessary, to select *the* best available foods, but it is always important to avoid potentially harmful foods. It is to be expected, and it appears to be the case, that evolution should have prepared animals in many and varied ways to solve the problems of food choice. Among these ways is taste-aversion learning (TAL).

When a rat consumes some food or drink and later feels ill, it associates the illness much more strongly with the food or drink than with any other, more recent stimuli (Garcia & Koelling, 1966). Also, it can associate taste with illness over delays much longer than the maximum delays for many other examples of learning (Garcia, Ervin, & Koelling, 1966). The same general tendencies are present in a wide variety of species and have quite evident adaptive value. If an animal feels sick, it is likely to gain an advantage by avoiding the recent foods it has eaten, particularly the novel foods. And if it is going to "blame" an illness on a food, it needs to be able to do so over substantial delays, as a toxic or deficient food may not make its effects felt until minutes or hours after the meal. For these reasons Rozin & Kalat (1971) inferred that the apparently special features of taste aversion were direct outcomes of natural selection pressures favoring modifications of the processes involved in learning.

There is, however, another point of view which holds that the learning mechanisms themselves are the same for all situations; the results for TAL differ only because the stimulus parameters are necessarily different. Taste cues have a slower onset and offset than lights and sounds and occur much less frequently during a day; illness has a slower onset and offset than electrical shock. Perhaps, the argument goes, taste-aversion learning appears to differ from other kinds of learning only because the stimuli are different, not because the learning mechanisms are different. Needless to say, I am simplifying this argument; for a fuller treatment see Revusky (1977), Krane (1980), or Krane & Wagner (1975), as well as Revusky's chapter in this volume.

This issue is not an easy one to resolve conclusively. To understand the difficulty of the issue, consider this analogous situation: Suppose someone has built a vehicle that can fly through the air, travel along the ground, and move like a submarine beneath the water. From the outside, these three kinds of travel differ in many ways including speed, maneuverability, fuel efficiency, and so forth. The question arises, are there different engine mechanisms or other mechanical specializations built into the vehicle for the three kinds of locomotion, or are the differences due strictly to the surrounding medium? We could imagine either answer as being correct. As long as we try to answer the question with strictly "behavioral" data, by collecting detailed lists of similarities and differences in movement through the three media, we cannot answer decisively the questions about underlying mechanisms. Similarly in the case of learning, it is difficult to compare the underlying mechanisms in two or more situations, because we do not really understand the mechanisms of learning in any situation.

With regard to the difficult issue of comparing mechanisms, I have little to add to an earlier review (Kalat, 1977). For the most part I sidestep the question of mechanism and focus on those characteristics of TAL that seem most relevant to problems that arise in nature. Indirectly, of course, this discussion does have some bearing on the question of mechanisms: If we found, for example, that the nature of some animal's learning is extraordinarily well adapted to the problems it faces in nature, and that different species show learning differences that correlate with differences in their natural environments, the implication would strongly favor the concept of evolutionary adaptations of the learning mechanism.

GENERAL STATEMENT ON THE APPLICATION OF ECOLOGICAL PRINCIPLES TO LEARNING

It is the position of this chapter that an ecological approach can be useful in studying TAL, at least as a heuristic for suggesting worthwhile experiments. I do not contend that this approach has in fact been consistently or very usefully applied in the past, nor that TAL affords a clear example of either the potential or the limitations of the ecological approach.

There are several reasons why much of the literature on TAL does not fit neatly into an ecological framework. First, there have been a great many experiments that deal with laboratory phenomena such as sensory preconditioning or higher order conditioning, which occur only after a sequence of events that must be very rare in nature. These experiments were not designed with ecological concerns in mind, nor are they easily interpretable in ecological terms.

Second, there has been very little interplay between TAL studies in the laboratory and field observations of feeding in the same species. For instance, one might like to know how frequently rats encounter poisons in nature, what are the most common poisons, what is the availability of vitamins and minerals, how frequently do rats sample new foods, and how do they react to seasonal variations in available food? There are many studies of rat feeding in captivity (e.g., Barnett, 1963; Rozin, 1969), but these do not answer all the critical questions. On the other hand, the whole concept of "the rat in nature" is so problematical that it is practically a fiction. For thousands of rat generations, many if not most rats have lived in proximity to humans. What we can say about the feral rat's habitat depends on whether we are examining rats on farms, in residential neighborhoods, near food processing plants, or in garbage dumps. Related problems apply to many other popular laboratory animals.

A third problem (which is almost a restatement of the second) is that many of the species that are most interesting from an ecological standpoint are difficult to study experimentally. For instance, it would be extremely interesting but very difficult to study the large predators. As Paul Rozin (1976) has noted, the only way a lion can become vitamin deficient is to eat vitamin-deficient herbivores. In one sense, the predators have the simplest problems; they can let the herbivores solve the food-selection and diet-balancing problems for them. In another sense, predators have the greatest problems; being at the top of the food chain, they concentrate many toxins whose presence in the diet they are almost helpless to control. If the ecological perspective is to be useful, it must predict that TAL will vary in at least a few parameters among predators, herbivores, omnivores, scavengers, insectivores, and extreme specialists such as the koala (which eats only eucalyptus leaves). However, lions, hyenas, and koalas are unpopular laboratory animals. With the outstanding exception of a few studies by Zahorik (Zahorik & Houpt, 1977) on grazing animals, we still have very little truly useful comparative data.

Because most studies of TAL deal with animals whose natural habitat and ecological niche are either spectacularly variable (rat, pigeon, mouse) or little known (hamster, guinea pig), the contributions of ecological and evolutionary thinking, up to the present time, have been largely speculative or post-hoc. This limitation is not damning in all cases; one does not need to observe rats in nature to know that there is some delay between ingestion and digestion, or that foods lead to illness more often than flashing lights do, or that avoidance of arsenic is evolutionarily adaptive. Still, we do run into problems when the research issues become more detailed.

Let me cite just one example of the kind of problem I mean, before getting into the literature review. Suppose a rat drinks one milliliter of unfamiliar solution

A and gets very ill. A week later, it drinks 10 milliliters of unfamiliar solution B and gets exactly as ill as it did after A. Another week later, the same rat is desperately thirsty and has available to it only the two solutions, A and B. Which should it prefer? A priori ecological, adaptive considerations suggest it should prefer B: If 1 milliliter of A is as bad as 10 milliliters of B, then B is the lesser of the evils. But in fact the results of Bond and DiGiusto (1975), Bond and Harland (1975), and Barker (1976) indicate the opposite: The rats apparently prefer A. In this and analogous situations we have three possible responses: We can look for a different way to conduct the experiments, possibly coming to a different conclusion (e.g., Kalat, 1976); we can concede that the ecological approach was not helpful in this case and that the behavior is evolutionarily maladaptive; or we can reexamine the ecology, to see whether our initial analysis overlooked something important. In other words, what we need is a give-and-take between field studies and laboratory studies. Without it, ecological considerations can still be useful in suggesting experiments, but we are at a loss to resolve any discrepancies that arise.

THE CHARACTERISTICS OF TAL

The remainder of this chapter covers a number of aspects of TAL, briefly in most cases, except where I have new information to present. I have not attempted a complete review of the literature; I have focused on those aspects of TAL that seem most relevant to problems likely to arise in nature.

Individual, Species, and Age Differences

The phenomenon of taste-aversion learning has proven to be a robust one not only for a variety of rodents but also for a wide variety of other species, including but not limited to quail (Wilcoxon, Dragoin, & Kral, 1971), bat (Terk & Green, 1980), catfish (Little, 1977), cow (Zahorik & Houpt, 1977), coyote (Gustavson, 1977), and slug (Gelperin, 1975). There have been only a few reports related to possible species differences. Visually oriented species such as birds and monkeys are more likely than rats to learn aversions to the appearance as well as to the taste of a food (Johnson, Beaton, & Hall, 1975). There is some evidence that taste-aversion learning is less reliable in grazing animals such as cattle than in rodents (Zahorik & Houpt, 1977).

There are measurable individual differences within a species in the intensity of learned aversions (Elkins, 1973a), and these differences appear to have a genetic basis. Furthermore, the genetic control of taste-aversion learning is not the same as the genetic control of shock-avoidance learning. Martin and Baettig (1980) compared TAL in two strains of rat, which had been selectively bred for high or low performance on shuttlebox shock avoidance. The strain that was worse on shock avoidance learned stronger taste aversions to a saccharin–glucose mixture, and extinguished more slowly, than the other strain. It is impossible to say, however, whether these differences reflected variations in learning per se or in sensory and motivational processes.

Age differences in taste-aversion learning have been extensively studied. Taste-aversion learning can occur even at one day of age in both rats (Gemberling & Domjan, 1982) and guinea pigs (Kalat, 1975). Learned food preferences, and learned discrimination between food and nonfood, are evident in newborn guinea pigs (Reisbick, 1973) and 2–3-day-old chickens (Hogan, 1973a,b). The precocity of this learning suggests that it does not depend on a long "learning-to-learn" process. There are some reports that taste-aversion learning may be somewhat weaker in young rats, even at age 23 days, than in fully mature rats (Baker, Baker, & Kesner, 1977; Klein, Domato, Hallstead, Stephens, & Mikulka, 1975; Martin & Alberts, 1979; Martin & Timmins, 1980). However, these results are consistent with an interpretation that the young rats learn just as well as the older rats but extinguish faster, perhaps because they are less able to tolerate fluid deprivation.

It is perhaps surprising that the ability to learn taste aversions matures so long before weaning, the time when an animal makes its first dietary selections. The role this ability plays early in life may be very different from its role later in life; it may, for instance, be involved in the infant's becoming familiar with certain ingredients in the mother's diet, which come through her milk (see Galef's chapter in this volume).

"Belongingness"

"Belongingness" is the concept that a given stimulus or behavior may be more associable with one outcome than with some other. The concept was introduced by E. L. Thorndike (1911) to describe the fact that cats could easily learn to make a variety of manipulations to escape a box but had great difficulty learning to scratch or lick themselves to escape the box. The latter associations were acquired very slowly and remained unstable even after many repetitions. Somehow, pulling a string "belongs" with opening a door, in a sense in which scratching one's self does not. Shettleworth (1972) reports some analogous results. Belongingness presumably relates to the actual relationship of two events to each other throughout a species' evolutionary history; that is, clawing and pushing frequently move barriers out of a cat's way; scratching and licking never do, except in laboratory experiments. Belongingness is not, however, a precise theory that allows one to predict new results with any confidence.

Belongingness plays a major part in TAL. Foods may give rise to gastrointestinal consequences; lights and sounds do not. Rats' learning seems to reflect this fact. Garcia and Koelling (1966) exposed rats to both a saccharin-flavored solution and a combination of loud noises and flashing lights prior to either x-rays or electric shock to the feet. They found that the rats given x-rays formed a strong aversion to the taste, but not the lights or sounds; the rats given shock formed an avoidance of lights and sounds, but not the taste. This general tendency has been replicated under slightly different conditions (Domjan & Wilson, 1972b; Miller & Domjan, 1981). Because the associability of the simultaneously presented taste, lights, and sounds varies depending on events that follow them, we cannot explain the selective association on the basis of variations in attention. Because similar results occur in rats as young as 5 days (Gemberling, Domjan, & Amsel, 1980) or 1 day (Gemberling & Domjan, 1982), they apparently reflect a built-in predisposition to learn some connections rather than others, rather than previous "learning to learn."

Initially it was believed that poisons were selectively associated only with tastes, because of convergence of taste and internal sensations in the medulla (Garcia & Ervin, 1968). However, under some circumstances animals can also learn poison-based aversions to olfactory stimuli (Hankins, Garcia, & Rusiniak, 1973) or visual stimuli (Best, Best, & Mickley, 1973; Braveman, 1975; Martin, Bellingham, & Storlien, 1977; Revusky & Parker, 1977; Rudy, Iwens, & Best, 1977).

The strength of a poison-based learned aversion to a nontaste stimulus depends on the experimental procedure. As discussed later, even aversions to taste cues depend on whether the substance was swallowed, and the same seems to be applicable for other kinds of stimulus also. If a visual or olfactory cue is merely presented, then followed by poison, the learned association is weak or absent. If, however, the nontaste cue is experienced in conjunction with ingestion, it may be strongly associated with poison.

If a rat experiences an odor alone, followed by poison, it develops little or no aversion. But if it gets the odor simultaneously with a taste that it ingests, followed by poison, it later shows a strong avoidance of both the taste and the odor (Domjan, 1973; Palmerino, Rusiniak, & Garcia, 1980). Similarly, rats poisoned after seeing a light avoid the light later only if they had a taste simultaneously with the light (Morrison & Collyer, 1974). Also, rats readily learn an avoidance of the appearance of a food capsule that was paired with poison, though they less readily learn an avoidance of the appearance of the food bin (Galef & Dalrymple, 1981).

Birds can associate the color of a substance with later poison, but the associability depends on several circumstances. Chickens readily associate the color of solid food with poison, much more strongly than they associate its taste with poison (Martin & Bellingham, 1979). However, they do not as a rule associate the color of a *liquid* with poison. One can get chickens to associate a colored liquid with poison either by putting it in an awkward container that requires much visual attention for drinking (Gillette, Martin, & Bellingham, 1980) or by giving the colored liquid a flavor as well (Lett, 1980; Westbrook, Clarke, & Provost, 1980). Additional comparative data, on a wide variety of species, would be welcome.

What all of this apparently means is that poison is primarily associated with ingested substances; the sensory modality for identifying the ingested substance can vary. An animal can associate the sight, odor, taste, or texture of an ingested substance with later consequences, provided that the animal attended to those stimuli at the time of ingestion. The same stimuli may be unassociable if the substance is not ingested. One might note that food aversions based on sight can differ in several ways from those based on taste. If an animal rejects a food on sight it need not spend time approaching it, chasing it, and so forth. On the other hand it risks missing an acceptable food that happens to resemble visually an unacceptable one, as in the case of Batesian mimicry.

Several experiments have explored possible modifiers of belongingness, particularly whether animals can associate illness with tastes that have special meanings to a species, giving rise to "instinctive" reactions. In general, the fact that a taste "belongs" with some other response does not seem to prevent its association with poison. Mother rats that were poisoned after eating their own placentas learned an aversion to placenta eating (Engwall & Kristal, 1977). Male hamsters poisoned after licking vaginal secretions learned a strong aversion to approaching and licking vaginal secretions (Johnston & Zahorik, 1975; Zahorik & Johnston, 1976). Later they showed some hesitance in mating with the female, but they did copulate (Emmerick & Snowdon, 1976; Johnston, Zahorik, Immler, & Zakon, 1978). Evidently the learned aversion is much stronger with regard to eating responses than to mating, even when both involve the same taste and odor.

A somewhat different rule applies to predatory attacks on prey, however. Coyotes learn not to attack sheep, based on subsequent poisoning (Gustavson, Garcia, Hankins, & Rusiniak, 1974), but for rats attacking mice (Berg & Baenninger, 1974; Krames, Milgram, & Christie, 1973) and grasshopper mice attacking insects (Langley, 1981), poisoning is more effective at inhibiting ingestion than at inhibiting the attack.

The Role of Swallowing

The reason that tastes are, and should be, associable with illness is that tastes signal the properties of the foods about to be ingested. If something is tasted but not swallowed, it cannot be harmful. Thus we should expect the act of swallowing to be related to TAL in some important way.

I wish I could say that these theoretical considerations stimulated my interest in the role of swallowing, but actually I first got involved in this issue by accident. A few years ago I was trying to test for taste-aversion learning in preweaning rats. I held each rat, force-fed it some sucrose, and 15 minutes later injected it with LiCl. I started with 10-day-old rats and moved up to successively older rats, hoping to find an age at which they shifted from nonlearners to learners. Although the rats were trained at various early ages, they were all tested for learned aversions after weaning. The first part of the experiment succeeded just as I had hoped: the 10-day-old rats failed to learn a strong aversion. Unfortunately, so did each older group, until I eventually discovered that not even adult rats learned much of an aversion under these circumstances. If they drank even one milliliter prior to poisoning, they learned an aversion, but they almost ignored the same or larger amount of the solution if it was force-fed. In fact, I noticed that they were closing off their esophagi, so that the force-fed solution dribbled out their mouths. Around this same time, Domjan and Wilson (1972a) also found that rats did not swallow a force-fed saccharin solution, nor did they learn aversions to it based on subsequent LiCl poisoning. However, Domjan and Wilson went on to demonstrate that if they force-fed the solution very slowly (10 ml in 10 minutes) to water-deprived rats, the rats would swallow it and would associate it with later poisoning. Thus, the critical determinant did not seem to be active approach to the solution versus force-feeding, but rather something having to do with swallowing. Later I found that guinea pigs would swallow a force-fed sucrose solution even if it was force-fed rapidly, and that they would form strong sucrose aversions based on later poisoning (Kalat, 1975). Together all these results indicate that animals can associate illness with a solution they tasted and swallowed, but not one that they tasted without swallowing.

The act of swallowing appears to be important in another context also, that of calorie regulation. If food is intubated directly to the duodenum, it suppresses the animal's appetite (Ehman, Albert, & Jamieson, 1971). The appetite-suppressant effect of food in the duodenum is enhanced if the animal had previously tasted and swallowed something, even if the solution leaked out through a fistula without reaching the stomach (Antin, Gibbs, & Smith, 1977).

How does the brain "know" whether the animal has swallowed something? There are at least two obvious possibilities. First, the brain may directly monitor the activity of the swallowing muscles. This hypothesis is plausible in light of the fact that the nucleus solitarius, one of the principal areas for taste perception, gets input from activity of the swallowing muscles (Car & Jean, 1971). Second, the animal may monitor the taste receptors in its mouth and some taste or volume receptors in the stomach, somehow altering its perception or retention of the mouth information depending on whether any of the tasted substance reaches the stomach.

To evaluate the second hypothesis, I poisoned rats with 5 mEq/kg LiCl 15 minutes after either a force-feeding of 1 ml of 10% sucrose (group FORCE SUC), or after an intubation of 2 ml of the sucrose solution directly to the stomach (group INTUBE SUC), or after both the force-feeding and the intubation (group FORCE SUC, INTUBE SUC). The hypothesis was that this third group should learn a much stronger aversion than the first two groups. On the basis of Smith and Balagura's (1969) data, little or no aversion was expected in the

INTUBE SUC group. For each of these three groups there was a control group that got the same procedure except that the LiCl was not administered until 24 hours later. The number of subjects was 17–20 for each of the six groups.

Five days after the training day, all rats were given a two-bottle test, sucrose solution versus water, for 2 hours. Percentage preference for sucrose was determined for each animal.

Fig. 5.1 presents the results. The differences among the three control groups were not statistically significant, according to a two-tail t-test. The FORCE SUC experimental group had a weak but significant aversion compared to its control group ($p < .05$). The INTUBE SUC and FORCE SUC, INTUBE SUC groups had aversions that were only marginally significant compared to their control groups ($.05 < p < .10$), but they also did not differ significantly from the FORCE SUC group.

In other words, an unswallowed taste is only weakly associable with poison, and an intubation of sucrose to the stomach potentiates the taste only slightly if at all. In fact, even if we ignore the statistics and take the results in Fig. 5.1 as

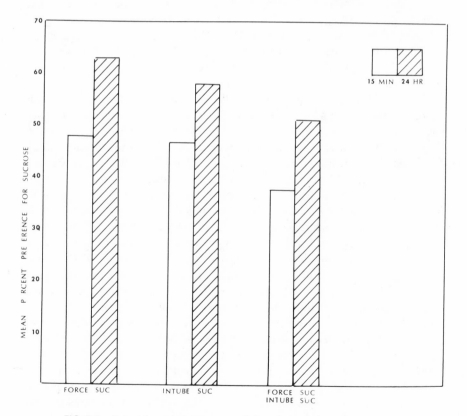

FIG. 5.1.   Learned aversions to sucrose solutions that were force-fed and/or intubated, prior to LiCl intubations.

indicating a stronger aversion in the FORCE SUC, INTUBE SUC group, it could be that the intubated sucrose added to the intensity of the poison rather than that of the taste. In any case, all these results contrast sharply with the results one commonly gets if rats actively drink 1 ml of solution 15 minutes before poisoning. In that case, rats learn an almost complete aversion to the solution.

By process of elimination, the suggested conclusion is that animals actively monitor the swallowing act and that they associate only swallowed substances with later illness or other outcomes. We may regard this conclusion as an extension of the belongingness concept; foods "belong" with illness only if they are ingested. An animal that sees, smells, or even tastes many foods is prepared to learn the consequences of only those foods that it actually swallows.

The Importance of Novelty

Novelty versus familiarity is an extremely important dimension concerning foods. Any new food requires caution, as it may be harmful. For this reason, animals usually sample very small amounts of a substance at their first encounter and increase their intake on later occasions. We see the same thing in our own behavior: What we refer to as "acquired tastes"—coffee, beer, and chili peppers, for example—are substances unfamiliar to us until adulthood. What we often forget is that everything is unfamiliar to infants and that to some extent all foods are acquired tastes.

It has long been recognized (Barnett, 1958; Rzoska, 1953) that rats are hesitant to approach novel stimuli or to consume novel foods. Their reactions to novelty play a major part in taste-aversion learning. Rats form a much stronger aversion to novel than to familiar solutions, when either is followed by poison (Elkins, 1973b; Farley, McLaurin, Scarborough, & Rowlings, 1964; Revusky & Bedarf, 1967). The associability of a taste with poison is significantly decreased by even a single previous exposure, 3 weeks before pairing it with poison (Kalat & Rozin, 1973; Siegel, 1974). The effect of familiarization occurs even with non-nutritive fluids tasted while not fluid deprived (Domjan, 1972). The effect can be very specific; an animal will more strongly learn an aversion to an unfamiliar concentration of a solute than to a familiar concentration (Kalat, 1974). Familiarization with one taste does, however, generalize somewhat to similar tastes (Holland & Forbes, 1980). The associability of a taste with poison is also affected by the novelty of the environment (Mitchell, Kirschbaum, & Perry, 1975; Mitchell, Winter, & Moffitt, 1980); Mitchell has argued that the critical determinant may be taste novelty *relative to* environment novelty—that is, whether the taste is more novel or less novel than the background environment.

Kalat and Rozin (1973) argued that the effect of familiarization on later associability is a learning process: During the first few hours after an exposure to a novel taste, if nothing unusual happens, the animal gradually learns that the taste is safe, or irrelevant, or meaningless, or nonpredictive. (See also Best, 1975; Bolles, Riley, & Laskowski, 1973; Nachman & Jones, 1974; Siegel, 1974.)

The Nature of the "Poison"

In discussing taste-aversion learning, most authors describe the event that follows the taste as poison, illness, or toxicosis. Unfortunately, the "illness" is very ill-defined. One can produce strong taste aversions by injections of LiCl, $CuSO_4$, red squill, or sodium fluoroacetate; however, one produces little or no aversion with equally toxic injections of thallium, warfarin, cyanide, and strychnine (Nachman & Hartley, 1975). One can get strong, reliable aversions based on low doses of x-rays that produce no easily observable effect on the animal (Garcia, Kimeldorf, & Hunt, 1961); by contrast, apomorphine makes animals look pretty miserable but induces only mild aversions. One can in fact get aversions without making the animal sick at all, just by leaving a rat that has eaten something in the company of another rat that had been poisoned (Lavin, Freise, & Coombes, 1980). In a related line, a blackbird can learn to avoid a food without eating it at all, after watching a conspecific eat it and then get sick (Mason & Reidinger, 1982).

Perhaps an even more striking piece of this puzzle is that rats will learn taste aversions based on injections of amphetamine, morphine, barbiturates, and other drugs that both humans and rats actively self-administer (Jacquet, 1973; Vogel, 1974; Vogel & Nathan, 1975). In fact, if a rat drinks a novel solution, then presses a lever for an injection of amphetamine, the self-administered amphetamine acts simultaneously as a positive reinforcement for the lever press and as a poison, inducing an aversion to the tasted solution (Cappell & LeBlanc, 1973; Wise, Yokel, & DeWit, 1976).

The effectiveness with which a treatment induces learned aversions apparently does not relate to stomach irritation. Taste-aversion learning is not affected by drugs that inhibit stomach motility (Smith & Morris, 1964), nor by cutting the vagus nerve (Keifer, Cabral, Rusiniak, & Garcia, 1980), which conveys information from the digestive system to the brain.

One possible unifying hypothesis has been offered by J. C. Smith and colleagues (e.g., Levy, Carroll, Smith, & Hofer, 1974): A large variety of treatments effective in producing learned aversions cause the body to release histamine, and antihistamines antagonize the acquisition of learned aversions.

Effects of Previous Familiarity with the Poison

A great number of experiments, varying in many details of procedure, concur in finding that a poison is less effective in inducing a learned taste aversion if the animal had previously experienced several unpaired presentations of that poison (Berman & Cannon, 1974; Cappell, LeBlanc, & Herling, 1975; Elkins, 1974; LeBlanc & Cappell, 1974; Revusky & Taukulis, 1975; Riley, Jacobs, & LoLordo, 1976; Suarez & Barker, 1976; Vogel & Nathan, 1976). One possible interpretation is that the animal develops a tolerance to the poison, so that the intensity of its effects on the body are, or seem, less than they did at first.

However, one finding that contradicts this interpretation is that previous exposures to the poison, if paired with some other taste, do not weaken its effectiveness as much as unpaired exposures (Cannon, Berman, Baker, & Atkinson, 1975; Mikulka, Leard, & Klein, 1977). If the phenomenon is just one of "getting used to the poison," it should not matter whether it was paired with a taste or not.

Another possible interpretation of the results is that after several exposures to a poison, the animal treats it as "unpredictable." Indeed, if one has repeatedly felt a particular type of illness without having eaten anything prior to the illness, the illness probably has some internal basis and ought not to be attributed to foods on a later occasion.

Learned Preferences

It is not known nor obvious which problem is more important for animals in nature, avoiding toxic foods or choosing foods containing some needed nutrient. Although most research has focused on avoidance of harmful foods, learning of positive preferences apparently occurs also. The classic work of Curt Richter (e.g., 1947a; Barelare, Holt, & Richter, 1938) demonstrated that rats demonstrate adaptive shifts in their food preferences, increasing their intakes of vitamin B when they are vitamin B-deficient, their intakes of protein and calcium when pregnant or nursing, and so forth. However, after Rozin (1967) demonstrated that many apparent preferences are really avoidances of the alternative, the question was reopened as to whether rats can learn a true preference for a food containing a needed nutrient. The alternative is that they merely learn which foods or combinations of foods are "safe," by process of elimination.

An adequate design must demonstrate that animals, after associating a distinctive taste with recovery from vitamin deficiency, or some other especially good result, will prefer that taste over other "safe" tastes that they experienced followed by neither illness nor an improvement of their condition. The most convincing demonstration of a true learned preference, in this sense, was reported by Zahorik (1977). Other demonstrations of a learned preference include Revusky's (1974) demonstration that rats learn an increased preference for tastes they have experienced when extremely thirsty, and Woods, Vasselli, and Milam's (1977) report that iron-deficient rats will work harder on a response that in the past had given them an iron-solution than on a response previously reinforced with other solutions.

Learning Over Long Taste–Poison Delays

For decades most experimental psychologists believed that learning required short delays, on the order of seconds, between the conditioned stimulus and the unconditioned stimulus. If this generalization were correct, without exceptions, it would be impossible to learn about the delayed consequences of food, except by means of a peripheral aftertaste—an explanation that many studies unambiguously disconfirm (Revusky & Garcia, 1970; Rozin & Kalat, 1971). Unfortunately there is no record that anyone predicted, on adaptive grounds, that animals should be capable of long-delay learning in this situation. However, after the fact was discovered, it certainly made a great deal of sense, adaptively. In nature, lights and noises generally predict events that occur within seconds, but ingested foods predict consequences delayed by minutes or hours.

If poisoned after consumption of an unfamiliar solution, depending on the nature of the taste, the poison, and the testing method, rats can learn aversions over delays of an hour (Garcia, Ervin, & Koelling, 1966), 6–12 hours (Smith & Roll, 1967), or even 24 hours (Etscorn & Stephens, 1973). When this phenomenon was first discovered it was resisted by many psychologists, and Garcia had difficulty getting some of his now-classic articles published (see Garcia, 1981). The phenomenon was, however, soon and extensively replicated.

It is difficult to know how frequently rats need to learn long-delay taste aversions in the wild. Many if not most poisons, after all, taste bad (Richter, 1950). The relevant abilities may have arisen partly to avoid vitamin-deficient diets as well as those containing toxins. Further studies of naturally occurring toxins could be valuable.

Role of Interference

If an animal gets ill after sampling two or more foods, it faces the problem of apportioning its aversion among them. One could imagine several possible solutions: (1) It could "play it safe" and acquire strong aversions to all the sampled foods. The cost of this strategy is the elimination of a food that may have been safe; (2) it could divide its aversion among all the choices and thus be cautious about all of them, but less so than it would have been about a single food that had preceded illness. The cost here is a significant likelihood of becoming sick again; (3) it could divide its aversion among the choices unequally, based on relative novelty, relative recency, and predispositions to "blame" some tastes more than others.

Because there are benefits and costs associated with each solution, an ecological approach to the problem cannot unambiguously predict which solution will be preferred. It may, however, suggest that the outcome may vary across species, depending on how many potential foods are ordinarily available and whether the risk of poisoning is worse than the risk of starvation. It also suggests that some animals may have evolved other, possibly unlearned, strategies to avoid the conflict altogether. For instance, Rozin (1969) found that rats confronted with a variety of novel foods usually eat a discrete meal of one of them, then sit and wait for several hours before eating either more of the same food or a different one. Seldom would a rat sample more than one or two novel foods within 1 hour.

If circumstances of limited availability force a rat to drink two solutions prior to poisoning, it assigns the aversion almost entirely to the novel solution, not to familiar ones (Revusky & Bedarf, 1967). If two solutions are unfamiliar, it learns an aversion to both (Kalat & Rozin, 1970). Some division of the aversion occurs, however; the rat learns a somewhat weaker aversion to each solution than it would to a single solution followed by poison (Bernstein, Vitiello, & Sigmundi, 1980; Revusky, 1971, 1977). The more a rat drinks of one solution, the more that solution interferes with learned aversion to the other (Der–Karabetian & Gorry, 1974). In spite of the interference effect, however, an animal is capable of learning aversions to a number of solutions that preceded a single poisoning. Rats that drank four novel solutions within 30 minutes prior to poisoning learned a strong aversion to the first solution (Kalat & Rozin, 1971), and presumably to the others also.

Overall, there seems to be a moderate amount of interference when two or more novel solutions precede a single poisoning. Is this amount the optimum amount? Armchair ecological or evolutionary speculation cannot help us here. Further data, particularly including species comparisons, could shed some light on the issue.

LEARNED AVERSIONS AND SELECTION AMONG SAFE FOODS

Most morphological and behavioral features of an animal have more than one use, and taste-aversion learning is no exception. The capacities involved in learning to avoid poisons are also potentially relevant to selecting among various safe foods and regulating the amounts eaten.

Rats display a phenomenon known as "sensory-specific satiety": After consuming a meal of one familiar substance, a rat tends to shift its preference toward another substance for its next meal (Holman, 1973; Morrison, 1974; Young, 1940). When we are dealing with a choice between two artificial flavors in the laboratory, the value of sensory-specific satiety may not be obvious, but in nature it can be a highly adaptive tendency. For instance, if there are a dozen foods available, each containing one or two important vitamins and minerals, the animal's survival requires it to rotate among foods (e.g., Richter, 1947a). Furthermore, most protein sources have a less than optimal balance of amino acids. Exclusive consumption of any one protein source would give an animal an excess of some amino acids and a deficit of others. Under some conditions, eating one protein exclusively can be worse than eating no protein at all (Harper, 1964; Simson & Booth, 1973). Thus, sensory-specific satiety tends to encourage a varied and balanced diet, at least for opportunistic omnivores like rats and humans. One would not expect to find this phenomenon in species with a limited, invariant diet.

Taste-aversion learning probably plays an important role in sensory-specific satiety. Richter (1947b, 1956) found that animals tend to drink about as much of a sugar solution as they can digest, and that additional intubated sugar, beyond the amount that the rats would drink, tended to show up in the urine and feces, undigested; that is, after one has consumed about as much of a nutrient as one can assimilate, additional amounts could be aversive. The establishment of a minimal, incipient aversion to the substance, based on the aversiveness of an excess, may play a role in ending a meal.

There are a number of results from both humans and rats that support this hypothesis. After repeatedly swallowing a sugar solution, people's ratings of the pleasantness of the taste declines steadily (the "sickening sweet" experience), whereas tasting but not swallowing the same amount of sugar does not affect the pleasantness of the taste (Cabanac, 1971; Cabanac, Minaire, & Adair, 1968). Overweight people, who may have a greater capacity to digest carbohydrates, can swallow a greater amount of sugar before they experience a decrease in pleasantness (Cabanac & Duclaux, 1970; Gilbert & Hagen, 1980). However, after intestinal bypass surgery, which decreases the amount they can digest, they become much quicker at reaching their limit for enjoyable consumption of sugar (Bray, Barry, Benfield, Castelnuevo–Tedesco, & Rodin, 1976). Similarly in rats, intubation of glucose to the stomach selectively decreases the number of carbohydrates a rat will consume, and similarly an intubation of proteins or fats decreases preferences for proteins or fats, respectively (Piquard, Schaeffer, & Haberey, 1975).

In a more direct test of the role of taste-aversion learning in sensory-specific satiety, I gave young rats (mean age 61 days) 10% sucrose to drink for 2½ minutes, then intubated each rat with 3 ml sucrose solution, 3 ml 0.9% NaCl solution, or an empty tube. After 2 recovery days, with water available for 1 hour and ½ hour, respectively, all rats were offered 2 bottles, one containing 10% sucrose and the other, tap water. Their percentage preference for sucrose was determined in a 30-minute test. Then the experiment was repeated with 0.9% NaCl substituted for sucrose as the test solution. (Rats were reassigned to groups to control the previous experience.)

Fig. 5.2 presents the results. A sucrose intubation produced a weak but significant aversion to the taste of sucrose ($p < .02$, Mann–Whitney U-test, 2-tail) but not to NaCl. Conversely, an NaCl intubation induced a weak, marginally significant aversion to the taste of NaCl ($.05 < p < .10$), but not to sucrose.

This is not a strong effect, nor would I expect it to be. It is consistent, however, with the idea that an additional amount of some nutrient can be aversive to an animal that has just consumed some of that nutrient. Doubtless, the size of this effect will depend on the substance. It is likely that this process plays an important part in sensory-specific satiety; it may also be involved in the regulation of meal size.

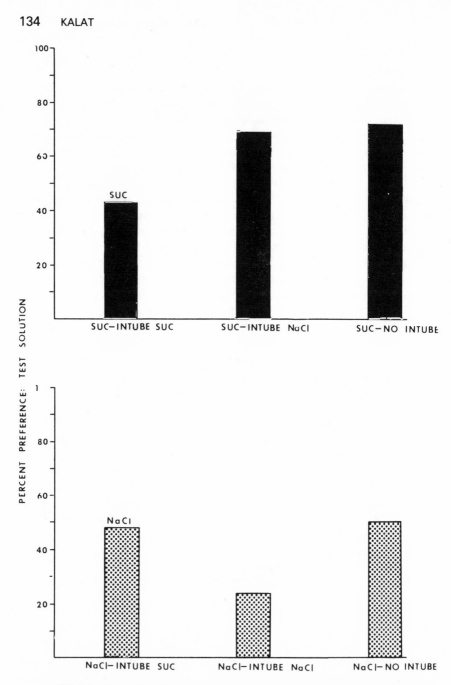

FIG. 5.2.   Learned aversions to sucrose and NaCl solutions based on contingent
intubations of sucrose and NaCl.

CONCLUSION

Some of the data on TAL conform neatly to what one might expect, based on ecological and evolutionary considerations. Learning can take place over long delays between taste and poison, much longer than the delays characteristic for other pairs of stimuli. Poison is more associable with foods than with other stimuli and can be associated with any sensory modality that is used to identify a food. The associability of a food with poison depends to a great extent on whether it is unfamiliar, and whether it is swallowed. Also, rats (and presumably others) can learn preferences as well as aversions and can use very mild aversions as a means of balancing their diet among safe but imperfect foods. On the other hand, there are some characteristics of TAL that one probably would not predict, based on our current understanding of the ecological circumstances. The ability to learn taste aversions arises much earlier in life than seems to be of any major use. The associability of a substance apparently increases with increased consumption of it, prior to poison. And the strength of the learned aversion apparently corresponds only weakly to the actual toxicity of the poison. We shall have to await further observations of feeding in the wild to know how seriously to take these discrepancies.

For an ecological approach to be useful, it is not necessary that all aspects of TAL prove to be maximally adaptive. After all, no machine, biological or otherwise, works perfectly under all circumstances; whatever mechanism is selected for achieving one goal will accidentally have some properties maladaptive for some other goal. Still, to maintain—as I do—that the learning mechanisms are evolutionarily adapted to meet specific ecological demands requires us to find a substantial number of specializations from one situation to another within a species and from one species to another within the same basic situation. The situational specializations within one species, such as the rat, are often difficult to interpret because the overall mechanisms of learning remain uncertain. The case for an ecological–evolutionary approach to learning is at this point most deficient in species-comparative data. It would be most helpful if future investigations would give more attention to detailed comparisons of TAL in different species, with different feeding habits and ecological niches.

REFERENCES

Antin, J., Gibbs, J., & Smith, G. P. (1977). Intestinal satiety requires pregastric food stimulation. *Physiology & behavior, 18,* 421–425.

Baker, L. J., Baker, T. B., & Kesner, R. P. (1977). Taste-aversion learning in young and adult rats. *Journal of Comparative and Physiological Psychology, 91,* 1168–1178.

Barelare, B., Jr., Holt, L. E., Jr., & Richter, C. P. (1938). Influence of vitamin deficiencies on appetite for particular foodstuffs. *American Journal of Physiology, 123,* 7–8.

Barker, L. M. (1976). CS duration, amount, and concentration effects in conditioning taste aversions. *Learning and Motivation, 7,* 265–273.

Barnett, S. A. (1958). Experiments on "neophobia" in wild and laboratory rats. *British Journal of Psychology, 49,* 195–201.

Barnett, S. A. (1963). *The rat: A study in behavior.* London: Methuen.

Berg, D., & Baenninger, R. (1974). Predation: Separation of aggressive and hunger motivation by conditioned aversion. *Journal of Comparative and Physiological Psychology, 86,* 601–606.

Berman, R. F., & Cannon, D. S. (1974). The effect of prior ethanol experience on ethanol-induced saccharin aversions. *Physiology & Behavior, 12,* 1041–1044.

Bernstein, I. L., Vitiello, M. V., & Sigmundi, R. A. (1980). Effects of interference stimuli on the acquisition of learned aversions to foods in the rat. *Journal of Comparative and Physiological Psychology, 94,* 921–931.

Best, M. R. (1975). Conditioned and latent inhibition in taste-aversion learning: Clarifying the role of learned safety. *Journal of Experimental Psychology: Animal Behavior Processes, 1,* 97–113.

Best, P. J., Best, M. R., & Mickley, G. A. (1973). Conditioned aversion to distinct environmental stimuli resulting from gastrointestinal distress. *Journal of Comparative and Physiological Psychology, 85,* 250–257.

Bolles, R. C., Riley, A. L., & Laskowski, B. (1973). A further demonstration of the learned safety effect in taste-aversion learning. *Bulletin of the Psychonomic Society, 1,* 190–192.

Bond, N., & DiGiusto, E. (1975). Amount of solution drunk is a factor in the establishment of taste aversion. *Animal Learning and Behavior, 3,* 81–84.

Bond, N., & Harland, W. (1975). Effect of amount of solution drunk on taste-aversion learning. *Bulletin of the Psychonomic Society, 5,* 219–220.

Braveman, N. S. (1975). Relative salience of gustatory and visual cues in the formation of poison-based food aversions by guinea pigs (Cavia porcellus). *Behavioral Biology, 14,* 189–199.

Bray, G. A., Barry, R. E., Benfield, J., Castelnuevo–Tedesco, P., & Rodin, J. (1976). Food intake and taste preferences for glucose and sucrose decrease after intestinal bypass surgery. In D. Novin, W. Wyrwicka, & G. Bray (Eds.), *Hunger: Basic mechanisms and clinical implications* (pp. 431–439). New York: Raven Press.

Cabanac, M. (1971). Physiological role of pleasure. *Science, 173,* 1103–1107.

Cabanac, M., & Duclaux, R. (1970). Specificity of internal signals in producing satiety for taste stimuli. *Nature, 227,* 966–967.

Cabanac, M., Minaire, Y., & Adair, E. R. (1968). Influence of internal factors on the pleasantness of a gustative sweet sensation. *Communications in Behavioral Biology, 1* (Part A), 77–82.

Cannon, D. S., Berman, R. F., Baker, T. B., & Atkinson, C. A. (1975). Effect of preconditioning unconditioned stimulus experience on learned taste aversions. *Journal of Experimental Psychology: Animal Behavior Processes, 1,* 270–284.

Cappell, H., & LeBlanc, A. E. (1973). Punishment of saccharin drinking by amphetamine in rats and its reversal by chlordiazepoxide. *Journal of Comparative and Physiological Psychology, 85,* 97–104.

Cappell, H., LeBlanc, A. E., & Herling, S. (1975). Modification of the punishing effects of psychoactive drugs in rats by previous drug experience. *Journal of Comparative and Physiological Psychology, 89,* 347–356.

Car, A., & Jean, A. (1971). Potentiels évoqués dans le rhombencéphale du mouton par la stimulation du nerf laryngé supérieur. *Journal de Physiologie Paris, 63,* 715–730.

Der–Karabetian, A., & Gorry, T. (1974). Amount of different flavors consumed during the CS–US interval in taste-aversion learning and interference. *Physiological Psychology, 2,* 457–460.

Domjan, M. (1972). CS preexposure in taste-aversion learning: Effects of deprivation and preexposure duration. *Learning and Motivation, 3,* 389–402.

Domjan, M. (1973). Role of ingestion in odor-toxicosis learning in the rat. *Journal of Comparative and Physiological Psychology, 84*, 507–521.

Domjan, M., & Wilson, N. E. (1972a). Contribution of ingestive behaviors to taste-aversion learning in the rat. *Journal of Comparative and Physiological Psychology, 80*, 403–412.

Domjan, M., & Wilson, N. E. (1972b). Specificity of cue to consequence in aversion learning in the rat. *Psychonomic Science, 26*, 143–145.

Ehman, G. K., Albert, D. J., & Jamieson, J. L. (1971). Injections into the duodenum and the induction of satiety in the rat. *Canadian journal of psychology, 25*, 147–166.

Elkins, R. L. (1973a). Individual differences in bait shyness: Effects of drug dose and measurement technique. *Psychological Record, 23*, 349–358.

Elkins, R. L. (1973b). Attenuation of drug-induced bait shyness to a palatable solution as an increasing function of its availability prior to conditioning. *Behavioral Biology, 9*, 221–226.

Elkins, R. L. (1974). Bait-shyness acquisition and resistance to extinction as functions of US exposure prior to conditioning. *Physiological Psychology, 2*, 341–343.

Emmerick, J. J., & Snowdon, C. T. (1976). Failure to show modification of male golden hamster mating behavior through taste/odor aversion learning. *Journal of Comparative and Physiological Psychology, 90*, 857–869.

Engwall, D. B., & Kristal, M. B. (1977). Placentophagia in rats is modifiable by taste-aversion learning. *Physiology & Behavior, 18*, 495–502.

Etscorn, F., & Stephens, R. (1973). Establishment of conditioned taste aversions with a 24 hour CS–US interval. *Physiological Psychology, 1*, 251–253.

Farley, J. A., McLaurin, W. A., Scarborough, B. B., & Rowlings, T. D. (1964). Preirradiation saccharin habituation: A factor in avoidance behavior. *Psychological Reports, 14*, 491–496.

Galef, B. G., Jr., & Dalrymple, A. J. (1981). Toxicosis-based aversions to visual cues in rats: A test of the Testa and Ternes hypothesis. *Animal Learning & Behavior, 9*, 332–334.

Garcia, J. (1981). Tilting at the paper mills of Academe. *American Psychologist, 36*, 149–158.

Garcia, J., & Ervin, F. R. (1968). Gustatory-visceral and telereceptor-cutaneous conditioning—Adaptation in internal and external milieus. *Communications in Behavioral Biology, 1* (Pt. A), 389–415.

Garcia, J., Ervin, F., & Koelling, R. (1966). Learning with prolonged delay of reinforcement, *Psychonomic Science, 5*, 121–122.

Garcia, J., Kimeldorf, D. J., & Hunt, E. L. (1961). The use of ionizing radiation as a motivating stimulus. *Psychological Review, 68*, 383–395.

Garcia, J., & Koelling, R. A. (1966). Relation of cue to consequence in avoidance learning. *Psychonomic Science, 4*, 123–124.

Gelperin, A. (1975). Rapid food-aversion learning by a terrestrial mollusk. *Science, 189*, 567–570.

Gemberling, G. A., & Domjan, M. (1982). Selective associations in 1-day-old rats: Taste-toxicosis and texture-shock aversion learning. *Journal of Comparative and Physiological Psychology, 96*, 105–113.

Gemberling, G. A., Domjan, M., & Amsel, A. (1980). Aversion learning in 5-day old rats: Taste-toxicosis and texture-shock associations. *Journal of Comparative and Physiological Psychology, 94*, 734–745.

Gilbert, D. G., & Hagen, R. L. (1980). Taste in underweight, overweight, and normal weight subjects before, during, and after sucrose ingestion. *Addictive Behaviors, 5*, 137–142.

Gillette, K., Martin, G. M., & Bellingham, W. P. (1980). Differential use of food and water cues in the formation of conditioned aversions by domestic chicks (*Gallus gallus*). *Journal of experimental psychology: Animal behavior processes, 6*, 99–111.

Gustavson, C. R. (1977). Comparative and field aspects of learned food aversions. In L. M. Barker, M. R. Best, & M. Domjan (Eds.), *Learning mechanisms in food selection*. Waco: Baylor University Press.

Gustavson, C. R., Garcia, J., Hankins, W. G., & Rusiniak, K. W. (1974). Coyote predation control by aversive conditioning. *Science, 184,* 581–583.

Hankins, W. G., Garcia, J., & Rusiniak, K. W. (1973). Dissociation of odor and taste in bait shyness. *Behavioral Biology, 8,* 407–419.

Harper, A. E. (1964). Amino acid toxicities and imbalances. In H. N. Munro & J. B. Allison (Eds.), *Mammalian protein metabolism* (Vol. 2). New York: Academic Press.

Hogan, J. A. (1973a). Development of food recognition in young chicks: I. Maturation and nutrition. *Journal of Comparative and Physiological Psychology, 83,* 355–366.

Hogan, J. A. (1973b). Development of food recognition in young chicks: II. Learned associations over long delays. *Journal of Comparative and Physiological Psychology, 83,* 367–373.

Holland, P. C., & Forbes, D. T. (1980). Effects of compound or element preexposure on compound flavor aversion conditioning. *Animal Learning & Behavior, 8,* 199–203.

Holman, E. W. (1973). Temporal properties of gustatory spontaneous alternation in rats. *Journal of Comparative and Physiological Psychology, 85,* 536–539.

Jacquet, Y. F. (1973). Conditioned aversion during morphine maintenance in mice and rats. *Physiology & Behavior, 11,* 527–541.

Johnson, C., Beaton, R., & Hall, K. (1975). Poison-based avoidance learning in nonhuman primates: Use of visual cues. *Physiology & Behavior, 14,* 403–407.

Johnston, R. E., & Zahorik, D. M. (1975). Taste aversions to sexual attractants. *Science, 189,* 893–894.

Johnston, R. E., Zahorik, D. M., Immler, K., & Zakon, H. (1978). Alterations of male sexual behavior by learned aversions to hamster vaginal secretion. *Journal of Comparative and Physiological Psychology, 92,* 85–92.

Kalat, J. W. (1974). Taste salience depends on novelty, not concentration, in taste-aversion learning in the rat. *Journal of Comparative and Physiological Psychology, 86,* 47–50.

Kalat, J. W. (1975). Taste-aversion learning in infant guinea pigs. *Developmental Psychobiology, 8,* 383–387.

Kalat, J. W. (1976). Should taste-aversion learning experiments control duration or volume of drinking on the training day? *Animal Learning & Behavior, 4,* 96–98.

Kalat, J. W. (1977). Biological significance of food-aversion learning. In N. W. Milgram, L. Krames, & T. M. Alloway (Eds.), *Food-aversion learning.* New York: Plenum Press.

Kalat, J. W., & Rozin, P. (1970). "Salience:" A factor which can override temporal contiguity in taste-aversion learning. *Journal of comparative and physiological psychology, 71,* 192–197.

Kalat, J. W., & Rozin, P. (1971). Role of interference in taste-aversion learning. *Journal of Comparative and Psychological Psychology, 77,* 53–58.

Kalat, J. W., & Rozin, P. (1973). "Learned safety" as a mechanism in long-delay taste-aversion learning in rats. *Journal of Comparative and Physiological Psychology, 83,* 198–207.

Keifer, S. W., Cabral, R. J., Rusiniak, K. W., & Garcia, J. (1980). Ethanol-induced flavor aversions in rats with subdiaphragmatic vagotomies. *Behavioral and Neural Biology, 29,* 246–254.

Klein, S. B., Domato, G. C., Hallstead, C., Stephens, I., & Mikulka, P. J. (1975). Acquisition of a conditioned aversion as a function of age and measurement technique. *Physiologial Psychology, 3,* 379–384.

Krames, L., Milgram, N. W., & Christie, D. P. (1973). Predatory aggression: Differential suppression of killing and feeding. *Behavioral Biology, 9,* 641–647.

Krane, R. V. (1980). Toxiphobia conditioning with exteroceptive cues. *Animal Learning & Behavior, 8,* 513–523.

Krane, R. V., & Wagner, A. R. (1975). Taste-aversion learning with a delayed shock US: Implications for the "generality of the laws of learning." *Journal of Comparative and Physiological Psychology, 88,* 882–889.

Langley, W. (1981). Failure of food-aversion conditioning to suppress predatory attack of the grasshopper mouse, *Onychomys Leucogaster, 33,* 317–333.

Lavin, M. J., Freise, B., & Coombes, S. (1980). Transferred flavor aversions in adult Rats. *Behavioral and Neural Biology, 28,* 15–33.

LeBlanc, A. E., & Cappell, H. (1974). Attenuation of punishing effects of morphine and amphetamine by chronic prior treatment. *Journal of Comparative and Physiological Psychology, 87,* 691–698.

Lett, B. T. (1980). Taste potentiates color-sickness associations in pigeons and quail. *Animal Learning & Behavior, 8,* 193–198.

Levy, C. J., Carroll, M. E., Smith, J. C., & Hofer, K. G. (1974). Antihistamines block radiation-induced taste aversions. *Science, 186,* 1044–1045.

Little, E. E. (1977). Conditioned aversion to amino acid flavors in the catfish, *Ictalurus Punctatus. Physiology & Behavior, 19,* 743–747.

Martin, G. M., & Bellingham, W. P. (1979). Learning of visual food aversions by chickens (*Gallus gallus*) over long delays. *Behavioral and Neural Biology, 24,* 58–68.

Martin, G. M., Bellingham, W. P., & Storlien, L. H. (1977). Effects of varied color experience on chickens' formation of color and texture aversions. *Physiology & Behavior, 18,* 415–420.

Martin, G. M., & Timmins, W. K. (1980). Taste-sickness associations in young rats over varying delays, stimulus, and test conditions. *Animal Learning & Behavior, 8,* 529–533.

Martin, J. R., & Baettig, K. (1980). Acquisition and extinction of gustatory aversion in two lines of rats selectively bred for differential shuttlebox avoidance performance. *Behavioral Processes, 5,* 303–310.

Martin, L. T., & Alberts, J. R. (1979). Taste aversions to mother's milk: The age-related role of nursing in acquisition and expression of a learned association. *Journal of Comparative and Physiological Psychology, 93,* 430–445.

Mason, J. R., & Reidinger, R. F. (1982). Observational learning of food aversions in red-winged blackbirds (*Agelaius phoenicius*). *Auk, 99,* 548–554.

Mikulka, P. J., Leard, B., & Klein, S. B. (1977). Illness-alone exposure as a source of interference with the acquisition and retention of a taste aversion. *Journal of Experimental Psychology: Animal Behavior Processes, 3,* 189–201.

Miller, V., & Domjan, M. (1981). Specificity of cue to consequence in aversion learning in the rat: Control for US-induced differential orientations. *Animal Learning & Behavior, 9,* 339–345.

Mitchell, D., Kirschbaum, E. H., & Perry, R. L. (1975). Effects of neophobia and habituation on the poison-induced avoidance of exteroceptive stimuli in the rat. *Journal of Experimental Psychology: Animal Behavior Processes, 104,* 47–55.

Mitchell, D., Winter, W., & Moffitt, T. (1980). Cross-modality contrast: Exteroceptive context habituation enhances taste neophobia and conditioned taste aversions. *Animal Learning & Behavior, 8,* 524–528.

Morrison, G. R. (1974). Alterations in palatability of nutrients for the rat as a result of prior tasting. *Journal of Comparative and Physiological Psychology, 86,* 56–61.

Morrison, G. R., & Collyer, R. (1974). Taste-mediated conditioned aversion to an exteroceptive stimulus following LiCl poisoning. *Journal of Comparative and Physiological Psychology, 86,* 51–55.

Nachman, M., & Hartley, P. L. (1975). Role of illness in producing learned taste aversions in rats: A comparison of several rodenticides. *Journal of Comparative and Physiological Psychology, 89,* 1010–1018.

Nachman, M., & Jones, D. (1974). Learned taste aversions over long delays in rats: The role of learned safety. *Journal of Comparative and Physiological Psychology, 86,* 949–956.

Palmerino, C. C., Rusiniak, K. W., & Garcia, J. (1980). Flavor-illness aversions: The peculiar roles of odor and taste in memory for poison. *Science, 208,* 753–755.

Piquard, F., Schaeffer, A., & Haberey, P. (1975). Effects de la perfusion de glucose, d'acides amines ou de lipides sur le choix alimentaire chez le rat. *Physiology & Behavior, 15,* 41–46.

Reisbick, S. H. (1973). Development of food preferences in newborn guinea pigs. *Journal of Comparative and Physiological Psychology, 85,* 427–442.

Revusky, S. (1971). The role of interference in association over a delay. In W. K. Honig & P. H. R. James (Eds.), *Animal memory.* New York: Academic Press.

Revusky, S. (1974). Retention of a learned increase in the preference for a flavored solution. *Behavioral Biology, 11,* 121–125.

Revusky, S. (1977). The concurrent interference approach to delay learning. In L. M. Barker, M. R. Best, & M. Domjan (Eds.), *Learning mechanisms in food selection.* Waco: Baylor University Press.

Revusky, S. H., & Bedarf, E. W. (1967). Association of illness with prior ingestion of novel foods. *Science, 155,* 219–220.

Revusky, S. H., & Garcia, J. (1970). Learned associations over long delays. In G. H. Bower & J. T. Spence (Eds.), *The psychology of learning and motivation* (Vol. 4). New York: Academic Press.

Revusky, S., & Parker, L. A. (1977). Aversions to unflavored water and cup drinking produced by delayed sickness. *Journal of Experimental Psychology: Animal Behavior Processes, 3,* 342–353.

Revusky, S., & Taukulis, H. (1975). Effects of alcohol and lithium habituation on the development of alcohol aversions through contingent lithium injection. *Behavior Research & Therapy, 13,* 163–166.

Richter, C. P. (1947a). Biology of drives. *Journal of Comparative and Physiological Psychology, 40,* 129–134.

Richter, C. P. (1947b). Carbohydrate appetite of normal and hyperthyroid rats as determined by the taste-threshold method. *Endocrinology, 40,* 455.

Richter, C. P. (1950). Taste and solubility of toxic compounds in poisoning of rats and man. *Journal of comparative and physiological psychology, 43,* 358–374.

Richter, C. P. (1956). Self-regulatory functions during gestation and lactation. In C. A. Villee (Ed.), *Gestation: Transactions of second conference.* Madison, NJ: Madison Printing Co.

Riley, A. L., Jacobs, W. J., & LoLordo, V. M. (1976). Drug exposure and the acquisition and retention of a conditioned taste aversion. *Journal of Comparative and Physiological Psychology, 90,* 799–807.

Rozin, P. (1967). Specific aversions as a component of specific hungers. *Journal of Comparative and Physiological Psychology, 64,* 237–242.

Rozin, P. (1969). Adaptive food sampling patterns in vitamin-deficient rats. *Journal of Comparative and Physiological Psychology, 69,* 126–132.

Rozin, P. (1976). The selection of food by rats, humans, and other animals. In J. S. Rosenblatt, R. A. Hinde, E. Shaw, & C. Beer (Eds.), *Advances in the study of behavior.* New York: Academic Press.

Rozin, P., & Kalat, J. W. (1971). Specific hungers and poison avoidance as adaptive specializations of learning. *Psychological Review, 78,* 459–486.

Rudy, J. W., Iwens, J., & Best, P. J. (1977). Pairing novel exteroceptive cues and illness reduces illness-induced taste aversions. *Journal of Experimental Psychology: Animal Behavior Processes, 3,* 14–25.

Rzoska, J. (1953). Bait shyness, a study in rat behavior. *British Journal of Animal Behaviour, 1,* 128–135.

Shettleworth, S. J. (1972). Stimulus relevance in the control of drinking and conditioned fear responses in domestic chicks (*Gallus Gallus*). *Journal of Comparative Physiological Psychology, 80,* 175–198.

Siegel, S. (1974). Flavor pre-exposure and "learned safety." *Journal of Comparative and Physiological Psychology, 87,* 1073–1982.

Simson, P. C., & Booth, D. A. (1973). Olfactory conditioning by association with histidine-free or balanced amino acid loads in rats. *Quarterly Journal of Experimental Psychology, 25,* 354–359.

Smith, D. F., & Balagura, S. (1969). Role of oropharyngeal factors in LiCl aversion. *Journal of Comparative and Physiological Psychology, 69,* 308–310.

Smith, J. C., & Morris, D. D. (1964). The effects of atropine sulfate and physostigmine on the conditioned aversion to saccharin solution with x-rays as the unconditioned stimulus. In T. J. Haley & R. S. Snider (Eds.), *Response of the nervous system to ionizing radiation: Second International Symposium.* Boston: Little, Brown.

Smith, J. C., & Roll, D. L. (1967). Trace conditioning with x-rays as an aversive stimulus. *Psychonomic Science, 9,* 11–12.

Suarez, E. M., & Barker, L. M. (1976). Effects of water deprivation and prior LiCl exposure in conditioning taste aversions. *Physiology & Behavior, 17,* 555–559.

Terk, M. P., & Green, L. (1980). Taste-aversion learning in the bat, *Carollia perspicillata. Behavioral & Neural Biology, 28,* 236–242.

Thorndike, E. L. (1911). *Animal intelligence.* Darien, CT: Hafner.

Vogel, J. R. (1974). Conditioning of taste aversion by drugs of abuse. In H. Lal & J. Singh (Eds.), *Neurobiology of drug dependence* (Vol. I). New York: Futura.

Vogel, J. R., & Nathan, B. A. (1975). Learned taste aversions induced by hypnotic drugs. *Pharmacology Biochemistry & Behavior, 3,* 189–194.

Vogel, J. R., & Nathan, B. A. (1976). Reduction of learned taste aversions by preexposure to drugs. *Psychopharmacology, 49,* 167–172.

Westbrook, R. F., Clarke, J. C., & Provost, S. (1980). Long-delay learning in the pigeon: Flavor, color, and flavor-mediated color aversions. *Behavioral and Neural Biology, 28,* 398–407.

Wilcoxon, H., Dragoin, W., & Kral, P. (1971). Illness-induced aversions in rat and quail: Relative salience of visual and gustatory cues. *Science, 171,* 826–828.

Wise, R. A., Yokel, R. A., & DeWit, H. (1976). Both positive reinforcement and conditioned aversion from amphetamine and from apomorphine in rats. *Science, 191,* 1273–1275.

Woods, S. C., Vasselli, J. R., & Milam, K. M. (1977). Iron appetite and latent learning in rats. *Physiology & Behavior, 19,* 623–626.

Young, P. T. (1940). Reversal of food preference of the white rat through controlled prefeeding. *Journal of General Psychology, 22,* 33–66.

Zahorik, D. M. (1977). Associative and nonassociative factors in learned food preferences. In L. M. Barker, M. R. Best, & M. Domjan (Eds.), *Learning mechanisms in food selection.* Waco: Baylor University Press.

Zahorik, D. M., & Houpt, K. A. (1977). The concept of nutritional wisdom: Applicability of laboratory learning models to large herbivores. In L. M. Barker, M. R. Best, & M. Domjan (Eds.), *Learning mechanisms in food selection.* Waco: Baylor University Press.

Zahorik, D. M., & Johnston, R. E. (1976). Taste aversions to food flavors and vaginal secretions in golden hamsters. *Journal of Comparative and Physiological Psychology, 90,* 57–66.

6

Social Learning in Wild Norway Rats

Bennett G. Galef, Jr.
Department of Psychology
McMaster University

In the decades before either comparative psychology or the study of animal behavior emerged as experimental disciplines, it was widely believed that learning by imitation was a central process in the acquisition of adaptive behavior by members of most vertebrate species. According to Morgan (1896):

> The young bird or mammal, especially in the case of gregarious species, is born into a community where certain behavior is constantly exhibited before its eyes. Through imitation it falls in with the traditional habits, and itself serves as one of the models for those that come after. There can be no question that this tradition is of great importance in animal life. (p. 184)

Instinct and imitation rather than instinct and learning were commonly considered the major alternative means of development of behaviors observed in natural circumstances. "Often we are unable to say in the present condition of our knowledge whether the performance of certain activities is due to heredity or tradition; whether they are instinctive or due to imitation" (Morgan, 1869, p. 184). Individual learning was treated as a modulator of instinct or antecedent to tradition rather than as a primary mode of behavior acquisition (Morgan, 1896, pp. 144–165; Romanes, 1884, pp. 220–229).

George Romanes, protégé of Charles Darwin, Fellow of the Royal Society, and a major influence in biology at the close of the Victorian era, was the foremost proponent of the view that learning by imitation is central to the development of behavior in animals. The importance of learning by imitation in Romanes' theory of behavior is clearly illustrated in his discussion of the causes of the perfection of instincts in allowing organisms to meet the challenges provided by their respective habitats.

Instincts were believed by Romanes (1884) to evolve in either of two ways: by Darwinian natural selection or "by the effects of habit on successive generations" (p. 177). Arguing by analogy, Romanes (1884) proposed that:

> Just as in the lifetime of the individual adjustive actions which were originally intelligent may by frequent repetition become automatic, so in the life-time of the species, actions originally intelligent may, by frequent repetition and heredity, so write their effects on the nervous system that the latter is prepared . . . to perform adjustive actions mechanically which in previous generations were performed intelligently. (p. 178)

In sum, intelligent behavior could modify instinct to increase its perfection and such learned modifications of behavior (now instinctive) could be inherited by future generations. One might expect Romanes to have argued, as had Darwin (1884) who held a similar view, that those learned behaviors that became instinctive were individually acquired. However, quite to the contrary, Romanes (1884) proposed "with animals, as with men, original ideas are not always forthcoming at the time they are wanted, and therefore it is often easier to imitate than to invent" (p. 219). For Romanes, the central process modifying instinct to ever greater perfection was imitation, particularly imitation of the behavior of members of one species by members of another.

Although such a model of the evolution of adaptive behavior may seem unnecessarily elaborate to the modern reader, we are fortunate in not having to attempt to explain the origins of species-typical behaviors as complex as those with which Romanes had to deal. The paucity of systematic observations of animal behavior available during the nineteenth century required Romanes to rely heavily on anecdotal accounts provided by correspondents for descriptions of relevant phenomena. Unfortunately, many of the reports of animal behavior provided by Romanes' contemporaries suggested that mammals were capable of achieving truly remarkable solutions to problems they encountered in their natural habitats. For example, mice in Iceland were said to store supplies of berries in dried mushrooms, to load these rations onto dried cow-paddies, and to launch and then steer such improvised, provisioned vessels across flooded rivers and streams using their tails as rudders in the rush of water. If one takes such an anecdote seriously, as Romanes did in consequence of his receiving two independent reports of the behavior (Romanes, 1881, p. 364), it suggests that the ability of animals to respond to environmental challenges is very sophisticated indeed. It is surely more parsimonious to hypothesize that mice first acquired such tricks by observing humans provision and steer boats and that the learned behavior became instinctive, than to assume that countless individual mice independently learned to provision, launch, and steer rafts; if such complex patterns of behavior can be learned by observation, it is surely reasonable to assume that simpler patterns of behavior can be acquired in the same way.

Perhaps the most historically important of the many instances of imitative learning in animals that Romanes discussed in his two major comparative texts, *Animal Intelligence* (1881) and *Mental Evolution in Animals* (1884), concerned a cat that belonged to Romanes' own coachman. This animal had learned, without formal tuition of any kind, to open a latched door in Romanes' yard by holding onto the latch guard with one forepaw, depressing the thumb-piece with the other, and simultaneously pushing at the doorpost with her hind feet. Romanes argued that the cat, in the absence of any other source of information, must have observed that humans opened the door by grasping the latch guard and moving the thumb-piece. Then, said Romanes (1881), the cat must have reasoned, "If a hand can do it, why not a paw?" (p. 422). Finally, the cat, strongly motivated by this insight, attempted to open the door in question, and succeeded.

Stephen Jay Gould (1977) has suggested (with tongue just barely in cheek) that Darwin's theory of evolution was conceived in response to the irritation provided by five years of forced conversation with the conservative, fundamentalist Robert Fitzroy, captain of *H.M.S. Beagle* and Darwin's constant dinner companion throughout their joint voyage of exploration. One might argue similarly that experimental animal psychology in North America arose from Edward Thorndike's irritation with excesses in Romanes' *Animal Intelligence:* its anecdotal method, its speculative conclusions, even its title (Thorndike, 1911, pp. 22–26, pp. 68–70). Thorndike pointed out that although accurate observation in nature may tell us what an animal does, observation alone cannot tell us how the observed behavior was acquired by its performer. The discovery of the processes underlying behavior acquisition, asserted Thorndike, can only come from examination in controlled and replicable situations of the behavior of subjects of known previous history. So in the late 1890s Thorndike brought the latch-opening behavior of cats, discussed by Romanes, into the laboratory and, under controlled conditions, observed the acquisition of the solution of problems similar to those posed by a latched garden gate. As is well known, Thorndike found that animals in general, and cats in particular, did not learn to operate mechanical devices by observing either other cats or humans do so. In fact, in some cases, observation of a trained demonstrator actually interfered with the gradual process of trial-and-error learning Thorndike believed necessary for naive individuals to acquire all rewarded responses. In 1898, when Thorndike published his now classic "Experimental study of associative processes in animals" in the *Psychological Review,* experimental psychologists began to turn away from the study of social learning in animals as a central concern and focused instead on the processes underlying individual acquisition of behavior.

Of course, as Thorndike (1911) emphasized, it cannot be inferred from the finding that observation of the performance of a trained individual does not facilitate response acquisition by naive individuals, that other types of social interaction might not prove important in the acquisition of adaptive behavior. Thorndike (1911, p. 76) discussed in some detail a number of ways in which behavior could be transmitted between individuals by processes he labeled "semi-" or "pseudoimitative." For example, he states (Thorndike, 1911):

> The young animal stays with or follows its mother from a specific instinct to keep near that particular object . . . It may thus learn to stay near trains, or scramble up trees, or feed at certain places and on certain plants. Actions due to following pure and simply may thus simulate imitation . . . more investigation and experimentation may finally reduce all the phenomena of so-called imitation of parents by young to the level of indirect results of instinctive acts. (pp. 77–78)

The possible role of such "indirect results of instinctive acts" in producing "semi-imitative" behaviors (a special case of incidental learning (Church, 1957) was largely ignored within psychology for the better part of a century. Psychologists turned from analysis of the mechanisms underlying behavior acquisition of animals in nature to study of acquisition processes in animals presumed analogous to those observed in humans. Learning by observation or imitation, assumed to underlie much of human learning (Bandura, 1962), was a phenomenon of interest to psychologists. Consequently, myriad experiments were undertaken (in large part unsuccessfully) to demonstrate learning by observation in mammals and birds. Learning incident upon close association with conspecifics was largely ignored, possibly because it was perceived to be irrelevant to processes underlying human learning.

There is, however, good reason to believe that social learning may be an important factor in the acquisition of adaptive behavior by free-living animals. Field biologists engaged in the systematic observation of mammals and birds in their natural habitats have described a variety of behavioral phenomena that seem to require explanation in terms of social learning of some kind. Comparison of the behavior of members of a single species living in nature in different social groups has frequently revealed that many of the members of one social group exhibit some pattern of behavior totally absent in other groups (see Galef, 1976, for a review). Those observng idiosyncratic behaviors typical of a social group have long assumed that such animal "traditions," as they are frequently called, are socially transmitted from individual to individual within a group as the result of imitation of one animal by another.

Although the fact that groups of conspecific animals may differ from one another in their behavior is well established, the role of either imitation learning or other social processes in the establishment and maintenance of such differences is not. As Thorndike stated, simple observation of an animal behaving in nature provides little useful information concerning the processes responsible for the development of the behavior observed. Field observers' reports of animal "traditions," thus, leave unanswered important questions concerning the necessary antecedent conditions for the development of idiosyncratic behaviors in groups of animals, questions that can only be answered under controlled conditions.

For the past decade my students and I have been studying the role of social process in the development of traditional patterns of feeding in wild Norway rats (*Rattus norvegicus*). In the remainder of the present chapter I briefly review two series of experiments in which my coworkers and I have attempted to determine the causes of colony-specific feeding patterns exhibited by groups of wild rats. Our methods have been similar in the two cases described. In each, we began with field reports of a traditional pattern of behavior in rats, then brought the phenomenon into the laboratory, and finally attempted to analyze its causes. In both cases, our analyses of potential social learning phenomena has been in terms of the observable behavior of the individuals comprising social groups. Consequently, our studies have been largely dependent on techniques developed within experimental animal psychology.

SOCIAL TRANSMISSION OF DIET PREFERENCE

Some years ago, Fritz Steiniger, an ecologist working in Germany, was studying the causes of difficulties experienced in controlling rat populations by means of poisoned baiting stations permanently placed in rat-infested areas. Steiniger (1950) had found that if a single poison bait were employed in a rat-infested area for an extended period of time, despite initial success, later acceptance of the bait was very poor. He noted, in particular, that young rats, born to those animals that had survived poisoning, rejected the poison bait without even sampling it themselves. These young fed exclusively on safe diets available in their colony territory. Steiniger attributed such avoidance of contact with potentially toxic baits by naive young animals to the behavior of experienced individuals which he believed disuaded inexperienced juveniles from ingesting poisoned food.

The tendency of juvenile wild rats to avoid ingesting diets that the adults of their colony have learned to avoid is a robust phenomenon that proved relatively easy to bring into the laboratory. In our basic experiment (Galef & Clark, 1971a), we established colonies of adult wild rats in 1 by 2 m enclosures like that illustrated in Fig. 6.1a. Water was continuously available in each enclosure and food was presented to each colony for 3 hours each day in two food bowls located about .8 m apart. Each food bowl contained one of two nutritionally adequate diets, each discriminable from the other in color, texture, taste, and smell. I refer to these two diets as Diets A and B in all that follows (Diet A was powdered Purina Laboratory Chow and Diet B consisted mainly of sucrose and casein. Naive rats strongly prefer Diet B to Diet A).

The adult members of our colonies were trained to eat one of the two diets presented each day and to avoid the other by introducing sublethal doses of poison (lithium chloride) into the samples of one of the diets offered to the colony during daily 3-hour feeding periods. Under these conditions our wild rats rapidly

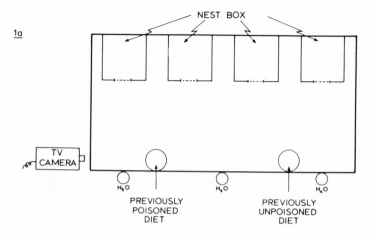

1a

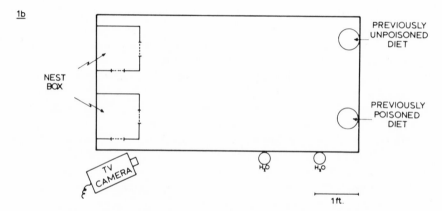

1b

FIG. 6.1.   One by two meter enclosures: (1a) housing adult colonies and their young and (1b) to which litters of weanlings were transferred. (Galef & Clark, 1971a. Copyright 1971 by the American Psychological Association. Reprinted by permission of the publisher and author.)

learned to avoid ingesting the poisoned diet, and, most importantly, they continued to avoid ingesting the previously poisoned diet for some additional weeks when offered uncontaminated samples of it.

The experiment proper began when litters of pups born to trained colony members left their nest-sites to feed on solid food for the very first time. We observed both adults and pups throughout daily 3-hour feeding periods on closed circuit television and recorded the number of times pups approached to within .1 m of each food bowl and the number of times pups ate from each food bowl, now containing uncontaminated samples of diet.

After a litter of pups had been feeding on solid food for a number of days, we transferred them to a new enclosure (illustrated in Fig. 6.1b),where, without the adults of their colony, they were again offered a choice between uncontaminated samples of Diets A and B. The amount of each diet eaten by the pups in this situation was determined by weighing food bowls before and after each feeding session.

Typical results of such experiments are presented in Figs 6.2 and 6.3. Figure 6.2a presents data describing the feeding behavior of a litter of wild rat pups born to a colony whose members had been trained to avoid ingesting the normally

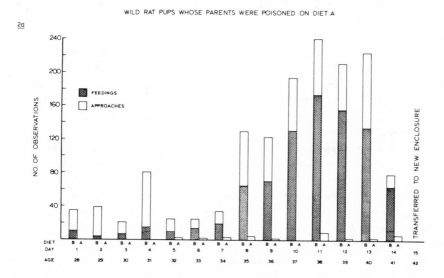

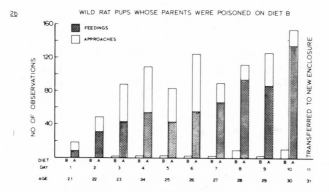

FIG. 6.2.   Number of observed approaches to and feedings from bowls containing Diets A and B by wild rat pups, the adults of whose colony had been poisoned A (2A) or Diet B (2B). (Galef & Clark, 1971a. Copyright 1971 by the American Psychological Association. Reprinted by permission of the publisher and author.)

preferred Diet B. The abscissa indicates both the age in days of the pups and the number of days they had been feeding on solid food. The ordinate indicates the number of times the pups approached and fed from each of the two food bowls. As is evidence from examination of Fig. 6.2a, pups born to a colony trained to avoid ingesting the normally preferred Diet B ate only Diet A, the diet that the adults of their colony had been trained to eat. Over the years, we have observed 36 litters in this condition and all but one has behaved similarly. Pups born to colonies trained to eat Diet A ate only Diet A and totally avoided eating Diet B.

Fig. 6.2b presents comparable data describing the feeding behavior of a litter of wild rat pups whose parents had been trained to avoid ingesting Diet A. As can be seen in Fig. 6.2b, again the pups ate only the diet that the adults of their colony have been trained to eat (Diet B) and totally avoided the alternative (Diet A) that their parents had learned to avoid. We have observed eight wild rat litters in this condition and all behaved identically. The data lead to the conclusion that, in the presence of adults of their colony, wild rat pups ingest only that diet that the adults of their colony are eating and avoid available alternatives that the adults are avoiding.

Furthermore, as shown in Fig. 6.3, the learned dietary preference of the adults of a colony continues to affect the feeding preference of their young for 8 to 10 days following transfer of the pups to an enclosure separate from those adults. Pups removed from colonies eating Diet A continued to eat Diet A, and those removed from colonies eating Diet B continued to prefer that diet, even in the absence of adults.

Taken together, our observations demonstrate, as Steiniger indicated, that adult rats can bias their offspring to feed solely on a safe diet in an environment containing food known by the adults to have been poisoned. The data also show that the food preferences learned in the presence of adults continue to affect the diet preference of pups for some time after the pups' removal from direct adult influence.

One obvious question arising from these observations concerns the process or processes responsible for pups weaning to that diet eaten by adults of their colony.[1] How do young rats come to know and prefer the foods their adult fellows are exploiting? The results of experiments conducted in my laboratory during the past several years have provided evidence of three ways in which adult wild rats can induce young conspecifics to wean to a specific food.

First, Mertice Clark and I (Galef & Clark, 1971b, 1972) have found that the physical presence of adult rats at a feeding site attracts pups to that site and markedly increases the probability of young rats weaning to the food located

---

[1]See Galef (1977) for discussion of the mechanisms responsible for continued pup avoidance of adult-avoided diets following removal of pups from direct adult influence.

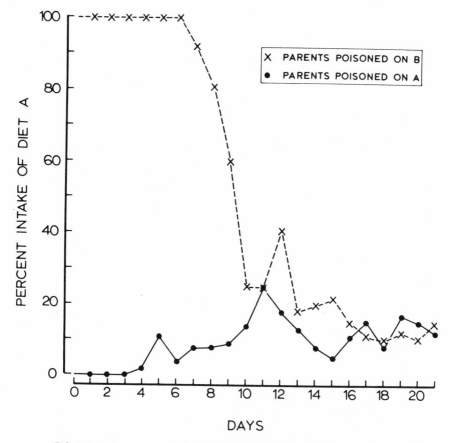

FIG. 6.3.   Mean amount of Diet A eaten, as a percentage of total intake, by pups on the days following their removal from the adult colony. (Galef & Clark, 1971a. Copyright 1971 by the American Psychological Association. Reprinted by permission of the publisher and author.)

there. If, for example, one establishes a colony of adult wild rats in a large enclosure like that illustrated in Fig. 6.4, makes Diet A available in two food bowls located behind the partition, and continuously monitors the area above the dotted line, one can determine the conditions under which each individual pup in a litter eats its very first meal of solid food. We have observed nine individually marked pups from three litters take their first meal of solid food, and each of the nine subjects ate its first meal under exactly the same circumstances. Each ate for the first time while an adult was eating and each ate at the same food-bowl as the feeding adult, not at the other food-bowl .5 m away. Given the observed temporal and spatial distributions of adult meals, the probability of pups eating their first meal under these conditions occurring nine of nine times by chance was less than four in a thousand. We concluded that the

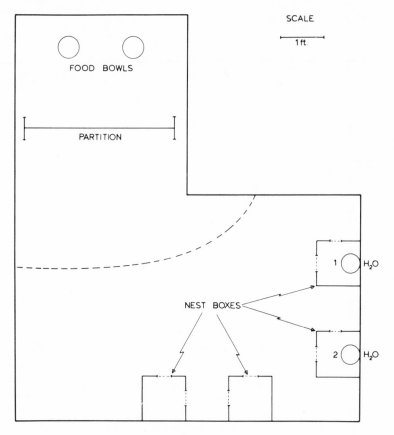

FIG. 6.4.   Large enclosure for continuous observation of a wild rat colony. (Galef & Clark, 1971b. Copyright 1971 by the Psychonomic Society. Reprinted by permission of the publisher and author.)

presence of an adult at a feeding site serves to attract pups to that site and to cause pups to initiate feeding there.

Second, Linda Heiber and I (Galef & Heiber, 1976) have found that adult rats deposit olfactory cues in areas that they visit and that these cues bias weaning pups' choice of areas for both exploration and initiation of feeding. Heiber and I confined a dam and litter for several days in the larger portion of the enclosure shown in Fig. 6.5. Then we removed this dam, her litter, and the partition from the enclosure and observed individual food-deprived pups from another litter feed for 3 hours each day in the open enclosure with Diet A available in both food-bowls. We found that pups ate 90% of their meals and spent 70% of their exloration time in the soiled end-third rather than clean end-third of the enclosure.

In addition to being able to influence a pup's choice of feeding site, and thus indirectly its food preference, the mother of a litter of pups can also directly

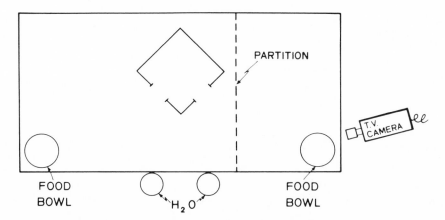

FIG. 6.5.   Enclosure in which the effects of residual olfactory cues on pup behavior were measured. (Galef & Heiber, 1976. Copyright 1976 by the American Psychological Association. Reprinted by permission of the publisher and author.)

influence her pups' dietary preference. Mertice Clark and I (Galef & Clark, 1972) conducted an experiment much like the very first experiment described previously (see Fig. 6.1a), but with one important difference. Colonies of adult rats were again housed in 1 by 2 m enclosures. However, in the present experiment, adults were removed to a separate cage where all were fed for 3 hours each day either Diet A or Diet B depending on the experimental condition to which their colony was assigned. While the adults were out of the colony enclosure, the pups were presented with two standard food-bowls, one containing an uncontaminated sample of Diet A and one an uncontaminated sample of Diet B. Fig. 6.6 presents data describing the amount of Diet A eaten by pups, the adults of whose colonies were fed either Diet A or Diet B. As is evident from examination of the figure, the diet eaten by adult colony members profoundly affected the food choice of pups, even though under the conditions of the present experiment adults and young had no opportunity to interact directly in a feeding situation.

David Sherry, Pat Henderson, and I (Galef & Henderson, 1972; Galef & Sherry, 1973) have provided evidence that the milk of a lactating female rat contains cues directly reflecting the flavor of her diet. Our data suggest that as the result of exposure during nursing to flavor cues present in mother's milk, weaning pups exhibit a preference for a diet of the same flavor as that which their mother eats during lactation. In one of our experiments, Sherry and I (Galef & Sherry, 1973) took rat pups nursing from a lactating female eating Diet A, force-fed them ½ cc of milk manually expressed from another lactating female eating Diet B, and then poisoned the pups by intraperitoneal injection of .12 molar Lithium chloride solution. At weaning we tested these experimental pups for their preference between Diets A and B. As is evident in Fig. 6.7, in

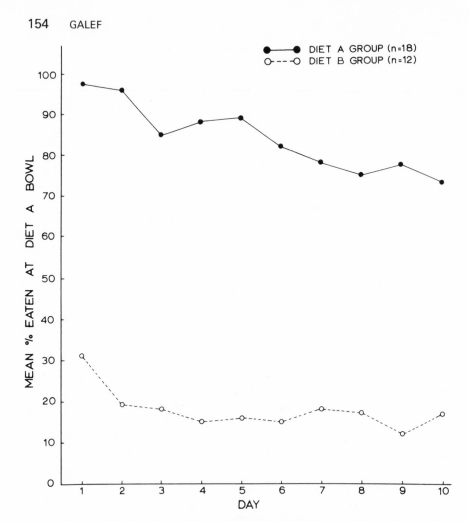

FIG. 6.6.   Mean amount of Diet A eaten by pups, as a percentage of total intake, when adults and pups have no opportunity to interact in a feeding situation and adults are eating either Diet A or Diet B. (Galef & Clark, 1972. Copyright 1972 by the American Psychological Association. Reprinted by permission of the publisher and author.)

comparison with a variety of controls, experimental pups (those that had received milk from a female eating Diet B prior to poisoning) exhibited an aversion to Diet B.

So the results of our research to date indicate the existence of three ways in which adults may bias the choice of diet by conspecific young at weaning. Both the physical presence of adults at a feeding site and residual olfactory cues deposited by adults in the vicinity of a food source influence pups' choice of a place at which to wean and, thus, indirectly their choice of diet at weaning.

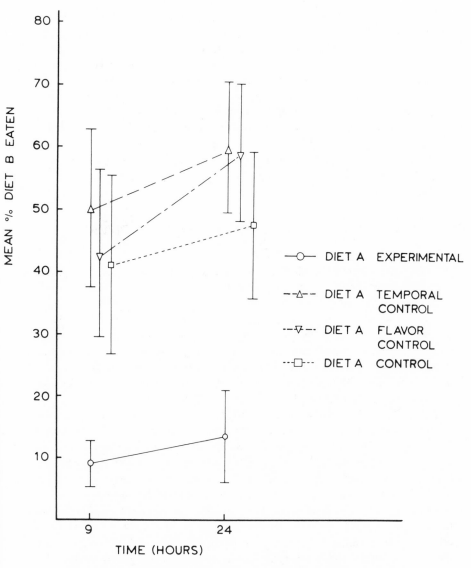

FIG. 6.7.   Mean amount of Diet B eaten at weaning, as a percentage of total intake, by pups poisoned after receiving milk from a mother eating Diet B and by controls. (Galef & Sherry, 1973. Copyright 1973 by the American Psychological Association. Reprinted by permission of the publisher and author.)

Cues contained in maternal milk have the potential to directly influence diet choice by pups at weaning.

Fritz Steiniger was right. The learned feeding preferences of adult wild rats can be socially transmitted to their young, reducing the probability that the young will ingest toxic food. Edward Thorndike was also right. The indirect results of what might be conceived of as instinctive acts, in this case the tendency of rat pups to suckle from their dam and to approach adults or their scents, can result in introduction of the young to diets eaten by adults of their colony and consequent simulated imitation of learned adult food preferences by young.

Of course, the finding that one pattern of behavior idiosyncratic to a particular social group of wild rats develops as the result of social interaction cannot be used to infer that all such "traditions" in wild rats are, in fact, the result of social processes, which brings us to the second series of experiments.

SOCIAL TRANSMISSION OF THE HABIT OF DIVING FOR FOOD

Wild rat colonies exhibit traditional variation not only in their food preferences but also in the motor patterns they employ in food acquisition. The range of feeding behaviors exhibited by different colonies of free-living Norway rats is very much greater than one might expect from observation of their fellows maintained in laboratory cages and eating pellets of rat chow. Members of some colonies of wild rats have been reliably reported to pursue and capture fingerling trout (Cottam, 1948), members of other colonies to stalk and kill sparrows and ducks (Steiniger, 1950), and members of yet other colonies to raid birds' nests for eggs and young (Austin, 1948; Norman, 1975).

Recently, two Italian field workers, Drs. Gandolfi and Parisi of the University of Parma, have reported that many members of some colonies of wild rats (*Rattus norvegicus*) living along the banks of the Po River in Northern Italy dive for and feed on molluscs inhabiting the river bottom, whereas no members of nearby colonies, having equal access to molluscs within their home-ranges, feed on them (Gandolfi & Parisi, 1972, 1973; Parisi & Gandolfi, 1974).

Gandolfi and Parisi interpreted their observations as indicating that exploitation of submerged prey spreads through a wild rat colony as the result of observational learning. If discovery of molluscs on the river bed by colony members is a rare event and if naive colony members readily learn to dive as a result of interacting with diving individuals, one would expect the observed bimodality in frequency of individuals diving in various colonies. Although the hypothesis that the habit of diving for food spreads by social learning is an attractive one, evidence adequate to support it would once again be extremely difficult to collect in the uncontrolled natural situation.

The series of experiments described in the following paragraphs (Galef, 1980) was, therefore, undertaken to assess the potential contribution of social processes to the development in rats of the habit of diving for food in shallow water. Although the present experiments involve laboratory analogues of the natural situation and cannot be extrapolated uncritically to the more complex natural situation, they do provide evidence relevant to the question of the necessity of invoking social learning as a mechanism to explain the observed distribution of the habit of diving for food among free-living rat colonies.

My subjects were sibling pairs of adult wild Norway rats (second and third generation laboratory-bred descendants of free-living animals captured on a garbage dump in southern Ontario), wild rat dams and their litters of young and sibling pairs of domesticated Long–Evans rats.

All subjects were housed and tested in *diving enclosures* like that illustrated in Fig. 6.8. Each diving enclosure was composed of three modules: first, a *living cage* providing harborage sites, ad lib water, and access to food for 3 hours each day; second, a *diving area,* consisting of a *caged patio* and glass-walled *diving pool;* and third, a *tunnel* providing access between the living cage and diving area. All behavior occurring on the patio or in the diving pool was recorded on a time-lapse video tape recorder and reviewed daily.

To begin, an individual adult rat was introduced into a diving enclosure and trained to dive for pieces of chocolate by starting with a dry diving tank with five pieces of chocolate on its floor and then, over a period of days, gradually raising the water level to 15 cm. The water level was maintained at 15 cm until

DIVING ENCLOSURE

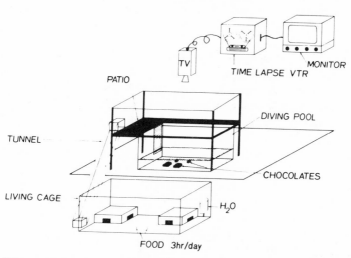

FIG. 6.8. The living cage, patio and diving-pool, and tunnel of the diving enclosure. (Galef, 1980. Copyright 1980 by the American Psychological Association. Reprinted by permission of the publisher and author.)

completion of the experiment, and any chocolates eaten were replaced twice daily. Once the trained rat was regularly diving, a naive sibling of the trained individual was shaved along its back for identification and introduced into the diving enclosure for 36 days. The dams of three litters of wild rat pups were also trained to dive for food in the same way as were other trained adults, and their pups were observed from 21 to 57 days of age to see if they exhibited diving behavior.

The main results are presented in Table 6.1, which indicates the number of wild and domesticated naive rats recovering one or more chocolates from the diving-pool floor during the 36 days each was present in the diving enclosure. As is evident from examination of the table, naive adults did not learn to dive as the result of interaction with a diving conspecific.

Although some juvenile rats in the experimental condition, (juveniles living with a diving mother) did learn to dive for food, an approximately equal proportion of those in the control condition (those whose mothers had not been trained to dive) also learned to dive.

The failure of naive rats to learn to dive could not be attributed to a failure on the part of their trained cage-mates to demonstrate diving behavior. Trained rats retrieved an average of 4.6 chocolates/day from the diving-pool floor on each of the days they co-occupied the diving apparatus with their naive partners. Similarly, the failure of naive subjects to learn to dive could not be attributed to their failure to observe their trained cage-mates diving. Naive subjects rapidly learned to await their diving cage-mate on the patio and frequently attempted to snatch retrieved chocolates from the diver, but naive subjects very rarely entered the water themselves. The results suggest that interaction with a diving conspecific is not in itself sufficient to induce either an adult or juvenile rat to dive for food.

Observation, both of naive subjects and of trained individuals early in the training process, suggested that a major impediment to acquisition of diving behavior was a reluctance to enter water. Thus, it seemed possible that rats that had learned to swim but not to dive might be socially induced to dive for food. I, therefore, initiated an experiment in which adult wild rats that had been trained

TABLE 6.1
Number of Naive Rats Diving or not Diving
for Food

Subjects	Diving	Not Diving
Adult wild rats	0	10
Adult domesticated rats	0	10
Juvenile wild rats (Expt'l)	4	14
Juvenile wild rats (Control)	3	15

to swim but not to dive were allowed to interact in the diving enclosure with a sibling who had been trained to dive. Unexpectedly, two of the six subjects trained to swim but not to dive began to dive in 15 cm of water and retrieve chocolates from the diving-pool floor before their diving-trained cage-mates had demonstrated diving behavior.

So the next experiment was undertaken to determine whether rats trained to swim would spontaneously dive and retrieve objects from beneath the water. Litters of pups were maintained in a *swimming enclosure,* a part of which is illustrated in Fig. 6.9. The swimming enclosure required subjects to cross a small body of water to acquire food. Although subjects were free to dive in the swimming pool, they received no extrinsic reinforcement for doing so.

Each subject litter of pups was taken from its dam and introduced as a group into the swimming enclosure at 30 days of age. The swimming pool was left empty until the litter had begun to feed at the food-bin and the pool was then gradually filled with water over a 1-week period to a depth of 20 cm. A litter was left undisturbed in the swimming enclosure for a month. Then each member of a litter was individually introduced into a diving enclosure with the diving pool already flooded to a depth of 15 cm and chocolates available on the diving pool floor. A bowl containing powdered Purina Laboratory Chow was placed in each living-cage for 3 hours on each of the 7 days each subject remained in its diving enclosure. Control subjects were treated identically to experimental subjects except that no water was ever introduced into their swimming pools prior to their transfer to diving enclosures. The results are presented in Fig. 6.10,

SWIMMING POOL

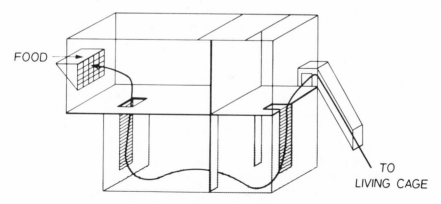

FIG. 6.9.   The swimming pool of the swimming enclosure. (Galef, 1980. Copyright 1980 by the American Psychological Association. Reprinted by permission of the publisher and author.)

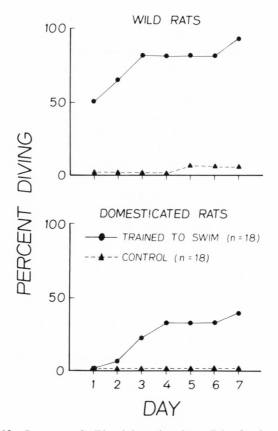

FIG. 6.10. Percentage of wild and domesticated rats diving for chocolates in the diving enclosure, on each of 7 days after either receiving or not receiving swimming experience in the swimming enclosure. (Galef, 1980. Copyright 1980 by the American Psychological Association. Reprinted by permission of the publisher and author.)

which shows the percentage of wild and domesticated experimental and control subjects retrieving one or more chocolates from beneath 15 cm of water in the diving enclosures on each of 7 consecutive days of testing. As can be seen in Fig. 6.10, swimming experience markedly facilitated diving behavior in both wild and domesticated rats.

The finding that swimming rats are effectively diving rats severely limits the role that social factors could play in the spread of diving behavior through a population. If rats learn to swim independently, and if swimming rats dive, social interaction could only serve to direct rats already prepared to dive to one locale rather than another. It is, however, also possible that social factors might indirectly result in the spread of diving behavior by facilitating the spread of swimming behavior.

The apparatus used to examine the role of social interaction in the development of swimming behavior is illustrated in Fig. 6.11. It consisted of a living cage attached to a 2–meter–long *swimming alley*. Food was available ad lib in a container mounted on a stand at the opposite end of the swimming alley from the living cage.

A mother and litter were introduced into the living cage on Day 2 postpartum and the dam was trained to swim for food. Water was continuously available in the living cage, and food was present there for 3 hours each day. Control litters were treated identically to experimental litters except that a partition with a small hole in it, which allowed pups but not dams access to the swimming alley, was placed in the tunnel between the living cage and swimming alley.

Figure 6.12 indicates the mean age of litters on the day one of their members first reached the food at the far end of the swimming alley from the living cage. As can be seen in the figure, wild rat pups will start to swim at an early age whether they are in the presence of a swimming adult rat or not, whereas Long–Evans rats will swim at a considerably earlier age in the presence than in the absence of a swimming adult.

These results are not consistent with the hypothesis that social interaction is necessary for the spread of swimming behavior. All litters of rats, regardless of whether they were exposed to swimming conspecifics, came to exhibit swimming behavior prior to reaching maturity.

The results of the experiments just described suggest that members of all groups of rats living near water will spontaneously learn to swim and therefore, with high probability, to dive. Taken together with Gandolfi and Parisi's field observations, indicating that in natural settings no members of many colonies exhibit diving behavior, our laboratory data suggest that in the field situation members of most rat colonies may acquire diving behavior, but that its subsequent performance is inhibited in some way in nondiving colonies.

SWIMMING ALLEY

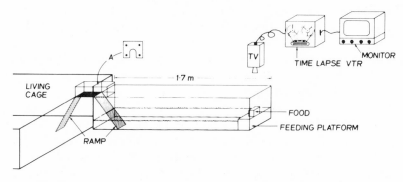

FIG. 6.11.   The swimming alley. (Galef, 1980. Copyright 1980 by the American Psychological Association. Reprinted by permission of the publisher and author.)

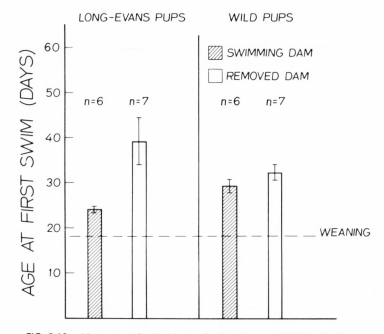

FIG. 6.12.   Mean age at first incidence of swimming to the feeding platform in the swimming alley by rat pups reared either by a swimming or nonswimming mother. (Galef, 1980. Copyright 1980 by the American Psychological Association. Reprinted by permission of the publisher and author.)

Clearly, the habit of diving for food is only one element in the feeding repertoires of the rats that exhibit it, and it is conceivable that rats would prefer not to dive in water for food if alternative sources of nutrition were available to them. In the next experiment the frequency of diving behavior in rats was examined as a function of the availability of alternative means of acquiring food. Each wild rat subject was placed in a diving enclosure and trained to dive for three chocolates per day in 15 cm of water while maintained on a 3-hr/day feeding schedule (Purina Laboratory Chow offered in its living cage). After each subject had learned to dive for chocolates, Purina Chow was made available ad lib in its living cage for 30 days. At the end of the period of ad lib feeding, each subject was returned to a 3-hr/day feeding schedule.

Fig. 6.13 shows the mean percentage of available chocolates eaten by subjects on each day of the experiment. As can be seen in the figure, even rats that have acquired the habit of diving for food will not do so if an adequate supply of food is available on land. This result is especially striking given that wild rats exhibit a strong preference for chocolate over Purina Laboratory Chow in a simple choice situation. The present result thus suggests that most rats living near water may, in fact, have acquired the habit of diving for food, but that they

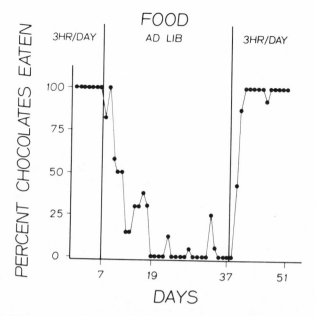

FIG. 6.13. Percentage of available chocolates retrieved from the diving-pool floor by wild rats on a 3 hr/day feeding schedule and while on ad lib food. (Galef, 1980. Copyright 1980 by the American Psychological Association. Reprinted by permission of the publisher and author.)

only exhibit diving behavior if they lack adequate alternative rations within their home ranges.

Although the data presented cannot be interpreted as showing that social learning of the behavior of diving in shallow water for food is unimportant in natural settings, they do suggest that the effects of environmental variables on diving behavior need to be examined in the wild before the social learning hypothesis is accepted. In particular, it would be valuable to know whether adult individuals trapped from nondiving colonies living along the Po River would spontaneously exhibit diving behavior in the laboratory when placed on a restricted feeding schedule. It would also be useful to know whether introduction of an alternative food source into the home-ranges of diving colonies along the Po would inhibit further diving.

Field observations are, in fact, consistent with the hypothesis that relative availability of alternative food sources within a colony's home range accounts for much of the intercolony variability in diving behavior. For example, Gandolfi and Parisi (1973) have reported that at those locations where predation on molluscs was observed, molluscs represent "one of the main sources if not the main source of food for rats" (p. 69). Gandolfi and Parisi (1974) have also found that "the time devoted by rats to mollusc capture depends greatly on the availability of other foods" (p. 102). Thus, laboratory data call attention to aspects of the field data that were not salient to the field observers themselves, field data that suggest that a nonsocial mechanism may underlie the observed intercolony variability in diving behavior observed in nature.

CONCLUSION

The message inherent in the preceding examples is that, although the existence of traditional patterns of behavior in social groups of free-living animals would seem to provide prima facie evidence of an important role of social learning in the acquisition of behavior, it is as true today as it was in Romanes' time that simple observation of behavior in nature is not adequate to determine its origins or causes. For example, recent observations are consistent with the view that one of the most frequently cited examples of culturally transmitted behavior in animals, the washing of sweet potatoes in salt water by the macaques of Koshima Island (Kawai, 1965; Kawamura, 1959), may be maintained and propogated by processes other than intraspecific social ones. Green (1975) has reported that the long-time caretakers of the Koshima Island monkeys, when showing the troop to researchers and tourists, preferentially present sweet potatoes to those troop members known to exhibit washing behavior. As sweet potatoes are only available to the island monkeys in this context, differential reinforcement by the caretaker rather than "culture" may be responsible for the maintenance of washing behavior in the troop. Green further suggests that, because the troop is spatially organized in matrilineal groups, the propagation of sweet potato washing along family lines may have been guided by the enhanced probability of relatives of "washers" remaining close to them and therefore coming close to the provisioner, the source of sweet potatoes and reinforcement for washing. The importance of a human agency in the propagation and maintenance of this "traditional" behavior remains to be determined.

Some of the intriguing differences in behavior to be found in different populations of a species may be the result of social processes, others are probably not. The only way to determine which is which is, as Thorndike proposed, to examine phenomena of interest in controlled settings.

Experimental animal psychology in North America began with analysis of the processes underlying acquisition of a pattern of behavior observed in free-living animals. In the intervening 80 years, the techniques and theory of experimental psychology have matured immensely; yet we know little more today of the determinants of the development of naturally occurring behaviors of interest than we did in 1894. It is time to return to study of some of the intriguing questions that were the proximal stimulus for the initiation of animal psychology as an experimental discipline.

ACKNOWLEDGMENTS

Preparation of this chapter was greatly facilitated by funds from the Natural Science and Engineering Research Council of Canada and the McMaster University Research Board. I thank the faculty and staff of the Department of Psychology of the University of Colorado at Boulder both for their warm hospitality and for provision of resources during the preparation of the manuscript. I also thank Jerry Rudy, Mertice Clark, and Jeffrey Alberts for their most helpful discussions of earlier drafts.

REFERENCES

Austin, O. L. (1948). Predation by the common rat (*Rattus norvegicus*) in the Cape Cod colonies of nesting terns. *Bird-Banding, 19*, 60–65.

Bandura, A. (1962). Social learning through imitation. In M. R. Jones (Ed.), *Nebraska Symposium on Motivation*. Lincoln: University of Nebraska Press.

Church, R. (1957). Transmission of learned behavior between rats. *Journal of Abnormal and Social Psychology, 54*, 163–165.

Cottam, C. (1948). Aquatic habits of the Norway rat. *Journal of Mammalogy, 29*, 299.

Darwin, C. R. (1884). Posthumous essay on instinct. In G. J. Romanes (Ed.), *Mental evolution in animals*. New York: D. Appleton & Co.

Galef, B. G., Jr. (1976). The social transmission of acquired behavior: A discussion of tradition and social learning in vertebrates. In J. S. Rosenblatt, R. H. Hinde, E. Shaw, & C. Beer (Eds.), *Advances in the study of behavior* (Vol. 6). New York: Academic Press.

Galef, B. G., Jr. (1977). Mechanisms for the social transmission of food preferences from adult to weanling rats. In L. M. Barker, M. Best, & M. Domjan (Eds.), *Learning mechanisms in food selection*. Waco: Baylor University Press.

Galef, B. G., Jr. (1980). Diving for food: Analysis of a possible case of social learning in wild rats (*Rattus norvegicus*). *Journal of Comparative and Physiological Psychology, 94*, 416–425.

Galef, B. G., Jr., & Clark, M. M. (1971a). Social factors in the poison avoidance and feeding behavior of wild and domesticated rat pups. *Journal of Comparative and Physiological Psychology, 75*, 341–357.

Galef, B. G., Jr., & Clark, M. M. (1971b). Parent–offspring interactions determine time and place of first ingestion of solid food by wild rat pups. *Psychonomic Science, 25*, 15–16.

Galef, B. G., Jr., & Clark, M. M. (1972). Mother's milk and adult presence: Two factors determining initial dietary selection by weaning rats. *Journal of Comparative and Physiological Psychology, 78*, 213–219.

Galef, B. G., Jr., & Heiber, L. (1976). The role of residual olfactory cues in the determination of feeding site selection and exploration patterns of domestic rats. *Journal of Comparative and Physiological Psychology, 90*, 727–739.

Galef, B. G., Jr., & Henderson, P. W. (1972). Mother's milk: A determinant of the feeding preferences of rat pups. *Journal of Comparative and Physiological Psychology, 78*, 213–219.

Galef, B. G., Jr., & Sherry, D. F. (1973). Mother's milk: A medium for the transmission of cues reflecting the flavor of mother's diet. *Journal of Comparative and Physiological Psychology, 83*, 374–378.

Gandolfi, G., & Parisi, V. (1972). Predazione su *Unio pictorum* L. da parte del ratto, *Rattus norvegicus* (Berkenhout). *Acta Naturalia, 8*, 1–27.

Gandolfi, G., & Parisi, V. (1973). Ethological aspects of predation by rats, *Rattus norvegicus* (Berkenhout) on bivalves, *Unio pictorum* L. and *Cerastoderma lamarcki* (Reeve). *Bollettino di Zoologia, 40*, 60–74.

Gould, S. J. (1977). Darwin's sea change, In S. J. Gould (Ed.), *Ever since Darwin*. New York: Norton.

Green, S. (1975). Dialects in Japanese monkeys. *Zeitschrift fur Tierpsychologie, 38*, 305–314.

Kawai, M. (1965). Newly acquired precultural behavior of Japanese monkeys. *Primates, 6*, 1–30.

Kawamura, S. (1959). Sub-culture propogation among Japanese macaques. *Primates, 2*, 43–60.

Morgan, C. L. (1896). *Habit and instinct*. London: Edward Arnold.

Norman, F. I. (1975). The murine rodents *Rattus rattus, exulans,* and *norvegicus* as avian predators. *Atoll Research Bulletin, No. 182*, 1–13.

Parisi, V., & Gandolfi, G. (1974). Further aspects of the predation by rats on various mollusc species. *Bollettino di Zoologia, 41*, 87–106.

Romanes, G. J. (1881). *Animal intelligence*. London: Kegan Paul.

Romanes, G. J. (1884). *Mental evolution in animals*. New York: D. Appleton & Co.

Steiniger, F. von. (1950). Beitrage zur Soziologie und sonstigen Biologie der Wanderratte. *Zeitschrift fur Tierpsychologie, 7*, 356–379.

Thorndike, E. L. (1911). *Animal intelligence:* An experimental study of association processes in animals. New York: MacMillan.

7 Restraints on Ground Squirrel Antipredator Behavior: Adjustments over Multiple Time Scales

Richard G. Coss and Donald H. Owings
Department of Psychology
University of California, Davis

Not only by migration intó other habitats, but also by changes, inorganic and organic, within its own habitat, does each species suffer from failures of adjustment. But mis-adjustment inevitably sets up re-adjustment. Those individuals in whom the likes and dislikes happen to be most out of harmony with the new circumstances, are the first to disappear. (Spencer, 1888, I, p. 281)

As used by Spencer, the term adjustment referred to both immediate and cumulative changes in organism–environment correspondence at the individual level and, with failures of adjustment, cumulative changes at the populational level. With the emergence of general process learning theory (Seligman, 1970) several decades later, Spencer's notion of adjustment had left its legacy in the theoretical development of associative learning, albeit stripped of its evolutionary and ecological context. This context, however, is presently being revived by a number of workers as more and more studies reveal differential predispositions for learning among various taxa (e.g., Bolles, 1970, 1975; Garcia & Koelling, 1966; Hinde, 1973; Marler, Dooling, & Zoloth, 1980; Rozin & Kalat, 1971; Seligman, 1970). These learning propensities are typically viewed as mediated by specific mechanisms that are the products of the process of natural selection. We, like Reed (this volume), are skeptical about the utility of this product–process dichotomy between proximate and ultimate explanations of behavior. An alternative is to view behavior as a facet of a process of adjustment over multiple time scales extending in a hierarchy from immediate to phylogenetic time. In such a view, the processes of immediate behavioral adjustment have been structured during phylogeny, but at the same time characterize the behavioral phenotype currently participating in the process of natural selection. Thus each level of the hierarchy is in two-way interaction with all other levels, i.e., proximate and ultimate considerations are inseparable (Hennessy, 1982; Webster & Goodwin, 1982; Wimsatt, 1980).

Learning is one level of behavioral adjustment that falls into the proximate realm. We contend that this level of adjustment can better be understood when treated as embedded in its ecological and evolutionary context. Our primary goal in this chapter is not to deal directly with learning per se, but to describe a context—ground squirrel antipredator behavior—in which learning can profitably be studied from an ecological perspective.

Ground squirrels adjust their antipredator behavior in appropriate and complex ways to the diversity of predators that eat them. Such diversity can be examined in natural and laboratory settings. Further, ground squirrel ecology, systematics, and evolutionary biology have been studied by a number of workers, thus providing the relevant background for assessing complex organism–environment relationships over multiple time scales.

ADJUSTMENTS OF ANTIPREDATOR BEHAVIOR OVER MULTIPLE TIME SCALES

North American ground squirrels are thought to have evolved from tree squirrels by the late Oligocene (Black, 1963, 1972) with more modern forms of *Spermophilus* appearing in the mid-Miocene (Bryant, 1945). Divergence from tree squirrels was probably a response to arid climatic conditions throughout the Miocene during which trees were replaced by extensive grasslands (Wolfe & Hopkins, 1967). By the end of the Miocene, 5 million years ago, ground squirrels had radiated extensively throughout North America and by mid-Pliocene times fossils with strong affinities to extant California populations (*Spermophilus beecheyi*) appeared in the Great Basin, ranging as far south as Arizona (Bryant, 1945).

Prairie dogs (*Cynomys* spp.) diverged from primitive spermophiles by late-Miocene times (Bryant, 1945), becoming more adapted to grassy savannah conditions well into Pliocene times. Essentially modern *Spermophilus* and *Cynomys* genera appear in the early to middle Pleistocene, one of which, (*Spermophilus beecheyi*) emphasized in this chapter, has retained archaic morphological traits similar to those of its mid-Pliocene progenitors.

A number of potential ground squirrel predators achieved relatively modern form by the late Pliocene and they appear with squirrels as sympatric fossils in a number of lower to middle Pleistocene field sites. These predators include rattlesnakes (Brattstrom, 1955; Klauber, 1972), hawks, falcons, wolves, bobcats, badgers, and weasels (Hansen & Begg, 1970; Miller, 1912). Some of these predators have constituted major sources of natural selection on ground squirrels for more than a million years and must have consistently shaped successful adjustments of antipredator behavior. Successful antipredator behavior by ground squirrels must in turn have acted as potent sources of selection shaping congruent predatory behaviors. This interplay of predatory and antipredatory behaviors ultimately produced a number of complex, coevolved predator–prey behavior systems. In this chapter we emphasize one of these systems—the antisnake behavior of ground squirrels. Our description of this system emphasizes adjustments in antisnake behavior over phylogenetic, ontogenetic, and proximate time scales.

Phylogenetic Adjustments

Antipredator behavior differs according to the type of coevolved predator–prey behavior system. For example, ground squirrels and snakes appear to have coevolved a number of unique interactive relationships since snakes began to act as major squirrel predators in the Miocene. In contrast to other predators of ground squirrels, snakes move slowly and depend almost exclusively on ambush. Because squirrels can approach snakes safely, encounters between squirrels and snakes may be prolonged in ways analogous in many respects to intraspecific agonistic interactions. During such interactions, variation in the form and application of antipredator behavior might differentially influence the outcome of the encounter. If such outcomes differentially affect inclusive fitness, selection would shape the squirrels' interactive styles although not necessarily to their optima (see Darlington, 1977; Gould, 1980, 1982; Gould & Lewontin, 1979: Lewontin & Levins, 1978; Van Valen, 1973). More importantly, long periods of selection by snakes over phylogenetic time might result in canalized development of antisnake behavior (Bateson, 1976; Coss, 1979a; Waddington, 1957), in such a way that the potential for antisnake behavior might survive intermittent intervals of relaxed selection, i.e., when snakes are absent. Such persistence of canalized epigenetic processes would act as a higher order restraint on ontogenetic and proximate adjustments. To study such persistence, one needs to compare the antisnake behavior of different genera, species, subspecies, and populations of ground squirrels with different histories of snake predation.

Our research on antisnake behavior has focused on comparisons among the following ground squirrel populations: (1) ground squirrels experiencing predation from both rattlesnakes and nonvenomous gopher and bull snakes; (2) ground squirrels experiencing gopher snake predation only; and (3) ground squirrels that have lived in a snake-free habitat for several million years. In addition to behavioral comparisons, we have used electrophoresis and fossil and geological time markers to generate a calibrated molecular clock for estimating times of population divergence (Smith & Coss, 1984; Smith, Bonn–Poran, & Coss, in preparation).

Ontogenetic Adjustments

The development of behavioral systems is an epigenetic process involving the dynamic interaction of genetic, physiological, morphological, and experiential factors (see Rosenblatt, Siegel, & Mayer, 1979). Epigenesis is in turn restrained by phylogenetic adjustments. An illustration of this type of restraint is the expectancy about song structure (auditory template) that guides the development of song in white-crowned sparrows (Marler, 1976).

Our laboratory studies indicate that snake-inexperienced ground squirrels have expectancies about snakes that guide their initial snake experiences and therefore probably affect the subsequent development of antisnake behavior (Coss & Owings, 1978; also see Marler, Dooling, & Zoloth, 1980). Newly weaned pups, for example, appear to expect snakes in particular types of appropriate microhabitats, e.g., tall grass and dark holes. When approaching these topographic features, these pups have a low threshold for signaling "snake" by tail-flagging. On occasions when snakes are present, this behavior can recruit the mother, whose intervention both protects the pup and provides a learning opportunity that moves the pup toward greater self-sufficiency in dealing with snakes. Although pups are not competent in dealing with snakes by the self-sufficient standards of adults, they are clearly quite adept at recruiting adult help during snake enounters. Pups are not imperfect adults but work very competently within the constraints of their current developmental stage. Thus, development is a hierarchical process of ontogenetic adjustment (Riedl, 1977), each stage of which has been shaped by natural selection (Chen, Coss, & Goldthwaite, 1983; Dobzhansky, 1956; Galef, 1981; Mason, 1979).

Proximate Adjustments

Within the hierarchy of time scales over which adjustment occurs, the most rapid range of adjustments occur at the proximate level. The proximate level itself can be subdivided into multiple rates of change that grade into the ontogenetic level. Like increases in heart rate on reaching alpine elevations, some proximate behavioral adjustments track their circumstances in very immediate ways. California ground squirrels, for example, change their pattern of calling when a mammalian predator switches from walking to running (Owings & Hennessy, 1984).

Other kinds of proximate behavioral adjustments require more time, in ways analogous to the somatic process of acclimation to alpine elevations (see Bateson, 1979, pp. 170–175). European blackbirds, for example, learn to treat an unfamiliar, nonthreatening bird as threatening after perceiving another blackbird mobbing it (Curio, Ernst, & Vieth, 1978). A series of such specific learning episodes can result in the learning of higher order rules, such as learning sets (Harlow, 1949). This longest term of the preceding three levels of proximate adjustment takes us into the realm of ontogeny. Such higher order rules place restraints on subsequent specific learning experiences. Therefore, specific proximate adjustments are restrained by prior ontogenetic adjustments that in turn are restrained by phylogeny, much as momentary changes in human speech are restrained by previous language learning that is guided by an innate syntax (Chomsky, 1965).

One of the major effects of phylogenetic change is to limit the total amount of adjustability in the form of behavior. Different phylogenetic histories can lead to different amounts of adjustability. A relevant comparison can be made between white-crowned sparrows and canaries that differ in their subsequent sensitivity to feedback from singing activity after their songs have stabilized during the first year (Marler, 1976).

Given such phylogenetic limitations on ontogenetic and proximate adjustability, each adjustment by an individual reduces the total remaining adjustability in the form of the behavior. Such declining adjustability is illustrated by the age-related decline in the mynah bird's ability to imitate sounds, which correlates with age-related reductions in neuroanatomical adjustability (Rausch & Scheich, 1982). Similar age-related reductions in neural plasticity appear in species as phylogenetically distant as honeybees and cichlid fish (Brandon & Coss, 1982; Burgess & Coss, 1981, 1982; Coss, Brandon, & Globus, 1980). This delimitation, based on the history of previous neural substrate adjustments, could conceivably stabilize the operation of behavioral "programs" by converting relatively "open" programs into relatively "closed" ones (see Coss & Brandon, 1982; Mayr, 1974, 1976; Plotkin & Odling–Smee, 1979).

Patterns of behavior that are used under conditions of great urgency are likely to have been shaped by selection for minimal initial adjustability so that they occur reliably on first use (Alcock, 1979; Coss, 1979a; Coss & Brandon, 1982; Owings & Coss, 1977). On the other hand, high adjustability of behavioral patterns is likely to have evolved for less urgent contexts (see Coss, 1979a). Such adjustability permits fine tuning of expectancies about environmental conditions of relatively high variability during phylogeny.

Phylogenetic restraints on adjustability are imposed at multiple levels of behavioral organization (Bateson, 1979), e.g., at the level of both form and application to specific environmental circumstances (Manning, 1979, p. 47). With respect to birds, the initial canalized learning of star patterns in the northern sky (Emlen, 1970) is subsequently applied to a canalized process of migration, which itself involves learning to navigate to specific overwintering sites (Perdeck, 1958, 1964). Similarly, the movements of ground squirrels following playback of "alarm" vocalizations suggests that they engage continually in the proximate adjustment process of keeping track of where they are relative to burrow refuges (Leger, Owings, & Boal, 1979). Such tracking of location probably involves the application of a "cognitive map" developed during the pups' active exploration of the topographic features of their home range (see Calhoun, 1962, p. 72; Menzel, 1978; Tolman, 1948). The ontogeny of cognitive maps, in turn, is likely to be guided by phylogenetic adjustments with respect to the valence of particular topographic features, such as burrows. Snake-inexperienced ground squirrels, for example, behave as though they expect to encounter snakes in burrows (Coss & Owings, 1978).

In the remainder of this chapter, we describe the relationship between ground squirrels and the snakes that eat them. The phylogenetic antiquity of these relationships suggests that the process of ontogenetic and proximate adjustments, such as learning, is likely to be deeply canalized. Such a system could provide ecological depth to the concept of biological boundaries of learning (Seligman & Hager, 1972).

GROUND SQUIRREL ANTISNAKE BEHAVIOR

We have studied squirrel–snake interactions in California ground squirrels (*Spermophilus beecheyi*), Arctic ground squirrels (*S. parryii ablusus*) from Alaska, and Black-tailed prairie dogs (*Cynomys ludovicianus*) in Oklahoma and Wyoming. Sympatric snake species selected for study were the Pacific gopher snake (*Pituophis melanoleucus catenifer*) and Northern Pacific rattlesnake (*Crotalus viridis oreganus*), both of which are common predators of California ground squirrels. The garter snake (*Thamnophis elegans*), which is not a predatory threat, was included for comparative purposes to avoid possible injury to young squirrels. Black-tailed prairie dogs were exposed to their probable snake predators, the Prairie rattlesnake (*C. v. viridis*), Western diamondback rattlesnake (*C. atrox*), and bull snake (*P. m. sayi*).

Although gopher snakes are active predators on young California ground squirrels, rattlesnakes inhabiting the Coast Range and Sierra foothills constitute the greatest danger (Fitch, 1948, 1949; Grinnell & Dixon, 1918; Linsdale, 1946). These snakes live in close association with squirrels because they enter squirrel burrows to forage, to regulate body temperature, and to escape potential danger (Klauber, 1972). Snakes tend to hunt as mobile ambushers, a predatory strategy dependent on surprise. Once detected by ground squirrels, snakes pose a distinct sort of threat because they are slow moving and easily circumvented. Although pups are most vulnerable to snakes, adult squirrels are also at risk. Large rattlesnakes, gopher snakes, and bull snakes are capable of eating adult ground squirrels; smaller rattlesnakes can kill ground squirrels too large to eat (unpublished observations). The risk goes both ways, however. Ground squirrels are known to kill small gopher snakes by pouncing on them and biting them, and to entomb large rattlesnakes and gopher snakes in burrows by plugging alleys and entrances (Fitch, 1948; Halpin, 1983; Merriam, 1901).

General Form of Antisnake Behavior

Our field studies typically employ portable video recorders and cameras equipped with telephoto zoom lenses (Hennessy, Owings, Rowe, Coss, & Leger, 1981; Owings & Coss, 1977; Owings & Owings, 1979). In addition to observing natural encounters with snakes, we also placed anesthetized snakes and tethered snakes near burrow systems (e.g., Hennessy et al., 1981).

When squirrels first detect snakes above ground, their posture rapidly changes into one in which the legs are positioned for evasive leaping. If it approaches the snake, the squirrel often elongates its body and advances cautiously, periodically bobbing its head to gather distance information. Sudden movement by the snake is followed by rapid withdrawal by the squirrel, often in a manner that permits continued visual monitoring of the snake's activity (Owings & Coss, 1977, 1981).

After a rattlesnake is detected by a lone California ground squirrel, the ensuing activity may attract other squirrels who approach cautiously, sniffing nearby burrow entrances as they advance. Lone snake-directed squirrels may attract other squirrels by vigorously moving their tails (tail-flagging) in temporally clumped bouts, each consisting of several cycles of back-and-forth movement (see Hennessy et al., 1981). As other squirrels arrive at the scene, their tail movements shift from periodic 1-cycle tail-flagging bouts to clumped multicycled bouts like those of the first squirrel. Once other squirrels are recruited and initiate close-range interactions with the snake, the squirrel who first detected the snake may retire, moving a short distance away while emitting periodic 1-cycle tail-flagging bouts indicative of less snake-directed behavior (Fig. 7.1). This squirrel, however, continues to monitor the activity of those squirrels nearest the snake that are vigorously tail-flagging. Tail-flagging is a variable signal that affords information about the snake's proximity and other details of any squirrel–snake

FIG. 7.1.   Harassment of a tethered rattlesnake by five California ground squirrels (reconstructed from video recordings). Squirrels on the far left and right are exhibiting elongate postures and vigorously tail-flagging. The top middle squirrel is kicking loose substrate repeatedly at the snake. The bottom middle squirrel, which is eating, was first to detect the snake and her subsequent harassment activity attracted the other squirrels.

interaction. Tail-flagging is therefore a clear example of behavior that is prox-
imately adjusted in accordance with changes in circumstances.

Snake-directed behavior by California ground squirrels has a number of features that clearly could be characterized as harassment. For example, squirrels
approach rattlesnakes and gopher snakes very closely with pilomotor-erected
pelage, especially the tail hairs. Approach movements often have stalking qualities, such as slow deliberate advances interrupted with pauses, head-bobbing,
and vigorous tail flagging. Some approaches to tethered rattlesnakes observed
in the field are so close that the squirrel's nose almost touches the snakes's snout.
Prolonged staring (Coss, 1978, 1979b) may enhance the intimidating appearance
of the squirrel who continues to approach until very close. However, such close
proximity with associated head-bobbing may actually entice striking; the squirrel
then jumps dramatically away from the snake (Fig. 7.2). Curiously, slow-motion
video analyses have revealed unequivocal evidence of contact by rattlesnakes,
but usually without evidence that the squirrel was envenomated. However, squirrels
can be killed if they fail to break away quickly from embedded fangs. Biochemical research has shown that California ground squirrels have evolved serum
components with venom-neutralizing properties, an adaptation that would protect

FIG. 7.2. California ground squirrel leaping back after being struck by the rattlesnake. The snake has just released the squirrel after holding on for 67 msec.
Such evasive leaping by ground squirrels, which limits the amount of enven-
omation, has coevolved with the ability to neutralize rattlesnake venom. Illustration
by Richard G. Coss.

squirrels struck briefly by rattlesnakes (Bonn–Poran, Coss, & Benjamini, in preparation).

Another strategy of snake harassment occurs when squirrels encounter snakes on loose dirt near burrow entrances. California ground squirrels approach in rapid lurching advances and kick loose substrate at the snake using the forepaws (Coss & Owings, 1978; Owings & Coss, 1977). Between bouts of substrate-kicking, the squirrel may gather more material by digging. Black-tailed prairie dogs are known to use their hind legs for kicking loose substrate at snakes (Halpin, 1983). Snakes hit by successive volleys of dirt or sand may strike wildly, usually missing the squirrel. Snakes strike more at young squirrels during substrate-kicking bouts than they do at adults, possibly because young squirrels approach more closely to kick substrate or kick less effectively. Because substrate-kicking is followed by jumping backwards or sideways, we infer that the squirrel anticipates the snake's striking at close range (Coss & Owings, 1978).

Systematic Experimental and Comparative Research

Our observations of squirrel–snake interactions prompted more systematic field and laboratory research. The following questions were formulated about ground squirrel antisnake behavior: (1) How does antisnake behavior differ among populations with different histories of selection from snakes? (2) Is the development of expectancies about snakes and their behavioral potential in different microhabitats highly canalized? (3) How do different genera of ground squirrels differ in antisnake behavior? (4) How do ground squirrels adjust their antisnake behavior to changes in circumstances?

Rattlesnake-Exposed Versus Rattlesnake-Free Populations. We compared adults from two populations of Douglas ground squirrels (*S. b. douglasii*). One population was trapped in the California Coast Range foothills (near Capay, Yolo Co.), an area abundant in both rattlesnakes and gopher snakes; the other population was trapped 48 km SE on the floor of the Sacramento Valley at field sites on the University of California, Davis campus. Rattlesnakes have never been reported on the floor of the Sacramento Valley, but gopher snakes are frequently observed in uncultivated fields. The Davis and Coast Range populations diverged about 3,000 years ago, an estimate derived from two calibrating time markers (Smith & Coss, 1984; Eugene Begg, personal communication). Divergence was probably initiated by the wetter climatic conditions that followed the dryer, stable period after the Wisconsin (Etkins & Epstein, 1982; Johnson, 1977; Shackleton & Opdyke, 1976) when Coast Range ground squirrels presumably dispersed onto the floor of the Sacramento Valley; barriers to further dispersal were maintained by periodic flooding and poor drainage of lowland areas separating the Davis and Coast Range populations. Prior to extensive flood control, Grinnell and Dixon (1918) reported that the floor of the Sacramento Valley contained only widely separated colonies of Douglas ground squirrels. Due to poor habitat conditions separating Davis and Coast Range ground squirrels, selection from rattlesnakes has probably been absent since the time of squirrel population divergence.

For comparative purposes, a third ground squirrel population was selected for study. This population comprised Fisher ground squirrels (*S. b. fisheri*), a closely related subspecies living in an area abundant in rattlesnakes and gopher snakes. These squirrels were trapped in the Sierra foothills at the San Joaquin Experimental Range (Madera Co.), where squirrels constitute 69% of the diet of rattlesnakes (Fitch, 1948). Separated by the Sacramento and San Joaquin rivers and concomitant flood plain, Douglas and Fisher ground squirrels diverged more than 0.5 million years ago (Smith, Bonn–Poran, & Coss, in preparation).

Laboratory studies of squirrel–snake interactions employed two experimental rooms (2.53 by 2.43 m and 2.43 by 2.9 m), each containing 5 cm of sand to simulate a natural substrate. Squirrels were given a 24-hour period of habituation to these rooms just prior to introducing the snake. Overhead wide-angle mirrors afforded close-up video recordings of 10-minute interactions with a Northern Pacific rattlesnake, Pacific gopher snake, and a California garter snake. The results of our initial experiment supported the contention that Douglas ground squirrels from Davis would show less conservative antisnake behavior indicative of phylogenetic adjustments to a rattlesnake-free habitat (Fig. 7.3; Owings & Coss, 1977). Compared with the more rattlesnake-adapted Douglas and Fisher ground squirrels, the Davis population experiencing relaxed selection typically approached all the snakes more frequently. Douglas ground squirrels from Davis were particularly aggressive toward their natural predator, the gopher snake, which they frequently pounced on and attempted to bite.

Because the above-ground squirrel populations were wild-caught, there was no way of knowing whether they had gained previous experience in dealing with snakes. We therefore decided to compare the behavior of lab-reared, rattlesnake-adapted Fisher ground squirrels with that of less adapted Douglas ground squirrels from Davis. As depicted in Fig. 7.3, wild-caught Fisher ground squirrels had shown the most conservative snake-directed behavior, whereas the Douglas ground squirrels from Davis were the least conservative. Assuming that selection from venomous snakes had shaped the conservative behavior of Fisher ground squirrels, lab-reared Fisher ground squirrels were expected to deal with snakes much more conservatively than lab-reared Douglas ground squirrels from Davis (Owings & Coss, 1977).

Young squirrels of each subspecies were born and reared in outdoor field pens. Prior to the experiment, they had no opportunity to dig or move sand. Because of their assumed vulnerability to gopher snakes and rattlesnakes, these young squirrels were exposed only to a California garter snake and an animate

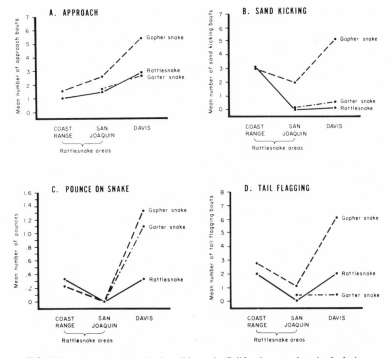

FIG. 7.3.   Antisnake behavior by wild-caught California ground squirrels during 10-minute interactions with snakes in a laboratory setting (N = 9 squirrels/group). Rattlesnake less-adapted Douglas (Davis) ground squirrels approached the gopher snake a significantly greater number of times than did the rattlesnake-adapted Douglas (Coast Range) ground squirrels (A, $p < .05$). Overall, the Davis ground squirrels attacked the snakes significantly more frequently than either the rattle-snake-adapted Douglas (Coast Range) or Fisher (San Joaquin) ground squirrels (C, $p < .05$).

control object, comprising a white rat in an amorphous green nylon bag. The bag was tied to a nylon string and could be jerked forward to stimulate the lurching movement of a striking snake. As in the initial experiment, each squirrel was given a 24-hour period to habituate to the novel experiment room conditions.

The results of this study revealed that snake-inexperienced pups exhibited antisnake behavior remarkably similar to that of wild-caught adults. As expected, rattlesnake-adapted Fisher pups acted very conservatively toward the garter snake compared with the less adapted Davis pups. In keeping with this conservative behavior, Fisher pups were also less likely than the Davis pups to approach the animate bag containing the white rat (Fig. 7.4). Compared with the bag condition, pups from both populations kicked sand much more often at the snake, a behavior that seems to characterize snake harassment.

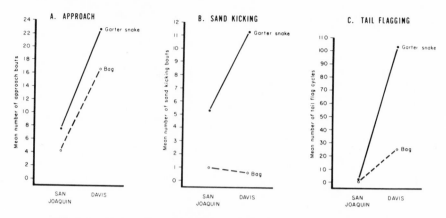

FIG. 7.4.   Comparisons of six young snake-inexperienced Fisher ground squirrels (San Joaquin), which are frequent prey of rattlesnakes and gopher snakes, and six Douglas ground squirrels (Davis) from a rattlesnake-free area during 10-minute encounters with a garter snake and a novel animate bag containing a rat. The behavior of the Douglas pups was relatively snake specific, i.e., they exhibited adult-like antisnake behavior significantly more to the snake than to the bag (B, $p < .05$; C, $p < .01$). For the snake condition only, Douglas pups (A) approached and (C) tail-flagged significantly more at the snake ($p < .025$) than the Fisher pups did.

Young Versus Adults.   We also compared the behavior of pups with adults from the same populations and found that pups engaged in many more sand-kicking and tail-flagging bouts (Fig. 7.5). On the basis of these laboratory results, we expected to find that pups in the field would also interact more readily with snakes than adults would. However, our expectations were not confirmed. In the field, pups were usually accompanied by adults and remained farther away while adults dealt directly with the snakes. The pups did participate by watching the adults, tail-flagging, and vocalizing. In this context, the adults provide the pups with potential sources of information about how to deal with snakes not unlike that observed for the cultural transmission of antipredator behavior in birds (Curio, Ernst, & Vieth, 1978) and perhaps primates (Seyfarth & Cheney, 1980).

The contrast between snake-directed behavior by young squirrels in the field and laboratory may be more profitably viewed as a proximate adjustment to differing situational restraints, rather than simply an aberrant product of laboratory conditions. Substrate kicking is a form of defensive burying behavior seen in other rodents in the absence of an effective escape route (see Pinel, Treit, Ladak, & MacLennan, 1980). It is therefore not surprising that ground squirrels, notably the young, kick sand vigorously at snakes in a small room. But not all lab–field differences are so readily viewed as cases of adaptive adjustability. Tail-flagging, for example, is as variable in the laboratory as in the field. As

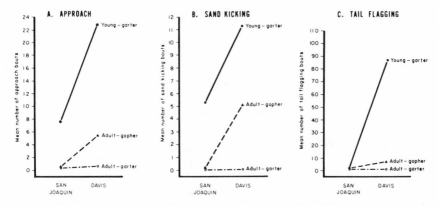

FIG. 7.5.   Comparisons of nine wild-caught Fisher ground squirrels (San Joaquin) and nine Douglas ground squirrels (Davis) described in Fig. 7.3 with the young snake-inexperienced Fisher and Douglas ground squirrels described in Fig. 7.4. The young squirrels (A) approached ($p < .005$), (B) sand-kicked ($p < .01$), and (C) tail-flagged ($p < .005$) significantly more during encounters with a garter snake than the adults did during encounters with either a garter snake or gopher snake.

mentioned earlier, in the field such variability has clear situational correlates. In the laboratory, such variability fails to correlate with changing situations, i.e., it is simply "noise." In keeping with these examples of differences in laboratory and field studies, it is important to consider the advantages and disadvantages of gathering data in each situation. For example, our laboratory video setup provided an unrestricted view of all reciprocal squirrel–snake activities, which could be quantified with much greater resolution than those provided by video recordings in the field. Laboratory study thus provides increased precision in analyzing squirrel–snake interactions at a cost of reduced ability to infer generality to naturally occurring conditions.

Encounters in Burrows.   There is one situational context in which laboratory research is imperative—the study of snake-directed behavior in burrows. Rattlesnakes and gopher snakes are burrow predators, at times taking squirrel pups prior to their emergence (Bill Longhurst, personal communication). Encounters with snakes in burrows would increase the risk to squirrels because of the loss of visual information so important for evasive maneuvers. Squirrels would not be able to judge distance as effectively using auditory and olfactory cues, and narrow burrows restrain movement.

Anecdotes from field observations indicate that squirrels quickly leave burrows or refuse to enter burrows containing rattlesnakes (Fitch, 1948; Linsdale, 1946; Klauber, 1972; Tevis, 1943). Snakes found in burrow entrances may be harassed by vigorous substrate-kicking into the burrow entrances. Both prairie dogs and

California ground squirrels have been observed to entomb snakes by plugging burrow entrances (Halpin, 1983; Klauber, 1972; Merriam, 1901). Plugging activity deeper in the burrow is also reported (Klauber, 1972; Linsdale, 1946).

We examined squirrel–snake interactions in this context by constructing an artificial burrow system comprising horizontal maze-like, sand-filled alleys and two exits that could be sealed (Coss & Owings, 1978). Behavior was recorded on video tape using a low-light infrared camera. An overhead mirror provided a plan view of the burrow alleys. Comparisons were made of behavioral organization of young snake-inexperienced Fisher ground squirrels under conditions in which a gopher snake and white rat, in separate trials, were introduced into the burrow. Exploratory research also examined the behavior of several squirrels encountering a rattlesnake. As in the previous experiments, each squirrel was given a 24-hour habituation period. Squirrels quickly adapted to the artificial burrow, moving quickly through the dark alleys without hesitation. During the night, they invariably plugged both burrow exits, a phenomenon observed in the wild that presumably functions to aid thermoregulation and to prevent squirrel odors and noise from attracting weasels and badgers.

During the formal experiment, a medium-sized gopher snake or a white rat was placed in the burrow and behavior was recorded for 10 minutes after the first interaction. Squirrel behavior directed at the gopher snake differed considerably from that directed at the white rat. For example, the squirrels behaved as if they were particularly sensitive to snake movement as compared with rat movement and they adjusted their proximity accordingly. After initial snake detection, the squirrel directed its efforts at trying to leave the burrow. It rarely did so after interacting with the rat (Fig. 7.6). Following vigorous digging at the sealed burrow exit, the squirrel shifted its behavior mode into one of snake harassment (Fig. 7.7). Typically, the squirrel approached the snake in an elongate posture, pausing intermittently to inspect the adjacent alley before proceeding. If the snake was in the adjacent alley, the squirrel would quickly turn the corner, kicking sand repeatedly in front of it. Concurrent with this aversive treatment, the gopher snake would strike, often hitting the squirrel as it quickly withdrew back to the adjacent alley. Surprisingly, the snake often advanced toward the squirrel and most of the squirrels retreated to the sealed exit to continue their escape attempts (Fig. 7.7D) In overall comparison with their behavior toward the rat, the squirrels' behavior toward the snake could be characterized as cautious and flight motivated, especially as illustrated by the squirrels' persistent efforts to leave the burrow.

Above-ground antisnake behavior by snake-inexperienced squirrels in laboratory settings shared features similar to those observed below ground, although some differences did emerge. For instance, kicking sand at the snake was more prevalent in the burrow, whereas tail-flagging, an above-ground signal, was rarely observed. Elongate postures during investigative approach were seen frequently both above and below ground. Also in both situations, squirrels were concerned about changes in the snake's location.

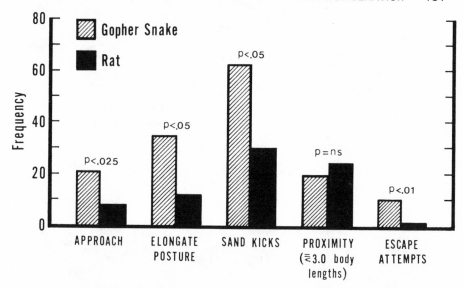

FIG. 7.6. Mean number of behavioral acts by six snake-inexperienced Fisher pups during 10-minute interactions with a gopher snake and rat in the artificial burrow.

Follow-up exploratory burrow research used a rattlesnake in place of a gopher snake. Under this condition, snake-inexperienced squirrels showed much greater alarm after detecting the snake; they exhibited slow deliberate movements followed by active sand-moving behaviors, culminating in the erection of a thick plug separating the animals (see Fig. 7.7E). Unlike the gopher snake condition which yielded burrow plugging in only 1 of 26 trials, burrow plugging occurred in all 3 rattlesnake trials. This preliminary finding suggests that burrow plugging under natural conditions may be a more prevalent response to slower moving, but venomous rattlesnakes, as compared with other snake species.

In summary, it is apparent that both snake-inexperienced young and wild-caught adult ground squirrels exhibited specialized antisnake behaviors. During their first encounter with a snake, young Douglas and Fisher ground squirrels exhibited antisnake behavior remarkably similar to that of wild-caught and presumably snake-experienced adults. The young, however, were much more persistent and this difference between young and adult squirrels may reflect ontogenetic adjustments. Similarities in antisnake behavior in the young and adults also raised questions about whether the observed behaviors were specialized adaptations to snakes and whether population differences were clear indices of phylogenetic adjustments. We considered the possibility that the snake's slow, smooth locomotion and sudden hissing, rattling, and striking behavior would foster approach–withdrawal activity by the squirrel (e.g., Schneirla, 1965). Because the bag containing the rat also displayed slow, undulating snake-like movements as the rat moved about, as well as lurching "striking" movements when squirrels

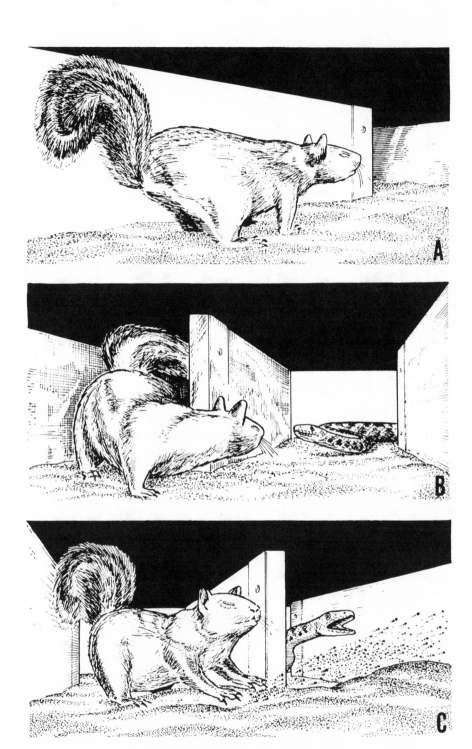

FIG. 7.7. Examples of antisnake behavior in the artificial burrow: A. elongate posture during investigative approach after a gopher snake is detected; B. cautious investigation of an adjacent alley; C. confirming the snake's presence by kicking sand around the corner, which entices gopher snake striking;

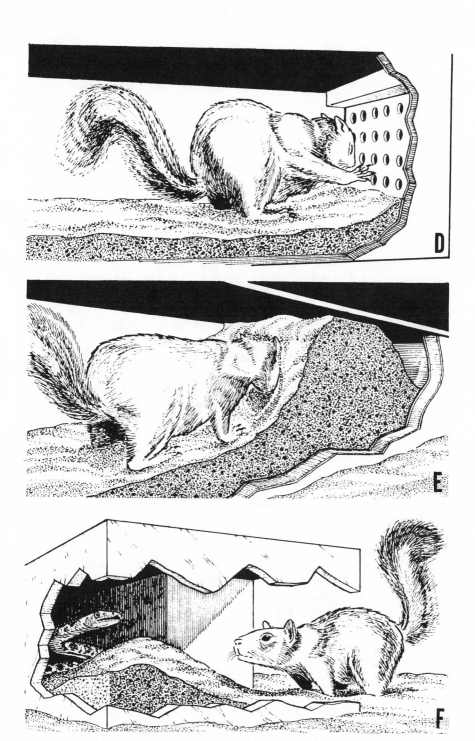

FIG. 7.7 (*continued*) D. attempt to escape from sealed burrow exist; E. plugging burrow alley by butting sand with head after detecting a rattlesnake; F. plugging burrow entrance containing a gopher snake. Illustrations by Richard G. Coss.

approached closely, we considered this to be the appropriate control object lacking in the obvious linear, sinusoidal, and voluted forms that characterized snakes. Despite these similarities in both slow and sudden movement, snake-inexperienced squirrels treated the animate bag differently than they did the snake (Fig. 7.4)

Population from a Snake-Free Habitat.   Another way to investigate phylogenetic specialization of antisnake behavior is to study a species of ground squirrels with no history of snake predation for the last several million years. To address this question, we selected another squirrel population for comparative study, the Arctic ground squirrel from snake-free central Alaska (see Howell, 1938). Arctic and California ground squirrels belong to different subgenera (*Spermophilus* and *Otospermophilus*, respectively) that had already diverged by late Miocene times according to the fossil record (Black, 1963, 1972).

Our electrophoretic analyses (Smith & Coss, 1984) corroborate the fossil evidence and show Arctic and California populations diverging about 5.2 million years ago during a period of late Miocene cooling (Bandy, 1968). We estimate that Arctic ground squirrels and their ancestors have not received selection from snakes for at least 3 million years because: (1) Even during this relatively warm (Holocene) period, no snake species are sympatric with Arctic ground squirrels (compare Burt & Grossenheider, 1964, and Stebbins, 1966); (2) Arctic squirrel–snake sympatry in North America was even less likely during the preceding late Miocene and mid-Pliocene to Holocene cold periods (Shackleton & Opdyke, 1977; Vail & Hardenbol, 1979); and (3) Ground squirrels of the subgenus *Spermophilus* were already cold adapted and crossing the Bering land bridge into Asia prior to 2 million years ago (Black, 1972; Repenning, 1980).

In further support for this argument, Arctic ground squirrels have no resistance to rattlesnake venom, whereas Davis and Coast Range populations share similar amounts of venom resistance despite 3,000 years of differential rattlesnake selection (Bonn–Poran, Coss, & Benjamini, in preparation).

We compared the snake-directed behavior of snake-inexperienced Arctic and Fisher ground squirrels during encounters with a gopher snake in the sand-filled room and artificial burrow (Goldthwaite, Coss, & Owings, in preparation). As before, a rat and an animate bag containing a rat were used as control objects in the burrow and room, respectively. In the room situation, Arctic ground squirrels used the same general classes of motor patterns as did the Fisher ground squirrels. The two species did not differ significantly in the frequency of tail-flagging and sand-kicking at the snake. However, the organization of their behavior with respect to the snake suggested that the Arctic ground squirrels were substantially less competent. Unlike the vigorous sand-kicking of Fisher ground squirrels, which faced the snake and pushed sand forward with their forepaws, Arctic ground squirrels turned around to deliver less forceful kicks with their hind paws. Turned around, the Arctic ground squirrels were much less able to evade snake strikes than were the Fisher ground squirrels. Moreover, the Arctic ground squirrels sometimes positioned themselves between the snake and a nearby wall, often hitting the wall as they jumped away during snake strikes. Fisher ground squirrels were never observed doing this. Fisher ground squirrels constantly faced the snake when they approached within striking distance. Arctic ground squirrels did so only about 90% of the time. Most of the time, however, Fisher ground squirrels kept out of striking range but rushed forward to deliver forceful sand-kicks. In contrast, Arctic ground squirrels spent more time near the snake.

Group differences in the artificial burrow reflected the same trend as the room comparisons. Arctic ground squirrels spent more time in the same alley as the snake, whereas Fisher ground squirrels spent more time in the adjacent alley. Both groups engaged in vigorous earth-moving behaviors. Fisher ground squirrels kicked sand at the snake, as described earlier in this chapter, but Arctic ground squirrels never did so, frequently building burrow plugs instead.

Behavior differences between Arctic and Fisher ground squirrels were much less apparent for the nonsnake conditions, i.e., the animate bag in the room and rat in the burrow. Compared with the Fisher ground squirrels, the Arctic ground squirrels were less cautious of the animate bag containing the rat. Several Arctic ground squirrels even climbed on the bag, withdrawing only when the bag moved suddenly. Unlike their interactions with the gopher snake, neither group sand-kicked at the bag. Group differences were even less pronounced for the condition with the rat in the burrow. Arctic ground squirrels showed little investigative or avoidance behavior, whereas the Fisher ground squirrels tended to avoid inter-acting with the rat. During interactions with the rat, neither group built plugs in the burrow.

In review, Arctic and Fisher ground squirrels used the same classes of motor patterns to deal with the snake, but Arctic ground squirrels applied these motor patterns less competently. Fisher ground squirrels harassed the gopher snake effectively in both room and burrow conditions, keeping their distance between bouts of harassment. Arctic ground squirrels also harassed the snake, but less effectively, spending significantly more time near the snake and sometimes turning away at close range. Unlike the room condition in which both species harassed the snake, Arctic and Fisher ground squirrels differed qualitatively in their treatment of the snake in the burrow. Here, Fisher ground squirrels actively harassed the snake by sand-kicking, whereas Arctic ground squirrels built defen-sive burrow plugs.

These results can be interpreted several ways. Because the novel animate bag was treated with mild caution by both squirrel groups, particularly the Fisher ground squirrels, similarities in elongate postures and tail-flagging might simply represent a generalized investigative behavior with adaptive value not exclusively centered around snakes. It seems reasonable to consider that these behaviors are multifunctional and may have utility for dealing with other predators and aggres-sive conspecifics. Earth-moving behaviors are also multifunctional and may be used for digging and modifying burrow systems, for burrow alley and entrance plugging to provide a barrier, and for harassment purposes. The question arises as to whether Arctic and California ground squirrels share a common pattern of antisnake behavioral organization. Ground squirrels of both species kicked sand at the snake and plugged burrow alleys near the snake. California ground squirrels were consistently more cautious than the Arctics during close-range snake interactions.

In this comparative context, it is difficult to state with certainty whether the behavioral organization of Arctic ground squirrels has specialized antisnake components that are 3–million-year-old remnants of previous snake selection. Furthermore, in the absence of continuous snake selection, one could never know whether these possible remnants had been modified somewhat from a more snake-adapted state, had been kept in stasis because of their canalized multifunctional attributes, had never evolved the more specialized features seen in California ground squirrels, or were constrained by any combination of these. The best evidence that the behavior of Arctic ground squirrels may include some antisnake behavior remnants is provided by their burrow-plugging activity. Although used to block burrow entrances and to inter conspecifics and mustelid predators (Armitage & Downhower, 1970; Henderson, Springer, & Adrian, 1970), plug building to block the progress of a predator would seem to have the greatest defensive utility if the predator were of the slow-moving, nondigging variety like gopher snakes and rattlesnakes. Congruent with burrow plugging, which uses both forepaws and hind paws to dig and move earth, above- and below-ground substrate-kicking by California ground squirrels appears to be an antisnake specialization only occasionally used to harass conspecifics (Levy, 1977) or deter burrow intruders (Coss & Owings, 1978).

Kicking substrate with the forepaws rather than the hind paws affords both well-aimed forceful substrate throwing and continuous monitoring of the snake's activities. Arctic ground squirrels occasionally used their forepaws to kick substrate at snakes above ground. In contrast, Arctic ground squirrels have been observed to throw loose substrate vigorously at a domestic cat using their forepaws (unpublished data). The well-developed expression of this behavior during exposure to a cat (resembling a bobcat), as compared with only incipient expression of this behavior during encounters with snakes, provides support to the supposition that the Arctics had never evolved the specialized application of motor patterns, like forepaw substrate throwing, to snake confrontation and harassment. It must be noted, however, that substrate-kicking is probably quite old in fossorial rodents and probably not specific to snakes. The appearance of defensive burying behavior in Norway rats (Pinel et al., 1980) suggests that such behavior has broad defensive utility. In light of this generality, variation in the form and application of Arctic ground squirrel behavior during laboratory encounters with snakes might be best viewed as comprising some of the raw material that may have characterized Miocene ground squirrels during the earliest phase of snake selection.

Black-Tailed Prairie Dogs.   Research on the antipredator behavior of Black-tailed prairie dogs, which are much more closely related to Arctic ground squirrels (Bryant, 1945; Howell, 1938) than they are to California ground squirrels, provides further insight into questions of homology and evolution of antisnake behavior (see Hodos & Campbell, 1969). For example, Black-tailed prairie dogs more closely resemble Arctic than California ground squirrels in their use of hind paws to kick loose substrate at snakes (Halpin, 1983). On the other hand, Black-tailed prairie dogs resemble California ground squirrels in their competency in dealing with snakes, which suggests that Black-tailed prairie dogs have also had a long history of snake predation. This competency reflects common expectancies about how to deal with snakes, which may well have homologous attributes derived from a common Miocene ancestor (Bryant, 1945). Such shared expectancies by these two species may account for the overall similarity in the organization ("grammar") of antisnake behavior even though divergent motor patterns ("words") are applied to the task of dealing with snakes. Both species, for example, recruit conspecifics while dealing with snakes: Black-tailed prairie dogs do so by "jump-yipping," California ground squirrels by tail-flagging (Owings & Owings, 1979).

   Detailed research on antisnake behavior of Black-tailed prairie dogs was conducted at field sites with low snake density (Devil's Tower National Monument, Wyoming), and high snake density (Wichita Mountains National Wildlife Refuge, Oklahoma), and in snake-free settings at the St. Louis Zoo, Missouri and the Oklahoma City Zoo. In separate trials, a medium-sized Prairie rattlesnake and a large bull snake were anesthetized with ketamine hydrochloride so that they were either immobilized or crawled about slowly. Each snake was placed within prairie dog coterie territories and the ensuing behavior was video taped. Like California ground squirrels, Black-tailed prairie dogs approached the snake slowly in elongate postures, paused intermittently to bob their heads, lurched backwards when the snake moved, and finally got close enough to sniff and even attack the snake. During this ongoing interaction with the snake, individuals would retreat one to several body lengths from the snake and emit one or more jump-yips. A prairie dog jump-yips by leaping from a quadrupedal to an extended bipedal stance, then immediately returning the forequarters to the ground. A two-syllable "yip" accompanies the leap. Jump-yipping often attracted other prairie dogs, who also began to harass the snake. After several individuals assembled in the vicinity of the snake, some fed and apparently observed the interactions, whereas others dealt directly with the snake, in ways similar to the behavior of California ground squirrels described earlier (see Fig. 7.1).

   Populations differed in ways that suggested that they had made different adjustments of antisnake behavior during ontogeny. The wild population experiencing frequent contact with snakes in Oklahoma harassed both mobile and immobile snakes. The snake-free populations in zoos harassed mobile snakes but seemed indifferent to immobile snakes, even though at least some of the zoo prairie dogs originated from stock living in areas of high snake density. The wild population of Black-tailed prairie dogs in Wyoming, an area with few snakes, also was unresponsive to immobile snakes, but harassed mobile snakes. It is possible that the behavior of the Wyoming population reflected both onto-genetic and phylogenetic adjustments (see Owings & Owings, 1979).

Risk Assessment

Previous discussion of interactions between ground squirrels and snakes has centered on the squirrel's contribution to the predator–prey behavior system, emphasizing adjustments in the organization of ground squirrel antipredator behavior rather than corresponding adjustments in the snake's predatory or defen-sive behaviors. Variation in the snake's behavior is implicit in this predator–prey behavior system and it strongly affects successive decision making by the squirrel. Thus, ground squirrel antipredator behavior involves not only immediate adjustments to the snake's behavior but also adjustments based on expectations of the snake's ensuing behavior. Furthermore, the squirrel's ability to assess the current situation, as well as to predict the consequences of its actions, is sharply limited by surrounding biotic and abiotic variables, such as the type of snake, its relative size, and the topographic features of the setting.

Discrimination.   Experimental analyses of these biotic and abiotic variables are beginning to provide some understanding of the complexity of the cognitive processes apparent in the organization of ground squirrel antisnake behavior. Laboratory research by Hennessy and Owings (1978) has shown that wild-trapped, rattlesnake-adapted adult Douglas ground squirrels differentiate the more dangerous Northern Pacific rattlesnake from the Pacific gopher snake. In a mod-ification of the experimental room procedure, squirrels were exposed to a gopher snake or a rattlesnake restrained in a sealed or perforated, transparent plastic bag. The squirrels stayed significantly farther away from the rattlesnake but remained oriented toward the rattlesnake more consistently than toward the gopher snake. Moreover, availability of olfactory cues from the perforated bag markedly enhanced squirrel cautiousness toward the rattlesnake. In addition to olfactory cues, auditory and visual cues appeared to be important for assessing the relative risks engendered by either snake species.

In further study of the importance of auditory cues in risk assessment, Rowe and Owings (1978) played back the sound of a large or small rattlesnake's rattle as ground squirrels entered an artificial burrow. These sounds were compared with amplitude-matched control tones. Analyses of antisnake behavior at the burrow entrance, such as sand-kicking, pausing, tail-flagging, and withdrawal, indicated that ground squirrels behaved more cautiously to the sound of a large rattlesnake than to the sound of a small rattlesnake.

Black-tailed prairie dogs also adjust their antisnake behavior to apparent risk, as indicated by the size and venomousness of the snake (Owings & Loughry, 1984). However, pups and adults adjust their behavior differently in ways that suggest that they differ in their perceptions of the dangerousness of particular snakes. At the Wichita Mountains Wildlife Refuge in Oklahoma, a region with many venomous and nonvenomous snakes, wild prairie dogs were exposed on separate trials to crawling, but partially anesthetized, large and small bull snakes and Western diamondback rattlesnakes. While dealing with the snakes, adults and pups were about equally likely to jump-yip, but pups "barked" much more often than adults. Because barks are usually used in more dangerous situations than jump-yips (Smith, Smith, Oppenheimer, & Devilla, 1977) and pups stayed farther from the snakes than adults did, we concluded that the more vulnerable pups were assessing snakes as more dangerous than adults were (see Fitch, 1948). The fact that pup yips were more bark like than adult yips also was consistent with the view that pups perceived themselves to be more vulnerable to the snakes than adults did. Our most remarkable finding was that pups were just as competent at differentiating among snakes as adults were, but pups and adults made different distinctions. Both pups and adults yipped differentially to all six pairs of sizes and species of snake except one. Pups failed to differentiate large and small rattlesnakes: Adults failed to differentiate large and small bull snakes. Such an outcome clearly indicates that prairie dogs adjust their antisnake behavior ontogenetically, but that the adjustments do not simply represent a gradual accumulation of adult levels of competency through learning (compare Seyfarth & Cheney, 1980). Instead, pups and adults appear to organize their antisnake behavior in equally competent, but distinctly different, ways. Such separation of ontogeny into different stages is in part a result of phylogenetic adjustment (see Galef, 1981).

Visual cues are especially important in estimating risk during squirrel–snake interactions. Black-tailed prairie dogs concentrate their activity around the head of an anesthetized rattlesnake or bull snake (Owings & Owings, 1979). In both laboratory and field, we have observed numerous examples in which the snake's head was treated as an important visual cue by California ground squirrels for directing their attention and adjusting their approach behavior.

In field settings with short-cropped grasses, small stones, and heterogeneous floral debris, stationary rattlesnakes can go undetected by nearby California ground squirrels for some time (unpublished observations). The scale patterns and coloration of rattlesnakes and gopher snakes are quite cryptic to human observers, blending evenly into the background terrain. The scales of rattlesnakes even have a low reflective mat surface that reduces highlights delineating the serpentine form. Snake movement, on the other hand, readily attracts the attention of nearby ground squirrels. We have observed ground squirrels to lose sight of the snake after a momentary distraction and even kick substrate at long sticks before rediscovering the snake's location (also see Linsdale, 1946). As discussed earlier, ground squirrels are hard pressed to detect immobile snakes on some surfaces. Recognition of immobile snakes seems to be an important cognitive ability enhanced by successive experience (Owings & Coss, 1977; Owings & Owings, 1979).

Cognitive Topography.   Our present research has yielded only a small amount of information about snake recognition processes, some of which are restrained by phylogenetic adjustments. We know even less about the adjustability of these processes over ontogenetic and proximate time scales. Several anecdotes of snake-directed behavior in the laboratory and field have prompted us to consider how varying microhabitat features might influence moment-to-moment decision making by ground squirrels. The following examples inspired us to speculate about the range of expectancies squirrels evince about the hunting strategies of their predators in different microhabitats, particularly that engendered without appropriate experience with specific predators and their use of specific topographic features.

In one remarkable observation, we saw a lab-reared Fisher pup leap back and tail-flag vigorously with an elongate posture moments after it started to enter the dark hole of its transfer box. Minutes before, this snake-inexperienced pup had investigated an immobile garter snake that was later removed at the end of the 10-minute trial. The squirrel behaved as if it suddenly "remembered" that the snake could lurk in the dark hole, even though the snake had not been in the transfer box, and the squirrel had never experienced a moving snake or a burrow system. The squirrel, or course, had learned the previous location of the immobile snake and was familiar with dark nest box holes; nevertheless, the squirrel appeared to make the ecologically relevant association between snakes and holes frequently seen in both newly emerged pups and snake-experienced adults in the field. In another example, we saw a snake-inexperienced Fisher pup pause in an elongate posture, tail-flag, and kick sand into our artificial burrow before entering (Coss & Owings, 1978). Unlike the previous observation, gopher snake and squirrel odors might have been present, because an aggressive squirrel–snake encounter had occurred in the burrow earlier that day.

As discussed earlier, feral ground squirrels dealing with wild or tethered snakes typically pause at burrow entrances, sniffing the substrate before entering. This behavior may persist for several hours after the snake leaves the area or is removed. Similar antisnake behavior is observed among ground squirrels near shady boulder crevices and ledges where snakes might go to thermoregulate or ambush passing prey. Newly emerged pups are especially cautious as they move through clumps of grass that could conceal a snake and sometimes pause and tail-flag when they encounter sticks and curled leaves. Ground squirrels thus appear to infer from different microhabitat conditions the relative risks of encountering a snake.

Experience with snakes in different settings among adult squirrels is likely to contribute to this form of risk assessment. On the other hand, young snake-inexperienced squirrels make inferences appropriate to the situation without the benefit of previous experience. Within a theoretical context, the nature of these expectancies could reflect the phylogenetic probabilities of injurious encounters with snakes in different settings. Moreover, these expectancies would have been constantly adjusted by selection to correspond to changes in the relative frequency with which ground squirrels failed to detect snakes, failed to recognize dangerous snakes, and failed to apply behaviors sufficiently well to survive these encounters. Adjustments in the cognitive processes supporting these expectancies might never achieve their optima on a phylogenetic time scale, but they would be expected to "track" the prevailing risks along gradients of varying microhabitat topography (Fig. 7.8 and 7.9; see Lewontin & Levins, 1978; Van Valen, 1973, 1974). Similar selection on ground squirrels by fast-moving avian and mammalian predators could conceivably shape a cognitive topography unique to the hunting strategies of each type of predator. As newly emerged pups explore their habitat, they would learn about the various microhabitat features, such as the location of burrows, rocks, trees, and edible plants. The information extracted on a proximate time scale would fuse into the higher order cognitive topography about relative risks. According to this theoretical framework, ground squirrels would possess several layers of predator-specific expectancies for different microhabitat conditions, some of which would share common assumptions. Burrows, for example, would be safe places of refuge during attacks by eagles, hawks, bobcats, and coyotes but might be dangerous places to hide from snakes, weasels, and badgers (Coss & Owings, 1978; Leger & Owings, 1978; Leger, Owings, & Boal, 1979; Leger, Owings, & Gelfand, 1980; Seyfarth, Cheney, & Marler, 1980).

In light of these emerging ideas about how ground squirrels adjust their behaviors in heterogeneous environments, we examined the location and behavior of Fisher ground squirrels at the San Joaquin Experimental Range (Leger, Owings, & Coss, 1983). We attempted to discover the size of the habitat area visually monitored by squirrels in relation to the number of burrows, rocks, and trees at specific distances from the squirrels. After sampling behaviors such as foraging, pausing while foraging, locomotion, vigilance, and grooming, we found that burrows, rocks, and trees were salient to the squirrels, accounting for up to 75% of the variance of some behaviors. For instance, pausing while foraging, locomotion, and vigilance increased with the number of nearby burrows, whereas locomotion and vigilance declined with an increasing number of nearby trees. This initial study demonstrates that some aspects of ground squirrel behavior are predictable in different microhabitats and may involve differential risk assessment.

CONCLUSIONS AND IMPLICATIONS

Interactions with Other Predators

Our review of ground squirrel antipredator behavior has emphasized the interactions with gopher snakes and rattlesnakes. These interactions typify situations with an intermediate level of urgency. As prolonged affairs, squirrel–snake interactions tend to occur in localized areas ideal for field study and laboratory

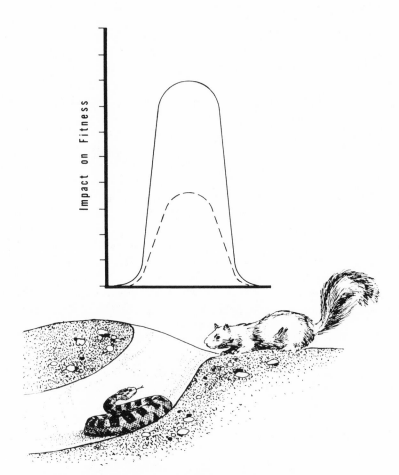

FIG. 7.8. Ground squirrel cognitive topography shown as a theoretical index of the relative risk of encountering rattlesnakes in burrow entrances. Abscissa corresponds with burrow entrance configuration. The solid contour line represents differential selection on a spatial gradient of varying proximity to the burrow entrance. This selection line characterizes the relative frequency with which squirrels had encounters with rattlesnakes that negatively affected fitness over the phylogenetic time scale. The dashed contour line, which "tracks" the selection line over phylogenetic time, represents the epigenetically structured maximum range of ontogenetic adjustments in squirrel expectancy of encountering rattlesnakes in burrows.

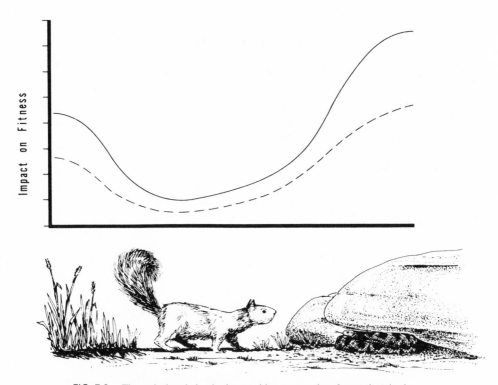

FIG. 7.9. Theoretical variation in the cognitive topography of ground squirrels, depicting the relative risks of encountering rattlesnakes along gradients of snake detectability as influenced by vegetation height and density as well as availability of rocky ambush sites. The solid contour line represents differential selection over phylogenetic time. The dashed contour line tracking the selection line represents the epigenetically structured maximum range of squirrel expectancy of encountering rattlesnakes in these different microhabitats.

simulation of natural settings. On the other hand, the study of ground squirrel antipredator behavior under situations of great urgency is much less amenable to detailed behavior analyses because interactions with fast-moving predators tend to be brief. Moreover, ground squirrel antipredator behavior is much less variable under conditions of great urgency than under conditions of intermediate urgency. For example, ground squirrels emit single-note calls after they are startled by low-flying raptors or suddenly appearing mammalian predators. Single-note call structure is not different for the two types of predators. On the other hand, chatter calls occur under conditions of intermediate urgency after these predators are spotted at a distance. The structure of chatters differs for raptorial and mammalian predators (Leger, Owings, & Gelfand, 1980; Owings & Leger, 1980).

The complexity of antipredator behavior varies considerably with level of urgency. Ground squirrels bolt quickly into their home burrows if a nearby low-flying raptor is approaching them. If, however, the raptor's trajectory appears unlikely to intersect the ground squirrel, it may remain at the burrow entrance and visually track the raptor's flight. When dealing with slower-moving mammalian predators, squirrels are more likely to interact distally with the predator. When a dog appears, for example, ground squirrels may mount promontories and call repetitively in ways that track the ongoing behavior of the dog. Only when the dog gets very close does the ground squirrel, seemingly reluctantly, abandon its promontory and enter its burrow (Owings & Coss, 1981; Owings, Gladney, Leger, & Hennessy, in preparation; Owings & Virginia, 1978). Appropriate decision making and execution of antipredator behavior is clearly restrained under conditions of great urgency, and it is not surprising to find much less behavioral variation when ground squirrels quickly seek refuge. Both the habitat structure and concomitant predator behavior impose these restraints which have selective properties only when squirrels fail to make correct decisions.

A Structuralist Approach

In a structuralist view, an organism is a network of processes restrained not only by their adaptation to the environment through ontogeny and phylogeny, but also by the relationships of each process with all other processes (Webster & Goodwin, 1982). Because each process is adapted not only to the environment but also to all the other processes that comprise the organism, each process is most understandable in the context of the organism's *overall* behavior in the animal's *normal* environment (see Pittendrigh, 1958). Such an approach has clear implications for the study of the processes of learning. The most useful starting point would involve studies of natural behavior in which correlations are sought between behavioral and situational changes. Strong correlations would guide the researcher's choice of the ecologically most relevant independent and dependent variables for experimental study (see Johnston, 1981; Johnston & Turvey, 1980).

A structuralist approach, with its emphasis on the origin and transformation of structure, is closely allied to an organismic view, which begins with the premise that process or change is primary and stability imposed (see Overton, 1976; Overton & Reese, 1973, 1981). In contrast, it seems to us that most of biology works within a mechanistic view, which begins with the premise that stability is primary and change therefore requires causal explanations (Meyer–Abich, 1964; Overton & Reese, 1981; Pepper, 1942; Varela, 1979; Webster & Goodwin, 1982). Efforts to understand processes, such as evolution, ontogeny, and learning, are likely to be most fruitful when pursued in a paradigm that emphasizes the primacy of change.

We began our work on the antipredator behavior of ground squirrels very much in a mechanistic tradition. Variation was quite apparent in our data from the beginning, and the concepts available in a mechanistic view seemed of limited utility in attempting to deal with such variation. The highly interactive nature of ground squirrel–snake relationships over multiple time scales seems much more manageable with the organismic concept of reciprocal causation, than with the concept of one-way causation most prevalent in a mechanistic view (Bateson, 1979). Variation in the species and behavior of a snake then is readily viewed as a major source of variation in ground squirrel antisnake behavior, which is in turn a major source of variation in the snake's behavior. Different facets of the ground squirrel's behavior change at different rates, but in ways that seem interdependent (see Moran, Fentress, & Golani, 1981). Thus the proximity of a pup to a snake changes in a dynamic way during an interaction with the snake. The outcome of this interaction probably influences the pup's slower, ontogenetic shift from using adults to self-sufficiency in dealing with snakes. This ontogenetic shift in turn results in the newly self-sufficient squirrel approaching the snake more closely than younger pups do. The concept of hierarchical organization, e.g., in time scales of change, stems readily from a structuralist tradition (Bateson, 1979; Overton & Reese, 1981). Hierarchical organization combined with reciprocal influence between hierarchical levels yields the concept of interdependent time scales of change that we have found so useful in dealing with behavioral variation (Hennessy, 1982).

With respect to our interests in how animals deal with predators, we consider learning to be an integral part of the ongoing process of structuring antipredator behavior. We propose that the most profitable studies of learning will deal with phylogenetically old and important contexts. One identifies such importance and antiquity through population and species comparisons. The utility of this comparative approach has been noted elsewhere (e.g., Curio, 1961, 1969, 1973; Lehrman, 1953; McPhail, 1969; Schneirla, 1965; Slater, 1974). As our future comparative studies of predator–prey relationships reveal more about the role of learning, we may choose to study learning in a structuralist framework.

ACKNOWLEDGMENTS

This research was supported by Faculty Research Grant D–922 and National Science Foundation Grants No. BNS–7906843 and BNS 84–06172 to Richard G. Coss and Faculty Research Grant D–819 and National Science Foundation Grants No. BNS–7817770 and BNS–8210065 to Donald H. Owings.

REFERENCES

Alcock, J. (1979). *Animal behavior: An evolutionary approach*. Sunderland: Sinauer Associates.
Armitage, K. B., & Downhower, J. F. (1970). Interment behavior in the yellow-bellied marmot (*Marmota flaviventris*). *Journal of Mammalogy, 51*, 177–178.

Bandy, O. L. (1968). Cycles in Neogene paleoceanography and eustatic changes. *Palaeogeography, Paleoclimatology, Palaeoecology, 5,* 63–75.

Bateson, G. (1979). *Mind and nature: A necessary unity.* New York: Dutton.

Bateson, P. P. G. (1976). Rules and reciprocity in behavioural development. In P. P. G. Bateson & R. A. Hinde (Eds.), *Growing points in ethology.* Cambridge: Cambridge University Press.

Black, C. C. (1963). A review of the North American Tertiary Sciuridae. *Bulletin of the Museum of Comparative Zoology, Harvard University, 130,* 109–248.

Black, C. C. (1972). Holarctic evolution and dispersal of squirrels (Rodentia: Sciuridae). In T. Dobzhansky, M. K. Hecht, & W. C. Steere (Eds.), *Evolutionary biology* (Vol. 6). New York: Appleton–Century–Crofts.

Bolles, R. C. (1970). Species-specific defense reactions and avoidance learning. *Psychological Review, 77,* 32–48.

Bolles, R. C. (1975). *Theory of motivation* (2nd ed.). New York: Harper & Row.

Bonn–Poran, N., Coss, R. G., & Benjamini, E. (in preparation). *Resistance of ground squirrels to rattlesnake venom: A study of adaptive variation.*

Brandon, J. G., & Coss, R. G. (1982). Rapid dendritic spine stem shortening during one-trial learning: The honeybee's first orientation flight. *Brain Research, 252,* 51–61.

Brattstrom, B. H. (1955). Pliocene and Pleistocene amphibians and reptiles from Southeastern Arizona. *Journal of Paleontology, 29,* 150–154.

Bryant, M. D. (1945). Phylogeny of Nearctic Sciuridae. *American Midland Naturalist, 33,* 257–386.

Burgess, J. W., & Coss, R. G. (1981). Short-term juvenile crowding arrests the developmental formation of dendritic spines on tectal interneurons in jewel fish. *Developmental Psychobiology, 14,* 389–396.

Burgess, J. W., & Coss, R. G. (1982). Effects of chronic crowding stress on midbrain development: Changes in dendritic spine density and morphology in jewel fish optic tectum. *Developmental Psychobiology, 15,* 461–470.

Burt, W. H., & Grossenheider, R. P. (1964). *A Field Guide to the Mammals.* Boston: Houghton Mifflin.

Calhoun, J. B. (1962). *The Ecology and Sociology of the Norway Rat* (Public Health Service Publication No. 1008). Washington, DC: U.S. Government Printing Office.

Chen, M. J., Coss, R. G., & Goldthwaite, R. O. (1983). Timing of dispersal in juvenile jewel fish during development is unaffected by available space. *Developmental Psychobiology, 16.,* 303–310.

Chomsky, N. (1965). *Aspects of the theory of syntax.* Cambridge: Massachusetts Institute of Technology Press.

Coss, R. G. (1978). Perceptual determinants of gaze aversion by the lesser mouse lemur (*Microcebus murinus*), the role of two facing eyes. *Behaviour, 64,* 248–270.

Coss, R. G. (1979a). Delayed plasticity of an instinct: Recognition and avoidance of 2 facing eyes by the jewel fish. *Developmental Psychobiology, 12,* 335–345.

Coss, R. G. (1979b). Perceptual determinants of gaze aversion by normal and psychotic children: The role of two facing eyes. *Behaviour, 69,* 228–254.

Coss, R. G., & Brandon, J. G. (1982). Rapid changes in dendritic spine morphology during the honeybee's first orientation flight. In M. D. Breed, C. D. Michener, & H. E. Evans (Eds.), *The biology of social insects.* Boulder: Westview Press.

Coss, R. G., Brandon, J. G., & Globus, A. (1980). Changes in morphology of dendritic spines on honeybee calycal interneurons associated with cumulative nursing and foraging experiences. *Brain Research, 192,* 49–59.

Coss, R. G., & Owings, D. H. (1978). Snake-directed behavior by snake naive and experienced California ground squirrels in a simulated burrow. *Zeitschrift für Tierpsychologie, 48,* 421–435.

Curio, E. (1961). Rassenspezifisches Verhalten gegen einen Raubfeind. *Experientia, 17,* 1–4.

Curio, E. (1969). Funktionsweise und Stammesgeschichte des Flugfeinderkennens einiger Darwinfinken (*Geospizinae*). *Zeitschrift für Tierpsychologie, 26,* 394–487.

Curio, E. (1973). Towards a methodology of teleonomy. *Experientia, 29,* 1045–1058.

Curio, E., Ernst, V., & Vieth, W. (1978). The adaptive significance of avian mobbing. II. Cultural transmission of enemy recognition in blackbirds: Effectiveness and some constraints. *Zeitschrift für Tierpsychologie, 48,* 184–202.

Darlington, P. J., Jr. (1977). The cost of evolution and the imprecision of adaptation. *Proceedings of the National Academy of Sciences, 74,* 1647–1651.

Dobzhansky, T. (1956). What is an adaptive trait? *American Naturalist, 90,* 337–347.

Emlen, S. T. (1970). Celestial rotation: Its importance in the development of migratory orientation. *Science, 170,* 1198–1201.

Etkins, R., Epstein, E. S. (1982). The rise of global mean sea level as an indication of climate change. *Science, 215,* 287–289.

Fitch, H. S. (1948). Ecology of the California ground squirrel on grazing lands. *American Midland Naturalist, 39,* 513–596.

Fitch, H. S. (1949). Study of snake populations in central California. *American Midland Naturalist, 41,* 513–579.

Galef, B. G. (1981). The ecology of weaning: Parasitism and the achievement of independence by altricial mammals. In D. J. Gubernick & P. H. Klopfer (Eds.), *Parental care in mammals.* New York: Plenum Press.

Garcia, J., & Koelling, R. A. (1966). Relation of cue to consequence in avoidance learning. *Psychonomic Science, 4,* 123–124.

Goldthwaite, R. O., Coss, R. G., & Owings, D. H. (in preparation). *Adaptive variation in antisnake behavior of California and Arctic ground squirrels: Above and below ground comparisons.*

Gould, S. J. (1980). Is a new general theory of evolution emerging? *Paleobiology, 6,* 119–130.

Gould, S. J. (1982). Darwinism and the expansion of evolutionary theory. *Science, 216,* 380–387.

Gould, S. J., & Lewontin, R. C. (1979). The spandrels of San Marco and the Panglossian paradigm: A critique of the adaptationist programme. *Proceedings of the Royal Society of London* (B), *205,* 581–598.

Grinnell, J., & Dixon, J. (1918). California ground squirrels. *The Monthly Bulletin, California State Commission of Horticulture, 7,* 9–59.

Halpin, Z. (1983). Naturally occurring encounters between Black-tailed prairie dogs (*Cynomys ludovicianus*) and snakes. *American Midland Naturalist, 109,* 50–54.

Hansen, R. O., & Begg, E. L. (1970). Age of Quaternary sediments and soils in the Sacramento area, California by uranium and actinium series dating of vertebrate fossils. *Earth and Planetary Science Letters, 8,* 411–419.

Harlow, H. F. (1949). The formation of learning sets. *Psychological Review, 56,* 51–56.

Henderson, F. R., Springer, P. R., & Adrian, R. (1970). The Black-footed ferret in South Dakota. *Publication of the South Dakota Department of Fish, Game and Parks.*

Hennessy, D. F. (1982). *Functional significance of variation in predator harassment.* Doctoral dissertation, University of California, Davis.

Hennessy, D. F., & Owings, D. H. (1978). Snake species discrimination and the role of olfactory cues in the snake-directed behavior of the California ground squirrel. *Behaviour, 65,* 115–124.

Hennessy, D. F., Owings, D. H., Rowe, M. P., Coss, R. G., & Leger, D. W. (1981). The information afforded by a variable signal: Constraints on snake-elicited tail flagging by California ground squirrels. *Behaviour, 78,* 188–226.

Hinde, R. A. (1973). Constraints on learning—An introduction to the problems. In R. A. Hinde & J. Stevenson–Hinde (Eds.), *Constraints on learning: Limitations and predispositions.* London: Academic Press.

Hodos, W., & Campbell, C. B. G. (1969). *Scala naturae:* Why there is no theory in comparative psychology. *Psychological Review, 76,* 337–350.

Howell, A. H. (1938). Revision of the North American ground squirrels, with a classification of the North American Sciuridae. *North American Fauna, 56,* 1–256.

198   COSS AND OWINGS

Johnson, D. L. (1977). The late Quarternary climate of coastal California: Evidence for an ice-age refugium. *Quaternary Research, 8*, 154–179.

Johnston, T. D. (1981). Contrasting approaches to a theory of learning. *Behavioral and Brain Sciences, 4*, 125–173.

Johnston, T. D., & Turvey, M. T. (1980). A sketch of an ecological metatheory for theories of learning. In G. H. Bower (Ed.), *The psychology of learning and motivation* (Vol. 14). New York: Academic Press.

Klauber, L. M. (1972). *Rattlesnakes* (2 vols.). Berkeley: University of California Press.

Leger, D. W., & Owings, D. H. (1978). Responses to alarm calls by California ground squirrels: Effects of call structure and maternal status. *Behavioral Ecology and Sociobiology, 3*, 177–186.

Leger, D. W., Owings, D. H., & Boal, L. M. (1979). Contextual information and differential responses to alarm whistles in California ground squirrels. *Zeitschrift für Tierpsychologie, 49*, 142–155.

Leger, D. W., Owings, D. H., & Coss, R. G. (1983). The behavioral ecology of time allocation in California ground squirrels (*Spermophilus beecheyi*): Microhabitat effects. *Journal of Comparative Psychology, 97*, 283–291.

Leger, D. W., Owings, D. H., & Gelfand, D. L. (1980). Single-note vocalizations of California ground squirrels: Graded signals and situation-specificity of predator and socially evoked calls. *Zeitschrift für Tierpsychologie, 52*, 227–246.

Lehrman, D. S. (1953). A critique of Konrad Lorenz's theory of instinctive behavior. *Quarterly Review of Biology, 28*, 337–363.

Levy, N. (1977). *Sound communication in the California ground squirrel.* Master's thesis, California State University at Northridge.

Lewontin, R. C., & Levins, R. (1978). Evoluzione. In *Enciclopedia, V: Divino-Fame.* Torino: Einaudi.

Linsdale, J. M. (1946). *The California ground squirrel.* Berkeley: University of California Press.

Manning, A. (1979). *An introduction to animal behavior* (3rd ed.). London: Addison–Wesley.

Marler, P. R. (1976). Sensory templates in species-specific behavior. In J. C. Fentress (Ed.), *Simple networks and behavior.* MA: Sinauer Associates.

Marler, P. R., Dooling, R. J., & Zoloth, S. (1980). Comparative perspectives on ethology and behavioral development. In M. Bornstein (Ed.), *The comparative method in psychology: Ethological, developmental and cross-cultural viewpoints.* Hillsdale, NJ: Lawrence Erlbaum Associates.

Mason, W. (1979). Ontogeny of social behavior. In P. Marler, & J. G. Vandenbergh (Eds.), *Handbook of behavioral neurobiology: III, Social behavior and communication.* New York: Plenum Press.

Mayr, E. (1974). Behavioral programs and evolutionary strategies. *American Scientist, 62*, 650–659.

Mayr, E. (1976). *Evolution and the Diversity of Life.* Cambridge: Harvard University Press.

McPhail, J. D. (1969). Predation and the evolution of a stickleback (*Gasterosteus*). *Journal of the Fisheries Research Board of Canada, 26*, 3183–3208.

Menzel, E. W. (1978). Cognitive mapping in chimpanzees. In S. H. Hulse, H. Fowler, & W. K. Honig (Eds.), *Cognitive processes in animal behavior.* Hillsdale, NJ: Lawrence Erlbaum Associates.

Merriam, C. H. (1901). The prairie dog of the great plains. *Yearbook of the United States Department of Agriculture*, 257–270.

Meyer–Abich, A. (1964). The historico–philosophical background of the modern evolution-biology. *Bibliotheca Biotheoretica, 10*, 1–170.

Miller, L. H. (1912). Contributions to avian palaeontology from the Pacific Coast of North America. *University of California Publications in Geology, 7*, 61–115.

Moran, G., Fentress, J. C., & Golani, I. (1981). A description of relational patterns of movement during 'ritualized fighting' in wolves. *Animal Behaviour, 29*, 1146–1165.

Overton, W. F. (1976). The active organism in Structuralism. *Human Development, 19*, 71–86.

Overton, W. F., & Reese, H. W. (1973). Models of development: Methodological implications. In J. R. Nesselroade & H. W. Reese (Eds.), *Life-span developmental psychology: Methodological issues.* New York: Academic Press.

Overton, W. F., & Reese, H. W. (1981). Conceptual prerequisites for an understanding of stability–change and continuity–discontinuity. *International Journal of Behavioral Development, 4,* 99–123.

Owings, D. H., & Coss, R. G. (1977). Snake mobbing by California ground squirrels: Adaptive variation and ontogeny. *Behaviour, 62,* 50–69.

Owings, D. H., & Coss, R. G. (1981). How ground squirrels deal with snakes. *Anima, 99,* 37–43.

Owings, D. H., Gladney, A. B., Leger, D. W., & Hennessy, D. F. (in preparation). Calling by ground squirrels at terrestrial predators can be both nepotistic and non-nepotistic.

Owings, D. H., & Hennessy, D. F. (1984). The importance of variation in sciurid visual and vocal communication. In J. O. Murie & G. R. Michener (Eds.), *Annual cycles, behavioral ecology, and sociality.* Lincoln: University of Nebraska Press.

Owings, D. H., & Leger, D. W. (1980). Chatter vocalizations of California ground squirrels: Predator- and social-role specificity. *Zeitschrift für Tierpsychologie, 54,* 163–184.

Owings, D. H., & Loughry, W. J. (1984). Variation in snake-elicited jump yipping by Black-tailed prairie dogs: Snake specificity and its ontogeny. *Zeitschrift für Tierpsychologie,* in press.

Owings, D. H., & Owings, S. C. (1979). Snake-directed behavior by Black-tailed prairie dogs (*Cynomys ludovicianus*). *Zeitschrift für Tierpsychologie, 49,* 35–54.

Owings, D. H., & Virginia, R. A. (1978). Alarm calls of California ground squirrels (*Spermophilus beecheyi*). *Zeitschrift für Tierpsychologie, 46,* 58–70.

Pepper, S. C. (1942). *World hypotheses: A study in evidence.* Berkeley: University of California Press.

Perdeck, A. C. (1958). Two types of orientation in migrating starlings, *Sturnus vulgaris* L., and chaffinches, *Fringilla coelebs* L., as revealed by displacement experiments. *Ardea, 46,* 1–37.

Perdeck, A. C. (1964). An experiment on the ending of autumn migration in starlings. *Ardea, 52,* 133–139.

Pinel, J. P., Treit, D., Ladak, F., & MacLennan, A. J. (1980). Conditioned defensive burying in rats free to escape. *Animal Learning and Behavior, 8,* 447–451.

Pittendrigh, C. S. (1958). Adaptation, natural selection, and behavior. In A. Roe & G. G. Simpson (Eds.), *Behavior and evolution.* New Haven: Yale University Press.

Plotkin, H. C., & Odling-Smee, F. J. (1979). Learning, change, and evolution: An inquiry into the teleonomy of learning. In J. S. Rosenblatt, R. A. Hinde, C. Beer, & M.-C. Busnel (Eds.), *Advances in the study of behavior* (Vol. 10). New York: Academic Press.

Rausch, G., & Scheich, H. (1982). Dendritic spine loss and enlargement during maturation of the speech control system in the Mynah bird (*Gracula religiosa*). *Neuroscience Letters, 29,* 129–133.

Repenning, C. A. (1980). Faunal exchanges between Siberia and North America. *Canadian Journal of Anthropology, 1,* 37–44.

Riedl, R. (1977). A systems-analytical approach to macro-evolutionary phenomena. *Quarterly Review of Biology, 52,* 351–370.

Rosenblatt, J. S., Siegel, H. I., & Mayer, A. D. (1979). Progress in the study of maternal behavior in the rat: Hormonal, nonhormonal, sensory, and developmental aspects. In J. S. Rosenblatt, R. A. Hinde, C. Beer, & M.-C. Busnel (Eds.), *Advances in the study of behavior* (Vol. 10). New York: Academic Press.

Rowe, M. P., & Owings, D. H. (1978). The meaning of the sound of rattling by rattlesnakes to California ground squirrels. *Behaviour, 66,* 252–267.

Rozin, P., & Kalat, J. W. (1971). Specific hungers and poison avoidance as adaptive specializations of learning. *Psychological Review, 78,* 459–486.

Schneirla, T. C. (1965). Aspects of stimulation and organization in approach/withdrawal processes underlying vertebrate behavioural development. In D. S. Lehrman, R. A. Hinde, & E. Shaw (Eds.), *Advances in the study of behavior (Vol. 1).* New York: Academic Press.

Seligman, M. E. P. (1970). On the generality of the laws of learning. *Psychological Review, 77,* 406–418.

Seligman, M. E. P., & Hager, J. L. (1972). *Biological boundaries of learning.* New York: Appleton–Century–Crofts.

Seyfarth, R. M., & Cheney, D. L. (1980). The ontogeny of vervet monkey alarm calling behavior: A preliminary report. *Zeitschrift für Tierpsychologie, 54,* 37–56.

Seyfarth, R. M., Cheney, D. L., & Marler, P. (1980). Vervet monkey alarm calls: Semantic communication in a free-ranging primate. *Animal Behaviour, 28,* 1070–1094.

Shackleton, N. J., & Opdyke, N. D. (1976). Oxygen-isotobe and paleomagnetic stratigraphy of Pacific core V28-239 late Pliocene to latest Pleistocene. In R. M. Cline & J. D. Hays (Eds.), *Investigation of Late Quaternary Paleoceanography and Paleoclimatology, Geological Society of America Memoir, 145,* 449–464.

Shackleton, N. J., & Opdyke, N. D. (1977). Oxygen isotobe and paleomagnetic evidence for early Northern Hemisphere glaciation. *Nature, 270,* 216–219.

Slater, P. J. B. (1974). A reassessment of ethology. In W. B. Broughton (Ed.), *The biology of brains.* London: The Institute of Biology.

Smith, D. G., & Coss, R. G. (1984). Calibrating the molecular clock: Estimates of ground squirrel divergence made using fossil and geological time markers. *Molecular Biology and Evolution, 1,* 249–259.

Smith, D. G., Bonn–Poran, N., & Coss, R. G. (in preparation). Genetic variation among four subspecies of California ground squirrels *(Spermophilus beecheyi).*

Smith, W. J., Smith, S. L., Oppenheimer, E. C., & Devilla, J.G. (1977). Vocalizations of the black-tailed prairie dog, *Cynomys ludovicianus. Animal Behaviour, 25,* 152–164.

Spencer, H. (1888). *The principles of psychology* (Vol. 1). New York: D. Appleton.

Stebbins, R. C. (1966). *A field guide to Western reptiles and amphibians.* Boston: Houghton Mifflin.

Tevis, L. (1943). Field notes on a red rattlesnake in lower California. *Copeia, 4,* 242–244.

Tolman, E. C. (1948). Cognitive maps in rats and men. *Psychological Review, 55,* 189–208.

Vail, P. R., & Hardenbol, J. (1979). Sea-level changes during the tertiary. *Oceanus, 22,* 71–79.

Van Valen, L. (1973). A new evolutionary law. *Evolutionary Theory, 1,* 1–30.

Van Valen, L. (1974). Molecular evolution as predicted by natural selection. *Journal of Molecular Evolution, 3,* 89–101.

Varela, F. J. (1979). *Principles of biological autonomy.* New York: Elsevier.

Waddington, C. H. (1957). *The strategy of the genes.* London: George Allen Unwin.

Webster, G., & Goodwin, B. C. (1982). The origin of species: A structuralist approach. *Journal of Social and Biological Structures, 5,* 15–47.

Wimsatt, W. C. (1980). Units of selection and the structure of the multi-level genome. *Philosophy of Science Association, 2,* 122–183.

Wolfe, J. A., & Hopkins, D. M. (1967). Climatic changes recorded by tertiary land floras in Northwestern North America. In K. Hatai (Ed.), *Tertiary Correlations and Climatic Changes in the Pacific, The Eleventh Pacific Science Congress, Symposium 25.* Sendai, Japan: Sasaki Printing and Publishing Company Limited.

8 An Ecological Approach to Development of Spatial Orientation

Nancy Hazen
Department of Home Economics
University of Texas

Herbert L. Pick, Jr.
Institute of Child Development
University of Minnesota

The study of the development of spatial orientation lends itself to an ecological approach. First, being spatially oriented is most critical for organisms when they are moving within natural, large-scale environments. All organisms have species-specific needs for achieving and maintaining spatial orientation, whether these be foraging for food, making seasonal migrations, or traveling to engage in economic concerns. To meet these needs, each species has evolved mechanisms or strategies for maintaining orientation that are particularly adapted to their ecology. Second, as organisms mature, the ecological context of their behavior changes and imposes different demands for spatial orientation. Orientation strategies must be developmentally adapted to such ecological changes. Finally, different individuals within a species encounter different ecological demands for orientation. These different demands may play a significant role in the development of individual variations in orientation ability within a species.

Surprisingly little research has systematically examined the development of spatial orientation in relation to ecological context despite the seemingly obvious connection. The study of spatial orientation has been approached by a variety of disciplines from different conceptual frameworks, addressing different questions and using different methods. Integration of findings is exceedingly difficult. And, whether studying human or animal spatial orientation, investigators have traditionally been concerned with *either* the perceptual and cognitive processes and structures that permit spatial orientation *or* the ecological contexts within which orientation occurs. Recently, though, the interdependence between orientation mechanisms and ecological contexts is beginning to be recognized.

THEORETICAL PERSPECTIVES IN THE STUDY OF
SPATIAL ORIENTATION

The dichotomy of interest in cognitive structures and processes versus ecological and environmental factors is evident among investigators of human spatial behavior and cognition. Investigators who take the former, *structuralist* perspective are concerned with analyzing the nature, operation, and development of underlying cognitive structures and processes; investigators who take the latter, *functionalist* perspective are more concerned with assessing how these structures and processes are adapted to tasks encountered in everyday ecological contexts. Among investigators of human spatial cognition and behavior, developmental and cognitive psychologists have largely had structural concerns, whereas cross-cultural and ecological/environmental psychologists have been more likely to have functional concerns.

In their investigations of the development of spatial orientation, developmental and cognitive psychologists have asked questions such as: "How is spatial knowledge mentally represented and organized?"; "how do people process information in order to make spatial judgments?"; and "what developmental changes occur in the representation, organization, and manipulation of spatial information?" Thus, their primary focus has been on the nature and development of abstract spatial concepts such as the ability to infer spatial relationships, to use objective reference systems, and to represent distance information. Their methods have generally concentrated upon the use of experiments in controlled laboratory settings.

Researchers taking this structuralist approach have made explicit attempts to "decontextualize" tasks as much as possible in order to infer abstract underlying spatial conceptions. Siegel (1981) stated that for developmental psychologists, "The fundamental problem in understanding the acquisition and development of cognitive mapping is the externalization of cognitive maps—getting the spatial knowledge out in some public medium, unconfounded by (theoretically) 'non-spatial' task load" (p. 168). Although developmental and cognitive psychologists have studied the effect of several kinds of environmental factors on the representation of spatial knowledge (e.g., the scale of environments, the presence of barriers, and the presence of landmarks), their concern has been more on how these factors affect the structural development of spatial concepts than on how spatial concepts function in everyday ecological contexts.

Although early research in the development of spatial cognition was characterized by the use of small-scale table-top models or paper-and-pencil tasks, over the past decade many researchers have turned to tasks set in large-scale environments, i.e., environments that surround the individual and cannot be entirely perceived from a single vantage point (Acredolo, 1981). A major reason for the shift toward using large-scale environments has been an ecological concern that the perceptual and cognitive processes used for spatial orientation in small-scale laboratory spaces may not generalize to orientation in large-scale, more natural spaces. Small-scale spaces can be viewed in their entirety from one vantage point whereas large-scale spaces surround and enclose individuals, requiring them to move through the space, integrating multiple perspectives in order to grasp all the spatial relations. (See Acredolo, 1981; Lockman & Pick, in press; and Weatherford, 1982, for a discussion of issues related to scale of space.)

This concern brings the developmental and cognitive psychologists a little closer to the ecological study of human development and behavior. The study of how humans develop and function in natural contexts is not new to psychology. Thirty years ago, Barker and Wright (1954) pioneered the ecological study of human development and behavior. Their detailed observations of children in their natural environments anticipated contemporary ecological approaches proposed by several environmental and cross-cultural psychologists (Bronfenbrenner, 1979; Cole, Hood, & McDermott, 1979; Wohlwill, 1976). Bronfenbrenner (1979) describes the emphasis in contemporary ecological, functionalist approaches as not being "on the traditional psychological processes of perception, motivation, thinking, and learning, but on their *content—what* is perceived, desired, feared, thought about, or acquired as knowledge, and how the nature of this psychological material changes as a function of a person's exposure to and interaction with the environment" (p. 9). For the most part, psychologists with strong ecological perspectives are thus concerned primarily with how environments affect children's and adult's attitudes toward, behavior in, and use of different environments rather than with how spatial orientation develops.[1] They have focused on cognition about *places,* or actual environments, whereas cognitive and developmental psychologists have concentrated on the fundamental cognitive concepts and processes used to orient within space in general.

In recent years these two areas have become increasingly integrated and are beginning to share research methods and theoretical perspectives. Both environmental and developmental psychologists are finding that spatial tasks such as model construction inevitably tap both knowledge of particular environments and knowledge about space in general (Liben, 1981). Siegel (1982), for example, has recently argued that a full understanding of structural cognitive development cannot be obtained without adopting a functionalist, ecological perspective:

> During the last twenty years, structural models of cognitive competence have been the core focus of the central research issues of cognitive development. It has been argued that the structural development of competence must be adaptive, but such arguments have been pretty vague about adaptation for *what*. With some exceptions, the research movements of the last decade have not seriously attempted to explore

---

[1]James Gibson's (1979) ecological approach is a very interesting and unique analysis of what the environment is. His approach was developed with particular reference to visual perception and deals in considerable detail with certain aspects of spatial orientation. The more cognitive aspects of spatial orientation, however, have not yet been incorporated within his perspective.

those contexts toward which adaptation is directed . . . We need a new functionalism that must include in some broad sense, an analysis and a theory of the
contexts of children's behavior. (pp. 84–85)

Interestingly, psychologists and biologists who have studied spatial orientation
of animals have also traditionally been more concerned with structural than with
functional questions. They too are increasingly integrating their findings within
an ecological perspective. Biologists, studying animal behavior from the conceptual framework of evolutionary theory, have traditionally emphasized the
importance of interpreting behavior from an ecological framework much more
than have psychologists. But although biologists have published many studies
in recent years on the mechanisms used for spatial orientation by various species,
especially birds, (see Able, 1980; Emlen, 1975a; Keeton, 1981; and Schmidt–
Koenig, 1975, for reviews), few have been interpreted within an ecological
framework. Brown (1975) notes that, until about a decade ago, ethologists
focused primarily upon the usefulness of behaviors as taxonomic characteristics
and devoted less attention to the study of the environments and selection pressures
that influenced the evolution of behaviors. More recently, biologists investigating
mechanisms for spatial orientation in animals have interpreted their research
from an ecological framework and have encouraged the further integration of
the areas of ecology and ethology (Emlen, 1975a).

Comparative psychologists, too, have been concerned primarily with investigating the mechanisms underlying a species' spatial orientation, preferring to
use experimental methods. Variations of maze problems are still being conducted,
but, whereas traditional studies were primarily concerned with explaining the
animal's spatial behavior in terms of general laws of learning and motivation,
current approaches focus on how perceptual and cognitive processes and structures are used to solve spatial problems. Typical of these approaches is the
research of Menzel (1978) and Olton (1979), who have studied the construction
and use of "cognitive maps" by chimpanzees and rats, respectively.

Olton (1979), for example, has suggested that spatial exploration patterns in
rats can be predicted from their foraging patterns, which in turn depend on the
ecological distribution of their food supplies. If the food supply of a particular
species is found in clusters, that species will probably use a *win–stay* foraging
pattern, returning to the area in which food has previously been found (Kamil
& Sargent, 1981). This strategy has been found in the English thrush and the
ovenbird, both of which feed on worms and grubs that cluster together (Smith,
1974; Zach & Falls, 1976). In contrast, if the food supply of a particular species
is scattered, that species will follow a win–shift pattern. Olton confirmed a win–
shift prediction for rats in a study in which animals fed in one arm of a three-
arm maze chose to go subsequently to a new arm rather than to the arm where
food had previously been found. A similar analysis and prediction was recently
confirmed for hummingbirds (Cole, Hainsworth, Kamil, Mercier, & Wolf, 1982).

These examples indicate why the ecological context of spatial behavior is important for predicting when particular spatial strategies are likely to be found in particular species. A general theory of spatial cognition and behavior that can be used to integrate data from diverse disciplines must address the *functions* of the relevant perceptual and cognitive structures and processes. An ecological approach focusing on the process of adaptation between organism and environment is a powerful perspective for ultimately explaining both universals and variations in the development of spatial orientation. Such an approach will also help relate the development of spatial orientation to other aspects of cognitive and social development.

Such a general, interdisciplinary perspective requires a systematic conceptual framework for organizing and interpreting different organism–environment relationships. In this chapter, we try to sketch a preliminary formulation of such a framework by outlining major categories of organism–environment relationships in the development of spatial orientation. We then use this framework to integrate and interpret some of the extant data on the development of spatial orientation, particularly in humans. We emphasize *human* spatial development in part because that is our area of research, and in part because there are few developmental studies on animal spatial orientation. However, we include a few examples from the animal literature to illustrate the broad applicability of the conceptual framework. Finally, we suggest future directions for the ecological study of spatial orientation.

AN ECOLOGICAL FRAMEWORK FOR STUDYING THE DEVELOPMENT OF SPATIAL ORIENTATION

We propose that, from an ecological perspective, the contribution of organism and environment to the development of spatial competencies be viewed as *transactional* rather than as additive or interactive. The transactional approach, originated by Dewey and Bentley (1949), implies that organism and environment are components of a system that are never encountered independently of each other and in fact cannot exist separately. Organism–environment transactions may be of two general types: They may be *universal within species* and thus critical for species-typical structural developments in spatial cognition, or they may be *specific to individuals* and hence result in within-species variations in the development of spatial competencies.

Throughout the evolutionary history of any species, species-typical developments in spatial competencies have become adapted to changes in the ecological contexts encountered by the species over the course of the life-span; that is, organisms develop more sophisticated spatial orientation competencies to meet increasing needs for spatial activity. At the same time, these developmental changes in ecology are not only adapted to developmental changes in spatial competencies, which permit the organism to range farther and remain oriented, but are also adapted to other types of developmental changes. For example, the development of motor skills that permit infants to stand and walk upright will change their view of the environment and thus affect the development of their spatial competencies. Thus, the environment and the organism continually exert mutual effects upon each other throughout the life-span.

Within-species variations result from organism–environment transactions specific to individuals within a species, rather than to the species as a whole. Whether these variations have their source in the individual or in the environments encountered by the individual, variations in one component of the system will affect the other component as well. For example, a blind infant will not encounter the same environments as a sighted infant, and a child who grows up in an apartment building is likely to develop different types of spatial competencies from a child who grows up in a rural area.

In the following two sections, we review what is known about organism–environment transactions involved in, first, species-typical developments in spatial competencies, and second, within-species variations in spatial competencies, particularly in humans. In our discussion of species-typical developments, we attempt to specify the relationship between the species-typical developments in perceptual and cognitive skills used for spatial orientation and the species-typical changes across the life-span in the ecological contexts that call for spatial orientation. We hope that such a specification of organism-environment relationships can lay the groundwork for investigations of whether particular normally encountered environmental contexts are necessary for the normal sequential development of particular species-typical spatial competencies. In our discussion of variations in development within species, we attempt to specify sources of variation in individuals and in environments that lead to variations in organism–environment transactions contributing to differential spatial competencies.

SPECIES-TYPICAL PATTERNS OF DEVELOPMENT IN SPATIAL COMPETENCIES

Unfortunately, few studies have been specifically designed to investigate the organism–environment transactions involved in universal developments in human spatial competencies. Instead, we must be content to relate what is known about developments in spatial cognition to what we know about changes in the contexts of development across the life-span. This account of possible organism–environment transactions in the development of human spatial competencies is necessarily speculative. Although we have learned a great deal in the last decade about developmental changes in acquisition and use of knowledge about large-scale environments, many questions remain unanswered. Furthermore, very few empirical data exist concerning changes in the spatial problems people encounter within various environmental contexts over their life-spans.

Developmental research on human spatial orientation has emphasized two major issues: changes with age in (1) the frames of references used to define spatial position, and (2) the mental representations of spatial layouts. *Frames of reference* may be either egocentric, in which spatial orientation is achieved with reference to loci on the body, or geocentric when achieved with reference to loci external to the body. Obviously, this is only a rough classification, because within each category there are numerous loci and ways of using them to define spatial position (Pick & Lockman, 1981). Spatial location could be egocentrically defined on the basis of sensory information indicating the position of an object relative to the perceiver, or on the basis of motor movements. Location could also be specified relative to the body as a whole or relative to certain parts of the body. For example, in typing, the location of the keys is defined in terms of motor movements of the individual fingers. Similarly, multiple geocentric reference systems are available. Geocentric cues can vary in their distance from the perceiver and from the target objects to be spatially located. They can also vary in the extent to which they are discrete objects or more pervasive features that could function as a "container" for locating other objects (Acredolo, 1976). "Container" frames of reference themselves may vary from small rooms to large geographic features like rivers or tree lines that define extensive areas. A further complication occurs in many way-finding situations when travellers must use a combination of reference systems contingently in order to remain oriented (Pick, Yonas, & Rieser, 1979). For example, a traveller may use a geocentric cue ("Go to the first light") to make an egocentric response ("Turn left").

Research on *spatial representation* has examined developmental changes in the type of spatial information that is represented, in its organization, and in the type of mental operations that may be performed on it. Reversing a known route and inferring relationships between spatial loci that have not been directly experienced are two operations of obvious importance in way-finding. A third operation often important in planning travel is perspective-taking. With age individuals are better able to integrate separately experienced locations and routes in memory due to developmental changes in ability to represent and operate on spatial information (Rieser, 1983). Spatial orientation can be viewed as a joint function of the traveller's spatial representation of a particular environment and choice of reference system within that environment. In the following sections we review what is known about the development of spatial orientation during each major phase of the life-span and then relate those developments to ecological changes characteristic of each of those phases.

Infancy

According to Piaget (1952, 1954; Piaget & Inhelder, 1967), during the first year of life the infant has little notion of objective spatial relations, in which objects exist in relation to each other, independent of his or her relation to them. Instead, the infant is unable to conceive of objects apart from his or her own actions on them and therefore must rely on an egocentric frame of reference to locate objects. By the final stage of sensorimotor development, around 18 months of age, the infant can conceive of space as a container in which the self and other objects are located in relation to each other, permitting the use of geocentric reference systems in simple spaces. Although many studies have confirmed that infants predominately use egocentric reference systems (cf. Acredolo, 1978; Bremner & Bryant, 1977), recent evidence indicates that infants under 1 year of age may respond geocentrically in specific situations.

The primary spatial behavior of infants during the first 2 months of life is the orienting of sense organs to environmental features, which is an egocentric adjustment (Pick, Yonas, & Rieser, 1979). About 3 months of age infants, become capable of visually guided reaching, but there is no evidence that they know the location of objects when they reach except in relation to their own bodies. Even at 6 months of age, infants depend primarily on egocentric reference systems. In a typical procedure, Acredolo (Acredolo, 1978; Acredolo & Evans, 1980) trained 6-month-old infants sitting in a small room to anticipate an event by looking at one of two identical windows located to either side. They were then carried to the opposite end of the room and turned around. Their anticipation in this new position was observed to be in the same egocentric direction as in the original position. However, if one window was very distinctively marked, e.g., by bright stripes and flashing lights, the infants could be induced part of the time to anticipate on a geocentric basis.

In a study similar in principle, Rieser (1979) trained 6-month-old infants to anticipate an event and then changed their position from 45° to right of upright to 45° to the left of upright. As in Acredolo's study, windows were located so that orienting in one direction would indicate egocentric responding and in another, geocentric responding. When gravity provided a possible external frame of reference, 6-month-old infants responded geocentrically. Because even newborns are sensitive to gravitational cues (Andre–Thomas & Autgaerden, 1966), such information may be used for establishing external frames of reference at a particularly early age.

By 9 months of age, infants extend their use of geocentric frames of reference to a wider variety of situations. Acredolo and Evans (1980) found that infants of this age used a geocentric reference system 100% of the time when the target location was directly marked by a highly salient landmark but still responded primarily egocentrically when no landmarks or only indirect landmarks (distinctive patterns on nontarget windows) were available. However, a study by Presson and Ihrig (1982) indicates that 9-month olds may be able to use their mother's position as an indirect landmark in order to code locations geocentrically. Presson and Ihrig used a procedure similar to that used by Acredolo and Evans (1980) but varied the position of the mother. When the mother moved with the infant on the test trials, the infant responded egocentrically, but when the mother remained in a fixed position, the infants responded geocentrically.

The mother may be one of the most salient and hence earliest used landmarks for the infant, albeit not a very reliable one because of her propensity to move around in naturalistic settings.

Search behavior of 9- and 10-month-old infants is of particular interest because at this age (Piaget's sensorimotor Stage IV) infants have learned enough about the continued existence of objects to search for them when they are hidden; yet interesting errors are still made. If an infant repeatedly views and retrieves an object being hidden at a location A, then sees it being hidden at location B, she or he will often continue to search for it at A. Piaget (1954) suggests that the infant does not yet completely understand that objects continue to exist independently of her or his actions on them; i.e., the infant conceives of the object as "the thing I find at A." Several recent investigations have indicated that patterns of search in the Piagetian Stage IV object concept task are related to the infant's spatial detection of the relationships of the hidden object to its surrounding environment (Bremner & Bryant, 1977; Lucas & Uzgiris, 1977).

Using a varient of this task, Bremner (1978a,b) presented infants with two distinctively marked screens and allowed them repeatedly to retrieve an object under one of the screens (A). As Piaget found, infants perseverated in searching under A when the object was moved to B. But when the object was hidden under A as usual and the infant was moved 180° with respect to the stimulus display, the infants chose the correct geocentric location. This suggests that the Stage IV search error may be a response to the geocentric cue of the object's cover, rather than an egocentric response based on past actions, as Piaget has assumed. But when it was the *background* on which the objects and covers were displayed that was differentiated, rather than the covers, infants were more likely to respond egocentrically after moving (Bremner & Bryant, 1977; Bremner, 1978a). This is in agreement with Acredolo and Evan's finding that 9-month olds reliably use geocentric landmarks when they *directly* mark a spatial location, but not otherwise.

Whether the covers or the background were distinctively marked, 9-month-olds were more likely to respond geocentrically when they were moved around the table than when the table itself was rotated (Bremner, 1978b). This may be because the infants' perception of their own movements allowed them to update their spatial position in relation to the geocentric cues provided by the stimulus display, or because they could only use the geocentric cues provided by the stimulus display in conjunction with geocentric cues in the environment external to the display. It is difficult to evaluate these alternatives, because there is currently no conclusive evidence that infants of this age can either update an egocentric reference system when they are passively moved or can use distal landmarks as a geocentric reference system. Apparently, egocentric and geocentric cues interact in complex ways to influence infants' choice of reference system, but investigations are only just beginning to address these interactions (Butterworth, Jarrett, & Hicks, 1982).

By 11 months of age, infants in Acredolo and Evans' (1980) study were able to use an indirect salient landmark as a geocentric reference. But when no landmarks were available, infants were not able to anticipate the correct window after being moved until 16 months of age (Acredolo, 1978). This is in agreement with the findings of a recent study by Rieser and Heiman (1982), who examined the ability of 18-month olds to find a hidden target object after they had moved in a space containing no relevant distinctive landmarks. These toddlers were able to adjust their egocentric response to the direction and magnitude of their own movement. There is a clear difference between this sophisticated updating of an egocentric response and the more primitive use of egocentric frames of reference used by the younger infant, who is unable to orient correctly to objects after movement. Rieser and Heiman (1982) prefer to call this more mature behavior a "self-reference" system to distinguish it from the less mature type of egocentric responding.

Clearly, more is happening during infancy than a simple development from egocentric to geocentric frames of reference. Rather, changes occur in the type of internal and external cues that may be used as reference systems, and in how these various cues interact. Use of an egocentric frame of reference is not necessarily "incorrect" or immature. As previously noted, use of self-reference can produce appropriate responding when used in conjunction with updating of position. Similarly, the use of geocentric cues is not necessarily more accurate or developmentally more advanced than the use of egocentric cues, because even young infants can use geocentric cues that directly mark a location. What develops in this domain seems to be the ability to use cues that are less salient and more distant from the target object and the observer (Pick, 1976), and to choose the reference system most adaptive for prevailing ecological conditions.

In contrast to the use of reference systems, the development of spatial representation in infancy has not been extensively studied. Researchers have tended to regard children as unable to symbolize spatial layouts mentally until Stage VI of the sensorimotor period (18–24 months of age). Although infants cannot yet infer on a mental, symbolic level spatial relationships that they have not directly experienced, they can do so on a practical behavioral level. Piaget (1954) has proposed that by Stage IV of sensorimotor development (8–12 months), the infant is capable of spatial *reversibility* (i.e., the knowledge that it is possible to return to a starting point by reversing a displacement), and by Stage V, (12–18 months), of spatial *associativity,* (i.e., detour knowledge, or the knowledge that it is possible to reach a particular spatial endpoint from a variety of routes). However, according to Piaget, before Stage VI such reversals and detours are only possible when the reversal or detour path can be perceived directly, because planning reversals or detours when any part of the path is out of view would require mental representation.

Is this practical knowledge of reversibility and associativity applied to all spaces at once? Recent work suggests not; instead, as development progresses, it is applied to spaces increasingly remote from the infant's body. Lockman (1984) tested infants between 8 and 12 months of age on their ability to perform reaching and locomotor detours. Infants were able to reach around an opaque barrier to retrieve an object by about 10 months of age but were not able to solve the detour problem by crawling around an opaque barrier until about 12 months of age. Because all infants were able to crawl before being given either detour task, the application of associativity to a reaching space before a crawling space was not due to motor limitations.

When spatial relationships must be established within environments that are not perceivable in a single act, mental representation of the parts of the environment that are out of view may need to be established. Lockman's (1984) detour data indicate that when the space is very close to the infant's body and the route is not complex, infants are capable of making detours well before Stage VI, even when they cannot perceive the detour route. In this task, the experimenter lifted an object over a high barrier. The infant was physically unable to retrieve the object by reversing its trajectory but was able to reach or crawl around the barrier in order to do so. Performance of this task, however, may not require a mental representation of the spatial layout, but only knowledge that the object is now behind the barrier, and knowledge of how detours around barriers can be made.

In contrast, the performance of detours in more complex or distal spaces does seem to require representation of the layouts of these spaces. In a recent study by Rieser, Doxsey, McCarrell, and Brooks (1982), children from 9 to 25 months of age were provided with aerial views of an L-shaped maze while their mothers sat on the opposite side of the maze. From the air, the child could see that one side of the maze had an open path to the mother, whereas the other was blocked. They were then lowered to the ground and motivated to find their mothers. Consistent movement to the open path side of the maze without trial and error would require that the child mentally represent the location of the barrier and coordinate this representation with her or his new location on the ground. Only the oldest (25-month old) children were able to perform correctly.

How, then, do these developments in infants' frames of references and capacities for spatial representation relate to the changing ecological contexts of infant development? Very young infants perceive and interact with only a very proximal world. They are not yet capable of changing their location except by being passively carried or by making lateral movements. An egocentric reference system is all that is needed while the infant establishes the spatial coordination of body parts with one another and reaches for objects in space from a fixed position. Disorientation could possibly occur if the infant rolled to one side, but at least by 6 months, and perhaps even sooner, infants can update their locations after lateral displacements by using gravitational cues.

Remaining oriented in space becomes more of a problem with initiation of crawling (8–9 months of age), because egocentric responses that are not updated will result in errors following movement. If it is true that 9-month-old infants use geocentric cues only when they rather directly mark a target location, infants of this age should experience problems in spatial orientation, because indirect cues are usually available in natural environments, whereas direct cues are not. Yet these infants do not seem to have difficulty remaining oriented in everyday situations.

One possible reason for their success may be that they have some ability to update spatial responses, at least within small-scale crawling spaces. Recall that infants in Bremner's (1978b) study could make geocentric responses using direct landmarks when their own bodies were rotated, but not when the display was rotated. Perception of their own movement is apparently important to maintenance of spatial orientation. It is unfortunate that no studies have examined reference systems used by crawling infants who move *by themselves* to new locations, because recent studies (Feldman & Acredolo, 1979; Hazen, 1982) have indicated that children who locomote actively are better oriented spatially than children who locomote passively (i.e., are led or carried by another). These studies were primarily with older toddlers and preschool children, but findings indicated that active exploration was most helpful to the younger children, and this factor may be even more critical for infants.

A second reason why infants may often behave egocentrically in the laboratory but not at home is simply because of the difference in familiarity. Acredolo (1979) found that, whereas 65% of searches for objects in a laboratory setting were egocentric, only 13% were egocentric when the same task was done at home. Further study indicated that infants will respond more geocentrically even in the laboratory when they are familiarized with the setting and the experimenter. Acredolo (1982) concluded that the stress of being in an unfamiliar setting distracted the infant from environmental cues available for spatial orientation. Perhaps the infant's use of the mother as a spatial landmark in Presson and Ihrig's (1982) study stems from attending closely to her movements in the unfamiliar situation of the laboratory and would be less likely to occur in the home.

The self-generated locomotion permitted by crawling provides infants with experiences that surely aid their developing abilities to update their egocentric responses in accordance with their movements, to use geocentric cues that are more distant from themselves and the target locations they seek, and to apply knowledge of spatial reversibility and associativity to spaces more distant from their bodies. The development of walking at about 13–15 months of age should affect these developments even more profoundly (Rieser & Heiman, 1982). Moving about in a standing position also gives the child a wider visual perspective of the surrounding environment. The ability of infants to pull themselves to a standing position by 10–11 months of age may account for the ability of 11-month olds in Acredolo and Evans' (1980) study to use indirect landmarks for orientation. Standing and walking also provide the infant with the opportunity to combine various perspectives (standing versus sitting, lying, or crawling) of the same environment.

Although the ability to walk increases opportunities for spatial learning, it also presents more difficult problems for spatial orientation as the child locomotes within increasingly larger and more unfamiliar environments. Thus, toddlers have both the opportunity and the need to develop the ability to update egocentric movements, to use more distal geocentric cues, to reverse routes and make detours, to mentally represent spatial layouts that are out of view, and to coordinate those developing abilities. Nevertheless, these developing spatial competencies can be applied successfully only within relatively small, room-sized, familiar environments, such as the home or very simple laboratory spaces.

Early Childhood

During the preschool years, children extend their developing spatial competencies to increasingly larger and more complex locomotor spaces. Although toddlers are able to detour directly around barriers in a relatively simple laboratory space (Reiser, Doxsey, McCarrell, & Brooks, 1982), they may fall back on trial-and-error detours when the space is more complex and requires them to keep track of several turns rather than just one. Hazen (1982) trained 2- and 3-year olds to learn one of two routes to a goal, each requiring two turns, through a layout consisting of three small rooms arranged in a triangular pattern. The children's ability to take detour routes to the goal was assessed by putting barriers at various points along the learned route as well as by asking the children to find their way from new starting points. Three-year olds were easily able to take the most direct detours to the goal, but the young toddlers had more difficulty, often reverting to trial-and-error strategies. The younger children were also less successful in reversing the learned route, especially when route reversal required using *opposite* turns to those used in walking the route in the forward direction. Thus, toddlers may fall back on using nonupdated egocentric reference systems when required to make difficult spatial transformations.

Hazen's subjects did not perform as well as the toddlers in the aforementioned Rieser et al. (1982) task who were given an aerial view first. Hazen's task may well be more difficult because it required subjects to generate a representation of the layout during exploration and then to coordinate this representation with their position when they confronted the barriers. The toddlers in Rieser's task, on the other hand, were able to perceive the layout of the maze directly from an aerial perspective and then needed only to coordinate their representation with their ground-level position. In addition, Hazen's layout was more complex than the one used by Reiser et al.

Research by Hazen, Lockman, and Pick (1978) also indicated that preschool children are easily able to walk a learned route in reverse but revealed that the spatial representations of preschool children are still limited in various ways. In this study, children aged 3 to 6 years of age learned a specific route through a series of small rooms, each of which contained a distinctive toy animal as a landmark. Once they had learned the route and the landmarks along it, they were tested on their ability to travel the route in reverse, and to infer relationships between parts of the environment they had not directly experienced.

Even though the 3-year olds were easily able to reverse routes on a motor level, it was not until 4 years of age that children were able to reverse the sequence of landmarks along a route, and not until 6 years of age that they were able to perform accurately on the spatial inference task. The children did not need to have an accurate mental representation of the space in order to reverse the route correctly but instead could do so by correctly updating a series of egocentric responses. However, successful performance in the inference task would require that the children accurately represent the shape of the spatial layout of the environment and also update their position in the environment in coordination with their representation of the environment, all in all a rather formidable task.

Children's ability to infer the overall configuration of this space was assessed by asking them to construct a model showing the overall shape of the space and the location of the landmarks within the space. Surprisingly, children did quite well on this measure by the age of 4, even though at this age they could not make accurate spatial inferences. In most cases, they seemed to generate the overall configuration of the space during the process of using the model to convey their knowledge of the route. Coordinating knowledge of the shape of the layout with the sequence of landmarks within it may need to be well established in order to infer spatial relationships accurately. The ability to do this, even in such a small space, does not seem to be present before the age of 6 years.

But what if the space is very familiar and has been experienced from numerous vantage points—such as the home? Can spatial inferences then be made at an earlier age? A recent study reported by Pick and Lockman (1982) indicates that they probably can. Children aged 4-to-6 and 8-to-9 years were asked to aim a sighting tube toward various target locations in their apartments from various station points within their apartments. Although the target locations were all out of view, even the 4-to 6-year olds, though imprecise, performed far better than chance, at least when target locations were on the same floor as the station point. Even 3- to 4-year olds, for whom the sighting task was too difficult, could generally answer questions about which rooms lay behind walls, although they had difficulty making spatial inferences about what lay above ceilings or under floors. Within very familiar environments, then, even young preschool children can make reasonable spatial inferences on a two-dimensional plane.

Thus, during the preschool years, children extend their ability to update egocentric responses to larger and more complex locomotor spaces, develop the ability to represent route sequences and the overall shape of routes mentally, and begin to coordinate their representations of spatial layouts with their movements through space in order to infer spatial relationships they have not directly experienced. However, these abilities seem to be limited to room-sized or house-sized environments and are less successfully applied when the environments are larger or are unfamiliar.

These developments are well matched to the ecological changes in spatial experiences that occur during the preschool years. In particular, children increase their territorial range during this period. In Barker and Wright's (1954) study of the ecology of a Midwestern town, preschool children spent an average of 1 hour per day more than infants in settings outside the home. Preschool children today probably spend even more time outside the home, because many more mothers work. Preschool children are also more often able to play with supervision in the area around their homes. Thus, they are presented with the need and the opportunity to extend their spatial competencies to larger areas beyond their homes, such as their yard and the neighbor's yard and their preschool classroom and playground.

Perhaps a more significant change is that preschool children are more likely to walk through unfamiliar environments, rather than being carried or pushed in a stroller. Recent studies have indicated that preschool children can more accurately remember spatial relationships within an environment when they walk rather ride through it (Herman, Kolker, & Shaw, 1982) or simply look at it (Cohen, Weatherford, & Byrd, 1980; Herman & Siegel, 1978).

Because they must walk through unfamiliar environments, preschool children might easily become lost if they ventured too far from their parents, so they must keep track of their parents' movements in relation to the rest of the environment as well as their own. Walking through unfamiliar environments thus gives children practice in integrating and remembering spatial experiences but also presents more difficult spatial orientation tasks. When the environment is more familiar to the child, e.g., a community playground, the parent may simply wait at a particular location and let the child explore freely, knowing that the child will be able to take direct routes to the parent from any location on the playground, even if the parent is out of view. More information about the types of environments experienced by preschool children and about parent–child interactions during the exploration of unfamiliar environments is badly needed, as is information about the effects of these experiences on developing spatial abilities.

Middle Childhood and Adolescence

A great deal of research on the development of spatial orientation has focused on middle childhood (5 to 13 years of age), whereas relatively little is known about developments between adolescence and early adulthood. Spatial orientation becomes more accurate with regard to distance and direction judgments during middle childhood and adolescence. Although preschool children have a general ability to update egocentric movements, to point to objects out of view, and to infer what is on the other side of a wall, they are often relatively inaccurate. In Piaget's terms preschool children rely primarily on topological relations (e.g., of proximity, continuity, and separation) to make spatial judgments and only by middle to late childhood become capable of using Euclidean concepts (in which all spatial relationships can be coordinated using an objective, metric system). Then, probably on the basis of more precise metric judgments, children's configurational knowledge of spatial layouts improves and can be extended to larger scale spaces, such as neighborhoods.

A series of studies reported by Siegel (1981) illustrates well the reliance of preschool children on topological cues to reconstruct a spatial layout, and the ability of older children to use Euclidean relations to do so. Children aged 5, 7, and 10 years walked three times through a large model town and were asked to reconstruct the town after each walk. When the town was laid out in a large gymnasium, the 5-year olds were much less accurate than the other two groups. The walls of the gymnasium were too remote to provide useful topological cues and the young children's estimate of the distances and directions of buildings relative to each other was poor. However, when the task was performed in a smaller classroom, the proximity of the walls enabled use of topological information and all age groups were equally accurate by the third construction. Similarly, preschool children have been found to remember the location of an event as well as 8-year olds in an environment containing distinctive landmarks, but not in an undifferentiated environment (Acredolo, Pick, & Olson, 1975).

Throughout middle childhood and early adolescence, children develop accurate configurational knowledge of familiar environments outside the home. Hardwick, McIntyre, and Pick (1976) found that 2nd-grade and 5th-grade children were all able to point to locations in a familiar library that were out of view, but absolute accuracy increased with age. Similarly, in a study in which 7- to 14-year olds pointed to out-of-view landmarks, Anooshian and Young (1981) found that all age groups could indicate correctly the general direction of the landmark, but the absolute accuracy of pointing increased between the ages of 7 and 11. Curtis, Siegel, and Furlong (1981) also found considerable improvement in children's ability to locate targets accurately and consistently from different station points between the ages of 6 and 11 years. Less improvement was found between the ages of 10 and 14 years. Taken together, these studies indicate that by about 10 years of age children can very accurately infer distance and direction between targets not directly experienced, at least in familiar environments.

The development of more accurate metric knowledge of spatial relationships, distances, and directions during middle childhood parallels the considerable extension of the child's territorial range during this period. In his ecological study of children's spatial activity and spatial knowledge of their New England neighborhood, Hart (1979) noted that it is generally after the age of 5 years that children's free range is extended beyond what is visually accessible from their home. This extension seemed to be related to attending school and making friends who live at a greater distance from home, as well as to maturational factors. By 4th to 6th grade, girls more than doubled the distance they could travel from their homes, whereas boys nearly tripled this distance. This significant increase in free range during preadolescence was influenced by children's increased use of bicycles for travel after 3rd grade. With parental permission, 6th-grade children (at least, boys) could go nearly anywhere within biking or walking distance. Barker and Wright (1954) also found that the amount of time children spend outside the home nearly doubles between the preschool and middle childhood years. Spatial orientation within extensive and often relatively undifferentiated environments would require more metrically accurate appraisals of distance and direction. Also, it is during middle childhood that children establish "secondary home bases" (e.g., school, friend's houses, a local playground, the "secret hideout") from which they venture forth (Barker & Wright, 1954). Children thus have the opportunity to construct accurate configurational knowledge of several familiar environments, which may increase their familiarity with Euclidean spatial properties.

Children of this age are also much more likely to guide themselves in exploring unfamiliar environments, whereas preschool children are more likely to be led or to follow adults. Several studies have indicated that self-directed exploration is associated with more accurate spatial knowledge than is other-directed exploration (Feldman & Acredolo, 1979; Hazen, 1982). Another ecological factor that probably has considerable impact on the development of Euclidean spatial concepts is school attendance (White & Siegel, in press). In school children are explicitly taught spatial and mathematical concepts, and perhaps most importantly, they learn how to read and make maps and models of spatial layouts, including maps of environments they have actually experienced. Children often seem to discover new relationships in familiar environments through their attempts to model externally the spatial layout of these environments (Hart, 1981; Hazen et al., 1978). Thus, experience with reading and making representational displays of actual environments may further enhance the accuracy of configurational spatial knowledge.

Adulthood

Although the most significant increase in ability to make spatial inferences occurs about the age of 10 years, precision continues to improve thereafter. Adults can more accurately point to objects out of view (Curtis et al., 1981; Hardwick et al., 1976; Pick & Lockman, 1982) and can more accurately estimate distances (Allen, Kirasic, Siegel, & Herman, 1979; Curtis et al., 1981) than can older children and adolescents. In addition, adults are much more accurate than children in pointing to spatial locations while taking imagined perspectives (Hardwick et al., 1976).

One would assume that adults also have greater knowledge than children about what environmental information is most useful for spatial orientation. Evidence for this has been provided by Allen et al. (1979). Second graders, 5th graders, and adults were shown a series of slides depicting a route and were then asked to select scenes that they felt would be most helpful to them in remembering their way along the walk. Nearly all of adults' choices were scenes that marked a turning point. Children were less likely to select such points of directional change.

Adulthood is often accompanied by profound changes in spatial ecology. Adults may travel widely and their travel is usually self-directed. They use modes of transportation, particularly cars, which extend their range of travel and may require the integration of spatial landmarks that may be miles apart. Their ability to estimate distances and direction and to infer configurational spatial relationships must be quite accurate, although systematic errors may still be made in distance estimation (Cohen, Baldwin, & Sherman, 1978), and in inferring directional relationships (Stevens & Coupe, 1978; Tversky, 1981), under certain environmental conditions.

Communicating spatial information, e.g., giving directions to others, is another common adult activity. The ability to localize targets from imagined points of view and to select the most critical spatial information for orientation would seem to be essential for good communication. As just described, these are late-maturing abilities, so one would not expect children to perform well in spatial communication. As with map or model construction, verbally communicating spatial information may lead the speaker to discover spatial relationships that were not previously realized.

As yet, relatively little research has examined spatial orientation abilities in younger versus older adults, but some recent data indicates that certain spatial orientation abilities decline in the elderly. Herman (1981), for example, found that 60- and 70-year-old subjects were less accurate than 20-year-old subjects in pointing to spatial locations from an imagined perspective in an unfamiliar environment.

Although both cognitive and perceptual abilities decline with advanced age, ecological factors may also play a role in the decline of spatial accuracy. Waddell and Rogoff (1981) found that elderly adults remembered the spatial locations of objects that were organized in a meaningful context as well as middle-aged adults. They did not perform as well when the objects were not contextually organized, leading the investigators to suggest that such lack of context was not typical of the everyday memory demands of elderly people. It is typical of tasks required in school-like situations, and older adults have had fewer years of formal schooling than younger adults, as well as less-recent schooling. Also, older adults travel less widely than younger adults (Barker & Wright, 1954), and their exploration may be less self-directed. They may be more likely to use public transportation than to drive themselves, which Appleyard (1970) found to be related to less-accurate spatial knowledge. These ecological changes in spatial activity could stem from a decline in general perceptual, cognitive, and motor abilities, as well as in specific spatial orientation abilities. Once established, these changes in spatial activity are likely to perpetuate the decline of spatial orientation abilities.

Comparative Development of Spatial Orientation

Nearly all reseach on mechanisms of nonhuman spatial orientation has focused on mature organisms. The strategy has been to examine the mechanisms used by adult members of different species or populations, or by adult individuals of a given species under particular ecological conditions. In a recent review of animal spatial orientation, Able (1980) noted that, "A small number of studies has revealed the power of a developmental approach to understanding orientation. Although new variables such as age and experience may obscure patterns, onto-genetic studies provide an excellent window through which to examine the plasticity characteristics of orientation mechanisms" (p. 363). Plasticity of ori-entation mechanisms has attracted increasing interest as researchers have come to realize that rather than having a single, built-in mechanism for orientation, a given species may have multiple mechanisms that can be adjusted to the situation at hand (Emlen, 1975a).

Because birds face particularly challenging spatial orientation demands, their orientation systems have been heavily studied. Early evidence that learning and development play a role in the migratory orientation of at least some bird species came from a classic series of studies by Perdeck (1958, 1967). Thousands of European starlings were displaced from their usual migratory route. Experienced adult starlings were able to correct for this displacement and arrive at or near their usual wintering area. In contrast, juvenile birds making their first migration did not correct for the displacement but continued to fly in the same direction, ending in a different area. In subsequent years, the young birds returned to the new wintering area. Thus, simple directional orientation seems to be innate in starlings, but the ability to correct a displacement requires experience. These studies specified neither the mechanisms involved nor the ecological circum-stances that might help explain this developmental sequence. Possibly young starlings avoid becoming displaced (and therefore lost) on their first migration by following adults.

A series of studies by Emlen (1975a,b) represents a more sophisticated attempt to analyze the ontogenesis of avian orientation. He first discovered that young indigo buntings cannot orient properly when they begin their first autumnal migration unless they have been exposed to the night sky during the preceding weeks. In fact, birds deprived of this exposure are never able to use the stars for orientation, indicating that there is a sensitive period in the development of star-compass orientation. Further studies indicated that during this early period, young buntings are predisposed to attend to the apparent rotational motion of the night sky. Emlen proposed that, because stars located near the axis of rotation move more slowly, through smaller arcs, birds can use them as a frame of reference. They may then use this frame of reference to calibrate other star patterns. Evidence for this hypothesis was obtained by exposing hand-reared young buntings to a planetarium sky rotating around an incorrect axis. These buntings oriented in the incorrect, predicted direction when exposed to a normal sky, and even after a year's exposure to a normal sky were unable to correct their star compass. Emlen suggested that the instability of star positions, except for those near the axis, would prevent the evolution of an innate mechanism for using star positions for orientation. Because large parts of the sky are often clouded over, an innate mechanism that depends on recognition and use of the stable star patterns would be less useful than a mechanism that permits the bird with experience to recognize all star patterns. Developmental work such as that of Emlen illustrates well the utility of an ecological approach to species-specific developments in spatial orientation. The considerable work done on the navigational achievements of mature members of migrating and homing species testifies to the variety of mechanisms used for orientation (e.g., Keeton, 1974); but a full explanation of these mechanisms will require further developmental studies (see Wiltschko, 1983).

WITHIN-SPECIES VARIATIONS IN SPATIAL COMPETENCY

An ecological approach to the development of spatial orientation should involve the systematic study of the organism–environment transactions that result in individual *variations* within a species as well as universals. We have already seen that variations in certain environmental factors will result in the use of different mechanisms for spatial orientation. The child's choice of spatial reference system or her or his ability to make spatial inferences depends not only on her or his developmental level, but also on the familiarity, size, and complexity of the environment, the geocentric cues available, the mode in which the environment is explored, and probably a great many other factors. We now examine in more detail the ways in specific organism–environment transactions can effect within-species variations in the development of spatial orientation.

Organism–environment transactions that vary within species can affect individual spatial behavior in either a *limited* or a *general* way. *Limited* variations are variations between individuals that are transitory, or specific to a particular time and place. Individuals traveling through rugged terrain, for example, may experience distances as greater than they actually are while travelling through that particular environment but may not permanently change their strategies for making spatial judgments.

In contrast, *general* variations result from variations in organism–environment transactions that permanently influence the ways in which organisms encode and organize spatial information. Such general variations lead to individual differences in spatial orientation strategies or competencies that to some degree are manifested across settings and retain some continuity over time. In practice, the distinction between general and limited variations may be fuzzy. When individuals repeatedly encounter specific spatial experiences, it may influence their general modes of spatial perception and cognition. For example, individuals who live in wide-open, barrier-free environments may develop different spatial competencies than individuals who live in environments that are divided into small areas. We define such variations as *general* ones, even though they arise from repeated limited experiences, because they result in general individual differences in styles of spatial perception and cognition. In this section we discuss organism–environment transactions that may result in both limited and general variations in spatial learning and development.

Limited Variations

Most research on variations in human spatial orientation has addressed limited rather than general variations. Although this research has indicated only which factors may produce transitory variations in spatial capacities, we review it here because it indicates which factors might lead to general variations if encountered repeatedly. The limited variations in human spatial orientation resulting from organism–environment transactions may be separated for the sake of convenience into two categories: variations due primarily to the individual and variations due primarily to the environment. Limited variations due to the individual include the amount and type of experience in environments, and any special training received. They also include the goals and emotions of the individual within specific spatial contexts. Limited variations due to the environment include availability and type of landmarks, the presence or absence of barriers and subdivisions, and task demands imposed by environments.

Limited Variations Due to the Individual

Amount of Experience. The amount of experience in a particular environment is probably the most obvious factor that can be expected to influence a person's spatial competence within that environment. Several investigations found that people who have resided in a neighborhood or city for longer periods of time can construct more detailed and accurate maps of these environments (Appleyard, 1970; Beck & Wood, 1976; Ladd, 1970). However, frequency of use of the environment rather than mere residence is probably the determining factor. Even newcomers to a city may have accurate knowledge of heavily used parts of the city, although their maps of the city as a whole are sketchy and poorly integrated (Appleyard, 1970). This relationship between amount of use of particular parts of the environment and spatial knowledge of these parts has also been found in children (Hart, 1979) and the elderly (Walsh, Krauss, & Regnier, 1981).

Because amount of experience in natural environments is inevitably confounded with other variables such as emotional significance of the environment (Acredolo, 1982), and because it is difficult to measure exactly the amount and nature of experience in such settings, amount of experience in laboratory studies has been defined as number of training trials or trips through a space. These studies have consistently found that repeated exposure to a laboratory space results in more accurate judgments about spatial relations within that space, for both children and adults (cf. Allen et al., 1979; Herman & Siegel, 1978).

Type of Experience.   Recent research indicates that type or quality of spatial experience, as well as its amount, influences spatial orientation. For example, *active* spatial exploration appears to result in more extensive and accurate spatial knowledge than *passive* exploration. Active and passive experience have been defined in two general ways: (1) in terms of the motor activity of the individual, and (2) in terms of the extent to which decisions about where to explore are made by the individual, or are guided by another.

Motor activity can facilitate spatial orientation depending on the developmental level of children and the difficulty of the spatial task. In a task in which children of two ages viewed a large model town either from a stationary position, while riding through it, or while walking through it, 3rd graders reconstructed the town equally well in all conditions, whereas kindergartners performed most accurately when they walked through the town (Herman, Kolker, & Shaw, 1982). However, when the environment cannot be viewed in its entirety from a single vantage point, or when the spatial task is more difficult (e.g., when barriers are present), motor activity may facilitate performance even for adults (cf. Cohen & Weatherford, 1980; Weatherford & Cohen, 1981).

Consider next active versus passive exploration defined as self-directed versus other-directed exploration. Studies done in natural environments (Appleyard, 1970; Beck & Wood, 1976) have indicated that adults who get around their home cities by driving (self-guided) construct more accurate maps of their cities than adults who get around by riding the bus (other-guided). However, this correlational finding is difficult to interpret, because it may be that people who drive do so because they have better spatial competencies to begin with. Also, drivers probably differ from bus riders not only in the number of decisions concerning spatial orientation they must make, but also in the extent of their geographic range.

Feldman and Acredolo (1979) experimentally isolated the effects of mode of exploration by taking preschool and 10-year-old children on a walk through unfamiliar halls to find a hidden object. Children were either led by the hand by the experimenter (passive condition) or walked by themselves with the experimenter following behind (active condition). Preschool children who explored actively were more accurate in remembering the location of the object than were preschoolers who explored passively, but the 9- to 10-year olds did equally well in both conditions.

Further evidence that self-guided exploration facilitates spatial orientation in young children is provided by correlational data from Hazen (1982). This study was designed to examine whether naturally occurring differences in young children's exploration were related to their spatial knowledge. Children aged 1½ to 3½ years were observed exploring in a museum room and in a maze-like laboratory environment. Children whose exploration of these two environments was primarily self-directed rather than guided by their parents performed better on detour and route-reversal tasks in the laboratory environment. Although these data do not resolve the causal direction of the relationship between self-guided exploration and more accurate spatial orientation, taken together with Feldman and Acredolo's (1979) data, they suggest that young children who actively guide their own exploration acquire more accurate spatial knowledge than children who are guided by others.

In contrast, Herman (1980) found that kindergartners and 3rd graders reconstructed a large model town more accurately when their motor activity and attention were guided by an experimenter rather than self-guided. This difference may be due in part to the fact that subjects in the studies by Feldman and Acredolo (1979) and Hazen (1982) were 4 years of age or younger, whereas children in Herman's (1980) study were older. Older children range may interpret the experimenter-guided situation as similar to experiences they have in school in which teachers provide specific information and later test children's knowledge of it. Feldman and Acredolo (1979) and Hazen (1982), however, did not inform children of the spatial task they would be required to do until after they explored. Even if they had been informed, children less than 4 years old would probably be unable to use this information to improve their spatial memory, as they have encountered few school-like testing situations. This example illustrates the importance of considering the everyday situations the child encounters in order to infer how the child may interpret the laboratory task. For younger children, self-guided exploration may serve to direct their attention to spatial relationships that might be ignored during adult-guided exploration, because they must make decisions about where to go and must monitor their position relative to other landmarks (including significant adults). For the older child, the advantages of self-guided exploration may be surpassed by the advantages of obtaining specific information from adults that is relevant to the spatial tasks to be encountered later.

Specific Spatial Training.   Herman's (1980) study indicates the possibility of improving spatial orientation through specific training, at least for older children and adults. Natural situations often include various kinds of training, from getting directions on how to get somewhere to formal lessons in map reading and other geographic concepts. Spatial training is involved in preparation for a variety of jobs, from driving a cab to being an air traffic controller, and for sports such as orienteering, hiking, or sailing. In spite of the widespread use of spatial training, little research has examined its effects.

As noted earlier, the act of creating a map or model—of trying to externalize one's knowledge of an environmental layout—seems to direct attention to spatial relationships not previously realized (Hart, 1981; Hazen et al., 1978). Training and practice in making and interpreting maps might also be expected to lead to improvement in their construction and use. Thorndyke and Statz (1980) trained poor map readers (adults) in several specific techniques designed to maximize the information they could acquire from maps. The trained subjects were able to acquire more knowledge from maps than were control subjects who continued to practice their own techniques. Studies investigating the effects of other types of training on spatial knowledge are badly needed, as they would provide information that would be useful for practical as well as theoretical reasons.

Affect and Motivation.   As Siegel (1982) has emphasized, spatial orientation occurs within social-emotional contexts. An ecological, functionalist perspective must take account of the emotional significance of the environment for the individual, and of the individual's goals and motivations within that environment. People encode spatial landmarks and relationships that are meaningful to them because of their importance in everyday activities. This is particularly true for young children, who are more likely to include personal rather than objective spatial information in their spatial representations. For example, Hart (1979) found that children's maps of their neighborhoods were largely composed of landmarks with personal meanings such as "the house with the dog that bites" and "the snow slide to the school bus" (p. 225). Children's spatial experience and hence knowledge may also be limited by emotional factors. Moore and Young (1978) have noted that children limit their range of exploration by avoiding places they fear, because of physical dangers such as heavy traffic, bodies of water, dangerous animals, or people who might hurt them; or because they are too far away or unfamiliar.

The spatial behavior and knowledge of nonhuman species is no doubt also effected by motivation and emotion. For example, Menzel (1978) carried chimpanzees around a field to show them the locations of hidden fruits and vegetables. When released, the chimps did not follow the experienced path but instead used a least-distance strategy to collect and eat all the fruits (which they prefer) before collecting the vegetables. Menzel also noted that the chimps quickly learned the types of locations used for hiding food. When they had previously seen food being hidden in a location, they would grab it immediately. However, when they saw a location that looked suspiciously like a hiding place for food but had not actually seen food being hidden there, they would approach cautiously, sometimes first poking the location with a stick to check for snakes or other dangers. Thus, chimps are able to encode spatial locations important to their survival and to integrate knowledge of these locations with knowledge of their emotional significance.

Finally, spatial orientation may be more accurate when the individual feels emotionally secure. Evidence for this comes from the previously cited study by Acredolo (1979), in which infants were more likely to accurately locate hidden objects using geocentric reference system when in their homes than when in a laboratory setting. Because this difference disappeared when infants were provided with an extended "get acquainted" period in the laboratory, Acredolo (1982) attributed the infant's poorer initial performance in the laboratory to emotional distraction.

Limited Variations Due to the Environment

Landmarks .   Probably the most obvious environmental factors that can be expected to influence an individual's spatial orientation are the amount, type, and location of the landmarks that differentiate the environment. As discussed in our review of universal developments in human spatial orientation, the availability of salient landmarks permits infants to use objective, geocentric frames of reference and to avoid egocentric errors (Acredolo & Evans, 1980; Bremner & Bryant, 1977; Rieser, 1979). Landmarks are also helpful to preschool children in reconstructing spatial layouts (Siegel, 1981), and in recalling spatial locations (Acredolo et al., 1975). As children grow older and develop the ability to use metric information to make distance and direction judgments, landmarks are not as necessary for spatial orientation.

Especially for young children, landmarks are most helpful when they are salient and when they mark locations directly. The *directness* of landmarks may be operationally defined as the distance between the landmark and the spatial location being sought, but it has been difficult to get beyond circular definitions of *salience*. An ecological, functional approach may be very valuable in dealing with issues such as this. Landmarks should be salient for individuals to the extent that they serve an important function in the individual's daily life. For example, chimpanzees appear to be extremely sensitive to the locations of objects in the environment (Menzel, 1978). They are able to remember the locations of up to 18 pieces of hidden food. They also take special notice of novel objects, objects that have been moved, and vertical structures. In contrast, wolves are less attentive to the nature and location of objects in their environment (Peters, 1973). They appear instead to use distal environmental features such as tree lines or rivers for spatial orientation.

These cross-species differences in landmark salience may be explained with reference to ecological factors. Chimpanzees inhabit highly differentiated environments containing a multitude of food and water locations. They therefore need to be very attentive to subtle variations in environmental features and to have a good memory for spatial locations. For safety, chimps are very attentive to environmental alterations that would signal the presence of predators or dangerous animals like snakes, and they always sleep in trees. This could account for their attention to novelty and to vertical structures. In contrast, many populations of wolves inhabit fairly undifferentiated habitats, and their food source has no permanent location. They range far from their home bases in search of food, and thus it is more adaptive for them to rely on large distal features rather than subtle proximal features. The differences in salience of landmarks between chimps and wolves is an example of *general* variations *between* species, which may account for *limited* variations *within* species.

Barriers and Subdivisions.   Individuals may overestimate the distance between locations if barriers prevent them from taking a straight-line route from one to another. Illustrative of this is a study by Kosslyn, Pick, and Fariello (1974), who taught preschool children and adults the locations of 10 objects in a room-sized square space. The space was subdivided into four quadrants by a transparent barrier in one direction and an opaque barrier in the other. Children tended to exaggerate the distance between pairs separated by either type of barrier, whereas adults only exaggerated the distance between pairs separated by the opaque barrier. Thus, distance judgments of both adults and children may be affected by functional considerations, i.e., the time and/or effort required to travel the distance, but adults may be able to overcome this bias when optical cues are available.

A study by Allen (1981) suggests an alternative explanation. Children and adults were presented with slides depicting a route and were asked to subdivide the route. They were then asked to estimate the distance between locations within and between subdivisions. Both children and adults overestimated distances *between* subdivisions more than distances *within* subdivisions. Thus, barriers may result in the overestimation of paths they intersect because they are used to subdivide spaces cognitively. This hypothesis is further supported by Newcombe and Liben (in press), who presented data indicating that children need to organize space into smaller subdivisions than adults because of more limited information-processing capacities, which accounts for the differential effects of barriers at different ages, e.g., in Kosslyn et al. (1974). When a cognitively less-demanding task was presented (i.e., paired distance judgment rather than rank orderings of all distances), children did not differ from adults in their performance. Also, when adults were presented with twice as many objects in the same space and were required to rank order the distances between all pairs of objects, they overestimated distances between locations separated by both transparent and opaque barriers. Thus, the biasing effect of barriers may be a joint function of the difficulty of the spatial judgments and the information-processing capacity of the individual.

Barriers and subdivisions may affect directional as well as distance judgments. Stevens and Coupe (1978) found that when one entire subdivision of a space was in a particular directional relationship to another entire subdivision, adult subjects tended to infer that this same directional relationship applied to all points within each subdivision. This strategy may result in errors of directional judgment. For example, because Nevada is east of California, people generally assume that Reno is northeast of San Diego, whereas it is actually northwest. Recent data from Acredolo and Boulter (1983) indicates that school-aged children also show such a bias.

Task Demands. Individuals given the same experiences in the same environment but presented with different spatial tasks may show different levels of spatial competency as a result of their attempts to use whatever competencies they possess to meet the demands of the task. For example, in the previously discussed study by Newcombe and Liben (in press), all children received the same type of training within the same environment to learn the objects' locations, but they differed in their representations of the distances between these objects as a function of the type of distance estimation task that was presented. In this example, different task demands did not affect the individual's knowledge of the environment, because this knowledge was acquired before the imposition of different tasks. Rather, the task demands affected which aspects of this knowledge they extracted, and how they extracted it.

Task demands can also directly affect spatial knowledge to the extent that they induce the individual to experience the environment in different ways. Instructions informing individuals that they will be required to remember spatial information would be expected to affect their acquisition of spatial knowledge. Children as young as 3 years of age remember more spatial information when they are informed of the task they will be given later (Acredolo et al., 1975). However, such information may be less helpful as the spatial memory task becomes more difficult (Herman et al., 1982). Instructions about the spatial task will result in better performance on the task to the extent that individuals are able to adapt their encoding of spatial information to meet task demands.

Similarly, the extent to which spatial experience is adapted to spatial task demands affects spatial performance. In a relevant study, Cohen, Weatherford, and Byrd (1980) trained 2nd and 6th graders to learn the locations of several objects either by walking between them (active acquisition) or by viewing them (passive acquisition). They were then asked to estimate the distances between these objects either by walking out the distance (active response) or by telling the experimenter how far to walk (passive response). Second graders performed more accurately when acquisition and response were congruent than when they were incongruent, although 6th graders performed equally well in both conditions.

Similarly, Siegel, Herman, Allen, and Kirasic (1979) found that children from 5 to 10 years of age reconstructed a model of a town more accurately when the scale of the model presented during acquisition was congruent with the scale presented during assessment.

Thus, task demands affect spatial *knowledge* to the extent that they affect the individual's acquisition of particular types of spatial information. They affect spatial *performance* to the extent that they induce the individual to extract certain aspects of their spatial knowledge, and to the extent that they shape the acquisition of spatial knowledge in ways that are congruent with the types of spatial performance that will be required later.

It is important to keep in mind that task demands and other environmentally imposed variations, such as landmarks and barriers, are affected by the individual's spatial competencies and interpretation of the particular spatial problems presented by environments. It is thus impossible to specify the effects of environmental variations without reference to the particular organism and its spatial goals. We have seen that even within a particular species, such as humans, we cannot make blanket statements about the effects of landmarks, barriers, or task demands on orientation. The effect of such variations depends on factors such as the individual's developmental level, past experiences, current goals, and perceptual and cognitive capacities. Between species, the effects of different environmental variations on spatial orientation are likely to be even more diverse. As we have noted, an undifferentiated and barrier-free environment would present very different sorts of spatial demands on a wolf versus a chimpanzee. Thus, when viewed from an ecological perspective, the limited effects of environmental variations must be analyzed in terms of the spatial problems they present to particular organisms.

General Variations

As we have noted, any limited variations in spatial orientation abilities may become general variations if the particular transactions involved in these variations recur to the extent that they affect the individual's general handling of spatial information. For example, individuals who are consistently very active in their spatial exploration, who travel extensively, or who receive extensive spatial training of some sort may develop general ways of processing spatial information that differ from those of individuals who lack these experiences. Similarly, individuals who live in environments that are highly differentiated may develop different general strategies for processing spatial information relative to individuals who live in relatively undifferentiated environments. Thus, whereas limited variations occur *within* individuals, general variations occur *between* individuals, or between entire populations, cultures, or species. Like limited variations, general variations may be due primarily to the individual or to the environment.

General Variations Due to the Individual

Because individuals exert influences over the ecological situations they encounter, any individual variations in processing environmental information can potentially affect the quality of the individual's life experiences in ways that may lead to general variations in spatial competencies (Wohlwill, 1981). Hence, individuals may acquire general variations in their spatial skill repertoires to the extent that they differ in their perception or cognitive processing of spatial information, in the types of spatial activities they habitually engage in, or in the types of environments they generally encounter. Individual characteristics that could lead to general variations in spatial competencies among humans include sex, physical and sensory handicaps, general cognitive abilities and cognitive styles, and individual differences in socioemotional factors.

Sex Differences.   A considerable number of studies indicate that males excel in certain types of spatial competence relative to females. For example, males have been found to be more accurate than females in their sense of direction (Koslowski & Bryant, 1977), their reconstruction of spatial layouts (Siegel & Schadler, 1977), and their ability to mentally rotate spatial arrays (Tapley & Bryden, 1977). These sex-related differences in spatial competency have been attributed to differences in both physiological factors such as sex hormones (e.g., Money & Erhardt, 1972) and brain lateralization (e.g., McGlone, 1978), and cultural factors such as the actual physical environments of boys and girls (e.g., Hart, 1979) and the types of toys and materials provided to boys and girls (e.g., Rheingold & Cook, 1975). Reviews of the relevant literature (Harris, 1981; McGee, 1982; Newcombe, 1982) suggest that no single cause can account for all the sex differences in spatial competency; it is more likely that a variety of factors are mutually reinforcing. As Wohlwill (1981) has noted, any incipient differences between sexes that affect their spatial behavior and processing of spatial information may generate differences in ecological contexts of early development.

Physical and Sensory Handicaps.   Because spatial orientation is facilitated more by active exploration of the environment than by passive exploration, physical handicaps that curtail motor ability, such as cerebral palsy and orthopedic handicaps, might be expected to be detrimental for developing spatial abilities. Similarly, sensory handicaps, such as blindness or deafness, should also affect developing spatial competencies, because these handicaps will affect the individual's spatial activity and encoding of spatial information. However, apart from a few recent investigations of the spatial competencies of blind children and adults, almost no empirical work has addressed these issues.

Longitudinal studies by Fraiberg (1977) have indicated that blind infants may be delayed in acquisition of the concept of object permanence. They were often delayed in their search for dropped objects and in their ability to use sound as a cue to locate objects. Such findings suggest that blind children may have more difficulty than sighted children in using objective, geocentric frames of reference.

Visual experience may also play an important role in the ability to construct spatial representations and to make spatial inferences. Vision permits individuals to detect the underlying invariant structure of spatial layout across optical transformations that occur with movement (Gibson, 1979). The blind are at a considerable disadvantage in perceiving this structure and thus may lack experiences important for development of the ability to form accurate representations of spatial layouts. Are the blind able to construct accurate, Euclidean mental representations of spatial layouts, or must their representations necessarily be route-like and highly influenced by functional distance? Rieser, Lockman, and Pick (1980) investigated this question by asking sighted, adventitiously blind, and congenitally blind adults to rank order both functional and straight-line distances between pairs of locations in a familiar environment. As expected, because of the familiarity of the layout, the functional distance judgments of the three groups did not differ much, but the congenitally blind subjects made less accurate straight-line judgments. They were likely to exaggerate straight-line distances when the functional distance between two points exceeded the straight-line distance. However, map-like representations generated from the straight-line judgments of the congenitally blind subjects did in fact resemble the actual environment to a considerable degree. Visual experience is thus very helpful, but not essential, for the formation of Euclidean spatial representations.

Cognitive Ability and Cognitive Style.   Individuals differ in their basic capacities for encoding, remembering, and using information—spatial or otherwise. It is not particularly interesting or useful to know that individual differences in general intelligence are related to individual differences in spatial capacities, but it would be interesting to know how individuals with particularly good spatial abilities adapt to various types of ecologically imposed spatial problems. Yet, surprisingly little is known about individual variations in spatial information processing. The previously discussed study by Thorndyke and Statz (1980) illustrates one promising approach. In order to design effective strategies to help individuals acquire information from maps, these investigators examined the processes used by people who were very good at map reading. When individuals with poor map-reading skills learned the attention, mnemonic, and control strategies used by the expert readers, their ability to extract information from maps improved relative to a control group.

Styles of processing spatial information could also lead to individual differences in spatial competencies. Most research in this area has examined the impact of fairly global individual differences in cognitive style (especially field dependence/independence) on various types of standardized spatial tasks (Liben, 1981).

Cognitive style has not yet been examined in relation to way-finding in large-scale environments, nor have the particular cognitive processes used by field-dependent and independent persons been examined. Studies examining the ecological factors that influence individual differences in styles of spatial information processing are also needed.

Socioemotional Factors.   To the extent that individuals differ across situations in their confidence about exploration and their habitual tendency to explore actively versus passively, individual differences in spatial competencies may result. Hazen (1982) found that mode of exploration of preschoolers was highly consistent across two very different settings (a museum and a laboratory playhouse), and children who explored more independently in the museum were likely to be more accurate in their ability to take direct detours and infer new routes within the laboratory playhouse.

Why might some children be consistently more active in exploration than others? Mode of exploration is probably influenced by parental restrictions and by the child's feelings about exploring away from the parent, and thus the parent–child relationship would seem to be an important factor in determining general variations in mode of exploration. In Bowlby's (1969) ethological theory of mother–child attachment, individual differences in security of attachment are defined to a large extent by the balance infants show between exploring and seeking proximity to their mothers. With this in mind, Hazen and Durrett (1982) investigated the relationship between early individual differences in infants' security of attachment and their later exploration and spatial orientation abilities. As predicted, 2½-year-old children who had been classified at 12 months of age as securely attached were more active, independent explorers and scored higher in spatial orientation tasks (i.e., taking detours around a barrier to find a goal and finding the goal from new starting points) than those classified as anxiously attached. Some children previously classified as anxiously attached were reluctant to leave their mothers to explore; others explored without apparent interest in their surroundings and therefore might not have encoded spatial information. These results suggest that individual differences in affective response to the environment may mediate styles of exploring and of encoding information about environments.

General Variations Due to the Environment

To the extent that variations in the physical environment and in the spatial tasks encountered as a function of this environment retain some consistency over the course of development, individuals may develop general differences in their strategies for processing spatial information and maintaining spatial orientation. Environmental variations would include both physical features of the environment (i.e., degree of differentiation, presence of barriers, and type of organization) and social contextual features (e.g., behaviors required to function in that particular environment, the social roles imposed, and cultural norms and practices).

In our discussion of the effect of specific environmental variation, we examined several investigators' attempts to isolate the specific effects of particular types of physical features and contextual task demands. Almost by definition, experimental laboratory investigations of the effects of environmental variations on spatial orientation must deal only with *limited* effects, because the environmental manipulations are confined to a very restricted time and place. Examination of the general effects of environmental variations almost necessarily requires that the investigator examine differences in spatial orientation between *naturalistic* contexts that differ in particular physical features and/or social task demands. Comparisons may be made between populations that inhabit different sorts of environments (e.g., urban versus rural areas), or between cultures that may differ not only in their physical environments but also in their norms and institutions for adapting to these environments. Finally, these comparisons may also be made between species, which differ not only in the types of environments they inhabit, but also in their basic perceptual and cognitive capacities for adapting to environmentally imposed problems of spatial orientation. Cross-cultural and cross-species comparisons of spatial orientation competencies and skills have been discussed in detail elsewhere (Hazen, 1983). Here we examine their relevance in our conceptual framework for organizing and interpreting organism–environment transactions affecting spatial orientation.

General Variations Between Populations and Cultures

Because spatial orientation is accomplished more easily and accurately in environments that are highly differentiated by landmarks and organized into predictable patterns, individuals who live in relatively undifferentiated, unpatterned environments should develop keen abilities to detect very subtle cues and patterns, and to use Euclidean representations of space to remain oriented. Support for this suggestion comes from a study by Norman (1980), who compared the map-drawing abilities of children living in a relatively undeveloped environment with little obvious spatial organization (rural Appalachia) and children living in highly differentiated and patterned urban and suburban environments. The rural children performed better than the urban and suburban children, despite their relatively impoverished backgrounds. Cross-cultural studies also indicate that individuals in less-differentiated environments may develop superior spatial abilities. Berry (1966, 1971) found that Canadian Eskimos who inhabit a relatively uniform and barren environment scored higher on standardized spatial tasks than the Temne of West Africa, who live in a colorful and highly differentiated jungle environment.

The use of cross-population and cross-cultural comparisons to examine the effect of variations in the physical environment on general spatial abilities poses problems of interpretation. Individuals who inhabit very different physical environments are usually subject to very different norms, roles, and technologies that affect their spatial behavior. For example, the Eskimos are hunters who have traditionally needed to travel far from their homes in search of food, whereas the Temne subsist by farming and therefore rarely travel beyond their villages. These differences in both physical environment and spatial task demands have also led to differences in each culture's technology for dealing with spatial orientation. The Eskimo language has many more words to describe spatial location than does the Temne language, and it includes labels for very subtle variations in winds, ice, and snow (Berry, 1966; Carpenter, 1973). The Eskimos are also able to make quite detailed and accurate maps of their environment, whereas the Temne generally do not make maps. Finally, the Eskimos have devised complex technologies for spatial orientation that must be transmitted through direct teaching. Their orientation system makes use of subtle variations in snow and ice texture, aqueous features, winds, and reflections from low-hanging clouds; as well as metric information determined by dead reckoning (Carpenter, 1973). Thus, Eskimo child-rearing practices must include the teaching of these systems and strategies for spatial orientation. It is difficult to separate the effects of variations in physical versus cultural environments, because cultural norms and technologies are likely to be adapted to the constraints imposed by the physical environments in which these norms and technologies evolved (Harris, 1979).

To date, cross-cultural studies of spatial orientation have for the most part made rather global comparisons of differences in general spatial abilities between cultures that exemplify ecological extremes. For example, the use of standardized spatial tests tells us little about the spatial representations and behaviors used by the Eskimos and the Temne to solve the particular spatial orientation problems they face. More interesting cross-cultural comparisons might involve naturalistic observation of how individuals from different cultures actually maintain spatial orientation, as well as an analysis of their respective ecologies. What is the difference, for example, between the navigation systems used by Canadian Eskimos, natives of the Caroline Islands, and Western navigators? What similarities and differences exist in the ways that navigators from these cultures represent and utilize spatial information? How do these navigators adapt their capabilities for processing spatial information to meet the task at hand?

A recent study by Hutchins (1980), which compared the conceptual frameworks of Caroline Island navigation and western navigation, makes a promising start toward examining some of these issues. The ecological problems faced by the Caroline Island navigators and the spatial behaviors they use to cope with these problems have been thoroughly documented by previous investigators (Gladwin, 1970; Lewis, 1972). Hutchins felt that the tendency of previous investigators to interpret the Caroline Island navigation system from a western perspective hampered their ability to understand thoroughly why this system functions so effectively.

Western navigation is a bicoordinate system, in which a grid is established using two or more factors such that one's precise position can be established without reference to where one has already been. This system requires the navigator to adopt a bird's-eye view in order to determine his position relative to the position of his surroundings. The navigator determine his bearings and relates them to a location on his chart. In contrast, the Caroline Island navigator define each voyage between islands in terms of a star path made up of about eight to 10 stars. A third island is used as a reference to express the distance traveled. The actual location of the reference island is never seen but only imagined. As the voyage progresses, the navigator imagines that the reference island is moving back under different star bearings, while the navigator, his canoe, and the stars remain stationary. As the navigator visualizes the reference island passing under a particular star, he knows that a certain proportion of the voyage has been completed.

It is because the Caroline Island navigators imagine islands as moving, Hutchins suggests, that they find the idea of adopting a bird's-eye view in order to locate islands on a map to be baffling and nonsensical. From the perspective of Western navigators, an orientation system involving the idea of moving geography—an idea not found in any examples of western spatial orientation—is equally baffling. Western reference systems are based on fixed reference points, such as objects, distal geographic features, or abstract spatial coordinates. It is necessary to understand thoroughly the organizing framework used by the Caroline Island navigators in order to understand their navigation system and to see how it enables them to make the types of spatial inferences they make.

But why do the navigators of the Caroline Islands use this particular system? Western navigation systems developed because advances in technology led to the development of instruments and techniques that permitted individuals to keep track of their spatial location without relying on large amounts of rote memorization. The Caroline Island system, in contrast, requires a tremendous memory load. Navigators must memorize the meaning of hundreds of subtle environmental cues (e.g., sea birds, marine life, swells, wind patterns, star patterns), and of numerous possible combinations of these factors. They must also keep track constantly of the amount of time that has gone by. The reference system of keeping track of "moving" islands probably developed because it provided an easily imaged framework for organizing all the information that had to be remembered.

As Gatty (1958) has pointed out, navigation systems that use a local reference point, such as the one used by the Caroline Island navigators, may be less elegant and more cumbersome than compass-based orientation systems, but they may also be safer. They have a great deal of built-in redundancy, and they function by maintaining constant orientation to known reference points. In contrast, mistakes in calculation using the compass-based system can cause the navigator to lose track of the point of departure. Thus, Caroline Island navigation is well adapted for its own particular purpose but could not be applied beyond the area well known to the navigator.

Besides providing experiences specifically designed to foster particular types of spatial orientation skills, cultures can also affect spatial orientation indirectly. For example, children's spatial competencies may be affected by the extent to which a particular culture encourages freedom of movement and exploration for young children. As mentioned previously, cultural norms may play an important role in sex differences in spatial competencies to the extent that normative sex roles prescribe different types of spatial activities for boys and girls.

Cross-species Comparisons

Differences in spatial behavior across species cannot be fully explained without reference to the ecological niche within which such behavior occurs. We have already noted many of the ecological factors that may play a role in the types of landmarks that are salient for chimpanzees versus wolves. Based on ecological differences in the environments within which they move, we might also expect that chimps would be more sensitive to three-dimensional spatial layouts than wolves, because chimps can and do move vertically much more easily than wolves. Also, chimps should rely on more proximal reference systems than wolves. Because chimps live in an environment so rich in landmarks, and because they are so skilled in encoding and utilizing them, it seems that they should rarely if ever have a need to use a more distal frame of reference than an object reference system. Wolves, in contrast, might often be required to use a more distal system in which object locations are encoded within an all-encompassing container system, defined by two-dimensional coordinates. These coordinates could be specified by large-scale geographic features, such as a river or tree line. An alternative adaptation to meet the problem of traveling across large expanses of relatively barren land would be to *create* landmarks that permit the use of an object reference system. In fact, wolves do scent-mark familiar paths and important locations (Peters, 1973). Differences in foraging patterns was suggested as another example of the utility of an ecological approach for predicting as well as exploring cross-species variations in spatial behavior.

Cross-species comparisons of spatial orientation may be made in two general ways. The two groups being compared may be either genetically similar but faced with different environmental problems or genetically diverse but faced with similar environmental problems. In the first case, we get an idea of the various ways in which groups that share certain physical, perceptual, and cognitive capacities can use these capacities to meet divergent environmental demands. In the second case, we get an idea of how groups that differ in their basic capacities can use what they have to solve convergent environmental problems.

In making cross-species comparisons, it is important to keep in mind that most, if not all, species have multiple means of staying spatially oriented (e.g.,

Emlen, 1975a; Keeton, 1981). Finding evidence that humans and wolves can create landmarks to stay oriented in undifferentiated terrain does not rule out the possibility that these species might use distal reference systems at the same time or in other circumstances. In fact, we know that humans can do both, and wolves probably can as well. Particularly difficult spatial problems often demand multiple perceptual and cognitive solutions. To the extent that one type of strategy cannot be used or could possibly fail, alternative strategies must be available. Thus, comparisons must be made between interrelated systems of behavior and the range of environmental problems to which they are adapted.

DIRECTIONS FOR THE ECOLOGICAL STUDY OF SPATIAL ORIENTATION

In this chapter, we have argued that an ecological approach can serve as a broad conceptual framework for integrating interdisciplinary research on spatial orientation and cognition. Such an approach brings together investigators concerned primarily with perceptual and cognitive mechanisms of spatial orientation and investigators concerned primarily with environments in which spatial behavior occurs. It also provides a common ground for researchers studying human and animal spatial orientation. The spatial behavior of all organisms, in all phases of their development, is viewed as both an adaptation to and an influence on the ecological contexts of development.

How might the ecological study of spatial orientation and its development proceed? We have noted two general approaches to the study of the organism–environment transactions involved in spatial orientation development. The first focuses on developments that are universal across species; the second on variations in development that occur within species or within individuals.

Although investigators have learned much about the various mechanisms of spatial orientation that develop universally in humans and in various nonhuman species, they are just beginning to consider the interplay between the ontogenesis of these orientation mechanisms and the spatial orientation problems that are encountered over an individual's life history. Longitudinal studies of the development of individuals' spatial abilities in conjunction with the ecological changes they experience would teach us more about these relationships. Almost no studies have examined human spatial orientation as it occurs in the real-life contexts in which it functions and develops. Indeed, several investigations have suggested that the study of human development is in need of a body of naturalistic, descriptive data that deals with children's adaptation to and influence upon the varied ecological contexts encountered over the course of their development (Bronfenbrenner, 1979; White & Siegel, in press; Wohlwill, 1981). A natural history of the ecological changes that accompany developments in spatial abilities is the

first step toward establishing an understanding of organism–environment transactions in species-specific spatial developments.

But knowing that a particular spatial development regularly coincides with a
particular ecological change still leaves unanswered questions about the extent
to which particular universal ecological changes exert causal effects on the
development of spatial orientation. For example, must human infants learn to
walk before they develop the ability to update egocentric movements in small
locomotor spaces, or does walking merely facilitate this development? Controlled
experiments would be most desirable to answer such questions. Of course tamper-
ing with universal ecological changes in the case of humans would be clearly
unethical and probably impractical, but the effects of infants' walking could be
studied, for example, by seeking out natural instances in which it does not
develop. Alternatively, experiences could be provided that produce ecological
effects similar to walking, but at an earlier age (e.g., giving infants experience
in walkers). Such studies are useful and suggestive but require caution in interpretation, because the processes of experimentally induced and naturally occurring development might be different (Wohlwill, 1973).

The relationship between spatial orientation and ecological factors can also
be studied by examining the extent to which variations in ecological factors are
correlated with variations in spatial orientation skills. We have noted that ecological variations can have either limited effects, resulting in variations in spatial
orientation abilities *within* individuals, or general effects, resulting in variations
between individuals. In the study of the development of human spatial orientation,
more research has focused on the former type of ecological variation, probably
because of an emphasis on laboratory tasks that isolate the effects of specific
environmental variations on spatial performance.

Little research, however, has examined how environmental variations that
retain some consistency over the course of an individual's development affect
spatial competence. For example, do individuals that inhabit fairly barren environments develop the ability to use more distal frames of reference than individuals who inhabit highly differentiated environments? Multiple research
strategies might be used to examine such questions. Two populations that inhabit
environments differing in some theoretically interesting way could be observed
performing orientation tasks that they encounter in their daily lives. From these
observations, hypotheses could be made concerning the cognitive processes and
strategies used to solve these tasks, and the environmental factors that may have
influenced their development. Such hypotheses could then be tested, using especially constructed experimental tasks.

Because individuals shape and influence the ecological contexts in which they
develop, variations between individuals can also result in variations in organism–
environment spatial transactions. As with environmentally based variations, variations due to individuals may also be limited or general. Again, less is known
about how differences in the ecological contexts of individuals who differ in

general ways (e.g., males vs. females or blind vs. sighted persons) affect the development of their spatial abilities than is known about how limited differences that occur within individuals (e.g., active vs. passive movement or feelings of security) affect spatial abilities.

Finally, it is important to note that adopting a functionalist perspective to the development of spatial orientation requires concomitant changes in traditional methods of evaluating human performance on spatial tasks. Spatial knowledge and abilities have generally been assessed by requiring subjects to produce some sort of external representation of their spatial knowledge via models, drawings, verbal distance and direction judgments, motor behavior, etc. The measure of such knowledge has been its "accuracy," with the usual standard of accuracy being a metrically accurate cartographic map (Downs & Siegel, 1981). Such evaluation leads to the conclusion that children become more accurate, therefore better adapted, as they mature (though even adults remain "inaccurate" when evaluated by cartographic maps). But the notion that children progress from a state that is poorly adapted to a state that is better adapted is contrary to a functionalist perspective, rooted in evolutionary biology, in which organisms are assumed to be adapted to ecological demands at all phases of their life-spans (Oppenheim, 1981). Clearly, individuals who are poorly adapted early in life should be less likely to survive until they can reproduce. Furthermore, we know that children's spatial orientation in everyday situations is overwhelmingly accurate (Downs & Siegel, 1981). They can generally locate what they need and rarely get lost. They only become inaccurate when their spatial orientation skills are pushed to the limits by psychological laboratory tasks.

Our purpose here is not to question the usefulness of experimental laboratory tasks. Indeed, precisely because children's spatial behavior in naturalistic settings is so uniformly accurate, we are limited in what we can discover about the nature of the cognitive structures and processes that permit spatial orientation unless we examine them under controlled conditions that tax their limits. Our point here is that, as many other developmental psychologists are coming to realize, we cannot fully understand or interpret human capabilities and limitations in spatial orientation, or how these change with development, without examining how people use spatial orientation strategies in the various ecological situations they encounter over their life-spans.

ACKNOWLEDGMENTS

Preparation of this chapter was partially supported by Program Project Grant No. HD050207 from NICHHD to the Institute of Child Development of the University of Minnesota. The authors are indebted to Bill Swann and Renee Baillargeon for constructive criticism of the manuscript.

REFERENCES

Able, K. P. (1980). Mechanisms of orientation, navigation, and homing. In S. A. Gauthreaux, Jr. (Ed.), *Animal migration, orientation, and homing.* New York: Academic Press.

Acredolo, L. P. (1976). Frames of reference used by children for orientation in an unfamiliar space. In G. Moore & R. Golledge (Eds.), *Environmental knowing.* Stroudsburg, PA: Dowden, Hutchinson, & Ross.

Acredolo, L. P. (1978). Development of spatial orientation in infancy. *Developmental Psychology, 14,* 224–234.

Acredolo, L. P. (1979). Laboratory versus home: The effect of environment on the 9-month-old infant's choice of spatial reference system. *Developmental Psychology, 15,* 666–667.

Acredolo, L. P. (1981). Small- and large-scale spatial concepts in infancy and childhood. In L. S. Liben, A. H. Patterson, & N. Newcombe (Eds.), *Spatial representation and behavior across the life-span.* New York: Academic Press.

Acredolo, L. P. (1982). The familiarity factor in spatial research. In R. Cohen (Ed.), *Children's conceptions of spatial relationships.* San Francisco: Jossey–Bass.

Acredolo, L. P., & Boulter, L. (1983). *Effects of "subdivision" organization on children's judgments of distance and direction.* Paper presented at the meetings of the Society for Research in Child Development, Detroit, April.

Acredolo, L. P., & Evans, D. (1980). Developmental changes in the effects of landmarks on infant spatial behavior. *Developmental Psychology, 16,* 312–318.

Acredolo, L. P., Pick, H. L., Jr., & Olson, M. G. (1975). Environmental differentiation and familiarity as determinants of children's memory for spatial location. *Developmental Psychology, 11,* 495–501.

Allen, G. L. (1981). A developmental perspective on the effects of "subdividing" macrospatial experience. *Journal of Experimental Psychology: Human Learning and Memory, 7,* 120–132.

Allen, G. L., Kirasic, K. C., Siegel, A. W., & Herman, J. F. (1979). Developmental issues in cognitive mapping: The selection and utilization of environmental landmarks. *Child Development, 50,* 1062–1070.

Andre–Thomas, C. Y., & Autgaerden, S. (1966). *Locomotion from pre- to post-natal life.* Lavenham Suffolk, England: Spastics Society with Heinemann Medical.

Anooshian, L. J., & Young, D. (1981). Developmental changes in cognitive maps of a familiar neighborhood. *Child Development, 52,* 341–348.

Appleyard, D. (1970). Styles and methods of structuring a city. *Environment and Behavior, 2,* 100–116.

Barker, R. G., & Wright, H. F. (1954). *Midwest and its children: The psychological ecology of an American town.* Evanston, IL: Row, Peterson.

Beck, R. J., & Wood, D. (1976). Cognitive transformation of information from urban geographic fields to mental maps. *Environment and Behavior, 8,* 199–238.

Berry, J. W. (1966). Temne and Eskimo perceptual skills. *International Journal of Psychology, 1*(3), 207–229.

Berry, J. W. (1971). Ecological and cultural factors in spatial perceptual development. *Canadian Journal of Behavioral Science, 3*(4), 324–336.

Bowlby, J. (1969). *Attachment and loss:* (Vol. 1) *Attachment.* New York: Basic Books.

Bremner, J. G. (1978a). Spatial errors made by infants: Inadequate spatial cues or evidence of egocentrism? *British Journal of Psychology, 69,* 77–84.

Bremner, J. G. (1978b). Egocentric versus allocentric spatial coding in 9-month-old infants: Factors influencing the choice of code. *Developmental Psychology, 14,* 346–355.

Bremner, J. G., & Bryant, P. E. (1977). Place versus response as a basis of spatial errors made by young children. *Journal of Experimental Child Psychology, 23,* 162–171.

Bronfenbrenner, U. (1979). *The ecology of human development: Experiments by nature and design.* Cambridge: Harvard University Press.

Brown, J. L. (1975). *The evolution of behavior.* New York: Norton.

Butterworth, G., Jarrett, N., & Hicks, L. (1982). Spatiotemporal identity in infancy: Perceptual competence or conceptual deficit? *Developmental Psychology, 18,* 435–449.

Carpenter, E. (1973). *Eskimo realities.* New York: Holt, Rinehart, & Winston.

Cohen, R., Baldwin, L. M., & Sherman, R. C. (1978). Cognitive maps of a naturalistic setting. *Child Development, 49,* 1216–1218.

Cohen, R., & Weatherford, D. L. (1980). Effect of route traveled on distance estimates of children and adults. *Journal of Experimental Child Psychology, 29,* 403–412.

Cohen, R., Weatherford, D. L., & Byrd, D. (1980). Distance estimates of children as a function of acquisition and response activities. *Journal of Experimental Child Psychology, 30,* 464–472.

Cole, M., Hood, L., & McDermott, R. (1979). *Ecological niche picking: Ecological invalidity as an axiom of experimental cognitive psychology.* New York: Laboratory of Comparative Human Cognition and Institute for Comparative Human Development, Rockfeller University.

Cole, S., Hainsworth, F. R., Kamil, A. C., Mercier, T., & Wolf, L. L. (1982). Spatial learning as an adaptation in hummingbirds. *Science, 217,* 655–657.

Curtis, L. E., Siegel, A. W., & Furlong, N. E. (1981). Developmental differences in cognitive mapping: Configurational knowledge in familiar large-scale environments. *Journal of Experimental Child Psychology, 31,* 456–469.

Dewey, J., & Bentley, A. S. (1949). *Knowing and the known.* Boston: Beacon Press.

Downs, R. M., & Siegel, A. W. (1981). On mapping researchers mapping children mapping space. In L. S. Liben, A. H. Patterson, & N. Newcombe (Eds.), *Spatial representation and behavior across the life-span.* New York: Academic Press.

Emlen, S. T. (1975a). Migration: Orientation and navigation. In D. S. Farner & J. R. King (Eds.), *Avian biology.* New York: Academic Press.

Emlen, S. T. (1975b). The stellar-orientation system of a migratory bird. *Scientific American, 233*(2), 102–111.

Feldman, A., & Acredolo, L. (1979). The effect of active versus passive exploration on memory for spatial location in children. *Child Development, 49,* 623–636.

Fraiberg, S. (1977). *Insights from the blind.* New York: Basic Books.

Gatty, H. (1958). *Nature is your guide.* London: Collins.

Gibson, J. J. (1979). *The ecological approach to visual perception.* Boston: Houghton Mifflin.

Gladwin, T. (1970). *East is a big bird.* Cambridge: Harvard University Press.

Hardwick, D. A., McIntyre, C. W., & Pick, H. L., Jr. (1976). The content and manipulation of cognitive maps in children and adults. *Monographs of the Society for Research in Child Development, 41* (3, Serial No. 166).

Harris, L. J. (1981). Sex-related variations in spatial skill. In L. S. Liben, A. H. Patterson, & N. Newcombe (Eds.), *Spatial representation and behavior across the life-span.* New York: Academic Press.

Harris, M. (1979). *Cultural materialism.* New York: Vintage.

Hart, R. A. (1979). *Children's experience of place.* New York: Irvington Publishers.

Hart, R. A. (1981). Children's spatial representation of the landscape: Lessons and questions from a field study. In L. S. Liben, A. H. Patterson, & N. Newcombe (Eds.), *Spatial representation and behavior across the life-span.* New York: Academic Press.

Hazen, N. L. (1982). Spatial exploration and spatial knowledge: Individual and developmental differences in very young children. *Child Development, 53,* 826–833.

Hazen, N. L. (1983). Spatial orientation: A comparative approach. In H. L. Pick, Jr. & L. P. Acredolo (Eds.), *Spatial orientation: Theory, research, and applications.* New York: Plenum.

Hazen, N. L., & Durrett, M. E. (1982). Relationship of security of attachment to exploration and cognitive mapping abilities in 2-year olds. *Developmental Psychology, 18,* 751–759.

Hazen, N. L., Lockman, J. J., & Pick, H. L., Jr. (1978). The development of children's representations of large-scale environments. *Child Development, 49,* 623–636.

Herman, J. F. (1980). Children's cognitive maps of large-scale spaces: Effects of exploration, direction, and repeated experience. *Journal of Experimental Child Psychology, 29,* 126–143.

Herman, J. F. (1981). *The assessment of spatial cognition in elderly persons: A synthesis of laboratory and field experiments.* Paper presented at the meetings of the Society for Research in Child Development, Boston, April.

Herman, J. F., Kolker, R. G., & Shaw, M. L. (1982). Effects of motor activity on children's intentional and incidental memory for spatial orientation. *Child Development, 53,* 239–244.

Herman, J. F., & Siegel, A. W. (1978). The development of cognitive mapping of the large-scale environment. *Journal of Experimental Child Psychology, 26,* 389–401.

Hutchins, E. (1980). *Conceptual structures of Caroline Island navigation.* Center for Human Information Processing (Report No. 93), University of California, San Diego.

Kamil, A., & Sargent, T. (Eds.). (1981). *Foraging behavior.* New York: Garland/STPM.

Keeton, W. T. (1974). The orientational and navigational basis for homing in birds. In Rubin (Ed.), *Recent advances in the study of behavior.* New York: Academic Press.

Keeton, W. T. (1981). The orientation and navigation of birds. In D. J. Aidley (Ed.), *Animal migration.* Cambridge: Cambridge University Press.

Koslowski, L. T., & Bryant, K. H. (1977). Sense of direction, spatial orientation, and cognitive maps. *Journal of Experimental Psychology: Human Perception and Performance, 3,* 590–598.

Kosslyn, S. M., Pick, H., & Fariello, F. R. (1974). Cognitive maps in children and men. *Child Development, 45,* 707–716.

Ladd, F. C. (1970). Black youths view their environment: Neighborhood maps. *Environment and Behavior, 2,* 64–79.

Lewis, D. (1972). *We the navigators.* Honolulu: The University Press of Hawaii.

Liben, L. S. (1981). Spatial representation and behavior: Multiple perspectives. In L. S. Liben, A. H. Patterson, & N. Newcombe (Eds.), *Spatial representation and behavior across the lifespan.* New York: Academic Press.

Lockman, J. J. (1984). The development of detour ability during infancy. *Child Development., 55,* 482–491.

Lockman, J. J., & Pick, H. L., Jr. (in press). Problems of scale in spatial development. In C. Sophian (Ed.), *Origins of cognitive skills.* Hillsdale, NJ: Lawrence Erlbaum Associates.

Lynch, K. (1973). Some references to orientation. In R. M. Downs & D. Stea (Eds.), *Image and environment.* Chicago: Aldine.

McGee, M. G. (1982). Spatial abilities: The influence of genetic factors. In M. Potegal (Ed.), *Spatial abilities: Development and physiological foundations.* New York: Academic Press.

McGlone, J. (1978). Sex differences in functional brain asymmetry. *Cortex, 14,* 122–128.

Menzel, E. W. (1978). Cognitive mapping in chimpanzees. In S. H. Hulse, H. Fowler, & W. K. Honig (Eds.), *Cognitive aspects of animal behavior.* Hillsdale, NJ: Lawrence Erlbaum Associates.

Money, J., & Erhardt, A. A. (1972). *Man & woman, boy & girl.* Baltimore: The Johns Hopkins University Press.

Moore, R., & Young, D. (1978). Childhood outdoors: Toward a social ecology of the landscape. In I. Altman & J. F. Wohlwill (Eds.), *Children and the environment (Human behavior and the environment,* Vol. III). New York: Plenum.

Newcombe, N. (1982). Sex-related differences in spatial ability: Problem and gaps in current approaches. In M. Potegal (Ed.), *Spatial abilities: Developmental and physiological foundations.* New York: Academic Press.

Newcombe, N., & Liben, L. S. (in press). Barrier effects in the cognitive maps of children and adults. *Journal of Experimental Child Psychology.*

Norman, D. K. (1980). A comparison of children's spatial reasoning: Rural Appalachia, suburban, and urban New England. *Child Development, 51,* 288–291.

Olton, D. S. (1979). Mazes, maps, & memory. *American Psychologist, 34,* 583–596.

Oppenheim, R. W. (1981). Ontogenetic adaptations and retrogressive processes in the development of the nervous system and behavior: A neuroembryological perspective. In K. J. Connolly & H. F. R. Prechtl (Eds.), *Maturation and development: Biological and psychological perspectives.* Philadelphia: Lippencott.

Perdeck, A. C. (1958). Two types of orientation in migrating starlings, *Sturnus vulgaris,* and chaffindnes, *Fringilla coelebs,* as revealed by displacement experiments. *Ardea, 46,* 1–37.

Perdeck, A. C. (1967). Orientation of starlings after displacement to Spain. *Ardea, 55,* 194–202.

Peters, R. (1973). Cognitive maps in wolves and men. In W. P. Preiser (Ed.). *Environmental design research* (Vol. 2). Stroudsburg, PA: Dowden, Hutchinson, & Ross.

Piaget, J. (1952). *The origins of intelligence in children.* New York: International Universities Press.

Piaget, J. (1954). *The construction of reality in the child.* New York: Basic Books.

Piaget, J., & Inhelder, B. (1967). *The child's conception of space.* New York: Norton.

Pick, H. L., Jr. (1976). Comments on the transactional-constructivist approach to environmental knowing. In G. Moore & R. Golledge (Eds.), *Environmental knowing.* Stroudsburg, PA: Dowden, Hutchinson, & Ross.

Pick, H. L., Jr., & Lockman, J. J. (1981). From frames of reference to spatial representations. In L. S. Liben, A. H. Patterson, & N. Newcombe (Eds.), *Spatial representation and behavior across the life-span.* New York: Academic Press.

Pick, H. L., Jr., & Lockman, J. J. (1982). Development of spatial cognition in children. In J. C. Baird & A. D. Lutkus (Eds.), *Mind child architecture.* Hanover, NH: University Press of New England.

Pick, H. L., Jr., Yonas, A., & Rieser, J. J. (1979). Spatial reference systems in perceptual development. In M. H. Bornstein & W. Kessen (Eds.), *Psychological development from infancy.* Hillsdale, NJ: Lawrence Erlbaum Associates.

Presson, C. C., & Ihrig, L. H. (1982). Using mother as a spatial landmark: Evidence against egocentric coding in infancy. *Developmental Psychology, 18,* 699–703.

Rheingold, H. L., & Cook, K. V. (1975). The content of boys' and girls' rooms as an index of parents' behavior. *Child Development, 46,* 459–463.

Rieser, J. (1979). Spatial orientation of six-month-old infants. *Child Development, 50,* 1078–1087.

Rieser, J. J. (1983). The generation and early development of spatial inferences. In H. L. Pick, Jr. & L. P. Acredolo (Eds.), *Spatial orientation: Theory, research, and applications.* New York: Plenum.

Rieser, J. J., Doxsey, P. A., McCarrell, N. S., & Brooks, P. H. (1982). Way finding and toddlers' use of information from an aerial view of a maze. *Developmental Psychology, 18,* 724–720.

Rieser, J. J., & Heiman, M. L. (1982). Spatial self-reference systems and shortest-route behavior in toddlers. *Child Development, 53,* 524–533.

Rieser, J. J., Lockman, J. J., & Pick, H. L., Jr. (1980). The role of visual experience in knowledge of spatial layout. *Perception and Psychophysics, 28,* 185–190.

Schmidt–Koenig, K. (1975). *Migration and homing in animals.* New York: Springer–Verlag.

Siegel, A. W. (1981). The externalization of cognitive maps by children and adults: In search of ways to ask better questions. In L. S. Liben, A. H. Patterson, and N. Newcombe (Eds.), *Spatial representation and behavior across the life-span.* New York: Academic Press.

Siegel, A. W. (1982). Toward a social ecology of cognitive mapping. In R. Cohen (Ed.), *Children's conceptions of spatial relationships.* San Francisco: Jossey–Bass.

Siegel, A. W., Herman, J. F., Allen, G. L., & Kirasic, K. C. (1979). The development of cognitive maps of large- and small-scale space. *Child Development, 50,* 582–585.

Siegel, A. W., & Schadler, M. (1977). Young children's cognitive maps of their classroom. *Child Development, 48,* 388–394.

Smith, J. N. M. (1974). The food searching behavior of two European thrushes: II. The adaptiveness of the search pattern. *Behavior, 49*, 1–61.

Stevens, A., & Coupe, P. (1978). Distortions in judged spatial relations. *Cognitive Psychology, 10*, 422–437.

Tapley, S. M., & Bryden, M. P. (1977). An investigation of sex differences in spatial ability: Mental rotation of three-dimensional objects. *Canadian Journal of Psychology, 31*, 122–130.

Thorndyke, P. W., & Statz, C. (1980). Individual differences in procedures for knowledge acquisition from maps. *Cognitive Psychology, 12*, 137–175.

Tversky, B. (1981). Distortions in memory for maps. *Cognitive Psychology, 13*, 407–433.

Waddell, K. J., & Rogoff, B. (1981). Effect of contextual organization on spatial memory of middle-aged and older women. *Developmental Psychology, 17*, 878–885.

Walsh, D. A., Krauss, I. K., & Regnier, V. A. (1981). Spatial ability, environmental knowledge, and environmental use: The elderly. In L. S. Liben, A. H. Patterson, & N. Newcombe (Eds.), *Spatial representation and behavior across the life-span.* New York: Academic Press.

Weatherford, D. L. (1982). Spatial cognition as a function of size and scale of the environment. In R. Cohen (Ed.), *Children's conceptions of spatial relationships.* San Francisco: Jossey–Bass.

Weatherford, D. L., & Cohen, R. (1981). *The influence of locomotor activity on spatial representation of large-scale environments.* Paper presented at the meetings of the Society for Research in Child Development, Boston, April.

White, S. H., & Siegel, A. W. (in press). Cognitive development in the time and space. In B. Rogoff & J. Love (Eds.), *Everyday cognition: Its development in social context.* Cambridge: Harvard University Press.

Wiltschko, R. (1983). The ontogeny of orientation in young pigeons. *Comparative Biochemistry and Physiology, A, 76*, 701–708.

Wohlwill, J. F. (1973). *The study of behavioral development.* New York: Academic Press.

Wohlwill, J. F. (1976). Searching for the environment in environmental cognition research: A commentary on research strategy. In G. T. Moore & R. C. Gollege (Eds.), *Environmental knowing.* Stroudsburg, PA: Dowden, Hutchinson, & Ross.

Wohlwill, J. F. (1981). Experimental, developmental, differential: Which way the royal road to knowledge about spatial cognition? In L. S. Liben, A. H. Patterson, & N. Newcombe (Eds.), *Spatial representation and behavior across the life-span.* New York: Academic Press.

Zach, R., & Falls, J. B. (1976). Ovenbird (Aves: Parulidae) hunting behavior in a patchy environment: An experimental study. *Canadian Journal of Zoology, 54*, 1863–1879.

9

Learning by Performing: An Ecological Theme for the Study of Vocal Learning

Meredith J. West
Department of Psychology
University of North Carolina

Andrew P. King
Department of Psychology
Duke University

> A patient one day presented himself to Abernethy; after careful examination the celebrated practitioner said, 'You need amusement; go and hear Grimaldi; he will make you laugh and that will be better for you than any drugs.' 'My God,' exclaimed the invalid, 'but I am Grimaldi!' (Lombroso, 1891, p. 24).

The ecological approach to the study of learning "seeks its general principles in the relationship between animals and their natural environments, rather than in the characteristics of the animal alone" (Johnston, 1981, p. 125). The ecological approach may also be captured by a series of "really" questions: What does the animal "really" learn?; where does it "really" learn it?; what is "really" picked up from the environment?; and how does the animal "really" learn it? As different methods are required to answer each question, another set of meta-ecological questions can be asked: How is the learning "really" studied?; what do the investigators "really" measure?; and what does the obtained outcome "really" signify?

In the chapter to follow, we ask these two kinds of questions about song learning in birds. What is really learned in song learning and how is song learning really studied? We attempt to answer the first question by reference to the second, i.e., to ask how the study of song informs us about the assumed nature of song learning.

We begin by describing briefly the qualities of bird song that have elevated it to its present status as the premier animal model of vocal learning. We note as well the historical context in which the study of song learning achieved prominence. What then follows is an evaluation of concepts and methods central

245

to the study of song learning. Their features are examined in general and specific terms, exploiting research on song learning in cowbirds for the latter purpose. We end by posing new questions for the study of song learning that highlight the need to consider the relationship between the song learner and its environment.

BIRD SONG: A NICHE FOR EVERYONE?

It's hard to think of a behavior more adapted to ecological analysis than bird song. The study of song affords an array of settings, species, and sounds to suit scientists of all persuasions. Moreover, its dependence on learning, heredity, maturation, climate, neuroanatomy, and the inclinations of the sexes invites diverse theorizing. And, if all else fails, watching and listening to birds cannot fail but to inspire us as we behold the vocal and aerial accomplishments of a "simpler" species.

The scientific charms of song have not gone unnoticed. Rather the opposite has occurred, as most recently stated by Hinde (1982):

> I would suggest that the study of bird song is the example *par excellence* of the ethological approach. It involves the study of a naturally occurring pattern of behavior against a background of natural history of the species concerned, but employs an experimental methodology. It involves questions about the causation, ontogeny, function, and evolution of the pattern in question, questions that are at the same time independent and interfertile. It is probably true to say that the study of bird song has done as much for the advancement of ethology as the study of any other specific aspect of behavior. (p. xvi)

How did the study of bird song achieve such status? First and foremost, the nature of song learning, like imprinting, demonstrated principles of learning not easily accommodated by behaviorism. Second, it not only implicated evolution in learning, but learning in evolution. Third, bird song unified genes and the environment at a time when empirical examples of such interactions were most needed. Predispositions and constraints for perceptual learning, for motor learning, and for adapting to different environments were evident. And finally, bird song offered a model for the study of human speech, as sufficient parallels existed to make profitable and probably heuristic analogies (Marler, 1970; Nottebohm, 1972; Petrinovich, 1972).

Given such contributions, what more can be said about the study of song? This chapter adds little to the chronology of past achievements as they have been recently and admirably reviewed (Kroodsma & Miller, 1982). Our focus is on what the study of song promises for the future. Thus, we choose to survey the issues and concepts that guided past efforts and to evaluate their potential for guiding prospective endeavors. We begin by briefly noting historical events that may have contributed to the views of learning implicit in the study of song acquisition.

SETTING THE STAGE

Although the structure and function of bird song had been intensively described for many years, the first thorough investigations of the role of learning only began in the late 1950s (Thorpe, 1958, 1961). This was a time when learning was typically the province of comparative psychology and instinct the province of ethology. As a result, song learning and related phenomena such as imprinting were often measured and defined against the standard set by the psychology of learning (Hess, 1970). At that time, however, the comparative psychology of learning was undergoing an indentity crisis about the nature and significance of its contributions to psychology and animal behavior (Eaton, 1970; Hodos & Campbell, 1969; Lockard, 1971). Diagnoses and possible therapies for comparative psychology abounded and perhaps none was so appealing as the "back to nature" remedy preferred by ethology. What better than to flee the laboratory and to be restored by the animal's "all natural" ecology? That ethology was enjoying considerable success in revealing the functions of animal behavior conferred added appeal to this proposed remedy for the problems of comparative psychology.

In retrospect, the proposals for revitalizing comparative psychology, from within and without the discipline, seemed to have focused more on curing symptoms than on identifying causes. Thus, the un-comparative nature of comparative psychology, the animal psychologist's reliance on a few "representative" species, tested with unnatural stimuli in artificial settings, was repeatedly targeted as responsible for its ills. If these methods could be changed, by raising investigators' phyletic consciousness, by beginning with ethograms, by selecting behaviors with regard to their evolutionary histories, by adopting the "ethological attitude" (Hess, 1970), the study of learning could proceed on a more ecologically valid course.

Although these changes have come to pass slowly but surely, it is unclear that they were accompanied or caused by changes in theoretical orientation. Studying new organisms in new settings did not insure the adoption of new assumptions about the nature of behavior analysis. "Natural" behaviors such as imprinting could just as readily be studied using unnatural stimuli and unecological settings as could key-pecking. Likewise, key-pecking or other familiar forms of conditioning could be approached as successfully from an evolutionary perspective as the phenomena of supernormal stimuli or innate releasing mechanisms could be explained in the language of operant conditioning (Staddon,

1975, 1983; Staddon & Simmelhag, 1971). Commitment to proximate or ultimate explanations for behavior still inspired different questions about the "same" phenomena.

Perhaps the area of greatest historical synthesis for psychology and ethology was the mutual recognition of constraints or biological boundaries for learning (Hinde & Stevenson–Hinde, 1973; Seligman, 1970; Seligman & Hager, 1972). The recognition of constraints reminded many in psychology that animals could not be programmed to learn at random and that healthy babies could not be routinely channeled into the vocation of their parent's choice. The natural limits to learning were thus emphasized. Others, however, particularly ethologists, emphasized that constraints provided barriers to prevent misdirected learning. As Marler (1970) noted in arguing for the closer study of the constraints affecting vocal learning:

> Any species whose biology depends in any fundamental way upon a series of complex learning processes can ill afford to leave the direction in which that learning will take place to chance. The capacity for learning can be as biologically harmful as it can be advantageous, in the wrong circumstances. (p. 672)

Concern over misdirected learning was probably in part a reaction to behavioristic claims of unlimited flexibility and in part a reflection of competing influences in ethology. Evolutionary biologists possess few models of nongenetic transmission of behavior and have reserved learning as an important isolating mechanism for few species other than man (Feldman & Cavalli-Sforza, 1976; Mayr, 1958). Likewise, phylogenies are generally constructed only on the basis of inherited traits (Payne, in press). A concern still present in the study of song learning is that of understanding how learning is restricted to the "right" songs of the "right" species, that is, to ask what "fail-safe" mechanisms protect the animal from the vagaries of its environment (Kroodsma, 1983; Marler, 1983). As in ethology in general, the study of song learning has not concentrated on delineating principles or mechanisms of learning itself, but in specifying the genetic programs that protect the organism by dictating when, where, and what can be learned.

The focus on misdirected learning may also have originated in more traditionally ethological ideas about the importance of innate, i.e., highly constrained, factors in development (Hess, 1970; Marler, 1979). Thus, learning was not and is not viewed in ethology as a very general adaptation—the view prevalent in the psychology of learning—but as a highly specific one, a view recently reiterated by Gould (1982):

> Animals are perhaps in some sense molded and shaped by their environments and experiences, but within a set of complex, species-specific rules that do not at all fit the model that classical behaviorists maintained. Learning . . . is one of the

standard, off-the-shelf programming tricks available to evolution and despite the usual dichotomy, this kind of learning is the epitome of instinct. (p. 275).

The presence of such different views as to the superordinate or subordinate role of learning as a mechanism of behavior captures many of the historical and current disctinctions between psychological and ethological approaches to behavior. Its superordinate status in psychology has, of course, been modified, humbled by the failures of S–R theories of learning. Its subordinate status in ethology has undergone less change, partly because of psychology's difficulties but partly because ethology had another theory, that of evolution, to provide a secure and enviable base from which to theorize. As Eaton (1970) noted:

> Biological (evolutionary) theory accounted for both innate and learned behavior determinants and their mutual roles in adapting the organism. It was biological theory in the hands of ethologists that led to a rapid growth of evidence on the importance of heredity in behavior, and this provided the long needed shot in the arm for comparative psychology. It is now apparent that several decades of research in comparative psychology were limited in progress by asking of inappropriate questions. (pp. 186–187)

Although one could argue about psychology's reaction to the putative inoculation from ethology or about how, if at all, inappropriate the questions of comparative psychology were, one cannot but be impressed that, despite such differences, phychologists and ethologists have found common ground. That their paths have crossed enough to achieve the level of communication present now does not, however, lessen the need to continue to ask meta-ecological questions about what each field is "really" trying to discover. As is evident in the study of song learning, birds were not, and largely have not been, investigated to continue the analysis of learning where comparative psychology left it but to answer questions derived from different paradigms. Bird song was and is not studied to demonstrate principles of learning first identified in psychological laboratories. That it could be remains to be discussed.

Our ultimate goal, however, is not to stress differences but to promote synthesis. We hope to indicate, by our analysis of bird song learning, a further point of convergence by showing that the study of song, largely the enterprise of ethologists, is now positioned at the same point in the road as was comparative psychology in the 1960s. It must now adjust its boundary conditions to achieve further progress. That the study of vocal learning can continue to advance our knowledge of general and specific behavioral mechanisms will not be challenged, but championed, given that new questions are posed. That ethology can profit from the past experience of comparative psychology would also provide reciprocal evidence of kinship between the two behavioral disciplines that Darwin's theory sired.

ESTABLISHING THE FACT OF SONG LEARNING

Methods and Concepts in Song Learning

Beer (1982a) recently commented that "what developmental study looks for depends on what is thought to be there to find, which depends on how the social communication system is viewed in its syntactic, semantic, and pragmatic aspects" (p. 300). We thus begin by examining concepts and methods central to the study of song learning as a means of highlighting what investigators have "thought to be there to find" in the analysis of song learning. The methods and concepts parallel those used by ethologists to study species-typical behavior in general, and fixed action patterns and innate releasing mechanisms in particular (Smith, 1977). Thus, emphasis was placed on identifying patterns of responsiveness to the environment in the absence or presence of auditory stimulation. These efforts can best be described by discussion of four features of the study of song: the use of isolation rearing as a technique for detecting the role of learning; the concept of the song template as a metaphor for song perception and production; the search for sources of vocal instruction; and the comparative analysis of species differences in song behavior and development. We consider each in general and specific terms.

The Interpretation of Isolate Song.   That song is learned or partially learned is established by demonstrating that a bird can imitate or copy vocalizations and/ or by showing that its song develops abnormally when reared in acoustic deprivation (Kroodsma & Baylis, 1983). The strongest case for vocal learning based on imitation comes from birds who normally copy conspecifics developing regional dialects (Nottebohm, 1969). The details of vocal copying are most often revealed through controlled rearing and, as such, they depend directly on the technique of species-atypical rearing, the "Kaspar Hauser" condition, which has been a major tool in confirming the environmental contribution to a diverse array of behaviors (Lorenz, 1950). With respect to bird song, the rationale was stated by Thorpe (1961) in his work with the chaffinch, *Fringilla coelebs*: The songs of isolates reveal the "inherited" or "innate" song of a species, the blueprint with which the environment must work. The same rationale remains operative today (Marler, 1983). Thus, isolate song is assumed to provide an entry point for identifying the role of the environment.

As powerful as isolation can be for implicating the environment in development, it cannot specify the effects of the genes, as might be implied by the term *innate* song. An animal in isolation is not in a neutral or environment-less state but is exposed to artificial circumstances of a completely asocial existence (Lehrman, 1953). The behavior resulting from such isolates should more properly be termed *behavioral neo-phenotypes* (Kuo, 1967): learned adaptations of the animal to an environment typically not encountered in nature. An even more precise term might be *autophenotype* as the predominant form of stimulation is self-produced (see Dennis & Dennis, 1941 for a similar concept labeled "auto-genous" behavior).

By any name, the outcome of isolation is difficult to interpret. In every passerine studied, although isolates produce songs that differ from those of their normally reared counterparts, the degree of deviation and its functional significance vary (Kroodsma, 1978). How such phenotypes relate to those developed normally is the problem. Thus, although the technique of isolation can detect the fact of learning, it can shed little light by itself on mechanisms as only negative evidence for learning is obtained (Bateson, 1976; Hinde, 1971; Kroodsma, 1983; Marler & Hamilton, 1966).

Isolate songs also pose difficulties because, although their acoustic outcomes can be measured, their functional significance is harder to assess. Are isolate songs also functionally abnormal? Do they elicit normal species-typical responses? The best test would be if the isolate subject were allowed to use his atypical song in a appropriate context such as during mating or territorial establishment or defense. In most cases, however, isolation produces an animal unable to compete. When the behavior of isolates or of birds singing abnormal songs has been studied, the results indicate substantial variability across species in the outcome with some birds holding territories and attracting mates and others being much less successful (Emlen, Thompson, & Rising, 1975; King & West, 1977; Rice, 1981). Thus, although structural abnormalities can be readily detected in many species, the same cannot be said for the functional consequences.

Species-Typical Filtering and Sensitive Periods.   Isolation has also been used to establish the selectivity of song learning: What songs will an isolate copy? In general the data point to innate predispositions that restrict memory and attention along species-typical lines (Dooling, 1982; Marler, 1976; Marler & Peters, 1977). Although such data establish perceptual preconditions for song imitation, another caution must be sounded as to the meaning of negative results: Birds that do not copy sounds in the laboratory may do so in other circumstances (Baptista & Morton, 1981; Dobkin, 1979; Kroodsma, 1983). Learning what these circumstances are represents a crucial step for developing knowledge about the mechanisms of song learning.

Along with imprinting, some of the best examples of sensitive periods come from songbird research (see especially Kroodsma & Pickert, 1980). Establishment of temporal constraints on learning necessarily also relies on isolation and tutoring and is thus subject to the constraints already discussed (Baptista, 1972; Baptista, Morton, & Pereyra, 1981). Recent evidence indicating the need for caution comes from Baptista and Petrinovich (1984), who have demonstrated that white-crowned sparrows (*Zonotrichia leucophrys*) will learn the songs of tutors (even nonconspecific tutors) with whom they can interact well past previously established critical periods that were defined by failures to incorporate tape-recorded songs after a certain age. The young sparrows learned noncon-specific songs even when they could hear appropriate conspecific song.

The increasing difficulties of interpreting the effects of isolation are best captured by Kroodsma (1982):

> For the field and evolutionary biologist, a simple caveat looms above the bewilder-ing array of data on vocal learning in the laboratory: what is actually happening in nature may not be reflected accurately by results of laboratory experiments. The complex physical and social processes occurring in nature cannot be duplicated in the laboratory. (p. 16).

Song Templates and Innate Releasers: Avian Machinery.   A further com-plexity in studying song is that one is really studying two processes, perception and production. The young bird's attention to species-typical stimuli, his filtering of other sounds, and his ability to reproduce what is heard must all be accounted for. The concepts of a sensory filter and of an innate releasing mechanism have been combined in the postulation of the song template (Marler, 1976). The template is a perceptual-motor guide used in the construction of song copies, where the bird may be copying only himself or other birds. The template is typically explained in terms of feedback loops but other types of metaphorical machinery are implied. Filters, often pretuned, must be presumed to explain differential attention to conspecific sounds. A tape recorder is called for to explain memory for songs sung and songs heard. The possibility of prerecorded passages on the recorder must also be considered given that many isolates sing recogniz-able, if incomplete, versions of their species' song. The entire system appears to be externally activated by the avian equivalent of electricity, that is, sex hormones that are in turn controlled by the environment.

As a perceptual filter, the template concept is most useful because it leads to testable hypotheses employing tutoring or tests of early perceptual responsiveness (Dooling, 1982; Marler & Peters, 1977, 1982). As a mechanism for song pro-duction, its utility is less clear. The template is said to provide a "crude" spec-ification of a species song, but the sense in which it is crude is not clear: Is it too broad? Too narrow? Does it contain only species-typical sounds? It is also assumed to be modifiable by postnatal experience. The mechanisms that control template modification are not clear: On what basis is it modified by one sound and not another? What filters the filter?

Not only do singers potentially need templates but listeners do as well (Bap-tista, 1975; King & West, 1983a). How do females, for example, recognize song? Moreover, as some females sing or can be induced to sing through hor-mones, female recipients may also normally possess production templates linked in some as yet unknown way with perception templates (Baptista, 1974; Falls, 1969; Konishi, 1965). Whether females' templates produce correlated outcomes, i.e., whether they sing what they like to hear, remains an open question. Two templates in one head or four templates inside two heads, however, are no better than a single template in one head without specification of coupling mechanisms. Although progress has been made on this link in insects and frogs (Doherty & Gerhardt, 1983; Hoy, 1974), the study of song calls for concepts describing the joint product of song development, communication (Smith, 1977).

Vocal Learning: Sources of Instruction.   A review of definitions of song learning quickly reveals that song learning has been exclusively viewed as a set of auditory tasks. Criteria for song-learning capacity and for song learning as well as for specifications of the template depend entirely on acoustic variables; i.e., vocal learning is the ability to use *auditory* information (including feedback) to modify or enhance vocal development and learning capacity is evidenced by abnormal vocal development under *acoustic* deprivation in the laboratory (Kroodsma, 1983; Kroodsma & Baylis, 1983; Marler, 1983; Nottebohm, 1972; Thorpe, 1961).

The rationale for focusing on a single modality was in part a theoretical consideration and in part an empirical conclusion. Thorpe (1961) argued for such an orientation on the basis of parsimony, saying that "while it is very difficult for a human being (and perhaps impossible for an animal) to see himself as others see him, it is much less difficult for him to hear himself as others hear him" (p. 79). He also stressed the role of simple vocal copying to rule out the need "to invoke self-consciousness, something of the intent to profit by another's experience" (p. 78). This view also derives from data providing convincing documentation of the role of sound as evidenced by the deficits in the singing performance of deafened birds (Konishi, 1965; Konishi & Nottebohm, 1969). There was and is no question that song development depends on adequate auditory stimulation.

Few data exist, however, regarding nonvocal effects, particularly the influence of purely social feedback (Beer, 1982b; Kroodsma, 1983). What data there are do favor social as well as vocal sources of instruction, (e.g., Baptista & Petrinovich, 1984; Immelmann, 1969, 1972; Kroodsma, 1974; Marler, 1975; McGregor & Krebs, 1982; Nicolai, 1959; Payne, 1981, 1983a; Price, 1979; Todt, Hultsch, & Heike, 1979; Waser & Marler, 1977). Collectively, these studies indicate that the incorporation of vocal sounds from others is socially mediated in many species; that is, the relationship between the tutor and pupil affects what is learned. What varies across species is the nature of the interaction required between the tutor and pupil. Although these data demonstrate the limitations of isolation rearing and the auditory template to capture the social dimensions of song learning, they do not, of course, question Thorpe's basic assumption that song learning is an auditory process. What they do contribute, however, is a proposed mechanism to explain why young birds attend to certain sounds and not others.

Because of the almost inevitable correlation between social and vocal stimulation in song learning, bird song has not been considered as a case of social learning (Galef, 1976). To qualify as the latter, purely social influences would need to be considered. Could a devocalized tutor affect song learning? Could social reinforcement modify development? As discussed later in this chapter, such influences need to be considered (King & West, 1983).

Could there be other nonvocal and nonsocial influences on song development? Few studies have considered the possibility (see, however, Mundinger & Waddick, 1972). At present, more arbitrary rewards such as food appear to have no influence, but it cannot be assumed that song learning is refractory to all external rewards.

Thorpe's hesitation regarding the possibility of multimodal effects on song contrasts with his quite pragmatic view of communication (1961). This pragmatic orientation continues today and most definitions of the broader concept of communication suggest the possibility of receptive influences on song learning. "Communication is said to occur," noted Dawkins and Krebs (1978), "when an animal, the actor, does something which appears to be the result of selection to influence the sense organs of another animal, the reactor, so that the reactor's behavior changes to the advantage of the actor" (p. 283). Marler (1967) speaks of "the occurrence of communication between two animals as . . . being found in the behavior of one upon its perception of a signal from another" (p. 769). Beer (1982b) offers that "a great deal of vertebrate communication is more readily regarded as action undertaken than as movement undergone" (p. 264). All stress the reciprocal and *active* nature of communication and emphasize the effects of the singer's song, effects that may not be excusively vocal in nature. A territorial song may be met with silent attack or flight, a courtship song may result in rebuff or mating. Are such nonvocal effects irrelevant to song learning?

Thus, the potential role of nonvocal stimulation can be considered at two levels. First, the social determinants of song perception must be integrated with the concepts of the template. This ought not to be difficult given current theories. Second, the possibility of higher order integration of information gained by singing must be dealt with. If birds can and do pay attention to more than the sounds of their songs, how are such perceptions coded? At this level, the concept of the template and the present acoustic boundary conditions for song learning may require study. At present, one need only worry about feedback loops and storage capacity for sound waves. If birds can also modify their song on the basis of nonvocal experience, how are such experiences registered, recorded, and recalled?

The focus on exclusively vocal effects may also derive from another concept, the view that song development is completed before song use. Although stages of vocal development have been noted and studied, the purpose has been to uncover the maturational program for vocal ontogeny and to document young birds' memories for song they heard when they themselves could not sing (Marler & Peters, 1982; Nice, 1943; Thorpe & Pilcher, 1958). Subsong or juvenile song has been and is typically viewed as noncommunicative, i.e., the song has no immediate effect or elicits no typical response from a listener. For species where the young bird's attention to and memory for song occurs before singing, such a characterization may be most useful and it was for such species that the template was derived (Marler, 1976). Not all birds, however, experience such a dichotomy between song perception and production, and recent data suggest the need to modify this view even in species for which the dichotomy was previously thought to hold, such as the white-crowned sparrow (Baptista & Petrinovich, 1984). Thus, more attention needs to be devoted to understanding the functional consequences of singing as a key to song ontogeny.

Species Differencies in Singing: Which Bird is the Best Model?

A count of references to different species in the 1982 volumes by Kroodsma and Miller on acoustic communication in birds revealed the sparrows to be the most frequently studied species and one representative, the white-crowned sparrow, *Zonotrichia leucophrys*, the most often cited of all species, giving it the dubious distinction of being to the study of song learning what the white rat is to the study of conditioning. In both cases, the effect has been mixed: On the one hand, much was learned in depth about song learning and conditioning, respectively; on the other hand, extrapolation to other species has preceded explanation of microphyletic differences (Kroodsma, 1978).

The white-crowned sparrow is frequently cited to illustrate the role of sensitive periods in song learning (see, however, Baptista & Petrinovich, 1984). Some songbird species, however, continue to learn past the first year, and others show periods of learning that coincide with their arrival on breeding sites rather than learning merely during the natal period (McGregor & Krebs, 1982; Payne, 1982; Slater & Ince, 1979). The function of the songs in different species also varies from strictly territorial defense to territorial defense and courtship or courtship alone. Birds also differ considerably in the diversity of their repertoires: The white-crown is in fact quite unusual in its one-song repertoire, a feature that has vastly enhanced its viability as an experimental subject. Even within families or genera, birds vary greatly in the geographic variation of their songs (Wiens, 1982). Lastly, the song environments of species differ considerably: Some species sing almost year round, most show refractory periods in the fall and winter, but song may not cease altogether. In others, juvenile song may be continuous with juvenile begging calls and may overlap with much adult song; in still others the amount of juvenile song may vary with hatching time or may overlap very little if at all with adult song (Armstrong, 1963; Saunders, 1947; Thorpe, 1961). Finally, birds other than songbirds have complex acoustic communication systems that vary considerably in their developmental determinants as compared to the sub-oscines (Beer, 1973; Gottlieb, 1971). Thus, the task of identifying the common features of song learning is a difficult one and that of choosing a representative songbird for macrophyletic analogies quite intimidating.

This is not to say that the considerable differences in the songs of passerines have gone unnoticed. In contrast to comparative psychologists, students of song have successfully exploited such diversity to demonstrate ecological and evolutionary adaptations and to make predictions about what behavioral and environmental factors might foster what developmental strategy. Some of the pertinent ecological variables that may contribute to differences in learning include migratory habits, latitude (and hence photoperiods), density of sympatric species, and the bioacoustics of the learner's environment (Kroodsma, 1978, 1983).

For theories of learning, however, the question of which species shall be chosen for comparative analyses remains. The point for psychology is not to repeat its own past and depend too heavily on species that fit our preconceptions or biases about the nature of learning. Preferably, information on many bird species should always be used but if, for argument's sake, or for simplicity, we must focus on model or modal species, the specific question we are trying to answer should guide our choices (Mook, 1983). Thus, if the question is the similarity between bird song and speech, one must consider not only characteristics of the learner but of the environment as well. Thus, one might want to choose an avian counterpart that, like humans, has a varied repertoire, year-round capacity for vocalization, frequent social interaction between and among juveniles and adults, and a vocal system in which immature vocalizations are communicative. It is possible to fulfill many of these requirements, as discussed below.

The Nature of Song Learning as Revealed by Methodology

To summarize, there can be no question that bird song affords opportunities for the study of learning. The degree to which mechanisms or processes of song learning can be revealed may, however, be constrained by the methods and concepts that characterize studies of song learning. As alluded to earlier, many of the problems in the study of song learning should be familiar to students of comparative psychology: extrapolation from artificial environments, e.g., isolation; testing with artificial stimuli, e.g., noninteractive; narrow boundary conditions for learning, e.g., defining song learning in solely acoustic terms; and reliance on generalizations based on a few "typical" species, e.g., the *Zontrichia* sparrows. These methods and concepts must now be adapted to facilitate progress and to accommodate new findings. As further demonstration of this need, let us now turn to an examination of song learning in cowbirds to indicate in fact what we have argued in principle.

THE COWBIRD: AN UNLIKELY BUT TIMELY MODEL?

Because the cowbird is a brood parasite, and hence an exception to the typical vertebrate rule of parental behavior, it might appear an odd choice for comparative analysis. As Lehrman (1974) first pointed out, however, it is precisely because of its exceptional status that comparative psychology and ethology must attend to its behavior. If early experience with nonconspecifics affects development in one avian species, such as the red-winged blackbird (*Agelaius phoeniceus*), but not in the cowbird, a member of the same *Icteridae* family, what conclusions can be drawn? Lehrman states: "Were we to be asked about the general question about whether early experience plays a role in determining species identification, intraspecies association, or mate selection in birds, we would reach entirely different conclusions from studies of the two species" (Lehrman, 1974, pp. 191–192). It is all too easy, argued Lehrman, to indulge in self-fulfilling analogies by selecting those species whose behaviors fit what we already think humans do and by ignoring those less easily assimilated into our schemas. Given the frequent extrapolations to humans of findings on imprinting, senstive periods, and attachment, Lehrman's cautions seem understated.

However, when Lehrman drew attention to the cowbird, little in fact was known about its development. A decade later, we now know that the cowbird's song ontogeny is exceptional, but not in ways that anyone had predicted (see West, King, & Eastzer, 1981a). Its vocal development exemplifies a learned communication system and suggests new parallels to human communication. If it were not for the sticky problem of foster parents, the cowbird might in fact be the model/modal species sought for earlier (although given human trends toward day care, we may not have long to wait). Cowbirds sing two to seven different song types, they show geographic variation in their songs, they sing throughout almost the whole year, they live and interact in mixed flocks of juveniles and adults, their song is clearly modified by social and auditory stimulation from conspecifics, and song is an integral part of social interactions (King, West, & Eastzer, 1980; West, King & Eastzer, 1981b).

Studying Song Learning in the Cowbird

The nature and significance of cowbirds' vocal learning is best illustrated by recourse to the aforementioned concepts of isolation, song templates, sources of information for vocal development, and species differences.

The Experience of Isolation.   When young male cowbirds are acoustically isolated but housed socially with nonsinging females or members of other species, they, like all passerines studied, produce atypical songs. This finding was at the time somewhat surprising as cowbirds had been assumed to manifest an entirely closed program for development to avoid learning the songs of their foster parents (Mayr, 1963, 1974). Even more surprising, however, were the functional properties of the isolates' songs which were tested by playing back their songs to female cowbirds, the song's natural recipient. Females of two subspecies responded with twice as many copulatory postures to the songs of isolates compared with those of normally reared males (King & West, 1977; King, West, & Eastzer, 1980; West & King, 1980).

The apparent superiority of isolate song was puzzling especially as it is clear that cowbirds are not acoustically deprived during song development but live in large flocks, a condition that in the laboratory leads to less effective songs. What does this finding then say about the effects of isolation in cowbirds? Simply that the experience of isolation as well as its outcome must be considered. In the case of the cowbird, although the males lacked an adult model, they had a captive and noncompetitive audience in the form of female or nonconspecific companions. Males reared with other males or with males *and* females, the normal state of affairs, were confronted with a more intimidating audience in that males singing very potent songs risk attack from competing males (West et al., 1981a). Isolation thus conferred on males by default the status of the dominant male. And like dominant males in a normal group, they could sing songs highly attractive to the female (West et al., 1981a).

A second study with this species clarified further the nature of the experience of isolation, namely, that its most obvious facet, lack of auditory experience, was not responsible for the functional outcome obtained. Here, males were maintained in a common auditory environment but exposed to different social experiences: Some males lived in a group of males and females; others lived with only females but could see the group; and others lived with females with only auditory access to the other birds. The results replicated those of the first study: The birds in visual isolation from other males but housed with females developed highly effective songs, whereas the males in a group or the males witnessing the group's interactions sang less effective songs. Cowbird song is thus highly dependent on a male's perception of the *social* consequences of singing. And that is indeed what isolation had altered, the consequences of singing a particular song. This is not to say that hearing songs does not matter: It does, especially for acquiring geographic markers, but hearing songs is not the exclusive source of vocal instruction.

The Cowbird Template: A Complex Form.   Given these findings on isolation, might it still be possible to reveal "innate" or "inherited" components of song production as discussed earlier? Yes and no. Examination of the acoustic structure of isolate song reveals that it contains "generic" structures for cowbird song. Such songs are geographically nonspecific: Males of the eastern subspecies, "*Molothrus ater ater* (AT), when reared out of contact with other males from 4–5 days after hatching, sing songs containing structures never found in normal eastern AT song but commonly found only in the songs of the southern subspecies, *M.a. obscurus* (OB). Young eastern males with only a brief exposure to eastern adult song, however, do not sing these structures, apparently deleting them early in ontogeny (King et al., 1980; King & West, 1983). Thus, the "innate" template probably contains an oversupply of material with which the male fashions an appropriate song. This view of the template is consistent with findings for other species (Marler & Peters, 1982; Thorpe, 1961).

Other data, however, revealed nonvocal influences on cowbird song learning less easily assimilated into the template concept. We were led to consideration of such influences by data revealing the male and female cowbirds' reciprocal contribution to the development of geographic variation in AT and OB males. For males, the data showed that juvenile AT became bilingual (singing clear renditions of both AT and OB variants) when exposed to OB males (West, King, & Harrocks, 1983). Adult AT males did not learn OB song when housed with OB males, but they did do so when housed with OB males *and* females. Moreover, adult AT and OB males substantially altered their repertoires when housed only with nonsinging females of the other subspecies. Thus, females appeared to affect song content. We tested this proposition directly by investigating the female's influence on juvenile males learning their song for the first time. Thus, hand-reared AT males were housed in acoustic isolation from other males but maintained with (1) other species; (2) AT females; or (3) OB females for their first fall, winter, and spring. The three groups of males developed significantly different vocal phenotypes from one another although none had ever heard cowbird song and all presumably had the same template. Analysis of their first-year songs reveals that males housed with other species show intermediate performance on acoustic and geographic measures of song content, AT males housed with AT females sing no OB song. Moreover, the two groups with females show nonoverlapping distributions on acoustic critical acoustic measures (King & West, 1983b). However the females effected this change, they did *NOT* do it by singing cowbird song. The most likely form of their feedback was in the form of regulating the distance between themselves and males as well as through responses such as visual attention and displays (King & West, 1983b). How males normally integrate such information with vocal feedback from their own singing and from other males provides an important challenge to current concepts of song learning.

Thus, for cowbirds, the guide or template for song development may take an external social form. For the female's part, her response to song appears less flexible (King & West, 1983a). Whether reared with other females, other species, or males of either subspecies, AT and OB females overwhelmingly prefer their native song variant. Thus, the cowbird template may not reside in the male's head but in the female's. How does the female, the silent partner, convey her "knowledge" of song? Probably through the responses cited earlier, by her attention and response to male singing. Much more needs to be learned, however, to explain how cowbirds, or any species, communicate about communicating.

Thus, although the female's response to song suggests that her behavior is explicable in terms of an auditory template, the male's development of his song is not. How does the male incorporate the outcomes of social encounters that contain no vocal correlates? The idea of song learning as "trial-and-error" shaping of a song has long been postulated, but the learning was presumed to relate to how a song sounded in relation to the template rather than in learning what effect a song had on the listener (Thorpe, 1961). It remains to be seen how amenable theories of song learning are to the incorporation of new sources of stimulation.

Cowbird Song Learning: Perceiving Sounds and Effects.   Just as these data raise questions for the interpretation of isolation and the template, they also clearly call for broader definitions of song learning to integrate vocal *and* social sources of instruction. A male's perception of song consequences may be as critical a source of information for song learning as is his ability to hear and repeat the sounds: Both sensory and performatory feedback may obtain (J. J. Gibson, 1966). Sensory influences would be those passively or actively obtained by singing and listening; following Gibson (1966), performatory feedback would derive from actions that "alter the environment in ways beneficial to the organism" (p. 57). Gibson also contrasted the terms by suggesting that sensory feedback accomplished the pickup of information, performatory feedback accomplished behavior in its usual sense.

The previously cited data on song learning by adult cowbirds also suggest interrelationships between sensory and performatory feedback. In several studies, we have housed adult AT males with adult OB males and monitored song learning to determine the adult's flexibility. As noted earlier, adults do not become bilingual under circumstances where juveniles do. For adults, access to an OB song model may be a necessary but not a sufficient condition for bilingualism. Access to female social stimulation is also required as the adults only developed bilingual repertoires when exposed to males *and* females. Why? We propose that it was because they had a model, the OB males, and a motive, the OB female. When the AT adults witnessed successful interactions between OB males and females, they perceived different effects of singing. Thus, sensory information alone may have different effects on juveniles or adults because of differences in the performatory experience each has had with song. Thus, what may change with maturity is the male's instrumental knowledge of song function, knowledge attainable only through performance.

Our studies of juveniles learning songs for the first time also highlight the need to distinguish levels of competence with respect to song development. In tracking the stages of song development in juvenile AT tutored with adult AT song, we have learned that juvenile males can copy the tutor song quite exactly early in their first year at least by early winter. These males cannot produce any original, i.e., nonshared or noncopied song, for at least two more months subsequent to their perfection of copied song. They continue in fact to subsing variable and poorly articulated original songs at the same time they produce clear copied song. Thus, juveniles are motorically capable of articulating full song long before the crystallization of their first year repertoires in April. Thus, whatever subsong is for, its occurrence does not mean that the singer is incapable of adult song or that his vocal apparatus is in an immature or refractory state.

Song development is thus clearly more than the acquisition of sensory-motor experience. The males have had sufficient experience by early winter to sing clear songs. However, whereas accuracy may be achieved by solitary rehearsal and auditory matching, efficacy may require performatory feedback obtainable only through social exchanges, exchanges that become more frequent as spring approaches. Beer (1982a) also noted the role of learning in gaining vocal proficiency (as apart from vocal content) in nonpasserine birds. It thus becomes necessary to specify in more detail specific tasks within the complex of song learning in order to understand the dynamics of its development. And it may turn out that not all parts of the song learning enterprise can be explained by concepts developed to explain highly stereotyped motor programs such as fixed action patterns or innate releasing mechanisms. Beer's (1982b) stress on the conceptual distinction between "movements undergone" and "actions undertaken" seems especially relevant to this point.

Is the Cowbird Idiosyncratic?

Over 90% of the songs cowbird males sing during the breeding season occur when they are very close to a male or female and when judged to be attempting to or actually interacting with the recipient. Similarly, in late winter and early spring, the males significantly increase the proportion of their songs delivered in a dyadic context (Kennedy, 1983). Cowbird song constitutes an *en face* signal highly sensitive to immediate and nonvocal responses. As such, it differs on yet another dimension from the songs of other well-studied songbirds where the song is typically broadcast over longer distances and thus where the responses may occur with a longer latency and be primarily of an auditory nature. Just as advertising strategies differ for sales displays and door-to-door salesmen, the demand characteristics of songs must differ considerably with proximity to a recipient.

Thus, before meaningful comparisons can be drawn between cowbirds and other songbirds, the species may have to be equated or classified on the basis of song use. At present, neither the cowbird's use nor development of song can be compared to other birds because the methods of investigation differ so markedly. But it may be that the differences described here are also a function of the ecological differences in how cowbirds use song. Understanding the ecology of singing represents a crucial next step to facilitate new and more accurate micro- and macrophyletic comparisons.

Kroodsma's warning about the interpretability of laboratory data also bears repeating at this point. With respect to the cowbird, although the data suggest new capacities for song learning, their actual expression in nature awaits investigation. Their value at this point is that they offer a new perspective on the study of song because the *pattern* of the cowbird's communication system appears to differ from that of other well-studied songbirds. By pattern, we hope to capture Johnston's (1981) sense of studying the *relationship* between animals and their environments. What the cowbird data say again and again is that their vocal ontogeny is an active system and that one cannot specify a priori what cowbirds do or do not learn without studying what their environments do or do not offer. In J. J. Gibson's sense (1966), we must understand how animals obtain information, not how it is imposed on them.

It is also at the level of patterns of behavior that Lehrman (1974) was most confident about the value of comparative analysis between species:

> And if, instead of comparing the equivalent processes, details or areas of behavior in the two (species) and thus incorrectly surmising what was going on in each, we were to compare the total pattern of life of each animal, including the process in question; then each pattern would give us some perspective about the organization of, and about the ecological significance of, the other pattern which would be more valuable than the perspective we could get about either by studying it alone. (pp. 192–193)

ECOLOGICAL THEMES FOR SONG LEARNING

To begin a summary, let us recall Johnston's definition of an ecological approach as one going beyond specification of characteristics of the animal to one joining the animal and its environment, the "pattern" analysis espoused by Lehrman. Viewed with such a perspective, it is clear that the study of song learning has focused most on the characteristics of the singer and it is here that the most progress has been made. How does one approach the task of forging the links between the learner and its environment? Some direction can be provided by recourse to Johnston's proposals for levels of ecological analysis (1981). These proposals indicate some of the steps that the study of song learning must take to realize its goals.

Johnston's first level of analysis requires a task description to determine what it is the animal actually learns in the course of development. As noted earlier, the study of song learning could greatly profit from the construction of behavioral taxonomies detailing, among other things, seasonal and contextual use of song, the *Umwelten* of the singer and the recipient prior to, during, and after song development, and more detailed functional distinctions among classes of songs. Useful distinctions might be made among descriptive, social, and expressive functions of song (Lyons, 1977). Is bird song comparable to a descriptive function of language, i.e., the transfer of information?; or communicating the "state" of the speaker, i.e., an expressive function?; or to the social goal of establishing and facilitating social relations? Although mutually exclusive distinctions would make no more sense for song than for language, they could facilitate the process of defining the tasks that constitute learning to sing as they have in understanding what is involved in learning to speak. Such categorizations have not been neglected (e.g., Armstrong, 1963; Smith, 1977), but they suffer from the lack of a coherent body of facts with which to evaluate their merits.

Likewise, some of the more proximate events surrounding song learning must be analyzed. Smith (1977) has commented that "what is missing in the traditional emphasis on individuals [in the study of communication] is the mechanics of their interaction—the interactions to which displays contribute, and in which social functions are achieved" (p. 11). As described earlier, when cowbirds sing, they often clearly engage in a social interaction as they turn and face a recipient who is typically less than a foot away. Songbirds vary greatly in the circumstances for singing and, yet again, information on such variables exists in only a piece-meal fashion. Gathering it together may provide as important an ecological dimension as species density or migratory habits.

Such information will also be critical to broader comparisons between song and speech, for example: When human babies vocalize, especially in *en face* contexts, adults or peers often reciprocate by imitating the immature sounds or by interpreting the utterances as intentional and communicative as evidenced by their behavior. Adult birds are not known to subsing to their young, and after the vocal begging stages parents may maintain no relationship at all with their young. Such potential differences in the species-typical social environments of birds and humans cannot be ignored as they constitute part of the task dimensions facing the learner. Interspecific comparisons must thus address the issue of contrasts in the context as well as in the content of vocal learning. Although the functions and circumstances of mature singing have been described (e.g., Andrew, 1961; Armstrong, 1963), such information has rarely been integrated with onto-genetic questions about acquisition.

As formidable as these taxonomic tasks may be, they probably represent the easier part of defining what is actually learned. The harder part is deciding what the animal is capable of learning and what the environment is capable of pro-viding, and then how, in nature, development is realized. Here, we may profit most from the experience of those who have redefined the concept of perceptual learning from the essentially subjective task of constructing reality into the objective activity of detecting, exploring, and differentiating a highly informative physical world (E. J. Gibson, 1969; J. J. Gibson, 1966, 1979). Approaches to perceptual learning that view the senses as active systems of environmental investigation hold the most promise for song learning, because they are based on the concept of an intimate relationship between understanding what there is to be perceived and what there is to be communicated (Dent & Rader, 1979; Smith, 1977; Verbrugge, in press). J. J. Gibson (1966) has argued that self-produced stimulation is "intrinsic to the flow of activity, not extrinsic to it, dependent on it, not independent of it" (p. 31). What better words to capture the instrumental nature of song learning in the cowbird and perhaps in other species? Thus, understanding what is learned in song learning has both sensory and performatory dimensions. Concepts of "learning by doing" (Anzai & Simon, 1979) or "learning what comes naturally" (Kaufman, 1975) also pertain in that they stress how actions may uncover information.

An even more radical task description might be one that tries to capture more than the final acoustic product, the song itself. One might want to consider the difference between asking how birds learn to *sing* and how they learn their *song*. The latter question has dominated the field reflecting, no doubt, the underlying concept of song as a fixed action pattern and as a behavioral organ from which and by which to construct phylogenies (Smith, 1977). What birds really do, however, is sing, not possess, a song. The cowbird's use of performatory feedback may pertain more to learning to sing than to learning a song. The focus in ecological perception of events speaks to the same issue (J. J. Gibson, 1979; Verbrugge, in press). Songs occur over space and time, physical facts our human senses and technology can only approximate. Thus, the activity of singing and, hence, the task of learning to sing needs to be defined even more broadly.

One also senses the spirit of ecological taxonomies for learning in recalling the functional psychology of the first half of the twentieth century, one of the schools of psychology most committed to evolutionary thinking. As Woodworth stressed, the proper subject matter for psychology is a *behaving* organism, not the *behavior* of organisms. It is the animal engaging its environment that must be explained. Woodworth (1940) further asserted that "since we shall be studying activities . . . we shall need one noun, individual, or organism, as the subject of all verbs" (p. 18). In the same vein, he cautioned that:

> . . . Like other sciences, psychology finds it convenient to transform its verbs into nouns. Then what happens? We forget that our nouns are merely substitutes for verbs, and start hunting for the things denoted by the nouns . . . but no such things exist; there is only the individual engaged in these different activities. (p. 19)

Thus, the task of describing how learning affects singing and vice versa promises to be both challenging and rewarding. It should be noted as well that such a task analysis will require experimentation as well as description. As the findings from the cowbird show, intuitions about what is learned may underestimate dimensions of both an animal's competence and performance. Both laboratory and field investigations are needed to distinguish what birds can and what they do learn.

The second level of analysis, according to Johnston, requires investigating the experiences that lead to skilled performance and the manner of their effects. As in many areas of development, knowledge of what happens during song development lags far behind knowledge of outcome. Although we can say early experience is important, we know little about what constitutes the *experience* of early experience. Some directions for remedial actions have already been described. First, we must specify what we are removing or adding when we rear an animal in the laboratory and study its singing. Replacement of the term *isolation* or *deprivation* with *biased rearing* (E. J. Gibson, 1969) is preferable as it denotes more clearly the complexity of this manipulation. Thus, we should not say we *isolated* the animal from x, y, or z but that we biased the animal toward or away from x, y, or z. The songs of isolates would be "biased" songs, not innate songs. Miller's terms of environmental transposition or controlled rearing also speak to the same concern (this volume).

One might also consider the alternative strategy altogether to identifying the role of learning: A behavior can be considered to be refractory to environmental influence if its nature remains the same when animals are reared in diverse environments (Keil, 1981; Marler & Hamilton, 1966; Marler & Peters, 1977). In this way, environmentally stable or labile elements can be revealed. It is in fact only through this method that we can approximate how the environment operates in a constructive as opposed to a destructive manner.

The role of the template as an explanatory mechanism also needs to be considered at this level of analysis. As a metaphor to describe how songs are stored during ontogeny, it may remain most useful in species where the young cannot imitate conspecific sounds at the time of critical exposure. The receptive properties of the template seem most amenable to experimental test. But, as we learn more about the subsequent modifiability of song perception, and as we learn more about birds' reliance on vocal and social stimulation during song production, the simplicity of the original concept is lost. In any case, its value has always been nominal: Its definition is no substitute for the search for proximate mechanisms of attention, memory, filtering, articulation, imitations, modification, and comprehension, to name only some. Perhaps, what needs to be considered most is what the template is really to explain.

Likewise, the search for experiences that affect vocal learning must be expanded beyond their present acoustic limits. Goffman (1964) has noted in the study of human language that we know most about those features of speech that are easily written. The same is true for song learning where our knowledge of the events affecting song has been influenced by the constraints of tape recorders to hear but not see what the animals do when they learn to sing. Similarly, the experience of a sound-attenuation chamber may preclude the manifestation of species-typical patterns of development fundamental to normal ontogeny. How open a species' program may be for song learning may at this point say more about the openness of the methods used to study it than the flexibility of the program itself (Lehrman, 1953).

Finally, Johnston specifies the goals of formulating local and general principles of adaptation. How should the task of micro- and macrophyletic comparisons be approached? As a starting point, the ecological taxonomy of song called for earlier could provide more precise points for comparison. Likewise, species could be compared on the kinds of experience needed for normal development. Given the diversity among songbirds, even local principles await further study.

More global principles require even more advances, particularly in the specification of what is to be compared. Most of the analogies that have been drawn between humans and birds necessarily refer to song and speech as if each were a unitary phenomenon. Just as birds do not sing in the same way, humans do not just speak: They talk, shout, chat, rap, argue, pronounce, whisper, cry, orate, and proclaim; not to mention sing, hum, whistle, and yodel. How many of these pertain to songs? The functional significance of such variations in vocal behavior must be considered before meaningful interspecific comparisons can be made.

With respect to global comparisons to humans, why not begin with the most literal sense, that is, to ask how birds' songs relate to humans' songs? It is intriguing to consider that memories for the melodies and the perception of melodic structure manifest an ease in coding perhaps comparable to the facility with which young birds store memories of songs (Ostwald, 1973; Pick, 1979). The natural tendencies of human babies to engage in and imitate melodies and to be manipulated by them also pertains (Papousek & Papousek, 1981). Finally, consider that the standards for effective singing vary greatly from those of effective speaking. Certainly, female songbirds must assess not only the song itself but its delivery. The question of what should really be compared promises to be as, if not more, fascinating than the comparisons themselves as it engages us directly in the task of pattern analysis.

Such analyses might also bring us closer to defining the kinds of "learning" presumed in the phrase "song learning" and therefore specify more directly the kinds of experience that would be relevant. Is there one kind of song learning possessed to different degrees by different species, or are there as many forms of learning as there are species with modifiable repertoires? This question is important not only to relate song learning to learning in other animals but also to aid in understanding general principles of behavior and development.

CLOSING THEMES: NATURE–NATURE–NURTURE

A major goal for the study of song learning is to extend the study of vocal learning beyond the characteristics of the singer and his or her song to that of the setting in which song ontogeny occurs. If we can resort to Galton's terms, we know much more about the nature of the singer than we do about the nurturant properties of his or her environment. Stated another way, we know what prevents misnurture, but not what constitutes nurture. Just as a bird's capacity for song learning may have been underestimated, the capacity of the species-typical environment to furnish its occupants with adaptive information may also not have been fully appreciated.

It is in fact somewhat unfortunate that Galton (1874, 1970) usurped the word "nature" for characteristics of the organism because it is also so appealing a word for the environment inherited by the organism. Is the Nature around any less real than that inside us? Are not songbirds as likely to inherit adults that sing in their presence as a syrinx with which to sing? Although the nature within us has more obvious boundaries, its contents are perhaps no less complex than those connoted by the external power of Nature (Fancher, 1979). The two senses of the word are worth contemplating given that the processes they represent have often been considered as opposing forces, when indeed they are complementary. Even in an era of nature *and* nurture, one senses a more lingering mistrust of nurture as a source of behavioral transmission than of nature (Gould, 1982; Marler, 1970; Mayr, 1963). The problem with nurture, as noted earlier, is the danger of misnurture. Innate programs are needed for the control of nurture by nature (Gould, 1982; Marler, 1982).

A skepticism regarding the role of learning in development may stem in part from the same set of biases that leads most theorists to reject the environment as a direct medium for perception. But as the Gibsons have articulated, it is in fact more parsimonious and biological to implicate the environment as a co-evolved partner of the perceiver rather than as an erratic and essentially unknowable force (E. J. Gibson, 1969; J. J. Gibson, 1979; Michaels & Carello, 1981).

Such distrust of learning may also have been a conditioned response to that era in comparative psychology when animals were expected to learn quite peculiar things and, of course, did. If birds can be taught to dance for food, what protects them in Nature from doing equally unlikely things? Such fears were unfounded, of course, and stemmed in part from misunderstandings about the questions that were being asked (Mook, 1983). If the emphasis in the study of vocal learning on the constraints and the genetic regulation of learning was partly a reaction to such events within the comparative psychology of learning, it is time for change. If ethologists dismissed learning because of the way it was studied, rather than for its intrinsic importance to the understanding of behavior, then a reexamination is in order. Hess (1970), for example, in a major review of the contributions of ethology to psychology, begins by stating that " 'learning' here refers to what the learning psychologists call learning" (p. 2). Times, however, and definitions of learning, have changed. The role of learning should never be dismissed on the grounds of guilt by association. Perhaps psychology has yet to capture its essence, but nothing in its history or that of ethology has diminished its potential value as a behavioral mechanism.

The progress achieved in understanding learning owes much to events during the era of "learning psychology." Studying higher order processes or intervening variables is a daunting task, and the continued study of the psychology of learning has contributed much at a conceptual and methodological level. Moreover, it remains to be seen whether processes such as conditioning, trial-and-error learning, or reinforcement are irrelevant to more "biological" processes such as vocal learning. To say that vocal development may involve principles of conditioning or reinforcement need not raise the spectre of a theory with no biological controls.

The time may then be right in the study of vocal learning to reassess in detail how principles of learning first revealed in arbitrary environments pertain to the more complex ones that animals normally inhabit. As this volume demonstrates, the struggle for survival of the psychology of learning has vastly improved its vision. And, as the cowbird, the species considered most unlikely to learn, shows us, our most formidable task continues to be to learn to see when we look at Nature–nature.

ACKNOWLEDGMENTS

We thank A. Nash for assistance with the references. C. Logan and H. Rheingold provided insightful reviews of the manuscript. Financial assistance was provided by NSF grant BNS 80–23108 and NINCD&S grant 1 KO4 NS 00676–01.

REFERENCES

Andrew, R. J. (1961). The displays given by passerines in courtship and reproductive fighting: A review. *Ibis, 103a*, 315–348.

Anzai, Y., & Simon, H. A. (1979). The theory of learning by doing. *Psychological Review, 86*, 124–140.

Armstrong, E. A. (1963). *A study of bird song*. London: Oxford University Press.

Baptista, L. F. (1972). Wild house finch sings White-crowned sparrow song. *Zeitschrift für Tierpsychologie, 30*, 266–270.

Baptista, L. F. (1974). The effects of songs of wintering White-crowned sparows on song development in sedentary populations of the species. *Zeitschrift für Tierpsychologie, 34*, 147–171.

Baptista, L. F. (1975). Song dialects and demes in sedentary populations of the White-crowned Sparrow (*Zonotrichia leucophrys nuttali*)I. *University of California Publications in Zoology*, 105.

Baptista, L. F., & Morton, M. L. (1981). Interspecific song acquisition by a White-crowned sparrow. *Auk, 98*, 383–385.

Baptista, L. F., Morton, M. L., & Pereyra, M. E. (1981). Interspecific song mimesis by a Lincoln sparrow. *Wilson Bulletin, 93*, (2), 265–267.

Baptista, L. F., & Petrinovich, L. (1984). Social interaction, sensitive phases and the song template hypothesis in the white-crowned sparrow. *Animal Behaviour, 32*, 172–181.

Bateson, P. P. G. (1976). Rules and reciprocities in behavioural development. In P. P. G. & R. A. Hinde (Eds.), *Growing points in ethology*, (p. 401–421). Cambridge: Cambridge University Press.

Beer, C. G. (1973). A view of birds. In A. Pick (Ed.), *Minnesota Symposium on Child Development*, (Vol. 7, p. 47–86). Minneapolis: Minnesota University Press.

Beer, C. G. (1982a). Conceptual issues in the study of communication. In D. E. Kroodsma & E. H. Miller (Eds.), *Acoustic communication in birds*, (Vol. 2, p. 279–310). New York: Academic Press.

Beer, C. G. (1982b). Study of vertebrate communication—its cognitive implications. In. D. E. Griffin (Ed.), *Animal mind–human mind*. (Dahlem Workshop Report 21). Berlin: Springer–Verlag.

Dawkins, R., & Krebs, J. R. (1978). Animal signals: Information or manipulation? In J. R. Krebs & N. B. Davies, *Behavioural ecology: An evolutionary approach*, (p. 282–309). Sunderland, Ja: Sinauer Associates.

Dennis, W., & Dennis, S. (1941). Infant development under conditons of restricted practice and minimum social stimulation. *Genetic Psychology Monographs, 147*, 149–155.

Dent, C. & Rader, N. (1979). A theoretical approach to meaning based on a theory of direct perception. In P. French (Ed.), *The development of meaning*, (p. 146–177). Hiroshima: Bunka Hyoron Publishing Co.

Dobkin, D.S. (1979). Functional and evolutionary relationships of vocal copying phenomena in birds. *Zeitschrift für Tierpsychologie, 50*, 348–363.

Doherty, J. A., & Gerhardt, H. C. (1983). Hybrid tree frogs: Vocalizations of males and selective phonotaxis of females. *Science, 220*, 1078–1080.

Dooling, R. J. (1982). Ontogeny of song recognition in birds. *American Zoologist, 22*, 571–580.

Eaton, R. (1970). An historical look at ethology: A shot in the arm for comparative psychology. *Journal of the History of the Behavioral Sciences, 6*, 176–187.

Emlen, S. T., Thompson, W. L., & Rising, J. D. (1975). A behavioral and morphological study of sympatry in the Indigo and Lazuli Buntings of the Great Plains. *Wilson Bulletin, 87*, 145–179.

Falls, J. B. (1969), Functions of territorial song in the white-throated sparrow. In R. A. Hinde (Ed.), *Bird Vocalizations* (p. 207–232). Cambridge: Cambridge University Press.

Fancher, R.E. (1979). A note on the origin of the term "nature and nurture." *Journal of the History of the Behavioral Sciences, 15*, 321–322.

Feldman, M.W. & Cavalli–Sforza, L. L. (1976). Cultural and biological evolutionary processes, selection for a trait under complex transmission. *Theoretical Population Biology, 9*, 238–259.

Galef, B. G. (1976). Social transmission of acquired behavior: A discussion of tradition and social learning in vertebrates. In J. S. Rosenblatt, R. A. Hinde, E. Shaw, & C. Beer (Eds.), *Advances in the study of behavior*, Vol. 6 (p. 77–100). New York: Academic Press.

Galton, F. (1874). On men of science, their nature and nurture. *Proceedings of the Royal Institution, 7, 227–236*.

Galton, F. (1970). English men of science: Their nature and nurture. London: Frank Cass & Co.

Gibson, E. J. (1969). *Principles of perceptual learning and development*. New York: Appleton–Century–Crofts.

Gibson, J. J. (1966). *The senses considered as perceptual systems*. Boston: Hougton–Mifflin.

Gibson, J. J. (1979). The ecological approach to visual perception. Boston: Hougton–Mifflin.

Goffman, E. (1964). The neglected situation. *American Anthropologist, 66*, (6), 133–136.

Gottlieb, G. (1971). *Development of species identification in birds*. Chicago: University of Chicago press.

Gould, J. L. (1982). *Ethology: The mechanisms and evolution of behavior*. New York: Norton.

Hess, E. H. (1970). Ethology and developmental psychology. In P. Mussen (Ed.), *Carmichael's manual of child psychology* (Vol. I, p. 1–38). New York: Wiley.

Hinde, R. A. (1971). *Animal behaviour: A synthesis of ethology and comparative psychology*. New York: McGraw–Hill.

Hinde, R. A. (1982). Foreword. In D. E. Kroodsma & E. H. Miller, *Acoustic communication in birds* (Volumes 1 & 2, p. xii–xvi). New York: Academic Press.

Hinde, R. A., & Stevenson–Hinde, J. (1973). *Constraints on learning: Limitations and predispositions*. New York: Academic Press.

Hodos, W., & Campbell, C. B. G. (1969). *Scala naturae:* Why there is no theory in comparative psychology. *Psychological Review, 76*. 337–350.

Hoy, R. R. (1974). Genetic control of acoustic behavior in crickets. *American Zoologist, 14*, 1067–1078.

Immelmann, K. (1969). Song development in the zebra finch and other estrildine finches. In R. A. Hinde (Ed.), *Bird vocalizations* (p. 61–74). Cambridge: Cambridge University Press.

Immelmann, K. (1972). The influence of early experience upon the development of social behavior in estrildine finches. *Proceedings of the XV Interenational Ornithological Congress*, 219–313.

Johnston, T. D. (1981). Contrasting approaches to a theory of learning. *Behavioral and Brain Sciences, 4*, 125–173.

Kaufman, I. C. (1975). Learning what comes naturally: The role of life experience in the establishment of species typical behavior. *Ethos, 3*, 129–142.

Keil, F. C. (1981). Constraints on knowledge and cognitive development. *Psychological Review, 88*, 197–227.

Kennedy, J. (1983). *Winter behavior of cowbirds.* Unpublished manuscript. University of North Carolina at Chapel Hill.

King, A. P., & West, M. J. (1977). Species identification in cowbirds: Appropriate responses to abnormal song. *Science, 192*, 1002–1004.

King, A. P., & West, M. J. (1983a)I. Female perception of cowbird song: A closed developmental program. *Developmental Psychobiology, 16*, 335–342.

King, J. (1983b). Epigenesis of cowbird song: A joint endeavor of males and feamles. *Nature, 305*, 704–706.

King, A. P., West, M. J., & Eastzer, D.H. (1980). Song structure and song development as potential contributors to reproductive isolation in cowbirds (*Molothrus ater*). *Journal of Comparative and Physiological Psychology, 94*, 1028–1036.

Konishi, M. (1965). The role of auditory feedback in the control of vocalization in the White-crowned sparrow. *Zeitschrift fürs Tierpsychologie, 22*, 770–783.

Konishi, M., & Nottebohm, F. (1969). Experimental studies in the ontogeny of avian vocalizations. In R. A. Hinde (Ed.), *Bird vocalizations* (p. 29–48). Cambridge: Cambridge University Press.

Kroodsma, D. E. (1974). Song learning, dialects, and dispersal in the Bewick's wren. *Zeitschrift für Tierpsychologie, 35*, 352–380.

Kroodsma, D. E. (1978). Aspects of learning in the ontogeny of bird song: Where, from whom, when, how many, which, and how accurately? In G. M. Burghardt & M. Bekoff (Eds.), *Ontogeny of behavior.* (p. 215–230). New York: Garland.

Kroodsma, D.E. (1982). Learning and the ontogeny of sound signals in birds. In D. E. Kroodsma & E. H. Miller (Eds.), *Acoustic communication in birds* (Vol. 2, p. 1–23). New York: Academic Press.

Kroodsma, D. E. (1983). The ecology of avian vocal learning. *BioScience, 33*, 165–171.

Kroodsma, D. E., & Baylis, J. R. (1982). Appendix A: A world survey of vocal learning. In D. E. Kroodsma & E. H. Miller (Eds.), *Acoustic communication in birds* (Vol. 2, p. 311–337). New York: Academic Press.

Kroodsma, D. E. & Miller, E. H. (1982). *Acoustic communication in birds* (Two volumes). New York: Academic Press.

Kroodsma, D. E., & Pickert, R. (1980). Environmentally dependent sensitive periods for avian vocal learning. *Nature, 288*, 477–479.

Kuo, Z. Y. (1967). *The dynamics of behavior development: An epigenetic view.* New York: Random House.

Lehrman, D. S. (1953). A critique of Konrad Lorenz's theory of instinctive behavior. *Quarterly Review of Biology, 28*, 337–363.

Lehrman, D. S. (1974). Can psychiatrists use ethology? In N. F. White (Ed)., *Ethology and psychiatry* (p. 187–196). Toronto: University of Toronto Press.

Lockard, R. B. (1971). Reflections on the fall of comparative psychology: Is there a message for us all? *American Psychologist, 26*, 168–;179.

Lombroso, Cesare. (1891). *The man of genius*. London: Walter Scott.

Lorenz, K. Z. (1950). The comparative method in studying innate behavior patterns. *Symposia of the Society of Experimental Biology, 4;*, 221–268.

Lyons, J. (1977). *Semantics* (Vol. 1). Cambridge: Cambridge University Press.

Marler, P. (1967). Animal communication signals. *Science, 157*, 769–774.

Marler, P. (1970). Birdsong and speech development: Could there be parallels? *American Scientist, 58*, 669–673.

Marler, P. (1975). On strategies of behavioural development. In G. Baerends, C. Beer, & A. Manning (Eds.);, *Function and evolution of behaviour* (p. 254–275). Oxford: Clarendon Press.

Marler, P. (1976). Sensory templates in species-specific behavior. In J. C. Fentress (Ed.), *Simpler networks and behavior* (p. 314–329). Sunderland, MA: Sinauer Associates.

Marler, P. (1979). Development of auditory perception in relation to vocal behavior. In M. von Cranach, K. Foppa, W. Lepenies, & D. Ploog (Eds.), *Human ethology: Claims and limits of a new discipline* (p. 663–681). Cambridge: Cambridge University Press.

Marler, P. (1982). Some ethological implcations for neuroethology: The ontogeny of birdsong. In J. P. Ewert, R. r. Capranica, & D. J. Ingle (Eds.), *Advances in vertebrate neuroethology* (21–52). New York: Plenum.

Marler, P. R., & Hamilton, W. J. (1966). *Mechanisms of animal behavior*. New York: Wiley.

Marler, P., & Peters, S. (1977). Selective vocal learning in a sparrow. *Science, 198*, 519–521.

Marler, & Peters, S. (1982). Subsong and plastic song: Their role in the vocal learning process. In D. E. Kroodsma & E. H. Miller (Eds.) *Acoustic communication in birds* (Vol. 2), p. 25–50). New York: Academic Press.

Mayr, E. (1958). Behavior and systematics. In A. Roe & G. G. Simpson (Eds.) *Behavior and evolution*. New Haven: Yale University Press.

Mayr, E. (1963). *Animal species and evolution*. Cambridge: Harvard University Press.

Mayr, E. (1974). Behavior programs and evolutionary strategies. *American Scientist, 62*, 650–659.

McGregor, P.K., & Krebs, J. R. (1982). Song types in a population of great tits (Parus major): Their distribution, abundance and acquistion by individuals. *Behaviour, 79* 126–147.

Michaels, C. F., & Carello, C. (1981). *Direct perception*. Englewood Cliffs, NJ: Prentice-Hall.

Mook, D. G. (1983). In defense of external validity. *American Psychologist, 38* 379–387.

Mundinger, P., & Waddick, L. (1972). *Song learning and ontogeny in cross fostered house finches*. Unpublished manuscript.

Nice, M. M. (1943). Studies in the life history of the song sparrow. II. The behavior of the song sparrow and other passerines. *Transactions of the Linnaean Society of New York, 6*, 1–324.

Nicolai, J. (1959). Familientradition in der Gesangentwicklung des Gimpels *(Pyrrhula phrrhula L.)*. *Journal of Ornithology, 100*, 39–46.

Nottebohm, F. (1969). The song of the chingolo, *Zonotrichia capensis*, in Argentina: Description and evaluation of a system of dialects. *Condor, 71*, 299–315.

Nottebohm, F. (1972). Origins of vocal learning. *American Naturalist, 106*, 116–140.

Ostwald, P. F. (1973). Musical behavior in early childhood. *Developmental Medicine and Child Neurology*, 367–375.

Papousek, J., & Papousek, H. (1981). Musical elements in the infant's vocalizations: Their significance for communication, cognition, and creativity. In L. P. Lipsitt (Ed.) *Advances in infancy research* (Vol. 1, p. 164–217). Norwood, NJ: Ablex. & Papousek.

Payne, R. B. (1981). Song learning and social interaction in indigo buntings. *Animal Behaviour, 29*, 688–697.

Payne, R. B. (1982). Ecological consequences of song matching: Breeding success and intraspecific song mimicry in indigo buntings. *Ecology, 63*, 401–411.

Payne, R. B. (1983a). Bird songs, sexual selection, and female mating strategies. In S. K. Wasser (Ed.), *Social behavior of female vertebrates* (p. 55–90). New York: Academic Press.

Payne, R.B. (In press). *Bird song and avian systematics*. Current ornithology, 3.

Petrinovich, L. P. (1972). Psychobiological foundations of language development. In G. Newton & A. H. Riesen (Eds.), *Advances in psychobiology* (Vol. 1, p. 259–285). New York: Wiley–Interscience.

Pick, A. D. (1979). Listening to melodies: Perceiving events. In A. D. Pick (Ed.), *Perception and its development*, (pp.145–168). Hillsdale, NJ: Lawrence Erlbaum Associates.

Price, P. H. (1979). Developmental determinants of structure in zebra finch song. *Journal of Comparative and Physiological Psychology, 93*, 260–277.

Rice, J. C. (1981). Behavioral implications of aberrant song of a red-eyed vireo. *Wilson Bulletin, 93*, 383–390.

Saunders, A. A. (1947). The beginning of song in spring. *Auk, 64*, 97–107.

Seligman, M. E. P. (1970). On the generality of the laws of learning. *Psychological Review, 77*, 406–418.

Seligman, M. E. P., & Hager, J. (Eds.) (1972). *Biological boundaries of learning*. Englewood Cliffs, NJ: Prentice-Hall.

Slater, P. J. B., & Ince, S. A. (1979). Cultural evolution in chaffinch song. *Behaviour, 71*, 146–166.

Smith, W. J. (1977). *The behavior of communicating*. Cambridge: Harvard University Press.

Staddon, J. E. R. (1975). A note on the evolutionary significance of "supernormal" stimuli. *American Naturalist, 109*, 541–545.

Staddon, J. E. R. (1983). *Adaptive behavior and learning*. Cambridge: Cambridge University Press.

Staddon, J. E. R., & Simmelhag, L. V. (1971). The "superstition" experiment: A re-examination of its implications for the principles of adaptive behavior. *Psychological Review, 78*, 3–43.

Thorpe, W. H. (1958). The learning of song patterns by birds,with special reference to the song of the chaffinch, *Fringilla coelebs. Ibis, 100*, 535–570.

Thorpe, W. H. (1961), *Bird Song*. Cambridge: Cambridge University Press.

Thorpe, W. H., & Pilcher, P. M. (1958). The nature and characteristics of subsong. *British Birds, 51*, 509–514.

Todt, D., Hultsch, H., & Heike, D. (1979). Conditions affecting song learning in nightingales (*Luscinia megarhynchos*). *Zeitschrift für Tierpsychologie, 51*, 23–35.

Verbrugge, R. R. (in press). Language and event perception: Steps toward a synthesis. In W. H. Warren & R. E. Shaw (Eds.), *Persistence and change: Proceedings of the First International Conference on Event Perception*. Hillsdale, NJ: Lawrence Erlbaum Associates.

Waser, M. S., & Marler, P. (1977). Song learning in canaries. *Journal of Comparative and Physiological Psychology, 91*, 1–7.

West, M. J., & King, A. P. (1980). Enriching cowbird song by social deprivation. *Journal of Comparative and Physiological Psychology, 94*, 263–270.

West, M. J., King, A. P., & Eastzer, D. H. (1981a). The cowbird: Reflections of development from an unlikely source. *American Scientist, 69*, 57–66.

West, M. J., King, A. P., Eastzer, D. H. (1981b). Validating the female bioassay of cowbird song: Relating differences in song potency to mating success. *Animal Behaviour, 29*, 490–501.

West, M. J., King, A. P., & Harrocks, T. H. (1983). Cultural transmission of cowbird song (*Molothrus ater*): Measuring its development and outcome. *Journal of Comparative Psychology, 97*, 327–337.

Wiens, J. A. (1982). Song pattern variation in the sage sparrow (*Amphispiza belli*): Dialects or epiphenomena? *Auk, 99*, 208–229.

Woodworth, R. S. (1940). *Psychology*. New York: Henry Holt.

III

THE ECOLOGY OF LEARNING: THEORETICAL PROBLEMS

Theoretical and empirical research go hand in hand in scientific progress. Theory without data is vacuous, but data without theory can easily become a meaningless collection of uncoordinated facts. The chapters in Part 3 address some of the ecological problems of learning from a theoretical rather than from an empirical perspective. Shaw and Alley consider the nature of learning curves and what they imply for the ecological study of learning. Their chapter illustrates the kind of rigorous treatment that may already be possible for some theoretical problems in the ecology of learning, despite the relatively undeveloped state of the area. The chapters by Schleidt and by Gray both address an issue of vital importance for the ecological approach that has been completely ignored by traditional approaches to the study of learning, namely the description of the environment in which learning takes place. Schleidt addresses that problem in general terms, adopting the viewpoint of classical ethological theory, especially as developed by the pioneer ethologist Jacob von Uexküll. Gray focuses on the more specific problem of developing ways to describe the dimensions that are important to an animal's behavioral relations with its environment. Only when we can describe the environment from the animal's perspective will we be able to analyze the ways in which the animal learns to deal with its environment. Gray's chapter describes one way in which we might tackle the first of those problems. Finally, Reed considers an issue that is fundamental to the ecological approach to learning, namely the ecological approach to behavior. Learning involves change in behavior, and the ecological coherence of our theories of learning will depend to a large extent on the ecological coherence of the theories of behavior on which they are, even if implicitly, built.

10 How to Draw Learning Curves: Their Use and Justification

Robert E. Shaw
Thomas R. Alley
Department of Psychology
University of Connecticut

"true rigor is productive, being distinguished from another rigor which is purely formal and tiresome, casting a shadow over the problems it touches"
—Emile Picard (cited in Kline, 1972, p. 1025)

INTRODUCTION: LEARNING AS A CUMULATIVE FUNCTION

Although learning theorists often disagree about what learning is, they agree that whatever the process is its effects are clearly cumulative and, therefore, may be plotted as a curve. By *cumulative* we mean that somehow the effects of experience carry over to aid later performance. This property is fundamental to the construction of "learning curves." The justification for drawing learning curves is the belief that such a cumulative function exists; that, mathematically speaking, the function is *well defined*. But is it? It is one thing to assume a function exists because you need it, and quite another to define it rigorously and justify its use.

This chapter examines this question, clarifies the definition of learning, and proposes a function whose existence justifies drawing learning curves. Finally, we show how this function may represent learning as a lawful process. This is important if we wish to justify the method for drawing learning curves rather than merely take it for granted.

The Cartesian Method for Drawing Learning Curves

All traditional techniques for drawing "learning curves" presume that successive data-points can be connected by a (smooth) curve. Typically, we use graphs to display such results because they provide a clear, succinct, and accurate way to reveal any cumulative effects over successive "trials" that may exist. What must we assume about learning to draw the corresponding curve?

Although there are a variety of methods for constructing "learning curves," they all assume that successive trials or episodes in a learning series may be plotted along the abscissa (x-axis), response characteristics along the ordinate (y-axis), and that the data-points distributed in the xy-plane may be legitimately *connected by a curve*. This is the Cartesian method. Everyone who draws learning curves tacitly assumes its validity (Kling & Riggs, 1971, p. 609). Using the Cartesian method to construct learning curves implies that learning is a function that maps values on the y-axis into values on the x-axis, and also that the mapping is *at least* continuous over the x-axis.

We say "at least" because, even though the function must be continuous over the x-axis if a curve is to be drawn, it may not also be continuous over the y-axis. Instead, it may be argued that learning is discontinuous over the y-axis (e.g., Greeno, 1974; Krechevsky, 1938). Under such an assumption, the function involved would still be represented by a continuously connected curve but the curve would be "stepped" over successive trials; that is, it would be a step function. Consequently, to appreciate what is at issue, one must not confuse stepwise-discontinuity over the response measure with topological continuity (connectivity) over successive trials. The latter assumption rather than the former underlies the Cartesian method for drawing learning curves of any sort—including those that fit an all-or-none hypothesis about learning (see Restle, 1965).

If learning curves are to be justified, there must be reason to believe that the x-axis represents a continuum, and trials a series of samples of that continuum. For if it is not a continuum, then how do we know whether the trials truly represent samples of the same phenomenon—whether there is a dimension called "learning" over which measurements might legitimately be taken? This is implied when we assume that successive episodes belong to the same *series*, as when we assume that a series of trials constitutes *one* experiment rather than a succession of distinct experiments. This also underlies our designation of experimental (independent) variables.

What guarantees that the successive samples do comprise a series? This is the crucial question for deciding whether or not the Cartesian method of curve drawing is justified for learning data. There are two answers to this question: One answer is that the successive samples may be connected because there is a *lawful* relationship among the samples (or data-points); a second answer is that the samples may be connected because there is some operationally defined *rule* for doing so. Such a law or rule for defining a series of relationships for connecting values (e.g., *xy*-values) is exactly what we mean by a *function*.[1] The mathematical justification of the Cartesian method requires only that a rule be found for defining the learning function, but much more is required to justify its scientific use.

Given the mathematical rule by which samples *may* be connected to form a curve, the question remains *should* they be so connected? Are the constraints on the system responsible for the learning data a reasonable expression of the rule used by the system, or of a law governing it? An answer to this question moves us one step closer to understanding how an animal "recognizes" that successive situations are sufficiently similar to belong to the same series, a series over which "savings" might accumulate in the manner revealed by a learning curve. What the "mechanism" of learning is remains a mystery until we discover how the learner perceives the relation that connects the successive trials into a continuous series (cf. Koffka, 1935).

We must be careful not to jump to the conclusion that the scientist's view of the task, from an *external* perspective, is necessarily the same as the organism's

---

[1]Historically, the most revolutionary proposal for how functions should be defined was made by the French mathematician Dirichlet in the 18th century. After witnessing many failures by others to provide completely satisfactory analytic or algebraic accounts of functions, he opted for liberalizing the concept so that it no longer lay in the exclusive province of mathematics but moved to the more general province of logic. He proposed that any value *y* be considered a function of a variable *x* whenever a precise principle of correspondence between *x* and *y* could be clearly stated. He no longer regarded it as indispensable that the principle of correspondence be defined by mathematical operations alone; rather, a purely verbal definition could suffice if it were logically precise. This compromise in rigor opened the door to the eventual development of a purely logical theory of functions, recursive function theory, on which the theory of computable functions is based, and by which a new interpretation is given to the meaning of "rigorous." The theory of computable functions provides an important alternative to the classical technique for rigorously formulating functions— an alternative, however, that exceeds the limits of traditional natural sciences such as physics.

Perhaps the notorious principle of complementarity owes its existence to this breach in the tradition of physics being the sole judge of how functions should be rigorously defined. This principle asserts that no description of phenomena in nature can be given completely using natural (dynamic) law but also will require the use of rate-independent linguistic variables. Hence all phenomena, especially those involving living systems, will require explanations that draw on both rule-defined (linguistic mode) and law-defined (dynamic mode) functions (Jammer, 1974; Pattee, 1979, in press).

Rule-defined functions provide the foundations for computer science, mathematical linguistics, and most major attempts in cognitive science to model the mechanisms responsible for psychological functions, such as perceiving, remembering, and learning. The tacit acceptance of Dirichlet's proposal is, most likely, a major reason for the close alliance we now witness being forged among these kindred disciplines.

The ecological approach to psychology is a notable exception that resists the rule characterization of function and, hence, of psychological functions. This approach prefers to redefine what is meant by law while conserving the original meaning of a function as the expression of some underlying law of nature. The purpose served by this strategy is that continuity between psychology and physics, biology and physics, and psychology and biology might be better preserved, and the paradoxes of mind–matter and mind–body dualisms might be avoided (see Turvey, Shaw, Reed, & Mace, 1981).

internal perspective. In designing an experiment, an experimenter can assume a vague, intuitive rule presumed to connect the trials into a series even if no such rule exists for the learner to follow, or if a different rule is actually used by the learner in perceiving the relationship over trials that links them to the same series. Because of this possibility, both theorists and experimenters may impute a simpler basis to the continuity over successive trials than is actually the case. Indeed, this may be the reason that so few questions have been raised about the continuity tacitly assumed to justify the drawing of learning curves. It is not enough simply to define operationally a function by which a curve might be drawn to fit observed data-points; one must also show why that particular function is a reasonable candidate for modeling the law- or rule-governed constraints actually responsible for the learning accomplished by the organism in a given context. Although we address the formal basis for relating members of learning series, explanation of the perceptual grounds by which certain temporally distributed events and not others join together to form a learning series is beyond the scope of this chapter.

Let us pause to summarize the steps that justify the use of the Cartesian method in drawing learning curves:

1. Plot the sampled data-points in an xy-coordinate space where the x-axis represents the independent variable and the y-axis the dependent response measure. This determines the discrete data-points to be connected.

2. Find a rule for operationally defining a function, $y = f(x)$, that describes a smooth curve that passes through every data-point. This is the function whose existence needs to be justified, for without it only discontinuous plots (e.g., bar graphs) would be justified.

Note that this second step is not a license for indiscriminately connecting adjacent data-points; rather it is a primary demand that before we connect the data-points we must first justify that the function assumed does in fact exist and, by existing, serves as a constraint that guides one's pen along a predetermined course for joining each point in a manner analogous to the law or mechanism that guides the learner through related learning episodes.

It is a popular but insidious mistake, a fallacy of method, to treat the learning curve (or any other curve for that matter) as having an existence independent of the function it expresses, or the function as having any reality apart from the law or mechanism that exhibits it. This is a dangerous tactic for science, for it risks mistaking a fiction for a fact. At best, the premature drawing of the curve serves only as the concretion of your hope or hypothesis, as the observer-turned-theorist, that the function will be found and scientifically justified—if not by you, then by someone else. Thus the final step toward justifying the production of learning curves is:

3. Specify the scientific constraints (e.g., the law or mechanism) that the learning function putatively expresses that make it more than a mathematical fiction.

Exactly how one should do this is a choice of method. Behaviorists will do it one way, cognitive psychologists another, and ecological psychologists still another. Where the behaviorist might search for the invariant relationship among reinforcement contingencies common over trials (a stimulus dimension), the cognitive psychologist might search for a rule associating common features (a mediating construct). The two approaches differ regarding the role that observables are believed to play in characterizing the dimension of "belongingness" by which successive trials form a connected series: Behaviorism emphasizes "external" states of the learning situation, whereas cognitive psychology emphasizes the "internal" states of the learner.

Learning as an Ecosystem Function

In sharp contrast to both of these approaches, ecological psychology seeks the required continuity in the covariation of two dimensions: one having its footing in the environment, the other in the organism. The fundamental postulate of the ecological approach is that these two dimensions are invariantly related by a pair of functions: perception and action. Gibson (1979) refers to this as the principle of organism-environment mutuality; a mutuality that might be modeled as a mathematical duality[2] (Shaw & Turvey, 1981; Shaw, Turvey, & Mace, 1982; Turvey & Shaw, 1979; Turvey, Shaw, & Mace, 1977). Let us consider briefly the relevance of the principle of mutuality, or duality, for the problem of characterizing learning.

Roughly speaking, perception is a mapping from the series of values taken by the environmental variable into the series of values taken by the organism variable, whereas action consists of the inverse mapping. There is, however, a

---

[2]A mathematical duality D is an operation that establishes a special isomorphic correspondence between one structure X (e.g., a series) and another structure Y (e.g., another series), so that for any function f that establishes a value in X there exists another function g that establishes a corresponding (dual) value in Y. Furthermore, a duality between the structures is not transitive, for if there exists another function h that putatively carries the image of X into another structure Z, then Z must equal X.

When D is its own inverse, it is sometimes said to establish "double" duals between X and Z. The ecological approach we are espousing postulates a doubly dual relationship between the values of X, taken as environmental properties, and corresponding values of Y, taken as organismic properties. We call the duality operation $f: X \rightarrow Y$, *perception*, and its values, *affordances*. We call the inverse duality operation $g: Y \rightarrow X$, *action*, and its values, *effectivities*. The double duality, D, consisting of the operations f and g, $D: X \leftrightarrow Y$, designates a system of constraints composing an *ecosystem*.

special relationship between the perceptual function and the action function that guarantees their covariation whenever the organism is successfully guided by perception through a series of felicitous regulatory acts (e.g., muscular adjustments) that achieve an intended goal (e.g., the grasping of an object). Under such felicitous circumstances, the two functions must become *duals* so that the course of values assumed by one constrains the course of values assumed by the other (see footnote 2) in an ongoing and mutual process:

$$P(t_0) \rightarrow A(t_1),\ A(t_1) \rightarrow P(t_2),\ P(t_2) \rightarrow A(t_3),\ \cdots$$

Thus perception and action operate on each other reciprocally, in a "closed looping" fashion rather than in a open-ended, causal chaining fashion. The covariation that results is properly termed *ecological* because it involves both environmental and organismic variables.

Finally, the perceptual and action series spiral through space–time intertwined like a double helix, tracing out a path determined by a logic of circular constraint. In this way, ecological events involving perceiving and acting determine "fat" world-lines in space-time (four-dimensional) geometry (see Kugler, Turvey, Carello, & Shaw, in press).

In this scheme, learning is a lawful operation that increases the coordination between perception and action series. Metaphorically, learning is a function that tightens the constraints on the double helix, bringing the perceptual "helix" (or series) into closer alignment with the action "helix" (or series). This view of learning assumes the existence of two series whose values can be coupled such that certain values in one series are potentially duals of certain values in the other series. "Affordances" and "effectivities" are just such duals.

Affordances and Effectivities as Duals.   An object that *affords* grasping by some organism is said to have the affordance property of "graspability" for that organism. The affordance property is a value that will appear in the perceptual series of a properly "attuned" organism (i.e., of an organism that has a "grasper" properly designed and controlled to accommodate the object in question). When an organism learns to use its grasper to achieve grasping of a given object, the affordance property also takes on a corresponding (dual) value in the action series. We call this dual value in the action series an *effectivity*.

These series are by no means simple; instead, they consist of higher order invariant properties of environmental situations and organismic states. The perceptual series is a series of affordances linked by the actions of an organism toward environmental objects. The action series is a series of effectivities linked by an organism's ongoing perceptions of environmental properties. Like affordances, effectivity values are complex, referring to the fact that for an organism to act, some appropriate effector organ must be connected to a repertoire of control constraints (e.g., muscular adjustments) suitable for determining an act (e.g., grasping of x) that realizes some affordance goal (the graspability of x).

Because of our endorsement of the principle of organism-environment mutuality, we, as ecological psychologists, require two of everything listed previously: two sets of data-points—one showing how the learner's perception of the task variables changed over time and one showing how the learner's action (response characteristics) changed as a function of the task variables; two learning curves must be justified—one showing perceptual learning in the task and the other action learning; two mathematical rules must be found for determining how the data-points are to be connected to form a series; two laws must be discovered to justify the scientific use of the pair of functions; and finally, in keeping with the concept of affordance, the two laws must be shown to "fuse" into a *dual* pair of reciprocal equations consisting of complementary variables—one equation to describe changes in the perceptual series and one to describe the dual changes in the action series. Here again the concept of dual is the mathematical one rather than the philosophical one and refers to a special relationship between two equations (or functions), so that the solution to (definition of) one specifies the solution to (definition of) the other.

We return to this discussion of duality in the ecological approach to learning toward the end of this chapter. In what follows now, we show how one might address each of the three points discussed earlier. Although our illustration is a serious attempt to provide a first pass on an ecological approach to learning theory, we hope that readers who disagree with that approach will, nevertheless, find some benefit for their own theories from an examination of the method used.

Step 1. Plotting Data-Points Sampled from a Continuum

Generally, we might define learning as a cumulative function, L, that determines a mapping between two series: a *perceptual* (stimulus) series and an *action* (response) series. The perceptual series consists of episodes (e.g., trials) on which the learning function applies to increase the value of some response characteristic of the organism over time. This means that we can analyze the global function L into a series of lesser functions that apply locally to give the exact increment to the y-values (response characteristics) at each x-value (trial) as follows:

$$L = f(x)_1 + f(x)_2 + f(x)_3 + \cdots = y_1 + y_2 + y_3 + \cdots, \qquad (1)$$

$$\text{or} \quad L = \int_a^b f(x)dx,$$

where a and b are first and last trials, respectively, in the series of trials run.

There is, however, a subtlety in this characterization of learning that should not be overlooked: The "trial" variable must be considered to be imbedded in a continuum or else no curve can be drawn to connect the data-points in the Cartesian manner (where each distinct data-point is an (x, y) value in the plane of the graph $y = f(x)$). The continuity requirement is satisfied, however, by the assumption that L is a function that is continuously summable (integrable) over x. This is tantamount to the claim that x is a continuous variable and, therefore, qualified to be an axis over which a time-varying process might be well defined. This assumption that the x-intercepts of all adjacent data-points are at least integrable over time guarantees, in principle, the connectability of the data-points into the desired learning curve. What kind of function must L be for this assumption to be justified?

In the next section we propose an answer to this question that accords with some of the most general facts known about learning.

Step 2. Defining Learning by Analogy to Dissipative Functions

Learning is not merely a simple accretion of a response tendency with repeated experience; often, if not always, specific and nonspecific changes in the general disposition to learn also accompany these changes in response characteristics. Therefore, any function used to represent learning must consist of two distinct parts: a "response" variable and a "state" variable (irrespective of whether the state variable is taken to be behaviorally, cognitively, or ecologically defined). The *response* variable expresses an "observable": the observed change in the behavior of the system. The *state* variable expresses a "dispositional": specific or nonspecific changes in the disposition of the system to learn. When this change in disposition is nonspecific, fosters learning, and persists over an extensive interval of time, we refer to it as the formation of a "learning set" (e.g., Harlow, 1949) or, more generally, as "learning to learn" (e.g., Bransford, Stein, Shelton, & Owings, 1981). Conversely, when the nonspecific transfer effect is increasingly negative (inhibiting learning), we call it "fatigue." Both of these generalized changes in the disposition of organisms to learn are *dissipative* parameters: Learning to learn can be considered the dissipation of inhibition (e.g., of distractions) and fatigue the dissipation of facilitation (e.g., of interest or energy).

Historically, the mathematical characterization of functions involving dissipative parameters has proven problematic. For instance, the classical treatment of the behavior of a spring under differential loadings assumed the validity of Hooke's famous law asserting that strain (stretching or compressing) is directly proportional to stress (restorative force). Unfortunately, the problem is more complicated than this because the coefficient of elasticity of the spring, a dispositional variable, tends (like the disposition to learn) to change with repeated use. Hooke's simple law fails to take this change into account. In Hooke's day, it was not mathematically possible to formulate a function that included the effects on the spring's behavior of both the stress force and the dissipation of elasticity arising from stress. In fact, the mathematics needed to provide a generalized version of Hooke's law did not become available until nearly two centuries later when Volterra, the great Italian mathematician, turned his attention to problems involving "hereditary" influences (Kramer, 1970). Dissipative changes in the disposition of a system to respond is but one among a class of influences that may operate persistently to alter dynamically the response characteristics of a system, be it living or not.

A formal analogy holds between the formulation of laws required to relate observable to dispositional variables in physics and those required to serve a similar function in learning theory. (Some of the historical and technical details of this analogy are contained in Appendix A.) We believe that the task of formulating learning functions will be made easier if we examine how physics solved the problem of designing a general form of Hooke's law for springs: one that included dispositional variables that change as a function of use. With this as a guide, we might formulate analogous functions for learning with nested dispositional variables that also lawfully change their values as a function of use (practice). Such a formulation would satisfy Step 3 of our procedure for justifying the drawing of learning curves by showing how the underlying function could be continuous over the x-axis.

Common abstract solutions to the two classes of problems arise because learning systems, like physical systems with dissipative parameters, are governed by *hereditary* laws: laws that express the effects of hereditary influences on the state (dispositional) variables of a system. If this is so, the problem of formulating rigorous laws of learning becomes an aspect of the more general problem of discovering the laws of what Picard (1907) called "hereditary mechanics." Picard coined this name for a new discipline to emphasize the fact that no existing form of mechanics yet included the study of laws involving hereditary influences; not classical mechanics, variational mechanics, quantum mechanics, or relativistic mechanics, for none of these approaches, in principle, can explain the behavior of systems that are governed even in part by dispositional variables that serve a "record-keeping" function (Jammer, 1974; Pattee, 1979, in press).

Psychology is reputed to be the science of systems that do keep "records" that influence current states, yet it has not developed the techniques needed for characterizing functions that incorporate dispositional variables: new functions whose courses of values are steered by hereditary influences. Instead, the field has concentrated on developing "mechanisms" founded either on old functions borrowed from the classical period of mathematical physics or on rules so intuitive that the functions they entail escape analysis.

Much help can be obtained by exploiting analogic connections to abstractly similar problems in older fields, like physics, where formal techniques and scientific methods may be better developed. Thus our problem may be better understood by analogy to the struggle of physics to define rigorously dissipative functions, a close analogue of our problem. Consequently, let us treat physics as a resource field from which certain formal tools might be borrowed. No reductionism is necessarily implied by such a strategy because the variables to be included in the learning function, the response variable and the dispositional variable, are psychological rather than physical. It is only the logical scheme, or syntax, of the law that we intend to borrow to help determine the type of function needed to model learning. We beg the reader's indulgence as we delve into unfamiliar matters drawn from the history of physics and mathematics. Although one half of the analogy, the resource field of hereditary mechanics, may be unfamiliar, the second half, the test field of learning theory, is not. Our intention is not to import psychology into physics nor physics into psychology, but to clarify the function by which learning might be defined by justifying learning curves.

Learning as a Problem for Hereditary Mechanics

A function constrained by a hereditary influence (e.g., a dissipative parameter) cannot be captured by the ordinary means available to traditional physics for expressing functions, or by the laws they may represent. The means available have traditionally been either differential or partial differential equations and their integral counterparts. But none of these will do. (For discussion of the reasons, see Appendix A.) Because the laws of classical (variational) mechanics depend exclusively on rigorous expression in differential (integral) form, dissipative phenomena (such as the effects of fatigue on the behavior of an elastic system), although perfectly lawful, failed to fit the form of any known laws. This can be seen in the case of elastic systems (e.g., springs) alluded to earlier.

Experimentation revealed that the behavior of elastic systems was not merely a function of its last initial condition, but also of the entire history of its initial conditions.[3] For instance, as pointed out earlier, a spring's behavior is not

---

[3]Traditionally, two forms of physical laws are recognized: those that map initial conditions (forward in time) into final conditions, and those that map final conditions (backward in time) into initial conditions. The mathematical form of the "forward" acting law was that of a differential equation, whereas that of the "backward" acting law was that of an integral equation (see Appendix A). Classical mechanics developed laws that were exclusively differential in form, whereas *variational mechanics* was the name of the discipline that was devoted to the development of laws that were integral in form. These two approaches to mechanics expressed two distinct philosophical, even theological, orientations. Briefly, their differing motivations can be explained as follows: Because causes necessarily precede effects, the differential form, as used by classical (Lagrangian) mechanics, was deemed the appropriate function for expressing "causal" laws. By contrast, because goal-directed systems are constrained by the final (often optimal) state toward which they tend, the integral form, as used by variational (Hamiltonian) mechanics, was deemed the appropriate function for expressing "teleological" laws. As discussed in Appendix A, however, the defense of this distinction is not so straightforward as might first appear.

predictable from Hooke's law, which asserts that *stress* (restorative force) is directly proportional to the *strain* (change in length) undergone; instead, careful experimentation showed stress to be a function of the entire history of the strains undergone by the spring on all previous occasions (Lindsay & Margenau, 1957). Hence, strain acts as a hereditary influence on an elastic system, exerting a cumulative fatigue effect on its later behavior. What makes systems that operate under hereditary influences impossible to explain by the ordinary laws of mechanics?

Hooke's law can be represented by the equation

$$y = -kx \tag{2}$$

where x is the strain behavior of the spring (i.e., how far it will stretch), y is the stress (the tendency of the spring to restore itself to its original length when stretched), and k is the coefficient of elasticity of the system. From this equation we see that elastic systems with high coefficients have greater restorative forces than those with lower ones. Therefore, after a spring with a high k-value is loaded, we would expect it to stretch much less than a comparably loaded spring with a low k-value. Furthermore, according to this equation, we should also expect springs with the same k always to stretch by the same amount under identical loadings, irrespective of the distance or number of times they had been stretched in the past. As noted previously, this was shown not to be the case. Frequency of use and style of use have cumulative (hereditary) effects analogous to practice in the case of learning. Elasticity (k) decreases according to some function not contained in Hooke's simple law. Hooke's law treats k as a constant when it is really a variable that exhibits a rather orderly change in value over time proportional to its history of use. This proportion also requires a function for its rigorous expression.

Stated more generally, we recognize that what is needed is a law statement involving two kinds of functions: an observable or behavioral function, and a dispositional or state function. Hooke provided us with a law statement involving only one function and a constant, but clearly there can be no generality to such an equation with respect to historical effects. Even if we make k a variable instead of a fixed value, we would have to determine its exact value empirically just before loading the spring for a new test of the law. Moreover, we would be unable to generalize to future uses of the spring because the test itself would have required loading of the spring, which would again alter the value of k: a vicious circle!

In learning theory this would be analogous to trying to express learning over a series of trials as the function of an unspecified variable whose behavior is not known, but which cannot be determined without running the subject in still another learning trial, which itself alters the value of the variable: another vicious circle! This unspecified variable, like the k in Hooke's law, is a dispositional term referring to an unspecified state of the system: the capacity to learn under the stipulated circumstances. If this unspecified variable can, like k, be treated as a fixed value (i.e., a constant), the equation predicting learning will be well behaved when the appropriate value is plugged in. On the other hand, should this value change as some linear or nonlinear function of exposure to the experimental variables, then, to that extent, the equation will fail to predict and will be an incomplete characterization. More importantly, learning will appear to be unlawful even though it is actually lawful. Thus, we may conclude that learning either is or is not law governed ony when we are sure that our equation is complete and that the behavior of *all* its terms is functionally specified.

The existence of learning to learn demands a search for the appropriate formal means of expressing the dispositional term as a well-behaved function. It will not do simply to treat the capacity of an organism to learn as fixed, for then any lawfulness that might exist will escape detection. Nor will it do to try to circumvent the problem by treating learning in terms of difference equations rather than the more demanding technique of functional analysis required in hereditary mechanics, for such difference equations are themselves not well behaved under circumstances where terms refer to functions of functions. This occurs, for example, where dispositional functions change their course as a function of behavioral functions (Greeno, 1974). Functions that are the function of other functions rather than of variables are called *functionals*. Strictly speaking, all hereditary functionals are in a sense nonlinear and, therefore, cannot be adequately expressed by linear equations; they can only be approximated. Moreover, as others (e.g., Herrnstein, 1979) have recognized, learning is better described by nonlinear than linear models. (See Appendix B.)

If, as we have argued, learning is a *functional* rather than merely a function, the linear equations typically used (as in traditional physics) will fail to capture the significant and necessary role played by hereditary influences. This suggests that a better understanding of the nature of this limitation may prove helpful in understanding the form that realistic formulations of learning must take if any lawfulness present is to be expressed.

In the parlance of mechanics, we express this limitation of traditional law statements by saying that laws must be "initialized"; that is, the *initial conditions* for a law are not themselves an intrinsic part of the equation of the law but must be added before the law can be applied.[4] This seems to make initial conditions

---

[4]Initial conditions are the values that must be given to the free parameters in the equation for a law statement in order to be able to predict final conditions (outcomes) dynamically. For instance, applying the laws of mechanics to predict the final resting places of all the billiard balls struck in a game of billiards requires that we specify the momentum of each ball in the chain reaction. But because momentum is equal to the mass of a ball times its velocity, and the momentum of each subsequently struck ball is determined ultimately by the impulse force (force × time) applied to the first ball, the mass and velocity terms are initial conditions that must be specified before the equations for the applicable laws of motion can be evaluated to predict the final locations of each ball after the chain of collisions.

an indispensable afterthought, something sorely needed for the practical application of the law but unencompassed by it. Then why not simply build laws that incorporate their initial conditions as an intrinsic component of the law statement? Why not simply construct equations for learning or mechanical laws out of functionals that incorporate functions of hereditary functions? Unfortunately, this is easier said than done.

Classical mechanics (and all other branches of science that choose differential equations for expressing laws) is prohibited from taking this course of action because there is formally no way to place initial conditions within a differential form and still have a solvable equation.[5] This is because a hereditary influence requires a separate and distinct form of expression. Thus to formulate a law that incorporates hereditary influences like learning, we must liberalize our concept of the mathematical form that law statements might take. We must look beyond simple differential or integral forms and entertain some other possibility. What might this new form for a law equation be?

To answer by way of a recapitulation, note that three properties of learning functions have been discussed:

1. Learning functions are *cumulative* (i.e., on the average, they increase monotonically).
2. The cumulative nature of such functions is, in general, positively (or negatively for aversive conditioning) *constrained by hereditary influences* on analogy to dissipative parameters.
3. The generic learning functional, most likely, will prove to be *nonlinear*, with linearity being a special, if important, case.

Taken together, these three properties suggest that learning functions must be characterized by a *nonlinear integro-differential form*. In the next section we

---

[5]Mathematically speaking, integral forms are opposite, or complementary to, differential forms: Whereas, under different initial values a differential equation specifies the values of individual points lying on a curve, an integral equation provides a general solution to the whole set of distinctly initialized differential equations, treated collectively and simultaneously, and thereby yields the curve itself. Thus, differential forms sample the curve piecemeal whereas integral forms exhibit the whole curve so that it might be sampled. For this reason, the solving of a differential equation requires integration whereas the solving of integral equations requires differentiation. The attempt to nest all the initial conditions needed to evaluate fully a law statement couched in differential form would be ludicrous, because this would require the law equation to be solved prior to its application; it would require solutions to a potentially infinite set of differential equations before any application could be made: an impossible demand.

The strategy of attempting to embed the final conditions under the law function in order to postdict the initial conditions, in the manner of (Hamilton's) variational mechanics, is similarly ill fated, for this would also require a priori knowledge of an inverse nonlinear hereditary functional on k: the very thing being sought. The proper strategy for avoiding this dilemma was taken by Volterra (see Appendix A).

discuss some of the problems that must be overcome before integro-differential equations can be made completely appropriate for characterizing learning.

Step 3. A Hereditary Law Form for Learning

Like the law forms of classical physics that ignored the dissipative parameters of elastic systems, the law forms adopted by classical learning theory, stochastic learning models, and cognitive approaches also fail to provide a principled place for the hereditary aspect of learning. This is not to say that learning equations have not been written. They have, but to our knowledge, no innovation in the construction of law forms has resulted from such attempts.

For example, neither reinforcement (causal) nor expectancy (teleological) theories succeeded in providing new law forms that can explain all types of learning. Their failure is analogous to the failure of their corresponding law forms in mechanics. As discussed earlier, because of their dependence on differential and integral law forms, neither classical ("causal") nor variational ("teleological") mechanics could provide a strictly lawful explanation of elastic systems. Apparently, some law form more powerful than either of these is needed.

It is not our purpose to develop the mathematics of hereditary systems, but we do wish to provide the abstract form of the functions defining the behavior of such systems because this, presumably, is the form that learning functions must take if the analogy proposed is valid. Consequently, here we present only the abstract equivalent to the actual mathematical expressions required. We would also like to contrast the form of functions that involve hereditary influences with those that do not.

INTEGRO-DIFFERENTIAL EQUATIONS AS THE LAW FORM FOR LEARNING

The abstract form of all hereditary laws, including learning, is that of an *integro-differential* equation. The general form of this equation is

$$y(t) = kx(t) + \int_a^b K(t,s)\, x(s)ds \tag{3}$$

The hereditary influence is defined over the temporal interval from time s to time t, as associated with the *occasions* (a to b) when samples of the x-series are taken (e.g., from Trial a to Trial b). Here $y(t)$ expresses the value of the *behavioral variable* (response characteristic) y observed at time t, whereas $x(t)$ is the value of the *dispositional variable* x also at time t. The constant k scales the initial value of the dispositional (state) variable (such as the elasticity coefficient or capacity to learn). Finally, $K(t,s)$ is an integral transform called the *coefficient of hereditary influence* which acts over the interval from s to t (of the trials continuum) and determines the series of values x assumes over that sampling interval. This change in the x variable is measured in units $x(s)ds$. Such equations may describe a *learning* function when $y(t)$ is, on the average, increasing, and a *decay* function (for habituation or fatigue) when $y(t)$ is, on the average, decreasing.

To simplify our presentation, we treat the integro-differential form algebraically in "operator" notation. An *operator* denotes a mathematical operation that converts one function, say $x(t)$, into another function, say $w(t)$. (Note that an operator is not itself a function; instead, functions are the "objects" of operators.) We use k as the special symbol for an operator. Using operator notation we can portray, abstractly, the major difference between the classical formulation of Hooke's law (Eq. 2) and the more general hereditary formulation known as the *generalized* version of Hooke's law. The major terms of this equation are represented by the algebraic operators that act as place holders for integral and differential forms as follows:

$$y = kx + K \tag{4}$$

In this equation, K can be called a "hereditary transform of k." Equation 4 asserts that strain x (of, say, a simple spring) is not simply proportional to stress, as claimed in Hooke's original formulation of his law (Eq. 2), but instead depends on all the values that x assumed from the time of application of initial stress to the time now being considered. In other words, K is a series of values (perhaps nonlinear; see Appendix B) that must be added to k to change its course of values over time; this, of course, changes the series denoted by the independent variable x.

With the hereditary formulations of Equations 3 and 4 in hand, the process of learning can at last be translated, through analogy, into a hereditary functional. For this analogy, learning situations may be viewed as placing a "stress" on an organism's general learning capacity (k), thereby causing a relatively permanent change in response tendency (y), as reflected in "strain" (average monotonic increase) of the relevant response characteristic (x), graphically shown as the amplitude of the learning curve. The hereditary influence, designated by the transform K, represents the cumulative effect of learning to learn over the series of trials; an effect not explained by the facilitative stress applied on each individual trial.

We urge learning theorists to consider adopting a hereditary law form for learning functions. No one can yet tell whether hereditary law forms will prove more adequate than their predecessors. We believe they will, because they can express the rather peculiar circularity (nonlinearity) of dispositional variables, like k, being dependent on the behavioral variables that they help to determine. Such "circular logic" (Turvey, Shaw, & Mace, 1977) for nonlinear learning laws stands in sharp contrast to the more traditional, "one-way" transitive logic of the classical attempts to formulate linear laws for learning. The potential power of the circular transitivity of the laws of hereditary mechanics is much like the recursive power of rule-defined learning functions favored by cognitive approaches that attempt to model learning formally, or by computer-driven simulation programs. We favor the hereditary functional formulation over the recursive rule formulation, because it permits the search for laws of learning to continue as an extension of the classical tradition while maintaining close ties, without reductionism, to other sciences (e.g., physics) that may continue to function as useful resource fields for our test field of psychology.

In the next section we discuss some more specific aspects of treating learning as a hereditary functional from the perspective of ecological psychology.

THE ROLE OF COMPLEMENTARITY AND DUALITY IN AN ECOLOGICAL PSYCHOLOGY OF LEARNING

An essential ingredient of an ecological theory of psychology, following the principle of organism–environment mutuality (Gibson, 1979; Turvey & Shaw, 1979), is the existence of a perception–action "loop" by which an organism is related to its environment. This mutuality principle asserts that an organism's perception of the environment provides control constraints for its actions, and, conversely, that an organism's controlled encounters with its environment (via its action system) provide constraints on the perceptual information that unfolds as a function of such encounters.

In the language of control systems engineering (see Nagrath & Gopal, 1982), such a loop between two variable-state systems constitutes a *duality* (i.e., a mutuality of constraints) of controllability and observability. *Controllability* is a property of a system when, given any initial state and any designated final state, there exists a time interval and an input that determine how the system moves from the initial state to the final state during the specified interval of time. *Observability* is a property of a system when, given any final state and any designated initial state, there exists a time interval and an output that determine how the system moves from the final state to the initial state during the specified time interval.

We have met this duality principle before in our discussion of the relationship between laws stated in the differential ("causal") forms of classical mechanics and in the integral ("teleological") forms of variational mechanics. The concept of duality is now sufficiently ubiquitous to call it a *fundamental* principle of all mathematical science. (See Lautmann, 1971; Patten, 1982; Shaw & Mingolla, 1982; Shaw & Todd, 1980; Shaw & Turvey, 1981 for examples of its applicability in fields ranging from physics to ecology and psychology.)

Duality and Ecosystems.   Because an ecosystem consists of both energy interactions and information transactions between organisms and their environment, one might argue that the principle of complementarity applies in psychology as well as in physics and biology. On the contrary, we suggest that in an ecosystem where perception and action are equal, concomitant, and intrinsic components, the principle of complementarity is usurped by the principle of duality. The principle of duality is the manifest constraint that permits an ecosystem model to circumvent the principle of complementarity of energy and information by construing these two concepts as a duality rather than a dualism. The principle of complementarity asserts that living systems may not be adequately explained by the dynamical (rate-dependent) laws but also require information (rate-independent) rules as well. We see the need for these two modes of description most emphatically in the apparent dualism of the enzyme-folding (dynamical) process by which DNA molecules replicate as contrasted with the double-helical code that provides the informational constraints that guide the replication process (Pattee, 1979, in press).

The concept of *control*, interpreted for ecosystems, corresponds to the *means* by which actions and perceptions are determined. Such means are the operators by which the organism processes energy to produce actions, on the one hand, and the operators by which the environment structures the energy distributions that are perceived, on the other. Let K_0 and K_E designate the organism and environment operators, respectively, and x and y their respective energy inputs. The corresponding control equations are $(y = K_0 x)$ and $(x = K_E y)$.

The concept of *observable,* interpreted for ecosystems, corresponds to the *goals* toward which actions are controlled and that perceptual information specifies. An *effectivity* is a goal-directed function that an organism might, in principle, realize. When the goal-directed function is also determined by the environment, it is called an *affordance*. The "observable" properties of an ecosystem are effectivities and affordances. Using this same operator notation, the information that renders each of these properties observable can be given by $(x = K_0^* y)$ for an effectivity goal and $(y = K_E^* x)$ for an affordance goal, when the energy control equations are also given. Figure 10.1 illustrates how the energy support for perception and action (control) and the information specification of affordances and effectivities (observables) come together to define an ecosystem as a *closed loop* over a pair of dual external states.

An ecosystem requires four equations for its complete specification: a pair of dual energy equations that are dual to a pair of dual information equations. Table 10.1 presents these equations in their generic integro-differential form (in contrast to their operator form as in Fig. 10.1). Because these equations involve hereditary transforms (K_0, K_E, K_0^*, K_E^*), they express the generic form of the hereditary law governing an ecosystem's history of energy interactions and information transactions. The operators designated by the asterisks denote the hereditary transforms of integrals that specify information transactions, and that run temporally counter to the causal direction of energy interactions (represented by the integral

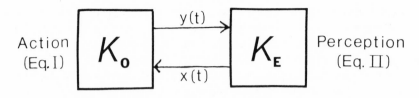

I. ENERGY (CONTROL) DUALS

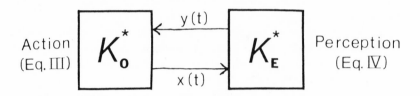

II. INFORMATION (OBSERVATION) DUALS

FIG.10.1 Diagram of the energy (control) and information (observation) duals shown in operator notation. The corresponding equations (denoted in parentheses) for perception and action are given in Table 10.1.

TABLE 10.1
Table of Duals

| | | Perspective Duals | |
		Organism-Perspective (Action)	Environment-Perspective (Perception)
Temporal Duals	Energy (Control)	$y(t) = \int_0^t K_0\ (t,s)\ x(s)ds$ (Equation I)	$x(t) = \int_0^t K_E\ (t,s)\ y(s)ds$ (Equation II)
	Information (Observation)	$x(t) = \int_0^t K_0^*\ (s,t)\ y(s)ds$ (Equation III)	$y(t) = \int_0^t K_E^*\ (s,t)\ x(s)ds$ (Equation IV)

Note: The symbols in these equations are explained in the text in connection with Eq. 3. The transforms whose kernels take the form $K(t,s)$ designate "past pending" integrals that sum energy interactions from some past state (s) to some future state (t). By contrast, those with kernels of the form $K^*(s,t)$ designate "future tending" integrals that sum information transactions from some potential future goal state (t) "backwards" in time to some current state (s).

equations whose operators have no asterisks). These dual information and energy integrals express a temporal symmetry analogous to the temporal contrast expressed by the equations of variational and classical mechanics, for there are both future- and past-pending forms. Where the energy integrals (Eqs. I and II in Table 10.1) express the *means* by which energy interactions between an environment and an organism provide the "drive" for the action and perception systems, the information integrals (Eqs. III and IV) specify the effectivity and affordance "*goals*" that the information transactions signify.

Nature must allow organisms to solve this predicament: Given a certain need state, how can an organism being showered only with the present energy (time-forward) interactions reach a stipulated future goal state in an optimal fashion? The answer is that it cannot! Intentional behaviors cannot be reduced to causal relations. Rather, the organism must learn to use hereditary influences and current information (time-backward) transactions to guide it optimally toward the required goal state. The arguments raised by supporters of teleological views against the causal approaches of classical mechanics and reinforcement theories were not so much off the mark as merely one-sided. Neither variational nor expectancy theories alone can be complete: A theory that incorporates the causal and intentional, energy and information, as dual forms of the same law, however, might be complete or, at least, completable in principle.

Because the four equations in Table 10.1 are intrinsically related by duality operations, the ecosystem can be said to be *self-controllable* and *self-observable*. These four equations in concert provide us with the two coordinated series needed for learning. Hence, if these series have solvable equations, then, contrary to the complementarity perspective, the learning functional coordinating them exists. If we identify the learning functional with the dual equations (Eqs. I and III) having K_0 as an operator, the composite functional provides a rigorous characterization of action (response) learning: With the dual equations (Eqs. II and IV) having K_E as an operator, it provides a rigorous characterization of perceptual learning.

Presumably, the overall learning series requires the sum of the hereditary influences of both perceptual learning and action learning: a summation performed by the learning functional. We might consider learning over the coordinated series to be complementary such that:

$$(K_0 x + K_E y = 1) \quad \text{for} \quad 0 \le K_0 < K_E \quad \text{or} \quad 0 \le K_E < K_0. \qquad (5)$$

Learning with respect to Equation I might be interpreted as improvement in biomechanical coordination so that energy resources are optimized. By contrast, learning with respect to Equation II might be interpreted as improvement in perceptual strategies producing a refined use of the energy patterns required to orient and detect. Similarly, learning with respect to Equations III and IV pertains to the selection of optimal paths from potentially attainable effectivity and affordance goals through the state-space of subgoals that define the current action state and perceptual state of the system, respectively. These four kinds of learning might contribute differentially to the overall change in response characteristics.

The amount of variance explained by each of these series can be experimentally ascertained by *within-subjects* designs with repeated measures where the subjects are brought to criterion on the perceptual displays incorporated in the learning, as contrasted with a similar design where subjects are permitted practice on the response measure. Overall, then, the process of learning will include three fundamental sources of variance: the dual (energy and information) perceptual learning series, the dual (energy and information) action learning series, and the learning-to-learn contribution over each of these series.

SUMMARY AND CONCLUSIONS

Learning theorists were once content to adopt the linearly causal law forms developed by traditional physics. Later, after seeing the failure of such law forms to explain all kinds of learning, and under a variety of incisive criticisms (see, e.g., Hinde & Stevenson–Hinde, 1973; Johnston, 1981; Seligman and Hager, 1972), many learning theorists abandoned altogether the quest for laws in favor of rule descriptions for learning functions. In this chapter we have offered reasons for reconsidering the case for learning laws. Let us close with an assessment of the formal analogy between our test field (learning) and our resource field (mechanics).

Our historical junket (Appendix A) has revealed considerable support for the proposed analogy between physics and psychology. The validity of the analogy is seen to be a consequence of a shared belief that laws are desirable, attainable, and capable of rigorous formulation. We have argued that strong analogical connections arose because of the mutual desire to formulate law-based equations in both fields. Both fields tacitly assumed that such laws must take on the analytic forms developed by classical physics: the familiar differential or integral forms. This analogy was strengthened by noticing that reinforcement theory stands to classical mechanics on the "causal" interpretation of differential forms as expectancy theory stands to variational mechanics on the "teleological" interpretation of integral forms of law (see Appendix A). The discovery of hereditary (dissipative) phenomena, not expressible in either of these forms alone, led us to consider the hybrid integro-differential forms required to express the laws of hereditary mechanics: laws that incorporate the historical series over which initial conditions are "updated" to reflect hereditary influences.

Acceptance of the proposed analogy between learning theory as our test field and hereditary mechanics as a resource field entails serious consideration of the integro-differential form as the law form appropriate for modeling learning functions. Because learning acts as a hereditary functional over trials, as evidenced by learning to learn, rather than as a simple linear function, only this law form can fully justify the drawing of learning curves.

ACKNOWLEDGMENTS

We are grateful to J. J. Jenkins, T. D. Johnston, P. N. Kugler, W. M. Mace, E. Mingolla, and M. T. Turvey for their helpful comments and discussion during the preparation of this chapter. The second author was supported by a Postdoctoral Fellowship from the National Institute of Dental Research (Grant DEO–7047).

APPENDIX A
Analogical Law Forms in Physics and Psychology

The classical period of mathematical analysis, the 17th and 18th centuries, gave birth to the optimistic view that physical science could soon be completed with mathematical rigor and its foundations secured with axiomatic certainty. Near the end of this period, Lagrange (1788) was confident enough to boast in his highly influential book, *Mécanique Analytique,* that he had developed Newton's mechanics to such a high state of mathematical rigor that he had banned forever from science the need for diagrams and (therefore) geometric intuition.

In the mid-20th century a similar optimism regarding the role of mathematical rigor in defining deterministic laws was entertained by learning theorists. Was there good reason for this similarity in scientific attitudes shared by physicists during the classical period of mechanics and psychologists during the classical period of learning theory? Why do scientific determinism and mathematical absolutism go hand in hand?

Analytic Functions as the Classic Law Form

Mathematicians of the 17th and 18th centuries knew only of functions that were *analytic*, a property of being represented by a convergent Taylor series: a particularly simple kind of series, known as the power series, which always converges (has a limit) over a continuous range. Consider the infinite series,

$$a_0 + a_1(x - k)^1 + a_2(x - k)^2 + a_3(x - k)^3 + \cdots,$$

in which $a_0, a_1, a_2, \cdots$ and k are arbitrary, fixed finite numbers, and x is variable. Note that the series is based upon successive integral powers of $(x - k)^n$—hence the name "power series." The power series always converges for the value $x = k$

because it then reduces to its first term, a_0. The series may also converge for other values of x, thereby defining a continuous range of values of x with the point $x = k$ occupying the center of the range. Within this range, the power series defines a continuous function whose derivatives are all continuous.

Because all functions dealt with by mathematicians of this era were expressible in terms of such series, they erroneously concluded that all mathematical functions were necessarily analytic (i.e., were expressible in terms of infinite series that are both convergent and continuous). It scarcely need be noted that geometric curves can be drawn using the Cartesian method to represent such functions graphically rather than numerically.

For the classical physicist, the belief that series of observations or measurements could be presented graphically via the Cartesian method, and that all such functions so represented could be expressed by Taylor series, gave mathematical expression to a strict determinism. Given a small set of observations, predictions and postdictions could be made by means of geometric intuitions or (later) by the rigorous application of the technique of analytic continuation. Hence the very concept of being *determined by law* became synonymous with being *expressible by analytic function*.

It should be obvious that an implicit, if little discussed, assumption that learning functions must be analytic functions (i.e., that learning series are Taylor series) lies behind the construction of learning curves: For how else could one justify extrapolating from discrete data points to a smooth continuous curve that converges on some criterial value as its limits? Little wonder then that a similar attitude of strict determinism prevailed among learning theorists of the mid-20th century, and that discovering laws of learning became synonymous with formulating the learning function in an analogous analytic manner.

For the process of drawing continuous curves from discrete data points to have greater justification than simply geometric intuition or ill-founded convention, another property of analytic functions must hold for learning: the property of *analytic continuation*. Gestalt psychologists recognized this property as a perceptually based, geometric intuition they called "good continuation," whereby any curve or line "carries its own law within itself" (Koffka, 1935, p. 175). This geometric intuition can be understood in a more rigorous fashion when expressed in terms of analytic functions.

The perceptual tendency to continue a curve from an arc can be attributed to the fact that a small arc generatively specifies a longer curve. An arc is mathematically equivalent to an interval of all values of x for some analytic function $f(x)$ from which the derivatives specifying a longer Taylor series may be extracted (d'Abro, 1951). Thus the Gestalt law of good continuation, intuitively used in the extrapolation of learning curves, has a legitimate basis so long as the curves are analytic and the series upon which the curves are based determine Taylor series. The analogy developed here between classical mechanics and learning theory is neither superficial nor accidental but is grounded in a common assumption that laws are deterministic because they involve functions that are analytic.

Causal and Teleological Determinism in Physics and Psychology

In classical mechanics, the laws of motion and change may be expressed in either of two ways: as *differential* equations that describe the process as it unfolds over time, or as *integral* equations that describe the complete time course of the process. The differential form of a law assumes that the process unfolds with infinitesimal continuity from a preceding state to its next successive state. For this reason, it is assumed to be expressing the dynamic laws of a system in terms of *efficient* cause (cause and effect). The integral form of the same process, because it defines each intermediate state in terms of the total process, can be seen as expressing the dynamic laws in terms of *final* cause. Mathematically speaking, these two forms of expressing dynamic laws yield identical quantitative results. Furthermore, the two methods are just complementary expressions of the fact that a system's continuous change or motions trace a continuous curve in space over time so that, given any intermediate arc of the curve, the procedure of analytic continuation (in principle, but not always in practice) allows the arc to be extended either backward or forward in time.

This property accounts for the reversibility of the laws of classical mechanics (cf. Overseth, 1969). These laws treat change in state of a mechanical system in terms of an infinite chain of states with infinitesimal links, where the direction of motion of the system with respect to time depends only on whether a past (initial) or future (final) state is specified. The same laws, therefore, permit two opposing philosophical interpretations of strict determinism: causality when the direction of change is fore, and teleology when the direction is aft. Either interpretation is mathematically legitimate because the laws are taken to embody change as an analytic function. Thus, the causal and purposive outlooks on physical reality are but complementary aspects of the mathematics selected to describe strict determinism.

That the philosophically complementary views are a consequence of the mathematics selected rather than the physics employed suggests that analogous consequences should be found in other sciences that (implicitly or explicitly) adopt similar mathematical methods for treating change as strictly deterministic. Classical learning theory offers just such an analogous case.

Classical theories of learning (e.g., those of Hull, Skinner, Thorndike, and Tolman) differed with respect to what conditions are required for learning to occur but tacitly agreed that the learning function can be graphed as a curve in the Cartesian manner. Behind this assumption sits the deeper assumption that learning curves are justified because they are analytic and, therefore, that strict determinism under the stipulated laws follows. In addition, the laws of learning, whether based on the belief in the necessity of reinforcement or mere continuity, were believed to be universal in two senses: in holding (1) over all contexts, and (2) over all stimuli and responses. Regarding this latter universal property, sometimes referred to as the "assumption of equipotentiality," Bolles (1975) observes:

> To be sure, it has always been recognized that some stimuli may be more salient or more vivid or have more ready access to the sensorium that others, and some responses may have had a higher initial rate of occurrence than others, but these considerations were always of minor theoretical importance. They only meant that in a given application *learning might start at a different point on the curve, but all learning followed the same basic curve.* (p. 253, our emphasis)

The implication that various types of learning may be abstractly equivalent in the sense of *following the same curve* clearly supports the contention that the learning series defines some mathematical function. That in spite of differences in application learning might be considered to start at different points *on the same curve* suggests that the function in question has the analytic property required for continuation. If so, then like classical physics, there should be two equally legitimate, mathematically complementary, alternative forms that the laws of learning might assume, each of which expresses a different temporal direction for determinism.

The two contrasting views are of course the *reinforcement* view and the *expectancy* view. Where Thorndike, Hull, Skinner, and other reinforcement theorists sought a system of empirical laws to explain later behavior in terms of past elements in a learning series, Tolman and other expectancy theorists sought laws to explain the association of prior elements in the series in terms of the "purposive" relationships to anticipated (future) elements in the series. Thus, as in the case of classical mechanics, the learning laws also took two forms: a differential (reinforcement) form that is *past pending* in that the future state of a learner depends on its past schedule of reinforcing events, and an integral (expectancy) form that is *future tending* in that the significance of experience is determined by the future usefulness of the expectancies created by this experience. For instance, in a contemporary version of the law of effect, Herrnstein (1979) has used a differential law form to predict the (behavioral) effects of reinforcement.

We have painstakingly drawn the analogy between classical mechanics and classical learning theory partially in order to prepare the way for understanding the current controversy between ecological psychologists with their penchant for law-governed learning, and the cognitive scientists with their rule-governed view of learning. Just as the attempts to give the same sort of rigorous formulation to laws can account for the mathematically complementary but philosophically opposing views, we propose that the current debate in both physics (see Pattee, 1979, in press) and psychology (e.g., Fodor & Pylyshyn, 1981; Turvey et al., 1981) over rule-governed versus law-governed views of phenomena can be best understood as a continuation of the analogy. This thesis can be supported, and the analogy strengthened, if both physics and psychology not only encounter the same difficulty in adhering to strict determinism as spelled out with analytic precision but seek resolution of the difficulty by drawing on the same formal means. There is reason to believe this is the case.

The Problem of Nonanalytic and Discontinuous Functions

To the extent that dynamic law proved analytic, physicists could ignore the causal and teleological interpretations of law, because on purely quantitative grounds it made no difference. But if one of the two properties required for such functions to be considered analytic (i.e., continuity and convergence) failed to hold, how could the corresponding law be rigorously formulated? If the data series derives from a discontinuous function, how can curves be extrapolated to make either predictions or postdictions? Likewise, if the series is continuous but fails to converge, how can derivatives be taken or integrations formed?

Although the functions dealt with by 17th- and 18th-century physicists in mechanical problems were typically analytic, many nonanalytic functions are encountered in physics. A classic example is the vibrating string. There is no analytic series that allows the V-shaped form of the string when plucked to be continuously mapped on to the other curves the string exhibits during its vibration. (In the mid-18th century, Bernoulli proposed a nonanalytic series of curves to handle this problem.) Likewise, the classical physicists assumed that essentially all physical change might involve *continuous* change and, therefore, that all functions underlying laws of change might be modeled (piecewise) by continuous functions. This turns out not to be the case: Rubber bands stretch and break, beams buckle, ice expands and cracks, and so on. Continuous variation, if pursued too far, inevitably leads to discontinuous changes in state. The 19th-century physicists were well aware of the need to address all such phenomenon but were not equipped with the appropriate mathematical tools for doing so.

Later, it was shown that certain restricted classes of discontinuous curves could be represented by Fourier series. Also, a formal understanding of some discontinuous series not integrable by Newton's method was provided by Riemann and Lebesque. Contemporary research in differential topology (e.g., catastrophe theory and bifurcation theory) provides even greater understanding of such functions.

The discovery of the limited applicability of analytic function theory to numerous physical changes forced mathematicians to recognize that the unity, symmetry, and completeness of relation between function and series were still wanting.

This forced them to liberalize the denotation of function along lines proposed by Dirichlet (see footnote 1). As argued earlier, adoption of his proposal that a function need not be analytic but might be a rule defined a branch-point in the history of attempts to give rigorous characterization to all functions. Rules may be formally rigorous, but they are not mathematically rigorous in the analytic sense originally intended.

During Dirichlet's era the only analytic forms for functions were the differential and integral forms. Hence, these were the only tools available to model laws. Physics needed laws, however, that went beyond these two forms. Thus, from necessity (the mother of invention) they became willing to entertain, for the first time, rule-defined laws (e.g., the so-called "delta" operators of Kronecker and, later, Dirac). With this innovation, three forms emerged for laws: the differential form, the integral form, and now the (recursive) rule form.

It is not too surprising, therefore, that with the recognition of discontinuities in learning series, such as in learning with prolonged delay of "reinforcement" (Andrews & Braveman, 1975; Garcia, Ervin, & Koelling, 1966), psychologists, like physicists, should also entertain nonanalytic characterizations for functions and should realize that learning rules should vie for dominance over learning laws. What analytic alternative was there?

Actually, there is an analytic alternative by which certain discontinuities in series might be modeled in a lawful manner without invoking nonanalytic rules; or, at least, by which such a breach in tradition might be forestalled: the integro-differential form compounded from the other two analytic forms; that is, perhaps laws should be considered as functionals rather than functions. This was Volterra's strategy, and the one we are endorsing. Whether it will prove to be only a means for postponing the inevitable remains to be seen, but at least the strategy deserves serious consideration because the rule strategy aborts the search for laws in favor of the search for mechanism. These are not equivalent theoretical goals, for rules require embodiments whereas laws do not (Feynman, 1965). The search for the mechanistic embodiments of laws has been fruitless in the extreme, as witness the history of failures to find convincing evidence for the mechanistic embodiments of laws of the electromagnetic field (ether), combustion (phlogiston), and motion (impetus).

APPENDIX B
Nonlinearity in the Learning Functional

Two independent variables are nonlinearly related if the course of values of one is constrained by the course of values assumed by the other; that is, of one of them appears in the argument of some more general function, whereas the other appears as a value in the range of that more general function. The subtlety is that whereas the pair of functions may be linear, the functional that relates them may be either linear or nonlinear. For instance, each value of k plays a linear role in determining the magnitude of the stress (restorative force), x, for a given strain, y, of a spring, and each stress value (x) plays a linear role in determining the magnitude of the strain. This is in accordance with the linear form of Hooke's law where k is treated as a constant because it is assumed to be independent of strain (y). Still, over the history of its use the strain variables (frequency and magnitude of strain) constituting y determine a nonlinear influence on the future course of k values and require, therefore, a generalized form of Hooke's law that is nonlinear. Thus, two linear functions may add up to a nonlinear functional!

We expect learning to be equally complex (i.e., a nonlinear hereditary functional). In fact, Grossberg (1980) has found it necessary to use nonlinear functionals in the design of neural nets that exhibit interesting forms of cooperativity and competition: a kind of learning. Because the hereditary influence (K) over learning series may not be linear, the learning functional (y) probably requires a hereditary law that is the sum of a linear function x and a nonlinear function K.

A simple test of linearity requires that

$$kx + K - y = 0. \tag{5}$$

If the learning-to-learn (or fatigue) effects introduce a nonlinear dissipative parameter such that

$$kx + K - y = d > 0 \quad \text{(or } d < 0 \text{ for fatigue)},$$

then the coefficient d provides a measure of the *linear deficiency* of the equation for the learning functional. Under such circumstances, the learning series would correspond to a *nonlinear* Volterra series defined over a set of simultaneous, multiple integral equations:

$$v(t) = kx(t) + \sum_{m=1}^{t} \underbrace{\int_0^t \cdots \int_0^t K(t,s_1)x(s_1)ds_1 \cdots K(t,s_m)x(s_m)ds_m}_{m \text{ times}} \tag{6}$$

In abbreviated operator notation Eq. 6 is represented by:

$$v = kx + K_1 + K_2 + \cdots + K_m. \tag{7}$$

From a computational viewpoint, this means that after solving for the learning function v on trial $n < m$ in a series of m trials, the entire computation must be repeated if the learning effect on $n + 1$ trials is desired. Hence, to determine the hereditary influence of K_m, one must solve for K_1, K_1, $+ K_2$, $\cdots$, $K_1 + \cdots +$ K_{m-1}. Little wonder that the laws of hereditary mechanics and learning may be difficult to formulate, their corresponding functionals hard to express, and the exact nature of the underlying data series as discretely sampled not readily revealing.

Furthermore, the theory of nonlinear integro-differential equations is still incomplete and no general approach yet exists. However, approaches do exist for determining the integrability of simple nonlinear series (e.g., Volterra series). Nonlinear Volterra series have been required for adequate characterization of a wide range of systems that exhibit hereditary effects, including pupillary reflexes (Sandberg & Stark, 1968), irradiated tissues (Iberall, 1967), competing populations of neural cells (Grossberg, 1980), and automatic control systems (e.g., Tsypkin, 1973). Consequently, one should not be surprised that so ubiquitous a strategy might emerge again in human and animal learning. If so, then psychologists, like the physicists, would be wise to incorporate integro-differential equations into their theories of learning and to admit openly allegiance to hereditary mechanics.

REFERENCES

Andrews, E. A., & Braveman, N. S. (1975). The combined effects of dosage level and interstimulus interval on the formation of one-trial poison-based aversions in rats. *Animal Learning and Behavior, 3,* 287–289.

Bolles, R. C. (1975). *Learning theory.* New York: Holt, Rinehart, & Winston.

Bransford, J. D., Stein, B. S., Shelton, T. S., & Owings, R. A. (1981). Cognition and adaptation: The importance of learning to learn. In J. H. Harvey (Ed.), *Cognition, social behavior, and the environment.* Hillsdale, NJ: Lawrence Erlbaum Associates.

d'Abro, A. (1951). *The rise of the new physics: Its mathematical and physical theories* (2nd ed.). New York: Dover.

Feynman, R. (1965). *The character of physical laws.* Cambridge, MA: MIT Press.

Fodor, J. A., & Pylyshyn, Z. (1981). How direct is visual perception? Some reflections on Gibson's "Ecological Approach." *Cognition, 9,* 139–196.

Garcia, J., Ervin, F. R., & Koelling, R. A. (1966). Learning with prolonged delay of reinforcement. *Psychonomic Science, 5,* 121–122.

Gibson, J. J. (1979). *The ecological approach to visual perception.* Boston: Houghton Mifflin.

Greeno, J. G. (1974). Representation of learning as discrete transition in a finite state space. In D. H. Krantz, R. C. Atkinson, R. D. Luce, & P. Suppes (Eds.), *Contemporary developments in mathematical psychology* (Vol. 1): *Learning, memory, and thinking.* San Francisco: W. H. Freeman.

Grossberg, S. (1980). Biological competition: Decision rules, pattern formation, and oscillations. *Proceedings of the National Academy of Science, 77,* 2338–2342.

Harlow, H. F. (1949). The formation of learning sets. *Psychological Review, 56,* 51–65.

Herrnstein, R. J. (1979). Derivatives of matching. *Psychological Review, 86,* 486–495.

Hinde, R. A., & Stevenson–Hinde, J. (Eds.). (1973). *Constraints on learning.* New York: Academic Press.

Iberall, A. S. (1967). Quantitative modelling of the physiological factors in radiation lethality. *Annals of the New York Academy of Sciences, 147*, 1–81.

Jammer, M. (1974). *The philosophy of quantum mechanics.* New York: Wiley.

Johnston, T. D. (1981). Contrasting approaches to a theory of learning. *Behavioral and Brain Sciences, 4*, 125–173.

Kline, M. (1972). *Mathematical thought from ancient to modern times.* New York: Oxford University Press.

Kling, J. W., & Riggs, L. A. (Eds.). (1971). *Experimental psychology* (3rd ed.). New York: Holt, Rinehart, & Winston.

Koffka, K. (1935). *Principles of gestalt psychology.* New York: Harcourt, Brace.

Kramer, E. E. (1970). *The nature and growth of modern mathematics.* New York: Hawthorn.

Krechevsky, I. (1938). The study of continuity of the problem-solving process. *Psychological Review, 45*, 107–133.

Kugler, P. N., Turvey, M. T., Carello, C., & Shaw, R. (in press). The physics of controlled collisions: A reverie about locomotion. In W. H. Warren Jr. & R. E. Shaw (Eds.), *Persistence and change.* Hillsdale, NJ: Lawrence Erlbaum Associates.

Lagrange, J.-L. (1788). *Mécanique analytique.* Paris: Chez la Veuve Desaint.

Lautmann, A. (1971). Symmetry and dissymmetry in mathematics and physics. In F. LeLionnais (Ed.), *Great currents of mathematical thought* (Vol. 1). New York: Dover.

Lindsay, R. B., & Margenau, H. (1957). *Foundations of physics.* New York: Dover.

Nagrath, I. J., & Gopal, M. (1982). *Control systems engineering.* New York: Wiley.

Overseth, O. E. (1969). Experiments in time reversal. *Scientific American, 221*(4), 88–101.

Pattee, H. H. (1979). Complementarity vs. reduction as explanation of biological complexity. *American Journal of Physiology, 236*(5), R241–R246.

Pattee, H. H. (in press). Cell psychology: An evolutionary approach to the symbol–matter problem. *Cognition and Brain Research.*

Patten, B. C. (1982). Environs: Relativistic elementary particles for ecology. *American Naturalist, 119*, 179–219.

Picard, E. (1907). La mécanique classique et ses approximations successives. *Revista di scienza, 1*, 4–15.

Restle, F. (1965). Significance of all-or-none learning. *Psychological Bulletin, 64*, 313–325.

Sandberg, A., & Stark, L. (1968). Functional analysis of pupil nonlinearization. In H. L. Oestreicher & D. R. Moore (Eds.), *Cybernetic problems in bionics.* New York: Gordon & Breach.

Seligman, M. E. P., & Hager, J. L. (Eds.), (1972). *Biological boundaries of learning.* New York: Appleton–Century–Crofts.

Shaw, R. E., & Mingolla, E. (1982). Ecologizing world graphs. *Behavioral and Brain Sciences, 5*, 648–650.

Shaw, R. E., & Todd, J. (1980). Abstract machine theory and direct perception. *Behavioral and Brain Sciences, 3*, 400–401.

Shaw, R. E., & Turvey, M. T. (1981). Coalitions as models for ecosystems: A realist perspective on perceptual organization. In M. Kubovy & J. Pomerantz (Eds.), *Perceptual organization.* Hillsdale, NJ: Lawrence Erlbaum Associates.

Shaw, R. E., Turvey, M. T., & Mace, W. (1982). Ecological psychology: The consequence of a committment to realism. In W. Weimer & D. S. Palermo (Eds.), *Cognition and the symbolic processes II.* Hillsdale, NJ: Lawrence Erlbaum Associates.

Tsypkin, Ya. Z. (1973). *Foundations of the theory of learning systems.* New York: Academic Press.

Turvey, M. T., & Shaw, R. E. (1979). The primacy of perceiving: An ecological reformulation of perception for understanding memory. In L.-G. Nilsson (Eds.), *Perspectives on memory research.* Hillsdale, NJ: Lawrence Erlbaum Associates.

Turvey, M. T., Shaw, R. E., & Mace, W. M. (1977). Issues in the theory of action: Degrees of freedom, coordinative structures and coalitions. In J. Requin (Ed.), *Attention and performance* (Vol. 7). Hillsdale, NJ: Lawrence Erlbaum Associates.

Turvey, M. T., Shaw, R. E., Reed, E. S., & Mace, W. M. (1981). Ecological laws of perceiving and acting: In reply to Fodor and Pylyshyn. *Cognition, 9,* 237–304.

11

Learning and the Description of the Environment

Wolfgang M. Schleidt
Department of Zoology
University of Maryland

Learning is a concept that has received much attention from psychologists, but little from biologists, whereas the opposite can be said for the concept of *environment*. Psychologists deal with human and animal behavior, predominantly in that order, whereas biologists are concerned with a great many aspects of a large number of species among which *Homo sapiens* is only one. When psychologists and biologists engage in a discourse, any concept used extensively in one field is likely to have a different connotation for a scientist in the other field, and misunderstandings are possible. When a psychologist talks about the need to describe the environment, he may have Gibson's (1977) concept of affordance clearly in mind; the biologist may nod in full agreement but may be thinking of Hutchinson's (1957) n-dimensional niche, which is a very different concept. In order to avoid such confusions, one might suggest that the biologist read Gibson (and that the psychologist read Hutchinson), but this will provide only temporary relief, for it does not resolve the basic problem, which is to come up with a format for the description of the environment that is equally useful to the psychologist and to the biologist, that can be used in the context of both learned and unlearned behavior, and that is applicable both to humans and to other kinds of organisms.

The invitation to write this chapter, and my acceptance of this invitation, may have been based on a misunderstanding of this kind. Johnston and Turvey (1980) have developed and proposed an ecological metatheory for theories of learning, and my confession, in commenting on a more recent presentation of these ideas (Johnston, 1981), that I did not understand exactly what was meant by the terms *learning, ecological approach,* and *environment* (Schleidt, 1981a), resulted in this opportunity to help clarify these issues. The comments I received on an earlier draft of this chapter alerted me to the possibility that a reader with a solid background in psychology may expect from the title a review of ecological psychology, a primer of Gibson's "theory of affordance," or a discussion of the current use of learning theory by the Environmental Protection Agency or by professional ecologists. I am not sufficiently well acquainted with these areas to provide such a thorough analysis, and at best I can only attempt to outline a proposal for describing organismic environments in a format that may be acceptable to both psychologists and biologists. Thus, this chapter does not deal specifically with learning, but rather with the environment in which populations of organisms evolve, and within which individual organisms can learn.

Organisms cannot exist without an environment, but the environment can exist without organisms. When the first organism evolved, it did so in an environment consisting solely of physico-chemical factors. From then on each organism became part of another organism's environment and each organism began to interact with its environment resulting in a strong interdependence between organism and environment, and among organisms. At this state, no specific mechanisms of *individual adaptation* to environmental changes have to be postulated. The behavior of the organism was not modified by its individual experience but changed over generations through the process of natural selection. Thus, the need for dealing with the environment, and for describing its specific features in reference to a specific organism, arises first in a purely evolutionary context, free of individual learning.

Learning, as the modification of the behavior of an individual organism through practice, training, or experience, is a special case of individual adaptation to particular environmental contingencies (Lorenz, 1965). The concept of learning is derived from specifically human abilities and is biased in favor of "higher" forms of adaptation that involve primarily the cortex of the brain as the main regulatory and information storage organ; it excludes simpler forms of adaptation that involve other organ systems (e.g., the increase in pigmentation of our skin in response to solar radiation) and noncortical parts of the brain (e.g., the adaptive response of the visual system to different luminances, or the accommodation of the eye to objects at different distances). This definite anthropocentric bias in our concept of learning has led to considerable confusion when the concept is applied to other species. The effects of this bias are likely to increase as a function of the genetic and neural dissimilarity between man and any other species we may choose to study.

If we restrict our attempt to describe the environment in which learning takes place to the human case, it may be possible to succeed without much concern for the issue of biological constraints. But if we strive for a more general understanding of the interaction between the individual organism and its environment and want to discuss this problem in the case of a primate, a rat, a bird, an insect, or a protozoon, the concept of environment has to be developed within a wider biological context. Therefore, I start with a sketch of the conceptual framework by locating the individual organism within a hierarchical system of "levels of organization," and by delineating the interface between organism and environment. Next, I pay homage to the pioneer ethologist Jakob von Uexküll and to his *Umwelt* concept, add a brief discussion of the diversity of environments and of the origin of the adaptation between organism and environment in the evolutionary process, and follow up on Brunswik's and Gibson's proposals for describing the environment in terms of objects. In the closing section, I propose a format for describing an organism's environment for behavioral studies in general, but one that is also suitable for the study of learning, perception, and related cognitive processes.

LEVELS OF ORGANIZATION

Most readers of this chapter will agree with me on the basis of their everyday experience that life is a complex affair, and that only rarely do we find a single factor that exerts sole control over a complex system. Nevertheless, we sustain a romantic belief in simplicity and nourish the hope that we may discover one factor or principle that explains everything, or nearly everything. The conditioned reflex may serve as example of such a monistic principle from the past, and the "selfish gene" has raised equally high hopes in recent years, until it was recognized that organisms cannot be reduced to mere "survival-machines" for our immortal genes (Dawkins, 1976, p. 25). Because of the complexity of the interaction between organisms, their parts, and their environments, it is important that we agree on a conceptual framework that incorporates at least the most salient variables of this interactive process. Even though I believe that the framework that I propose is the most parsimonious, it is hypothetical in nature, and therefore I present it as a set of reasonable assumptions.

Each organism is a system, composed of subsystems (organ systems, organs, tissues, cells, etc.) and is itself part of other systems (family, population, ecosystem, etc.). Thus, I accept the notion of hierarchical *levels of organization* (Novikoff, 1945). I do not believe that a particular feature on a (higher) level can be explained solely by simpler phenomena on a lower level, as the orthodox "ontological reductionists" assume. Instead, I want to stress the importance of higher levels affecting lower ones ("downward causation"; Campbell, 1974), of cyclic interactions between levels (Riedl, 1975), and of the punctuation of the evolutionary process and the subsequent differentiation of the hierarchical structure by the sudden appearance of new system featurers ("fulguratio"; Lorenz, 1977, 1981). The evolutionary process cannot be explained or understood by reference to any one level but requires at least the levels of ecosystems, populations, organisms, and genes (Schleidt, 1981b). But the majority of causal interactions among entities appear to occur *within the same level of organization*. The uncritical use of a concept on a level other than that for which it was created can result in a confusion of issues. Therefore, we have to restrict some concepts only to that level on which they are clearly applicable and adequate (*niveau-adequate Terminologie*; von Holst & von St. Paul, 1963). In summary, the hierarchical schema of integrative levels of organization serves as a supporting conceptual framework within which to discuss the evolution of the relations between organisms and environments.

ORGANISM AND ENVIRONMENT

The environment in which learning takes place is the environment of an individual organism. Even though the learning process involves entities within the organism, the interactions between living systems and their environments must be clarified first on the organismic level. When I use the term organism, I do not want to limit myself to animals similar to man but include all kinds of animals, plants, and unicellular creatures with the ability to maintain their integrity over a span of time (survival) and with the potential for propagating information in a generative process (reproduction). I hasten to admit, however, that even though I attempt a clear delineation among groupings, and among concepts, some borders remain "fuzzy." For instance, I see no reason to exclude bacteria or viruses from the category of organisms, even though they do not show a cellular organization, or a worker ant, even though it cannot reproduce. The facts that in a particular case or at a particular moment the border between two organisms may not be clearly defined (as in a colony of bryozoa), that any one organism and its environment constitute a system, and that the precise location of the boundary between organism and environment may vary with the method we use to detect it, should not keep us from making statements about organisms and environment that are valid in most cases.

The setting of the organism in its environment can be sketched as follows (Schleidt & Crawley, 1980):

> Assuming Euclidian space, each organism consists of a three-dimensional body which is separated from the rest of the universe by a two-dimensional surface, its interface with the environment. Topologically this implies an *inside*, a *surface*, and an *outside*. At any moment this body occupies a discrete *location*, and assumes a particular *orientation* in reference to the space coordinates. The body's surface regulates the flow of matter, energy, and information from the inside of the organism to the environment and from the environment to the inside. (p. 3)

Even though this delineation between organism and environment appears to be generally acceptable today, the concept of environment has been used with different meanings in the past, especially within psychology, and so a brief etymological discourse may be enlightening. According to the Oxford English Dictionary (1971), environment is akin to surroundings: "That which environs;

the objects or region surrounding anything," or "the conditions under which any person or thing lives or is developed; the sum-total of influences which modify and determine the development of life or character" (p. 880). The first meaning is one of topology and geometry, whereas the second evokes a dynamic process and implies time and causal effects. All definitions of "environment" include the idea of something *outside* something else. The earliest use of the term that I can document to include something *inside* is found in Watson's *Behaviorism* (1924):

> *"our 'environment'—our world of stimuli—is thus not only one of external objects, sights, sounds, and smells; it is one of internal objects as well—hunger contractions, bladder distensions, palpitating heart, rapid breathing, muscular changes and the like"* (p. 59, italics in the original).

Thus, it appears that Watson, in his attempt to collect all behavior-controlling stimuli into one general category, combined the common meaning of surroundings with Claude Bernard's *milieu interne*, producing a concept that gained widespread acceptance in psychology, but that did not leave any clear alternative to the environmental domain. As everything had become environment, the concept had lost its usefulness as a scientific tool. Therefore, although Watson's definition must be noted in the context of the history of science, because it is the basis for the behaviorist's belief that behavior is *completely under environmental control* (necessarily, because what else is left?), I think it should be abandoned in favor of the original meaning of something outside, "the objects or region surrounding an organism."

ENVIRONMENT VERSUS *UMWELT*

Jakob von Uexküll (1909, 1957) was the first to investigate systematically the differences among the environments of different species, and to point out that each organism interacts only with a selected part of the universe, the selection being based on the particular sensory and motor capabilities of the individual organism. Von Uexküll (1957) stated: "The *Umwelt* of any animal that we wish to investigate is only a section carved out of the environment which we see spread around it—and this environment is nothing but our own world. The first task of *Umwelt* research is to identify each animal's perceptual cues among all the stimuli in its environment and to build up the animal's specific world with them" (p. 13). Even though it is difficult at times to provide solid data for such a reconstruction of what another animal may see (e.g., von Uexküll & Brock, 1927), the *Umwelt* concept has provided us with important insights and has guided our attention to the close match between an animal's structure and its environment.

For von Uexküll, the close match between an animal and its *Umwelt* was an expression of a preestablished harmony of creation, based on a divine design (a *Bauplan* or blueprint), which insures that the *Umwelten* of different species interlock like the gears of a divine clockwork, akin to the heavenly spheres, the *harmonia mundi*. It is strange that von Uexküll was able to see the dynamic interactions between organism and *Umwelt* so well but was compelled to reject the dynamic process of natural selection as utterly absurd, and to suppress in his mind even the interactions between organisms (von Uexküll, 1920): "For each animal its functional cycles form a world of its own in which it leads its *existence in complete isolation*" (p. 96, emphasis added). This attitude led him into a preoccupation with description as a form of worship of the infinite wisdom of nature and blinded him to the *evolutionary* significance of competitive interactions among organisms, and to that of the interaction between organism and *Umwelt*.

The rejection of natural selection is only one reason why it is impossible for me to embrace the *Umwelt-Lehre* in its original and orthodox form. Von Uexküll's representation of the interaction between animal and *Umwelt* in the "functional cycle" diagram (*Funktionskreis*) anticipated modern control theory but was linked to interpretations that went beyond the experimental evidence. He claims that the action of the animal extinguishes the "perceptual cue bearer" (*Merkmal*, the features of the eliciting object), thus destroying its *Umwelt* as long as it is active; action ceases only in the absence of further perceptual cue bearers. Following this logic we must conclude that the animal at rest has no *Umwelt*, clearly an unacceptable consequence. Therefore, I hesitate to accept the term *Umwelt* as synonymous with the environment of the individual animal and propose instead a new definition in the spirit of von Uexküll: *An organism's environment is that part of its surroundings between its surface and infinity that is affected by, or affects, this organism.*

HOW DIFFERENT ARE THE ENVIRONMENTS OF DIFFERENT ORGANISMS?

I was born and raised as a protanope and still am one, even though I have learned to compensate for the effects of this heritable ailment by attending more closely to texture. Thanks to my excellent vision (better than 20/20), I rarely confuse spinach with tomato sauce now, but red objects remain relatively inconspicuous for me: Even though I love wild strawberries, I can walk past a patch without noticing it is loaded with ripe berries. My hearing was excellent, especially for high-pitched sounds, until I was drafted into the army and exposed to an environment that was excessively noisy at times; consequently I suffered, among other ailments inflicted by this environment, a permanent hearing loss of 60 dB, centered at 4kHz, in both ears. Therefore, high-pitched bird song now escapes my attention, and I am oblivious to chirping insects that get on the nerves of people standing next to me. Fortunately, my hearing loss did not impair my sensitivity to extremely high frequencies, and I noticed high-pitched calls in small rodents (Schleidt, 1948) that had apparently escaped the attention of other investigators, became aware of the "22-kHz call" of the rat several years before it was reported in the literature, and invented and built a "bat detector" (Schleidt, 1950), not only to expand my own sensory range, but to demonstrate to colleagues with less acute hearing what I was able to hear with my unaided ear. I reveal these aberrations in my sensory abilities, not only to give credence to my great admiration for von Uexküll and his ideas, but also to exemplify how strongly the senses can influence our particular *Umwelt*, and how different the *Umwelten* can be even between the members of one species. The sensory capacities of our dearest pets (such as dogs, cats, hamsters, and parakeets) and our worst pests (such as mice, rats, starlings, pigeons, roaches, and germs) are vastly different from those of our own species, and therefore it is safe to assume that their evironments are equally different from ours. Based on our knowledge of individual differences in the sensory capacity of humans and of laboratory animals, we can infer that even different individuals of the same species perceive different environments, and that perception can change during the life of the individual. Thus the question raised in the title of this section can be answered: Different organisms are likely to perceive their environment very differently.

The environment of a particular organism can be reconstructed, however, not solely and not only by analyzing its sensory capacities. The shape of a claw or an extremity and the particular behaviors in which these anatomical structures are used can reveal features of the species-specific environment much more strikingly than the particular form or function of the retina or the eye. For a more detailed discussion I refer the reader specifically to the first chapter in Lorenz (1981), "Thinking in Biological Terms," and for more examples to Wainwright, Biggs, Currey, and Gosline (1976). Von Uexküll never failed to emphasize that the whole organism is adapted to its environment, and his attempts to depict a particular *Umwelt*, for instance, a village street as seen by man, by a fly, and by a mollusc (von Uexküll, 1957) must not be taken to mean that the *Umwelt* is only a visual or sensory concept. In fact, contemporary ecological studies of the different "niches" occupied by different species rarely use the organism's perceptual specializations but concentrate on the actual resources that the organism uses, such as the type of food eaten, or on the organs that serve for their procurement (e.g., the size and shape of the beak in competing species of birds).

Let us delay the discussion of how to measure in detail the features of the environment, agreeing only that such measurements must utilize adaptations of both receptor and effector systems, and that they must include not only static features but dynamic, behavioral features as well. Then we can formulate several hypotheses concerning the differences between the environments of different individual organisms, depending on their taxonomic relations. For a general metric, we can adopt Hutchinson's concept of the niche as a location in a conceptual hyperspace (Hutchinson, 1957).[1] Each dimension represents a particular environmental feature, for instance, the wavelength of electromagnetic radiation, or the size of objects, and the width of the niche is represented by that portion of each dimension that a particular organism can perceive and handle. Thus, in the example given, the niche might be defined in part by the wavelengths that are visible to a bird as light, and by those objects it can handle with its beak. The axes can be marked in standard units of the metric system, or in relative units, e.g., the band width of a particular species or individual, or the standard deviation of multiple measurements on one individual, and differences between points in the hyperspace can be expressed by the Euclidian distance between them. When we set out to construct such a hyperspace, we will notice that the number of dimensions we have to introduce to represent the relevant environmental variables with any degree of completeness will be amazingly high; so high, in fact, that we may be inclined to abandon this project immediately. If we continue, however, at least to achieve a first approximation, we are likely to find that those species shown to be most ancient ("primitive" species such as algae, flagellates, and horseshoe crabs) will require fewer variables than those "advanced" species that have evolved relatively recently in a burst of evolutionary radiation, such as songbirds and primates. Thus, the evolutionary process leads to an increase in the number of relevant environmental variables and ultimately results in a closer match between the organism and its environment.

THE EVOLUTIONARY ORIGIN OF THE MATCHING BETWEEN ORGANISM AND ENVIRONMENT

Physical or chemical systems change over time toward a state of lower energy and order. Ultimately, they burn out like the flame of a candle after all the wax has been consumed, the high state of chemical energy converted to the low state of radiation, and the complex order of its mechanical and chemical structure replaced by a cloud of water vapor and carbon dioxide that disappears in the random motion of the atmosphere's gas molecules. Living systems speed up this process on a global scale, but within their local domain they are able to create and maintain a higher level of energy and order. Access to energy is of fundamental importance for the maintenance of life and for the evolutionary process,

---

[1] I must emphasize that although I have borrowed Hutchinson's concept, I am using it in a different sense. Hutchinson uses the hyperspace to represent a particular physical environment, in which the niches of individuals are plotted. In my usage, the hyperspace contains all possible environments, and the environment of an individual is represented as a point or local region.

and the *creation of order* is an integral part of these processes. The maintenance of order is dependent on the availability of *information about the environment*, in the sense that the individual organism with specific information concerning how and where to obtain necessary resources (such as food, shelter, and mates), and to avoid hazards (such as predators, competitors, and dehydration), is more likely to survive than one that leaves any of these matters to chance. Thus, natural selection favors those individuals within a population that have the most detailed information about the environment and encodes this information in the gene pool of each species.

Without going into the details of the evolutionary process and of the coding of genetic information in sequences of base pairs within a strand of DNA, we can say that on the individual level the end result of evolution is a specific structure of the organism, and a specific set of programs (instructions, algorithms) that are applied to environmental contingencies. Any such program is valid primarily within the environment within which the ancestral forms of this organism have evolved. Mutations, randomly occurring mistakes in the genetic coding system that result in a modified or completely new program, are weeded out if the new program is a failure but spread within the population if the program is a better match to the environmental contingencies. As a consequence, the gene pool of a species accumulates successful programs, and the stored information must correspond, in some way, to a record of the collective historical environments of the species. Even the single zygote, and the particular organism that develops from it, must show some correspondence between genome, ancestral environments, and programs for future environments. There will always be some information lost in each generation, because the gametes carry only half of the parental chromosome set, and the effects of genetic information that conflicts with the demands of the current environment (due to the results of selection in different former environments) must be amended in some way.

The gradual improvement in the match between organism and environment by the evolutionary process is best explained by considering a simple organism from our earliest evolutionary history, soon after the origin of life. Such a hypothetical organism may have been similar to some of the simplest bacteria or algae of today and probably consisted mainly of a short strand of DNA, combined with some biochemical machinery for the extraction of energy to fuel its replication. The environment of such a simple creature is very simple and can be described by a very few variables: the range of concentration of essential resources, the kind of medium (water), and the ranges of a few basic physical variables within which life can be maintained (such as temperature and pH). This brief description can be contrasted with the nearly infinite list of agents and variables that are irrelevant, a list that could equally well be constructed but that would be utterly impracticable. Even those agents that are potentially harmful for the maintenance of the organism's existence are too numerous, at first, to be considered in detail. As soon as an organism shows the ability to detect a particular noxious agent and to avoid or counteract its effects, the features of this agent become an essential part of the environment and must be added to the list of variables that describes the environment. As the evolutionary process progresses, and the size of the genome of the organism is increased, more alternative genetic programs can be stored, and the match between the organism and particular environmental features is improved.

Even though we can trace clear "progress" in the evolution of organismic complexity, and in the complexity of the environmental contingencies the individual organism can handle, the details of this evolution are still a matter of research and controversy (see, e.g., Brown, 1975; Mayr, 1963; Williams, 1966). But it is an undisputed fact that ever since the Cambrian period (from which we have an abundant fossil record) some 500 million years ago, new habitats were invaded, new species with larger genomes have appeared, and the overall diversity of species and their environments has increased substantially.

PATTERNS IN THE ENVIRONMENT:
STIMULI OR OBJECTS?

If we would express the richness of an organism's environment by the number of variables it can distinguish, this number would range from a few in the case of an alga or bacterium to the thousands, even millions in the Norway rat, in the song thrush, or in man. Ever since von Uexküll's attempt to depict the richness of different environments (von Uexküll & Brock, 1927), it has been tempting to assume that the differences in the richness of the perceived environment are mainly a matter of acuity. An animal with more receptors in its retina must see more details than the animal with a lesser number. However, the relation between the grain size of the perceived environment and sensory acuity is simply a necessary by-product of the widely varying abilities of organisms to deal effectively with complex space–time entities in their environments, and especially of their abilities to detect and classify patterns in space and/or time, e.g., objects and events.

Biologist and psychologists alike were always aware of the complexity of the subjects of their scientific inquiry, but the great success of the Cartesian analytical method in physics and chemistry encouraged them to seek explanations couched in the simplest—and often most simplistic—terms. Thus, the concept of the stimulus, a causal factor quite appropriate to physiological investigation at the level of cells and sensory organs, was adopted as *the* elementary unit of environmental effects on the whole organism. The stimulus concept in psychology owes much of its success to the explanatory appeal of the conditioned reflex paradigm and was adopted with modifications by both behaviorists and ethologists: Watson (1924) made the stimulus the cornerstone of his creed "Our environment—our world of stimuli" (p. 59), whereas Lorenz (1935, 1970, 1981) added a special category, the key stimulus, for more complex environmental contingencies. The ability of organisms to respond to complex environmental contingencies was never disputed (indeed it was emphasized by many investigators, including von Uexküll, Lorenz, and the proponents of Gestalt psychology), and the simplistic use of the stimulus concept was criticized by psychologists like Brunswik (1937) and J. J. Gibson (1960, 1979). However, the prevailing attitude was, and still is, that the stimulus *is* the elementary unit of environmental description, and that "the real problem" is posed by the question of how the organism synthesizes simple stimuli into a concept of a complex pattern.

I propose that the stimulus concept has put us on the wrong track and has led us into an unresolvable conflict between evidence from different levels of organization. The physiological concept of the stimulus concerns the transfer of *energy* from a simple, physical environment into the substrate of a receptor and is only appropriate at the level of the cell or sensory organ. In the multicellular organism no direct correspondence exists between the domain of stimuli and that of the flow of *information* from the very complex environment to the organism as a whole. In our hierarchical schema of levels of organization such a flow of information concerns the level of organisms. A correspondence may exist for very simple organisms up to the cellular level, but it is lost as the complexity of organismic organization increases. The process of natural selection rewards pragmatic solutions and is indifferent to epistemological eloquence. Even on the level of advanced unicellular organisms it is unlikely that the individual has a taste for particular chemical compounds that support its livelihood, or the desire to find a particular strand of DNA; rather, it will be rewarded for the ingestion of objects that contain the essential chemicals and for choosing the most successful mate in conjugation or copulation. Thus, organisms have been adapted since the dawn of life to deal with complex environmental space–time entities, notably objects (including conspecific organisms). The simplicity of their dealings with such entities lies in the fact that the features that signify them are in many cases very simple. Sensory organs were not created by natural selection to become perfect instruments for the measurement of physical energy or chemical structure, but to serve the organism in its pursuit of longevity and reproductive success by detecting and classifying space–time entities in its environment. Based on these considerations, I propose the thesis that *the fundamental unit of the environment is not the "stimulus," but the biologically relevant space–time entity*. Examples of such space–time entities are most notably "objects" (things, alive or inanimate, that contrast with the background), "locations" (places with certain geographic or geometric features), "events" (specific temporal changes in the state of objects or locations), and "situations" (specific coincidences of objects, locations, and/or events). A more detailed discussion of this thesis will be presented in a separate publication (Schleidt, in preparation). The most important consequence of the thesis is that the puzzling problem of how a complex entity (the notion of an object or of an event) can be synthesized from simple stimuli can be laid to rest. Instead, we can ask: Which are the space–time entities that are of significance for the survival and reproductive success of the members of a particular taxon, and what are the significant feature variables of each of these entities?

I am puzzled by the simplicity of this resolution of an ancient problem and cannot quite understand why I should have been the first one to find it. Brunswik (1934, 1937) tried to redefine psychology as the "science of objective relations" but failed to find a good argument for why we should attend to the features of objects as wholes. J. J. Gibson (1979), who has contributed so much to our understanding of the texture of our environment, cloaks the issue in the animal's "perception of affordance," which, as far as I can see, is a revival and refinement of von Uexküll's concept of "functional tone."

Because organisms are adapted to deal with space–time entities in their environment, a detailed description of the environment in terms of physical and chemical stimuli is useless and inappropriate, except for the most ancient and simple creatures. Therefore, any measure of the richness of the particular environment of more advanced organisms must not only convey its general graininess but must also include specifications of the organism's ability to detect space–time entities, notably objects, against a noisy background, to distinguish them from irrelevant clutter (in the sense of Gibson, 1979), and to classify them according to their "functional tone" or "affordance."

When I emphasized earlier that organisms are adapted to deal with space–time entities, I meant not only patterns or objects that are detectable by one single sensory system but also multisensory entities that are experienced within a coherent space. For instance, a cat hears the scraping sound of a gnawing mouse, locates the mouse by ear first, then by sight, then handles it with its paws and ultimately chews on it. Thus the cat employs four different senses for the detection of one object without any difficulty, and without any indication that it is dealing with four different types of stimuli. Kittens spend many hours playing with mouse-like objects and may well learn to coordinate, or calibrate, the coherence of their auditory, visual, and tactile spaces. That such coherence of different sensory spaces can be preprogramed without requiring prior learning, or calibration processes, is known from the study of crickets, which pursue a rival or mate first by sound and at closer distance by vision and touch. A turkey hen, sitting on egg dummies in a state of broodiness for the first time in her life, responds to the sound of peeping young by raising her body and looking at the eggs, regardless of the direction from which the peeping sound comes. Thus, the actual spatial coordinates of the sound source are ignored and the sound is projected to the location of tactile stimulation, which is then checked and the presence of eggs confirmed visually. Within the narrow view of sensory modalities, intersensory perception and sensory integration may pose complex problems, but many animals can handle this task very well, as can humans who are not made aware of the existence of separate senses.

THE DESCRIPTION OF
AN ORGANISM'S ENVIRONMENT

The closing statement of my remarks (Schleidt, 1981a) on Johnston's (1981) paper on "Contrasting approaches to a theory of learning" reads: "It will take great epistemological skill and sophistication to devise a useful format with which to describe the environment where learning, as an adaptive process, takes place" (p. 159). I now present a format for the description of an organism's environment, but I may fail on several counts. My presentation of the conceptual framework may lack the necessary epistemological skill and/or sophistication, or my earlier predictions may have been overstated. However, I hope that the format that I present is useful and provides guidance in the design of new experiments and inspiration for where to look for interesting observable facts.

Considering the dominant role in learning attributed to the environment by psychologists, it is amazing how little research has been done on this topic, and how narrowly attention has been focused on the "nature–nurture" problem, on human learning, and on learning in single sensory domains. Even though the biological bases of behavior are recognized in principle, the consequences of such recognition have not been fully realized. For instance, J. J. Gibson, who has pioneered and advocated *an ecological approach* to the problem of perception, centered his ideas on human perception and in particular did not coordinate his views with the results of contemporary work in biology (e.g., no reference to von Uexküll, Lorenz, Tinbergen, Odum, Hutchinson, Klopfer, McArthur, or other authors of studies in animal behavior or ecology are given in Gibson, 1979). Similarly, the human case and the role of perception are commonly ignored by ecologists. Von Uexküll's *Umwelt-Lehre* stands as a lone monument in honor of its creator, acknowledged and venerated by ethologists, but resisting incorporation into the mainstream of thought, presumably because of its anti-evolutionary trimmings. Therefore, we have here an unexpected chance to widen our perspective, to trace proposed connections and find new ones, to gain new insights, and ultimately to achieve a better understanding of the interrelation between organism and environment.

Most importantly, we must recognize the great diversity of organisms and the great diversity of adaptations that were obtained by their ancestors during the evolutionary process. Thus, any attempt to formulate general rules for the description of one particular organism's environment will have to take into consideration not only the individual history but also the specific adaptations that are characteristic of this group, i.e., the taxon, of which it is a member. In the case of a "lower" animal, the important environmental contingencies may be rather limited in number. These contingencies may be sufficiently characterized by simple features that are practically synonymous with physiological stimuli. The organism's ability to adapt may be restricted to habituation and fatigue. In the case of "higher" animals, such as birds and mammals, taxa that have radiated into a vast variety of geographic regions and habitats (Eisenberg, 1981), the relevant environmental contingencies are likely to be not only more numerous, but also more complex "space–time entities," that can be classifed as specific objects, locations, events, and situations. To call them "stimuli" is an absurd and misleading simplification (Schleidt, in preparation). In higher animals, the potential for adaptive modification of the individual's behavior is vastly increased, both in terms of the ability to learn to detect and classify specific space–time-entities in the environment, and in terms of learning specific skills to deal with them. In man the ability to adapt, to learn, has evolved much further, even though not quite to the extent that it has freed him of all biological constraints (as some behaviorists had assumed). Because I am trying to clarify these issues especially for the psychologically inclined reader, I do not discuss the environmental setting of lower organisms any further and instead concentrate on those features of the environment that are most relevant to members of our own species, and of other species of higher animals, notably birds and mammals, that may be of interest for comparison.

The format that I suggest for the description of the *environment* of a higher animal corresponds closely to the format that had been designed earlier for the description of *behavior*, or more precisely, for the description of "patterns in the behavior of organisms" (Drummond, 1981; Schleidt, 1982; Schleidt & Crawley, 1980). In an earlier section of this chapter I have delineated the border between the particular organism and its individual environment (p. 308) I and have elaborated on the evolutionary origin of the matching between organism and environment. As we can look at the organism from a vantage point *outside its skin* and describe *behavior* as change, in time, of the organism's location and orientation in space and of its surface structure (Schleidt & Crawley, 1980), so we can choose as a vantage point for the description of the *environment* the particular *location of the organism* and search for patterns in environmental features that appear on this organism's surface. Thus, we can phrase the description of the environment in an identical formalism, composed of the location in reference to the space coordinates of the environment, the orientation as space vector of the main axis of the organism, and a set of feature maps, i.e., mappings of the environment on the organism's surface. The *patterns* in the environmental feature variables can be detected and classified according to algorithms that have been developed in the field of computer science (e.g., Duda & Hart, 1973). They are the *space–time entities* that I have postulated earlier as the relevant units of environmental description (objects, locations, events, situations; p. 315). In the case of the higher animals, various structures and processes have evolved that extend the reach of the organism into the depth of the environment, for instance, by mechanically probing with an appendage, or by triangulating the location of distant sources of feature variables. Whereas in unicellular and lower animals we may consider the environment to have the dimensionality of a *plane* that wraps around the organism's surface, in higher animals, including man, the environment becomes a *space* between the organism's surface and some plane at a finite distance, the background. In this space the space–time entities are detected as adhering either to the background (like in the ancient belief of stars attached to the firmament), on the organism's skin (a flea on my foot), or in between (the fly screen in my window, between myself and the sky). The "empty" space between skin and background that fills the void constitutes the medium. The particular part of the background that supports the organism may constitute a separate entity as floor, perch, or as substrate in general. This view of the environment is consistent with the proposed definition at the end of the section "Environment versus *Umwelt*" (p. 310) and formally akin to the concepts proposed originally by von Uexküll (1909, 1957) and by Gibson (1979). What is new is the insight (if I interpret these authors properly) that the specification of the location and orientation of an organism *must* be part of the environmental description, and my hypothesis that the algorithms of pattern detection and pattern classification are sufficient for the definition of complex space–time entities.

The environment of an organism cannot be described without the specification of *temporal* features. The environment in which the individual organism lives is nearly always changing in time, and the environment of its ancestors has changed quite dramatically from the beginning of life to the present. Thus, a picture postcard of the environment is as useful or as useless as a single photograph of a behavior pattern. For instance, *objects* and *locations* are characterized by their *relative permanence*, in contrast to passing events and situations. Once a particular object or location has been detected and classified on the basis of a particular set of feature variables, this relative permanence of an object or location makes the continued monitoring unnecessary. An occasional updating of the status is sufficient. An anthropocentric example illustrates this point: When I sit around a table with some friends in the evening, and the light goes out, nonvisual cues are sufficient to keep me informed about the continued presence of the people in the room, cues that may not be sufficient for a speedy identification for someone just entering the room. The fact that we can rely on a relative permanence of objects and locations is the feature that enables even organisms with rather limited neurosensory capacities to recognize a morsel of food, a predator, a mate, or the location of a nest under conditions of a continuously varying sensory input without having to resort to complicated mechanisms of gestalt perception or of cognitive psychology (e.g., constancy phenomena, cross-modal transfer). Invoking Occam's razor, we may be able to explain the persistence with which even higher animals engage in continuing activities with a particular object or return for the execution of certain behaviors to the same location as a result of these animal's "knowledge" of the relative permanence of objects and locations.

Events and situations are especially marked by their temporal features. Their duration is usually limited, even though their effects may be lasting. However, as in the case of objects and locations, the permanence does not remove the constraint of time; events and situations are also linked to features of space, especially to locations. At least in the human mind the remembering of a particular event, or confronting a new event of a particular kind, may evoke memories of the local geography, as revisiting a particular geographic location may evoke memories of events, situations, or "objects" we had encountered there many years ago. Thus, my proposal that we think of the environment in terms of space–time entities may provide an impulse to cognitive psychologists or researchers in the field of "artificial intelligence" to explore the presence of such combinations of space–time features in our basic concepts.

When we confront the task of describing the environment of a particular type of organism, for instance, of a newly hatched mallard duckling, I propose to compile a more or less complete repertoire of the organism's space–time entities, each entity being specified by a set of spatial and temporal features and labeled with a code name that is somewhat compatible with our anthropocentric world. What constitutes an entity for the duckling depends on its behavior. In other words, any set of feature variables that maintains or elicits one specific behavior pattern, or several different, alternative patterns, can be assumed to constitute a discrete space–time entity. For instance, a solid substrate supports ("affords" in the terminology of Gibson 1977) standing, walking, running, food pecking, etc., whereas a liquid substrate supports swimming, darting, diving, dabbling, etc., whereas other activities (e.g., preening) can occur on either substrate. Thus, for the duckling we have to assume the existence of two discrete types of substrate, "land" and "water" (as substrate), whereas the space–time entity "perch" is utterly meaningless to the duckling, or, for that matter, for a chick of the migratory quail. Next, we may inquire about the features of the medium and will find certain essential features that define its optimal range (in terms of composition of gasses, presence of particulate matter, temperature, radiation, etc.) and note that the behavior changes as we approach the limits of the optimal range. Low temperature will elicit shivering and a specific type of calling, high temperature will elicit panting, low oxygen or high carbon dioxide levels elicit gasping, etc. Next, we may search for the correlation between particular behaviors of the duckling and particular objects, locations, events, and situations in its environment. We find that *small objects*, especially if contrasting with the background and moving, elicit feeding behavior, if close to the ground (land or water), but "alert immobility," if seen against the sky. Learning sets in within minutes, new feature variables are added for edible objects, and new classes of different food objects and inedible objects are formed, whereas alert immobility eliciting objects may loose their conspicuousness due to selective habituaton. Again, for comparison, I want to point out that a young turkey may "hunt" for a fast-moving small object in the sky, but respond by crouching, if the object moves slowly (Schleidt, 1961). *Larger objects*, if within a certain distance and size range, elicit the "following response" in the newly hatched mallard duckling and initiate the process of imprinting (Hess, 1973; Lorenz, 1935, 1970, 1981).

In a natural setting, the primary object of imprinting is the mother duck, but the siblings may also be subject to an imprinting-like process, as the individual features of both the mother and the siblings are most likely also subject to conventional learning. Mother and sibling constitute, however, discrete, separate categories. We may want to remember the nearly forgotten concept of "companion" (Lorenz, 1935, 1970) for different kinds of social objects and make use of it. There may be other types of objects of particular significance to the duckling. A rather interesting one, at least for the philosopher, is the object of "self," in the form of the duckling's body surface, subjected to extensive preening behavior. I do not want to enter into a philosophical discussion of the experience of "self" in animals, but as a challenge I claim *scabo, ergo sum* has a rather sensible priority over *cogito, ergo sum*. Geographic *locations* appear to be irrelevant in the life of the young duckling, and so are *situations*, in the sense of particular, complex sets of contingencies. Significant *events* are numerous, however: Changes in the ambient temperature, illumination, and noise elicit specific behaviors, features that we may file either in the context of the medium or each as separate space–time entity. The latter is especially justified in the cases of social signals, e.g., different types of alarm calls. When we tally this nearly complete repertoire of environmental space–time entities of the newly hatched duckling, we find roughly estimated 10 types of "objects" and maybe 10 types of "events." The sexually mature mallard duck will have added by maturation and by learning a few more objects and events and will have learned several specific geographic locations (e.g., a nesting site) and possibly some situations (e.g., the assembly of males engaged in their characteristic social courtship).

The number of duck-specific space–time-entities are well within the range of comprehension of a research scientist dealing with the behavior of this species. As we are used to compile an "ethogram" for a species to lay down the basic repertoire of behavior patterns, so will we have to face the necessity to compile an "ecogram" (or "environgram"?) for each species' basic space–time entities. As in the case of the ethogram, such a task may be quite tedious at first, and boring, but, just as already existing ethograms provide a convenient framework for a taxonomically related or similar species, so ecograms of related species, or of species that live in a similar environment, will be quite similar in structure, but sufficiently diverse to make the task interesting. As the comparison of ethograms, or sections thereof (e.g., social "displays"; Moynihan 1970), becomes an interesting problem in its own right, so could the comparison of ecograms reveal new insights in the evolutionary process of increasing fidelity of the match between the behavior of an organism and its environment.

Because psychologists are ultimately interested in man, I want to touch on some aspects of the human environment and its description in terms of space–time entities as the fundamental "unit." What is a unit? Weiss (1971) says: "A unit is a composite fragment of the Universe which in our experience has proved to retain sufficient identity over a given period of time to deserve a name—a conservative array of measurable properties amidst the continuously and erratically changing 'background' phenomena that reveal no recognizable pattern" (p. 9). Thus, a dictionary of the nouns of the English language constitutes a first approximation to the ecogram of English-speaking (and English-thinking) people. Does it? Maybe, if we define a taxon of *Homo britannicus*. On the level of the individual, we have to restrict ourselves to that selection of nouns that name meaningful concepts. My personal ecogram does contain, however, quite a few concepts that I share with the members of my family, with my scientific colleagues in my specialties, with the members of certain trades or crafts, but that are *not* common to all of us. Only if we concentrate on those nouns that are shared by all mentally competent, mature members of the taxon *Homo britannicus* (the nouns of a dictionary of pidgin English?) will we come close to a "working ecogram" for this taxon. If we draw a comparison with the example of the mallard duck and the mallard duckling, it will be obvious that the development of the ecogram, starting with the "first words" of the human baby, constitutes an interesting topic for the new field of ecological psychology and is not just an absurd obsession of developmental or cognitive psychologists.

I would not dare to predict the response my proposal for the format of the description of the environment, especially the call for the compilation of ecograms, will get from my colleagues in biology and psychology. The proposal may well be accepted in principle but fail in its implementation, because of the laborious investigations that are necessary in order to obtain what may be considered a minor gain. There are striking formal similarities between ecogram and ethogram, and therefore we may learn from the history of the latter and avoid past oversights that ultimately proved to be very costly in terms of wasted efforts and fruitless discussions. The concept of ethogram was first proposed by H. S. Jennings (1906) under the label *action system* and applied to lower animals. G. F. Makkink (1936) apparently coined the term *ethogram* and used it in the title of his study of a bird, the European avocet. Through the establishment of ethology in the 1950s, facilitated by the teaching of Lorenz and Tinbergen, the need for the compilation of ethograms was finally realized. However, the prose of ethograms is about as boring to the average reader as the poetry of DNA sequences, and the compilation of the data is rather tedious. Therefore, only few ethograms are close to complete, and most of them are used as "in-house documents" but are not available in print. Only recently has a more systematic approach been proposed, especially by using the methods of electronic data processing (e.g., Schleidt, Yakalis, Donnelly & McGarry, 1984). As long as it was an acceptable assumption that "a single representative example . . . the white rat" (Skinner, 1938, p. 47) is sufficiently similar to man to permit investigation of the fundamental principles of behavior, no need existed to dwell on the obvious differences. Much time and grant money has been wasted because of this assumption before it was realized to be unwarranted. Under the doctrine of the "empty organism" it was even overlooked that the primary surface of interaction between organism and environment in the Skinner box was *not* that of the animal, but the surface of the keys and the food magazine. Thus, the measurements did not even concern the input/output relations of the organism, but the output/input relations of the experimental setup. The environment in the classical Skinner box is restricted to space-time entities on the background and an empty medium. Only as it becomes generally accepted that different entities in the environment may activate different behaviors and utilize different forms of learning does it become interesting to explore the effect of alternative configurations of environmental features on the behavior of an organism of a particular species. Because the need to address the issue of taxon-specific ecograms does coincide with the already existing awareness of the need for ethograms, both issues may be resolved concurrently.

The environment within which learning takes place is in no way different from the environment within which the animal acts and responds by unlearned behavior. Therefore, all the preceding points should be considered *before* learning is investigated and interpreted. Thus, a knowledge of the environment is as relevant to the study of learning as the knowledge of biochemistry is to the study of drug effects, or the knowledge of acoustics to the study of psychoacoustics. Learned behavior remains conceptually the antithesis of unlearned behavior and constitutes a discrete alternative of individual, adaptive modification to unlearned adaptations, achieved by selection acting in populations of interbreeding individuals (Lorenz, 1965, 1981). Nonetheless, in man as well as in other species (at least in higher animals), survival to reproductive age and subsequent reproductive success depend on the *integration of both types of adaptation*. From the study of genetic and phenotypic diversity within breeding populations, we know that different combinations of traits can result in the same life expectancy or number of offspring. Similarly, it is very likely that different adaptations to the particularities of a specific environment can be fully equivalent. Therefore, we should start to investigate the *diversity* of learning and not only track the unfolding of particular innate programs and their integration with learned programs during the life of an individual but also search for alternative routes that the individual may take within the same taxon-specific environment.

REFERENCES

Brown, J. L. (1975). *The evolution of behavior*. New York: Norton.

Brunswik, E. (1934). *Wahrnehmung und Gegenstandswelt - Grundlegung einer Psychologie vom Gegenstand her*. Leipzig: Deuticke.

Brunswik, E. (1937) Psychology as a science of objective relations. *Philosophy of Science, 4*, 227–260.

Campbell, D. T. (1974). "Downward causation" in hierarchically organized biological systems. In F. J. Ayala & T. Dobzhansky (Eds.), *Studies in the Philosophy of Biology* (pp. 179–186). London: Macmillan.

Dawkins, R. (1976). *The selfish gene.* New York: Oxford University Press.

Drummond, H. (1981). The nature and description of behavior patterns. In P. P. G. Bateson & P. H. Klopfer (Eds.), *Perspectives in ethology* (Vol. 4, pp. 1–33). New York: Plenum.

Duda, R. O., & Hart, P. E. (1973). *Pattern classification and scene analysis.* New York: Wiley.

Eisenberg, J. F. (1981). *The mammalian radiations: Analysis of trends in evolution, adaptation, and behavior.* Chicago: University of Chicago Press.

Gibson, J. J. (1960). The concept of stimulus in psychology. *American Psychologist, 15,* 694–703.

Gibson, J. J. (1977). The theory of affordances. In R. Shaw & J. Bransford (Eds.), *Perceiving, acting and knowing: Towards an ecological psychology* (pp. 67–82). New York: Lawrence Erlbaum Associates.

Gibson, J. J. (1979). *The ecological approach to visual perception.* Boston: Mifflin.

Hess, E. H. (1973). *Imprinting.* New York: Van Nostrand Reinhold.

Holst, E. von, & Saint Paul, U. von, (1963). On the functional organization of drives. *Animal Behaviour, 11,* 1–20.

Hutchinson, G.E. (1957). Concluding remarks. *Cold Spring Harbor Symposia on Quantitative Biology, 22,* 415–427.

Jennings, H. S. (1906). *Behavior of the lower animals.* New York: Columbia University Press.

Johnston, T. D. (1981). Contrasting approaches to a theory of learning. *Behavioral and Brain Sciences, 4,* 125–173.

Johnston, T. D., & Turvey, M. T. (1980). An ecological metatheory for theories of learning. In G. H. Bower (Ed.), *The psychology of learning and motivation,* Vol. 14, pp. 147–205. New York: Academic Press.

Lorenz, K. (1935). Der Kumpan in der Umwelt des Vogels. *Journal für Ornithologie, 83,* 137–215, 289–413.

Lorenz, K. (1965). *Evolution and modification of behavior.* Chicago: University of Chicago Press.

Lorenz, K. (1970). *Studies in animal and human behaviour.* Cambridge, Ma: Harvard University Press.

Lorenz, K. (1977). *Behind the mirror.* London: Methuen.

Lorenz, K. (1981). *The foundations of ethology.* New York: Springer–Verlag.

Makkink, G. F. (1936). An attempt at an ethogram of the European avocet (*Recurvirostra avosetta L.*) with ethological and psychological remarks. *Ardea, 25,* 1–60.

Mayr, E. (1963). *Animal species and evolution.* Cambridge, MA: Harvard University Press.

Moynihan, M. (1970). Control, suppression, decay, disappearance and replacement of displays. *Journal of Theoretical Biology, 29,* 85–112.

Novikoff, A. B. (1945). The concept of integrative levels and biology. *Science, 101,* 209–215.

Oxford English Dictionary, Compact Edition. (1971). Oxford: Oxford University Press.

Riedl, R. (1975). *Die Ordnung des Lebendigen.* Hamburg: Parey.

Schleidt, W. M. (1948). Töne hoher Frequenz bei Mäusen. *Experientia, 4,* 145–146.

Schleidt, W. M. (1950). Überlagerungsverstärker für Ultraschall. *Radiotechnik, 26,* 11–12.

Schleidt, W. M. (1961). Reaktionen von Truthühnern auf fliegende Raubvögel und Versuche zur Analyse ihrer AAM's. *Zeitschrift für Tierpsychologie, 18,* 534–560.

Schleidt, W. M. (1981a). Adaptive modification of behavior: Processing information from the environment. *Behavioral and Brain Sciences, 4,* 158–159.

Schleidt, W. M. (1981b). The behavior of organisms, as it is linked to genes and populations. In P. P. G. Bateson & P. H. Klopfer (Eds.), *Perspectives in Ethology* (Vol. 4, pp. 147–155). New York: Plenum.

Schleidt, W. M. (1982). Stereotyped feature variables are essential constituents of behavior patterns. *Behaviour, 79*, 230–238.

Schleidt, W. M. (in preparation). Stimulus or object?

Schleidt, W. M., & Crawley, J. N. (1980). Patterns in the behaviour of organisms. *Journal of Social and Biological Structure, 3*, 1–15.

Schleidt, W. M., Yakalis, G., Donnelly, M., & McGarry, J. (1984). Ethogram of the Bluebreasted Quail (*Coturnix chinensis*). *Zeitschrift für Tierpsychologie, 64*, 193–220.

Skinner, B. F. (1938). *The behavior of organisms*. New York: Appleton.

Uexküll, J. von (1909). *Umwelt and innenwelt der tiere*. Berlin: Springer.

Uexküll, J. von (1920). *Theoretische biologie*. Berlin: Paetel.

Uexküll, J. von (1957). A stroll through the worlds of animals and men. In C. H. Schiller (Ed.) *Instinctive behavior* (pp. 5–80). New York: International University Press.

Uexküll, J. von, & Brock, F. (1927). Atlas zur Bestimmung der Orte in den sehräumen der Tiere. *Zeitschrift für vergleichende Physiologie, 5*, 167–178.

Wainwright, S. A., Biggs, W. D, Currey, J. D., & Gosline, J. M. (1976). *Mechanical design in organisms*. New York: Wiley.

Watson, J. B. (1924). *Behaviorism*. New York: Norton.

Weiss, P. A. (1971). *Hierarchically organized systems in theory and practice*. New York: Hafner.

Williams, G. C. (1966). *Adaptation and natural selection*. Princeton, NJ: Princeton University Press.

12 The Environmental Dimensions that Influence Behavior

Lincoln Gray
Department of Otolaryngology—Head and Neck Surgery
University of Texas Medical School

The environment provides myriad cues in the form of physical attributes such as sounds, colors, and distances that an animal can use to its advantage. Kangaroo rats, for example, that do not respond to the weak low-frequency vibrations of owls' wings are more likely to be eaten (Webster, 1962). Male sage grouse that select territories close to the center of a communal mating center achieve more copulations than those on the periphery (Wiley, 1973). Suitable nesting habitat for small woodland birds is probably indicated by the density of leaves at various heights above the ground (Orians, 1971). Such examples of lawful responsiveness to environmental cues can be found throughout the animal kingdom. At one extreme the ocean's simplest animals, zooplankton, rise and descend in daily response to light. At the other extreme, the complicated behaviors of human consumers often depend on combinations of cues such as price and quality.

Animals' well-being thus depends on appropriate responses to environmental cues. One interesting class of cues are those that vary continuously between two extremes. For example, the "freezing" response of young ducklings to avoid potential predation is influenced by the repetition rate of their mother's call (Miller, 1980). Fish are influenced by size in selecting their prey (Werner & Hall, 1974). Bees are influenced by distance and tend to fly from one flower to a near-neighboring flower (Waddington & Heinrich, 1981). These physical continua are termed environmental dimensions.

Consideration of the environmental dimensions that influence an animal's behavior provides a framework for examining issues in the ecological study of learning. Diverse theories from zoology and psychology come together in an analysis of these critical dimensions. Studies of evolution, genetics, community ecology, and ethology contribute to our understanding of *what* dimensions are important (Johnston, 1981). Studies of psycho physics, learning, development, and the nervous system indicate *how* animals might come to respond to these dimensions. This endeavor is important because animals' survival depends in part on their ability to attend to relevant environmental cues.

Animals' responses to environmental dimensions can often be analyzed as if there were subjective dimensions that were created by the perception of physical cues. Our subjective scale of loudness, for example, is related to the amplitude of an acoustic stimulus, pitch is related to frequency, etc. These subjective dimensions describe the animal's perception of its environment. As suggested by von Uexküll's concept of the *Umwelt* (see Klopfer, 1974, pp. 136–137), animals' perceptions of the world around them depend on these relationships between physical and subjective dimensions.

The purpose of this chapter is to show how subjective dimensions of animals' perceptions can be inferred from their behavior and then related to physical dimensions in the environment. Hopefully, some ideas from ecology and psychology that have previously been considered separately will be united. The chapter is organized into three main parts to briefly review the theories, techniques, and mechanisms that relate subjective and environmental dimensions.

In the first part two theories about the nature of dimensions that influence behavior are discussed. Optimal foraging theory from the ecological literature is reviewed to show how natural selection may organize behavior along an underlying dimension. Single-peaked preference theory from the psychological literature is reviewed to show how commonly observed functions of preference may be derived from an underlying dimension. Not surprisingly, these two theories are essentially identical. This similarity between theories about the ecological dimensions that influence behavior and the psychological dimensions that underlie behavior suggests that an analysis of such influential dimensions may further an ecological theory of learning. These concepts are then extended to more realistic but complicated situations where multiple dimensions may affect an animal's behavior.

In the second part of this chapter two psychophysical scaling techniques that can be used to identify influential dimensions are explained. Animals are obviously influenced by ecologically relevant dimensions in their environment, and these techniques may provide ways to identify those dimensions solely from the animals' naturally occurring responses.

In the third part various mechanisms that might establish the influence of particular environmental dimensions are reviewed. This involves brief summaries of some evolutionary and learning theory. Experience can play many roles in the development of the relationship between environmental and perceptual dimensions. Learning can be critically important in establishing animals' responsiveness to ecologically relevant cues. Gottlieb (1981), for example, has shown that young Peking ducklings learn the repetition rate of their mother's call from only a few minutes of exposure to sibling vocalizations. In other animals learning may be relatively unimportant in determining the control of environmental cues. Garter snakes from different populations, for example, are born with different ontogenetically stable preferences for slugs (Arnold, 1981). Thus, an intriguing integration of both genetic and experiential influences produces the relationships between environmental and perceptual dimensions. For example, the effects of food-related cues on the foraging behavior of deer mice depend more on an interaction between genetic and environmental influences than on either learning or heritable differences alone (Gray, in preparation).

THE THEORETICAL FOUNDATIONS OF INFLUENTIAL DIMENSIONS

The point of this chapter is that an interesting phenomenon occurs when perceptual and environmental dimensions are related; that is, subjective continua inferred from animals' responses can sometimes be closely related to physical continua. The term *influential dimensions* might be used to express this congruence. Influential dimensions link something in the environment with a corresponding quality in animals' perceptions. Although we refer to these dimensions by some physical description (such as hue, size, or density), they are really fundamental attributes of the organisms that use them. Influential dimensions derive their importance first because they succinctly describe a larger set of an animal's responses, and second because they are ecologically relevant. The first part of this chapter attempts to show the theoretical relationship between environmental and perceptual dimensions by comparing the ecological theory of optimal foraging with the psychological theory of single-peaked preferences.

Optimal Foraging

Animals probably convert their "ultimate" goal of leaving more genes in future generations (i.e., increasing "fitness") into more "proximate" goals of finding nutritious food, fecund mates, safe refuges, etc. (Lewontin, 1979). It is likely that these searches for suitable resources are influenced by a limited number of critical environmental dimensions. According to this hypothesis of proximate cues, there is some optimal preference along any critical dimension (Pyke, Pulliam, & Charnov, 1977). Desert rodents, for example, optimize their diets through preferences for various seeds (Reichman, 1975). Natural selection may lead toward curves of preference that rise to a relative maximum along critical environmental dimensions (Cody, 1974).

Single-peaked Preferences

Psychologists recognize that functions of preference are most commonly single peaked; that is, along most subjective continua (such as saltiness or loudness) there is a value that is most preferred, and preferences decrease on either side of this ideal point. Young Peking ducks, for example, show a maximum preference for pulses of sound at 4 per second, like their mother's call, and show decreasing preferences for faster and slower pulses (Gottlieb, 1981). This fundamental form of preferences can be derived from only a few basic assumptions about how positive and negative aspects of available choices are integrated, as shown in Table 12.1. Based on these assumptions, powerful techniques have been developed for uncovering the underlying structure from a set of animals' preferences.

Congruence

According to optimal foraging theory (Schoener, 1971), the form of animals' preferences should be predictable from environmental conditions. According to single-peaked preference theory (Coombs & Avrunin, 1977), a consistent structure underlying preferences should be derivable from sets of animals' responses. Influential dimensions arise when these predicted and derived dimensions coincide. Not surprisingly, these ecological and psychological theories that address the critical dimensions of behavior are similar. The behavioral processes ecologists believe should evolve through natural selection resemble the behavioral processes psychologists believe underlie commonly observed preferences.

A formal link between ecological and psychological theories of selective influence is established below. The mathematical conditions derived from assumptions of optimal foraging and those conditions assumed to generate single-peaked preference functions are essentially identical. As shown in Table 12.1 and explained later, each theoretical model has three equivalent steps: (1) ordering the available choices along a critical dimension, (2) describing the costs and benefits of the available choices as a function of the underlying dimension and, (3) solving for an optimal preference.

The first step is to order the choices. Psychologists recognize that single-peakedness depends on the ordering of choices and so suggest that the ordering be done independently of preferences. In their example of preferences for vacations of different durations, Coombs and Avrunin (1977) ordered the choices by time because it seemed reasonable. To ecologists, ordering the choices requires choosing a dimension to be optimized. This dimension should affect fitness (that is the number of future offspring) and is usually closely related to net energy intake. For a general model, time spent foraging is a dimension that is likely to influence behavior (Schoener, 1971). Thus, for typical foraging choices, the options should be ordered as a function of time expended.

The second step is to determine how costs and benefits relate to the underlying dimensions. Ecologists have successfully applied economic theories to biological systems to provide a unified view of choice behaviors. The general relationship between costs (including maintenance of body weight, temperature, and activity) versus the benefits of more food are shown in Fig. 12.1 (Hainsworth & Wolf,

TABLE 12.1
Equivalence of Single-Peaked Preference Theory and Optimal Foraging Theory

Steps Toward Equivalence	Single-Peaked Preference Theory (Coombs & Avrunin, 1977)	Optimal Foraging Theory (Schoener, 1971)
Goal of theory.	Derive the conditions that must exist for the single-peakedness of commonly observed preferences to occur.	Derive the behaviors that will evolve if natural selection favors the strategy that leaves the most offspring.
Example of the general problem.	What duration of vacation will maximize overall enjoyment?	How long should an animal feed so as to maximize fitness (i.e. future offspring)?
Step I. Choose a dimension along which to order available choices.	Order options along any dimension that is measured independently of preferences. Vacations can, for example, be ordered by duration or time, t.	Pick some currency redeemable in future offspring. The energy yield from feeding for some amount of time (T) is always useful in describing optimal foraging.
A. Equivalent dimensions.	Choices are ordered over a single dimension, time (t).	Choices are ordered over a single dimension, time (T).
B. Minor difference.	Small letter t used for time.	Capital letter T used for time.
C. Equivalent terms for the influential dimension.	Attribute.	Currency.
Step II. Define the cost and benefit functions.	What feels good and bad.	What increases and decreases future offspring.
A. Define the benefit or positive attribute.	The good consequences of traveling are the stimulation and novelty of new experiences. This hedonic function over time is $\phi_1(t)$.	Maximum reproductive output, G, is a function of available energy, E. Energy yield, in turn, is a function of time spent foraging $E = F(T)$. Total potential benefit is thus G(F(T)), if no time is lost in feeding.
1. How does this benefit relate to the dimension?	Good things satiate. For example, the longer one travels, the more the benefits accumulate, but as traveling continues our interest in new places wanes. Therefore, we see functions of benefit over time that are increasing but negatively accelerating. See ϕ_1, or utility for the good, on the left of Figure 12.	More energy is gained with more time spent foraging, but the gain slows down over time as food gets harder to find. More offspring are produced with more energy, but this gain also levels off. Both functions, and therefore their product, have positive but decreasing first derivatives as seen at the right of Figure 12, $(dF/dT)(dG/dF)$.

TABLE 12.1 (continued)
Equivalence of Single-Peaked Preference Theory and Optimal Foraging Theory

Steps Toward Equivalence	Single-Peaked Preference Theory (Coombs & Avrunin, 1977)	Optimal Foraging Theory (Schoener, 1971)
2. Approximate Equivalence.	Humans get less and less additional enjoyment out of more and more of something good.	Animals get fewer and fewer additional offspring the more time they spend foraging.
3. Equivalent terms for benefit function.	Utility, Approach attribute, Positive value.	Potential reproduction, r max.
B. Define the cost or negative attribute.	The longer the vacation, the more it costs in money and in the effects of being away from one's home, garden and business. The sum of these negative effects, while small at first, becomes more and more serious.	Loss is the difference between potential and actual reproduction, given that the animal has to spend time feeding rather than doing something else.
1. How does this cost relate to the dimension?	Costs increase with time and grow more and more rapidly. Perceived utility is decreasing and negatively accelerating over time. See ϕ_2, or utility for the bad in Figure 12.	Losses, or $L(T)$, start out small but increase with time at an ever increasing rate. The first derivative of loss as a function of time, dL/dT, is therefore positive and increasing, as seen at the right of Figure 12.
2. Minor difference.	An unattractive dimension is said to have negative utility and to decrease as things get worse. Cost is the inverse of the utility of a bad dimension. We multiply by -1 to make decreasing utility equivalent to increasing costs; $-\phi_2(t)$ increases with time as seen in Figure 12.	Costs increase as things get worse. Negating the utility of an unattractive dimension makes it equivalent to cost. $L(T) \approx -\phi_2(t)$.
3. Equivalent terms for cost function.	Negative utility, Avoidance attribute.	Deficit, Predation, Competition.
Step III. Solve for the optimum.	How long to vacation.	How long to feed.
A. Determine how costs and benefits are combined.	The sum of those two utility functions $\phi(t) = \phi_1(t) - \phi_2(t)$ is necessarily a single-peaked function over time.	We wish to maximize $(G - L)$ or the actual reproductive output.

Steps Toward Equivalence	Single-Peaked Preference Theory (Coombs & Avrunin, 1977)	Optimal Foraging Theory (Schoener, 1971)
B. Solve for the optimum.	There is some duration that is optimum in that the total preference, $\phi(t)$, is maximum and falls off as the duration increases or decreases.	There is some foraging time (T_{op}) that is optimum in that the total fitness is maximum and falls off as foraging time increases or decreases.
C. Equivalence.	Preference or utility $\phi(t)$ is a single-peaked function over time, as seen in the left panel of Figure 12.	Actual reproduction or fitness, $(G - L)$, is a single-peaked function over time, as seen in the right panel of Figure 12.
D. Equivalent terms for the single peak along the critical dimension.	Point of greater preference.	Point of maximum fitness.

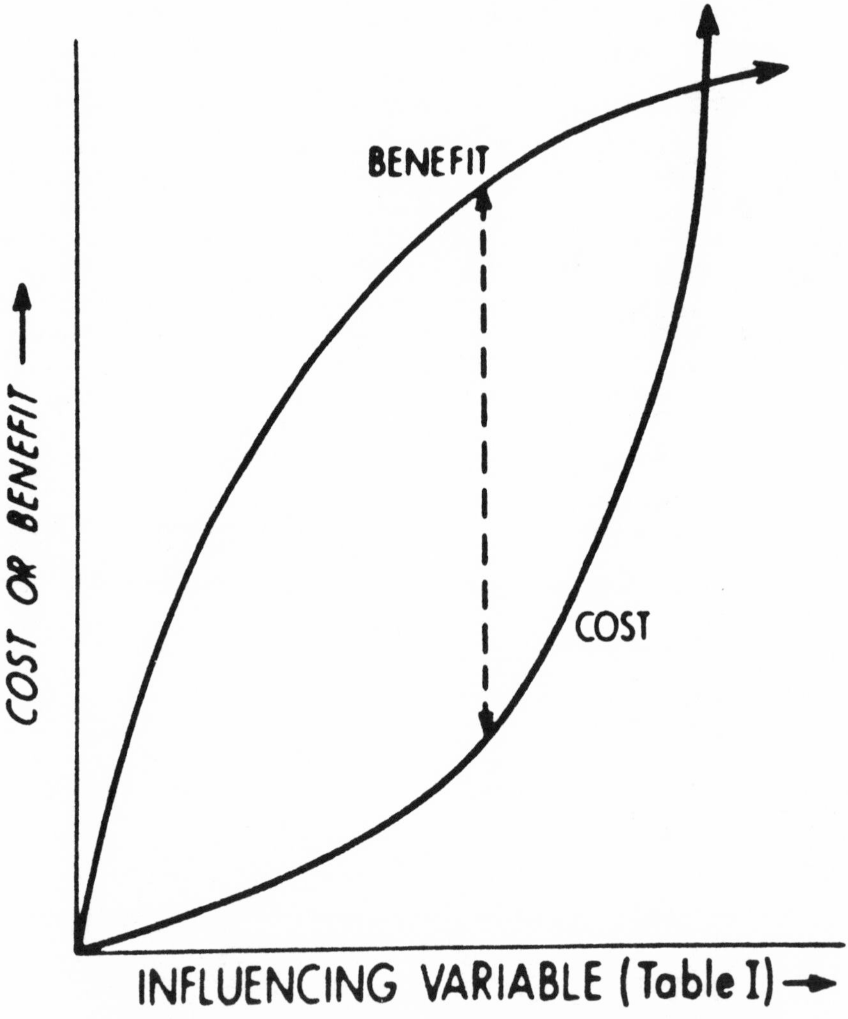

FIG. 12.1   General relationships among costs and benefits and a single influential dimension. Notice that the benefits asymptote and the costs escalate as the value of the dimension increases. Ignore the reference to Table I. (Reprinted, with permission, from Hainsworth & Wolf, 1979; copyright by Academic Press.)

1979). Psychologists recognize a basic principle that seems to be the source of commonly observed preferences. This principle is that good things satiate and bad things escalate (Coombs & Avrunin, 1977); that is, as we get more and more of the things we like, we seem to enjoy the increments less and less. Conversely, increments of the things we dislike seem to grow more and more unpleasant as they accumulate. This general principle for assessing pleasure and pain seems reasonable from common experiences with food, sex, and money.

The third step is to solve for an optimum. This is relatively easy given the ranking and cost/benefit relations determined in the previous steps. As shown in Table 12.1, the theory of single-peaked preferences (Coombs & Avrunin, 1977) matches the theory of optimal foraging (Schoener, 1971) step for step. The concluded similarity is shown graphically in Fig. 12.2: the psychological theory by the functions of preferences over the influential dimension, the ecological theory by derivatives of fitness over the critical environmental dimension.

The resemblance shown in Table 12.1 and Fig. 12.2 means that assessing peak preference and optimizing fitness, as currently defined in psychological and ecological theories, respectively, are similar. The ideas of fitness and preferences are certainly very different, but these theories suggest that animals will behave in a similar way to maximize preference and fitness. This similarity comes from

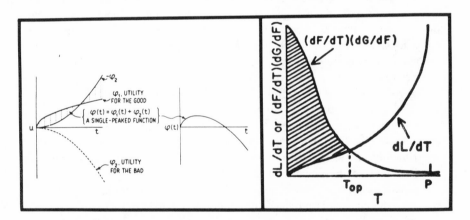

FIG. 12.2   Graphic equivalence of single-peaked preference theory and optimal foraging theory. The left panel is from Coombs, C., and Avrunin, G. (1977). Single-peaked functions and the theory of preference. *Psychological Review, 84*, 216–230. Copyright 1977 by the American Psychological Association, reprinted by perission of the authors. The right panel is from Schoener, 1971; reprinted, with permission, from the *Annual Review of Ecology and Systematics* (Vol. 2); © 1971 by Annual Reviews, Inc. As outlined in Table 12.1, these two figures depict equivalent theories of how positive and negative effects combine. Both the curves on the left and the first derivatives on the right produce a single peak along the underlying dimension.

the theoretical influence of preferences on fitness and vice versa; that is, the choices animals make based on preferences influence their reproductive success (fitness); additionally, preferences have been affected by the relative fitnesses of animals in previous generations. Animals are thus predicted to show single-peaked preferences when making choices that affect their offspring, and optimal utilization functions from ecological studies are expected to be single peaked. These diverse theories are seen to be equivalent when we consider a single influential dimension.

Niche Dimensions

An important consequence of the equivalence of optimality theory and single-peaked preference theory is that it might be possible to identify niche dimensions from subjective dimensions of preference. The general theories of optimal foraging and niche dimensions both refer to the "ultimate" goal of fitness. Animals, however, probably respond on an immediate or proximate level to more specific dimensions, such as the size of food or the location of activity. The concept of an ecological niche is thus becoming increasingly identified with patterns of resource utilization (Pianka, Huey, & Lawlor, 1979). Resources are pictured as ordered on a line (MacArthur, 1972) and niche relationships are modeled as single-peaked curves along a spectrum of resources (Roughgarden, 1974). Niche dimensions may thus be predicted by dimensions of preference. An empirical approach that follows from this hypothesis is to determine an underlying structure from psychological analyses of preferences and attempt to relate these dimensions to an ecological analysis of environmental utilization.

Two competing species of birds, for example, might segregate their feeding according to height above the ground and size of prey as shown in Fig. 12.3. This is a typical example of competitive exclusion (MacArthur, 1972), the often-stated hypothesis that no two species can occupy the same niche at the same time (Hutchinson, 1959). These niche dimensions are clearly equivalent to single-peaked preferences over two influential dimensions.

A superb example of how natural selection might affect both perceptual and ecological dimensions is provided by Arnold (1981). He measured the preferences of coastal and inland garter snakes for pieces of slugs and showed that these preferences are correlated with a genetically determined (heritable) difference in responsiveness to slug odors. When the slug-eating propensity of newborn snakes was quantified, most individuals either consistently ate or consistently ignored slugs. These preferences permit a simple classification of snakes into a slug-eating morph and a slug-refusing morph. These distinct feeding morphs emerge from variation in the responsiveness to the odors of slugs. Figure 12.4 shows the strong correlation between a slug chemoreceptive score and the probability of eating slugs. The perception of possible prey is thus quantitatively

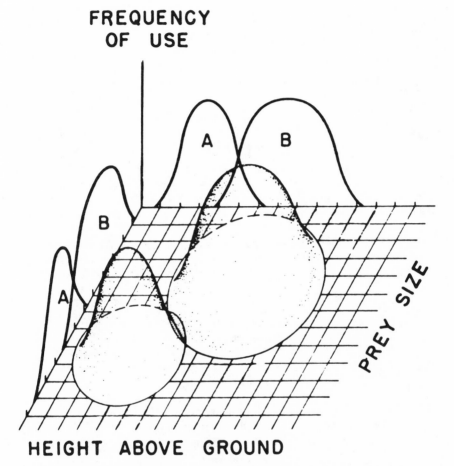

FIG. 12.3   Resource utilization surfaces for two hypothetical species, A and B, along two different niche dimensions. Silhouettes of these peaks on either resource axis alone overlap, but true multidimensional overlap is slight. (Reprinted from "Niche Segregation in Desert Lizards," by Eric R. Pianka, Raymond B. Huey, and Lawrence R. Lawlor, in *Analysis of Ecological Systems,* edited by David J. Horn, Gordon R. Stairs, and Rodger D. Mitchell. Ohio State University Biosciences Colloquia, No. 3. Copyright, © 1979, by the Ohio State University Press. All rights reserved. Used by permission of the authors, editors, and publisher.)

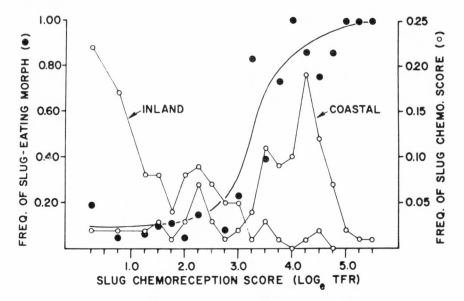

FIG. 12.4   A heritable difference in responsiveness to an influential dimension, slug odor. (The responsiveness of garter snakes for the odor of slugs was measured by tongue-flick rates, TFR. The "Slug Chemoreception Score" was measured as the natural logarithm of a snake's tongue-flick rate to a cotton swab dipped in an extract of slug. The solid circles show the frequency of actually eating slugs as a function of the chemoreception score: the higher the tongue-flick rate, the greater the proportion of slug-eating snakes. The open circles show the frequency of the chemoreception scores in both inland and coastal snakes. Interestingly, the inflection points in these distributions are correlated. Inland and coastal populations of snakes thus show differences in responsiveness to slugs. From Arnold, 1981, copyright by Garland Publishing, Inc.; reprinted with permission.)

different between two geographically isolated populations and is in part heritable. Arnold (1981) showed further that this perceptual difference between coastal and inland populations correlated with available prey. Slugs are abundant in the moist coastal habitat but rare at inland sites. The example thus shows that a perceptual and an environmental dimension can coincide closely.

Multidimensional Theory

Although ecological niche theory is usually framed in terms of a single principal dimension, it is rare for real plants and animals to differ in their use of only one resource. Animals are, for example, thought to separate resources temporally, spatially, and trophically (Pianka, 1973); that is, by when, where, and what they eat. Pairs of species often show moderate overlap along two or more dimensions (Pianka, Huey, & Lawlor, 1979). Thus, a fundamental question for a realistic theory of community ecology is how many and which dimensions are important in separating species (Pyke, Pulliam, & Charnov, 1977; Schoener, 1971).

The role of learning in the development of control by multiple ecologically relevant dimensions has, to my knowledge, never been investigated. Thus a possible direction for research toward an ecological theory of learning is to investigate how hierarchies of species-appropriate cues develop and how those multiple influential dimensions relate to the animals' environment.

Summary of Part I

This section has shown that identification of the dimension(s) that influence animals' choices provides a useful classification of both ecological and psychological aspects of behavior. Influential dimensions reflect niche relationships as well as learned preferences. Current operational concepts of fitness and preference are equivalent when there is a single influential dimension. For realistic theories of ecology and learning, however, multiple dimensions must be more seriously studied.

TECHNIQUES: HOW TO IDENTIFY INFLUENTIAL DIMENSIONS

Psychophysical scaling techniques can be used to identify the important dimensions that affect animals' choices. This scaling uncovers subjective dimensions that can then be related to physical dimensions. The process simultaneously allows learning theorists to derive an animal-relevant description of the environment (Johnston & Turvey, 1980) and allows ecologists to take the animal's viewpoint into account in determining niche relationships (Colwell & Futuyma, 1971).

Two independent analyses of animals' responses are useful in psychophysical scaling: calculations of dominance and proximity. Dominance relationships reflect an ordinal ranking of preferences. If one choice is preferred over another, it is said to dominate. Such an ordinal scale shows only how the subjects rank the choices from most to least preferred (Stevens, 1975). Dominance is a binary relationship; it describes only whether a choice is or is not preferred over another choice. Proximity relationships, on the other hand, reflect perceived similarities or differences between choices. Proximity is not a measure of preference, but can be inferred from two preferences. Choices that are perceived as similar are said to have high proximity, whereas choices that appear different to the subject are said to have low proximity. Proximities are sometimes thought to have interval-scale properties (Carroll & Arabie, 1980; Stevens, 1975); that is, the amount of proximity, from low to high values, can be a meaningful measure. Often the same data from each animal can be interpreted as either dominances or proximities. For example, a 51 to 49% division of preferences between two choices shows dominance of the first choice over the second and high (or close) proximity. A 100 to 0% division of preferences between these two choices shows the same dominance of the first choice but low proximity. A 0 to 100% division would show the same proximity but the opposite dominance. For human subjects statements such as "A looks a lot like B" reflect high proximity. Statements such as "A is much better than B" reflect both a dominance and low proximity.

One classification of psychophysical scaling methods includes analyses of dominances or proximities in one or many dimensions. Two of these techniques for identifying influential dimensions are reviewed in the next two sections. The first technique, unfolding, uses dominance data and is useful for identifying a single underlying dimension. The second technique, multidimensional scaling, uses proximity measures to identify multiple dimensions.

Unfolding

In unfolding, a single underlying dimension is identified from a set of preference rankings (Coombs, 1976; Gray, 1979b). The technique is useful when there is a single overriding dimension that affects the preferences of several animals. Unfolding could be used to verify an assumption that animals are influenced by a particular dimension. In these studies the investigator would present choices that varied along the dimension predicted to be relevant. Unfolding could also be used to identify which one of many dimensions might be important to various animals. In these studies the investigator would collect preferences for choices that varied in many different respects. In either situation, two conditions must be met for an unfolded dimension to be meaningful. First, all the preferences must have been primarily affected by a single dimension. Second, different animals must have different preferences in a pattern described later. The investigator must collect and rank the preferences of several individuals or species for a common set of choices.

The most important step in unfolding, identifying the critical dimension, is simple. An illustration follows this brief explanation. The two choices that are most frequently preferred the least are noted. This is accomplished by counting the items that appear *last* in the preference rankings of all individuals. Only two different items should be the last choice of all animals. These disliked items should, however, also be the first choice of some animals. Two and only two different preference rankings should begin with one of these least preferred choices and end with the other, and these two rankings should be mirror images of each other. This ranking determines the important dimension. (More complicated aspects of unfolding are discussed in Carroll & Wish, 1974; Coombs, 1976; and Gray, 1979b.)

Suppose, for example, that we unfold the preferences of various people for steaks. We wish to determine a single dimension from which all these preferences can be derived. The ordinal rankings of the preference of seven individuals, from most to least preferred, are shown in Table 12.2. Various people are observed to have different preferences. The "bloodthirsty" individuals like their steaks rare; "squeamish" individuals like their steaks well done; and those in the "silent majority" dislike extremes. We quickly notice that only two types of steaks are ever least preferred: rare and well-done. Then we notice that only two ordinal rankings begin with one of these two types of steaks and end with the other. These mirror images are the first and last rankings in Table 12.2: rare to medium-rare to medium to well-done and vice versa. This ranking indentifies the underlying dimension and is easily recognized as consistent with the physical dimension of doneness.

To summarize, in unidimensional unfolding a single subjective dimension is uncovered from dominance data. Ordinal rankings of preferences are used to identify a single influential dimension.

Multidimensional Scaling

Multidimensional scaling includes several methods that use proximity data to identify one or more important dimensions. For analyses with multidimensional scaling the investigator collects measures of how similar various choices are perceived to be by the subjects. Large measures of proximity should reflect similar stimuli as perceived by the animals. Small measures of proximity should reflect large perceived differences among stimuli.

TABLE 12.2
Example of Unfolding

Part 1. The Raw Data

Different Individuals	*Preference Rankings Most Preferred to Least Preferred*			
#1 (Bloodthirsty)	Rare	Medium-rare	Medium	Well-done
#2	Medium-rare	Rare	Medium	Well-done
#3	Medium-rare	Medium	Rare	Well-done
#4 (Silent Majority)	Medium	Medium-rare	Rare	Well-done
#5	Medium	Medium-rare	Well-done	Rare
#6	Medium	Well-done	Medium-rare	Rare
#7 (Squeamish)	Well-done	Medium	Medium-rare	Rare

Part 2. The Identified Influential Dimension

Rare	Medium-rare	Medium	Well-done

Suppose, for example, that we wanted to know what environmental dimensions affect the foraging of birds in trees. Suspecting that there might be two important dimensions, height above the ground and distance from the trunk of the tree, we might offer captured birds choices between pairs of 10 bird feeders that differ in these two dimensions, as shown in Fig. 12.5A. There are 45 possible pairs of these choices, one of which is shown in Fig. 12.5B. It seems reasonable that equal feeding from two feeders would indicate a high degree of perceived similarity between the choices. We would know that the two choices are similar along dimensions to which the animals attended. It also seems reasonable that unequal feeding from the two choices would indicate a perceived difference along some dimension. Feeding diversity (Gray, 1979a) is one measure that increases as preferences become more equivalent; measures of feeding diversity are, accordingly, appropriate as input for multidimensional scaling (Gray & King, in press).

Multidimensional scaling would use these 45 measures of proximity among 10 choices to position 10 points in a space of any dimensionality in such a way that distances between points in the space correspond to the measures of proximities derived from the feeding experiments. Choices that were judged to be similar by the animals are represented by points that are close together in the imaginary space. Choices judged to be more different are more distant in the space. Axes in this imaginary space are interpreted as influential dimensions. A possible two-dimensional solution from the birds' proximity data is shown in Fig. 12.5C. The two axes are recognizable as height above ground and distance from trunk, which were originally predicted to be the critical dimensions.

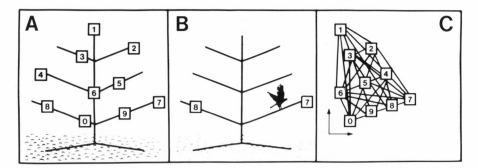

FIG. 12.5 A hypothetical example of multidimensional scaling in an ecologically relevant experiment. (Part A shows 10 bird feeders that differ along two dimensions: distance from the ground and from the trunk. Subjects are given choices between all possible pairs of these feeders. Part B shows one of these 45 tests; the bird is expected to use both feeders almost equally. Proximity measures derived from the behaviors are subjected to multidimensional scaling and a possible two-dimensional solution is shown in Part C. The orthogonal axes are interpretable as distances from the ground and trunk. Note that the horizontal dimension is "folded.")

As an analogy to the scaling process, suppose that plastic rods were cut in proportion to observed proximities. There would be short rods for large prox- imities, and longer rods for smaller proximities. (If, for example, the proximity of feeders 7 and 8 was high, as predicted because they are nearly the same height and distance from the trunk, this relationship would be represented by a short rod.) Because each proximity was measured from a pair of choices, the ends of the bars could be labeled for each choice. Because proximities refer only to the magnitude and not the direction of preferences, it would not matter which end was labeled for which choice in the pair. The ends of the rods could be connected, as in the construction of a geodesic dome. In this analogy, all the identically numbered ends would be connected. Forty-five rods have 90 ends that form 10 connections of 9 ends each. These connections are shown in Fig. 12.5C by the squares, and the fine lines in the figure represent the rods. The positions of these connections represent a two-dimensional scaling solution: The squares represent the 10 choices, and the orthogonal axes in this space represent the influential dimensions.

With imperfect data the rods would have to be heated so that they would stretch or shrink in order to make all the ends meet. Similarly, mathematical methods used in multidimensional scaling programs change distances as little as possible to make them match with the measured proximities. Configurations of points can be calculated in any number of dimensions. Using the plastic rod analogy, a three-dimensional configuration could be heated and forced between two plates to create a two-dimensional configuration. Mathematically, the sum of squares between a linear transformation of distances and the input proximities is minimized. Any data will fit better and better in more and more dimensions and will fit perfectly in one fewer dimensions than there are points. The number of dimensions to which the animals likely attended in making their choices is indicated by a relatively large increase in the goodness of fit as one more dimen- sion is allowed in the configuration of points.

To use multidimensional scaling, we would select approximately 10 choices that vary along several dimensions that the animals might notice. Values of the various dimensions should not be correlated across the set of choices. Ten is a reasonable number of choices to analyze because there are only 45 pairs of 10 choices, and the relative distances between points in a solution of three or fewer dimensions are likely to be meaningful if there are at least 10 choices (Young, 1970). We then present all possible pairs of these choices, one pair at a time, to one or more subjects and derive some index of proximity from the responses. The calculated matrix of proximities is submitted to a computer program for multidimensional scaling, and we obtain solutions with different numbers of dimensions. We can graph the imaginary positions of the choices along the resulting dimension that explains most of the variance and see if that ranking is consistent with any physical continuum. This examination can be continued for dimensions that explain less and less of the variance. There are two indications of the correct number of dimensions to include in an analysis: first, the largest number of interpretable dimensions; and second, the number of dimensions after the last relatively large increase in goodness of fit of the entire solution as one more dimension is added.

To summarize, multidimensional scaling uses multiple proximity measures to create a spatial model of available choices. Axes in this model are interpretable as influential dimensions.

Uses of Unfolding and Multidimensional Scaling

One Dimension.   Unfolding was used to uncover a single dimension that affected the selection of seeds by deer mice (Gray, 1979b). The identified dimension, seed size, is consistent with other ecological data on the critical dimension in these animals' niches (Brown & Lieberman, 1973; Mares & Rosenzweig, 1978). An analysis of proximity measures from these data identified the same dimension, seed size, as the critical dimension (Gray, in preparation). This analysis involved calculations of feeding diversity (as in Gray, 1979a), rather than the more complicated analysis of multidimensional scaling, and showed that seed size was a significant factor in determining the extent to which mice perceive different seeds as similar. These two studies show that, in one example where there is a single influential dimension, dominances and proximities are equally useful in identifying that dimension.

Unfolding worked well to uncover a single interpretable dimension to which flatworms (Adams, in review) and spiders (Adams, in press) respond in selecting their prey. Ordination analysis, based on proximity measures, failed to yield an interpretable one-dimensional solution for the flatworm data.

Although multidimensional scaling techniques could theoretically be used to identify a single dimension, I know of no such application.

Two Dimensions.   I know of no examples where multidimensional scaling techniques have been used to identify two ecologically relevant dimensions in animals. Unfolding can also, theoretically, be extended to two dimensions (Carroll & Wish, 1974) but I know of no application of multidimensional unfolding to an ecological problem. Two dimensional analyses would be particularly intriguing because both multidimensional scaling and unfolding could extract two influential dimensions from proximity and dominance data, respectively. Such a comparison would be of theoretical and practical importance.

Three Dimensions.   One version of multidimensional scaling, called INDS-CAL, successfully uncovered three influential dimensions from proximity measures derived from the behaviors of 45 wild deer mice (Gray & King, in press). Ten habitats were created to vary along three dimensions to which deer mice would be likely to respond. The preferences of captured mice were used to indicate the similarities among all possible pairs of habitats. The multidimensional scaling program created a three-dimensional configuration of 10 points where the axes were clearly interpretable as the three physical dimensions.

Analyses of dominance relationships in these data showed that there were consistent dimensions to which the mice responded, but those dimensions could not be identified from the ranked preferences. Therefore, whereas multidimensional scaling using proximity measures worked well to identify three influential dimensions, analyses of dominances failed to give interpretable results in three dimensions.

Four Dimensions. Ecologists frequently represent niche spaces in four or more dimensions. Multidimensional scaling should, in theory, be able to analyze data in any number of dimensions, up to one less than the number of choices.

Why Analyses of Dominance Data Fail in Three Dimensions

There are two fundamental psychological principles of preference (Coombs & Avrunin, 1977): (1) the law of diminishing returns, discussed earlier, that the pleasure of good things satiates as the choices become better and the aversion to bad things escalates as the choices become worse; and (2) the principle that excluded options are ignored. This exclusion principle (which will be explained later) only operates when animals attend to multiple dimensions and predicts that subjects may totally eliminate some choices from consideration when those choices are worse than others along all relevant dimensions. The combination of these two principles indicates that single-peaked preference functions will be very rare when there are three or more influential dimensions. This in turn means that analyses of ranked preferences are unlikely to be fruitful in identifying multiple dimensions.

As an example of the exclusion principle, suppose that there were two influential dimensions, one good and one bad. The exclusion principle states that, for every viable choice among consumers' selections, increases along the good dimension must be offset by increases along the bad dimension. Consider stereos that differ in price (a "bad" dimension) and fidelity (a "good" dimension). There are many stereo systems available that differ in price and fidelity. The exclusion principle predicts that any system that offered a lower fidelity for a higher price would be totally eliminated from consumers' choices and would not appear in any preference ranking. The requirements for inclusion in a preference ranking are actually even more stringent. A "dominated" choice is one that offers only a small increase in fidelity for a large increase in price and may be excluded. Mathematically, viable choices for psychophysical scaling must lie along a convex line in a plot of price versus fidelity. This insures that the options are ranked the same way on both dimensions, and this means that unfolding can uncover the influential dimensions.

When there are three influential dimensions, the principle that excluded options are ignored does not insure that the choices are ranked in the same order on all dimensions. These differences in orderings make single-peaked functions of preference very rare and mean that analyses of dominance data are unlikely to yield interpretable dimensions. For example, suppose that car buyers were influenced by three dimensions in selecting their automobiles: size (a "good" dimension, price (a "bad" dimension) and frequency of repairs (a "bad" dimension). If all excluded options were ignored (e.g., less size for more price and more repairs) and even if all dominated options are ignored (e.g., small increase in size for large increase in price and small decrease in repairs), a consistent ranking along all three dimensions is still not insured. For example, suppose that Volvos are more reliable than Cadillacs than Vegas, that Cadillacs are bigger than Volvos than Vegas, and that Vegas are cheaper than Volvos than Cadillacs. There is no consistent ranking of choices, and not all individual consumers will have single-peaked functions of preference over any ordering of automobiles. Analyses of dominance in three or more dimensions will not, according to this theory, yield interpretable dimensions. See Coombs and Avrunin (1977) for more details of this analysis.

Summary of Techniques

In this section, two of the most promising psychophysical scaling techniques for identifying influential dimensions, unfolding and multidimensional scaling, have been reviewed. Unfolding uncovers a single underlying dimension from the preference rankings of several animals. Unfolding uses dominance data, works well for one dimension, may work for two dimensions, and will probably fail for three dimensions. Multidimensional scaling techniques create a spatial model of available choices from matrices of data reflecting the perceived similarity between all possible pairs of available choices. Multidimensional scaling uses proximity data and should work for any number of dimensions. This technique has been effective in uncovering three ecologically relevant dimensions.

The theoretical importance of studying influential dimensions was established in the first part of this chapter. Techniques for identifying these dimensions were reviewed in the second part. The third part briefly reviews data that contribute to our understanding of how these influential dimensions arise.

MECHANISMS: HOW GENETIC AND EXPERIENTIAL DIFFERENCES AFFECT INFLUENTIAL DIMENSIONS

Influential dimensions, like any phenotype, arise from an interaction of genes and the environment during development. At issue in an ecological study of learning is the extent to which experiential and genetic differences contribute to differences in which dimensions affect behavior. This part of the chapter discusses these differences in three sections. First, some effects of early experience on the influence of environmental dimensions are reviewed. Second, the effects of genetic differences are considered. Third, an example of how genetic and experiential differences can interact to determine which dimensions affect behavior is given.

Experiential Effects

Perceptual Development

As developing organisms become responsive to physical dimensions in their environment, preferences narrow (Balaban, 1975; Bateson, 1971; Gray & Tardif, 1979; Hailman, 1967; Lehrman & Rosenblatt, 1971), generalization gradients steepen (Kerr, Ostapoff, & Rubel, 1979; Mednick & Lehtinen, 1957; Rubel & Rosenthal, 1975), and discriminations improve (Gibson & Gibson, 1955; Zolman & Becker, 1968). This age-related change has been termed differentiation (E. Gibson, 1969; Gottlieb, 1971), specificity (Gottlieb, 1976), and perceptual sharpening (Rubel & Rosenthal, 1975).

A connection between this age-related perceptual development and changes in the dimensions of perception was made in a study of how young chicks responded to acoustic stimulation (Gray & Rubel, 1981). Chicks were presented with the onset of a tone and then a change in the frequency of that tone. Newly hatched chicks responded similarly to the start of a tone and to a subsequent change in the frequency of that tone; that is, responses to changes in intensity and frequency were significantly correlated. Similar responses to these two very different types of acoustic signals suggest that these neonates did not separate the two dimensions of auditory stimulation. The similarity of responses to onsets and changes was significantly lower in 4-day-old chicks, suggesting that older birds can separate the two dimensions of intensity and frequency. Perceptual development can thus involve a separation of the dimensions that influence behavior.

Maturation may have different effects on different dimensions. Huddling in rat pups, for example, is initially under the control of many dimensions: thermal, olfactory, tactile, and visual (Alberts, 1978). As these animals develop, however, olfactory and visual cues become less important.

In summary, animals may become more responsive to a single dimension as they develop, and the dimensions to which they respond may change. Studies of multidimensional aspects of perceptual development have lagged far behind studies of perceptual development along a single dimension. Normally-occurring age-related changes in influential dimensions lead directly to testable predictions about the roles of early experience in the animals' responsiveness to various dimensions.

Roles of Early Experience

It is likely that some experience with cues that vary along a continuum is necessary before animals will respond to that dimension (Gans, 1968; Lashley & Wade, 1946). For example, animals reared in monochromatic light show flatter generalization gradients to hue than do animals reared in white light (Mountjoy & Malott, 1968; Peterson, 1962; Rudolf, Honig, & Gerry, 1969; Tracy, 1970), and chicks reared in silence show flatter generalization gradients to frequency than normal (Kerr, Ostapoff, & Rubel, 1979). Animals reared in the dark show poorer visual acuity (Dews & Wiesel, 1970; Fantz, 1965; Walk & Bond, 1968) and show more diverse color preferences than normal animals (Fischer, Davis, & Nord, 1975). These studies all indicate that deprived animals are not influenced by sensory dimensions with which they have had no experience.

One Dimension.   According to one view (Gans, 1968), passive exposure to changes along a critical dimension may be sufficient for animals to respond to that dimension. In another view (Jenkins & Harrison, 1960; Sutherland & Mackintosh, 1971), differential reinforcement between two values along a dimension is necessary before animals will respond to that dimension. There are data in the literature of experimental psychology to support both views. A question for an ecological study of learning is to determine the necessary species-typical conditions for the development of behavioral control by appropriate dimensions.

Passive exposure to differences along possible influential dimensions must be commonplace in the field. Desert rodents, for example, are exposed to seeds of different sizes, and this exposure could affect the influence of this important niche dimension on the animals' foraging preferences (Brown & Lieberman, 1973). Gottlieb (1981) has shown that young ducklings will later respond to differences in the repetition rate of the notes in their mother's call after only a few minutes of embryonic exposure to the calls of their siblings.

Differential reinforcement may also be important in determining influential dimensions. In laboratory tests, both domesticated rats and captive wild birds learned quickly to use available cues in order to forage efficiently (Kaufman & Collier, 1981; Krebs, Erichsen, Webber & Charnov, 1977). Such learning is also likely to be of importance in the field (Goss–Custard, 1981; Reichman, 1981; Zach & Smith, 1981).

Multiple Dimensions.   The role of learning in establishing the relative importance of multiple dimensions is fundamental to an ecological study of learning. Learning can have different effects on different dimensions. When pigeons, for example, were trained to discriminate red triangles from green circles, some individuals learned the discrimination by color and others by shape (Reynolds, 1961). Additionally, the effect of learning a response to one stimulus dimension depends on the animals' attentions to other dimensions (Rescorla & Wagner, 1972). For example, pigeons responded to the velocity of airflow toward the back of their head, but only when the key they were trained to peck was not lighted (Van Houten & Rudolph, 1972).

Early experience may play different roles in the development of different influential dimensions. For example, cats deprived of form vision for 14 weeks could later learn brightness discriminations but not discriminations between moving and nonmoving forms (Riesen & Aarons, 1959). Rats reared in a soundproof room could learn frequency but not pattern discriminations (Tees, 1976).

Thus, a critical area for future research is to determine how early experience and differential training affect the dimensions that influence behavior. Comparative studies of discrimination learning using several independent and species-typical environmental dimensions are needed. For example, the influence on foraging birds of two dimensions, distance from the ground and from tree trunks (MacArthur & MacArthur, 1961; Williamson, 1971), may be learned. Some kangaroo rats might learn to forage for clumped seeds (Reichman & Oberstein, 1977), whereas other rodents in the same environment might learn that seed size (Brown & Lieberman, 1973) or the proximity of bushes (Rosenzweig, 1973) is important. Animals may learn both about what dimensions are critical and about what values along those dimensions are to be preferred. Animals may, in general, learn about their ecological niches.

Genetic Effects

The effects of natural selection on influential dimensions are clear. Animals exhibit selective responsiveness to their environment (King, 1970). The ability of bats to hear their high-frequency echoes or bees to see ultraviolet colors on flowers has little to do with learning. On a finer level, laboratory-reared deer mice from Arizona selected their diet based on seed size, whereas lab-reared mice of the same species from Alberta were not influenced by this dimension (Gray, in preparation). Thus, genetic differences between geographically separated subspecies can result in a different amount of influence by certain cues.

The role of natural selection in the evolution of these influential dimensions is very clear in Arnold's (1981) study of garter snakes. As discussed previously, the inland snakes had a stronger preference for slugs than their coastal conspecifics. This preference was congenital, ontogenetically stable, and genetically heritable; in other words, "innate." Not surprisingly, there are more slugs in the inland habitats than on the coast, and the garter snakes have been able to expand their range by including slugs in their diet. Natural selection favored preferences for available prey.

Interaction of Genetic and Experiential Differences

The preceding sections have shown that both experiential and genetic differences can affect the dimensions that influence behavior. It is not, of course, productive to dichotomize dimensions into those that are "innate" and those that are "learned," because the dimensions to which each animal responds result from an interaction between its genes and environment over development. This interaction is evident in studies of feeding diversity.

Generalist feeders behave as if they perceive little difference among the foods they eat; they sample broadly from available foods. Proximities among available foods are high for generalists. Specialist feeders, on the other hand, behave as if the foods they eat are very different; they consume only a few types of food and ignore the rest. Proximities are low for specialists. Accordingly, differences along the continuum from generalists to specialists can be used as measures of psychophysical proximity among available foods (Gray, in preparation).

Genetic differences can affect these proximities (Gray, 1979a). A difference in feeding diversity between two genetically different groups of deer mice, reared under the same conditions, is due to a difference in responsiveness to one dimension, seed size (Gray, in preparation). Early experience can also affect feeding diversity (Gray & Tardif, 1979). A group of mice reared with a predictable diet became specialists, whereas littermates reared with an unpredictable diet became generalists. Of most interest is how these genetic and experiential effects interact.

Wild-caught deer mice from Michigan are more diverse than their laboratory-reared offspring. An experiential difference between the laboratory and the field was probably the cause of this difference in perceived proximities among available foods (Gray & Tardif, 1979; Tardif & Gray, 1978). Wild-caught deer mice of another species from Nevada, however, fed with the same diversity as their laboratory-reared offspring (Gray, in preparation). No experiential differences between our laboratory and the Nevada desert affected proximities in this species. The interaction between genetic and experiential differences is clear: Early experiences affect some influential dimensions in one species of mice and have no effect on the behavior of another species.

SUMMARY AND CONCLUSIONS

Early experiences and genetic differences interact as animals develop to produce the influence of particular environmental dimensions on animals' behavior. Various psychophysical scaling techniques can be used to identify those dimensions, as subjectively perceived by the animals. These dimensions are important not only because they are the basis of animals' choices but also because they affect the fitness of individuals and determine interactions among species. In some situations these critical dimensions may be more easily identified from the animals' behavior than from changes in fecundity along environmental gradients. Multiple influential dimensions may form a subjective map or an internal representation of an animal's ecological niche. This relationship between environmental and behavioral dimensions may be learned.

The ideas just summarized hopefully apply to a wide variety of ecologically relevant behaviors: foraging, habitat selection, mate choice, predator avoidance, conspecific recognition, etc. A consistent structure in mature animals' behaviors could first be identified with one of the two psychophysical scaling techniques reviewed in this chapter. Comparisons among competing species should show a separation of influence either within or between the identified dimensions, thus supporting the hypothesis that these dimensions are both ecologically relevant and important to several animals. Comparisons of closely related groups living in different environments would further strengthen any ecological interpretation of these dimensions. Normal age-related changes in these dimensions could then be observed by scaling the preferences of younger and older animals.

Examples where animals are likely to attend to two dimensions should be more fully explored. Because both analyses of dominances and proximities can be used to identify two influential dimensions, comparison among the available psychophysical scaling techniques would be instructive. Confidence in these methods must come from simple but realistic multidimensional analyses.

The role of early experience in determining which of several possible cues become overriding dimensions should be more fully investigated. Do the same developmental principles that apply within dimensions apply for perceptual development among dimensions? What determines how many dimensions will control behavior?

Taken together, these studies should lead to testable predictions about the mechanisms through which influential dimensions arise. They may be learned. The learning may be passive, or it may require much trial and error with successes and failures. The animal's natural environment probably provides the cues and rewards with which animals establish these relationships between environmental and subjective dimensions.

ACKNOWLEDGMENTS

Much of this chapter was written while the author was at the University of Virginia and was supported by the National Institutes of Health (NS17320). I thank T. Johnston for valuable editing and S. Stinson for assistance in preparing this manuscript.

REFERENCES

Adams, J. (in press). The habitat and feeding ecology of woodland harvestmen (*Arachnida, Opiliones*) in England. *Oikos*.

Adams, J. (in review). The structure of ecological guilds can be defined by a psychophysical unfolding model. *Journal of Animal Ecology*.

Alberts, J. R. (1978). Huddling by rat pups: Multisensory control of contact behavior. *Journal of Comparative and Physiological Psychology, 92*, 220–230.

Arnold, S. J. (1981). The microevolution of feeding behavior. In A. C. Kamil & T. D. Sargent (Eds.), *Foraging behavior: Ecological, ethological, and psychological approaches*. New York: Garland STPM Press.

Balaban, M. (1975). Behavioural ontogeny. In E. S. E. Hafez (Ed.), *The behavior of domestic animals*. Baltimore: Williams & Wilkins.

Bateson, P. P. G. (1971). Imprinting. In H. Moltz (Ed.), *The ontogeny of vertebrate behavior*. New York: Academic Press.

Brown, J. H., & Lieberman, G. A. (1973). Resource utilization and coexistence of seed-eating desert rodents in sand dune habitats. *Ecology, 54*, 788–797.

Carroll, J. D., & Arabie, P. (1980). Multidimensional scaling. *Annual Review of Psychology, 31*, 607–649.

Carroll, J. D., & Wish, M. (1974). Multidimensional perceptual models and measurement methods. In E. C. Carterette & M. P. Friedman (Eds.), *Handbook of Perception* (Vol. II). New York: Academic Press.

Cody, M. L. (1974). Optimization in ecology. *Science, 183*, 1156–1164.

Colwell, R. K., & Futuyma, D. J. (1971). On the measurement of niche breadth and overlap. *Ecology, 52*, 567–576.

Coombs, C. (1976). *A theory of data*. Ann Arbor, MI: Mathesis Press. (Original publication, 1964.)

Coombs, C., & Avrunin, G. (1977). Single-peaked functions and the theory of preference. *Psychological Review, 84*, 216–230.

Dews, P. B., & Wiesel, T. N. (1970). Consequences of monocular deprivation on visual behavior in kittens. *Journal of Physiology, 206*, 437–455.

Fantz, R. L. (1965). Ontogeny of perception. In A. M. Schrier, H. F. Harlow, & F. Stollnitz (Eds.), *Behavior of nonhuman primates: Modern research trends* (Vol. 2). New York: Academic Press.

Fischer, G., Davis, S., & Nord, J. (1975). Prehatch color stimulation effects on color pecking preferences and color discrimination learning in white leghorn chicks. *Developmental Psychobiology, 8*, 525–531.

Gans, L. (1968). An analysis of generalization behavior in the stimulus-deprived organism. In G. Newton & S. Levine (Eds.), *Early experience and behavior: The psychobiology of development*. Springfield, IL: Charles C. Thomas.

Gibson, E. J. (1969). *Principles of perceptual learning and development*. New York: Appleton–Century–Crofts.

Gibson, J. J., & Gibson, E. J. (1955). Perceptual learning: Differentiation or enrichment? *Psychological Review, 62*, 32–41.

Goss–Custard, J. D. (1981). Feeding behavior of redshank, *Tringa totanus*, and optimal foraging theory. In A. C. Kamil & T. D. Sargent (Eds.), *Foraging behavior: Ecological, ethological, and psychological approaches*. New York: Garland STPM Press.

Gottlieb, G. (1981). Roles of early experience in species-specific perceptual development. In R. N. Aslin, J. R. Alberts, & M. R. Peterson (Eds.), *Development of perception* (Vol. 1). New York: Academic Press.

Gottlieb, G. (1976). The roles of experience in the development of behavior and the nervous system. In G. Gottlieb (Ed.), *Studies on the development of behavior and the nervous system. Vol. 3: Neural and behavioral specificity*. New York: Academic Press.

Gottlieb, G. (1971). *Development of species identification in birds: An inquiry into the prenatal determinants of perception*. Chicago: University of Chicago Press.

Gray, L. (in preparation). Cues that influence feeding diversity in deer mice: Analysis of psychophysical proximities. *Journal of Comparative Psychology*.

Gray, L. (1979a). Feeding diversity in deer mice. *Journal of Comparative and Physiological Psychology, 93*, 1118–1126.

Gray, L. (1979b). The use of psychophysical unfolding theory to determine principal resource axes. *The American Naturalist, 114*, 695–706.

Gray, L., & King, J. A. (in press). The use of multidimensional scaling to determine principal resource axes. *The American Naturalist.* (Provisionally accepted pending revision)

Gray, L., & Rubel, E. W (1981). Development of responsiveness to suprathreshold acoustic stimulation in chickens. *Journal of Comparative and Physiological Psychology, 95,* 188–198.

Gray, L., & Tardif, R. R. (1979). Development of feeding diversity in deer mice. *Journal of Comparative and Physiological Psychology, 93,* 1127–1135.

Hailman, J. P. (1967). The ontogeny of an instinct: The pecking response in chicks of the laughing gull (*Larus atricilla* L.) and related species. *Behaviour, Supplement, 15,* 1–159.

Hainsworth, F. R., & Wolf, L. L. (1979). Feeding: An ecological approach. *Advances in the Study of Behavior, 9,* 53–96.

Hutchinson, G. E. (1959). Homage to Santa Rosalia *or* Why are there so many kinds of animals? *The American Naturalist, 93,* 145–159.

Jenkins, H. M., & Harrison, R. H. (1960). Effect of discrimination training on auditory generalization. *Journal of Experimental Psychology, 59,* 246–253.

Johnston, T. D. (1981). Contrasting approaches to a theory of learning. *Behavioral and Brain Sciences, 4,* 125–173.

Johnston, T. D., & Turvey, M. T. (1980). A sketch of an ecological metatheory for theories of learning. In G. H. Bower (Ed.), *The psychology of learning and motivation* (Vol. 14). New York: Academic Press.

Kaufman, L. W., & Collier, G. (1981). The economics of seed handling. *American Naturalist, 118,* 46–60.

Kerr, L. M., Ostapoff, E. M., & Rubel, E. W (1979). Influence of acoustic experience on the ontogeny of frequency generalization gradients in the chicken. *Journal of Experimental Psychology: Animal Behavior Processes, 5,* 97–115.

King, J. A. (1970). Ecological psychology: An approach to motivation. In W. J. Arnold & M. M. Page (Eds.), *Nebraska Symposium on Motivation* (Vol. 18). Lincoln: University of Nebraska Press.

Klopfer, P. H. (1974). *An introduction to animal behavior; Ethology's first century* (2nd ed.) Englewood Cliffs, NJ: Prentice Hall.

Krebs, J. R., Erichsen, J. T., Webber, M. I., & Charnov, E. L. (1977). Optimal prey selection in the great tit (*Parus major*). *Animal Behaviour, 25,* 30–38.

Lashley, K. S., & Wade, M. (1946). The Pavlovian theory of generalization. *Psychological Review, 53,* 72–87.

Lehrman, D. S., & Rosenblatt, J. S. (1971) .The study of behavior development. In H. Moltz (Ed.), *The ontogeny of vertebrate behavior.* New York: Academic Press.

Lewontin, R. C. (1979). Fitness, survival, and optimality. In D. J. Horn, G. R. Stairs, & R. D. Mitchell (Eds.), *Analysis of ecological systems.* Columbus: Ohio State University Press.

MacArthur, R. H. (1972). *Geographical ecology: Patterns in the distribution of species.* New York: Harper & Row.

MacArthur, R. H., & MacArthur, J. W. (1961). On bird species diversity. *Ecology, 42,* 594–600.

Mares, M. A., & Rosenzweig, M. L. (1978). Granivory in North and South American deserts: Rodents, birds, and ants. *Ecology, 59,* 235–241.

Mednick, S. A., & Lehtinen, L. E. (1957). Stimulus generalization as a function of age in children. *Journal of Experimental Psychology, 53,* 180–183.

Miller, D. B. (1980). Maternal vocal control of behavioral inhibition in mallard ducklings (*Anas platyrhynchos*). *Journal of Comparative and Physiological Psychology, 94,* 606–623.

Mountjoy, P. T., & Malott, M. K. (1968). Wavelength generalization curves for chickens reared in restricted portions of the spectrum. *Psychological Record, 18,* 575–583.

Orians, G. H. (1971). Ecological aspects of behavior. In D. S. Farner & J. R. King (Eds.), *Avian biology* (Vol. 1). New York: Academic Press.

Peterson, N. (1962). Effect of monochromatic rearing on the control of responding by wavelength. *Science, 136*, 774–775.

Pianka, E. R. (1973). The structure of lizard communities. *Annual Review of Ecology and Systematics, 4*, 53–74.

Pianka, E. R., Huey, R. B., & Lawlor, L. R. (1979). Niche segregation in desert lizards. In D. J. Horn, G. R. Stairs, and R. Mitchell (Eds.), *Analysis of ecological systems*. Columbus: Ohio State University Press.

Pyke, G. H., Pulliam, H. R., & Charnov, E. L. (1977). Optimal foraging: A selective review of theory and tests. *Quarterly Review of Biology, 52*, 137–154.

Reichman, O. J. (1981). Factors influencing foraging in desert rodents. In A. C. Kamil & T. D. Sargent (Eds.), *Foraging behavior: Ecological, ethological, and psychological approaches*. New York: Garland STPM Press.

Reichman, O. J. (1975). Relation of desert rodent diets to available resources. *Journal of Mammalogy, 56*, 731–751.

Reichman, O. J., & Oberstein, D. (1977). Selection of seed distribution types by *Dipodomys merriami* and *Perognathus amplus*. *Ecology, 58*, 636–643.

Rescorla, R. A., & Wagner, A. R. (1972). A theory of Pavlovian conditioning: Variations in the effectiveness of reinforcement and nonreinforcement. In A. Black, & W. F. Prokasy (Eds.), *Classical conditioning II: Current research and theory*. New York: Appleton–Century–Crofts.

Reynolds, G. S. (1961). Attention in the pigeon. *Journal of the Experimental Analysis of Behavior, 4*, 203–208.

Riesen, A. H., & Aarons, L. (1959). Visual movement and intensity discrimination in cats after early deprivation of pattern vision. *Journal of Comparative and Physiological Psychology, 52*, 142–149.

Rosenzweig, M. L. (1973). Habitat selection experiments with a pair of coexisting heteromyid rodent species. *Ecology, 54*, 111–117.

Roughgarden, J. (1974). Niche width: Biogeographic patterns among *Anolis* lizard populations. *American Naturalist, 108*, 429–442.

Rubel, E. W, & Rosenthal, M. (1975). The ontogeny of auditory frequency generalization in the chicken. *Journal of Experimental Psychology: Animal Behavior Processes, 1*, 287–297.

Rudolf, R. L., Honig, W. K., & Gerry, J. E. (1969). Effects of monochromatic rearing on the acquisition of stimulus control. *Journal of Comparative and Physiological Psychology, 67*, 50–57.

Schoener, T. W. (1971). Theory of feeding strategies. *Annual Review of Ecology and Systematic, 2*, 369–404.

Stevens, S. S. (1975). *Psychophysics*. New York: Wiley.

Sutherland, N. S., & Mackintosh, N. J. (1971). *Mechanisms of animal discrimination learning*. New York: Academic Press.

Tardif, R. R., & Gray, L. (1978). The feeding diversity of resident and immigrant *Peromyscus leucopus*. *Journal of Mammalogy, 59*, 559–562.

Tees, R. (1976). Perceptual development in mammals. In G. Gottlieb (Ed.), *Studies on the development of behavior and the nervous system. Vol. 3: Neural and behavioral specificity*. New York: Academic Press.

Tracy, W. K. (1970). Wavelength generalization and preference in monochromatically reared ducklings. *Journal of the Experimental Analysis of Behavior, 13*, 163–178.

Van Houten, R., & Rudolph, R. (1972). The development of stimulus control with and without a lighted key. *Journal of the Experimental Analysis of Behavior, 18*, 217–222.

Waddington, K. D., & Heinrich, B. (1981). Patterns of movement and floral choice by foraging bees. In A. C. Kamil & T. D. Sargent (Eds.), *Foraging behavior: Ecological, ethological, and psychological approaches*. New York: Garland STPM Press.

Walk, R. D., & Bond, E. K. (1968). Deficit in depth perception of 90-day-old dark-reared rats. *Psychonomic Science, 10*, 383–384.

Webster, D. B. (1962). A function of the enlarged middle ear cavities of the kangaroo rat, *Dipodomys. Physiological Zoology, 35*, 248–255.

Werner, E., & Hall, D. (1974). Optimal foraging and the size selection of prey by the Bluegill sunfish *(Lepomis macrochirus). Ecology, 55*, 1042–1052.

Wiley, R. H. (1973). Territoriality and non-random mating in sage grouse, *Centrocercus uvophasianus. Animal Behavior Monographs, 6*, 87–169.

Williamson, P. (1971). Feeding ecology of the red-eyed vireo (*Vireo olivaceous*) and associated foliage-gleaning birds. *Ecological Monographs, 41*, 129–152.

Young, F. W. (1970). Nonmetric multidimensional scaling: Recovery of metric information. *Psychometrika, 4*, 35, 455–473.

Zach, R., & Smith, J. N. M. (1981). Optimal foraging in wild birds? In A. C. Kamil & T. D. Sargent (Eds.), *Foraging behavior: Ecological, ethological, and psychological approaches.* New York: Garland STMP Press.

Zolman, J., & Becker, D. (1968). Spatial discrimination learning in young chicks. *Psychonomic Science, 10*, 361–362.

13

An Ecological Approach to the Evolution of Behavior

Edward S. Reed
Center for Research in Human Learning
University of Minnesota

This chapter is an analysis of the biological bases of behavior from a novel point of view. Ever since the time of Descartes, scientists have taken the biological bases of behavior to be the physiological mechanisms and anatomical structures involved in behavior. This traditional view is rejected here in favor of the idea that the biological bases of behavior are ecological. I argue that what makes a particular behavior occur as it does is a result of how that behavior has evolved in a complex and changing environment. The claim being pursued here is that animals can perceive the resources for behavior—which I call *affordances*, after Gibson (1979, Ch. 8)—surrounding them, and that animal behavior is based on this ability to appreciate what the environment offers. Thus, what makes a particular behavior the kind of behavior it is is how it functions as a mode of resource usage. The physiological mechanisms and anatomical structures involved in that resource usage are, of course, of tremendous importance, but they do not constitute the behavior; indeed these mechanisms and structures vary with the functional tasks of the animal. Therefore valid general theories of behavior must take the functional ecological facts of behavior as primary—or so the ecological approach being promoted here proposes.

The present chapter is one of a series of papers attempting to recast the concepts traditionally used to describe and explain behavior into an ecological framework (Kruse & Reed, 1981; Reed, 1981, 1982a,b; Reed & Jones, 1982; Turvey, Shaw, Reed, & Mace, 1981). Behavioral scientists frequently admit that their science contains many confusions and is in need of new approaches; but, because psychology is supposedly a "young" discipline, there is considerable patience with current ideas, despite the difficulties they produce. My own research in the history of psychology (Reed, 1982c; Reed & Jones, 1979) shows that the psychological sciences are at least as old as modern physical science (i.e., more than 350 years) and that the current inadequate concepts are not new but merely rehashes of centuries-old ideas. For this reason I urge behavioral scientists seriously to consider abandoning the restrictions of traditional assumptions, and to make a break with these inadequate ideas. To be sure, any novel ideas must be more adequate to the facts of behavior, and more productive of testable hypotheses and applications than previous nations. The final proof of the ecological approach will emerge only from subsequent test and debate, and not from methodological or philosophical discussion.

In order to begin such a debate I take a radical stand in what follows, rejecting two fundamental assumptions of existing behavioral research, using examples to illustrate both the reasons for rejection and the possibilities of the novel approach. First, the assumption that there is a useful distinction to be drawn between proximate and ultimate causes of behavior (cf. Hinde, 1970) is rejected. This distinction is pernicious because it blocks the study of the components of behavior from an evolutionary or functional point of view merely by assuming that the causes most relevant to components of behavior are proximate. It is often asserted, usually without evidence, that the muscle movements involved in, say, foraging behavior, can be studied without concern for the functions the movements serve. On the contrary, I assert that a full understanding of why certain neuromuscular mechanisms are involved in a behavior requires understanding the evolved function of that behavior. This leads to the second assumption to be rejected: that meaningful generalizations about mechanisms "underlying behaviors" can be made independently of functional analysis. I argue that physiology and anatomy do not provide the entire biological basis of behavior, and that evolutionary ecology provides us with the tools to understand the biological bases of behavior. (These points are both argued at length with respect to the study of motor control in Reed, 1982a.)

The preceding statements are all highly contentious ones that I do not pretend to justify in full, as that would require (at least!) an entire book. The purpose of this chapter is simply to raise the possibility that such a radical attack on tradition will have the positive effect of opening up new questions, lines of research, and conceptual developments. To avoid mere methodologizing, I do not argue for these points in an abstract way, but instead develop a few novel ideas not based on traditional asssumptions and suggest how these ideas can be pursued fruitfully. Briefly, the primary benefits of the ecological approach are *generalizability, testability,* and *functional relevance.* Currently, behavioral scientists are haunted by an inability to develop testable general hypotheses, especially hypotheses about function (see Johnston, 1981; Plotkin & Odling–Smee, 1979, for reviews). The ecological approach encourages the development of just such general hypotheses and suggests methods (especially comparative ones) for testing them. This fruitfulness is the best argument for taking a radical ecological approach to the study of behavior: Even if all the particular functional hypotheses discussed in this chapter are falsified, the study of behavior will have been advanced from its present state simply by the increased testing of functional and evolutionary hypotheses. Only by testing such functional hypotheses can the novelty of the ecological approach be appreciated. Much lip-service is given in behavioral research to evolutionary and ecological ideas, but rarely is behavior itself treated as a mode of resource usage—as an ecological (not anatomical or physiological) fact. The concepts of the ecological approach, especially the concepts of affordance, information, and functional specificity are intended to promote the kind of research and thinking that will encourage scientists to treat behavior as an ecological fact.

The study of learning can only be furthered by adopting an ecological approach; that is, by treating learning as a change in the functional relations of an animal to its surroundings. The widely acknowledged failure to find "laws of learning" may be due to the fact that the laws being sought were all mechanical or structural. The shortcomings of the search for these laws gave rise to the current idea that biological function constrains biological mechanism—that there are constraints on learning processes derived from the unique biological context of each species. But if there are no lawful learning mechanisms, constraints on those mechanisms must be equally fictitious. We should rather rethink our whole approach to learning, not merely patch up the old approach. It is my contention that functional laws of learning can and will be discovered as the ecological approach to behavior is further developed. Of course this claim is sheer speculation at present, but it is an exciting and well-founded suggestion to which I hope the present chapter lends some credence.

RESOURCES, BEHAVIOR, AND FUNCTIONAL SPECIFICITY

The unifying principle of modern biology is the theory of evolution by means of natural selection (Ghiselin, 1969; Reed, 1978). The key concepts underlying this unity are *resources* and the various processes involved in *competition* for resources. All forms of behavior, however much else they differ, are modes of competition for the use of some resource and have therefore evolved by means of natural selection. This does not mean that all behaviors are genetically determined, nor that they are all adaptive, nor even that they are all components of fitness (see Reed, 1981, for more on natural selection). It simply means that behaviors are the kinds of things that are, first and foremost, processes of resource use. A biologically adequate theory of behavior will therefore start from the concept of resources and work toward an understanding of what makes behavior a special mode of resource usage. Unfortunately for behavioral scientists the concept of a resource is almost nowhere explicity defined, although recent work suggests that a general account of resources and their usage will be necessary for an adequate understanding of all levels of biology (see Ghiselin, 1981; Hull,

1980; Plotkin & Odling–Smee, 1981). The following is a brief summary of such a general theory of resources and competition for resources. It should be noted that the theory is very tentative and in need of development.

I define a *resource* as *anything that can be incorporated into, and thereby contribute to, the furtherance of a biological process*. This definition is intentionally general, to allow for various kinds of resources at different levels (whose definition it is the task of further research to elucidate). A few comments on the definition will clarify it. A resource is a potential: It *can*, but it *need not*, become incorporated into a process. Oil is an energy resource even when it is lying untapped beneath the ground. However, a resource that is not being used nevertheless has actual *value*, not merely potential value. Just as oil is valuable even when untapped, so is a cache of food valuable, even when uneaten.[1] Finally, although resources exist independently of the processes they promote, what makes something a resource is its relation to such a process, its causal power to further that process, or type of process (hence all biological processes may be categorized as modes of competition for resources). A *potential* resource is therefore something that has a causal power to further a biological process, or a type of biological process, that has not yet evolved. The atmospheric medium surrounding the earth is a resource for aerial locomotion (but outer space is not); however, until flying creatures had evolved, this was merely a potential resource.

A satisfactory taxonomy of resources will await an adequate classification of the most important types of biological processes (i.e., the various modes of competition for resources). Table 13.1 attempts to categorize some of the more important kinds of resources and processes they support, without making any attempt at completeness.

The relation of a resource to the process it supports is termed *specificity*. There can be degrees of specificity, from uniquely to multiply specific. For example, some metabolic processes may require the support of a particular metabolite, whereas for other processes there may be alternate pathways for achieving the needed result. Only those resources that are specific to a given process can support that process, although, in cases where there are many resources multiply specific to the process, some of the resources may promote the process more efficaciously than others. Most vertebrates eat at least a small variety of foods but, under normal conditions, exhibit some preferences for certain foods; however, under marginal conditions these same animals will utilize marginal foods (see Wiens, 1977). Of course, no animals utilize nonfoods as food: you can't make a silk purse out of a sow's ear, and you can't use something as a resource if it is not specific to the process in need of support. Marginal or even

---

[1]Marx (1867/1977) stated: "It appears paradoxical to assert that uncaught fish, for instance, are a means of production in the fishing industry. But hitherto no one has discovered the art of catching fish in waters that contain none" (p. 287, note 7; cf. Cohen, 1978, p. 345).

TABLE 13.1

Types of Processes Supported	Types of Resources Competed for by Those Processes
1. Cellular growth & reproduction	*Metabolites:* Inorganic macromolecules; specificity of tertiary molecular structure.
2. Respiration	*Media:* Containing oxidizers; specificity of energy release.
3. Ingestion	*Food:* Objects containing nutrients; specificity to digestion.
4. Behavior	*Affordances:* Objects (animate and inanimate), places, and events; specificity to postures and movements.
5. Perception	*Information:* Energy distribution in media; specificity to other resources.

rotten foods (which contain significant amounts of nutrients) can be used as food, but sand cannot—there being no available nutrients in it.

It was James Gibson (1960, 1966, 1979) who first extended the concept of specificity from the molecular level to perceptual and behavioral processes. Information, Gibson argued, is able to support perception only to the extent that it specifies environmental resources.[2] Where there is a lack of information specific to the resources of the environment and the tasks of the animal, perception breaks down. Extending some of Gibson's ideas, I have argued that adaptive behavior requires both information specific to the function of the behavior and information specific to the movements and postures that must be coordinated to achieve that function (Reed, 1982a).

Most research in behavioral ecology has focused on energy efficiency, dealing with all kinds of resources as though they are reducible to, or at least measureable in terms of, specificity of energy use at the metabolic level. Whereas strong arguments have been made against such a reductionism (e.g., Orians, 1980), no positive approach can replace this "energy currency" view unless kinds of resources like food, affordances (resources supporting behavioral processes), and information (resources supporting perceptual processes) are explicity distinguished, and researchers begin to study how animals use those resources. The contributions of those behavioral ecologists who have studied the energy-economics of behavior are significant, but they need to be supplemented and amended by a study

---

[2]In fact, Gibson tended to go further and argued that perception is based on information uniquely specific to the affordances of the environment—but this is a secondary hypothesis outside the scope of the present discussion.

of behavior itself as a mode of resource usage, not merely as a means of obtaining and expending resources specific to metabolic processes.

The ecological approach treats behavior as *intrinsically* functional, as opposed to intrinsically *mechanical* and *extrinsically* functional. By this I mean that behavior itself is a mode of using resources, not merely a series of physiological processes whereby resources supportive of metabolic processes are obtained. Thus the adaptive or maladaptive value of a behavior is as much a part of any behavior as the mechanisms involved in the behavior. By and large, behavioral scientists have treated behaviors as composed of mechanisms leading to movements that attain a functional value only when inserted into a biological context from which metabolic or genetic value is obtained (see Hinde, 1975, for a good statement of this view of function). The idea that function is external to behaviors, which themselves are mechanical movements with no intrinsic function outside of a biological context, is consistent with the widely held view that questions of "ultimate" causality (evolutionary function) must be addressed separately from questions of immediate or proximate causality (see Hinde, 1970; Tinbergen, 1951). I have argued elsewhere that even reflexes cannot be understood in isolation from their functional context (Reed, 1982a). To oversimplify a detailed argument: Animal movements and postures considered independently from their ecological context do *not* comprise behaviors. Animals control and coordinate movements and postures into functional acts on the basis of their perception of the affordances of their surroundings, thus making the function of any behavior as integral to it as are the mechanisms underlying its component movements.

I am denying neither the utility nor the aptness (for certain purposes) of mechanical analyses of behavior. The analysis of the neural and other processes involved in animate movements and postures is an important aspect of behavioral research. However, such mechanical analyses—especially when conducted as laboratory exercises under "controlled" conditions in which most biological verisimilitude is necessarily eliminated—are not analyses of behavioral acts, although they are often mistaken for such. Both mechanical and functional analyses provide us with hypotheses about the nature of behaviors, hypotheses that must subsequently be tested. All too often it is assumed that, if *a* mechanism is found to yield a particular movement (under certain conditions), this is *the* biological substrate for all acts in which that movement figures. This particular assumption requires testing under a variety of functional regimes. In the area of motor control, where a number of such tests have been performed, I have shown that the hypothesis that a single mechanism underlies a variety of functional acts indifferently is untrue (Reed, 1982a). Far from being indifferent to changes in function, movements and postures (and their underlying mechanisms) are often precisely attuned to the animal's "motor problem." Thus I proposed the hypothesis that behaviors are *functionally* specific (i.e., supported by resources specific to behavior, by affordances) as a counter to the traditional hypothesis that behaviors are functionally indifferent (or mechanically specific, which comes to the same thing). It should be remembered that *both* of these views are hypotheses, requiring much further consideration. I am merely proposing that behavioral scientists begin to consider seriously the hypothesis that lawful regularities in behavior can be discovered—by focusing on behaviors as modes of resource use involving movements and postures, and not the other way around.

Surprisingly, even behaviors that appear to be mechanical often turn out to reveal sophisticated functional organization. Von Frisch (1975, pp. 95f.) reports several experiments on hive building in bees that vividly illustrate the role of functional specificity in perception and behavior. The orientation of the cells in a beehive is structurally crucial to the hive. The bees possess a gravity-sensing system in their "neck" that enables them to detect the orientation of cells under construction. By coating these bristle-like sense organs with hardening resin, von Frisch was able to create an entire hive of workers disoriented with respect to the gravitic vertical. These bees then clustered together and prepared to build a hive; however, they built only three "pitiful little cells" of irregular shape in 2 weeks, despite the fact that they moved normally and produced adequate amounts of wax. The bees, according to von Frisch, "behaved like workmen whose tools had been confiscated." After a heat wave melted the resin, the bees again built normal cells. A disruption of a mechanism underlying cell building did not inhibit the process of building; rather, it blocked the functional specificity of the process. A disrupted mechanism, such as a car engine, will function partially in some cases, but it will never *try* to function and *fail* (unlike the person using it). Although we must rely on von Frisch's powers of observation to believe that these bees were attempting to achieve a functionally specific goal, behaving more like a worker than like a tool in this experiment, a second experiment illustrates the same point even more forcefully.

In building cells, bees must determine the thickness of the cell walls very precisely, for this thickness is the basis of the sexual differentiation of the hive. Drones are larger than workers, so the queen bee lays drone eggs in the thicker and larger cells. Worker bees must therefore produce a group of cells for future workers with a wall thickness of 0.073mm and for future drones of 0.094mm, according to observations made by von Frisch. Even slight errors of thickness would be disastrous to the precise shape and energy requirements of a hive and would also interfere with the sex ratio. Bees perceive the thickness of the cell walls by means of active touch (see Gibson, 1962, 1966, Ch. 6). Using their mandibles, workers roll a ball of wax out into a thin sheet. While doing this, the worker presses sections of the sheet with her mandibles while simultaneously feeling for its elastic response with the tips of her antennae (which contain a very sensitive and specialized tactile organ). Because the hive is kept at a constant temperature (35°) and because all cells are the same shape, the recovery time of the cell wall from deflection uniquely specifies the thickness of the wall. When von Frisch amputated the tips of the workers' antennae, the bees continued to produce cells, but these cells had highly irregular wall thicknesses, and there were occasional holes in the wall (which never happens otherwise). In von Frisch's first experiment the bees stopped working not because their behavioral mechanism were inhibited, but because they were so disoriented that they literally could not perceive where to begin building. In the second experiment the bees were adequately oriented, but were unable to perform with precision a task that nevertheless had to be done.

Von Frisch's experiments suggest that bees' architectural behavior is functionally specific: intrinsically and not extrinsically functional. If bees are mechanisms triggered to act by stimuli, why did the removal of sensory input not halt behavior in *both* cases? If bees are mechanisms impelled by drives (instinctive or otherwise), why do they build very imperfect cells in experiment two, but not in experiment one? No purely mechanical hypothesis can explain in a consistent manner why disruption of sensory mechanisms in one case causes a "halt to production" and in a second case causes inferior quality production. At the very least a *functional* distinction must be introduced between two modes of sensory control of behavior (i.e., between sensory input that initiates *versus* input that guides behavior). According to the ecological approach, von Frisch's experiments show that the bees' perceptual ability to use functionally specific information in guiding their actions was entirely removed in the first experiment and severely limited in the second experiment. Bees that are disoriented with respect to gravity are capable of making all the movements necessary to build cells and hives—and even make desultory efforts to do so—but are incapable of organizing their behavior in any functionally appropriate manner. Bees that have reduced tactile sensitivity in their antennae are capable of inadequate control over cell wall thickness. The bees act like creatures trying to use available resources (and trying to create a new resource, the hive) and not like machines triggered to act by stimuli or impelled to act by drives or instincts.[3]

One of the great advantages of treating behavior as a mode of resource use is that one can formulate testable general hypotheses. General hypotheses about resource use need make no reference to specific mechanisms, or even to specific animals, but can nonetheless be tested if the claim is made sufficiently concrete and explicit. In fact, it is possible to formulate *laws* of resource usage, which

---

[3]Of course a proponent of mechanism might claim that bees (or any animal) are the sort of machines that are designed to utilize specific resources. This is the sort of ad hoc response that proves the increasing bankruptcy of mechanism as a research program: As yet, there are no machines in existence that use specific resources independently of workers guiding that usage. Machines, even modern computer-aided servomechanisms, are not designed to use resources; they are designed to eliminate certain steps in the use or fabrication of items by people. "The machine," Marx (1867/ 1977) explains, "is a mechanism that, after being set in motion, performs with its tools the same operation as the worker formerly did with similar tools" (p. 495). Machines are precisely the sorts of things whose goal is to perform certain motions (or operations), whereas, or so I argue, animals are the sorts of things whose goal is to discover and use resources in their environment.

apply across considerable variations in morphology and behavior.[4] In the following three sections of this chapter I discuss such laws. First, I review some recent work on the foraging energetics of hummingbirds, which beautifully illustrates how the interaction of two or more laws of resource usage can explain biological variations—in this case behavioral and morphological biogeographical variation. Then I present some laws of burrowing, focusing on the biophysics of substrates to show that there are laws of what affords burrowing that are generalizable across a number of phyla. Third, I sketch out several laws of predation and its perceptual guidance, emphasizing the use of information specific to the tasks of locating and pursuing prey.

THE BIOGEOGRAPHY OF RESOURCE USE

Competition among animals for food may take either of two forms: behavioral *interference*, in which one individual prevents others from gaining access to food (e.g., by defending a territory); or *exploitation*, in which the food source is shared, but some animals get more of it by virtue of more effective foraging strategies. The cost of behavioral interference with other animals as a mode of competition for food is usually measured as a correlate of the energy allotted to the various components of the competition processes (Case & Gilpin, 1974). The benefit of interference competition is more or less exclusive access to preferred resources (Miller, 1967), which may, in turn, yield a reduction in foraging time/unit of food (Schoener, 1971). Thus, under ideal circumstances, there will be selection for interference modes of foraging where exploitation modes lead to excessively long foraging bouts and/or excessive inability to obtain preferred resources.[5] In other words, ideally there is some cost measure, M_C, that is

---

[4]The term *law* as I use it designates a general *hypothesis* (not necessarily true). Laws are general by virtue of stating, as precisely as possible (for purpose of testing), a relation that invariably holds between two properties. For example, the laws of optical refraction state that the geometric properties of light rays (viz., angles of incidence and refraction) are a precise function of the optical density of the materials through which the light is propagating. For purposes of clarity I have stated that all laws in this chapter in a deterministic fashion, although some may prove to be probabilistic. Those who dislike terms like *laws of behavior* may substitute *hypothesis* or *rule*. However, it should be noted that following a rule implies knowledge of the rule, whereas following a law of nature does not. I discuss laws in biology at greater length elsewhere (Reed, 1981), and Gibson (1979, pp. 232–233) provides a useful discussion of rules and behavior.

[5]Cody (1974) and others have treated the alternative between interference and exploitative competition as involving optimization processes. This involves the gratuitous assumption that a more or less persistent selection pressure exists for optimizing energy expenditure; that is, that the "point of limiting returns" on Charnov's (1976) investment curve is continually being pushed toward increasing efficiency. There are few or no data to support this assumption, so I follow Ghiselin (1974, p. 87) in treating the general case as one of variable proportions among several costs and benefits. This leads to treating selection as operating *against* "excessive inefficiency" (defined over

correlated with the ratio between duration of foraging per unit quantity of obtained food and the benefits of foraging for that food. Selection will operate differentially depending on whether M_C is above or below some critical value, k. Thus

$$f(M_c) = \frac{\text{Duration of foraging/unit of food}}{\text{Benefit of foraging for that food}}$$

and

$$M_c > k \rightarrow \text{ selection favoring interference foraging}$$
$$M_c > k \rightarrow \text{ selection favoring exploitation foraging}$$

Because M_C is a function of both the duration and the benefit of foraging for a particular kind of food, either or both of these factors may be involved in selection favoring interference or exploitation modes of foraging. Biogeographical variations in the benefits of a given food item may thus change M_C and thereby change the selective forces on foraging. Feinsinger, Colwell, Terborgh, and Chaplin's (1979) study of the relation between the energetics of hummingbird flight and foraging in tropical hummingbirds provides an excellent example of how M_C varies with biogeographical variation (in this case, elevation changes).

Hummingbirds engage in interference competition for food by bouts involving extended hovering flight, whereas their exploitative mode of foraging decreases the need for such extended hovering. Territorial competition for food in hummingbirds thus produces selection pressures for flight with energy expenses as low as commensurate with competitively efficacious maneuverability. On the other hand, selection on exploitative foragers (other things being equal) will emphasize energy conservation over maneuverability.

Feinsinger and his colleagues show that for hovering flight such as is found in hummingbirds, there is a strong relationship among power required to hover, air density, and wing-disc loading. Wing-disc loading is the ratio of a bird's body weight to its wing-disc area (the area of a circle whose diameter is the bird's wing span). The energetic cost of hovering (i.e., power required to hover) increases both as wing-disc loading increases and as atmospheric density decreases. Maneuverable flight is an important requirement for territorial hummingbirds, leading to selection for relatively short wing spans. Short-winged birds, however, expend relatively more energy in hovering flight; therefore, competitive flight (which requires much hovering) is more costly for territorial than exploitative foragers. Note that a behavioral factor, in this case a foraging mode, can have an effect on selection pressures relating to morphology—a point emphasized long ago by Darwin (see Ghiselin, 1973) and Mayr (1942) but often neglected.

---

the relevant cost/benefit measures) and remaining agnostic concerning whether there exists selection "optimizing" any one cost/benefit proportion. Wiens (1977) claims, with some justification, that selection in variable (i.e., real) environments is more likely to operate in an intensively negative than in an intensely positive fashion.

From the previous discussion and the empirically verified proposition that most tropical communities contain about equal populations of territorial and exploitative foragers it follows that, as elevation increases, nonterritorial species will have on average lower wing disc loading than territorial hummingbirds. Also, the highest absolute value of wing-disc loading should decrease with elevation (to cut down on the costs of hovering in more rarefied atmosphere). Further, if resource availability does not change with altitude (so that the benefits of foraging are unchanged), the threshold value of wing-disc loading above which selection favors interference foraging should not change. Thus, those hummingbirds with similar wing morphology living at higher altitudes are more likely to engage in interference foraging than those living at lower altitudes. Also, on the average, wing-disc loading should decrease across all species as altitude increases. There is evidence to support both these propositions, although, as Feinsinger et al. (1979) note, more direct evidence is needed to establish the former claim.

Even if the several assumptions and hypotheses presented by Feinsinger and his colleagues turn out to be false, their statement of the two laws concerning energy efficiency in hovering flight will remain of value. For instance, it is likely that the threshold value of wing-disc loading above which territoriality is favored will change with altitude. If so, then predictions could be made about systematic changes in M_C with altitude that would relate the changing benefits of consuming a particular nectar at different altitudes to the changing energetics of flight at different altitudes, thus relating these two important biological processes.

The real value of this study lies in its suggestions for future research. Would it be possible to quantify foraging modes other than hovering flight in ways analogous to wing-disc ratio? If so, threshold values for different regimes of selection could be predicted and tested. For example, Huey and Pianka (1981) have argued that variations in foraging mode cause specific and systematic changes in selection pressure on lizard foraging. The next step would seem to be to attempt to formulate some general laws of foraging efficiency that could be applied to various species, using different modes of behavior, and then to test them on the model of Feinsinger et al. (1979) by measuring systematic variations in behavior and morphology as a function of variations in efficiency of resource use, and resource availability. The ecological approach proposed here offers a coherent conceptual framework into which such ecological studies of behavior can be placed and also suggests further tests of the hypotheses thus developed.

THE LAWS OF BURROWING

Behavioral and perceptual factors make as significant a contribution to the nature, intensity, and distribution of selection pressures on an evolving population as does competition for resources at other levels. In ecological terms, the niche of any species includes affordance and information variables as well as physico-chemical variables. Whereas the latter can often be measured in terms of energetic cost and benefits, we are only beginning to understand how to measure the affordances and information available to an animal species. Yet, if we are to take an evolutionary and ecological approach to behavior we must measure behavior as a mode of resource usage, and therefore we must analyze the kinds of resources I have labeled affordances and information. In this section I show that there are a number of general principles concerning what affords burrowing, and how that resource (the affordance of "burrowable-into") is realized. To achieve adequate generality but also sufficient concreteness, it seems necessary to amalgamate biophysical and behavioral studies of substrates and burrowers. It is also necessary to consider how information resources are used, but I delay discussion of the laws of information use until the next section, where they are discussed with reference to predation.

A large number of vertebrate and invertebrate animals burrow. This behavior has a variety of functions: Earthworms, for example, burrow in order to obtain nutrition from the soil and to protect their sensitive skins from desiccation. Many animals burrow in order to lay eggs or build a habitation. A substrate affords burrowing only if its surface and substance permit both *penetration* and further *extension* into the substrate without collapse. Burrowing should be distinguished from *boring* (Trueman, 1975, p. 87). In boring, a solid substance must be penetrated, whereas in burrowing it is a shifting or unstable substrate that must be penetrated. There is little difference between penetration and extension in boring (in fact, a "drilling" movement has evolved independently a number of times to facilitate boring), whereas many burrowing animals have specialized adaptations allowing them to "cement" and secure the walls of their burrows. Despite the tremendous variety of mechanisms in the myriads of animals that burrow, and despite the considerable variety of substances and surfaces into which these animals burrow, several general laws of burrowing can be suggested. These are laws of resource usage—laws concerning the realization of the affordance of burrowable-into.

The laws of burrowing are special cases of biophysical laws. Burrowing follows the laws of hydraulic penetration into a more or less viscous substrate by a system that has a limited degree of tolerance of variation in pressure, temperature, and friction. The laws of burrowing are general hypotheses about the kinds of movements and postures required to realize the affordances of a substrate, allowing for the realization of the various functions subserved by burrowing. As mentioned previously, burrowing has two phases: initial penetration and extension or progression through the substrate. This progression can be compared to the locomotory cycle of terrestrial animals (the "step cycle"). The following discussion is a simplification and slight revision of Trueman's (1975, Ch. 3) comprehensive analysis.

Penetration can be a problem for animals that have little mass and are not able to produce considerable leverage. Thus, the initial phase of burrowing may often be weak, slow, and somewhat ineffectual. Trueman (1975, p. 70) points out that this widespread biomechanical problem has led to equally widespread adaptations for entry into surfaces. Especially important is the ability to make a quick and efficient re-entry into the substrate or into a preexisting burrow when being pursued by a predator. These adaptations may be either anatomical (e.g., special cilia) or behavioral (e.g., rapid undulation). This conjunction of factors has apparently given rise to some selection pressure for place learning. It is widely reported (for example, by Reaka, 1980, discussing mantis shrimp) that burrowing animals can make a "'beeline' for their burrow. They behave as though they know the habitat, rather than hiding among the nearest coral" (p. 113).

The progressive phase of burrowing exhibits lawful regularities, especially in the digging cycle. First, there is a *necessary alternation of terminal and penetration anchors*. Forward motion of a nonrigid body in a substrate cannot proceed without some anchoring. This is a variant of stepping, as Trueman (1975) explains: "Essentially the principle of anchorage of part of the body to sustain backthrust while another part extends [forward] is common to all forms of locomotion by all animals, but the principle can nowhere be seen so clearly as in the movement of soft-bodied animals through soft substrates" (p. 72). The penetration anchor allows as much force as possible to be exerted against the substrate; if this anchor is weak, then if the animal were to exert great pressure against the substrate, it might actually slide backwards. Once the animal has penetrated the surface and has an anchor against it sufficient to allow it to push onwards, it forms a terminal anchor. This is done by exerting sufficient pressure outwards (at the sector of the body that has penetrated the substrate furthest) to begin to pull the rest of the body along via longitudinal muscles. The terminal and penetration anchors of a schematic soft-bodied burrower are illustrated in Fig. 13.1. The burrowing cycle is the alternate application of these two kinds of anchors, with a very gradual progression into the substrate. Because a substrate is so much more resistant than a medium, the "step length" in a burrowing cycle is a much smaller proportion of body length than in a step cycle, but otherwise there are remarkable similarities between the two modes of locomotion.

The second biophysical law of the digging cycle is the *necessity for scraping or displacing substrate material in the locomotory path*. A number of species have developed specialized scrapers, but soft-bodied animals have an alternate means of displacing material. In order to anchor effectively (and to pack down the burrow walls), many soft-bodied animals are capable of producing high-pressure pulses, usually by contraction of longitudinal muscles in conjunction with relaxation of circular muscles, allowing the body to dilate. Where the proboscis forms part of the body cavity, pressure pulses can protrude the proboscis with considerable force by *simultaneous* contraction of longitudinal and circular muscles. Thus a hole can be "punched" into the substrate, so that contraction of the proboscis retractor muscles along with forward anchoring will pull the creature into the hole. That this is a general affordance of substrates is illustrated by its being found in different phyla (Trueman, 1975, p. 73).

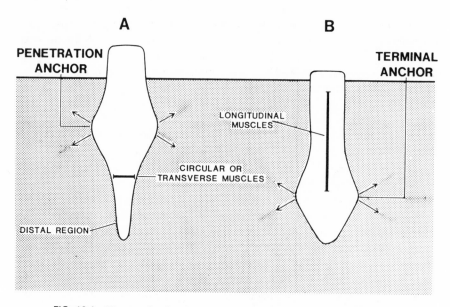

FIG. 13.1 Diagram showing the two principal stages in the burrowing process for a generalized soft-bodied animal: (A) formation of the penetration anchor that holds the animal when the distal region is elongated by contraction of the circular muscles; (B) dilation of distal region producing a terminal anchor that allows contraction of longitudinal muscles to pull the animal into the substratum. After Trueman (1975, Fig. 3.1).

Furthermore, the law of "punch and pull" applies even to some hard-skeletoned creatures. Trueman (1975, p. 74) cites a study of mole crabs who burrow backwards: These creatures use their uropods and the fourth pair of thoracic limbs in a proboscis-like way and follow it with a rowing-like pulling motion with their other legs. The division of labor between penetration and progression would thus seem to be a general law of burrowing, instantiated by a variety of mechanisms.

A further law of burrowing that is as widespread as the two listed earlier is: *Maintain a tunnel-width slightly larger than one's diameter throughout the tunnel.* Achieving this goal is very important for animals that inhabit their tunnels for any length of time. In his studies on earthworm burrowing, Darwin (1882/ 1904) showed that worms maintained burrow diameter by a mixture of "tamping down" (via continued dilation of the worms' bodies) and secretion (via excretions of earth that had been moistened). The lining thus produced is structurally stable and affords excellent points of support throughout. Darwin also observed that worms build up such linings in regions of rough soil, protecting their skins from excessive friction.Worms also pull leaves into the mouths of their burrows to line them especially well. To test whether the worms' behavior was an adaptive response to the resource variations of soil quality, Darwin (1904) deposited glass beads and bits of tile along with pine needles near some worm burrows. The worms responded by constructing burrow mouths in which:

> The pine leaves had all been drawn in by their bases; and the sharp points of the needles had been pressed into the lining of the voided earth. Had this not been effectually done, the sharp points would have prevented the retreat of the worms into the burrows. . . . The skill shown by these worms is noteworthy and is the more remarkable as the Scotch pine is not a native of this district. (pp. 114–115)

Whether such precisely adapted behaviors, specific to resource variations of different substrates, are widespread among burrowers is an unanswered question well worth pursuing experimentally. In the century since Darwin's death, behavioral biologists have neglected experiments in which resource parameters (especially affordance parameters) have been varied. Therefore, many basis questions about behavioral function remain unanswered. Darwin's careful and systematic functional analyses of earthworm behavior might still serve as a valuable model for future research (see Reed, 1982b, for an overview of Darwin's scores of experiments on earthworm behavior).

Finally, it should be mentioned that many burrowing animals build "chambers" in their burrows that are larger than the average burrow diameter. Such chambers may serve a number of functions, such as egg laying, food storage, or habitation. Where such chambers exist, it is important for them to be built at an appropriate depth. An affordance and information-based analysis of the control of chamber building would be most useful, because single factors (e.g., temperature, moisture) do *not* explain how animals determine the depth of their burrows (Brockmann, 1980; Darwin, 1882/1904, pp. 115–117; Grow, 1981). It should be noted that according to Brockmann (1980), "the depth at which a particular temperature, light, or moisture level occurs differs markedly over the day" (p. 443). The specific property of a locale that affords chamber building for a given animal and function is probably an invariant combination of at least these several factors, and the question is: What information is available to a burrower that specifies this unique combination of factors? Perhaps this question could be studied by following Darwin's method of varying resource factors related to the hypothesized functions of the behavior.

The laws proposed here concerning burrowing are ecological, and not merely physiological or biophysical. Burrowing itself is an ecological relation between an animal and a place in its habitat; namely, the substrate (for more on acts as relations, see Reed, 1982a). The biophysical, anatomical, and physiological parameters of burrowing are important, but should not be allowed to obscure the specificity of burrowing as a mode of resource usage; that is, as a specific use of the affordances of a substrate for behavior. The laws I have described are about these affordances–not about abstract biophysical parameters of either the animal or the substrate, but about how these parameters combine in the specific ecological relation that substrates afford burrowing to certain animals.

THE LAWS OF PREDATION

In discussing burrowing my emphasis was on general biophysical factors that constrain almost any burrowing animal. There are equally general laws of predation, but they are laws of information usage more than laws of affordance usage. Because of the diversity of predator and prey alike, there are few universal laws of predatory action followed by all animals. Yet there are a number of principles connecting the perceptual and action aspects of predation. I deal with these laws under three headings, reflecting the three universal stages of the predation process: (1) search and general orientation (2) orientation to prey and (3) pursuit and capture. In all these stages there is an intimate relation between perception and action; the ability of a predator to use information specific to its task of predation is a major constraint on the predator's skill.

Search and General Orientation

Predators must use information specific to a variety of affordances of both their prey and the habitat in which the predator and prey are found. Ecologists have long believed that species partition habitats according to resource usage (Hutchinson, 1959). However, without an explicit taxonomy of resources, direct tests of these ideas have been difficult and controversial. Furthermore, the idea of resources at a behavioral level (affordances) or a perceptual level (information) has barely been developed, much less tested. Gibson (1979, *passim*) suggests that affordances be divided into the affordances of places, events, and objects (animate and inanimate). I use this classification throughout this section.

Places. Studies of resource partitioning have often implicated selectivity of place as an important factor in competition. For example, Emmons' (1980) recent monograph on nine species of African rain forest squirrels showed that nearly two-thirds of their ecological diversity could be accounted for in terms of sub-habitat specialization, and that all these specializations also correlated with feeding specialization. Huey and Pianka (1981) argue that "foraging mode"—roughly, the style of behavior used in general search for prey—has a strong influence on lizards' choice of places from which to predate. In an important study, Moermond (1979) demonstrated that *Anolis* lizards select predation sites by locating places that afford both a good vantage point and accurate jumping. Moermond (1979, pp. 151–154) was able to define several different types of foraging zones on the basis of these two affordances. (In fact, one of the affordances—a good vantage point—should really be analyzed in terms of the information thereby made available to the lizard, but this was not done.) Using his affordance-based analysis, Moermond was able to confirm several predicted behavioral consequences of the differences among the foraging zones. Especially relevant here is Moermond's finding that both visual scanning patterns and overt behavior of seven *Anolis* species correlated more with the affordances of the different foraging zones than with the morphology of the lizards. Moermond's is one of the very few studies in which predictions from a functional analysis are directly tested against more reductionist or mechanistic predictions. Many more such studies are needed to improve and refine these competing approaches.

The law concerning predation and places is straightforward: *Seek places from which prey can be observed and pursued* (i.e., seek places at which there is likely to be useful information specific to pursuit of prey). Natural selection will always favor predators who can do this, and, where costs are high, selection will favor those predators whose choice of predation sites yields energetically efficient information uptake, search, and pursuit (some evidence for this may be found in Huey & Pianka, 1981, and Moermond, 1979). Curio (1976, pp. 54f.) reviews a number of studies showing that predators differentiate places in relation to the likelihood of prey being in them. Many predators, such as dragonfly larvae and carrion crows, will fixate particular locales from which pray have gone out of sight. This ability to maintain orientation to temporarily hidden prey is widespread. In an ingenious series of experiments, Hill (1979) showed that Salticid spiders remain precisely oriented to hidden places as well as hidden objects and guide their movements accordingly. The optical information specifying occluded surfaces has been described by Gibson (1979, Ch. 11). Apparently some predators can orient not just to particular places, but to *kinds* of places (this seems to be a perceptual-motor prerequisite of foraging modes). Krebs, MacRoberts & Cullen (1972, cited in Curio, 1976, p. 79), report that great tits that had fed on meal worms taped to trees subsequently searched in similar places for prey. Field workers have also reported predators having preferences for specific kinds of places. For example, Eckhardt (1979, p. 136) found that warblers and flycatchers showed markedly different preferences for perch sites within the same habitat. Finally, as Curio (1976, p. 55) notes, most predators avoid places not likely to be frequented by prey.

Events. The orientation of predators to specific events and to specific kinds of events has been implicitly acknowledged under the somewhat misleading hypothesis that some predators are very sensitive to "motion." However, it has been shown repeatedly that mere "motion" is rarely enough to elicit predatory responses; rather, most predators respond to highly specific configurations of animate movements. For example, in a number of experiments, Ewert has shown that toads are highly selective in their responses to moving objects, limiting their predatory attempts to configurations of movement more or less specific to types of prey, such as worms (review in Ewert, 1980). Curio (1976, p. 119) claims that vertebrate predators are capable of detecting "oddities" of prey movement, specifying panic or illness, and may use this to select which prey to pursue. Owls will not strike at dead prey that are artificially moved and several insectivores have been shown to strike most reliably at objects with jerking limb-like movement and continual fluttering (Rilling, Mittelstaedt, & Roeder, 1959, cited in Curio, 1976, pp. 89–90). The ability to detect prey as objects embedded within even larger events than animate movements and postures has also been reported. Many predators attend to the aggregation of prey, or to the likelihood of prey availability at different times of day or even season. Honeybees selectively forage on different flowers at different times, depending on the availability of nectar.

Orientation to Prey (As Animate Objects)

The orientation of predators to likely objects is usually discussed under the "search image" hypothesis. This can be somewhat misleading: An image is a two-dimensional representation on a surface of a solid object or three-dimensional scene. A prey, of course, is an object and not an image. It is an *animate* object, and its movements and postures may be just as specific as its shape. The widespread ability of predators to orient to and search out a particular kind of prey out of many kinds, or to locate temporarily hidden prey is sometimes taken to prove the existence of an "image" of the prey to be searched for, (a mental image, one must assume). This confuses one possible mechanism of visual memory (the storage of some sort of image) with the more general function of visual memory (the ability to maintain orientation to hidden surfaces). As it is likely that many mechanisms mediate visual memory in different predators, such a confusion of particular mechanisms with general functions of a process is to be avoided.

Most researchers studying the search image hypothesis do not theorize explicitly in terms of mental images and are aware of the argument of the preceding paragraph. Nevertheless, these same scientists still confuse recognition or learning via *pictorial images* of prey with the perception of prey as such (see for example the important experiment of Pietrewicz and Kamil, 1979). The ability to recognize and even learn from an image (or other *representation*) of a prey animal is an important fact, but it should not be confused with the ability to learn to recognize the prey itself, or with the storage of some sort of image of the prey by the predator. The point of the search-image researchers is that predators are able to orient in highly specific ways to their prey and (more or less) only their prey, even under conditions that might induce confusion, distraction, or misorientation. This functional specificity has come to be called a *search image* by some; however, to the extent that this name implies a particular mechanism mediating the functionally specific ability, it is a misleading expression.

A second misleading hypothesis about predatory behavior is that predators attend to *cues* that are correlated with the presence of prey. Curio (1976, *passim*), for example, seems to hold this view. If the cue hypothesis is interpreted as meaning that *predators seek whatever information is available that specifies their prey*, it would seem to be a potentially valuable law, worth testing. However, the idea of cues is more often than not interpreted to mean something like the hypothesis that predators have some sort of mechanism that, when exposed to a feature commonly found on or associated with a prey, produces predatory behavior. Taken literally, there are myriads of problems with this hypothesis. There are at least six good reasons to think that the detection of prey is not a mechanical process, based on the triggering of certain feature detector mechanisms by certain cues, or stimulus features.

First, hidden prey cannot be detected by a feature detector; nevertheless, many predators orient to hidden prey. Second, "cues" are often not sufficient to elicit predatory behavior (they certainly do not "trigger" such behavior). If a predator does not perceive its prey at an appropriate time or in an appropriate place (see examples given earlier), it may not pursue it. Moreover, many perceptible prey are *not* attacked (Curio, 1976, p. 59). Third, no cues are necessary for eliciting predation. The elimination of one cue may diminish intensity or accuracy of responding but rarely or never completely stops predation (Curio, 1976, p. 100). There are many examples showing that individual cues or features are not necessary: Trigger fish predate sea urchins and will attack dummies only if they are both round and have spines. Yet a buried sea urchin can elicit an attack merely by moving its semivisible spines through the substrate, even though its round shape is at that time invisible. Moreover, although all known cues are only probabilistic indicators of prey, combinations of cues seem to produce higher, not lower, probabilities—which seems to be a paradox, inexplicable even by the most sophisticated of cue theorists. If the independent probabilities of each cue are merely combined, then a cluster of cues should have a *lower* probability of specifying the prey than a single cue. Of course the separate cue probabilities might be weighted and integrated—but on the basis of what information? How can a predator know the probabilities of a certain cluster of cues co-occurring without having independent information about the cause of that co-occurrence (i.e., the desired object itself)? But if such independent information is available, why bother with probabilistic cues in the first place? This is not a mere verbal paradox, but an important conundrum at the heart of any cue theory of perception: It is a merely verbal solution to state that a cue is a good predictor of the presence of a prey. How did the cue come to have this value for the predator? There seems to be no alternative but to seek ecological laws of how information resources specifying environmental resources, such as food, come into existence and are used.

Fourth, perception of prey is frequently not limited to a single sensory channel (it is multimodal or "amodal"). Salamanders, for example, use both olfaction and vision in predation and change the sense they rely on depending on whether the prey is static (reliance on olfaction) or moving (reliance on vision) (Roth & Luthardt, 1980). Drummond (1979, Table 7) has experimentally analyzed the intricate coordination of vision, smell, and mechanoreception in water snake predation. The rule seems to be that detection of potential prey via one perceptual system elicits the subsequent orientation of other perceptual systems to that locus. At best, cues or feature detection could be only one small part of such a complex multimodal system. Fifth, highly specific movements and postures can elicit predation but are not necessary for prey recognition (Curio, 1976, p.85). Sixth, predators do not wait for cues but actively seek information (Gibson, 1966, Ch.2) and, if such information is not available, predators often desist from hunting temporarily. For example, kingfishers will stop hunting if rain makes the water surface nontransparent (Curio, 1976, p.94). Individually, each of these six problems with the cue-mechanism hypothesis might be answerable. Taken together, they suggest that something like the cue-as-specific-information idea is far more plausible.

Predation is not *triggered* by stimulus features, nor is it even *guided* like a missile with a pre-established goal. Predation is an action that is highly specific to an animal's situation. This specificity requires that predators detect and use information specific to the tasks of predation. The various cue hypotheses current encourage us to treat predators as machines waiting to be stimulated; the various search image hypotheses encourage us to think of predators as some sort of guided missile. Yet the evidence is that predators are neither: They actively seek information and are able to rely on very different sorts of information and adjust their actions to particulars of situations. Behavioral ecologists should try to understand the principles guiding the active search processes, and the information being searched for, in predation.

Pursuit and Capture of Prey

"There are three general laws of pursuit that I will discuss:

1. Move so as to have the prey object getting closer at an acceptable rate. For convenience, this can be called *interception*.
2. In following the law of interception, use movements and postures that will be nonalarming (or even nonperceptible) to prey. This is *stalking*.
3. Finish the movements involved in interception by locating oneself in a position from which the prey object is catchable. This is *pouncing*.

The generality of these procedures of pursuit and capture have been noticed by Land (1974) and by Forster (1982), who have shown in great detail that these (and many other) behaviors are shared by hunting spiders and mammals— a remarkable convergence of function between two types of animals shose neural mechanisms are radically different.

Interception. A predator must be able to approach a prey quickly enough not to waste too much time and energy on each pursuit. Therefore, it is plausible to hypothesize that predators search for two kinds of information: first, information specifying whether the predator can catch up quickly enough to make the pursuit worthwhile; and second, information specifying the time to this catching-up point. D. N. Lee (1980) has shown that any predator with a visual system has access to information specifying "time to contact" between the predator and any surface in its environment. The inverse of the instantaneous rate of separation of two optical elements projected from any surface in the environment specifies the time to contact between the moving observer and that surface at their current velocities. Behavioral strategies based on this time-to-contact information have been shown to be of great value in the precise timing and coordination of a variety of motor skills. For example, Lee and Reddish (1981) have argued that diving sea birds use this time-to-contact information to control their wing retraction prior to entering the water to catch fish. Curio (1976, pp.148–149) reports that many vertebrate predators are able to intercept the course of a prey. Collett and Land (1978) have shown that hoverflies are able to intercept the intricate path of another fly, and H. Wagner (1982) has demonstrated that flies use a time-to-contact strategy to control landing on static horizontal surfaces. Thus it is possible that invertebrate predators use time-to-contact strategies as well, although this has yet to be demonstrated directly. Turvey, Shaw, Reed, and Mace (1981) speculate that all predators might use information based on time to contact to decide whether to initiate attempts to catch prey, because predators need to know both whether a given run is fast enough, and if their approach is advantageous in speed and direction. These speculative extensions of Lee's ideas need to be tested and refined, but they are very provocative. It may be possible, by extending Lee's work, to determine empirically whether a given predator has information available to it that specifies the energetic costs of bouts of predation. Thus, the various assumptions about "perfect knowledge" often made in work on foraging behavior could be replaced by empirically determined assays of the perceptual control of predation. Kruuk (1972; cited in Curio, 1976, p. 128) reports that some mammalian carnivores seem to "test" their quarry by making short runs at them—as if to choose a particular prey that would not be too costly to catch. Studies of this sort of "testing" behavior would be an excellent place to begin bringing together Lee's theory of information use and theories of optimal foraging.

Stalking. Like information for the detection of prey, information for stalking is amodal, although here it is the prey that is trying to perceive the predator trying to deceive the prey. Predators try to reduce all their perceptible properties, whether visual, audible, or chemical. They crouch, so as to look smaller, they are careful to reduce noise, and they often choose a head-on-path, so as to minimize their visibility. (In a cluttered environment, lateral motion produces considerably more occlusion and disocclusion of background—one of the most salient kinds of visual information—than does head-on motion.) Cade (1967; cited in Curio, 1976, p. 136) reports that some birds, such as great shrikes, are capable of flying low to the ground in such a way as to hide themselves in a sort of stalking flight path! Forster (1982) reports that Salticid spiders stalk in ways strikingly analogous to cats: crouched down, but with an alert head and eyes, leading to a final prepounce crouch with at least one forelimb at the ready. Detouring, so as to go temporarily out of sight of one's prey, is very common (Curio, 1976, p. 137), which may explain why most predators are able to orient to temporarily hidden prey.

Pouncing. If a pounce is made from a running start, information based on time to contact could be used both for initiating the pounce and for controlling movements prior to the pounce. If a pounce is made from a relatively static posture (as is often the case), then information functionally equivalent to time to contact is available visually. This is what Lee (1974) calls "body-scaled information"; that is, information about how many body-lengths (or step-lengths) stand between a static observer and some surface in the environment. Although this hypothesis has not been tested directly in predation, there is some evidence that such information is used by predators. For example, Forster (1982) showed that Salticid spiders never initiate stalks for prey more than 20 body-lengths away, and that the overwhelming majority of pounces are initiated between 1.5 and 3.3 body-lengths (with an average of about 2). Because different predators will use different means to immobilize or debilitate their prey, there may be specializations that require more tightly controlled pouncing. Because Salticids must land on their prey and quickly pierce them with their fangs, they may be put at a severe disadvantage anytime they do not land fully and squarely on their target. The diving gannets (*Sula bassani*) studied by Lee and Reddish (1981) have a different problem: They must dive so as to break the water's surface with sufficient velocity to dive through and under a shoal of fish, spearing their prey on their way back up to the surface. Thus, when initiating their pounce (which is, in this special case, a power dive), they may require information about their projected velocity on reaching the water.

Yet all these specializations of predation are not mechanical in the sense of being responses caused by any prey as a stimulus, or movements determined by features of stimulation. There are clear examples of adaptive adjustments from pounce to pounce, and also when different types of prey are being attacked. After analyzing 1,500 predatory bouts of Salticid spiders, Forster (1982), emphasized "that spiders can adjust their hunting behavior and the order in which [its] various units are performed as the occasion demands. Such reactions necessitate the immediate perception of appropriate information" (p. 169). Olive (1980, p. 1134 and Table 2) has shown that different types of prey elicit specific and different types of attacks, appropriate to the size, shape, and behavior of both the spider and its prey.

CONCLUSIONS

There are no laws concerning behavioral mechanisms of learning that are widely applicable throughout the animal kingdom. The traditional question of what is the mechanism underlying a behavior can rarely be answered, because it is a leading question, a question that begs what is at issue—whether there is one and only one mechanism underlying a particular functional act. Given the vicissitudes of evolution and ecology, there rarely is "the" mechanism of a kind of behavior: Flying, seeing, predating, communicating—all these and more have evolved independently many times, under a number of different specific circumstances. The overwhelming lesson of behavioral ecology is that *variable* mechanisms and factors are required to achieve *unique* functional results under the changing environmental conditions surrounding most animals. The idea that there could be laws of S–R connections, of reinforcement, of hierarchies of drives, of learning, or of genetically predetermined acts has either to be seriously qualified by the concept of "biological constraints" or simply rejected (Johnston, 1981).

Whether there are true laws of behavior considered as resource usage no one yet knows. However, the possibilities and fruitfulness of this approach are illustrated throughout this chapter. If the concepts of affordances (resources for action) and information (resources for perception) can be further developed, refined, and tested, then behavioral research may take its place as an autonomous and important discipline within the life sciences.

The limitations of the present account cannot be overstressed, although I do not think these limitations so great as to mitigate against the idea of taking an ecological approach to behavior. Most of the hypotheses developed herein require significant further testing and refinement. Many of the statements are too general for I have repeatedly made general claims and supported them merely with citations of scattered instances. Some of these flaws are due to space limitations, and many of my general claims should be supported or refuted by more extensive reviews of the relevant literature. Other flaws are due to the inadequate development of the concepts of resource and functional specificity. It should be quite obvious that much more research needs to be done in which resource variables for behavior and perception are studied. It is one thing to postulate a general law of burrowing behavior with reference to comparative zoology; it is much more difficult to follow this up with a careful experimental analysis of the resource parameters hypothesized to explain that behavior. Where possible, I have suggested concrete directions for future research, but *much* more work needs to be done. My goal has not been to prove a particular theory of behavioral function (an approach is not a theory) but to stimulate further research and theorizing about the ecological and functional facts of behavior. To do this we need an adequately evolutionary and ecological conceptual framework to help us understand and ask questions about behavior. It has been my goal here to begin the construction of such a framework,

Little has been said in this chapter about learning. Yet the concepts of behavior and perception as the realization of affordances as guided by perception based on information has many implications for the study of learning. Eleanor Gibson (1969, 1982) has developed a theory of perceptual learning from an ecological point of view. She argues that perceptual learning is a process of an animal's refining its abilities to use perceptual information. This can involve an increasing ability to use more and more specific information for a given task, or an increasing efficiency in information usage, or an ability to use a greater quantity of information than previously. There is impressive support for this theory of perceptual development (substantiating all three of these trends) from studies on human development, but few comparative studies have addressed any of these theoretical issues. As for action learning—the processes whereby an animal comes to be able to realize new affordances, or to use older ones more efficiently, or in a novel way (i.e., via different specific postures and movements)—there are only a few scattered results. The emphasis of sociobiologists and behavioral ecologists on the costs (in terms of fitness or energy) of learning (see Johnston, 1982, for review) has obscured the need to understand *what* it is that animals learn. All the laws mentioned earlier leave some room for learning: An animal may have to learn to seek out information relevant to a task, or learn to perceive some affordances, or learn how to realize some affordances, or learn how to realize a particular affordance effectively.

In addition to promoting useful and integrative research, the ecological approach proposed here has several theoretical advantages, not the least of which is that it treats behavioral studies as both an autonomous discipline and a part of evolutionary life science. Only if behavior is treated as a mode of resource usage can there be an autonomous science of behavior that is both biologically sound and not reductionist. Only if taxonomies of resource use (including affordance and information use) are developed and tested will the role of behavior in evolution and of evolution in behavior be susceptible to test without misleading confusions and separations of levels. Only by developing functional taxonomies of behavior as modes of affordance use (see Reed, 1982a, for a detailed example) will we be able to formulate and test concrete generalizations about kinds of behaviors. Without such functional taxonomies we will have to rest content with building a detailed model for every particular biobehavioral mechanism we discover. The findings of comparative zoology concerning biological variation force us to realize that such models can never converge into some general principles or laws. The only way we will ever achieve a sound but generalizable science of behavior is by treating behavior itself an an autonomous biological process.

For these reasons and for the many empirical reasons discussed previously, we must reject the traditional assumptions of biobehavioral studies: Behaviors are not based on proximate mechanisms that only have functions when considered in evolutionary contexts. Behaviors are modes of resource usage and are intrinsically functional. The question is how to study this mode of resource usage and function in the most effective way.

ACKNOWLEDGMENTS

A number of people commented on earlier versions of this manuscript and gave me much valuable advice: Tim Johnston and Sandy Pietrewicz both wrote copious and well-thought-out critiques of a number of my bad ideas or poorly expressed thoughts, and the chapter is much better for their aid. Charles Torrey also made several helpful suggestions. I am very grateful that Peter Feinsinger took the trouble to correct my reporting of his and his colleagues' research, as well as to make some helpful general suggestions. Richard Lewontin also made a number of most helpful suggestions, especially in forcing me to be more clear about the problem of behaving adaptively in an environment whose resources are continually changing. Naturally, none of these individuals are responsible for any of the incorrect ideas or infelicitous style still remaining in this chapter. Correspondence should be addressed to: Department of Humanities and Communication, Drexel University, Philadelphia, PA 19104.

REFERENCES

Brockmann, H. J. (1980). The control of nest depth in a digger wasp (*Sphex ichneumeneus* L.) *Animal Behaviour, 28*, 426–445.

Cade, T. J. (1967). Ecological and behavioral aspects of predation by the northern shrike. *Living Bird, 6*, 43–86.

Case, T. J., & Gilpin, M. E. (1974). Interference competition and niche theory. *Proceedings of the National Academy of Sciences (U.S.A.), 71*, 3073–3077.

Charnov, E. L. (1976). Optimal foraging: The marginal value theorem. *Theoretical Population Biology, 9*, 129–136.

Cody, M. L. (1974). Optimization in ecology. *Science, 183*, 1156–1164.

Cohen, G. A. (1978). *Karl Marx's theory of history: A defense.* Princeton: Princeton University Press.

Collett, T. S., & Land, M. F. (1978). How hoverflies compute interception courses. *Journal of Comparative Physiology A, 125*, 191–204.

Curio, E. (1976). *The ethology of predation.* Berlin: Springer–Verlag.

Darwin, C. (1904). *The formation of vegetable mould through the action of worms.* New York: D. Appleton. (First published by John Murray of London in 1882.)

Drummond, H. (1979). Stimulus control of amphibious predation in the Northern Water Snake (*Nerodia s. sipedon*). *Zeitschrift für Tierpsychologie, 50*, 18–44.

Eckhardt, R. C. (1979). The adaptive syndromes of two guilds of insectivorous birds in the Colorado Rocky Mountains. *Ecological Monographs, 49*, 129–149.

Emmons, L. H. (1980). Ecology and resource partitioning among nine species of African rain forest squirrels. *Ecological Monographs, 50*, 31–54.

Ewert, P. (1980). *Neuroethology*. Berlin: Springer–Verlag.

Feinsinger, P., Colwell, R., Terborgh, J., & Chaplin, S. (1979). Elevation and the morphology, flight energetics, and foraging ecology of tropical hummingbirds. *American Naturalist, 113*, 481–497.

Forster, L. (1982). Vision and prey-eating strategies in jumping spiders. *American Scientist, 70*, 165–175.

Ghiselin, M. T. (1969). *The triumph of the Darwinian method*. Berkeley: University of California Press.

Ghiselin, M. T. (1973). Darwin and evolutionary psychology. *Science, 179*, 964–968.

Ghiselin, M. T. (1974). *The economy of nature and the evolution of sex*. Berkeley: University of California Press.

Ghiselin, M. T. (1981). Categories, life, and thinking. *Behavioral and Brain Sciences, 4*, 269–313.

Gibson, E. J. (1969). *Principles of perceptual learning and development*. New York: Appleton–Century–Crofts.

Gibson, E. J. (1982). The concept of affordances in development: The renascence of functionalism. In W. A. Collins (Ed.), *Minnesota Symposia on Child Psychology*, (Vol. 15), *The concept of development*. Hillsdale, NJ: Lawrence Erlbaum Associates.

Gibson, J. J. (1960). The information contained in light. *Acta Psychologica, 17*, 23–30. Reprinted in E. S. Reed & R. K. Jones (Eds.), *Reasons for realism: Selected essays of James J. Gibson*. Hillsdale, NJ: Lawerence Erlbaum Associates.

Gibson, J. J. (1962). Observations on active touch. *Psychological Review, 69*, 477–491.

Gibson, J. J. (1966). *The senses considered as perceptual systems*. Boston: Houghton–Mifflin.

Gibson, J. J. (1979). *The ecological approach to visual perception*. Boston: Houghton–Mifflin.

Grow, L. (1981). Burrowing behavior in the crayfish, *Cambarus diogenes diogenes* Girard. *Animal Behaviour, 29*, 351–356.

Hill, D. E. (1979). Orientation by jumping spiders of the Genus *Phidippus* (Araneae: Salticidae) during the pursuit of prey. *Behavioral Ecology and Sociobiology, 5*, 301–322.

Hinde, R. A. (1970). *Animal Behavior* 2nd Ed. New York: McGraw–Hill.

Hinde, R. A. (1975). The concept of function. In G. Baerends, C. Beer, & A. Manning (Eds.). *Function and evolution in Behaviour*. Oxford: Oxford University Press.

Huey, R. B., & Pianka, E. R. (1981). Ecological consequences of foraging mode. *Ecology, 62*, 991–999.

Hull, D. L. (1980). Individuality and selection. *Annual Review of Ecology and Systematics, 11*, 311–332.

Hutchinson, G. E. (1959). Homage to Santa Rosalia, or why are there so many kinds of animals? *American Naturalist, 93*, 145–159.

Johnston, T. D. (1981). Contrasting approaches to a theory of learning. *Behavioral and Brain Sciences, 4*, 125–173.

Johnston, T. D. (1982). Selective costs and benefits in the evolution of learning. *Advances in the Study of Behavior, 12*, 65–106.

Krebs, J. R., MacRoberts, M. H., & Cullen, J. M. (1972). Flocking and feeding in the great tit, *Parus major*—an experimental study. *Ibis, 14*, 507–530.

Kruse, J., & Reed, E. S. (1981). The ecological approach to learning. (Commentary) *Behavioral Sciences, 4*, 125–173.

Kruuk, H. (1972). *The spotted hyena*. Chicago: University of Chicago Press.

Land, M. (1974). A comparison of the visual behavior of a predatory arthropod with that of a mammal. In F. Schmitt & F. Worden (Eds.), *Neurosciences: Third study program*. Cambridge, MA: MIT Press.

Lee, D. N. (1974). Visual information during locomotion. In R. McLeod & H. Pick (Eds.), *Perception: Essays in honor of James Gibson*. Ithaca, NY: Cornell University Press.

Lee, D. N. (1980). Visuo-motor coordination in space–time. In G. Stelmach & J. Requin (Eds.), *Tutorials in motor behavior*. Amsterdam: North Holland.

Lee, D. N., & Reddish, P. E. (1981). Plummeting gannets: A paradigm of ecological optics. *Nature, 293*, 293–294.

Marx, K. (1977). *Capital*. New York: Viking. (Originally published in German in 1867.)

Mayr, E. *Systematics and the origin of species*. New York: Columbia University Press.

Miller, R. E. (1967). Pattern and process in competition. *Advances in Ecological Research, 4*, 1–74.

Moermond, T. C. (1979). The influence of habitat structure on *Anolis* foraging behavior. *Behaviour, 70*, 147–167.

Olive, C. (1980). Foraging specializations in orb-weaving spiders. *Ecology, 61*, 1133–1144.

Orians, G. H. (1980). Foraging behavior and the evolution of discriminatory abilities. In A. Kamil & T. Sargent (Eds.), *Foraging behavior*. New York: Garland Press.

Pietrewicz, A. T., & Kamil, A. C. (1979). Search image formation in the blue jay (*Cyanocitta cristata*). *Science, 204*, 1332–1333.

Plotkin, H. C., & Odling–Smee, F. J. (1979). Learning, change, and evolution: An enquiry into the teleonomy of learning. *Advances in the Study of Behavior, 10*, 1–41.

Plotkin, H. C., & Odling–Smee, F. J. (1981). A multiple-level model of evolution and its implications for sociobiology. *Behavioral and Brain Sciences, 4*, 225–268.

Reaka, M. L. (1980). On learning and living in holes by mantis shrimp. *Animal Behaviour, 28*, 111–115.

Reed, E. S. (1978). Darwin's evolutionary philosophy: The laws of change. *Acta Biotheoretica, 27*, 201–235.

Reed, E. S. (1981). The lawfulness of natural selection. *American Naturalist, 118*, 61–71.

Reed, E. S. (1982a). An outline of a theory of action systems. *Journal of Motor Behavior, 14*, 98–134.

Reed, E. S. (1982b). Darwin's earthworms: A case study in the evolution of behavior. *Behaviorism, 10*, 165–185.

Reed, E. S. (1982c). Descartes' corporeal ideas hypothesis and the origin of scientific psychology. *Review of Metaphysics, 35*, 731–752.

Reed, E. S., & Jones, R. K. (1979). James Gibson's ecological revolution in psychology. *Philosophy of Social Science, 9*, 189–204.

Reed, E. S., & Jones, R. K. (1982). Introduction to Part IV. In E. S. Reed & R. K. Jones (Eds.), *Reasons for realism: Selected essays of James J. Gibson*. Hillsdale, NJ: Lawrence Erlbaum Associates.

Rilling, S., Mittelstaedt, H., & Roeder, K. O. (1959). Prey recognition in the praying mantis. *Behaviour, 14*, 164–184.

Roth, G., & Luthardt, G. (1980). The role of early sensory experience in the prey-catching responses of *Salamandra salamandra* to stationary prey. *Zeitschrift für Tierpsychologie, 141*–148.

Schoener, T. W. (1971). Theory of feeding strategies, *Annual Review of Ecology and Systematics, 2*, 369–404.

Tinbergen, N. (1951). *The study of instinct*. Oxford: Oxford University Press.

Trueman, E. (1975). *The locomotion of soft-bodied animals*. London: Arnold.

Turvey, M. T, Shaw, R. E., Reed, E. S., & Mace, W. M. (1981). Ecological laws of perceiving and acting: A reply to Fodor and Pylyshyn. *Cognition, 9*, 237–304.

von Frisch, K. (1975). *Animal architecture*. New York; Harcourt, Brace, Jovanovich.

Wagner, H. (1982). Flow-field variables trigger landing in flies. *Nature, 297*, 147–148.

Wiens, J. A. (1977). On competition and variable environments. *American Scientist, 65*, 590–597.

IV

ALTERNATIVES TO THE ECOLOGICAL APPROACH

The ecological approach to learning is a fairly recent endeavour and it would be unfair to leave the reader of this volume with the idea that there are no criticisms to be made of it. The two chapters in Part IV present cogent defenses of two alternatives to the ecological approach. Bolles describes some of the history of the biological boundaries approach to learning, the important and seminal criticism of traditional learning theory that revolutionized the field in the early 1970s and out of which the ecological approach evolved. Together with Kalat's chapter in Part II, Bolles' chapter will alert the reader who is not already familiar with this literature to the important contributions that the biological boundaries theorists made to our understanding of animal learning. Revusky's final chapter presents a reevaluation of the general process view of learning in the light of recent research within that tradition. He defends the position that learning is a general psychological process against the claims of both ecological and biological boundaries theorists that learning is to be better (or only) understood in relation to the specific environments of particular animal species. Although Revusky's position is at variance with that adopted by the other contributors to this volume, it is a position that is representative of a wide body of psychological opinion, and his defense of it serves to sharpen our appreciation of many of the fundamental issues involved in the ecological approach to the study of animal learning.

14

The Slaying of Goliath: What Happened to Reinforcement Theory

Robert C. Bolles
Department of Psychology
University of Washington

It has become fashionable these days to say unkind things about the biological boundaries movement (e.g., Johnston, 1981, this volume; Logue, 1979). So, let me set the history of the movement straight. And let me begin by pointing out that those of us who participated in the movement in the beginning, about 1970, we were the good guys. After all, we were the ones who saved us all from the Philistines.

The Philistines worshiped false gods; they believed in a strict S–R associationism, they adhered to a universal principle of reinforcement, and they had a monolithic view of behavior in which everything psychological, whether it was animal behavior or human personality, was interpreted in terms of learned S–R connections. They were a dangerous and barbarous lot. Keller and Marion Breland (1961, 1966) were perhaps the first to see the danger. They saw that there was something fundamentally wrong with the pervailing overemphasis on associationism, and with psychology's overinvestment in empiricism. They saw that learning in the animal kingdom was not universal and monolithic. They argued that a particular species of animal might be obliged to learn some things, e.g., about social relationships with conspecifics, that another species would not be obliged to learn. Horses, which live in herds, for example, should be expected to be, and in fact are, much more sensitive to social signals than are cats, which are solitary hunters. Try to teach a cat to move forward when you touch its flank, and you will discover what the Brelands were talking about.

John Garcia also saw the problem, but he saw it from a different angle. There were at that time a number of well-established laws of learning, one of which was that learning does not occur if reinforcement is delayed more than a few seconds. That had been established by Grice (1948) in the laboratory, and by Spence (1947) on theoretical grounds. It was a well-established principle, but

Garcia called it into question. He knew that if a rat becomes ill an hour or two after eating a novel food, it has *got* to be able to associate that illness with that novel food. If such long-delayed learning were not possible, rats could not survive. Because rats are omnivores, eating a variety of foods opportunistically, and because they are frequently in danger of being poisoned by people, they have to be capable of learning about the consequences of what they eat. They have to be proficient at learning to avoid those substances that make them sick. If that were not so, there could be no small rodents that are parasitic on human culture; that niche would be empty. The data (Garcia & Koelling, 1966) showed that Garcia was right; rats could indeed learn to associate the distinctive taste of a novel food with a subsequent illness. Moreover, this learning occurred, as it had to, under "impossible" conditions, that is, after just one or two learning trials and with an hour or two intervening between the cue (taste) and the consequences (illness).

But paradigms shift slowly (Kuhn, 1970). The establishment (the Philistines) saw some puzzles and recognized some problems that had been around for years, but they paid little attention to what was happening. The problems were seen, but they were not seen as serious, surely not sufficiently so to constitute a looming crisis. But there were a few individuals with better vision; mostly they resided at the University of Pennsylvania. There was Rozin and his student Kalat (Rozin & Kalat, 1971), and there were Seligman (1970) and Shettleworth (1972), all proclaiming in different ways that the general laws of learning were not homogeneous; sometimes different rules seemed to apply. And learning occurred much more readily in some circumstances than in others.

Other Pennsylvanians (Williams & Williams, 1969) were active participants in the big problem that was emerging for the learning establishment in the autoshaping phenomenon. What was at stake here was nothing less than the validity of the concept of reinforcement. Tradition had it that pigeons first learn to peck the food key in the Skinner box through a series of behavior "approximations." The experimenter first reinforces looking at the key, then approaching it, then making tentative movements, and so on, thus gradually "shaping" the desired response through the powerful automatic response-strengthening effect of reinforcement. But the Williamses had found that reinforcement had little to do with it, and the experimenter did not even have to be there. The birds would shape themselves (become autoshaped) as long as a light on the key signaled the arrival of food. The Pennsylvanians were very perceptive in those days. They could see that there was something terribly wrong with the learning principles that everyone had taken for granted. They told us that there were limits to the generality of the general laws of learning. They told us that some things might be learnable by a given species and some things might not be.

Relatively independently of these developments, but at just about the same time, I was discovering that there were grave problems for the prevailing view of learning and the empiricistic dogma in the area of avoidance behavior (Bolles,

1970). It had become apparent that avoidance learning did not follow the established rules. It was another problem that would contribute to the crisis for the established paradigm. The truth of the matter was that animals survive by avoiding predators and other dangers without benefit of the kind of universal reinforcement learning mechanism that Thorndike and Hull and Skinner and many others had depended on to explain all adaptive behavior. I had understood the message from Garcia: Animals had to be innately equipped in some way to avoid danger, or else they could not survive. If our theories of learning could not account for this behavior, then our theories of learning must be wrong. Ethologists were, of course, always sensitive to species differences in behavior, but they were too wrapped up in the analysis of fixed (innate) behavior patterns at that time to be much concerned with the species-specificity of learned behaviors. One suspects that because it was the psychological learning theorists who created the concept of a universal and uniform reinforcement mechanism, those same psychological learning theorists would have to dismiss the concept as inadequate. And that is just what was beginning to happen back in the early 1970s.

It is hard to believe the changes that have occurred in the animal learning area in the last 10 or 15 years. Some of us older citizens of the community can remember when reinforcement used to be a discrete event. It was controlled by and meted out by the experimenter, and it was used to strengthen a response. That is what a reinforcer was in 1970. But it is all different now. A reinforcer is no longer a discrete event; it is a schedule of events. And it is no longer necessarily controlled by the experimenter; the animal can provide itself with its own reinforcers (Herrnstein, 1970). Herrnstein proposed, in effect, that when the food pellet does control behaviors, that is well and good—the food was the reinforcer. Where it momentarily does not control the behavior, that is because there are other reinforcers controlling competing behaviors. Thus, the animal may look away from the task because exploration is reinforced, or it may groom because scratching is reinforced. A reinforcer no longer strengthens a response; it simply provides a schedule whose probability is matched by the animal's behavior. It does not control behavior: the animal just matches its occurrence (Baum, 1973). And behavior in those days was all S–R. It was the response itself that was learned. But today it is stimulus–stimulus associations that are learned, and instead of explaining behavior, what we do is explain representations. In present day experiments we dig out the memories of events, and we study the associative process, rather than changes in behavior. So, learning is assumed to involve a totally different process than we had then, and the elements that are associated are quite different. Animal learning has undergone a total renovation in the last few years.

I suspect that all uf us who jumped into the biological boundaries protest in the early 1970s are stupefied at the changes that have occurred. We would like to claim some credit for the changes, but at the same time, it is hard to believe that we have accomplished so much. We had the impression that we had puny weapons; primarily, we had a conviction. We find to our amazement that our puny slings have slain a Goliath. We knew all along we were right, but we are somewhat stunned by the apparent power of our righteousness. We are as surprised as David must have been that Goliath has fallen.

Actually, we did not do it all. More realistically, what happened is that at the very time we were slinging our stones at the enemy, they, the reinforcement people, had other problems as well. The old paradigm collapsed in part because of the autoshaping phenomenon, the reanalysis of superstitious behavior (Staddon & Simmelhag, 1971) and other internal problems. Because their high-powered weapons were not working very well, they withdrew and reorganized. And that is the history of the biological boundaries movement.

Note that the issue was not just whether there are biological boundaries to learning; it involved other questions as well. Part of the question at issue, and perhaps what the movement was really about, was how we should understand behavior. Are we to approach behavior from evolutionary considerations or are we to simply apply the prevailing associationistic principles? For example, if we attempt to train a rat to engage in a certain kind of behavior and it fails to perform, are we to say, "we have a rat here, and a rat has its own proclivities," or are we to say as the empiricists are wont to do, "there is something wrong with this animal's history of reinforcement." They believed that learning is just learning (they spoke of "arbitrary" responses, as though all respones were interchangeable) and that to control the animal you only need to control its reinforcers; to understand the animal you only need to understand your schedule of reinforcement. I think that is what the battle was about.

NEW BATTLES

The enemy has not conceded defeat, not by any means. But the lines are new ones, drawn on new frontiers. Several issues can be distinguished. Those of us who are sensitive to the biological implications of learning, who do not view it as *just* a general process, have the advantage of being functionally oriented. By that I mean we ask "why" questions. Why is it possible to get extraordinarily facile learning in one situation, such as that described by Garcia, and yet extraordinarily difficult to get learning in other situations such as the bar-press avoidance task. Rats, who are so proficient at pressing a bar to obtain little food pellets, have a terrible time acquiring the same response if it is programmed to avoid an electric shock. Many experimenters must have looked for such a thing, but is was not reported in the literature until Meyer, Cho, and Wesemann did so in 1960, by which time hoards of rats everywhere had bar-pressed for millions of food pellets. And the Meyer et al. paper was notable not for the success but for the troubles they reported. The pure associationists ("pure" in that they do not concern themselves with biological considerations) have no real answer. They have to find that there is a higher operant level in the one situation than the other, or that the stimuli are more salient, or that there is a generalization decrement, or competing responses, or some such argument. The associationist is at a total loss to explain why it is so easy to teach a rat a manipulatory response to obtain food and so difficult to teach the same rat the same response to avoid shock.[1]

The good guys can also be identified by their concern with the relevance of learning. We are functional in this second sense also. The true associationist, of course, is not in the least interested in the relevance of the behavior that he or she investigates. The ideal response is one like the nictitating membrane reflex in the rabbit. It serve no useful function. The animal has no voluntary control over it. As behavior goes, it is a pretty worthless response, but the true associationist loves it. The functionalist would ask why does the rabbit have a nictitating membrane? What purpose does it serve? The associationist does not care about that. The more purposeless the response is, the better he likes it. The functionalist is inclined to look to the situation in which the animal evolved and to ask what kind of things the animal might be adept at learning because of the selection pressures that have forced it to cope with the problems that exist in its real world. A rat, for example, ought to be able to solve spatial problems because a rat's world is a very spatial world, in which food lies over here, danger lies over there, home back yonder, and so on. Then, behold, when one tests a rat's spatial sense using extraordinarily difficult spatial discriminations, one finds that the rat is unbelievably good at solving them (Olton & Samuelson, 1976). That is the functionalist's approach.

A third virtue of the biologically oriented theorist is that we are interested in behavior for its own sake. It is behavior, after all, that makes contact with reality, and that must pay off in terms of the animal's survival. Everyone claims to be a behaviorist, and I think the biological boundary people really are behaviorists, but I am not so sure about the associationists. Contemporary preeminant associationists do not seem to be concerned with explaining behavior. They are concerned with looking at the associative process. Because they assume one process for all learning and are so concerned with studying it, it does not matter much to them what the behavior is. What matters is how this gets connected with that. We see this bias in the paradigms that now prevail in the experimental literature. The real associationist uses second-order conditioning in order to show that a first-order association had been established. Indeed, the beauty of the second-order procedure, we are told, is precisely that it lets the associative process be studied without it being obscured by the animal's behavior (Rescorla, 1980).

---

[1]Note that on the other side of the new battle lines, the enemy has changed identity somewhat. We, the good guys, are no longer at arms with reinforcement theorists; we won that battle. Now we have to do battle with modern style associationists and with all sorts of empiricists, i.e., those who would attribute everything psychological to experiential factors.

The thorough-going associationist studies everything in the world to get at the basic nature of what he takes to be the associative process, but he does not concern himself much with behavior.

The biological boundaries people can also claim the virtue of having discovered a number of new phenomenon. It was we who discovered the Garcia effect, and SSDRs, and the great alacrity with which rats solve spatial problems. It was George Collier (who I like to think of as one of us) who started studying the relationships among foraging, searching for food; attack, the obtaining of food; and eating, the consumption of food. Collier (1982) has discovered that these are independent sorts of behavior, which follow different rules. Thus, the animal's solution of the foraging problem may be quite different from its solution of the seizing or the consumption problem. And the manner of solution of all these problems depends on the animal's species identity.

The associationists have not been idle, of course. There are a lot of associationists and some of them are very shrewd. Some associationists (e.g., LoLordo, 1979) have argued that the biological boundaries people have not been able to make their case. We have not run the right experiments. We have not run the right control groups. And even if we had done everything right, all we would be capable of showing is that some stimuli are more associable than others. The fundamental associationistic principles, they would contend, are still intact. Some associationists would argue that we are even losing ground. For example, whereas imprinting was once heralded by Lorenz as a unique form of learning, which was uniquely adapted to serve an evolutionary function for certain animals, it may turn out, after all, to be not so unique and not so functional. It may also be subject to an associationistic account.

My reaction to these arguments is that it is quite irrelevant whether the associationistic doctrine can accommodate itself to our new findings, whether it can bend to handle the facts. Such malleability is to be expected. The remarkable transformation that has occurred in the concept of reinforcement in recent years has already been noted briefly. One wonders what it means to be a reinforcement theorist if what is believed in can be allowed to change so much. One wonders what an associationist can believe in if the principles and the very stuff of associationism are so undependable. But there is an underlying theme, a common thread. When all their differences are sifted out, associationists have always seemed to believe in a couple of things. One is the *uniformity* of learning. The laws of association, whatever they may be at the moment, apply uniformly to all learning, whatever the elements or the content of learning may be at the moment. There may be two kinds of learning (e.g., operant and respondent), or there may be just one that is fashionable, but there is only some such very small number of varieties. New kinds of learning, such as language learning, imprinting, perceptual learning, and taste aversions, cannot be allowed to be exceptions; they have to be reduced to the familiar formulas. I have shifted over at this point to a second thing associationists always seem to believe in, and that is the *sufficiency* of their principles. Their principles may not be eternal, but they are generally taken to be sufficient to explain any and all instances of learning. No further considerations are needed.

One defense of this assumption is to argue that the difference in learning between, say, Garcia's situation and other kinds of situations is really only a matter of degree. It is a quantitative difference not a qualitative one (Logue, 1979). The quantity is considerable, of course, about 1000 to 1; that is, conditioned taste aversions can be demonstrated with delays about 1000 times longer than can be tolerated by rats on a black–white discrimination (Grice, 1948). But it is only a quantitative matter. My comment on that is to offer an analogy. From reading about snakes, it is my understanding that one sees no leg bones on snake skeletons, but that one does see on the skeletons of some snakes little bumps on certain vertebrae where the legs might be if the snake had legs. They are pelvic bumps, and it is my understanding that these bumps may be 1 or 2 mm in size. And I would observe that although a 1- or 2-mm leg is not much of a leg, it is actually about 1/1000th the length of the legs of a race horse. So the difference in legs between a snake and a race horse is really only a matter of degree.

A thousand to one difference in any kind of biological system is never just a quantitative difference, never just a new value of some parameter. It has to represent a wholly different style of functioning. A 1000-lb animal that falls off its feet is in fatal danger of breaking bones; a 1-lb animal can take any kind of fall with impunity (Schmidt–Nielsen, 1972). Thus, horses have to have reflexive defenses against falling down, whereas a squirrel can safely fall out of a pine tree. (Thus, squirrels climb trees, whereas horses do not.) By the same token, conditioned taste aversions have to represent a different "style" of learning than the conditioning of the nictitating membrane response.

Thus, the question is not whether the associationists can fit some new parametric value to a new instance of facile learning or difficult learning. The real question is *why* are there such marked differences? The chief defect in the associationist position is that it can provide no convincing reason why one thing is easier or harder to learn than another. A biological point of view suggests immediately that fear conditioning and taste aversions should be acquired more readily than a conditioned nictitating membrane response, but the associationist has no grounds for predicting such a thing. As long as associationists concern themselves exclusively with discovering the principles of association formation, as long as they reject other sorts of behavioral considerations, they are not going to have much understanding of behavior. Or of animals.

If one wants to know something about learning in animals, one has to follow the Brelands' (1966) admonition to look at the animal. Determine what kind of life it lives. Ask what kind of thing it would be useful for that species of animal to be able to learn. What does it need to know? What kind of thing would it be inconsequential for the animal to learn? The mothers of some species recognize their young, but in some species they do not. Those that do not do not have to, because it does not make any difference, I would suppose. Perhaps the nest is isolated, and all the mother has to learn is where the nest is. But for animals that grow up in colonies it is essential for mothers to be able to identify their young from among all the other young that are wandering around (Beecher, 1981). If an animal's world is a spatial one, one must expect it to be able to solve spatial problems with proficiency. If the animal's world is not so much spatial as it is social, then one should expect the animal to be able to learn social relationships with facility.

So, the message should be clear: Know thine animal. There is, unfortunately, sometimes difficulty in reading the message and interpreting correctly the animal's place in the overall scheme of things. Let us consider some of these difficulties.

GENERAL VERSUS SPECIFIC ADAPTATIONS

Some of the adaptations we see in animals are just common, but unrelated, evolutionary adjustments to common circumstances. The phenomenon is called convergence, and color vision is an illustration of it. Full-spectrum color vision pops up here and there in the evolutionary tree. There is no evident continuity to it because it appears in some mammals, in most birds, in some fish, and in some of the arthropods. Animals in between are more or less color-blind. It decorates the evolutionary tree like a bunch of apples hanging here and there. One way to think of color vision is that it has been discovered or invented several times independently, presumably because in each case it conferred an advantage to animals evolving into a particular life style. Those who are highly mobile in trees or who try to discriminate flowers, for example, are well served by color vision. So color vision evolved again and again. So did wings and sexual dimorphism. There is something reversible about such adaptations; you may have color vision but your evolutionary descendents may not.

But some adaptations are evidently not reversible. Once bilateral symmetry evolved, all descendents were bilaterally symmetrical. There has been no reversion to amorphous or radial or other forms that animals might have. The evolution of the heart among higher animals is another one-way street. Once the two-compartment heart was developed there were no reversions to anything simpler. So some adaptations are permanent commitments and others are not. Consider feathers. All feathered animals have two legs and wings (even though they can't all fly), a wishbone, a high metabolism, and the ability to lay eggs with hard shells. Other kinds of animals might have feathers, but they do not. Only birds have feathers. But the feather idea was apparently stupendously successful, because there are no birds without feathers. Once feathers came upon the scene, that was it, all descendants were stuck with feathers. Some birds (e.g., penguins) have funny feathers, but there are no furry birds and there are no bald birds. It is trivial but nonetheless remarkable: All birds have feathers. Apparently once in possession of feathers, there is no set of environmental conditions that makes it possible to give them up. They may change shape and size and color and waxiness and so on, but evidently if you have feathers you can depend on all your descendents having feathers. There is no way back.

The questions I'm working up to is this: Is associative learning like feathers? Is the ability to learn such a stupendous advantage that once in possession of it there is no way back? You cannot give up learning because to do so would put you at such a disadvantage relative to everyone else that you could not survive under any circumstances. Is learning such an adaptation? If you and I and the rat and the pigeon all learn on the basis of the contiguity of stimuli, is the possession of such an attribute such a great advantage that we can depend on all our descendants possessing it too? Is it possible, after all, that there are universal associative mechanisms that have evolved, and that once in possession of them there is no way that they can be abandoned. Or is associative learning more like color vision? Does learning just modify itself according to the animal's life style? One animal can learn this kind of thing, another animal can learn that kind of thing. And so perhaps learning changes shape from one species to the next just as birds' beaks change shape, so that there are small beaks, large beaks, sharp ones, dull ones, and so on.

I cannot speak for the biological boundaries people as a whole, but my own view of the feather question is that associative learning probably is something like feathers. There is a structural aspect to it that is invariant. Feathers are all made of the same kind of stuff; they grow and become erect and fall out and so on in essentially the same way in all birds. I would make that concession.[2] But at the same time, I would insist that if one knew everything there was to know about feathers, if one had at their disposal all knowledge of how feathers were grown, nourished, and constructed, one would at that point know very little about birds. And how well can one really understand feathers without knowing something about birds? The message again: Know thine animal.

CONTINUING PROBLEMS

It has to be noted that the biological boundaries position does have its own problems. I have just conceded that associative learning may not be the specific kind of adaptation that, say, color vision is; it may be more like feathers. Let

---

[2]Garcia was led to discover the remarkable properties of conditioned taste aversions at least in part because of the biological idea that an omnivorous rat had to be capable of such learning. Smart thinking. But the corollary is that other animals, those with quite different foraging strategies, should *not* be capable of such learning. When we find, then, that cattle and koala bears also show conditioned taste aversions, it is clear that something has gone wrong. Perhaps Garcia was more lucky than smart. It remains possible, however, that, even though rats may not be so different from koala bears as we had thought, conditioned taste aversions may still be different from other kinds of conditioning. They may be a distinctive kind of feather.

me now play the part of the devil's advocate, turning traitor for the moment to my true cause, and note a couple of other problems that must be dealt with by a biological approach. One problem is that, whereas one might be tempted to look at a habitat and infer something about the inhabitant's psychology, the inference is apt to fall somewhat short of reality. Even inferences about the animal's morphology are hazardous. Suppose we were to have observed the supply of food available in Africa a few million years ago, and we saw that the tops of trees were not being eaten. Birds were there but they were not eating the leaves; they were eating bugs and things. The herbivores were generally only eating the lower reaches of the trees. Would it have been reasonable to suggest that there might develop a herbivore with a very long neck and very long legs that would be able to reach the tops of the trees? We might conclude that were evolution to take the right turn, an unexploited niche could be filled. The question is whether these observations would have led us to predict anything as silly as the giraffe coming about?

Suppose, observing the same habitat, we noted that many herbivores were being heavily predated. We might have concluded that what was needed to survive in the African environment was an extraordinarily large, powerful animal, with armor plate and some impressive weapon to defend against large cats. Now, even if we had seriously considered the possibility several million years ago, would we have been able to predict the evolution of the rhinoceros? Would we have anticipated, e.g., that he would carry his weapon on his nose instead of a more reasonable place? Who would have predicted such ridiculous animals as giraffes and rhinoceroses?

But suppose we had been that clever, and over time we witnessed the giraffe getting taller and taller, and the original puny rhinoceros getting bigger and tougher and more predator resistant. Would we ever have predicted that the giraffe would become voiceless or that the rhinoceros would become so irascible? What is it about being a large, armor-plated herbivore that makes it so irritable? In general, how does one make predictions from the kind of niches that are available to the kinds of creatures that evolve? And having figured out something about the size and shape of the animal, how does one make predictions about its psychology, the kinds of things that it is capable of learning and the kinds of motivational systems it has? In short, how can a description of the niche enable us to specify anything about the psychology of the animal? That is one problem that has to be faced.

A second problem has been described most eloquently by Boice (1977). This is the problem he calls surplusage. The idea is that in terms of whatever characteristics animals have that give them an advantage, they tend to be over-equipped. They have a surplus of whatever their special adaptation is. If the hawk's competitive advantage is keen sight, that makes sense. But we find that hawks not only have keen sight, they have unbelieveably keen sight. We have already noted that it is of some advantage to a rat to be able to localize things in space. But when we examine the rat's spatial ability we find an astonishing ability to learn spatial problems. Its ability must be far in excess of anything the rat needed in the course of its evolutionary history. If we look at the ability of subhuman primates to solve conceptual problems, oddity problems, and matching-to-sample problems, we find that their ability is greatly in excess of anything that might reasonably be required of them in nature. Where amid all the complications of a monkey's social life is the ability to solve oddity problems or delayed-matching-to-sample problems a real force in their natural environment? The surplusage problem reaches its climax, of course, in the case of the human. There is little reason to suppose that the human intellect has advanced materially in the last several thousand years, since at the time we were living in caves and obtaining foods by clubbing animals to death. There is no reason to suppose that the mean IQ has gotten any higher, because there is no reason to suppose that there has been further selection pressure on intelligence. So caveman must have been inherently as intelligent as we are today. But if we can play chess, program computers, play musical instruments, and learn new languages, and if caveman was really no less intelligent than we are, then he could do all our present-day tricks too. How in the world did he come by this extraordinary degree of intelligence, which was vastly superior to anything that was demanded of him in his niche. Our niche is the urban world, which is quite different, but we have not evolved into it; we built it and moved into it.

How did the human species develop this enormous surplusage of intelligence? If Cro-Magnon man or some other primitive man of 30,000 years ago was perfectly capable of computer programming, playing chess, and learning the English language, how did he become that intelligent. Even if we could see, 30,000 years ago, that there was a place in the world for a very intelligent primate, there were simply no grounds for predicting a primate intelligent enough to play chess and speak English. The problem, then, is that, because some adaptive specializations are carried to such excess, we cannot in general predict them from current selection pressures.[3]

The third point I raise, playing the devil's advocate, is that any evolutionary argument can be pushed this way or that. There is an alarming element of untestability about any evolutionary argument (which is too bad because it is evolutionary arguments that enable us to do battle with the associationists). When Denis Mitchell was a graduate student at the University of Washington, he wrote a short paper addressing the question of why pygmies are so small. How was it

---

[3]One answer to the surplusage problem is that giraffes do not compete with other animals, they compete primarily with other giraffes, so it is the giraffe with the longest neck that can do better what giraffes do best. And so it is with humans. It was not gorillas and chimpanzees we were competing with; it was other humanoids. And because they were rather clever, too, it took surplus of intelligence on our part to prevail over them. We also thrived because of our peculiar social system, which put a premium on intelligence (Symons, 1979).

possible for a race of humans to be physically so different from all the rest of us? He argued that it was all a matter of environmental setting. Because pygmies lived in the jungle, it was essential that they be mobile. There was also selection pressure with regard to hiding from their enemies. They also had to minimize food requirements because of the uncertainty of food supplies in the deep jungle, and on and on. Mitchell was able to enumerate an array of arguments for why it was advantageous for pygmies living in their world to be so small. In his conclusion he was able to pose the following question. Given all these more or less convincing advantages of smallness, the real question must be why pygmies are so big.

CONCLUSIONS

So it is clear that even good guys can have problems. but it is also clear that we have accomplished a great deal. Over the last 10 or 15 years there have been enormous changes in the learning paradigm, and we can claim some credit for having helped to bring these changes about. One assumes that changes are always beneficial and advantageous, so we tend to think of ourselves as the good guys because we have helped things along in what we took to be the right direction.

There is an enormous amount of work yet to be done, of course. We have been just moving along in the right direction without any real sense of fulfillment or completion, and unfortunately, without being able to answer many of the important questions. We still do not know how reasonable or profitable it is to look at an animal's learning ability in terms of the selection pressures acting on it. We still have no good answer to the question of surplusage. We still do not know why pygmies are as big as they are.

But at the same time, we can celebrate the fact that Goliath has fallen. The learning establishment that existed 10 or 15 years ago is now pretty well disintegrated. Different processes are now conceived, different elements are now assumed to be associated. There is fairly widespread and growing recognition of the fact that learning must have biological significance, in addition to adhering to the general associationistic formula. Perhaps more than anything else, we have engendered a search for the answers to a wide variety of behavioral questions that heretofore simply had not been raised. It is apparent that those of us who originally defended the idea that biological considerations are relevant to learning have every reason to rejoice.

REFERENCES

Baum, W. M. (1973). The correlation-based law of effect. *Journal of the Experimental Analysis of Behavior, 20,* 137–153.

Beecher, M. D. (1981). Development of parent–offspring recognition in birds. In R. Aslin, J. Alberts, & M. Petersen (Eds.), *Development of perception* (Vol. 1). New York: Academic Press.

Boice, R. (1977). Surplusage. *Bulletin of the Psychonomic Society, 9*, 452–454.

Bolles, R. C. (1970). Species-specific defense reactions and avoidance learning. *Psychological Review, 77*, 32–48.

Breland, K., & Breland M. (1961). The misbehavior of organisms. *American Psychologist, 16*, 681–684.

Breland, K. & Breland, M. (1966). *Animal behavior.* New York: Macmillan.

Collier, G. H. (1982). Determinants of choice. *Nebraska Symposium on Motivation.* Lincoln: University of Nebreska Press.

Garcia, J., & Koelling, R. A. (1966). Relation of cue to consequence in avoidance learning. *Psychonomic Science, 4*, 123–124.

Grice, G. R. (1948). The relation of secondary reinforcement to delayed reward in visual discrimination learning. *Journal of Experimental Psychology, 38*, 1–16.

Herrnstein, R. J. (1970). On the law of effect. *Journal of the Experimental Analysis of Behavior, 13*, 243–266.

Johnston, T. D. (1981). Contrasting approaches to a theory of learning. *Behavioral and Brain Sciences, 4*, 125–173.

Kuhn, T. S. (1970). *The structure of scientific revolution.* Chicago: University of Chicago Press.

Logue, A. W. (1979). Taste aversion and the generality of the laws of learning. *Psychological Bulletin, 86*, 276–296.

LoLordo, V. M. (1979). Selective associations. In A. Dickinson, & R. A. Boakes (Eds.), *Mechanisms of learning and motivation.* Hillsdale, N. J.: Lawrence Erlbaum Associates.

Meyer, D. R., Cho, C., & Wesemann, A. F. (1960). On problems of conditioned discriminated lever-press avoidance responses. *Psychological Review, 67*, 224–228.

Olton, D. S., & Samuelson, R. J. (1976). Remembrances of places past: Spatial memory in rats. *Journal of Experimental Psychology: Animal Behavior Process, 2*, 97–116.

Rescorla, R. A. (1980). *Second-order conditioning.* Hillsdale, N. J.: Lawrence Erlbaum Associates.

Rozin, P., & Kalat, J. W. (1971). Specific hungers and poison avoidance as adaptive specializations of learning. *Psychological Review, 78*, 459–586.

Schmidt–Nielsen, K. (1972). *How animals work.* London: Cambridge University Press.

Seligman, M. E. P. (1970). On the generality of the laws of learning. *Psychological Review, 77*, 406–418.

Shettleworth, S. J. (1972). Constraints on learning. In D. S. Lehrman, R. A. Hinde, & E. Shaw (Eds.), *Advances in the study of behavior*, (Vol. 4). New York: Academic Press.

Spence, K. W. (1947). The role of secondary reinforcement in delayed reward learning. *Psychological Review, 54*, 1–8.

Staddon, J. E. R., & Simmelhag, V. L. (1971). The "superstition" experiment: A reexamination of its implications for the principles of adaptive behavior. *Psychological Review, 78*, 3–43.

Symons, D. (1979). *The evolution of human sexuality.* New York: Oxford University Press.

Williams, D. R., & Williams, H. (1969). Automaintenance in the pigeon: Sustained pecking despite contingent nonreinforcement. *Journal of the Experimental Analysis of Behavior, 12*, 511–520.

15 The General Process Approach to Animal Learning

Sam Revusky
Department of Psychology
Memorial University of Newfoundland

This is a negativistic chapter. I disagree strongly with the traditional behavioristic approaches to animal learning. But I also disagree with the naturalistic approaches that are offered as an alternative to it by most of the other authors in this book. These tend to suggest greater species and situational differences in learning than exist. Evolutionary contraints have made learning a general biological process in about the same sense as respiration. The differences in the overt course of learning exhibited by different mammalian phyla are due to relatively minor adjustments in this underlying process. This general process ought to be the main subject matter for most of those with a primary interest in animal learning. These points are explained in more detail later in the chapter.

THE IDEOLOGY OF TRADITIONAL BEHAVIORISM AND ITS SCIENTIFIC INADEQUACY

Nowadays behaviorism is taken to be any belief that psychological functions are a result of biological processes. Thus it often is used as a synonym for scientific virtue rather than to denote a specific scientific approach. This overinclusive definition would define as behaviorists many psychologists who lived in the nineteenth century prior to the advent of behaviorism and many who combated the early behaviorism. A meaningful analysis of behaviorism requires that it be described in terms of what was unique to the behavioristic approach.

In this chapter, the term behaviorism is narrowly defined with regard to the study of animal learning as the insistence that learning is acquisition of a change in behavior. Any neural change involved in learning must be supposed to follow the same rules as changes in muscular and glandular behavior. Behavioristic theories of learning as defined here deny the existence of any acquisition of knowledge that does not follow rules of classical conditioning or instrumental learning obtained through the study of overt animal responses.

The Main Objection to Behaviorism

Essentially, behaviorism translates the concept of acquisition of knowledge into the concept of acquisition of behavior. Behaviorism arose at the turn of the twentieth century, when there were few physical models, such as computers, for the acquisition of knowledge. Hence knowledge seemed like a Platonic concept too closely aligned with traditional mind–body dualism to serve as a meaningful scientific concept. In classical behavioristic approaches, informational encoding in the nervous system was tacitly excluded from the definition of a change in behavior to combat the historical tendency to treat the nervous system as a surrogate for the metaphysical mind (Kantor, 1947). In contrast, a change in an animal's behavior was measurable, at least in principle, in the same way as part of its anatomy.

When the behaviorist did refer to neural changes during learning, he or she tended to assume that these were exactly parallel to the acquisition of overt behavior. This is roughly equivalent to the theory that each cell contains mechanisms that parallel lungs, teeth, and a mouth to permit absorption of oxygen and of nutrients from the blood. It has been ridiculed by W. K. Honig (unpublished manuscript) as follows:

> It may be attractive to think that behavioristic principles can account for nonbehavioral activity, but it is gratuitous to assume that the empirical paradigm for behavior should be incorporated, somehow, into the functioning of the nervous system. What separates the sciences are discontinuities in mechanism—those boundaries at which a set of facts *cannot* be explained by reference to terms of processes based upon the paradigm within which these facts were gathered and organized. I have called the postulation of little theoretical stimuli and responses the creation of a "behaviorunculus" with which behaviorists replaced the "homunculus"—the little man inside the big man—that they were trying to get rid of. The role of behavior, little or big, overt or covert, in the explanation of intellective processes has to be established by observation and not postulation.

Honig is sarcastically mimicking behavioristic polemics to make the point that the. behaviorists were guilty of fallacies similar to those against which they preached. *Homunculus* is a pejorative term used by behaviorists to refer to a mentalistic proclivity for naming internal processes instead of explaining behavior. *Behaviorunculus* is the name of a system inside the animal with exactly the same properties as the observed behavior.

Behaviorunculus theory has historically been characteristic of behaviorism although a small minority did define behaviorism as broadly as some define it today, as a more moderate commitment to objective scientific method. E. C. Tolman (1932), who called himself a cognitive behaviorist, is the most prominent example. Like thorough-going behaviorists such as Guthrie (1952), I am unwilling to define him as a behaviorist because he had a concept of knowledge independent of behavior. He is better considered a functionalist, like E. L.Thorndike or John Dewey.

I tend to use examples from the Hullian tradition because they are a bit extreme and thus illustrate my points clearly, but I do not mean to restrict my scope to Hullian psychology. One reviewer of an earlier draft of this chapter was apparently a follower of B. F. Skinner and claimed that my objections to behaviorism do not apply to his work. It is true that Skinner shares Tolman's molar approach to behavior and has come to emphasize molar performance more than learning. Nevertheless, Skinner is emphatic in his insistence that behavior is to be explained in terms of other behavior rather than in terms of underlying processes. This is clear from his work on schedules of reinforcement (Ferster & Skinner, 1957). Skinner's (1957) book on verbal behavior shows that he was committed to the view that all thought must follow the rules of classical or instrumental conditioning. This is philosophically closer to classical behaviorism than to Tolman.

Tabula rasa Theory

Although Woodworth and Sheehan (1964) were right to insist that extreme environmentalism is not *logically* a corollary of behaviorism, dogmatic environmentalism has been so closely intertwined with the behavioristic approach to the study of animal learning that it may be considered one of its defining characteristics. Learning was never initiated by the animal. Instead external reinforcement from the environment produced learning in a passive animal. Traditional students of learning have tended to be such extreme environmentalists that they treat the animal as a black box, an instrument with controls operated by the environment. Why such an odd doctrine?

The main cause of this environmentalist bias was a theory that predates behaviorism, the *tabula rasa* model of the mind. This is the doctrine that the mind is like a blank slate written upon by experience. Presumably, the mind takes impressions that objectively reflect the outer world, just as soft wax takes impressions that objectively reflect the object to be copied. Because learning is an adaptation to those causal relationships in biological environments that are very changeable, such a flexible system seems at first to be scientifically reasonable. Cues valid in one time or place may become invalid at another time or in another place or may even change meaning. A mind like a ball of wax, continually remolded by experience, may seem like a good model for the learning process.

Still, as Barzun (1972) has explained, the tenacity with which *tabula rasa* theory was held by its early popularizers, the 17th- and 18th-century British empiricists, is attributable to its importance as a rationale for the Age of Reason. For Reason to take the place of inherited authority and religion as an objective guide, it always must lead to the same valid conclusions regardless of who does the reasoning. If different minds were to come to different conclusions after similar experiences, the mind would not be an objective instrument and reason would not be an infallible guide. The *tabula rasa* doctrine that the mind translates sequences of sense impressions into conclusions in a straightforward way predetermined by the environment guarantees that all reasonable people will reach the same conclusions.

The *tabula rasa* doctrine had a related implication that was also politically loaded: the perfectability of mankind through changes in the environment. Translated into behaviorism, this doctrine led to the conjecture of John B. Watson (1919), that with a proper environment any healthy child could be reared to any skilled profession, such as medicine or law. In another form, this doctrine was to allow B. F. Skinner (1948) to suggest how the environment could be arranged to produce a Utopia to bring out the best in man.

The world would be a worse place without the social benefits that have resulted from the ideology that man can be improved by improving his environment. But the price for these benefits has been a distortion of scientific approaches to animal learning. If behavior is conditioned by the environment like a lump of clay, then the biology of the animal is not important for understanding how to control behavior. Hence there has been almost an antibiological bias in animal learning theory (Hinde, 1973; Pavlov, 1932). This bias is reinforced by the professional interests of those students of animal learning, like myself, with minimal backgrounds in the biological sciences.

Despite its apparent plausibility, the *tabula rasa* doctrine as developed through traditional learning theories implied a very inadequate learning system. The real learning system allows use of inherited information. For instance, animals selectively associate between feeding cues and sickness rather than between external cues and sickness (Garcia & Koelling, 1966). Animals without such an associative predisposition would be unlikely to learn that eating a particular food produces sickness hours later, because they would be confused by all the extraneous information with which they are bombarded during the delay. There are many instances for selective association in addition to those involved in feeding behavior (LoLordo, 1979), and the *tabula rasa* approach is to blame for the past failure of behaviorists to look for them or even to consider that they might exist.

Furthermore, the habits of thought generated by the *tabula rasa* doctrine resulted in a tacit assumption that would have seemed weird had it been made explicit. It was that all classes of animals (at least among the vertebrates) would somehow come to the same conclusions as a result of the same experiences. In other words, intelligence was seen as something that developed as a function of the phylogenetic scale, but there was no consideration of the possibility that animals in specific ecological niches might develop a specific intelligence to fit these niches. As already indicated, I strongly believe in the existence of a general learning process, which is a general intelligence. Nevertheless, the nearly complete neglect of specific intelligence among traditional animal learning theorists must be attributed to the *tabula rasa* doctrine.

Uselessness of the Behavioristic Definition of Learning

Behavioristic dogmaticism was so pronounced as to prevent development of a useful definition of learning. To illustrate this, I use the definition from what is generally recognized to be the best empirically oriented, advanced learning text of the 1960s: Kimble's (1961) revision of Hilgard and Marquis' *Conditioning and Learning*: "Learning is a relatively permanent change in behavioral potentiality which occurs as a result of reinforced practice" (p.6). It is fair to use this as a behavioristic definition because it is probably the most widely used single behavioristic definition of learning and does not illustrate behavioristic dogmaticism in its heyday but a much-moderated later form of it. I am innocent of selecting a careless definition to use as a straw man. In 1967, Kimble wrote an essay about its implications that shows how he carefully wrote the definition with a view to overcoming the shortcomings of earlier behavioristic definitions of learning. From my point of view, this same essay shows how the basic behavioristic approach to learning prevents rigorous scientific analysis.

Dogmas Inculculated by Kimble's Definition

Learning Defined as a Change in Behavior. Early behavioristic definitions of learning specifically stated that learning must be considered a change in behavior. Kimble tried to liberalize this doctrine by using the weaker term, *change in behavioral potentiality*, to describe learning. But the dogmaticism inherent in behaviorism made this difficult to accomplish. Kimble explained why he felt the traditional definition needed to be liberalized in his 1967 essay:

> Learning is commonly defined as simply a "change in behavior." This statement seems incomplete, however, because it is obvious that learning may occur when there is no change in behavior. We learn from school books, motion pictures, demonstrations, lectures, maps, and the gossip of our colleagues, but there is no immediate translation of such learning into performance. (p.86)

It was "obvious" to Kimble "that learning may occur when there is no change in behavior" because he unconsciously believed that learning is the acquisition of knowledge. If it is *obvious* that learning can occur in violation of the traditional behavioristic criteria, the real criteria for the occurrence of learning are not the alleged behavioristic criteria. If behavioristic definitions were definitions in, say, the same sense as mathematical definitions, learning without a change in behavior would be as inconceivable as a triangle with four angles. Kimbel's acceptance that learning can occur contrary to its definition was typical of behaviorists. According to older definitions of learning, considerably more restrictive than that of Kimble, learning could not occur without environmental reinforcement or without responses by the learner. But when it appeared that animals had acquired knowledge without reinforcement or responding, it was *obvious* to behaviorists that learning had occurred in apparent violation of the "scientific" definition. Their behavioristic ideology then led them to look for hidden reinforcements and/or hidden responses to explain the occurrence of learning. By their own avowed standards, they were closet mentalists because their real criterion for the occurrence of learning was the acquisition of knowledge. Because they fooled themselves into believing that they had behavioristic criteria for distinguishing between learned and unlearned changes in behavior, behaviorists never developed explicit and genuinely useful criteria.

Later in his essay on the definition of learning, Kimble (1967) almost apologized for his heretical reference to behavioral potentiality rather than behavior itself in his definition. He reaffirmed that a definition of learning should, as much as possible, insure that learning be considered as an acquisition of reactions. Only as a last resort, after all conceivable alternatives had been carefully considered, ought there to be any divergence from behavioristic right thinking (Kimble, 1967):

> In the case of certain concepts, the psychology of learning seems implicitly to have rejected certain elements of this definition. It has described as learned certain states of the organism such as inhibition, motivation and reinforcement which are neither behaviors nor potentialities for behavior. A wiser course might have been to pay closer attention to the reactions which serve as symptoms of those states and to consider the possibility that those reactions are those that are learned. (p.98)

To restate this stricture in Honig's sarcastic terminology, Kimble was demanding that before referring to learned states of the organism, one should carefully look for a behaviorunculus ("consider the possibility that those reactions are those that are learned"). As many behaviorist ideologues would have interpreted such advice, the time to cease looking for behavioruncuculi would have been indefinitely long in coming. In fairness, I should point out that Kimble himself ceased looking relatively early. Note, by the way, Kimble's flat refusal to consider inhibition, certainly a neural change, as a change in behavior. To be defined as a change in behavior, something had to be much like a classical response or an instrumental motor act.

Reinforcement as Necessary for Learning.   The belief that reinforcement from the environment is necessary if learning is to occur may be regarded as a mechanism that allows the environment to be responsible for learning in conformity with the *tabula rasa* doctrine. Traditionally, reinforcement was identified with obvious rewards and punishments or, occasionally, with other biologically important events. Kimble (1967) was trying to get away from that in order to be able to deal with effects like latent learning but failed because he was not willing to abandon his behavioristic framework. His definition of learning as a "change in behavioral potentiality which occurs as a result of reinforced practice" clearly implies that reinforcement is a necessary condition for learning.

To be able to deal with instances in which learning occurs without biologically important reinforcements, Kimble (1967) stated that the type of event that reinforces learning is an empirical question; it need not be a reinforcement in the traditional sense. Notice that this liberalization presupposes that learning cannot occur without some event (presumably from the external world) to reinforce it. Thus an indefinitely large number of conceivable hidden reinforcements are suggested so that it is harder than ever to disprove that reinforcement is necessary if learning is to occur. It was simply inconceivable to most traditional behaviorists that it is simply the nature of animals to learn about their environments in the same sense that it is their nature to grow, breathe, and reproduce. Rather, than must always be a reinforcing event from outside to make learning occur. This is still another type of antibiological bias.

Restriction to Associative Learning.   The dogma that an external reinforcing event is necessary for learning to occur also created confusion by restricting the definition of learning to associative learning. Learning about single events was excluded because it was assumed there could be no such thing as learning involving only a response or a CS in the absence of reinforcement. This effectively removed extinction from the category of learning because extinction, by definition, involves the occurrence of a response without later reinforcement.

The thoroughness with which the presupposition that learning depends on reinforcement pervaded all of Kimble's thinking about learning is illustrated by his (1967) claim that it is necessary to define learning as dependent on reinforcement on an empirical ground: If reinforcement were absent from the definition, extinction might be defined as a type of learning. He did not recognize that this "empirical ground" was really only a different form of the behavioristic dogma that learning depends on reinforcement. Similarly, effect such as habituation and sensitization, which also involve learning about single events not followed by reinforcement, were so thoroughly excluded from the definition of learning that they were regarded as artifacts in experiments about learning. Of course, habituation and sensitization are artifacts in studies of associative learning, and it is important to distinguish between associative learning and other types of learning. However, there is no empirical reason to restrict the definition of learning to include only associative learning.[1]

---

[1] From a classical standpoint, the material in this paragraph is distorted. In the traditional behaviorism, the animal did not learn an association or that two events occur in sequence. It learned only to emit a response. In the S–R behaviorism, it learned to emit this response in the presence of a

Inability to Eliminate Dogma even while Trying.   Material already quoted from Kimble's essay about the definition of learning shows that he was trying to liberalize traditional behaviorism by subsuming learning through observation in his defintion. Nevertheless, his adherence to a behavioristic framework forced him inadvertently to reaffirm the traditional dogma. He claimed learning was a result of "reinforced practice." In daily usage, "practice" implies overt activity; for example, practicing the piano is playing it, not listening to it. The term "reinforced" also implies the involvement of motor activity. Reinforcement was defined by Kimble (1961, p.5) in the usual manner as an event that follows a response and increases its subsequent probability. Hence, both words in the phrase "reinforced practice" imply that responding must be involved in learning. For Kimble to say what he seemed to want to say would have required him to refer to "experience," a term long considered mentalistic.

Inability even to Recognize Dogma.   Kimble's short definition of learning is as concerned with dogmas and with the interpretation of dogmas as a religious credo. Yet he asserted (Kimble, 1967) that it is "factual or empirical," suggesting a lack of strong arbitrary or ideological components. Such was the sway of behaviorism that, until recently, most learning psychologists would have agreed with him. In one sense, Kimble was right because he was contrasting his definition with definitions of learning in terms of underlying physiological processes. Still, only within the context of a strong, shared ideology would anyone claim such a definition was factual.

Inability to Function as a Definition

I have already alluded to the fact that behavioristic definitions were never used to determine when learning occurred. Now I demonstrate more completely how useless they were by comparing Kimble's definition relative to the following "unscientific" definition of learning: "Learning is the acquisition of knowledge through experience." This is a commonsense definition that an intelligent layman might casually offer without worrying about exact operational definitions of terms like *knowledge* and *experience*. Behaviorists used to humiliate their undergraduate students by various sophistical arguments when they offered similar "unscientific" definitions. However, although the layman's definition does not cover the acquisition of motor skills, it otherwise distinguishes between learned

---

stimulus because later reinforcement strengthened the stumulus–response bond. However, from a present-day vantage point, this type of learning may be considered to involve an association between a response and a reinforcement. Thus, if I were strictly accurate, I would state that the dogma that an external reinforcing event is necessary for learning restricted the definition of learning to *what I would call* associative learning. However, such extreme precision is tedious and I hope that this footnote makes it unnecessary.

behavior and unlearned behavior far more effectively than behavioristic definitions. Behavior that follows an experience can unequivocally show that the animal has acquired knowledge, although there was no change in behavior while the animal was being subjected to the original experience.

Controls for Learning.   The principles underlying the control procedures needed in the study of associative learning are quite simple in terms of something like the layman's definition of learning. Associative learning is learning (acquiring knowledge) that two events occur in sequence. Thus, a good control procedure is one in which the major elements of the associative learning procedure are present but are rearranged so the two events do not occur in sequence. If the same change in behavior is still obtained, there is no evidence for learning. For instance, if a tone precedes a shock on a number of occasions and, as a result, the animal exhibits fear to the tone, it seems to have learned that the tone precedes the shock. However, to be sure this interpretation is correct, one should rearrange the elements of this situation so that the animal experiences both the tone and the shock, but the tone does not regularly precede the shock. If the animal becomes just as fearful to the tone in the absence of tone–shock pairings, the fear to the tone resulting from the tone–shock pairings cannot be attributed to learning that the tone precedes the shock.

Of course, control procedures may contain extraneous features absent in the experimental procedure. Such features may make a definitive conclusion difficult, but the principle underlying the use of controls is clear. Changes in behavior due to sensitization, habituation, fatigue, and motivational changes are artifacts in an experiment about associative learning because they do not result from exposure to the sequential occurrence of the two events that the animal is to associate. Behaviorists cannot put things so simply because they insist that their primary concern is with the acquistion of responses and thus they confuse themselves thoroughly. Thus, to exclude such artifacts, Kimble (1967) added the phrase *relatively permanent* to his definition of learning. This circumlocution, like other circumlocutions (Rescorla, 1967), does not work. Learning can be very temporary—ask any teacher; motivational effects can be very long lasting—ask any psychotherapist.

Behavioristic Definition Yields False Claims of Learning.   The layman's definition of learning is superior to that of Kimble by yet another criterion. Some phenomena that fit Kimble's definition but do not fit the layman's definition are not considered instances of learning by anybody, even behaviorists. Suppose a middle-aged man in poor physical shape is reinforced daily with $20 after jogging 2 miles. As a result, his physical condition improves and he develops greater endurance in a variety of motor activities. This example fits Kimble's definition of learning because it is a "a relatively permanent change in behavioral potentiality which occurs as a result of reinforced practice," but nobody would call this learning. The real reason is that the change in behavioral potentiality is not due to any acquisition of knowledge. Of course, the man may be learning to jog better but his improved physical endurance is mainly due to an improvement in his health. This would be an instance of learning according to Kimble's definition.

It is clear that behavioristic definitions of learning exclude phenomena that ought to be included and include phenomena that ought to be excluded to a far greater extent than does a casual layman's effort. This proves that they are not scientific definitions at all but credos of a dogmatic theology. Of course, as in the case of outmoded religious dogmas, it may be possible to reinterpret behaviorism so that it would be acceptable today. But Kimble's failure to do this successfully shows how risky it is. I do not think it is worthwhile.

Retardation of Scientific Development by Behavioristic Dogma

It is common to claim that behaviorism was a boon for the study of animal learning because it resulted in the organized collection of data. I don't accept this. It is incorrect to give credit to a scientific approach for all discoveries made under its aegis. A theory can only be given credit for discoveries that could not reasonably be expected to have been made under the aegis of competing or alternative theories. I am certain that basic parametric studies, like those of the effects of amount of reward and deprivation on performance, would have been accomplished regardless of what theory was available. Many of these were direct developments of the work of Thorndike (1911) and of Pavlov (1927) and were not due to the specific behavioristic ideology I have described. To give specific credit to behaviorism for such discoveries seems silly to me. As McCullough (1979) has pointed out, it is even sillier to give credit for such discoveries to a specific behavioristic theory, such as that of Hull.

In general, theories do not usually generate research although they may channel it in a particular direction. The main factors generating the production of scholarly work are the activity levels and ambitions of individuals, the facilities available to them, and, in addition, perhaps, tenure and promotion policies of universities. Rarely, if ever, is any theory exciting enough to induce a person to do research, where he or she otherwise would have done none. Thus, the crucial question in evaluating theories is not whether they generated research, but whether they improved the quality of the research that was bound to have been done.

I admit that some important work, such as that on schedules of reinforcement (Ferster & Skinner, 1957) was probably advanced by the behavioristic ideology. However, my judgment is that overall, behaviorism interfered with progress in the area of learning by preventing undogmatic analysis of experimental findings.

Of course, I cannot prove this. But I can supply a number of examples of powerful resistance to inconvenient facts on the part of behaviorists.

Refusal to Accept Real Nature of Learning

By reasonable standards, the burden of proof upon traditional behaviorism became unacceptably heavy when Brogden (1939) showed that when a dog hears a buzzer and sees a light at the same time, it learns that the buzzer occurs together with the light even though there is no reinforcement or obvious change in behavior. To demonstrate this, Brogden devised the sensory preconditioning (SPC) method. Using dogs previously subjected to buzzer–light pairings, he paired the light with a shock so that the light elicited a defensive leg flexion. When the buzzer was presented in the absence of the light, it also elicited a leg flexion although it had never been directly paired with shock. Because the electric shock reinforcement had not been presented after the earlier buzzer–light pairings, this showed that the dogs had learned the buzzer–light association without reinforcement.

The discovery of SPC meant that neither a response nor a reinforcement is necessary for learning unless these terms are given meanings very different from those prevailing during the time the behaviorist approach to learning was developing. The obvious implication, that any reference to a response or reinforcement in the basic definition of learning is gratuitous, was resisted by fantastic demands that various far-fetched alternative explanations be excluded. We have seen an example in Kimble's (1967) claim that the event that reinforces learning is an empirical question. Others postulated important properties for the anticipatory and investigatory reactions that auditory and visual stimuli are likely to produce. Excessive ingenuity was used to avoid dealing with facts.

The Temporal Contiguity Dogma

The dominant behavioristic belief was that temporal contiguity (or near contiguity) between two events was necessary if associative learning was to occur. Presumably animals could not retain information for long enough to associate between events separated by as little as 10 seconds (Kimble, 1961). All instances of association over substantially longer delays were explained away in terms of some sort of indirect temporal contiguity. The most frequently used explanation was secondary reinforcement. A cue seemingly associated with a delayed primary reinforcer was supposed, in reality, to be associated with a secondary reinforcer that was, in turn, associated with a primary reinforcer. Hence what appeared to be association over a delay was explained away in terms of a combination of temporally contiguous associations.

The intuitive feeling that temporal contiguity is necessary for learning probably developed originally out of the *tabula rasa* doctrine, that the mind functions like a blank slate devoid of any innate propensity for selective association between particular types of events. This implies that the life of any animal is a chaotic confusion of sense impressions and hence makes it seem intuitively unreasonable that an animal should be able to connect a pair of them separated by a long delay. Later supports of the temporal contiguity doctrine were the belief that the animal learned like a very simple machine and the unwillingness of assume any type of memory except for a stimulus trace.

That dogmaticism underlay the temporal contiguity doctrine is shown in the very first sentence of what was long considered the best analysis of delayed reward, that of Kenneth Spence (1947): "One of the most puzzling problems facing the learning theorist has been that of explaining how a reward or goal situation which occurs after a stimulus response event (S–R connection) is apparently able to work back and strengthen it" (p. 1). How the reward works backward in time to strengthen the S–R connection is a problem only if it is tacitly assumed that several seconds after a stimulus–response coincidence, there is nothing stored in the animal's nervous system that can become affected by the delayed reward. What a fantastic assumption to make about an animal with billions of neurons in it! That this assumption was a result of a disciplined dogmatic refusal to consider obvious biological possibilities is shown by Spence's specific objections later in the same paper to any explanation of delay learning in terms of the nervous system. This would be "physiologizing," making indirect statements about the nervous system on the basis of behavior. Anybody who considered it obvious that the nervous system could store information was "physiologizing."

As explained in detail elsewhere (Revusky, 1977b), the experimental findings used to reinforce the temporal contiguity dogma really showed that animals cannot solve insoluble problems. It is unreasonable to expect an animal, moved into a strange laboratory apparatus loaded with sense impressions, to associate between two arbitrary sense impressions separated by a delay of as little as a minute when it is given minimal information as to which cues are to be associated. Any device that might have made the problem logically soluble was excluded, typically on the grounds that it produced secondary reinforcement.

The result was that ample evidence for long-delay learning typically was ignored by being labeled as though it were irrelevant to the study of associative learning (Revusky, 1977a; Revusky & Garcia, 1970). For instance, there was the delayed-reaction experiment (Tinklepaugh, 1928; Yerkes & Yerkes, 1928) which showed that monkeys and chimpanzees could remember over long delays which of two cups had been baited with food. Woodworth, a functionalist rather than a behaviorist, devoted two pages to discussing this in his 1938 text "Experimental Psychology." In a 1971 revision of this text, Kling and Schrier covered this material in a single sentence which suggested that 5 minutes was the maximum delay over which association was obtained. In fact, Tinklepaugh (1928) clearly referred to associations over delays of many hours. There also were findings that rats in runways and T-mazes could associate from one trial to another over long delays (Estes & Schoeffler, 1955; Petrinovich & Bolles, 1957; Tyler, Wortz, & Bitterman, 1953; Walker, 1956). Subsequent developments are described elsewhere (Lett, 1979; Lieberman, McIntosh, & Thomas, 1979).

Ignorance of Natural Behaviors

The followers of B. F. Skinner misinterpreted the key-peck of the pigeon as a model operant response for over two decades because they, like other behaviorists, were opposed to explaining behavior in terms of instincts and hence rarely were familiar with the natural behaviors of their animals. Following up Brown and Jenkins (1968) and Williams and Williams (1969), Moore (1973) and Jenkins (1973) have convincingly argued that the key-peck is not an operant at all but a classical response in which an instinctive peck is redirected from an innate releaser (or US in Pavlovian terms) toward a key. It is clear that much of what was considered evidence that "operant conditioning shapes behavior as a potter shapes a lump of clay" (Skinner, 1953) really depended on elicitation of key-pecking, a normal feeding reaction in pigeons, under circumstances in which food is obtained. Many of the triumphs of operant conditioning, like teaching a pigeon to bowl, involve, in reality, the elicitation of reactions exhibited by pigeons under natural conditions.

The work of E. R. Guthrie (1952), the worst example of a learning theorist dedicated to the proposition that animals function like extremely simple machines, illustrates the same point. The main evidence he offered to support his approach to learning was observations of the behavior of cats (Guthrie & Horton, 1946). Moore and Stuttard (1979) have shown that these cats were not learning at all but exhibiting an instinctive rubbing reaction in response to the presence of humans. In retrospect it is hard to imagine how anybody with any acquaintance with cats could have made the mistake Guthrie did. Guthrie's theory is still regarded as being of sufficient importance to merit a chapter in the most highly regarded single textbook on learning theory (Bower & Hilgard, 1981).

Only within a tradition in which biological factors were almost totally ignored could errors like these be perpetuated for decades.

INADEQUACY OF NATURALISTIC APPROACHES TO LEARNING

The deficiencies of the behavioristic general process approaches to learning have elicited various demands that the study of learning be based on the natural ecological roles of behavior. Presumably, just as the webbing on a duck's foot is adapted to the requirements of its ecological niche, so is a bit of behavior related to what the animal must do in its usual ecological niche. Given such a framework, investigators would be unlikely to mistake, for instance, an instinctive feeding reaction in the pigeon for a behavior shaped by reinforcement.

The main reason I oppose naturalistic approaches to learning is that I strongly believe in the existence of the general learning process described in the next section of this chapter. If there were no such general process, I would agree that learning ought to be studied in a naturalistic fashion, but I would not consider it a subject matter in itself. Rather, the subject matter would be ecology or the study of adaptive complexes, and "learning" would be a convenient word taken from ordinary lay language but would have no specific scientific meaning. That this is the underlying attitude of many of those who advocate naturalistic approaches to learning is illustrated, in my view, by T. D. Johnston's (1981) remark that his ecological approach to learning "deliberately blurs the distinction between development and learning" (p.135). Johnston would have been more exact if he had indicated that his approach eliminates this distinction at a scientific level so that learning is no longer a basic psychological or biological process. In fact, E. O. Wilson (1975) made exactly this claim: "The process of learning is not a basic trait that gradually emerges with the evolution of larger brain size. Rather it is a diverse array of peculiar behavioral adaptations, many of which have evolved independently and repeatedly in different animal taxa" (p.126).

Although my main disagreement with naturalistic approaches to learning centers on the factual question of whether a general learning process exists, I now explain how naturalistic approaches also are loaded with dogmas.

The Antiphysiological Bias

One does not have to deny the existence of a general learning process to oppose the general process approach to learning. In an extreme instance, Lorenz has claimed (Evans, 1974) that the general learning apparatus "is pretty much the same in cephalods, in crustaceans, in insects, and in vertebrates" (p.89) but that it is a simple feedback process of little importance. This claim was made in the context of an attack on Skinner and hence should not be taken quite literally, but it illustrates the active dislike of naturalists for the general process approach.

I don't think there is any underlying disagreement between Wilson, who claimed there is no general learning process, and Lorenz, who claimed that there is one but that it is relatively unimportant. They both don't like the approach. I think that, in addition to the deficiencies of traditional general process approaches as explained at the beginning of this chapter, professional biases are responsible. Ethologists and sociobiologists are naturalistic biologists who tend to dislike physiological methods and enjoy the analysis of biological diversity. They are veterans of the continuing Civil War in biology between naturalists and physiologists and do not like the artifical experimental devices of their opponents. The study of learning is typically as artificial as the most rarified physiology without the saving grace of being based on hard sciences.

Lorenz's naturalistic bias is much more extreme than that of most naturalistic students of behavior, but it supplies an insight into their mores. He feels that to deal with a subject matter, a scientist ought to be an expert on it through field observation rather than through experimental means. According to Lorenz (1970), to be an expert on behavior, one must "bring himself to stare at a fish, a bird or an ape with the unremitting persistence which is necessary in order to perceive the governing principles prevalent in the behavior of the animal" (p.xvi). He specifies that one cannot become an expert on behavior by experimentation: "In the study of behavior, more than in any other biological science, the modern contempt for purely descriptive observation and the tendency to premature experimentation does much damage by preventing young research workers from ever becoming experts and scientists" (p.xv). I infer that Lorenz regrets that the most prestigious biology is conducted by geneticists and molecular biologists devoid of naturalistic interests. I think a similar naturalistic bias is evident in the sociobiology movement, which seems to me much like an attempt to infuse greater prestige into the traditional biological topics that have been eclipsed by the high prestige of "unbiological" biologists. Many of the specific points about learning made by people with naturalistic mores (especially Lorenz, 1965) are absolutely correct. But because I think learning is best analyzed like a physiological process, I believe those motivated by a strong dislike of physiological methods are ill-equipped by temperament to offer a useful *general* approach to its study.

The Bias against Artificial Experimental Situations

When students of learning try to take on ethological mores, they get into untenable positions. An example is Schwartz's (1974) comment on the capacity of pigeons to learn sophisticated schedules of reinforcement in a Skinner Box:

> Thus, the general principles obtained in the laboratory may not apply to the species under study. However, these principles may well apply to man. It is odd, but perhaps reassuring, to think that by studying the behavior of pigeons, in arbitrary situations, one learns nothing about the principles which govern the behavior of pigeons in nature, but a great deal about the principles that govern the behavior of people. (p.196)

The valid core of Schwartz's argument is that experimentally oriented students of animal learning can strongly bias results by mistaking artificial experimental contrivances for basic facts about nature. This danger of all biological experimentation is especially great in the case of learning. Operant conditioning can become a study of tasks of interest primarily because they are clever inventions of experimenters. None have made this point as eloquently as Schwartz (particularly Schwartz, Schuldenfrei, & Lacey, 1978).

Nevertheless, Schwartz overstated this point by suggesting that abstract principles of learning demonstrated in a Skinner box may tell us "nothing about the principles which govern the behavior of pigeons in nature." Like the belief of early evolutionary theorists (Boice, 1977) that learning is not important in nature, this is incompatible with a reasonable approach to evolution. Only minor and relatively unimportant characteristics of animals (like the color of the internal organs) are likely to be unrelated to adaptation. I do not see how one can even imagine that performance under complex schedules of reinforcement can be unrelated to adaptation. Such a performance might involve, for instance, shifting from a high rate of response to a low rate depending on recent feedback.

If Schwartz is right in suggesting that the learning of schedules of reinforcement by the pigeon may have nothing to do with the pigeon, we have a burden of explaining why such performance occurs. Can it be an epiphenomenon resulting from the neural organization necessary for visual perception, an ability the pigeon certainly uses in nature? Can it be that whenever the nervous system becomes highly organized for any reason whatsoever, the capacity to learn reinforcement schedules automatically develops in spite of the fact that it is not specifically adaptive? Or perhaps the answer is simpler. The pigeon might have evolved from an ancestor for which such learning was adaptive. This intelligent ancestral bird might then have moved into an environment in which such learning was not adaptive (!!) and evolved into an animal that, in the Skinner box, somehow illustrates "principles that govern the behavior of people" but "may not apply to the species under study."

Of course, Schwartz means nothing like this but these ludicrous implications follow from his position and illustrate the danger of attempts to accommodate the naive view of learning usually held by naturalists. Schwartz certainly knows that discriminations based on temporal cues and on cues generated by the animal's own behavior govern performance on schedules of reinforcement (Ferster & Skinner, 1957). It is unreasonable to suppose that the pigeon does not use such cues under natural conditions. However, nature is not set up to illustrate this discrimination process, which can better be studied through schedules of reinforcement.

In general, the artificiality of learning experiments is nowhere as damning as naturalists may suggest. An experimental procedure creates a phenomenon that makes the principles underlying natural phenomena easier to understand, but it need not be natural. For instance, muscle tetanus seldom occurs in nature, but, like learning in a Skinner box, the principles it demonstrates apply to the species under study. Is a medical blood test invalid because the blood is treated in an unnatural way? In the case of the study of learning, there is an extra advantage in studying it under unnatural conditions. The learning mechanism has evolved particularly so that animals can adapt to changing conditions. Changing conditions are likely to differ from those with which the animal is familiar and, in that sense, they are less natural. It may be an advantage for analytic purposes when an experimental apparatus is far beyond the range of natural conditions for an animal. After all, that is the principle of the superstimulus, a perfectly respectable ethological device.

Oddly enough, I believe that the way in which learning in the Skinner box is a distortion of nature is exactly the opposite of the way naturalists think it is distorted. Not only is learning not an artifact of the experimental apparatus, but, like memory (Olton, 1979; Shettleworth, 1983), it is faster and more efficient under natural conditions than under artificial conditions. Under natural conditions, learning is made more useful by such adaptations to natural conditions as instinctive behaviors (Brown & Jenkins, 1968; Moore, 1973) and selective association (Garcia, McGowan, & Green, 1972). These may produce maladaptive learning under artificial conditions (McKearney, 1969; Morse, Mead, & Kelleher, 1967). On this basis, pigeons should be expected to use the proprioceptive and temporal cues responsible for learning in a Skinner box more effectively under natural conditions. Skinner boxes slow learning that is so fast under natural conditions that it is hard to observe. Even if learning were not so fast, field observation would be a poor method by which to observe it unless extremely careful precautions were taken. This methodological difficulty coupled with the lack of interest of ethologists in learning is probably responsible for the paucity of naturalistic investigations of learning that have encouraged the widespread opinion that learning is unimportant under natural conditions. Observing university students naturalistically would suggest that learning is as unimportant for them as it seems to be for the pigeon under natural conditions.

The Bias in Favor of Diversity

A more serious casualty than Schwartz of an attempt to approach learning from a naturalistic vantage point was Lockard (1971), who exaggerated the differences between different mammalian orders to the point of claiming that similarities in learning between rodents and primates are superficial because they "either nearly or completely fail to show a common ancestor" (p.174). This illustrates how radically specialized-adaptation approaches to learning can differ from traditional biology. Just as both rodents and primates have similar heart–lung-circulation systems, both have similar nervous systems indicative of common ancestry. Of course, Lockard did not mean exactly what he wrote, which would imply a return to the theory of separate creation. He meant that rats and primates are so distantly related that it makes no sense to extrapolate from one to the other. But, in fact, much of biology is based on such extrapolations. Despite this, some seem to take Lockard's entertaining polemics literally.

Overemphasis on evolutionary diversity at the expense of general principles in evolution is correlated with an overestimate of the speed of evolution. Faster evolutionary changes mean more diversity and greater importance of ecological factors. Lockard (1968) claimed that the albino rat has become degenerate as a result of selection for contingencies in breeding laboratories and/or by lack of evolutionary selection, and that substantial evolution of this type had occurred in only 10–25 generations. He assumed (Lockard, 1968) that the albino rat was so degenerate "as to be an indefensible choice not only in the realm of species-typical behavior, but also for diet and taste preferences (*albinus* may now eat whatever does not bite back), motivational mechanisms, and so on" (p. 739). It is now clear that the albino rat can select food quite well because it will associate between food and a sickness that occurs hours later (Revusky, 1968). There are only small differences in this respect between albino and half-wild rats (Rozin, 1968). However, Lockard's (1968, personal communication) reaction to such facts was not to admit that he had understated the generality of biological processes, but to postulate some new type of diversity. He claimed that the rat is unusually skilled at food selection because it is an omnivore and a scavenger. Thus, he proceeded from one theory to the opposite theory on the basis of a bias in favor of diversity that is characteristic of naturalistic students of behavior. This type of bias has been so influential that, for instance, many texts treat food-aversion learning as a species-specific adaptation in spite of the overwhelming evidence that it occurs in a very similar form throughout the vertebrates (Revusky, 1977a).

LEARNING AS A GENERAL BIOLOGICAL PROCESS

A general biological process exists when a wide variety of animals have evolutionarily related organ systems with similar functions that are partly determined by the nature of the environment. Mammalian respiration as described in basic textbooks of biology is a model of such a process: Oxygen is taken from the air, exchanged for waste products in the lungs, and then distributed by the action of the heart through the circulatory system where it is again exchanged for waste products in the cells. The similarity of these factors for all mammals defines mammalian respiration. Respiration differs in different species as a function of their ecologies and biological classes, but, as naturalists setting up a model for learning often forget, these are secondary to the general process.

The argument made in this section is that, contrary to E. O. Wilson's (1975) view that learning "is a diverse array of peculiar biological adaptations" (p. 126), mammalian learning can be considered general biological process in much the same sense as respiration.

Environmental and Biological Determinants

The main difference between the present approach and most of the ecological approaches likely to appear in this volume is in what is being adapted to. I see the learning processes as primarily an adaptation to principles of causality that allow causal inference and predictions about the future in nearly all biological environments. The adaptations to specific environments that naturalistic thinkers regard as the main basis for learning involve, at most, modifications of and superimpositions upon this basic process. These would correspond to the modifications of the mammalian respiratory process that allow a whale to function almost like a fish.

General principles of inference are valid for all biological environments. If this were not so, the first step for a biologist might be to develop a separate logic valid for inferences about the environment he is studying. In fact, methods of inference do not differ markedly from one biological situation to another, or even from one science to another. This common pattern of causal relationships means that common principles of learning can function effectively throughout the wide variety of ecologies and species in which learning occurs. Of course, animals do not use human verbal logic, but the same causality that permits human logic to function is responsible for the evolution of the portion of the nervous system responsible for learning. Thus causality has a role for learning parallel to the role of the similarity in mammalian gaseous environments for mammalian respiration.

Present Approach to Learning

According to the present point of view, the function of learning is the detection of causal relationships so that the animal can behave in a manner that anticipates the future. This allows animals to adapt to conditions that may change with the age of the animal, the season, or the ecology of a species (which is not absolutely fixed but may change from millenium to millenium).[2]

The aspect of learning that will concern us most is what I call the acquisition of knowledge through experience. Because the concept of knowledge cuts across many specific situations and responses, the acquisition of knowledge is a subject matter more abstract than either that of behaviorists or of ethologists. The role of behavior is to indicate that knowledge has been obtained. For instance, if a dog salivates to a tone after the tone has been paired with food and does not salivate to the tone under various control conditions, there is behavioral evidence that the dog has learned that the tone is followed by food. The particular behavior used as an indicator that the knowledge has been acquired is not critical. Of course, performance variables are a legitimate part of the study of learning but acquisition of knowledge is not a change in performance. Rather it is a process that underlies many different changes in performance.

I am innocent of structuring my task so as to make it trivially easy. I have emphasized a very psychological and apparently very unbiological aspect of

---

[2]Learning mechanisms may also be involved in the encoding of behavior that is entirely constant for a species. In embryology, it is found that certain characteristics are genetically encoded to develop as a result of interactions with the environment that are bound to occur. The same may apply to certain instinctive behaviors. But it is tedious to make such qualifications in the text.

learning, the acquisition of knowledge. Hence, unlike most behaviorists and ethologists, I have not distorted the nature of learning to implement my approach. I have also deliberately selected an unusually well-defined biological process, respiration, as a model. So I am not distorting biology to make it easier to treat the acquisition of knowledge as a biological process.

Evidence for the Existence of General Process Learning

So far, only one fact to support the existence of a general process for the acquisition of knowledge has been supplied. This is the existence of principles of causality in biological environments. I now show that the results of learning experiments support the existence of such a process. Furthermore, the principles of information processing required for a general learning process are easily within the known capacity of vertebrate nervous systems. I organize these points by means of a story but emphasize that its implications are backed by scientific facts throughout.

The story is that an imaginary logician gets sick and tries to acquire knowledge of what caused the sickness. He is a very clever fellow who goes about his task as well as feasible. Although our example involves detection of the cause of sickness, the principles of inference illustrated by the story apply to nearly all learning environments in much the same sense that the principles of a formal logical system are transsituational. Each step our logician takes is paralleled by a principle of animal learning that has been experimentally shown to apply to a variety of mammals in a variety of situations. These known principles of learning are of a type that can easily be modeled by a simple computer and hence ought to be within the capacity of the nervous system, which is far more complex. In fact, the case I make probably applies to vertebrates in general, not only mammals.

Our logician gets sick at 4:00 P.M. and wants to find out why. His activity may be divided for analytic purposes into two parts. The first part corresponds to what have traditionally been called parametric effects in learning; our man thinks about the sickness itself and all prior events, selecting all information relevant to the question of what caused the sickness. The second part of the learning process involves putting all this information together and coming to a tentative decision (or hierarchy of decisions).

Basic Parametric Effects

History with Sickness and with Foods Consumed before Sickness.   If our logician had experienced the same sickness on a number of occasions in the past, he might suspect that it is a chronic sickness and be less likely to attribute it to any particular precursor, such as the consumption of food. For instance, if he eats peppermint ice cream for the first time and then gets a migraine headache for the first time, he might attribute the headache to the ice cream, but he is less likely to do so if he has been getting headaches for years. Rats function in a similar way. When the same sickness has repeatedly occurred without being preceded by feeding cues, it is less likely to become associated with such cues (Braveman, 1977; Cappell & LeBlanc, 1977; Revusky & Taukulis, 1975). The same basic effect, called US habituation, applies to the capacity of shock to become associated with prior external cues both in rats (Rescorla, 1973) and in rabbits (Mis & Moore, 1973). It is reasonable to suppose that US habituation reflects evolutionary adapation to the fact that if an effect has repeatedly occurred in the absence of prior cues, the occurrence of such cues prior to that aftereffect on later occasions is likely to be due to chance.[3] Because such inference is valid for most animals in most environments, there is no reason for it to be species-specific or situation-specific. Hence it is probably a characteristic of the mammalian nervous system.

Similarly, if our logician has eaten peppermint ice cream regularly in the past without getting sick, he believes that it is unlikely to be responsible for the sickness. This illustrates a general principle of inference that is valid for all animals in all situations: A familiar cue is unlikely to be responsible for a novel aftereffect. Learning reflecting this principle is called latent inhibition. Lubow (1973) has documented that this process occurs in many species and many situations. There are no known situations in which it fails to occur. Of course, latent inhibition is never complete because a cue that did not predict an afteraffect formerly may, due to natural changes, come to predict that aftereffect. Thus the latent inhibition effect may be overridden by repeated trials.

Physical Intensity of Cues.   Our logician knows that the flavor of a food is an indicator of its chemical nature and that a strong flavor, on the average, indicates a higher concentration of important chemicals than a weak flavor. Hence he is more likely to blame a strong-tasting food for sickness than a bland food. This stimulus intensity principle holds not only in the poison-avoidance situation (Dragoin, 1971; Garcia, 1971) but in a wide variety of other situations (Hull, 1943; Pavlov, 1927), and, as far as is known, for all vertebrate species. It seems likely that under natural conditions stronger cues, such as loud sounds, are more important than weaker cues. For instance, although some predators have learned to be very silent, bigger animals tend to make more noise and to be more

---

[3]US habituation may conceivably be due to some sort of mechanism by which the US is associated with extraneous cues that happen to occur during the US-alone presentations. The effects of learning parameters can be analyzed either in terms of mechanism or in terms of adaptiveness, and one analysis does not invalidate the other (although sometimes it may trivialize it).

dangerous than smaller animals. Of course, the usual intuitive explanation of stimulus intensity effects is that stronger stimuli are bound to affect sensory systems more than weaker stimuli can. This cannot be denied and must be part of any explanation. However, because animals can perceive very weak stimuli perfectly well, it is unreasonable to suppose that stimulus intensity effects have their prominent role in learning mainly because animals cannot respond to weak stimuli. It is much more reasonable to suppose that stimulus intensity effects occur at least partly because they are usually adaptive.

Learning Trials.   Of course, the likelihood that our logician will attribute his sickness to the food is bound to increase with the number of past experiences in which the same food has been consumed prior to sickness. One pairing of a particular food with sickness could well be due to chance, but a number of such pairings indicate a causal relationship. Improvement in learning over trials is the general case for animals; contrary reports results from measurement techniques insensitive, for various reasons, to graded changes in learning (Mackintosh, 1974).

The adaptive value of the trials effect is not as widely recognized as it ought to be because students of learning are ontogenetically adapted to the ecology of universities where the desideratum is to learn instantaneously: Truth is the response that will be rewarded by the teacher, and everything he or she says and/or that appears in a textbook is true. Often it is possible to succeed in university courses by having the mind of a tape recorder. It is no wonder that professors habituated to this state of affairs suppose instantaneous learning is intelligent learning. In contrast, nature often lies to men and animals because events can occur together without being causally related. An ideal logician will notice a single occurrence of two events in sequence and act very tentatively on this basis, but he will remain uncertain about the existence of a causal relationship in the absence of additional experience. Similarly, it can be very important for an animal not to learn perfectly. For example, if an animal were to learn taste aversions perfectly to each food consumed during the hours preceding sickness, it might well develop so many aversions as to starve to death. Also, an animal that suffered pain and immediately associated it with all previous events might become so afraid of its normal environment as to be incapacitated. The same is true for humans also. Psychotherapists dealing with neurotics are likely to be more concerned with maladaptive learning that has occurred than with adaptive learning that has not occurred.

From a physical and/or chemical standpoint, instantaneous and complete learning can very simply and easily be accomplished. It is unreasonable to expect that evolution cannot produce a similar function if it is adaptive. All we know about machines that handle information indicates that fast, indiscriminate learning without forgetting is so simple to accomplish that it is characteristic of our cheapest devices: switches that have two states, on and off, and "remember" their preceding state until it is changed. Devices analogous to the slow selective learning of animals require more sophisticated mechanisms. Of course, I am referring only to the speed of learning and not to what an animal can learn.

The trials effect is only one of a number of cases in which apparent imperfections in learning or memory should be considered adaptive in nature rather than due to limitations of the learning process. The tendency to treat the learning process as though it were an indiscriminate absorption of information has resulted in an unfortunate underestimate of its intricacy.

Forgetting and Extinction.   Forgetting is an adaptation to the fact that the greater the duration of time since the original learning, the more likely it is that the original learning is no longer valid. Our logician would give more weight to recent experiences than to earlier experiences in his assessment of what is responsible for the sickness. Animals react in a similar way both in taste-aversion learning (McLaurin, Farley, & Scarborough, 1963) and in other learning tasks (Spear, 1978). Because the simplest physical and chemical devices remember indefinitely, there is no reason to doubt that perfect memory would have evolved had it been adaptive. Animals forget because, for instance, what is true in the spring may become false by autumn. Luria (1968) showed how maladaptive a perfect memory can be for a human. If a child forget nothing as it grew to adulthood, it would never have to relearn and hence would continue to understand everything from the perspective of a child.

Of course, extinction occurs more readily than forgetting because the animal has evidence that the situation has changed. There is no need to say more.

Temporal Proximity.   Our logician is more likely to attribute his sickness to something eaten just before the sickness than to something eaten long before it. Philosophical fine points aside, closeness in time is a useful criterion for a cause–effect relationship. The enhancement of learning by temporal proximity is so well documented that specific instances are unnecessary. There seems to be an additional rule, the temporal contiguity principle, that two events actually coinciding in time are substantially more likely to be associated than two events separated by only a 0.5 second gap (Kamin, 1965). This temporal contiguity principle is probably an adaptation to the causal nature of biological environments, because there is no doubt of the ability of animals to retain information for 0.5 sec. Sensations that occur at the same time are more likely to be different aspects of the same event than sensations separated by a split second.

Selective Association.   The logician in our story is far more concerned with what he ate than with other events preceding sickness. Like all mammals, he acts as if sickness is more likely to be due to what is eaten than to external events. This supposition is wired into the nervous system (Garcia & Ervin, 1968) because it is valid in the vast majority of environments. It is hard to imagine how, for instance, a rat could associate sickness specifically with a food eaten hours earlier if it did not possess selective association to keep it from confusing itself by considering all the visual and auditory cues experienced during the preceding hours. Also, Lett (1979) has pointed out that if animals associated all stimuli equally well with sickness, an instance of sickness might be falsely associated with environmental cues with the absurd result that the animal might be driven out of its usual ecological niche. This is not to say that selective association is so complete that external stimuli can never become associated with sickness. However, such association requires repeated pairings and optimal parametric conditions.

Because the occurrence of selective assocation does not fit the *tabula rasa* model, it has often been labeled as a biological constraint upon learning. This label tacitly makes the absurd suggestion that the remainder of the learning process is not biologically constrained. Even if learning adhered to the *tabula rasa* model, it would depend on an inherited nervous system adapted to the causal nature of the environment and would thus be biologically constrained. To avoid having an attempt at a scientific description of learning marred by echoes of irrelevant philosophies, I have deliberately classified selective association as a parameter of learning, not as an exception to the usual principles of learning.

My refusal to admit there is anything special about selective association would be a type of obsfucation if selective associations were highly species-specific or situation-specific and the main determinant of the course of learning. Then it might be desirable to study learning mainly in ecological terms with the general process as an afterthought. In fact, however, selective association between tastes and sickness, the most pronounced type of selective association, probably occurs in all mammals. Although it speeds up taste-aversion learning greatly, it in no way nullifies the effects of the other parameters of learning except for allowing associations over long delays (Revusky, 1977b).

There is some variation among mammals in the extent to which cues other than taste are associated with sickness. For instance, guinea pigs associate the appearance of drink with sickness much more readily than rats (Braveman, 1974), but it would be a great exaggeration to suggest that individual species easily develop special types of selective association. In many cases and perhaps in most cases, avoidance of nontaste feeding stimuli on the basis of experience with sickness is potentiated by taste associations, which are primary. Although birds might be expected, on the average, to use vision for the purpose of feeding more than mammals, many bird families develop aversions to the color of food as a secondary result of learned taste aversions (Clarke, Westbrook, & Irwin, 1979; Garcia & Rusiniak, 1980; Gillette, Martin, & Cunningham, 1980; Lett, 1980). The complexities of selective association in feeding behavior are reviewed by Lett (in press).

I do not know to what extent other types of selective association are specific to limited classes, orders, or species of mammals because there have been few studies outside of the feeding system. LoLordo (1979) and his colleagues have done substantial work on selective association in pigeons involving vision and audition, and there probably are similar effects in different families of mammals.

Integration of Information

Now we come to a property of learning that is more interesting than parametric effects, the integration of information. Just as the process of visual perception organizes the light energy that impinges on the eye into meaningful entities, so does the process of learning organize experience. In the visual system, the reaction to any particular light stimulus depends on the entire pattern of stimulation. The same applies to individual stimulus events in the learning system. To speak of learning about a single event or about an association between two events is a simplification for analytical purposes. The animal is, as it were, always considering all the relevant facts.

A major principle of organization in the learning system is concurrent interference (Revusky, 1971). It resembles the denouement of a detective story. As the story ends, the reader suspects different characters to different extents, but when the detective unmasks X as the murderer, the reader immediately loses his or her suspicion of the other characters. If X is the murderer, the other suspects must be innocent. Although such a rule occasionally leads to a false conclusion (as with conspiracies), it is generally useful. Our logician will use the same rule: If he got sick shortly after breakfast and had only eggs, he will consider the possibility that the eggs were responsible for the sickness even though he might have consumed eggs without sickness for many decades. But if he had caviar for the first time in his life at breakfast in addition to his eggs, he will almost certainly attribute the sickness to the caviar. Thus, our logician's suspicion of the eggs will be inversely related to his suspicions of other potential causes of the sickness.

In general, concurrent interference is the reflection in learning of the following principle: The likelihood that X is the cause of Z is inversely related to the likelihood that some other event is the cause of Z. During learning, the initial likelihoods, prior to adjustment by the operation of concurrent interference, are determined by the parametric principles of learning. Although concurrent interference is described heuristically here, it has also been expressed in a number of more rigorous ways and been studied extensively (Rescorla & Wagner, 1972; Revusky, 1971, 1977b). As far as is known, it is present in all animal learning although, like almost any other biological effect, it can be overridden in special cases (Kelleher & Gollub, 1962; Lett, in press).

Although concurrent interference results in what seems like a very cognitive mental process, the comparison of all causes likely to produce an effect, it is easily understandable in terms of neural principles. If a learned association occurs due to a connection between neurons that carry information about the events to be associated, concurrent interference must inhibit that connection. Inhibition of a neural connection by another connection involving one of the same neurons is commonplace. For instance, it is accepted that inhibitory processes in vision degrade redundant sensory input to highlight features that make visual experience more meaningful. Similarly, concurrent interference degrades confusing or redundant associations that might interfere with perception of a meaningful causal environment. I also like to compare concurrent interference to the operation of those radio circuits (automatic frequency control) that degrade weaker signals in order that the stronger signals will be heard clearly.

Conservatism of the General Learning Process

The preceding material demonstrates great similarities in learning in a wide variety of animals and similarity in the causal structures of a wide variety of biological environments. Arguments that may be used to dispute the implication that learning is a general biological process have, as far as I know, no real parallel in the discussion of any other biological process. Ethologists, with their great emphasis upon evolutionary diversity, may tend to suppose that the similarities in learning of different animal classes might have evolved independently due to similar evolutionary pressures. They might take the similarity of causal structures in many biological environments as the cause of independent evolution of different learning mechanisms with similar functions, just as similar environmental pressures caused flying to evolve independently in bats and birds. But although logically defensible, this type of argument is unconvincing when applied to mammalian (and even vertebrate) learning. Independent evolution usually occurs when there is a need for a function in one species but not in related species. But when, as is the case of learning, all species in a large category make use of the same biological function, it tends to be controlled by the same basic process with modifications for special situations. Furthermore, flying in bats and birds must have evolved independently because each depends on a different organ system. In contrast, all vertebrate learning is dependent on the same basic nervous system.

It may be thought that my use of the nervous system to help define the general learning process is not valid, because the nervous system does not define learning as rigidly as the lungs define respiration. By this argument, small changes in the nervous system over different mammalian orders may well yield substantially different learning processes. But this is a gratuitous presupposition of diversity under conditions where evolution tends to be conservative. The similarity in causal relationships in different environments means there is no need (that is, no evolutionary pressure) for different learning processes in different mammalian orders. Under such circumstances, one would expect the same basic nervous system to result in the same basic learning process. Of course, there may be variations in this mammalian learning process similar to those in mammalian respiration.

There is another class of evidence that it is unreasonable to regard learning as a number of specific adaptations that have all taken the same form due to similar environmental pressures rather than as a general process. Learning simply is not tailored to very specific situations in the way it would have to be if it were a set of specific adaptations. A general biological process differs from specific adaptations in that it can be maladaptive in particular situations. For instance, the same immune reactions that protect animals against sickness can be so maladaptive as to produce harmful allergies and perhaps some cancers. In much the same way, the generally adaptive learning process can be maladaptive in specific instances. These instance are of little importance in nature but can be demonstrated in the laboratory and elucidate the learning process in the same way that optical illusions elucidate the general perception process. If learning had the almost limitless plasticity implied in the writings of naturalistic students of learning, these instances of minor maladaptiveness would not exist.

One example, described in more detail elsewhere (Revusky, 1977a), is the occurrence of sensory preconditioning (SPC) in the feeding situation: A rat consumes, for instance, saccharin solution prior to or together with vinegar solution and then it is made sick after drinking vinegar solution in the absence of any saccharin. A subsequent test reveals a learned aversion to saccharin solution (Lavin, 1976). This aversion is slightly maladaptive because it is a near certainty that, under natural conditions corresponding to those of the SPC experiment, the substance with the role of saccharin would be safe for the animal because it consumed the saccharin solution during the saccharin–vinegar pairing without getting sick. Indeed, the most reasonable inference is that saccharin is an antidote to the sickness that usually follows consumption of vinegar solution. Most likely the occurrence of SPC in the feeding situation is a spillover from its adaptiveness in other situations. For instance, if a sound and a visual cue coincide in a normal environment, probably the same animal is responsible for both. If the animal later learns that pain follows one of these cues, it is adaptive for it to be fearful of the other cue. Presumably the general learning process makes a similar inference in the case of feeding behavior, although it is slightly maladaptive. An alternative possibility is that SPC is not specifically adaptive by itself but is an epiphenomenon of the general associative learning process. But this also contradicts the view that learning is a grab bag of specific adaptations because different specific adaptations should not all yield a similar epiphenomenon.

Revusky (1977a) has also described how the procedural difference between latent inhibition and conditioned inhibition, which at first blush seems trivial, has similar effects in food-aversion learning and in other types of learning (Reiss & Wagner, 1972; Taukulis & Revusky, 1975). This is not specifically adaptive in the feeding situation and would not make much sense if learning were a grab bag of situation-specific adaptations.

Response Acquisition

I have paid less attention to response acquisition than to the acquisition of knowledge because it is not as well understood as the acquisition of knowledge, despite having been regarded by behaviorists as the main subject matter for students of learning for the better part of a century. Still, it is certain that there are at least two types of response acquisition, each of which is obtained in many classes of vertebrates.

One of these is instrumental learning, in which the animal seeks out what improves its circumstances; that is, if it has acquired the knowledge that a response will get it what it needs, the animal will make the response. I know this description seems rather vague but it is not possible to be more precise right now. As far as is known, instrumental learning only occurs in mammals (Jenkins, 1973).

There is also a Pavlovian type of response acquisition in which a CS association with a US comes to elicit a response similar to that elicited by the US. Moore (1973) has summarized how this can produce motor performance in animals ranging from monkeys to fish. It is also responsible for smooth-muscle and glandular responses and for at least some conditioning involving physiological responses (Eikelboom & Stewart, 1982). It has one mark of a general biological process in that it is usually quite adaptive but occasionally can be maladaptive. Moore (1973) suggested that the instances of self-punitive behavior, in which monkeys come to shock themselves repeatedly (McKearney, 1969; Morse, Mead,& Kelleher, 1967), is a specific situation in which such Pavlovian conditioning leads to maladaptive results.

I presently incline to Eikelboom and Stewart's (1982) belief that those instances in which Pavlovian CRs appear to be opposite to their URs are artifacts of incorrect identification of the UR. If this turns out to be correct, the feedback loop in which the CR imitates the UR has remarkable generality. However, even if there is a separate type of Pavlovian conditioning in which the CR opposes the UR (Solomon, 1980), there is more than enough generality to response acquisition to mandate a general process approach.

SUMMARY

The traditional behavioristic approach to learning is unworkable. Naturalistic approaches would be preferable if learning were a set of peculiar behavioral adaptations. However, there is good evidence that learning is a general biological process adaptive to the causal relationships inherent in natural environments.

There may be instances of learning in vertebrates that are not due to the general learning process. I do not know enough about birdsong to venture an opinion about its relationship to a general process. But the existence of instances of behavior categorized as learning that are not due to the general process is not evidence against the general process. All biological general processes have limitations of this type.

ACKNOWLEDGMENTS

Laurel Furomoto, Peter Harley, Lois Hayweiser, Michael Lavin, Bow Tong Leti, Alexandra Logue, Horace Marchant, Bill Montevecchi, Richard Pohl, and Abraham Ross improved the present chapter by criticizing earlier versions of some of its sections. I am particularly grateful for the very helpful comments made by the editors of this volume, Drs. Johnston and Pietrewicz.

REFERENCES

Barzun, J. (1972). The enlightenment. In J. A. Garraty & Peter Gay (Eds.), *The Columbia history of the world*. New York: Harper & Row.

Boice, R. (1977). Surplusage. *Bulletin of the Psychonomic Society. i,* 452–454.

Bower, G. H., & Hilgard, E. R. (1981). *Theories of learning* (5th ed.). Englewood Cliffs, NJ: Prentice-Hall.

Braveman, N. S. (1974). Poison-based avoidance learning with flavored or colored water in guinea pigs. *Learning and Motivation, 5,* 182–194.

Braveman, N. S. (1977). What studies on preexposure to pharmacological agents tell us about the nature of the aversion inducing treatment. In L. M. Barker, M. R. Best, & M. Domjan (Eds.), *Learning mechanisms in food selection*. Waco, TX: Baylor University Press.

Brogden, W. J. (1939). Sensory preconditioning. *Journal of Experimental Psychology, 25,* 323–334.

Brown, P. L. & Jenkins, H. M. (1968) Autoshaping of the pigeon's key-peck. *Journal of the Experimental Analysis of Behavior, 11,* 1–8.

Clarke, J. C., Westbrook, R. F., & Irwin, J. (1979). Potentiation instead of overshadowing in the pigeon. *Behavioral and Neural Biology, 25,* 18–29.

Eikelboom, R., & Stewart, J. (1982). Conditioning of drug-induced physiological responses. *Psychological Review, 89,* 507–528.

Estes, W. K., & Schoeffler, M. S. (1955). Analysis of variables influencing alternation after forced trials. *Journal of Comparative and Physiological Psychology, 48,* 357–362.

Evans, R. I. (1974). Lorenz warns: "Man must know that the horse he is riding may be wild and should be bridled." *Psychology Today, 8*(6), 83–93.

Ferster, C. B., & Skinner, B. F. (1957). *Schedules of reinforcement*. New York: Appleton–Century–Crofs.

Garcia, J. (1971). The faddy rat and us. *New Scientist and Science Journal, 59,* 254–256.

Garcia, J., & Ervin, F. R. (1968). A neuropsychological approach to appropriateness of signals and specificity of reinforcers. *Communications in Behavioral Biology, 1,* Part A, 389–415.

Garcia, J., & Koelling, R. A. (1966). Relation of cue to consequences in avoidance learning. *Psychonomic Science, 4,* 123–124.

Garcia, J., McGowan, B. K., & Green, K. F. (1972). Biological constraints on conditioning. In A. H. Black & W. F. Prokasy (Eds.), *Classical conditioning* (II). New York: Appleton–Century–Crofs.

Garcia, J., & Rusiniak, K. W. (1980). What the nose learns from the mouth. In D. Muller–Schwarze & R. M. Silverstein (Eds.), *Chemical signals*. New York: Plenum Press.

Gillette, K., Martin, G. M., & Cunningham, W. P. (1980). Differential use of food and water cues in the formation of conditioned aversions by domestic chicks (*Gallus gallus*). *Journal of Experimental Psychology: Animal Behavior Processes, 6*, 99–111.

Guthrie, E. R. (1952). *The Psychology of learning* (rev. ed.). New York: Harper.

Guthrie, E. R., & Horton, G. P. (1946). *Cats in a puzzlebox*. New York: Rinehart.

Hinde, R. A. (1973). Constraints on learning: An introduction to the problem. In R. A. Hinde & J. Stevenson–Hinde (Eds.), *Constraints on learning*. London: Academic Press.

Jenkins, H. M. (1973). Effects of the stimulus-reinforcer relationship on selected and unselected responses. In R. A. Hinde & J. Stevenson–Hinde (Eds.), *Constraints on learning*. London: Academic Press.

Johnston, T. D. (1981). Contrasting approaches to a theory of learning. *Behavioral and Brain Sciences, 4*, 125–139.

Kamin, L. J. (1965). Temporal and intensity characteristics of the conditioned stimulus. In W. F. Prokasy (Ed.), *Classical conditioning: A symposium*. New York: Appleton–Century–Crofts.

Kantor, J. R. (1947). *Problems of physiological psychology*. Granville, OH: Principia Press.

Kelleher, R. T., & Gollub, L. R. (1962). A review of positive conditioned reinforcement. *Journal of the Experimental Analysis of Behavior, 5*, 543–597.

Kimble, G. A. (1961). *Hilgard and Marquis' conditioning and learning* (2nd ed.). New York: Appleton–Century–Crofts.

Kimble, G. A. (1967). The definition of learning and some useful distinctions. In G. A. Kimble (Ed.), *Foundations of learning and conditionin*. New York: Appleton–Century–Crofts.

Kling, J. W., & Schrier, A. M. (1971). Positive reinforcement. In J. W. Kling & L. A. Riggs (Eds.), *Woodworth and Scholosberg's experimental psychology*. New York: Holt, Rinehart, & Wonston.

Lavin, M. J. (1976). The establishment of flavor–flavor associations using a sensory preconditioning training procedure. *Learning and Motivation, 7*, 173–183.

Lett, B. T. (1979). Long-delay learning: Implications for learning and memory theory. In N. S. Sutherland (Ed.), *Tutorial essays in experimental psychology*. Hillsdale, NJ: Lawrence Erlbaum Associates.

Lett, B. T. (1980). Taste potentiates color-sickness associations in pigeons and quail. *Animal Learning and Behavior, 8*, 193–198.

Lett, B. T. (in press). Taste potentiation in poison avoidance learning. In M. L. Commons, R. J. Herrnstein, & A. R. Wagner (Eds.), *Quantitative analysis of behavior:* (Vol. 3), *Acquisition*. Cambridge, MA: Ballinger Press.

Lieberman, D. A., McIntosh, D. C., & Thomas, G. V. (1979). Learning when reward is delayed: A marking hypothesis. *Journal of Experimental Psychology: Animal Behavior Processes, 3*, 243–257.

Lockard, R. B. (1968). The albino rat: A defensible choice or a bad habit. *American Psychologist, 23*, 734–742.

Lockard, R. B. (1971). Reflections on the fall of comparative psychology: Is there a lesson for us all? *American Psychologist, 26*, 168–179.

LoLordo, V. M. (1979). Constraints on learning. In M. R. Bitterman, V. M. LoLordo, & M. Rashotte (Eds.), *Animal learning: Survey and analysis*. New York: Plenum.

Lorenz, K. (1965). *Evolution and the modification of behavior*. Chicago: University of Chicago Press.

Lorenz, K. (1970). *Studies in human and animal behavior* (Vol. 1). (R. Martin, Trans.). London: Methuen.

Luria, A. R. (1968). *The mind of a mnemonist*. New York: Basic Books.

McCullough, M. L. (1979). The primacy of the experiment: Some reservations. *Bulletin of the British Psychological Society, 32,* 409–412.

McKearney, J. W. (1969). Fixed interval schedules of electric shock presentation: Extinction and recovery of performance under different shock intensities and fixed-interval durations. *Journal of the Experimental Analysis of Behavior, 12,* 301–313.

McLaurin, W. A., Farley, J. A., & Scarborough, B. B. (1963). Inhibitory effect of preirradiation saccharin habituation on conditioned avoidance behavior. *Radiation Research, 18,* 473–478.

Moore, B. R. (1973). The role of directed Pavlovian reactions in simple instrumental learning in the pigeon. In R. A. Hinde & J. Stevenson–Hinde (Eds.), *Constraints on learning.* London: Academic Press.

Moore, B. R., & Tuttard, S. (1979). Dr. Guthrie and *Felix domesticus* or: Tripping over the cat. *Science, 205,* 1031–1033.

Morse, W. H., Mead, R. M., & Kelleher, R. T. (1967). Modulation of elicited behavior by a fixed-interval schedule of electric shock presentation. *Science, 157,* 215–217.

Olton, D. S. (1979). Mazes, maps, and memory. *American Psychologist, 34,* 583–596.

Pavlov, I. P. (1927). *Conditioned reflexes.* (G.V. Anrep, Trans.). Oxford: Oxford University Press.

Pavlov, I. P. (1932). The reply of a physiologist to psychologists. *Psychological Review, 39,* 91–127.

Petrinovich, L., & Bolles, R. C. (1957). Delayed alternation: Evidence for symbolic processes in the rat. *Journal of Comparative and Physiological Psychology, 50,* 363–365.

Reiss, S., & Wagner, A. R. (1972). A CS habituation effect produces a "latent inhibition effect" but no active "conditioned inhibition." *Learning and Motivation, 3,* 237–245.

Rescorla, R. A. (1967). Pavlovian conditioning and its proper control procedures. *Psychological Review, 74,* 71–80.

Rescorla, R. A. (1973). Effect of US habituation following conditioning. *Journal of Comparative and Physiological Psychology, 82,* 137–143.

Rescorla, R. A., & Wagner, A. R. (1972). A theory of Pavlovian conditioning: Variations in the effectiveness of reinforcement and nonreinforcement. In A. H. Black & W. F. Prokasy (Ed.), *Classical conditioning* (II). New York: Academic Press.

Revusky, S. H. (1968). Aversion to sucrose produced by contingent X-irradiation: Temporal and dosage parameters. *Journal of Comparative and Physiological Psychology, 65,* 17–22.

Revusky, S. (1971). The role of interference in association over a delay. In W. K. Honig & P. H. R. James (Eds.), *Animal memory.* New York: Academic Press.

Revusky, S. (1977a). Learning as a general process with an emphasis on data from feeding experiments. In N. W. Milgram, L. Krames, & T. W. Alloway (Eds.), *Food aversion learning.* New York: Plenum Press.

Revusky, S. (1977b). The concurrent interference approach to delay learning. In L. M. Barker, M. R. Best, & M. Domjan (Eds.), *Learning mechanisms in food selection.* Waco, TX: Baylor University Press.

Revusky, S., & Garcia, J. (1970). Learned associations over long delays. In G. H. Bower & J. T. Spence (Eds.), *The psychology of learning and motivation: Advances in theory and research* (Vol. 4). New York: Academic Press.

Revusky, S., & Taukulis, H. K. (1975). The effects of alcohol and lithium habituation on the development of alcohol aversions through contingent lithium injection. *Behaviour Research and Therapy, 13,* 163–166.

Rozin, P. (1968). Specific aversions and neophobia resulting from vitamin deficiency or poisoning in half-wild and domestic rats. *Journal of Comparative and Physiological Psychology, 66,* 82–88.

Schwartz, B. (1974). On going back to nature: A review of Seligman and Hager's "Biological Boundaries of Learning." *Journal of the Experimental Analysis of Behavior, 21,* 183–198.

Schwartz, B., Schuldenfrei, R., & Lacey, H. (1978). Operant psychology as factory psychology. *Behaviorism, 6*, 229–254.

Shettleworth, S. J. (1983). Memory in food-hoarding birds. *Scientific American, 248*, 102–110.

Skinner, B. F. (1948). *Walden two.* New York: Macmillan

Skinner, B. F. (1953). *Science and human behavior.* New York: Macmillan.

Skinner, B. F. (1957). *Verbal behavior.* New York: Appleton–Century–Crofts.

Solomon, R. L. (1980). The opponent-process theory of acquired motivation: The cost of pleasure and the benefit of pain. *American Psychologist, 35*, 691–712.

Spear, N. E. (1978). *The processing of memory: Forgetting and retention.* Hillsdale, NJ: Lawrence Erlbaum Associates.

Spence, K. W. (1947). The role of secondary reinforcement in delayed reward learning. *Psychological Review, 54*, 1–8.

Taukulis, H. K., & Revusky, S. (1975). Odor as a conditioned inhibitor: Applicability of the Rescorla–Wagner model to feeding behavior. *Learning and Motivation, 6*, 11–27.

Thorndike, E. L. (1911). *Animal intelligence.* New York: Macmillan.

Tinklepaugh, O. L. (1928). An experimental study of representative factors in monkeys. *Journal of Comparative Psychology, 8*, 197–236.

Tolman, E. C. (1932). *Purposive behavior in men and animals.* New York: Appleton–Century.

Tyler, D. W., Wortz, E. C., & Bitterman, M. E. (1953). The effect of random and alternating partial reinforcement on resistance to extinction in the rat. *American Journal of Psychology, 66*, 57–65.

Walker, E. L. (1956). The duration and course of the reaction decrement and the influence of reward. *Journal of Comparative and Physiological Psychology, 49*, 167–176.

Watson, J. B. (1919). *Psychology from the standpoint of a behaviorist.* Philadelphia: Lippincott.

Williams, D. R., & Williams, H. (1969). Automaintenance in the pigeon: Sustained pecking despite contingent nonreinforcement. *Journal of the Experimental Analysis of Behavior, 12*, 511–520.

Wilson, E. O. (1975). *Sociobiology: The new synthesis.* Cambridge, MA: Belknap Press of Harvard University.

Woodworth, R. S. (1938). *Experimental psychology.* New York: Henry Holt.

Woodworth, R. S., & Sheehan, M. R. (1964). *Contemporary schools of psychology* (3rd ed.). New York: Ronald Press.

Yerkes, R. M., & Yerkes, D. N. (1928). Concerning memory in the chimpanzee. *Journal of Comparative Psychology, 8*, 237–271.

Author Index

Page numbers in *italics* show where complete bibliographic references are given.

A

Aarons, L., 349, *354*
Able, K. P., 204, 219, *239*
Acredolo, L. P., 202, 203, 207, 208, 210, 212, 216, 217, 222, 223, 225, 227, *239, 240*
Adair, E. R., 133, *136*
Adams, J., 344, *351*
Adrian, R., 186, *197*
Albert, D. J., 126, *137*
Alberts, J. R., 123, *139,* 347, *351*
Alcock, J., 171, *195*
Allen, G. L., 217, 218, 222, 226, 228, *239, 242*
Allison, J., 88, *93*
Amsel, A., 124, *137*
Anastasi, A., 3,12, *18*
Andre-Thomas, C. Y., 208, *239*
Andrew, R. J., 263, *268*
Andrews, E. A., 300, *302*
Angell, J. R., 4, *18*
Anooshian, L. J., 216, *239*
Antin, J., 126, *135*
Anzai, Y., 264, *268*
Appleyard, D., 219, 221, 222, *239*
Arabie, P., 339, *352*
Armitage, K. B., 186, *195*
Armstrong, E. A., 255, 263, *268*

B

Arnold, S. J., 15, *19,* 329, 336, 338, 349, *352*
Aslin, R. N., 17, *19*
Atkinson, C. A., 130, *136*
Austin, O. L., 156, *165*
Autgaerden, S., 208, *239*
Avrunin, G., 330, 335, 345, 346, *352*
Ayala, F. J., 65, *70*

B

Baenninger, R., 125, *136*
Baerends, G. P., 89, *93*
Baettig, K., 122, *139*
Baker, L. J., 123, *135*
Baker, M. C., 17, *19*
Baker, T. B., 123, 130, *135, 136*
Balaban, M. 347, *352*
Balagura, S., 126, *141*
Baldwin, L. M., 218, *240*
Bandura, A., 146, *165*
Bandy, O. L., 184, *196*
Bannikov, A. G., 106, *116*
Baptista, L. F., 11, *19,* 251, 252, 253, 255, *268*
Barelare, B., 130, *135*
Barker, L. M., 122, 130, *136, 141*
Barker, R. G., 4, *19,* 203, 215, 217, 218, *239*
Barnett, S. A., 121, 127, *136*

433

Subject Index

A

action, 279n, 280, 290, 322, 380
adaptability, behavioral, 81, 170-171
adaptation, 2, 59-61, 169, 194, 307, 311
  hierarchy of, 167-168
  in history of psychology, 59-60
adaptationist fallacy, 15
adaptive correlation, method of, 14, 15
adaptive zone, 67n
affectional responses, development of, 51
affordance, 279n, 280-281, 291, 306, 316, 357
  in environmental description, 8, 9, 305,
    367-368, 372
Age of Reason, 404
anagenesis, 59-69, 314
  definition of, 63, 65
  examples of, 65
  as modern concept, 61
animal as actor, 7, 9
animal-environment relationship, (*see*
  organism-environment relationship)
Anolis lizard, predatory behavior of, 372-373
antipredator behavior
  in ground squirrels, 167-195
  in burrows, 172, 179-184
  development of, 169, 176-179, 189
  harrassment in, 174-175, 178, 185, 186
  risk assessment in, 188-191
  sensory cues used in, 188, 189

signals used in, 170, 173, 178, 184, 193
  towards snakes, 172-195
  in prairie dogs, 187, 188-189
aposematic coloration, 108
appetitive behavior, 48
artifacts, laboratory, 90
association, selective, 411, 417, 420-422
attention, 251, 254
autophenotype, 251
autoshaping, 108, 110, 388, 390

B

bee-wolf, orientation in, 45
bees, hive-building in, 363-364
behavior
  anecdotes about, 144
  as animal-environment relation, 5
  description of, 7, 74, 78, 318
  development of, 3, 50, 51, 143, 171
  evolution of, 29-30, 63, 65, 88
  evolutionary grades of, 64, 68
  functional analysis of, 362, 364, 373, 390
  mechanisms of, 357-358, 362, 379
  proximate vs. ultimate causes of, 358, 362
  as resource usage, (*see* resources,
    biological)
behavioral capability, (*see* effectivity)
behavioral neophenotype, 82, 87-88, 250
behaviorism, 5, 36, 246, 279, 314, 401-413